PAUL AND PERSEVERANCE

D1082334

PAUL AND PERSEVERANCE

STAYING IN AND FALLING AWAY

Judith M. Gundry Volf

Westminster/John Knox Press
Louisville, Kentucky

TO MIROSLAV

Published in Germany by J. C. B. Mohr (Paul Siebeck) Tübingen

First American edition

Published by Westminster / John Knox Press
Louisville, Kentucky

PRINTED IN THE UNITED STATES OF AMERICA
9 8 7 6 5 4 3 2 1

Library of Congress Cataloging-in-Publication Data

Gundry Volf, Judith M.
   Paul and perseverance : staying in and falling away / Judith M. Gundry Volf. — 1st American ed.
        p.   cm.
   Reprint. Originally published: Tübingen : J.C.B. Mohr, c 1990. Originally published in series: Wissenschaftliche Untersuchungen zum Neuen Testament. 2. Reihe ; 37.
   Revision of the author's thesis (Ph.D. — University of Tübingen, 1988)
   Includes bibliographical references and index.
   ISBN 0-664-25175-7

   1. Perseverance (Theology) — Biblical teaching.   2. Bible.   N.T. Epistles of Paul — Criticism, interpretation, etc.   I. Title.
BS2655.P53G85 1991
234 — dc20   90-19724

Preface

The present study is a slightly revised version of a doctoral dissertation accepted by the Evangelisch-Theologische Fakultät of the University of Tübingen in 1988. Prof. Dr. Otfried Hofius inspired me to work on the problem of perseverance and falling away in Paul's thought and supervised the project. His critical interaction with my thinking in the course of the investigation always proved invaluable, and his warmth and great personal interest added pleasantness to the task. One cannot wish for much more from a *Doktorvater*—thus, my heart-felt gratitude. The years of research in Tübingen were made possible to a large extent by the Diakonisches Werk of the Evangelische Kirche Deutschlands through its scholarship program for international students. During my time as a *Stipendiatin* I enjoyed the fine hospitality and resources of the Evangelisches Stift in Tübingen. My sincere thanks goes to both organizations.

A teaching post then took me to Yugoslavia, where my writing and, later, revisions were completed. By that time I had had the benefit of the reactions of others to the results of my research. I would like to thank those individuals here. Prof. I. Howard Marshall, whose expertise in my topic is well-known, kindly read various parts of the first draft and took the time to give helpful feed-back in conversation and correspondence. Prof. Robert H. Gundry read the entire first and final drafts of the dissertation and provided thorough and detailed comments—an accomplishment which owes no less to fatherly love than to academic enterprise. I benefited greatly from his insights. Prof. Dr. Peter Stuhlmacher read the dissertation as *Korreferent* and his extensive and provocative comments figured significantly in my thinking as I revised the manuscript for publication. Prof. Hans Dieter Betz kindly read the dissertation and made suggestive new observations which I was unfortunately unable to pursue and develop in the revisions. The one who perhaps knows more than any other how this book took shape and whose interaction also left its important traces on the text is Prof. Miroslav Volf, my husband. His theological interest and competence were a boon to me throughout. I remember gratefully the breakfast, mid-afternoon, and late night talks about whatever I was working on just then and the many helpful insights they brought. Not only my mind was fed, but my soul as well by his confidence-inspiring manner. It is fitting that this book is fondly dedicated to him, for it incorporates some of the fruits of our life together.

Finally, I express my appreciation to Prof. Dr. Martin Hengel and Prof. Dr. Otfried Hofius for accepting this book in the WUNT 2 series. Thanks also go to Mr. David Sielaff, Ms. Carey Wallace, and Ms. Sandy Bennett of the Word Processing Department of Fuller Theological Seminary for their mammoth effort and expertise in reformatting the better part of my text for this publication, and to Mr. Simon Seitz of the Wilhelm-Schickart-Institut für Informatik of the University of Tübingen for his extraordinary helpfulness at the critical stage of producing a laser print-out of my manuscript.

October, 1989   Judith M. Gundry Volf
Tübingen

CONTENTS

Preface   v

Introduction   1

PART ONE

THE ESCHATOLOGICAL TENSION

AND STAYING IN   7

I. Continuity in Salvation   9
God's Saving Works and Final Salvation
   Romans 8:29, 30   9
   2 Thessalonians 2:13, 14   15
   1 Thessalonians 5:9   21
The Spirit As Guarantee
   Romans 8:23; 2 Corinthians 1:22; 5:5   27
Finishing the "Good Work"
   Philippians 1:6   33

II. Tension in Continuity   49
"Hope That Does Not Disappoint"
   Romans 5:1–11   49
Victory in Trials and Tribulation
   Romans 8:28, 35–39   56
Salvation at the Last Judgment
   Romans 8:31–34   65
"God Is Faithful!"   69
   2 Thessalonians 3:3; 1 Corinthians 10:13   70
   1 Thessalonians 5:23, 24   74
   1 Corinthians 1:8, 9   76

Conclusion to Part One   80

PART TWO

CONDUCT AND FALLING AWAY 83

III. "Destruction" of the Weak 85
Romans 14:1–23; 1 Corinthians 8:7–13

IV. Punishment of the Disobedient 99
To "Eat" and "Drink" Judgment
1 Corinthians 11:27–34 99
Excursus: Divine Chastisement in
OT-Jewish Thought and the NT 107
Deliverance to Satan
1 Corinthians 5:1–5 113
Beware Not to Fall!
1 Corinthians 10:12 120

V. Exclusion of Evildoers from the Kingdom 131
1 Corinthians 6:9–11 132
Galatians 5:19–21 141

Conclusion to Part Two 155

PART THREE

FAITH AND FALLING AWAY 159

VI. Israel, the Gentiles, and the Gospel 161
Israel's Unbelief
Romans 9–11 161
Gentiles' Boasting
Romans 11:17–24 196

VII. Believers' Turning Away 203
Justification by Law and Falling from Grace
Galatians 5:1–4 203
Failing the Test of Faith
2 Corinthians 13:5 217

Conclusion to Part Three 226

PART FOUR

FINAL OUTCOME OF MISSION   231

VIII. Paul's Hope   233
Passing the Test
   1 Corinthians 9:27   233
Becoming the Gospel's Partner
   1 Corinthians 9:23   247
Attaining the Final Goal
   Philippians 3:11, 12   254

IX. Paul's Labor and Christians' Faith   261
Laboring in Vain
   Philippians 2:16; 1 Thessalonians 3:5; Galatians 2:2; 4:11   262
Believing in Vain
   1 Corinthians 15:2   271
Receiving Grace in Vain
   2 Corinthians 6:1   277

Conclusion to Part Four   281

General Conclusion   283

Bibliography of Works Cited   289

Index of References to Biblical and Other Ancient Sources   313

INTRODUCTION

An interest in re-examining fundamental aspects of Paul's gospel has characterized more recent New Testament scholarship. One of these aspects, to which in particular the work of E. P. Sanders has devoted considerable attention, is Paul's view of "staying in" salvation.[1] Using this terminology, Sanders put forward the thesis that for Paul as well as for Palestinian Judaism "salvation is by grace but ... works are the condition of remaining 'in'."[2] The ensuing debate has focused primarily on Paul's relationship to Judaism as regards the question of staying in salvation. The present book is interested in the same question but narrows the subject to *Paul's* teaching on staying in salvation; and instead of attempting a comparative religions study, this work is primarily exegetical-theological in nature. Further, it seeks to know not only *how* one remains in salvation according to Paul but also, more fundamentally, *whether* one necessarily does so.

If the present investigation bears a relation to the contemporary New Testament debate on Pauline soteriology, it is also, and even more closely, related to the centuries-old theological debate on the perseverance of the saints. Since Augustine this doctrine has served as a theological framework within which theologians have wrestled with the question of whether and how one remains in salvation. Augustine introduced the idea of a *donum perseverantiae:* as a divine gift the perseverance of the saints in grace was certain.[3] Calvin later championed the doctrine by affirming the perseverance of believers through the power and faithfulness of God.[4] The Reformed confessions, in particular, the *Canons of Dort*, emphatically espoused the perseverance of the saints by denying that they could totally or finally fall away.[5] Down through history, nevertheless, a chorus of

---

[1] See especially his major works, *Paul and Palestinian Judaism* and *Paul, the Law, and the Jewish People.*

[2] Sanders, *Palestinian Judaism*, 543.

[3] See Augustine, *De dono perseverantiae; De correptione et gratia* XII.33.

[4] See Calvin, *Institutes* III.2.15–28, 38–40; III.24.6–8.

[5] On the systematic-theological debate, see esp. Moltmann, *Prädestination und Perseveranz;* Berkouwer, *Faith and Perseverance.*

criticism has been heard against perseverance. Out of a wide variety of theological concerns the voices of dissent have offered an alternative: in the final analysis, remaining in salvation hinges on believers themselves, who may or may not persevere to the end, depending on the degree of steadfastness in their faith and practice.

In the discussion Paul's epistles have assumed a prominent position. Calvin drew scriptural arguments for the teaching of perseverance primarily from them, but they have served others well enough to affirm that Christians can "fall from grace" and "lose salvation." Interpreters have not only paid varying degrees of attention to a given Pauline text relating to perseverance. They have also come up with conflicting interpretations of the same text. The current debate on "staying in" carries on these efforts to show where Paul stands on the matter. The intersection of the contemporary discussion with the traditional debate calls for a reassessment of Paul's teaching related to perseverance.

Does Paul assume that Christians will remain in salvation? If so, on what basis? What, if anything, can disrupt this continuity, and to what extent can it do so? I will attempt to answer these and related questions through a detailed exegetical analysis of the relevant texts. The magnifying glass of rigorous exegesis will, I hope, let Paul's meaning prevail over our dogmatic prejudices, whatever they be. Moreover, no full-scale critical treatment of the Pauline passages related to perseverance is available, to my knowledge. Sanders' treatment in his two major works is neither comprehensive nor exegetically thoroughgoing—perhaps because his investigation is guided by a special interest in comparative religions—and the conclusions he draws are often, for this author, unsatisfyingly hesitant.[6] I. H. Marshall's chapter on Paul in his book *Kept by the Power of God* stands out as an important contribution to serious New Testament study of the problem, yet it suffers from brevity. We therefore need to expend a good deal of effort at the exegetical grindstone if we are to understand better Paul's thought on staying in salvation. Both the comparative religions side of the debate and the systematic-theological side stand to profit from this kind of study.

As the reader will discover, the exegetical conclusions reached here through in-depth analysis of the texts tend toward the classical Reformed doctrine of perseverance. Nevertheless, this study was not undertaken to confirm that doctrine; nor is the book meant to function as an exegetical defense of it. Rather, my intent is to uncover what Paul, unaware of

---

[6] See esp. *Law*, 105–113; *Palestinian Judaism*, 515–518.

theological systems formed after his time, believed about continuity in Christians' salvation. I have tried to let Paul set the agenda and determine how it is carried out. The material in his texts, not the internal requirements of a dogmatic treatise, gives the study its shape. The apostle himself raises the issues to be discussed here. For the most part, the degree of emphasis and amount of attention he devotes to a particular aspect of the problem will determine even the degree of its prominence in my investigation. And despite the aforementioned tendency, the conclusions drawn from the exegetical discussions will not invariably fit the Reformed position. Needless to say, the highly developed doctrine of perseverance that comes out of the sixteenth-century is not a mirror image of Paul's first-century teaching on continuity in individual salvation. It is the latter in its distinctiveness and pristine fullness which I purpose to investigate here. I will leave to others the task of applying the results of this study to dogmatic theology and comparative religions.[7]

Some readers will wonder however whether I have not set too ambitious a goal in attempting to organize Paul's thoughts on the question of remaining in salvation into a more or less unified whole. Can we speak of a Pauline view of staying in or falling away, or, for that matter, of Pauline theology at all? Or do not such conflicting thoughts flow from the apostle's pen that it is hard to attribute to him a "theology" in the strict sense? It is true, on the one hand, that Paul's epistles, occasional documents that they are, do not together constitute a comprehensive or watertight theological system. Therefore we can hardly expect them to set forth a systematically worked out, tightly argued position on a problem such as continuity in individual salvation. On the other hand, the presupposition that Paul was prone to blatant contradictions seems just as problematic. We do best to expect a certain coherence and consistency in his thought until the texts, whose contingency we have thoroughly taken into account, prove otherwise. The following study will support the reasonableness of this presupposition with exegetical evidence.

The epistles to the Thessalonians, Galatians, Corinthians, Romans and Philippians, whose Pauline authorship is widely and successfully defended,[8] constitute the sources for this investigation of Paul's thought on continuity in salvation. Although examination of all the pertinent texts in Ephesians, Colossians and the Pastoral Epistles would doubtless enrich the discussion, whether or not they are authored by Paul, for lack of time and

---

[7] For a view of the relationship between Paul and Judaism on continuity in salvation different from Sanders' and critical of it, see Gundry, "Grace," 1–38.

[8] On the question of the authenticity of 2 Thessalonians, see p. 15, n. 35.

space I have limited my comments to the most significant parallels.

I have arranged the texts under investigation topically instead of chronologically. This arrangement does not overlook the possibility that Paul's epistles reflect a general development in his theology. But other factors affecting interpretation—especially historical and literary contexts—seem in this case to unlock more doors to Paul's meaning than do chronological considerations. Besides, Pauline chronology itself is a matter of debate. The topical arrangement which I have used does not assume too much with regard to chronology. Further, the grouping of texts with common *topoi* lets their parallelism, nuances and contrasts come to light more easily. To avoid an artificial systematization by this kind of arrangement, however, careful attention is paid to immediate and overarching contexts.

The discussion of Paul's teaching on staying in salvation opens with an analysis of texts in which Paul announces and expounds fundamental theological truths about God's saving work in Jesus Christ, present and future, for Christian believers (Part One). In the first group of texts (Chapter I) Paul indicates the relation of various divine saving initiatives to each other and especially to final salvation. These texts reveal whether Paul believes in principle that a sure continuity exists in the individual's salvation,[9] so that aspects of God's saving work which have already benefited believers are integrally connected to the future consummation of their salvation.

The second group of texts (Chapter II) addresses the question of remaining in salvation in the light of the eschatological tension as characterized by Paul. Not only must believers endure in faith and hope the interval between present salvation and its future consummation. Until that day they also face tests and tribulation in which antagonistic forces threaten their continuance in salvation. The eschatological distress and final judgment raise the possibility of failing to remain in salvation to the end. Thus those passages where Paul's fundamental theological assertions on continuity in salvation meet with the concrete realities of present Christian existence provide yet deeper insight into the apostle's view of staying in salvation.

Parts Two, Three and Four seek to refine Paul's meaning further by analyzing texts in which the concrete problems Paul faced in his ministry touch the question of staying in salvation. These texts are often taken to have negative implications for the idea of sure continuity in Christians' salvation. They fall fairly neatly into two familiar categories: the first group deals with the problem of ethical failure as a possible reason for exclusion

---

[9] As the analysis of the texts will reveal, Paul can conceive of salvation as a work of God in *individual* Christian believers, not just as God's saving activity *among* them in the Christian community. Cf. Sanders, *Palestinian Judaism*, 547.

from salvation (Chapters III–V), and the second concerns the possibility of falling away through unbelief or abandonment of belief in the gospel (Chapters VI and VII). The last group of texts, in which the dangers are formulated more generally, deal with the final outcome of Paul's ministry for himself and his converts (Chapters VIII and IX).

Finally, the Conclusion will summarize the basic findings of the exegetical discussions and relate them to each other in an attempt to show how Paul answers the question whether and on what basis one "stays in."

PART ONE

THE ESCHATOLOGICAL TENSION

AND STAYING IN

In his fundamental theological expositions of God's saving work in Jesus Christ for Christian believers Paul can distinguish between various aspects or stages of salvation. Further he indicates that some of these divine saving initiatives have already benefited believers, but others lie yet in the future. The temporal separation between present and future aspects of salvation raises the question whether the blessings of salvation experienced now will certainly be followed by the coming ones. Is there a connection between them, and if so, what is it? Paul deals with this matter of the interrelationship of God's saving initiatives toward believers as he announces and explains to them basic theological truths about their Christian existence. First I will look at the most important Pauline texts in which the relation of present to future aspects of salvation comes to light and try to answer the question whether Paul there presupposes or asserts an underlying, sure continuity in Christians' salvation in view of which it will definitely reach completion (Chapter I). Then I will take up the same question where it surfaces in the context of the eschatological distress and final judgment. When Paul is dealing with end-time threats to the full accomplishment of Christians' salvation, how then does he portray the interrelationship between its present and future aspects (Chapter II)? What grounds does he put forward for his view?

I. CONTINUITY IN SALVATION

God's Saving Works and Final Salvation

Romans 8:29, 30. In the "golden chain" of Rom 8:29, 30 Paul names in succession various aspects of God's saving work in Christians. "Whom he foreknew, he also predestinated to be conformed to the image of his Son, that he might be the firstborn among many brethren; and whom he predestinated, these he also called; and whom he called, these he also justified; and whom he justified, these he also glorified." What is the goal of God's saving work portrayed here as a chain of divine actions leading up to a final climax? How are the individual links of the chain related to the goal?

The "beginning" of Christians' salvation lies in God's eternal counsel, according to Paul. He develops the notion of the divine πρόθεσις at 8:28b in the next verse with the use of the terms προγινώσκειν and προορίζειν.[1] According to God's eternal purpose, Christians are "foreknown" and "predestinated." προγινώσκειν denotes God's prior choice, not prior knowledge (so also 11:2; for the idea, cf. 9:11).[2] προορίζειν refers to God's eternal determination of the elect to a goal.[3] Pre*destination* thus expresses the goal-oriented aspect of divine election. Paul explains the goal of divine predestination here to be conformity to the image of God's Son: προώρισεν συμμόρφους τῆς εἰκόνος τοῦ υἱοῦ αὐτοῦ. Interpreters have understood the expression "conformed to the image of God's Son" in different ways. Does it refer to conformity to Christ in baptism (cf. Phil 3:10; also Rom

---

[1] V. d. Osten-Sacken, *Römer 8*, 279; Wilckens, *Röm* II, 163.

[2] BAGD, s. v. προγινώσκω: "choose beforehand." Cf. Schmithals, *Anthropologie*, 164: "Der Weg zum Heil beginnt also damit, daß Gott sich in freier Wahl die Menschen auserwählt, die er zum Heil führen will, nicht aber erkennt er nur im voraus diejenigen, die sich aufgrund ihres eigenen Verhaltens das Heil verdienen werden." Cf. also Bultmann, προγινώσκω, *TDNT* 1, 715; Calvin, *Institutes*, III.21.5; below, p. 167 with n. 27. Cf. the semitic use of ידע. The textual history of Rom 8:29, 30 suggests that προγινώσκειν and προορίζειν are so similar in meaning that they could be substituted for each other (Schmidt, προορίζω, *TDNT* 5, 456). In v. 30 προέγνω is the variant reading (A) for προώρισεν.

[3] See Michel, *Röm*, 277; Luz, *Geschichtsverständnis*, 253; Hofius, "Hoffnung," 9; Marshall, *Kept*, 102. Cf. 1 Cor 2:7: προώρισεν...πρὸ τῶν αἰώνων.

6:3–5)?[4] Is it rather a present, on-going process (cf. 2 Cor 3:18) in imitation of the Son's obedience in suffering?[5] Should we take it as a reference to the eschatological transformation (cf. Phil 3:21)?[6] Or is it used more broadly to connote the whole Christian life as participation in Christ (cf. 1 Cor 1:9)?[7] What is the goal of divine predestination described as conformity to the image of God's Son?

Paul can think of Christian conformity to Christ as both conformity in present mortal existence (συμμορφιζόμενος τῷ θανάτῳ αὐτοῦ, Phil 3:10)[8] and in the future glorified life of the resurrection (μετασχηματίσει τὸ σῶμα τῆς ταπεινώσεως ἡμῶν σύμμορφον τῷ σώματι τῆς δόξης αὐτοῦ, Phil 3:21). There is even present transformation (μεταμορφούμεθα) "from glory to glory" (2 Cor 3:18). Thus there are various aspects of conformity to Christ for Paul. Which aspect is meant in Rom 8:29?

The standard of conformity in Rom 8:29 is the εἰκὼν τοῦ υἱοῦ αὐτοῦ. Paul uses the phrase εἰκὼν θεοῦ elsewhere to designate Christ as the image of God in whom God's glory and essence shines forth (2 Cor 4:4, 6; cf. Col 1:15, 19). τὴν αὐτὴν εἰκόνα at 2 Cor 3:18 must also, in the light of 4:4, 6, refer to Christ as the image of God.[9] For Paul, δόξα characterizes Christ as the εἰκὼν θεοῦ (2 Cor 3:18; 4:4, 6). We see then that Paul uses the term εἰκών of Christ with reference to Christ's divine glory. The standard of conformity to which Christians are predestinated, therefore, is the Christ of glory.

This view gains support from 1 Cor 15:49, where Paul makes a sharp distinction between ἡ εἰκὼν τοῦ ἐπουρανίου, which "we will bear," and ἡ εἰκὼν τοῦ χοϊκοῦ, which "we have borne." The "image of the heavenly" refers to Christ,[10] and the future bearing of Christ's image, to the resurrection life, as the context makes clear.[11] Christians will be made like unto the image of the heavenly one, the resurrected and glorified Christ. This association of the resurrection with the image of Christ may form the background to Paul's formulation in Rom 8:29. For here Paul says that Christians will be conformed to the image "of his Son" (τοῦ υἱοῦ αὐτοῦ),

---

[4] Paulsen, *Römer 8*, 159.

[5] Calvin, *Rom, ad loc.*; Cranfield, *Rom*, 432; Bruce, *Rom*, 178. Cranfield and Bruce, however, do not exclude a future conformity.

[6] Michel, *Röm*, 277; Thüsing, *Per Christum*, 126, 127.

[7] Wilckens, *Röm* II, 164; similarly, v. d. Osten-Sacken, *Römer 8*, 284–286.

[8] The present tense of the participle does not permit a reference to baptism, however (Grundmann, σύν μετά, *TDNT* 7, 788, 789).

[9] Larsson, *Christus*, 277; Barrett, *2 Cor*, 125.

[10] Conzelmann, *1 Cor*, 287, 288; Grosheide, *1 Cor*, 389; Schlatter, *Bote*, 441; Jervell, *Imago Dei*, 191.

[11] Cf. Schlatter, *Bote*, 441; Grosheide, *1 Cor*, 389.

which suggests that they will attain the expected "sonship" (υἱοθεσία), namely, ἡ ἀπολύτρωσις τοῦ σώματος ἡμῶν (Rom 8:23), at the resurrection in becoming like the Son.[12] Phil 3:21 also interprets Christians' conformity to Christ as resurrection to glorified somatic existence like Christ's (σύμμορφον τῷ σώματι τῆς δόξης αὐτοῦ). In summary, the standard of conformity in Rom 8:29 is not Christ in an earthly state of humility but in a glorious state.[13] The attainment of such conformity will take place in the future resurrection. Then the ultimate goal of the predestination of Christians will be achieved.[14] προώρισεν has this final goal in view.[15]

Paul also reveals the purpose of Christians' predestination: εἰς τὸ εἶναι αὐτὸν πρωτότοκον ἐν πολλοῖς ἀδελφοῖς. Those whom God has predestinated to be conformed to the image of the Son will also be the Son's sisters and brothers. Without sacrificing the preeminence of Christ, here called πρωτότοκος,[16] Paul now relates Christians to Christ in such a way that implies their inheritance with Christ.[17] The goal of God's predestinating activity thus encompasses Christians' reception of the eschatological inheritance into which Christ as our elder brother has already entered, and Christians' relation to Christ as brothers and sisters in this glorified state. Paul has already prepared us for this understanding of the text in 8:17: "[We are] fellow heirs with Christ, since we suffer with him so that we might also be glorified with him."[18]

Paul began the "golden chain" in Rom 8:29, 30 by showing that the salvation of Christians, from its very origin in God's eternal counsel through God's predestinating activity, is moving toward final completion as conformity to the glorified Christ. He ends the chain on the same note of glorification: τούτους καὶ ἐδόξασεν. The aorist tense of ἐδόξασεν at first seems an unlikely choice to denote *future* completion of salvation. But the other references to glorification in the context (δόξα at 8:18, 21, and συνδοξασθῶμεν at 8:17c, also an aorist) refer clearly to future glorification (cf. also the future δόξα in Phil 3:21; 1 Cor 15:43; 2 Cor 4:17; 3:18; Rom 5:2;

---

[12] Cf. Michel, *Röm*, 277; Grundmann, σύν μετά, *TDNT* 7, 788, 789. Cf. Eph 1:5, προορίσας ἡμᾶς εἰς υἱοθεσίαν.

[13] With Michaelis, πρῶτος, *TDNT* 6, 877, n. 37; Jervell, *Imago Dei*, 277. Hofius ("Hoffnung," 9) explains: "Wir sollen Anteil bekommen an der Fülle der Herrlichkeit, die der auferstandene Herr besitzt. *Das* heißt, ihm gleich zu sein."

[14] Cf. Wiederkehr, *Berufung*, 161; Jervell, *Imago Dei*, 277; Grundmann, σύν μετά, *TDNT* 7, 788, 789.

[15] With Marshall, *Kept*, 102.

[16] Cf. Hofius, "Hoffnung," 9.

[17] Michel, *Röm*, 278; Wilckens, *Röm* II, 164; Cranfield, *Rom*, 432; Michaelis, πρῶτος, *TDNT* 6, 878; v. d. Osten-Sacken, *Römer 8*, 75.

[18] Cf. Wilckens, *Röm* II, 164; Hofius, "Hoffnung," 9.

2:7, 10). Has Paul taken over baptismal tradition in 8:30, preserving the aorist tenses while intending his readers to assume the usual future connotations of δοξάζειν/δόξα?[19] Indeed ἐδόξασεν would have had such a future connotation even in an original baptismal setting, for the baptismal tradition "stellt ... die Taufgemeinde ... unmittelbar in das zukünftige Offenbarungsgeschehen der Endzeit hinein."[20] Or there are other explanations of Paul's use of the aorist here. Some take ἐδόξασεν as an ingressive aorist denoting the glorification which begins through justification and culminates in the consummation of salvation.[21] Others see a proleptic aorist which encourages suffering Christians by triumphantly anticipating the future glorification as certain to come to pass.[22] Paul may use the aorist to depict Christians' glorification as so certain, from the perspective of divine predestination, that it can be spoken of as already true of believers, though its historical realization is yet to come.[23] All these explanations of the aorist tense of ἐδόξασεν share the implication that it includes future eschatological glorification.

In summary, the goal of God's saving work in Rom 8:29, 30 is Christians' final salvation. Paul both begins and ends the "golden chain" on this note. God has predestinated Christians to be conformed to the image of God's resurrected, glorified Son. Like unto the Son as brothers and sisters, they too will receive their eschatological inheritance. God will complete their salvation in final glorification.

Through divine calling (ἐκάλεσεν) and justification (ἐδικαίωσεν) present progress is being made toward that final goal. As the gospel is preached, God calls to salvation those whom God has elected.[24] This calling is effectual: it works faith in Christ unto salvation.[25] The goal of divine election thus becomes manifest historically in divine calling.[26] Another aspect of the historical realization of God's eternal purpose toward the elect is their justification. They are not only called through the gospel to believe in Jesus Christ, but, having faith in Christ, are also justified.

---

[19] For this view, see Schille, "Liebe Gottes," 242; Käsemann, *Rom*, 244, 245; Paulsen, *Römer 8*, 161; Jervell, *Imago Dei*, 273ff.; v. d. Osten-Sacken, *Römer 8*, 67ff.

[20] Wilckens, *Röm* II, 165. Cf. Schnackenburg, *Heilsgeschehen*, 199.

[21] Marshall, *Kept*, 102, 103; Wiederkehr, *Berufung*, 165; Schlier, *Röm*, 273.

[22] Barrett, *Rom*, 170; Calvin, *Rom*, *ad loc.*; Spicq, *Agape* I, 251; v. d. Osten-Sacken, *Römer 8*, 283; cf. Hofius, "Hoffnung," 10: "Die Wahl der genannten Zeitform ist vielmehr Ausdruck der unbedingten Heilsgewißheit."

[23] Hofius, "Hoffnung," 10; Cranfield, *Rom*, 433; Michel, *Röm*, 278; Bruce, *Rom*, 178; Leenhardt, *Rom*, 134; Mayer, *Heilsratschluß*, 165.

[24] Hofius, "Hoffnung," 9; Klein, "*KALEIN*," 64.

[25] Hofius, "Hoffnung," 9.

[26] Hofius, "Hoffnung," 9; Klein, "*KALEIN*," 63.

The goal of God's saving work toward Christians, final glorification, is integrally related not only to God's prehistorical initiatives for their salvation but also to these historical manifestations of God's saving purpose in calling and justification. Formal considerations suggest a close interconnection between the divine initiatives in Christians' salvation in 8:29, 30. The structure in each member of the chain is almost identical: οὓς (δέ) + aorist indicative, τούτους καί + aorist indicative. After a long expansion of the first member in v. 29, Paul ticks off the rest with rhythmic simplicity. The chain gains momentum not only from the repetitious, rhythmic structure but also from the themes announced in the verbs which advance from one aspect of salvation to the next until they reach the climax: God foreknew, predestinated, called, justified, glorified! Paul portrays salvation as a series of divine initiatives snowballing toward fullness. He links these initiatives so tightly that each is born of the former and bears a promise of the one which follows.[27] Glorification is thus the finishing touch on the indivisible divine work of salvation which originated in God's foreknowledge and predestination of Christians and has come to historical expression in their calling and justification.[28] These verses truly do form a "chain" of interconnected divine salvific works and so imply a continuity in Christians' salvation.

Paul attributes this continuity implicitly to God's activity. God is the subject of salvation throughout the chain; the saved appear only as objects. Their activity (e.g., in believing) is not negated, nevertheless, it is not mentioned.[29] Rather, the string of aorists points to the certainty of God's continued action in salvation.[30] The text wants to focus on God's work because therein lies the guarantee of continuity. What *God* undertakes will come to pass.[31]

Paul shows not only the continuity in God's initiatives in salvation. He

---

[27] Wiederkehr, *Berufung*, 168; Mayer, *Heilsratschluß*, 163.

[28] Cf. Hofius, "Hoffnung," 9.

[29] Cf. Sanders, *Palestinian Judaism*, 446: "It is true that Paul can describe God's saving action virtually without reference to the believing response of man. Thus Rom. 8.28–30, 33...." While Paul presupposes faith as a correlate of the divine work of salvation here, he does not define their relation as one in which faith is the condition of salvation, nor does he contemplate whether unbelief could disrupt continuity in salvation. The text resists discussion of such ways of reading it (cf., e.g., Marshall, *Kept*, 103; Lagrange, *Rom*, 217).

[30] Luz, *Geschichtsverständnis*, 255.

[31] Cf. Luz, *Geschichtsverständnis*, 254: "Skopus der Aussage von V. 29f. ist: Was Gott einmal zum Heil begonnen hat, das führt er auch unweigerlich zu Ende." Similarly, Schmithals, *Anthropologie*, 166, 167; Wiederkehr, *Berufung*, 166, 167; Thüsing, *Per Christum*, 121.

also makes clear that the objects of God's saving activity are the same from start to finish. The continuity between the stages of salvation is thus not general but specific: it applies to the salvation of individual Christians. "*Whom* he foreknew, *these* he also predestined...; and *whom* he predestined, *these* he also called; and *whom* he called, *these* he also justified; and *whom* he justified, *these* he also glorified." The οὒς δέ...τούτους καί construction identifying the objects of one divine initiative as the objects of the next pounds like a drumbeat through the text. With this rhetorical device of "climax"[32] Paul posits a continuity in the beneficiaries of salvation from its first manifestation in God's eternal counsel to its final one in glorification.

J. Wesley, however, cautions that "St. Paul does not affirm, either here, or in any other Part of his Writing, that precisely the same Number of Men are called, justified, and glorified.... He only affirms, that this is the Method whereby God leads us Step by Step toward Heaven."[33] While it is true that Paul does not speak of numbers here, it is also true that he could hardly have identified more clearly the objects of the divine initiatives in salvation as the same at every step. Wesley's view suffers from an oversight of Paul's use of "climax," by which the apostle intends to show the continuity in the beneficiaries of God's saving acts.[34]

In conclusion, the "golden chain" of Rom 8:29, 30 shows Christians' salvation to have continuity by portraying it as a series of interconnected divine initiatives leading to conformity to the Son of God in glorification and inheritance with Christ as the final goal of this salvation. Paul inspires in his Christian readers certainty that their salvation will be fully realized because each manifestation of God's saving work toward them leads with certainty to that final goal. God as the author of salvation guarantees its continuity.

---

[32] See *BDF* §493, 3.

[33] Wesley, *Notes*, 406.

[34] Lagrange (*Rom*, 217) introduces a false distinction when he argues that Rom 8:29, 30 gives assurance of the final salvation of Christians as a group, but not as individuals. For Paul the individual Christian is always a member of the Christian community and the community always made up of individuals. There can be no certainty for the group then without certainty for its individual members. Cf. Luz, *Geschichtsverständnis*, 253. See also Schmithals, *Anthropologie*, 198, against the view taken by Lagrange.

2 Thessalonians 2:13, 14.[35] In 2 Thess 2:13, 14, Paul's thanksgiving for his converts encompasses the whole gamut of God's saving work toward them. His thought begins with God's choice of them "from the beginning for salvation" and culminates in God's calling them "unto obtaining the glory of our Lord Jesus Christ." The sequence election – calling – glory recalls Rom 8:29, 30, where the same stages in salvation—eternal choice, historical realization in calling and justification, future eschatological glorification—are linked together in an unambiguous affirmation of continuity in Christians' salvation. Here also the argument intends to strengthen the readers' certainty of final salvation, in spite of suffering, by rooting it in God's pre-historical choice and in God's historical calling to final salvation. The Thessalonians should remain undaunted by persecution since they know that their future rests secure in the fulfillment of God's saving purpose for them.[36] In the following discussion I will examine the motifs of

---

[35] The authenticity of 2 Thessalonians has become widely disputed during the past two decades. The major objections arise from a comparison with 1 Thessalonians and are both formal and theological in nature. Yet the difficulties are not insurmountable. The somewhat less personal tone of 2 Thessalonians is not without parallel in Paul's epistles and seems justified here in view of the seriousness of the problem addressed. To put down the false teaching that the Day of the Lord had already come, 2 Thessalonians argues that certain other events must precede it. 1 Thessalonians does not necessarily contradict these points, however, by its stress on the imminence of the parousia and its unexpected timing. It is even conceivable that the first letter (presumably 1 Thessalonians) could have contributed to the development of a situation which required the different teaching given in 2 Thessalonians. The new situation calls for particular doctrinal and parenetic emphases, and other topics are left aside so that "characteristic" Pauline doctrines do not appear. Their absence may also indicate that Timothy and esp. Silvanus played a significant role in the co-authorship of the epistle (cf. 2 Thess 1:1; see Bruce's discussion on authorship, *Thess*, xxxii–xlvii). The similarities in structure and wording of the epistles need not imply that a pseudonymous author used 1 Thessalonians to compose 2 Thessalonians, but can be attributed to close proximity in date of composition, similarity of subject matter, and adherence to epistolary convention. Other literary arguments are also not compelling. The reference to the temple as still standing in 2 Thessalonians 2 as well as other indications of the epistle's primitive character combine with the improbability that a pseudonymous letter written in Paul's name would have circulated before his death to favor Pauline authorship. The argument for authenticity, besides not crumbling under recent criticisms, has early church tradition on its side. This is not the time or place to examine the individual arguments in detail. For a fresh and much fuller discussion which comes down on the side of Pauline authorship, see, e.g., Marshall, *Thess*, 28–45 (for the same view, see also Kümmel, *Einleitung*, 228–232). In view of the strong case which can be made for the authenticity of 2 Thessalonians, I will proceed to draw upon it as a source for Paul's thought on perseverance and falling away.

[36] Marshall (*Thess*, 205) describes the function of the thanksgiving as follows: "This expression is meant to have a teaching and reassuring function over against any doubts that they might have regarding the possibility of their apostasy from the faith, and so it serves as a basis for the encouragement in v. 15 to stand fast in what they have been

election, calling and obtaining glory and their implications for the Thessalonians' final destiny.

The address itself in 2:13, ἀδελφοὶ ἠγαπημένοι ὑπὸ κυρίου,[37] anticipates the theme of election which it introduces.[38] Divine love comes to expression in election (cf. 1 Thess 1:4; also Rom 1:7; Jude 1) and forms a bond between God and God's elect. The perfect tense of the participle ἠγαπημένοι points to the enduring quality of God's love toward those chosen[39] and thus parallels the thought in Rom 8:35–39, where election is also a predominant motif, that "nothing can separate us from the love of God in Christ Jesus."

The rare εἵλατο,[40] drawn from the rich variety of Paul's predestinarian vocabulary,[41] denotes the act of election here. This election takes place in God's eternal counsel. The antecedent nature of election is often denoted by the prefix προ- in predestinarian vocabulary, as in προγινώσκειν, προορίζειν, προτίθημι. Or it can become explicit in an explanatory phrase (e.g., πρὸ τῶν αἰώνων, 1 Cor 2:7; cf. Eph 1:4).[42] In 2 Thess 2:13 most exegetes see the pre-historical dimension of election expressed by ἀπ' ἀρχῆς: "God chose you from the beginning (of time)." Those who prefer the variant reading ἀπαρχήν, however, would of course fail to find an explicit reference to the pre-historicity of election. Both variants can claim strong MS support, ἀπ' ἀρχῆς, however, perhaps better.[43] Further, the statement which results from the text-critical decision for ἀπαρχήν—"God chose you as firstfruits"—is difficult. To say that the Thessalonians were "first converts" (in their region) would not make good sense in the context,

---

taught."

[37] ὑπὸ κυρίου refers to the Lord Jesus Christ and thus associates Christ's love for the elect with God's electing love (so Marshall, *Thess*, 206; *et al.*). Cf. the reference to God the Father's love in 2:16.

[38] Cf. Trilling, *2 Thess*, 120.

[39] Best, *Thess*, 71; Morris, *Thess*, 237; v. Dobschütz, *Thess*, 69.

[40] With the present meaning, only here in the NT. Cf. its use in Deut 26:18 LXX for God's election of Israel; so also προαιρεῖσθαι at Deut 7:6–8; 10:15 LXX. The last cited references combine the motif of election with that of divine love, as in 2 Thess 2:13.

[41] For the variety of terms used, see, e.g., Rom 8:29, 30; 1 Cor 1:27, 28; 1 Thess 1:4; 5:9; cf. Eph 1:4, 5, 11.

[42] Cf. Hofius, "Erwählt," 123–128, for a study of the notion of a pretemporal or premundane election in early Christianity and ancient Judaism.

[43] ἀπ' ἀρχῆς is supported by ℵ D K L Ψ most minuscules it d,g,61,86 syr p cop sa arm eth *al* (Metzger, *Textual Commentary*, 636). ἀπαρχήν can also claim good support, including the impressive witness of B, though its authority is not as great with respect to Pauline, as to gospel, texts. Since the decision between variants is not easy to make on the basis of textual evidence, other arguments will have to bear the weight of the final decision.

nor is it historically accurate—the Philippians preceded them. We ought therefore to reject the reading ἀπαρχήν as a scribal error, possibly arising from the substitution of a familiar Pauline word for a phrase unknown in Paul's other writings.[44] The decision for ἀπ' ἀρχῆς then makes election explicitly eternal here.

Some who read ἀπ' ἀρχῆς, however, identify ἀρχή as a beginning in history, namely, the beginning of the Christian missionary movement, or the preaching in Thessalonica itself (cf. Phil 4:15).[45] But the context strongly favors a reference to a beginning *before* history. For the readers' historical calling through the gospel in v. 14 presupposes and makes manifest God's *pre*-historical choice.[46] In our text Paul intends to build the Thessalonians' certainty of salvation on the most immovable ground, God's election in eternity.[47] To say less is to weaken Paul's argument significantly. It appears, therefore, that we should understand the phrase ἀπ' ἀρχῆς here as in Matt 19:4; 1 John 2:13; Isa 63:16; Sir 24:9 (cf. John 1:1, 2) to designate the beginning of time.[48]

God's election of believers from the beginning of time is an election "unto salvation."[49] σωτηρία encompasses the entire work of salvation here[50] but looks forward especially to future completed salvation (cf. 1 Thess 5:8, 9).[51] The persecuted Thessalonian Christians' ultimate destiny contrasts with the condemnation at the Lord's coming of "those who did not believe in the truth" and "who are [already] perishing" (2:10–12).[52] εἰς

---

[44] See, further, Marshall, *Thess*, 207; also v. Dobschütz, *Thess*, 298, n. 3; Morris, *Thess*, 238, n. 48.

[45] For representatives of this view, see v. Dobschütz, *Thess*, 298.

[46] Marshall, *Kept*, 101.

[47] V. Dobschütz, *Thess*, 298: "Diese Erwählung wird durch ἀπ' ἀρχῆς als eine ur-anfängliche, von Ewigkeit her bestehende, und darum durch nichts zu erschütternde bezeichnet." Similarly, Marshall, *Thess*, 207. See v. Dobschütz's criticisms of the other view. Best (*Thess*, 312) observes that "the Thessalonians' assurance of salvation does not rest on their own decision or conversion but on the fact that God chose them."

[48] With Marshall, *Kept*, 101; *idem*, *Thess*, 207; v. Dobschütz, *Thess*, 298; Morris, *Thess*, 237, 238; Trilling, *2 Thess*, 121; O'Brien, *Thanksgivings*, 188; Rigaux, *Thess*, 683, 684.

[49] Marshall's scepticism about a "pre-mundane election of particular individuals to salvation" (*Kept*, 239, n. 11) seems to ignore the precise wording of the text he is commenting on: εἵλατο ὑμᾶς ὁ θεὸς ἀπ' ἀρχῆς εἰς σωτηρίαν. His later commentary, however, may reflect a different understanding: "The present verses...treat of God's election of the readers to salvation" (*Thess*, 206).

[50] Marshall, *Thess*, 207; Trilling, *2 Thess*, 120; v. Dobschütz, *Thess*, 298; Best, *Thess*, 314.

[51] Cf. O'Brien, *Thanksgivings*, 188.

[52] Marshall sees a deliberate contrast (*Thess*, 207; *Kept*, 101). It should be noted that the text does not trace the destiny of *unbelievers* to God's eternal counsel.

περιποίησιν δόξης in v. 14 parallels εἰς σωτηρίαν in v. 13; thus the final aspect of salvation is attainment of the same eschatological glory ascribed to the risen Lord (δόξης τοῦ κυρίου ἡμῶν Ἰησοῦ Χριστοῦ).[53]

The purpose of election will not reach fulfillment until Christians' obtain this glory.[54] περιποίησις points to the future acquisition of glory by the elect.[55] In 1 Thess 5:9 God "appoints" (ἔθετο) believers εἰς περιποίησιν σωτηρίας διὰ τοῦ κυρίου ἡμῶν Ἰησοῦ Χριστοῦ. In this close parallel, God's election of Christians will issue in their gaining full possession of salvation at the day of the Lord.[56] Similarly, according to 2 Thess 2:13, 14, God will reach the ultimate goal of the election of the Thessalonians to salvation when they enter into full possession of the glory of Christ.

As W. Trilling observes, this text presents the Christian life as unfolding between the two poles of election and salvation.[57] Whatever happens between these poles in present experience—persecution, etc.—two things are certain: God has elected Christians from the beginning of time and he will finish their salvation. Election to salvation therefore offers certain hope to the Thessalonian Christians that not the trials of the present moment but the eternal saving purpose of God is the all-important reality in their lives.

Between the two poles there is a mid-point at which God's sovereign hand upon believers is also evident. It is the point where eternal election becomes manifest in history and where the salvation which will culminate in glory becomes part of human experience in divine calling. "He called you through our gospel" denotes God's effectual calling of believers when they respond in faith to the preached gospel.[58] εἰς ὃ immediately precedes ἐκάλεσεν ὑμᾶς. Most probably, Paul means to connect the thought of calling with that of election to salvation (εἰς σωτηρίαν)[59] by indicating that God is working out God's salvific purpose in election as God calls the elect to salvation (εἰς ὃ [καὶ] ἐκάλεσεν) through sanctification and faith. "To this (end)[60] he called you" thus adds another reason for the Thessalonians to be certain of their final salvation.

---

53 O'Brien, *Thanksgivings*, 188.

54 Best, *Thess*, 316; similarly, Trilling, *2 Thess*, 121.

55 Cf. 1 Thess 2:12, ὁ καλῶν ὑμᾶς εἰς...δόξαν; also, Rom 8: 28b–30, where Paul connects election with final glorification. "Obtaining the glory of Christ" at 2 Thess 2:14 harks back to 1:10: ὅταν ἔλθῃ ἐνδοξασθῆναι ἐν τοῖς ἁγίοις αὐτοῦ (Marshall, *Thess*, 208; cf. Rom 8:17).

56 See treatment of 1 Thess 5:9 below, pp. 21–27.

57 Trilling, *2 Thess*, 120.

58 Morris, *Thess*, 239; similarly, Best, *Thess*, 315, 316; Marshall, *Thess*, 208.

59 For εἰς ὃ as a construction connecting two thoughts, cf. 1:11. It has this function here (with v. Dobschütz, *Thess*, 300; Trilling, *2 Thess*, 122, n. 520).

60 So Marshall, *Thess*, 208.

In summary, 2 Thess 2:13, 14 lays a firm foundation for Christians' salvation by emphasizing God's own action toward this end. God loves the Thessalonians. God has chosen them from the beginning of time. The intention of divine election is their salvation. God has called them, and now they believe in the gospel and already enjoy its benefits. God purposes to complete their salvation; they can therefore look forward confidently to eschatological acquisition of glory.

Is it one-sided, however, to make only God's action toward believers the ground of their assurance of salvation in this text? Does the text in fact also draw attention to the readers' own part in ensuring that present salvation leads to its fulfillment? Should we see an exhortation to human effort in the phrase περιποίησις δόξης (v. 14), or a reminder that Christians must cooperate with God in the words ἐν ἁγιασμῷ πνεύματος καὶ πίστει ἀληθείας (v. 13), which follow σωτηρία? In short, does the text give assurance of salvation based on God's action under the condition that believers meet the requirements placed on them?

Undoubtedly, περιποίησις is used here as a *nomen actionis* in which Christians are the subjects of "obtaining."[61] This observation, however, does not necessarily lead to the conclusion that περιποίησις denotes human effort toward obtaining glory. Rather, as I. H. Marshall comments, "the phrase simply means 'to obtain possession' and allows (but does not demand) human cooperation with God in attaining that goal."[62] Elsewhere Christians do not earn glory; God bestows it on them (Rom 8:17c, 18, 30; 9:23; 2 Cor 3:18).[63] Instead of indicating that believers must do something to obtain glory,[64] περιποίησις "may be meant to stress the reality of the possession of this glory in face of the fact that some in Thessalonica all too readily became downhearted."[65] The future event of inheriting the glory to which they are heirs[66] pictured in the expression περιποίησις δόξης should give them renewed confidence of their final salvation.

ἐν ἁγιασμῷ πνεύματος καὶ πίστει ἀληθείας describes how God's

---

[61] O'Brien, *Thanksgivings*, 191; *et al.*

[62] Marshall, *Thess*, 209. Marshall's comment is aimed against Trilling, who claims, "Die eigene Aktivität des Menschen ist in jedem Fall angesprochen" (*2 Thess*, 123), and concludes, "Müßten wir bei dem Verfasser vielleicht doch eine Unklarheit über die kompromißlose paulinische Gnadenlehre mit einbeziehen?" (123). Similarly, Rigaux, *Thess*, 686.

[63] Selwyn, *1 Peter*, 167. Cf. 1 Thess 5:9, where περιποίησις σωτηρίας is traced to God's action: διὰ τοῦ κυρίου ἡμῶν Ἰησοῦ Χριστοῦ (see pp. 25, 26 below). Cf. also Col 3:4; 2 Tim 2:10.

[64] Against v. Dobschütz, *Thess*, 300.

[65] Morris, *Thess*, 239. Similarly, O'Brien, *Thanksgivings*, 191.

[66] Cf. this language in Rom 8:17.

election to salvation is worked out in the Christian life.[67] πνεῦμα is not the human spirit as the object of sanctification here (the genitive is not objective) but God's Spirit who sanctifies the elect (the genitive is subjective).[68] In the text, "sanctification by the Spirit" comes before "faith in the truth,"[69] a punctual action,[70] and for that reason probably refers to the initial "setting apart" of the convert (cf. 1 Cor 6:11; 1:2; also Eph 5:26)[71] rather than to the ongoing sanctifying activity of the Spirit.[72] Commentators generally make the observation that attention shifts from God's action in sanctifying by the Spirit to human action in πίστις ἀληθείας. This comment is appropriate in that Paul never conceives of salvation apart from human faith. The order of the actions here, however, may suggest that the work of the Spirit gives rise to human faith.[73] The reference to human faith therefore does not introduce ambiguity about the Thessalonians' final salvation.[74] For God not only elects to salvation but also supplies the means to realize this purpose, namely, sanctification and faith.[75] Attributing the means to salvation to God matches the text's strong emphasis on God's activity as the ground of assurance of salvation.[76]

In conclusion, 2 Thess 2:13, 14 bolsters Christians in persecution by showing that God's will to save them overarches their whole existence. They can trace it to the beginning of time. They can see it in their own calling through the gospel, their sanctification and faith in the truth. And they can therefore hope confidently for its completion through their future acquisition of the glory of Christ. With this assurance they will be able to "stand fast" (v. 15).

---

[67] So v. Dobschütz, *Thess*, 299; Trilling, *2 Thess*, 121.

[68] Cf. 1 Cor 6:11, ἡγιάσθητε; 1 Thess 4:7, 8; also 1 Pet 1:2. So, Trilling, *2 Thess*, 121; Marshall, *Thess*, 207; Morris, *Thess*, 238; Rigaux, *Thess*, 684, 685; *et al.* See Morris' arguments against taking πνεύματος here as an objective genitive (238).

[69] ἀληθείας is best taken as an objective genitive in view of the parallelism with 2:12, where ἀλήθεια is the object of faith (οἱ μὴ πιστεύσαντες τῇ ἀληθείᾳ, see, e.g., Best, *Thess*, 315; v. Dobschütz, *Thess*, 299). Here ἀλήθεια means the gospel as God's revealed truth (cf. Gal 5:7; so, e.g., Marshall, *Thess*, 207; Morris, *Thess*, 238).

[70] Cf. Best, *Thess*, 315.

[71] Cf. Chrysostom, *Hom. in ep. II ad Thess.*, 488.

[72] Otherwise the sequence is odd. But v. Dobschütz (*Thess*, 300) sees both. Contrast Best, *Thess*, 315.

[73] So v. Dobschütz, *Thess*, 299; O'Brien, *Thanksgivings*, 186, 187, n. 122; cf. Marshall, *Thess*, 207.

[74] So, apparently, Marshall (*Kept*, 101): "But although this has been God's purpose all along for them, it depends upon their sanctification and faith."

[75] So v. Dobschütz, *Thess*, 299; O'Brien, *Thanksgivings*, 188.

[76] Cf. O'Brien, *Thanksgivings*, 186.

1 Thessalonians 5:9. In 1 Thess 5:9 Paul declares in no uncertain terms what Christians' final destiny will be: "God has not appointed us to wrath but to obtaining salvation."[77] Paul formulates his assertion both negatively and positively for emphasis. The favorable final outcome of salvation is attributed to divine appointment: οὐκ ἔθετο ἡμᾶς ὁ Θεὸς εἰς ὀργὴν ἀλλὰ εἰς περιποίησιν σωτηρίας.[78] τιθέναι εἰς denotes divine determination unto something, as also in Acts 13:47 (Isa 49:6 LXX); 1 Pet 2:8 (cf. John 15:16, τ. ἵνα). In the present instance, the verb comes close in meaning to "predestine" or "elect" (cf. προορίζειν, προγινώσκειν, or ἐκλέγεσθαι[79]).[80] God has a set purpose toward believers which God will most assuredly carry out in accomplishing their salvation.[81] Though Paul does not specify where divine "appointing" takes place, we might locate it in God's eternal counsel[82] or in the act of baptism.[83] In either case, the notion of divine appointment to salvation serves to make the outcome of Christians' salvation certain.

According to God's fixed purpose, God has exempted Christians from the eschatological wrath to be poured out at the "day of wrath" associated with the last judgment (cf. Rom 2:5). As Paul has already told the Thessalonians in 1:10, "Jesus...saves us from the coming wrath."[84] God's determining that Christians should not suffer the future wrath comes to realization in the action of Christ, ὁ ῥυόμενος ἡμᾶς ἐκ τῆς ὀργῆς τῆς ἐρχομένης. Thus, in 5:9, 10a Paul does not fail to note that "God has appointed us not to wrath but to obtaining salvation διὰ τοῦ κυρίου ἡμῶν Ἰησοῦ Χριστοῦ τοῦ ἀποθανόντος ὑπὲρ ἡμῶν." Through the cross of Christ the judgment of God's wrath gives way to the hope of salvation (ἐλπὶς σωτηρίας, 5:8)[85] for Christians. This happens in fulfillment of God's plan.

---

[77] Mattern (*Gericht*, 78) notes here that "alle Christen ohne Ausnahme sind zur περιποίησις σωτηρίας prädestiniert."

[78] Morris, *Thess*, 160.

[79] Cf. the parallelism in John 15:16: ἐξελεξάμην ὑμᾶς καὶ ἔθηκα ὑμᾶς ἵνα....

[80] So Harnisch, *Existenz*, 147; Maurer, τίθημι, *TWNT* 8, 157; Schlier, *Apostel*, 91 v. Dobschütz, *Thess*, 212; Mattern, *Gericht*, 78; Morris, *Thess*, 160.

[81] Schlier (*Apostel*, 91) comments that τιθέναι "meint hier die göttliche Bestimmung und Setzung, die göttlicher Gedanke, Wille und Tat in einem ist."

[82] V. Dobschütz (*Thess*, 212) explains τιθέναι as the "vorweltliche Bestimmung Gottes."

[83] So Thüsing, *Per Christum*, 203.

[84] For the future eschatological wrath, see also Rom 2:8; 5:9; possibly also Rom 12:19; cf. also Col 3:6; Eph 5:6. On ὀργή as eschatological in 1 Thess 1:10 and 5:9, see Best, *Thess*, 216, *et al.*

[85] On the relation between οὐκ ἔθετο ἡμᾶς ὁ Θεὸς εἰς... (5:9) and the immediately preceding ἐλπὶς σωτηρίας (5:8), see p. 27 below.

God's fixed purpose toward Christians includes their obtaining final salvation (περιποίησις σωτηρίας). The antithetical parallel to exemption
from *future* wrath in 5:9 is participation in the *future* completion of salvation.[86] σωτηρία has a final sense at 5:9, as it does at 5:8, where Paul speaks
of Christians' "hope of salvation" (ἐλπὶς σωτηρίας).[87] In 5:10 Paul describes this future salvation as life with Christ, who "died for us so that
we...might live with him" (σὺν αὐτῷ ζήσωμεν, cf. 4:17; Rom 6:8; 2 Cor
4:14; Phil 1:23).[88] The fact that Paul applies to those who "sleep," i.e., the
dead, as well as those who "watch," i.e., the living, this promise of life with
Christ shows that he is thinking of the consummation of salvation at the
end time.

Paul juxtaposes "wrath" and "obtaining salvation" when he specifies
his readers' divine appointment: οὐκ...εἰς ὀργὴν ἀλλὰ εἰς περιποίησιν
σωτηρίας. The antithetical parallel is inexact, however. In the first member
believers are the implied *objects* of ὀργή. But Paul makes them the implied
grammatical *subjects* of the *nomen actionis*, περιποίησις, in the second
member.[89] With the formulation περιποίησις σωτηρίας he switches perspectives from "us" (ἡμᾶς) as objects to "we" as subjects of obtaining. This
grammatical shift raises the question whether περιποίησις σωτηρίας includes human effort. E. v. Dobschütz thinks that Paul wants to call attention
to the "notwendige Beteiligung seitens des Menschens" in the "Erwerbung
des Heils."[90] Thus the verse would mean that God appoints believers to *act
so as to gain* salvation—far short of an appointment to be beneficiaries of
salvation! Moreover, Paul's call to vigilance and sobriety in the context
(5:6, 8) is seen to serve this activistic understanding of περιποίησις[91] and
thus to suggest the possibility of losing salvation instead of gaining it. In
the words of E. Best: "Salvation may be lost through lack of vigilance but
it will not be gained by its exercise alone, except by those who have
already responded to the gospel."[92]

---

[86] Thüsing, *Per Christum*, 203.

[87] With Thüsing, *Per Christum*, 203; cf. Mattern, *Gericht*, 81; v. Dobschütz, *Thess*,
213.

[88] Harnisch, *Existenz*, 149; Mattern, *Gericht*, 81; Marshall, *Thess*, 141. In the light
of 4:17, we must judge the infrequent interpretation of ζήσωμεν as referring to the present ethical life of Christians to have clearly missed Paul's point. See, further, Harnisch's
criticisms, 150, 151; also v. Dobschütz, *Thess*, 213.

[89] Contrast the absolute use of περιποίησις (1 Pet 2:9) which denotes the object
possessed ("possession, property"; see BAGD, s.v. περιποίησις, 3).

[90] V. Dobschütz, *Thess*, 212 with n. 3. Similarly, Marshall, *Thess*, 139; Schlier,
Apostel, 92; Friedrich, *1 Thess*, 246; Neil, *Thess*, 117.

[91] So, e.g., v. Dobschütz, *Thess*, 212.

[92] Best, *Thess*, 217. See also Rigaux, *Thess*, 569, 571.

Does Paul thus here fall short of saying that God's appointment of Christians certainly entails their final salvation and that they can expect without a doubt to gain full possession of it? Instead does he view his readers as appointed to acquire salvation actively, lest they lose it? Just what does περιποίησις mean here, and what should we make of the fact that the Thessalonians are the implied grammatical subjects of περιποίησις σωτηρίας at 1 Thess 5:9?

Although περιποίησις can have the passive meaning "possession," as translated in absolute usage (see 1 Pet 2:9),[93] commentators generally do not take it to designate Christians as God's "possession" here, where it is followed by the genitive σωτηρίας.[94] Instead, the term is understood as a *nomen actionis* and translated "acquiring, obtaining, gaining possession of."[95] Further περιποίησις is usually taken to refer not simply to the act of taking possession but to effortful acquisition on the part of the acquirer.[96] Thus Paul would mean that the Thessalonians' gaining possession of salvation occurs on account of their own exertion. In the following discussion I will address the question whether Paul considers his readers to be active or passive subjects of περιποίησις σωτηρίας.[97]

Word usage shows that περιποίησις σωτηρίας need not entail the Thessalonians' own action toward acquisition of salvation. περιποίησις c. gen. at 2 Thess 2:14 does not necessarily imply that the subject acts in order to obtain.[98] Nor do extra-biblical uses always require such a connotation.[99] The word itself says nothing about the *means* of gaining possession but says only *that* possession is gained by the grammatical subject of περιποίησις, whether through the expenditure of the subject's own effort or through the effort of another. I. H. Marshall's cautious judgment on περιποίησις at 2 Thess 2:14 is worth repeating here: "The phrase simply means 'to obtain possession' and allows (but does not demand) human co-operation with God in attaining that goal."[100]

---

[93] But see p. 24 below on Eph 1:14.

[94] So Thüsing, *Per Christum*, 203, n. 103; Best, *Thess*, 216, 217. But see Schlier, *Apostel*, 92.

[95] See BAGD, s.v. περιποίησις, 2; LSJ, s.v. περιποίησις; Best, *Thess*, 217, *et al.*

[96] For the latter view, see n. 90 above.

[97] Rigaux (*Thess*, 571) seems to make this distinction between active and passive subjects when he says: "Nous voudrions cependant donner à περιποίησις non pas le sens d'obtention, d'acquisition, mais de possession du salut, la propriété du salut."

[98] See p. 19 above. Heb. 10:39 is not a parallel, for there περιποίησις c. gen. means "preservation, protection."

[99] Cf. P. Tebt. 317.26 (see Preisigke, *Wörterbuch* II, s.v. περιποίησις 1: "das Übrig-sein, Erwerb, Besitz"); Vett. Val. 85.16; Justinian *Edict* 13.15.

[100] Marshall, *Thess*, 209.

An example of the use of περιποίησις as a *nomen actionis* with a *passive* subject might be present at Eph 1:14, where the term appears in the absolute. This verse speaks of the Spirit as the ἀρραβὼν τῆς κληρονομίας ἡμῶν, εἰς ἀπολύτρωσιν τῆς περιποιήσεως. R. Schnackenburg argues that the active meaning here, "Inbesitznahme," (so at 1 Thess 5:9; 2 Thess 2:14) is preferable to the passive "Eigentum," which the readers could have understood only with difficulty, and which would not refer to the people of God (as his "possession," so 1 Pet 2:9), since Ephesians lacks this concept. Therefore, he interprets the phrase to mean "die Erlösung, nämlich die Inbesitznahme (des Erbes)."[101] This understanding of περιποίησις here as taking possession of one's *inheritance* excludes the idea of exerting effort toward possession. For an heir *receives* the inheritance on the basis of *status*—not activity—because she *is* an heir. Eph 1:14 thus could provide an example of the interpretation of περιποίησις as a *nomen actionis* which does *not* imply the subject's activity.

The same use of περιποίησις at 1 Thess 5:9 is suggested by the context. Here Paul makes the Thessalonians' *identity* significant for the coming of the day of the Lord. He describes them as υἱοὶ φωτός and υἱοὶ ἡμέρας (5:5; cf. ἡμεῖς δὲ ἡμέρας ὄντες, 5:8). "You are not in darkness, so that the day should overtake you as a thief" (5:4). Because Christians are "of the day" they can anticipate taking possession of salvation "at the day of the Lord," to which God has appointed them. It is God's making them to be such people that results in their obtaining salvation.

Thus word usage does not lead to the conclusion that περιποίησις σωτηρίας envisages the Thessalonians' effort to obtain salvation; instead it allows that their obtaining takes place without their own effort. This understanding finds further support from the context of 1 Thess 5:9. Paul's statement that "God has not appointed us to wrath" relativizes human action. For it makes believers exempt from divine wrath on the basis of God's action toward them, namely, God's graciousness in spite of their sinfulness. The negation οὐκ ἔθετο ἡμᾶς ὁ Θεὸς εἰς ὀργήν "macht...die dem Christen bestimmte σωτηρία als ein sich *sola gratia* ereignendes Geschehen verständlich."[102] Paul's negative formulation of Christians' destiny provides an essential clarification of his positive formulation by showing "daß die Prädestination der Glaubenden zur περιποίησις σωτηρίας auf einem Akt göttlicher χάρις beruht, d.h., 'das gnädige Handeln des Richters' an der ὀργή verdienenden Menschheit darstellt."[103]

---

101 Schnackenburg, *Eph*, 65, 66.
102 Harnisch, *Existenz*, 146; cf. Mattern, *Gericht*, 81, n. 141.
103 Harnisch, *Existenz*, 146.

In 1 Thess 5:9 Paul sets up a contrast between ὀργή and περιποίησις σωτηρίας. God has not appointed Christians to the former but to the latter. Since God is the subject of ὀργή, we expect him also to be the subject of the counterpart to ὀργή. And Paul's formal switch in perspectives from human objects of wrath to human subjects of obtaining salvation will not fool us into abandoning this expectation. For, although the antithetical parallel is formally inexact, it is not so materially. Paul wants the Thessalonians to know what to expect from *God's* hand at the last day. They will not receive wrath, but the fulfillment of their salvation. Thus, God is the actual "subject" of περιποίησις σωτηρίας in bringing Christians into full possession of salvation.

What is implied in the contrast οὐκ εἰς ὀργὴν ἀλλὰ εἰς περιποίησιν σωτηρίας is made explicit in the immediately succeeding prepositional phrase διὰ τοῦ κυρίου ἡμῶν Ἰησοῦ Χριστοῦ. God has appointed us to obtain salvation "through our Lord Jesus Christ." Most interpreters take the phrase to qualify περιποίησις σωτηρίας and thus deduce, rightly, Christ's mediating role in the gaining of final salvation.[104] Paul's identification of Christ as ὁ ἀποθανὼν ὑπὲρ ἡμῶν (5:10) clarifies how Christ mediates our obtaining of salvation: because Christ died for us we gain salvation.[105] Paul has in view here not only present but also completed salvation as the benefit of Christ's death. For, as he goes on to say, Christ died for us "so that (ἵνα) we might live with him (5:10)." At the parousia he will make us participate in his glorious life—the ultimate goal of his death for us[106]—and so mediate in the fullest sense our gaining possession of salvation.[107] Through Christ's death (and, implicitly, resurrection) Christians have a guarantee of their final salvation.[108] Paul thus attributes believers' eschatological acquisition of salvation to Christ's action. I. H. Marshall summarizes: "The obtaining of salvation takes place 'through our Lord Jesus Christ'; it rests on what he has done, and not on anything that we may do. From start to finish salvation depends on God's act in Jesus."[109] If salvation indeed depends

---

[104] So, e.g., v. Dobschütz, *Thess*, 212; Mattern, *Gericht*, 79; Fuchs, "Hermeneutik," 50. Differently, Harnisch (*Existenz*, 147, 148), who sees διὰ τοῦ κυρίου ἡμῶν Ἰησοῦ Χριστοῦ more broadly as qualifying the entire statement beginning with ἔθετο.

[105] Contrast Neil (*Thess*, 117), who sees Christians to gain salvation through the present indwelling power of Christ.

[106] Harnisch, *Existenz*, 149; Mattern, *Gericht*, 79.

[107] Thüsing, *Per Christum*, 204; v. Dobschütz, *Thess*, 212.

[108] Rigaux, *Thess*, 573. Too weakly, Schlier, *Apostel*, 92: Christ "ermöglicht" περιποίησις σωτηρίας.

[109] Marshall, *Thess*, 140. Nevertheless, Marshall's interpretation of περιποίησις σωτηρίας seems activistic: Christians must "do what is necessary to acquire salvation." Marshall sees paradox at the point of the relation of God's plan to human action (139).

entirely on God's initiative, there is no room for "sittliche Bedingtheit der Heilserlangung."[110] In summary, while the phrase περιποίησις σωτηρίας relates to the subjects of acquiring salvation—Christians—the phrase διὰ τοῦ κυρίου ἡμῶν 'Ιησοῦ Χριστοῦ identifies whose effort makes their acquisition possible—Christ's work for Christians. The view that believers obtain salvation through their own effort rides roughshod over the explicit wording of the text.

Nevertheless, some data from the context seem to support the activistic interpretation of περιποίησις σωτηρίας. Paul exhorts his readers to vigilance and sobriety in 5:6, 8. Yet this argument has little force. γρηγορῶμεν and νήφωμεν do not invoke human activity toward acquisition of salvation, but passive attentiveness in expectation of receiving salvation as a gift.[111] Not only believers who "watch" but also those who "sleep," i.e. the dead in Christ, who cannot exercise effort toward acquiring salvation, will obtain eternal life: "Whether we watch or whether we sleep we will at the same time live with him" (5:10).[112] σὺν αὐτῷ ζῆν interprets the σωτηρία of v. 9 to consist in the eschatological transformation which enables sharing life with Christ.[113] At the parousia, the dead in Christ will enter into this eschatological life[114] "simultaneously" (ἅμα; cf. 4:17)[115] with Christians who remain.[116] Human expenditure of effort in the acquisition of salvation is not in view here.

In summary, contextual considerations strongly discourage us from reading human effort into the term περιποίησις in 1 Thess 5:9. The subjects of this *nomen actionis* remain passive in their obtaining, for the obtaining is made possible through the effort of their Savior.[117]

---

110 Against v. Dobschütz, *Thess*, 212.

111 Best (*Thess*, 217) can say no more on the basis of the text than that Christians might "miss what is offered" if they are not watchful, though "the necessity of this vigilance does not imply that Paul is suggesting that man enters salvation through his own efforts."

112 Paul intends to assure Christians that final salvation is certain not only for the living but also for those who have died before the parousia (εἴτε γρηγορῶμεν εἴτε καθεύδωμεν). Cf. Eckart, "Thessalonicher," 42, n. 3.

113 Cf. Harnisch, *Existenz*, 150; Mattern, *Gericht*, 80.

114 ζήσωμεν is an inceptive aorist: "begin to live." See Best, *Thess*, 218, 219.

115 On ἅμα with σύν as temporal, see BAGD, s.v. ἅμα, 2. With Harnisch, *Existenz*, 150 with n. 43; Rigaux, *Thess*, 573; Best, *Thess*, 218.

116 With Best (*Thess*, 218) on the timing: at the parousia.

117 On this interpretation, cf. Morris, *Thess*, 161: "To adopt this understanding of it [περιποίησις σωτηρίας] is not to maintain that man is saved by works, but simply that the Christian is to make his salvation his own by entering fully into his possession. That nothing in the way of human merit or initiative is meant is made very clear by the following 'through our Lord Jesus Christ'." Cf. also Fuchs, "Hermeneutik," 50 ("Gott

The notion that God has appointed Christians not to wrath but to obtaining salvation through Christ's work (5:9, 10) grounds (ὅτι) their "hope of salvation" (ἐλπίδα σωτηρίας, 5:8).[118] Divine appointment to salvation is probably also meant to support the preceding cohortatives.[119] The certainty that believers will obtain salvation gives them reason to watch attentively for its coming.[120] We see thus that Paul's exhortations are grounded in Christians' divine appointment to salvation, not *vice versa*.[121] In conclusion, the Thessalonians should await the day of the Lord in confident hope. For they know "daß die ἡμέρα κυρίου nicht über ὀργή und σωτηρία urteilt, sondern daß dieses Urteil in der Prädestination Gottes bereits gefällt ist und der Tag des Herrn für die Christen σωτηρία bedeutet."[122]

The Spirit As Guarantee

Romans 8:23; 2 Corinthians 1:22; 5:5. In the passages to be considered in this section, Paul reveals the significance of the indwelling Spirit for Christians' future, final salvation. For Paul, the Spirit represents the eschatological factor in present Christian experience. Through the Spirit the future begins to invade the present.[123] The present indwelling of the Spirit in Christians thus becomes a guarantee that the future blessings of salvation will belong to them.[124] This significance of the indwelling Spirit comes to expression in Paul's characterization of the Spirit as ἀπαρχή (Rom 8:23) and ἀρραβών (2 Cor 1:22; 5:5; cf. Eph 1:14) and in his view that God

---

selbst hat uns das Heil erworben"), who nevertheless remained unclear on the philological problem.

[118] Mattern, *Gericht*, 78; v. Dobschütz, *Thess*, 212; Frame, *Thess*, 188.

[119] Harnisch (*Existenz*, 143) notes the difficulty of restricting the supportive function of the ὅτι-clause to a single member of the preceding section. ὅτι may also introduce the grounds for the preceding cohortatives (vv. 6, 8; so Jüngel, *Paulus und Jesus*, 67) or even the indicatives (vv. 4, 5). For representatives of these various views, see Harnisch, 143 with nn. 2, 3, 4.

[120] For Paul, God's appointment to salvation does not make human obedience superfluous; rather, obedience alone is appropriate in view of Christians' destiny. Divine determination of their destiny does not necessarily force us into saying that human beings are automatons or that exhortations are nonsensical (see esp. the discussions in Parts Two-Four). Cf. Marshall's discussion of this question, *Thess*, 139, 140.

[121] So Mattern, *Gericht*, 82. Cf. Schlatter, *Erläuterungen zum NT* 2, 104.

[122] Mattern, *Gericht*, 81.

[123] Barrett, *Gal*, 66.

[124] Sanders (*Palestinian Judaism*, 447) comments that the "conviction that Christians possess the Spirit as the present guarantee of future salvation" is one of the two most certain and consistently expressed elements in Paul's thought.

"seals" Christians with the Spirit ($\sigma\phi\rho\alpha\gamma\iota\zeta\epsilon\iota\nu$, 2 Cor 1:22; cf. Eph 1:13; 4:30). In the following discussion I will attempt to show how these metaphors illuminate the relation between the present gift of the Spirit to Christians and their future, completed salvation.

In Rom 8:18–25 Paul speaks of the anticipatory element in salvation: the "coming glory to be revealed to us" (v. 18), the awaited "sonship, the redemption of our body" (v. 23), the "unseen hope" which "we wait for with endurance" (v. 25). The terse statement $\tau\hat{\eta}$ $\dot{\epsilon}\lambda\pi\dot{\iota}\delta\iota$ $\dot{\epsilon}\sigma\dot{\omega}\theta\eta\mu\epsilon\nu$ at v. 24 sums up this characterization of present salvation well. And because Christians "are saved *in hope*" they "groan," longing for redemption (v. 23). Their groaning is not an expression of hopelessness, for they have the Spirit as an $\dot{\alpha}\pi\alpha\rho\chi\dot{\eta}$ (v. 23),[125] a "firstfruits" of the salvation yet to be completed. As $\dot{\alpha}\pi\alpha\rho\chi\dot{\eta}$ implies, they can expect this completion with confidence. They groan then in expectant and confident longing for the fullness of salvation which they have but tasted through the firstfruits of the Spirit—and *because* they have tasted it.[126]

Paul can use the term $\dot{\alpha}\pi\alpha\rho\chi\dot{\eta}$ to bring out the integral connection between the firstfruits and the complete whole from which it originates. Speaking metaphorically of Israel in Rom 11:16, he argues that the whole lump of dough is "holy" if the $\dot{\alpha}\pi\alpha\rho\chi\dot{\eta}$ is "holy."[127] Using $\dot{\alpha}\pi\alpha\rho\chi\dot{\eta}$ for Christ in 1 Cor 15:20, 23, Paul draws out the necessary implication of Christ's resurrection from the dead as $\dot{\alpha}\pi\alpha\rho\chi\dot{\eta}$ $\tau\hat{\omega}\nu$ $\kappa\epsilon\kappa\omicron\iota\mu\eta\mu\dot{\epsilon}\nu\omega\nu$ for "those who are of Christ." Their resurrection will follow Christ's: $\dot{\alpha}\pi\alpha\rho\chi\dot{\eta}$ $X\rho\iota\sigma\tau\dot{\omicron}\varsigma$, $\ddot{\epsilon}\pi\epsilon\iota\tau\alpha$ $\omicron\dot{\iota}$ $\tauο\hat{\upsilon}$ $X\rho\iota\sigma\tauο\hat{\upsilon}$ $\dot{\epsilon}\nu$ $\tau\hat{\eta}$ $\pi\alpha\rhoο\upsilon\sigma\dot{\iota}\alpha$ $\alpha\dot{\upsilon}\tauο\hat{\upsilon}$ (1 Cor 15:23). Paul is not merely giving a sequence of events here, but suggesting the relationship between them. The resurrected Christ as the "firstfruits" of those who have died functions as the guarantee of Christians' own resurrection. P. Stuhlmacher explains the sense of $\dot{\alpha}\pi\alpha\rho\chi\dot{\eta}$ here: "In der Auferweckung Jesu hat sich Gott also allen Christen schon unwiderruflich verbürgt und sie zur Hoffnung auf ihre eigene Auferstehung erst eigentlich ermächtigt."[128]

Not only is Christ the $\dot{\alpha}\pi\alpha\rho\chi\dot{\eta}$ for believers, whose resurrection is thereby guaranteed. The Spirit of Christ is the $\dot{\alpha}\pi\alpha\rho\chi\dot{\eta}$ *in* them (Rom 8:23). Because the Spirit of the resurrected Christ dwells in them, they are assured of that for which they groan, the "redemption of our body." Both in 1 Cor

---

[125] $\tauο\hat{\upsilon}$ $\pi\nu\epsilon\dot{\upsilon}\mu\alpha\tauο\varsigma$ is a genitive of apposition to $\dot{\alpha}\pi\alpha\rho\chi\dot{\eta}$, with Michel, *Röm*, 270; Käsemann, *Rom*, 237; Cranfield, *Rom*, 418.

[126] Cf. Hofius, "Hoffnung," 7.

[127] On this verse, see pp. 185–187 below.

[128] Stuhlmacher, "Gegenwart und Zukunft," 444–445. Cf. also Sand, $\dot{\alpha}\pi\alpha\rho\chi\dot{\eta}$, *EWNT* 1, 278.

15:20, 23 and Rom 8:23, where the context is the consummation of Christians' salvation, Paul introduces the metaphor of the "firstfruits." In each instance, ἀπαρχή supplies the crucial thought of a divine guarantee that present salvation will issue in future final salvation. By giving the Spirit to believers and thereby catching them up in God's work of salvation, God pledges faithfully to bring that work to completion in their lives.[129]

If any doubt remains about the precise significance of the metaphor ἀπαρχή as applied to the Spirit, Rom 8:11 clearly dispels it. There Paul states in the plainest terms the significance of the indwelling Spirit for Christians' future resurrection.[130] "If the Spirit of the one who raised Jesus from the dead dwells in you, he who raised Christ from the dead will make alive your mortal bodies also through[131] his Spirit who dwells in you." E. Käsemann sees the Spirit's function here, too, as a "pledge that we shall be made like the resurrected Christ."[132]

Further, Paul can borrow commercial terminology to express essentially the same significance of the Spirit as a pledge of final redemption. In 2 Cor 1:22 and 5:5 he calls the Spirit given to Christians an ἀρραβών, or "deposit."[133] The term refers literally to the downpayment on a purchase, which as a rule effected the transfer of that object to the purchaser and thereby obligated the latter to full payment.[134] Paul finds the image appropriate to describe Christians' redemption, the beginning of which is marked by God's "giving the deposit of the Spirit in our hearts" (2 Cor 1:22) and thus making them God's possession to no less a degree than in the commercial transaction alluded to. Just as the delay of full payment does not make the purchase any less valid, so the present incompleteness of Christians' redemption does not leave their status in question. "Der Getaufte *ist* rechtskräftig gekauft, losgekauft, hat einen neuen Herrn und ist seines

---

[129] Cf. Cranfield, *Rom*, 418: "What the believer has already received is a foretaste and a guarantee of what he has still to hope for."

[130] ζωοποιεῖν at Rom 8:11 does not have an ethical meaning, with Cranfield, *Rom*, 391; Wilckens, *Röm* I, 134; *et al.*; against Calvin, *Rom, ad loc.*

[131] If we prefer the accusative reading διὰ τὸ ἐνοικοῦν αὐτοῦ πνεῦμα with B and other reliable MSS, we will take the Spirit to be the "guarantee" (Michel, *Röm*, 255) of future resurrection. Since this is the function Paul gives the Spirit in the verse as a whole, however, the decision between readings makes little material difference (cf. Käsemann, *Rom*, 225).

[132] Käsemann, *Rom*, 237.

[133] Käsemann (*Rom*, 237) claims this meaning for ἀπαρχή also in Rom 8:23. For him and others (e.g., Stuhlmacher, "Gegenwart und Zukunft," 445; Dinkler, "Taufterminologie," 114), the meanings of ἀπαρχή and ἀρραβών mesh in Paul's description of the Spirit. At 2 Cor 1:22, τοῦ πνεύματος is a genitive of apposition to ἀρραβών, with Dinkler, 114.

[134] Dinkler, "Taufterminologie," 115; Sand, ἀρραβών, *EWNT* 1, 379.

Schutzes sicher. Und doch ist der Loskaufsprozeß nicht abgeschlossen."[135]

Not only does the downpayment of the Spirit sufficiently secure Christians as God's own. The Spirit given to believers also functions as a divine promise and guarantee that the redemptive process will be completed.[136] Final salvation is as certain to follow the gift of the Spirit as full payment must by law succeed the deposit for a purchase. Paul drives home the message of God's faithfulness in the work of salvation by using the familiar language of legally binding business transactions which alludes to the practice of the handing over of an *ἀρραβών* with its ensuing financial obligations. Believers have in the indwelling Spirit, then, a sign that God is committed to their full redemption. This outcome is entirely dependent on God's faithfulness, as the metaphor implies.[137] Thus, although Christian experience reflects the eschatological tension of the dawn of salvation, believers nevertheless live in confident hope based on a divine guarantee.[138]

In 2 Cor 1:22 Paul gains further inspiration from the commercial metaphor as he elucidates the gift of the Spirit with the term *σφραγίζειν*. In the ancient world an object was sealed primarily to indicate ownership and guard against theft or falsification.[139] The seal thus provided both authentication and protection. Paul says here that God has "sealed us and gives us the downpayment of the Spirit in our hearts." Ephesians gives us a more precise explanation of the connection between sealing and the Spirit. At Eph 1:13 we read that Christians "have been sealed with the Holy Spirit of promise." And 4:30 speaks of "the Holy Spirit of God with whom you have been sealed."[140] By putting the Spirit in believers God marks them out as a divine possession and places them under divine protective care.[141]

---

[135] Dinkler, "Taufterminologie," 115.

[136] Bruce calls this function of the Spirit "Paul's distinctive contribution to the NT doctrine of the Holy Spirit" (*Eph*, 266). Dinkler ("Taufterminologie," 114) finds the unspoken but understood reason why the Spirit is given as an *ἀρραβών* according to 2 Cor 1:22; 5:5—namely, for eschatological salvation and full reception of the inheritance—to be expressed in Eph 1:14, where the Spirit is the "down-payment of our inheritance for the redemption of [God's own] possession." See, further, Sand, *ἀρραβών*, *EWNT* 1, 379.

[137] Baumert (*Sterben*, 211) presses the analogy too far by speaking of "beidseitige Verpflichtung."

[138] Cf. Dinkler, "Taufterminologie," 115. Paul associates the Spirit as *ἀρραβών* directly with Christians' "groaning" under the weight of mortality in 2 Cor 5:4, 5 (on this relation, see Sand, *ἀρραβών*, *EWNT* 1, 379; Balz, *Heilsvertrauen*, 56).

[139] See Fitzer, *σφραγίς*, *TWNT* 7, 940, 941; Barrett, *2 Cor*, 79.

[140] Cf. Isa 44:3, 5 LXX, where the Lord's promise to "pour out my Spirit on your offspring" parallels the motif of eschatological sealing: "Another will write, 'Belonging to God'." BAGD, s.v. *σφραγίζω*, 2.b., lists this text among the references to eschatological sealing.

[141] Do the sealing and giving of the *ἀρραβών* as well as other motifs in 2 Cor 1:21,

For the discussion of perseverance the protection guaranteed by the seal is of utmost importance,[142] especially since this function of the seal recurs in eschatological contexts in both OT-Jewish and Christian literature. The angels of Revelation 7 must "seal (σφραγίσωμεν) the servants of our God upon their foreheads" before they "harm the earth and the sea and the trees" in execution of divine judgment (v. 3). Those marked with the "seal of the living God" (σφραγίς, v. 2; cf. ἐσφραγισμένοι, vv. 4, 5, 8) are then kept safe from the eschatological wrath.[143] We also find the concept of sealing as an eschatological safeguard in Ezek 9:4–6, where the Lord commands the messengers of punishment to "put a mark[144] on the foreheads of the people who sigh and groan over all the abominations which are being committed" in Jerusalem and "not [to] touch anyone on whom is the mark" when they strike the city with judgment.[145] According to *Ps. Sol.* 15:10–12, the inheritance of sinners is destruction and darkness, and they will perish in the day of the Lord's judgment; but "the seal[146] of God is upon the righteous εἰς σωτηρίαν" (*Ps. Sol.* 15:6). In these texts the purpose of sealing is the eschatological preservation of God's own (cf. also 4 Ezra 6:5, 6; 8:51ff.).[147]

This eschatological orientation of the protective sealing is also prominent in the notion of sealing with the Spirit in Ephesians. The very designation "Holy Spirit of promise" (Eph 1:13) to denote the Spirit with which believers are sealed expresses this orientation. The genitive τῆς ἐπαγγελίας probably refers to the promise of future glory for those indwelt by the Holy Spirit.[148] The parallel description of the Holy Spirit in v. 14 as the "ἀρραβών of our inheritance" favors this view. Moreover, Ephesians tells us that the sealing of Christians with the Spirit reaches its ultimate goal in their final redemption. Those who have believed are "sealed (ἐσφραγίσθητε) with the Holy Spirit of promise...εἰς ἀπολύτρωσιν τῆς

---

22 recall the event of baptism, as Dinkler argues ("Taufterminologie," 103)? Barrett thinks Dinkler has "exaggerated" the evidence (*2 Cor*, 80, 81).

[142] Marshall (*Kept*, 108) pays too little attention to the protective aspect of sealing.

[143] Cf. Schippers, "Seal," *NIDNTT* 3, 500; Fitzer, σφραγίς, *TDNT* 7, 951.

[144] Ezek 9:4–6 LXX has σημεῖον for "seal," just as Paul uses the word with this meaning in Rom 4:11, cf. BAGD, s.v. σημεῖον, 1.

[145] Cf. Zimmerli, *Ezech*, 226.

[146] Here σημεῖον. See n. 144 above.

[147] Lampe (*Seal*, 16) comments that "it is against this background of the sealing of God's people with a sign which marks them as His own, assures them of salvation in the day of wrath and judgment, and protects them from divine condemnation and from the malignant powers of evil, that we must set St. Paul's reminder to his converts that they have been 'sealed for a day of redemption.' "

[148] So Bruce, *Eph*, 265.

περιποιήσεως" (1:13, 14). Christians are "sealed (ἐσφραγίσθητε) with the Holy Spirit εἰς ἡμέραν ἀπολυτρώσεως for the praise of his glory" (4:30).[149] The completion of salvation is the intent of sealing and also its certain outcome.

The strong eschatological flavor of the aforementioned references to sealing with the Spirit also permeates the context of 2 Cor 1:22, where Paul describes God as "the one who sealed us and who gives us the ἀρραβών of the Spirit in our hearts" (v. 22).[150] Many of the same terms we have already seen associated with sealing and final redemption occur here too: ἀρραβών (v. 22), ἐπαγγελία, δόξα (v. 20). But perhaps the strongest evidence in this passage that sealing implies eschatological deliverance is the participle βεβαιῶν, parallel to σφραγισάμενος. It denotes God as the one who continually establishes believers firm in Christ[151] and thus makes their salvation secure until the day of its completion. 1 Cor 1:8 shows clearly the eschatological orientation of this term. There Paul assures the Corinthians that God "will establish you until the end (βεβαιώσει ὑμᾶς ἕως τέλους), blameless on the day of our Lord Jesus Christ."[152] Those who have been sealed with the Spirit thus come under divine protection until the end, when God will fully redeem God's own possession.[153] Thus, in 2 Cor 1:18–22 Paul tries to convince the Corinthians that his apostolic word is reliable— "not 'yes' and 'no' " (v. 18)—just as God's promise to finish their redemption is fully trustworthy in accordance with the guarantee consisting in the seal of the Spirit.[154]

---

[149] Bruce (*Eph*, 364) interprets ἀπολύτρωσις at 4:30 in the light of 1:14 as God's "redemption of [his own] possession," i.e., God's people. Differently, Schnackenburg (*Eph*, 66, 214) sees Christians' gaining possession of their inheritance in both verses. The important point for the present study, however, is that each interpretation takes ἀπολύτρωσις as final redemption.

[150] Paul's terse formulation here should not leave us in doubt that he means sealing *with the Spirit*. With his quick progression from σφραγισάμενος to δούς Paul lets one reference to the Spirit suffice for both participles.

[151] Cf. Col 2:7, βεβαιούμενοι τῇ πίστει.

[152] See pp 76–79 below.

[153] Cf. Barrett, *2 Cor*, 79. Dinkler ("Taufterminologie," 110, 111) takes σφραγίζειν in 2 Cor 1:22 as both eschatological (sealing for the end time) and juridical (legal transfer to Christ through baptism). See, however, above, n. 141.

[154] Fitzer (σφραγίς, *TDNT* 7, 949) also relates the contextual themes of certainty, reliability of the promise, and being established securely to being sealed with the Spirit and becoming God's "own inviolable possession." Marshall (*Kept*, 108) rightly denies the idea that there is "anything automatic, still less anything magical, in the fact that a divine seal is placed upon believers." This comment, however, does not take away from believers' certainty that God will fully redeem God's possession which has been sealed for this purpose. For the guarantee of the seal rests in God's faithfulness, not in some process at work outside of God.

In conclusion, God's Spirit who indwells believers not only brings the blessings of salvation into present experience but also guarantees the future completion of salvation. The metaphors used to describe the Spirit given to Christians—the Spirit as first-fruits, downpayment, and seal—have this meaning. Like divine calling and justification, the gift of the Spirit is for Paul a divine saving initiative already realized in present Christian experience which bears the promise of the completion of God's work of salvation in believers. Indeed, in comparison with other aspects of present salvation which point to its future consummation, Paul seems to attach greater significance to the indwelling Spirit. Perhaps the powerful experience of the Spirit in his communities accounts in part for the degree of importance this gift has in his thought as a confirmation of continuity in salvation.

Finishing the "Good Work"

Philippians 1:6. Paul is confident concerning the Philippian Christians that "the one who began a good work in you will complete it until the day of Christ Jesus" (Phil 1:6). This verse is often cited as evidence that Paul thought of the final salvation of the Philippian Christians as certain. Paul's statement itself, however, is rather vague. The term "good work" (ἔργον ἀγαθόν) is the *crux interpretum*. Does it denote the work of salvation which God has begun in the Philippians and which will be consummated at the last day? If so, this verse portrays Christians' salvation as having a sure continuity. The crucial term will be studied in the following discussion so as to clarify the significance of Paul's assertion for perseverance.

ἔργον ἀγαθόν has no uniform meaning in Paul's generally uncontested epistles.[155] In Rom 13:3 it alludes to the conduct of a good citizen who lives a lawful life. In Rom 2:7 it takes on religious overtones: the reward for ὑπομονὴν ἔργου ἀγαθοῦ (cf. ἐργάζεσθαι τὸ ἀγαθόν, v. 10)[156] is eternal life. Similarly, good works (as well as good words) should characterize the Christian life in 2 Thess 2:17. The context of charity to the poor at 2 Cor 9:8[157] makes πᾶν ἔργον ἀγαθόν there have a yet narrower religious sense and refer to charitable deeds, especially material aid (cf. v. 9

---

[155] Compare the scant use of the term in these epistles with the liberal use of ἔργον ἀγαθόν/καλόν and ἔργον/a καλόν/a in the pastorals (1 Tim 2:10; 3:1; 5:10, 25; 6:18; 2 Tim 2:21; 3:17; Tit 1:16; 2:7, 14; 3:1, 8, 14). Cf. also Eph 2:10; Col 1:10.

[156] Cf. Gal 6:10. Cf. also ποιεῖν τὸ καλόν (Rom 7:21; 2 Cor 13:7; Gal 6:9).

[157] On πᾶν ἔργον ἀγαθόν at 2 Cor 9:8, see p. 38 below.

and the larger context).[158] Paul can thus use ἔργον ἀγαθόν for behavior commendable in a socio-political or religious sense, including the practice of charity. What light do these parallels shed on the meaning of ἔργον ἀγαθόν at Phil 1:6?

ἔργον ἀγαθόν at Phil 1:6 stands out from Paul's use of the expression elsewhere in that here *God*, not a human being, does the good work. Or does God? The fact that Rom 2:17; 13:3; 2 Cor 9:8; 2 Thess 2:17 use ἔργον ἀγαθόν to refer to *human* action has led to the view that Phil 1:6 likewise refers to human action. The attributive adjective ἀγαθόν and the absence of the article are advanced as arguments in favor of this view.[159] It is contended that if Paul had intended ἔργον ἀγαθόν to signify a divine good work, he would have written τὸ ἔργον ἀγαθόν. On the other hand, this argument presupposes the existence and familiarity of such a phrase which denoted the divine good work in mind. If such a phrase were not in use, however, Paul need not have included the article. Moreover, the article in τὸ ἔργον ἀγαθόν would have suggested an identification of the good work with the preceding ἡ κοινωνία ὑμῶν εἰς τὸ εὐαγγέλιον (v. 5): the good work just mentioned, i.e., your participation in the gospel.[160] In order to avoid this confusion Paul would have had to specify his meaning further: τὸ ἔργον αὐτοῦ τὸ ἀγαθόν. This construction, however, is clumsy. The simple and emphatic anarthrous construction seems preferable, and so, we can reason, Paul would have used it instead, leaving the subject of the good work unexpressed. The absence of the article, thus, does not rule out a divine subject of ἔργον ἀγαθόν.[161]

But what is the force of the use of the adjective ἀγαθόν in Phil 1:6? Does it allow only a human good work? Although Paul attributes to God an ἔργον at Rom 14:20—where it denotes a work which God has brought into being—ἔργον ἀγαθόν in Paul always denotes something done by a human being. It would not have been without precedent, however, for Paul to attribute to God a "good work." The OT-Jewish tradition of good works (cf. Exod 18:20; Mic 6:8)[162] does so. In the literature influenced by this tradition various deeds of God fall into the category of good works, or the obligations of the righteous Jew.[163] In fact *b. Soṭah* 14a deliberately fits the di-

---

[158] Cf. Barrett, *2 Cor*, 237.

[159] Zahn, "Altes und Neues," 192.

[160] For ἡ κοινωνία ὑμῶν εἰς τὸ εὐαγγέλιον as the Philippians' activity, see n. 189 below.

[161] On the whole argument, see Ewald, *Phil*, 50, 51.

[162] These good works, מַעֲשִׂים טוֹבִים, consisted in almsgiving, צְדָקָה or מִצְוָה, and works of charity, גְּמִילוּת הַסָּדִים.

[163] For examples of these good works, see below; further, Str-B 4.1, 559–610.

vine deeds into this tradition in order to make God the supreme example in performing charitable deeds:

> What means the text, *Ye shall walk after the Lord your God* ?...but to walk after the attributes of the Holy One,.... As He clothes the naked, for it is written, *And the Lord God made for Adam and for his wife coats of skin, and clothed them*, so do thou also clothe the naked. The Holy One...visited the sick, for it is written, *And the Lord appeared unto him by the oaks of Mamre*, so do thou also visit the sick. The Holy One...comforted mourners, for it is written, *And it came to pass after the death of Abraham, that God blessed Isaac his son*, so do thou also comfort mourners. The Holy One...buried the dead, for it is written, *And he buried him in the valley*, so do thou also bury the dead.... Torah begins with an act of benevolence and ends with an act of benevolence. It begins with an act of benevolence, for it is written, *And the Lord God made for Adam and for his wife coats of skin, and clothed them*; and it ends with an act of benevolence, for it is written, '*And he buried him in the valley*'.[164]

1 Clement also speaks of the exemplary character of divine good works.

> What shall we do, then, brethren? Shall we be slothful in well-doing ($\dot{a}\gamma a\theta o\pi o\iota\acute{\iota}a$) and cease from love? May the Master forbid that this should happen, at least to us, but let us be zealous to accomplish every good deed ($\pi\hat{a}\nu\ \check{\epsilon}\rho\gamma o\nu\ \dot{a}\gamma a\theta\acute{o}\nu$) with energy and readiness. For the Creator and Master of the universe himself rejoices in his works ($\dot{\epsilon}\pi\grave{\iota}\ \tau o\hat{\iota}\varsigma\ \check{\epsilon}\rho\gamma o\iota\varsigma\ a\dot{v}\tau o\hat{v}$).... Let us observe that all the righteous have been adorned with good works ($\dot{\epsilon}\nu\ \check{\epsilon}\rho\gamma o\iota\varsigma\ \dot{a}\gamma a\theta o\hat{\iota}\varsigma$); and the Lord himself adorned himself with good works ($\check{\epsilon}\rho\gamma o\iota\varsigma\ \dot{a}\gamma a\theta o\hat{\iota}\varsigma$) and rejoiced. Having therefore this pattern let us follow his will without delay, let us work the work of righteousness with all our strength (33:1, 2, 7, 8).[165]

1 Clement records an early Christian prayer to God to perform a number of traditional good works toward God's people:

> We beseech thee, Master, to be our 'help and succour.' Save those of us who are in affliction, have mercy on the lowly, raise the fallen, show thyself to those in need, heal the sick, turn against the wanderers of thy people, feed the hungry, ransom our prisoners, raise up the weak, comfort the faint-hearted (59:4).[166]

---

[164] Epstein, *Nashim VI Nazir Soṭah*, 72, 73. Cf. *Sipre Deut.* 11, 22 §49 (85ᵃ); *Midr. Ps.* 25 §11 (107ᵃ), cited in Str-B 4.1, 561.
[165] *Apostolic Fathers* I, 62–65.
[166] *Apostolic Fathers* I, 112, 113.

The *Testament of Joseph* [167] pictures a series of divine actions belonging to the tradition of good works.

> I was sold into slavery, and the Lord of all made me free:
> I was taken into captivity, and his strong hand succoured me.
> I was beset with hunger, and the Lord himself nourished me.
> I was alone, and God comforted me:
> I was sick, and the Lord visited me:
> I was in prison, and the Savior[168] showed favour unto me;
> In bonds, and he released me;
> Slandered, and he pleaded my cause;
> Bitterly spoken against by the Egyptians, and he delivered me;
> Envied by my fellow-slaves, and he exalted me (1:5-7).[169]

The OT-Jewish tradition of divine good works also found its way into the New Testament.[170] Both Matthew's and Luke's Jesus teaches the certainty that God will feed the hungry and clothe the naked (works of charity) since God even feeds the birds and clothes the lilies (Matt 6:25–33; Luke 12:22–31).[171] Mary also testifies of divine nourishment of the hungry in the Magnificat (Luke 1:53).

Paul's letters also show influence of this tradition. Encouraging the Corinthians to contribute liberally to the collection for the Jerusalem saints in 2 Corinthians 8, Paul puts forward a divine example of generosity. Christ "became poor, though he was rich, in order that you might be made rich by his poverty" (8:9). The preexistent Son of God ($\pi\lambda o\acute{u}\sigma\iota o\varsigma$ $\H{\omega}\nu$)[172] "gave generously" to the "poor" by being incarnated and dying on the cross

---

[167] The question of the origin, Jewish or Christian, of the *Testaments of the Twelve Patriarchs* does not significantly affect the present argument.

[168] I have substituted this divine title for Charles' "my God" on the basis of the editions listed below in n. 228.

[169] *APOT* II, 346.

[170] The NT testifies to the early Christian practice of traditional works of charity and almsgiving by naming examples of such good works (see esp. Matt 6:1–4; 25:35, 36; see Jeremias, "Salbungsgeschichte," 75–82) and by using the technical designations $\dot{\epsilon}\lambda\epsilon\eta\mu o\sigma\acute{u}\nu\eta$ and $\kappa\alpha\lambda\dot{\alpha}/\dot{\alpha}\gamma\alpha\theta\grave{\alpha}$ $\check{\epsilon}\rho\gamma\alpha$. Paul's letters abound with examples of traditional good works. Agape meals, which provided for the poorer church members, were a form of feeding the hungry (1 Cor 11:33). Christians should practice this work of charity not only toward fellow Christians but also toward enemies (Rom 12:20) in imitation of OT spirituality (Prov 25:21, 22 LXX). Paul exhorted his readers to practice hospitality and to provide material assistance for others (Rom 12:13), including travellers (Rom 15:24; 1 Cor 16:6; 2 Cor 1:16). On the collection for Jerusalem as almsgiving, see n. 180 below.

[171] See Wikenhauser, "Liebeswerke," 371.

[172] $\pi\lambda o\acute{u}\sigma\iota o\varsigma$ $\H{\omega}\nu$ refers to Christ's life as the preexistent Son of God (Windisch, *2 Kor*, 252, 253).

(ἐπτώχευσεν)[173] to bring salvation (ἵνα ὑμεῖς τῇ ἐκείνου πτωχείᾳ πλουτήσητε, 8:9).[174] Here Paul portrays the divine work of salvation in Christ as a good work of almsgiving which Christians should emulate in their generosity[175] to the poor. In fact the Macedonian Christians had already followed the divine example in doing good works by "giving themselves" (ἑαυτοὺς ἔδωκαν, 8:5), just as Christ gave himself (τοῦ δόντος ἑαυτόν, Gal 1:4).[176]

Taking the metaphor for salvation in 2 Cor 8:9 as almsgiving to the poor fits the context well. For Paul draws on the tradition of good works throughout his discussion of the collection in 2 Corinthians 8 and 9. In 9:7 he supports his plea for a generous voluntary contribution to the collection by quoting Prov 22:8a LXX: ἱλαρὸν γὰρ δότην ἀγαπᾷ ὁ θεός. This proverb praises the generous almsgiver who "gives...bread to the poor" (Prov 22:9 LXX).[177] Paul applies the figure of sowing and reaping from wisdom literature (cf. Prov 11:24 LXX) to Christian almsgiving at 2 Cor 9:6: ὁ σπείρων φειδομένως φειδομένως καὶ θερίσει, καὶ ὁ σπείρων ἐπ' εὐλογίαις ἐπ' εὐλογίαις καὶ θερίσει. According to this maxim, liberality or stinginess will correspond in greatness to the future "reward" (cf. Rom 2:7, 8). Paul has incorporated into a Christian setting the Jewish teaching of almsgiving and its consequences.[178]

The context of 2 Cor 8:9 not only has allusions to the OT-Jewish tradition of works of charity and almsgiving. The appropriate terminology for such good works also appears. At 9:9 Paul quotes Ps 111:9 LXX in which the term δικαιοσύνη has the technical meaning "almsgiving" (cf. Matt 6:1; Tob 12:9).[179] The term reappears at 9:10 with reference to the Corinthians'

---

[173] ἐπτώχευσεν refers to Christ's incarnation and crucifixion (Barrett, *2 Cor*, 223; Windisch, *2 Kor*, 253).

[174] ἵνα ὑμεῖς...πλουτήσητε refers to eschatological salvation (Windisch, *2 Kor*, 253), called God's "indescribable gift" in 9:15 (cf. Barrett, *2 Cor*, 220). For the metaphor of salvation as riches, cf. also 2 Cor 6:10; 9:11; Rom 11:12; 1 Cor 1:5.

[175] Barrett (*2 Cor*, 222) translates χάριν at 8:9 as "generosity." Windisch (*2 Kor*, 250) interprets ταύτῃ τῇ χάριτι at 8:7 as "das Liebeswerk für Jerusalem." Paul's use of χάρις for both Christ's and the Corinthians' good work creates an obvious comparison between the two. Human examples from the OT also provided inspiration for the practice of good works in early Christianity (cf. Heb 13:2; *1 Clem* 10:7; 11:1; 12:1–8; see Wikenhauser, "Liebeswerke," 375).

[176] Windisch (*2 Kor*, 247) suggests: "Aus Gal 1,4 τοῦ δόντ. ἑαυτόν könnte man folgern, daß P. schon hier auf das Vorbild des Herrn anspielt (vgl. v. 9), dem die Maz. nacheifern."

[177] Cf. *Lev. Rab.* 34,9 (131b); Sir 35:7–10.

[178] Windisch, *2 Kor*, 276. Paul relates the same figure of sowing and reaping to the doing of good in Gal 6:7–10. This connection is also found in *3 Apoc. Bar.* 15:2, 3.

[179] Jeremias, "Salbungsgeschichte," 79, 80.

almsgiving. God's abundant provision will enable them to exercise even more generosity and thus "enlarge the harvest of your δικαιοσύνη." Paul especially has in mind the particular occasion for almsgiving at hand, the collection for the poor Christians in Jerusalem.[180] But the Corinthians should take every opportunity to abound in πᾶν ἔργον ἀγαθόν (2 Cor 9:8). Here Paul uses another technical term denoting traditional good works. The parallelism with δικαιοσύνη, almsgiving, at 9:9, 10 suggests that ἔργον ἀγαθόν at 9:8 has the connotation of almsgiving.[181]

In summary, the motifs and terminology from the tradition of works of charity and almsgiving which appear in 2 Corinthians 8 and 9 and the paralleling of Christian almsgiving and Christ's becoming poor to make others rich support the view that Paul intentionally characterizes the salvation event in 8:9 as a divine good work. This verse thus provides a Pauline example of a divine good work (almsgiving) which parallels the divine good works seen in other early Christian literature and in Judaism. Since Paul can conceive of God doing a good work belonging to the tradition of good works, it seems likely that he could also have used a technical term from this tradition to characterize a divine good work. We can now ask whether he has in fact done so at Phil 1:6 with the term ἔργον ἀγαθόν.

The term ἔργον ἀγαθόν at Phil 1:6 denotes either a human or a divine good work. Which does the context favor? ἔργον ἀγαθόν here is the object of ὁ ἐναρξάμενος, which all interpreters agree designates God.[182]

---

[180] Panikulam (*Koinonia*, 36–38): "In Judaism contemporary to...early Christianity, contributory practices were prevalent. In realizing his collection project it is probably [*sic*] that Paul was influenced by these practices. In its form and significance a striking correlation is perceptible.... But the Pauline collection in its institution and working was entirely different from the Jewish practices." Acts 24:17 uses ἐλεημοσύνη for the collection. The secondary literature refers to the collection more often as a work of charity ("ein Liebeswerk," Windisch, *2 Kor*, 250; "an act of love for the benefit of those who were in material need," Barrett, *2 Cor*, 28) than as almsgiving. But a sharp distinction between the two is unnecessary: "Streng genommen gehörten natürlich auch die Almosen (Werke der Wohltätigkeit) zu den 'Liebeswerken'" (Str-B 4/1.559). On financial contributions to poor churches similar to the Pauline collection, see v. Harnack, *Mission*, 205ff. The most thorough and valuable record of such material support of sister churches from the first three centuries, a letter from Cyprian of Carthage to Numidian bishops in 253 C.E., demonstrates that these financial contributions continued to be consciously placed within the tradition of good works: "Denn wenn der Herr in seinem Evangelium sagt: 'Ich bin krank gewesen, und ihr habt mich besucht', wie wird er erst zu weit größerer Belohnung unseres Almosens sagen: 'Ich bin gefangen gewesen, und ihr habt mich losgekauft'.... Endlich danken wir euch, daß ihr uns an eurem Kummer und an diesem so guten und notwendigen Liebeswerke Anteil nehmen ließet"(v. Harnack, *Mission*, 210).

[181] Jeremias, "Salbungsgeschichte," 79, 80.

[182] Elsewhere also Paul can substitute θεός with a participial construction drawing

ἔργον ἀγαθόν also functions as the object of ἐπιτελέσει, whose subject is God. That is, ἔργον ἀγαθόν is the grammatical object of two *divine* actions.[183] Further, Paul describes the Philippians as those who benefit from the good work—it happens ἐν ὑμῖν—not those who perform it.[184] The data of the text point to the view that ἔργον ἀγαθόν is a good work *of God*.[185]

Some, however, claim that both God and the Philippians are the subjects of ἔργον ἀγαθόν in Phil 1:6.[186] In support of a dual subject, J. B. Lightfoot points to 2:12, 13 as proof that Paul can conceive of God and humans as subjects of the *same* action.[187] The parallel breaks down, however, since there is no evidence for a dual subject in 1:6: here Paul makes no mention of a human subject of ἔργον ἀγαθόν to match the explicit reference to the divine subject.[188]

But could a dual subject, though not explicit, be implied? Only if ἔργον ἀγαθόν is identified with some clearly human activity in the context. For example, if κοινωνία ὑμῶν εἰς τὸ εὐαγγέλιον at 1:5, which denotes a human activity,[189] can be identified with ἔργον ἀγαθόν at 1:6, we could conclude that the κοινωνία which Paul describes as the Philippians' doing is shown to be ultimately God's work.[190] Nevertheless, the text offers no compelling reasons to identify κοινωνία ὑμῶν εἰς τὸ εὐαγγέλιον with ἔργον ἀγαθόν.[191] Rather, a differentiation between the two seems more

---

attention to the particular activity of God in view (cf. Rom 4:5, 17, 24; 8:11; Gal 1:6; 2:8; 5:8; 1 Thess 5:24).

[183] Ewald, *Phil*, 52.

[184] "To do something to someone" is expressed by ποιεῖν (ἐργάζεσθαι) τι ἕν τινι, εἰς τινα, τινι, BDF §206, 3.

[185] Against Schlier, *Phil*, 16. Barth (*Phil*, 15) comments: "Nicht Paulus hat 'das gute Werk angefangen' in Philippi, noch die Philipper selbst mit ihrer Bekehrung. Gott hat angefangen."

[186] So Lightfoot, *Phil*, 84; Zahn, "Altes und Neues," 192; Bonnard, *Phil*, 16; Michaelis, *Phil*, 18; Bertram, ἔργον, *TWNT* 2, 640.

[187] Lightfoot, *Phil*, 84.

[188] Cf. Ewald, *Phil*, 53, n. 1.

[189] Some maintain that κοινωνία ὑμῶν εἰς τὸ εὐαγγέλιον is not an activity of the Philippians but their fellowship in the gospel through faith (see Seesemann, *KOINΩNIA* 73–79). On the other hand, O'Brien (*Thanksgivings*, 24) argues that in Philippians κοινωνία is used mostly as a *nomen actionis* describing Paul's or the Philippians' involvement in the furtherance of the gospel (cf. ἐκοινώνησεν, 4:15).

[190] Even those who do not explicitly argue that Paul intended ἔργον ἀγαθόν to refer to both human and divine action often couple an interpretation of κοινωνία ὑμῶν εἰς τὸ εὐαγγέλιον as the *Philippians'* activity with the view that ἔργον ἀγαθόν also refers to the *Philippians'* activity. Cf. Schlier, *Phil*, 15, 16; Zahn, "Altes und Neues," 192.

[191] Zahn ("Altes und Neues," 191, 192) argues: "Da aber schon in V. 5 der Grund dieser Freudigkeit angegeben war, so ergibt sich, daß die Zuversicht V. 6 sich auf eben das beziehen muß, was V. 5 als Grund jener Freudigkeit genannt war." But Zahn fails to take into account the possibility that Paul might have wanted to express more than one

apparent. Paul omits the most natural means of connecting them grammatically with a demonstrative adjective (τοῦτο τὸ ἔργον τὸ ἀγαθόν), which would yield the meaning, "this good work, namely, the one just mentioned."[192] Even T. Zahn, who understands both phrases as activities of the Philippians, notices this lack of grammatical connection and finds it thus necessary to differentiate between ἔργον ἀγαθόν and κοινωνία ὑμῶν εἰς τὸ εὐαγγέλιον.[193] The difference in time spans of the activities (ἄχρι τοῦ νῦν, v. 5, but ἄχρι ἡμέρας Χριστοῦ Ἰησοῦ, v. 6) also speaks for a differentiation between the phrases. In short, Paul appears not to identify ἔργον ἀγαθόν in Phil 1:6 with any human activity in the context.

Other details of the context resist the interpretation of ἔργον ἀγαθόν as a human activity. ἐπιτελέσει, whose implied object is ἔργον ἀγαθόν, presupposes that the "good work" begun is moving toward a particular *telos*. When used together with a reference to the *beginning* of the action (as here with ἐνάρχεσθαι) ἐπιτελεῖν acquires the nuance of *final* completion and is translated "finish" (2 Cor 8:6, 11; Gal 3:3; cf. Rom 15:28 where the beginning [of the collection] is presupposed).[194] But to what activity which the *Philippians* had begun and were certain to finish could Paul be referring here? Not a financial contribution, for Paul had just received a gift from the Philippians and can now say, "I have everything and abound, I have been filled" (4:18).[195]

---

ground for his joyful and constant intercession. Ewald (*Phil*, 54) sees just such a "weitere Begründung" in v. 6. O'Brien (*Thanksgivings*, 23) comments that in 1 Thess 1:3, 4 we find a similar affirmation of unceasing intercession followed by multiple grounds. Thus κοινωνία ὑμῶν εἰς τὸ εὐαγγέλιον and ἔργον ἀγαθόν at Phil 1:5, 6 need not refer to the same thing. Gnilka (*Phil*, 46) correctly differentiates between the two phrases: "Aber diesmal wird nicht die Aktivität der Gemeinde in den Vordergrund gestellt wie in V. 5, vielmehr wird der gute Stand der Philipper auf ihren eigentlichen Grund hin durchleuchtet und so als göttliches Gnadenwirken erkannt." See also Ewald (*Phil*, 54): "Der Apostel leitet daraus, daß die Leser sich von Anfang bisher in der beschriebenen speziellen Richtung bewährt haben, die Gewißheit her, daß Gott seinem bei ihnen angefangenen guten Werk, von dem jenes stete κοινωνεῖν bis heute Zeugnis gibt, die Vollendung nicht fehlen lassen werde." Similarly, Martin, *Phil*, 60, 61; Hendriksen, *Phil*, 51; Calvin, *Phil*, *ad loc*.

[192] Ewald, *Phil*, 54.

[193] Zahn, "Altes und Neues," 192.

[194] See BAGD, s.v. ἐπιτελέω, 2. Cf. Ewald, *Phil*, 52: "Ja in Fällen, wo, wie hier, der Gegensatz eines ἐνάρχεσθαι vorliegt, ist diese Vorstellung [eines τέλος] sogar direkt vorherrschend ("zu *Ende* bringen, dem *Ziele* zuführen")." Because *1 Clem* 33:1—πᾶν ἔργον ἀγαθὸν ἐπιτελεῖν—lacks the corresponding reference to the beginning of the action, it is only formally, not materially, parallel to Phil 1:6. Without the companion verb ἐνάρχεσθαι, ἐπιτελεῖν can mean simply "perform, bring about," with no connotations of the attainment of a goal (cf. *1 Clem* 33:1; 2 Cor 7:1; see BAGD, s.v. ἐπιτελέω, 2).

[195] For the use of the verbs (προ)ἐνάρχεσθαι and/or ἐπιτελεῖν in connection with

For lack of a fitting *single* human work, interpreters have identified the human ἔργον ἀγαθόν as a repetitious, commendable practice—evangelization,[196] furtherance of the gospel,[197] cooperation with and affection for Paul[198]—or as the doing of good in general.[199] But such repeated or ongoing activity lacks the notion of a final completion or climax which ἐπιτελεῖν (in combination with ἐνάρχεσθαι) requires in Phil 1:6. Paul's confidence (πεποιθώς...ὅτι) reaches beyond a mere future continuation of this ἔργον ἀγαθόν[200] and stretches all the way to its completion.

Paul envisions the completion of the good work ἄχρι ἡμέρας Χριστοῦ Ἰησοῦ. This temporal reference[201] poses an additional problem for the interpretation of ἔργον ἀγαθόν as an ongoing human activity. For the death of individual Christians puts a stop to their good works whereas Phil 1:6 portrays the good work as continuing until its completion at the day of Christ Jesus, i.e., his parousia.[202] Human good work is not "ein auf ein mit der Parusie zusammenfallendes τέλος gewissermaßen zulaufendes."[203]

In summary, no convincing evidence from the context can be adduced to

---

the collection for Jerusalem, cf. 2 Cor 8:6, 10, 11; Rom 15:28. Paul's use of ἐνάρχεσθαι and ἐπιτελεῖν with human subjects in Gal 3:3 does not parallel Phil 1:6, for here the verbs are transitive but there, absolute. See BAGD, s.v. ἐπιτελεῖν, 2; s.v. ἐνάρχομαι. Moreover, the beginning and completion (of the Christian life) in Gal 3:3 is attributed not to the readers' activity but to the activity of the Spirit or the flesh, as the instrumental datives πνεύματι and σαρκί indicate (cf. Schlier, *Gal*, 123).

[196] Schlier, *Phil*, 16.

[197] Meyer, *Phil*, 13; Vincent, *Phil*, 8. Vincent also includes the reception of the gospel and Christian fellowship in his understanding of ἔργον ἀγαθόν.

[198] Lightfoot, *Phil*, 84; cf. Bonnard, *Phil*, 16, who includes also faith; cf. also Michaelis, *Phil*, 14.

[199] Zahn, "Altes und Neues," 192, with nn. 1, 2: "Dagegen bestätigt aller Sprachgebrauch, daß ἔργον ἀγαθόν entweder menschliches Guthandeln überhaupt, oder ein einzelnes gutes menschliches Werk bezeichne."

[200] Zahn ("Altes und Neues," 192) wrongly sees in Phil 1:6 a mere continuation in good works which (in the church) "bis an den Tag Christi fortdauern werde."

[201] ἄχρι ἡμέρας Χριστοῦ Ἰησοῦ is primarily a temporal reference (Michael, *Phil*, 13) in view of its parallelism to ἀπὸ τῆς πρώτης ἡμέρας ἄχρι τοῦ νῦν in v. 5. The thought of "testing" may also be present (Lightfoot, *Phil*, 84) as in εἰς ἡμέραν Χριστοῦ, 1:10 and 2:16 (Michael, *Phil*, 13; Vincent, *Phil*, 13).

[202] Delling, ἡμέρα, *TWNT* 8, 956; Vincent, *Phil*, 8.

[203] Ewald, *Phil*, 52. Zahn ("Altes und Neues," 192) argues that the *church as a whole* will continue to do good til the Lord comes, although individual Christians will die and cease from good works before this point. But Zahn gets around the problem posed by ἄχρι ἡμέρας Χριστοῦ Ἰησοῦ only by interpreting ἐπιτελεῖν to mean "continue." On the contrary, ἐπιτελεῖν must mean here "bring to an end, finish" (see above). Some scholars argue that Paul still considered the parousia to be imminent at the time he wrote Phil 1 (e.g., Vincent, *Phil*, 8; Meyer, *Phil*, 15). But this is unlikely (cf. e.g. Lightfoot, *Phil*, 84), and therefore cannot provide a solution for the problem of how to understand the completion of human good work ἄχρι ἡμέρας Χριστοῦ Ἰησοῦ.

support the view that ἔργον ἀγαθόν has a dual subject, both God and the Philippians. None of the proposed interpretations of ἔργον ἀγαθόν as a human work fits Paul's characterization of it as an activity which achieves its *telos* with the parousia. Therefore, God is the only subject of ἔργον ἀγαθόν in Phil 1:6.

What is the good work which God has begun and will complete at the day of Christ Jesus? We have already seen that Paul can characterize the salvation event as a divine good work of almsgiving (2 Cor 8:9) in order to draw a parallel with the Corinthians' contribution to the collection. Now we must consider the possibility that Paul intended to parallel in a similar way the Philippians' financial contribution to his ministry—which formed a main occasion for this epistle (cf. 4:10–19)[204]—i.e., their good work, and God's good work of salvation in their lives (ἐν ὑμῖν).[205] Paul seems to allude to their financial gift both in 1:3, ἐπὶ πάσῃ τῇ μνείᾳ ὑμῶν,[206] and in 1:5, κοινωνίᾳ ὑμῶν εἰς τὸ εὐαγγέλιον.[207] His thanksgiving for their good work of sending a contribution through Epaphroditus parallels his expression of confidence in 1:6 that God will also carry out the good work begun in the Philippians' conversion[208] until it is completed at the day of Christ Jesus. Similarly, when Paul speaks of the Philippians' contribution in 4:14–20 he compares their material "gift" to him with the spiritual "fruit abounding to your account" (4:17). He has "been filled" (πεπλήρωμαι) through their offering (4:18), and now he prays that they might "be filled

---

[204] The Philippians had recently performed not just one but two good works toward the apostle: they contributed to his material needs and sent an emissary to visit him in prison.

[205] ἐν ὑμῖν can mean either "in you" (so Vincent, *Phil*, 8) or "among you" (so Gnilka, *Phil*, 46).

[206] Though the prepositional phrase is often translated "in all my remembrance of you," a better translation is "for every (actual) expression of your remembrance of me" (so Schubert, *Form*, 74; with this sense also, Martin, *Phil*, 64, following Moffatt; Zahn, "Altes und Neues," 187, 188). In favor of this translation, ἐπί with the dative in Paul's other epistles always introduces the cause of thanks (so Schubert, *Form*, 71–82).

[207] Zahn ("Altes und Neues," 191), following Chrysostom, argues "daß die Betheiligung der Philipper vor allem in der Beisteuer zu den Kosten des Missionswerk bestanden habe...ohne daß man κοινωνία durch 'Mittheilung von Geldbeiträgen' an den Apostel zu übersetzen hätte." κοινωνία may allude to other forms of cooperation in the furtherance of the gospel in addition to material aid (cf. Bonnard, *Phil*, 16; Collange, *Phil*, 45; Martin, *Phil*, 47; Iwand, *Predigtmeditationen* II, 160; Lightfoot, *Phil*, 83). The facts that κοινωνία can have the technical meaning "contribution, almsgiving" (as in Rom 15:26; Heb 13:16; cf. 2 Cor 8:4; 9:13) and that the thought of financial assistance is already present in the Philippian thanksgiving (1:3) undergird the view that κοινωνία in Phil 1:5 includes the idea of material aid. Cf. also ἐκοινώνησεν εἰς λόγον δόσεως καὶ λήμψεως, 4:15.

[208] Dibelius, *Phil*, 63; Martin, *Phil*, 61.

(πεπληρωμένοι) with the fruit of righteousness through Jesus Christ" (1:11). Paul thus parallels filling with material goods and filling with spiritual fruit. At 1:11 he cleverly uses a word for spiritual goods, δικαιοσύνη, which can also have the material sense, "almsgiving."[209] The Philippians have practiced δικαιοσύνη toward Paul; they will receive the δικαιοσύνη which comes through Christ. Thus Paul intentionally parallels human good works with God's work of salvation in the Philippian introduction and in the process uses the same terminology for both (while carefully distinguishing them, however; cf. 4:17).

The parallelling of almsgiving and salvation in 2 Corinthians 8 (see esp. 8:9) is particularly significant for the interpretation of Phil 1:6. Both contexts have the verb combination (προ)ἐνάρχεσθαι and ἐπιτελειῦ.[210] God who began (ὁ ἐναρξάμενος) a good work will complete it (ἐπιτελέσει, Phil 1:6). The Corinthians have begun (προενήρξασθε) and should complete (ἐπιτελέσατε) their part in the Pauline collection (2 Cor 8:10, 11; cf. v. 6). The object of the Corinthians' action is a good work, namely, almsgiving. Thus the objects of the actions of beginning and completing in the two passages are also parallel. Whereas Phil 1:6 uses the technical term ἔργον ἀγαθόν for the direct object, 2 Corinthians 8 and 9 simply portray the object as a good work.[211]

These similarities between 2 Corinthians 8 and 9 and Phil 1:6 lend support to the view that Paul drew the term ἔργον ἀγαθόν in Phil 1:6 from the tradition of good works and used it to denote God's salvific activity in the same way that he depicted the salvation event as a good work of almsgiving in 2 Cor 8:9. This figure of speech for salvation occurred to Paul in both instances when he sought to parallel Christians' good work of financial contributions with God's work of salvation which benefits them. Perhaps the parallel seemed opportune to Paul because it put Christians'

---

[209] On the technical use of δικαιοσύνη for almsgiving, see pp. 37, 38 above.

[210] An "ältere Prägung" may account for Paul's coupling of the verbs (so Dibelius, *Phil*, 63). But the frequent use of these two verbs in a technical sense related to ritual and the action of offering a sacrifice (see BAGD, s.v. ἐπιτελέω 2; s.v. ἐνάρχομαι) can hardly provide the motive for Paul's combination of the verbs in Phil 1:6 (Michael, *Phil*, 13; Ewald, *Phil*, 52, n. 1; against Lightfoot, *Phil*, 84).

[211] Instead of using the more general term ἔργον ἀγαθόν as in Phil 1:6, Paul represents the Corinthians' contribution to the collection with the more specific term τὴν χάριν ταύτην (2 Cor 8:6) and the articular infinitives τὸ θέλειν...τὸ ποιῆσαι (2 Cor 8:10, 11a) as direct objects of (προ)ἐνάρχεσθαι and ἐπιτελεῖν. Nevertheless his use of ἔργον ἀγαθόν in 2 Cor 9:8 for all forms of generosity which the Corinthians ought to practice shows that Paul considered contributions to the collection to be good works. The object of the Corinthians' beginning and completing was therefore a good work in the technical sense.

good works in the framework of God's prior, saving work in their lives[212] and also showed forth their works as evidence that God is continuing to work out God's saving purpose in them.[213]

The thought of the Philippians' salvation as God's good work is not out of place in the Philippian introduction. Other Pauline introductions show that the apostle often reflects on God's saving work in his converts at this point in his epistles. 1 Cor 1:4, 7, 8; 1 Thess 1:5, 6, 10; 2 Thess 1:10; 2 Cor 1:14; Phlm 5, 6 (cf. Eph 1:13, 14) allude to the readers' salvation (their present stance in salvation or the beginning and/or end of their salvation).[214] References to the "day of Christ Jesus," as in Phil 1:6, or other expressions connoting the end time often appear in connection with final salvation in these introductions (2 Cor 1:14; 1 Cor 1:7; 1 Thess 1:10; also 2 Thess 1:7). Thus in Phil 1:6 Paul makes his customary introductory reference to the start and finish of his converts' salvation.

The time of final completion of the divine good work, ἄχρι ἡμέρας Χριστοῦ Ἰησοῦ is compatible with the view that ἔργον ἀγαθόν refers to salvation. The motif of final salvation in 3:20, 21 also incorporates a reference to the coming of Christ, who will appear as σωτήρ to transform believers to the state of his glorification by his ἐνέργεια. Phil 1:6 and 3:20, 21 have not only the motif of the parousia in common but also that of divine activity: ἐνέργεια (3:21) is a cognate to ἔργον. 3:21 thus fleshes out the metaphorical ἔργον ἀγαθόν in 1:6.[215] Phil 1:9–11, which also describes God's saving work leading up to the day of Christ (εἰς ἡμέραν Χριστοῦ, 1:10), sheds further light on the completion of the divine good work of salvation. In the last verses of the Philippian introduction Paul intercedes on his converts' behalf for their progress in sanctification εἰς ἡμέραν Χριστοῦ, in preparation for the day of Christ[216] and the testing

---

[212] In both Phil 1:3–5 and 2 Cor 9:11–13 the financial contribution is seen to have an integral connection with the givers' stance in faith: as the Jerusalem saints will interpret the Pauline collection from the perspective of the givers' "obedience to [their] confession of the gospel of Christ" (2 Cor 9:13), so Paul sees the Philippians' contributions in the context of their salvation and sanctification (Phil 1:6–11). Windisch (*2 Kor*, 283) identifies the "Christenstand der Spender" and the "Liebeswerk der Spender" as the two reasons for the giving of praise and thanks to God in 2 Cor 9:13.

[213] O'Brien, *Thanksgivings*, 26.

[214] Martin, *Phil*, 61; Gnilka, *Phil*, 47; O'Brien, *Thanksgivings*, 26. Hauck (κοινός, *TWNT* 3, 809), observes "[daß] Paulus in den Briefeinleitungen gewöhnlich für den guten Glaubensstand der Leser dankt."

[215] This argument presupposes the unity of Philippians, a discussion which time and space prevent me from entering here. See the arguments in favor of unity advanced by Kümmel (*Introduction*, 332–335).

[216] For εἰς as "for, against," not "till," see Vincent, *Phil*, 14; Ewald, *Phil*, 70; similarly, O'Brien, *Thanksgivings*, 35.

associated with that day. Vv. 9–11 supply the content of Paul's δέησις (1:4):[217] constant increase in love practiced with wisdom, blamelessness, purity and filling with the fruit of righteousness through Jesus Christ. Since these qualities of the Christian life are gifts of God (cf. Rom 5:5; Gal 4:22, 23)[218] they are properly objects of petition.[219] And God, by bestowing these gifts, will complete God's sanctifying work in believers and thus make them ready for the ἡμέρα Χριστοῦ. This aspect of God's salvific activity, the completion of sanctification εἰς ἡμέραν Χριστοῦ (1:10), further specifies what is entailed in the completion of the divine good work of salvation.[220] ἔργον ἀγαθόν should be understood broadly to include God's working in the believer now up to the future resurrection life.[221] Wesley captures this broad sense of ἔργον ἀγαθόν when he interprets: "He who justified You, has begun to sanctify You and will carry on this Work til it issue in Glory."[222]

The designation of salvation as a "good work" at Phil 1:6, however, has seemed impossible to some interpreters: "Niemand hat es zu rechtfertigen gewußt oder auch nur versucht, daß hier das eine, in allen Christen gleiche Heilswirken Gottes als ein 'gutes Wirken' oder das im Werden begriffene Resultat desselben als 'ein gutes Werk' Gottes bezeichnet sein sollte."[223] Admitting the rarity of this manner of referring to salvation as a "good work," E. Lohmeyer nevertheless attempts to defend this interpretation. When the influences of tradition are at play, he suggests, as in Rom 14:20; 1 Cor 3:13–15; 9:1, Paul can use ἔργον for "faith." Lohmeyer finds elements of liturgical style mirroring "eine archäische Gottesformel" in Phil 1:6, which clinches the argument for him that Paul, influenced by tradition,

---

[217] O'Brien, *Thanksgivings*, 29; Gnilka, *Phil*, 51.

[218] Gnilka, *Phil*, 51, 53; Barth, *Phil*, 20.

[219] The fact that Paul prays for the sanctification of the Philippians does not imply uncertainty but "complete dependence on the power of God's mercy" and recognition of "the freedom and faithfulness of God's grace" (Berkouwer, *Faith and Perseverance*, 128, 130); similarly, O'Brien, *Thanksgivings*, 41.

[220] God will bring believers to entire sanctification ultimately unto his own praise and glory (v. 11) as the finisher of their salvation (so Gnilka, *Phil*, 53; Vincent, *Phil*, 15; Lohmeyer, *Phil*, 35).

[221] Thus ἐπιτελέσει seems best taken as a linear future, implying that the action will be in progress in future time (Burton, *Syntax*, §60). Vincent (*Phil*, 8) gives ἐπιτελέσει a "pregnant" meaning: "carry on toward completion and finally complete." But see Moule, *Idiom*, 10; cf. O'Brien, *Thanksgivings*, 28, n. 43.

[222] Wesley, *Notes*, 531. Similarly, Martin (*Phil*, 61): redeeming and renewing work; Michael (*Phil*, 13) and O'Brien (*Thanksgivings*, 26): the operation of divine grace. Narrower, Gnilka (*Phil*, 46): "Glaubensstand"; Lohmeyer (*Phil*, 20): "Glauben"; Barth (*Phil*, 16): reconciliation; Ewald (*Phil*, 54): sanctification.

[223] Zahn, "Altes und Neues," 192.

used ἔργον ἀγαθόν to refer to the faith which God worked in the Philippians.[224] But Lohmeyer's solution does not solve the real problem. At Phil 1:6 we face the question how Paul can call salvation a *good* work, ἔργον ἀγαθόν, not simply ἔργον. The problem is not, as Lohmeyer thinks, that ἔργον belongs to the terminology of the faith-works antithesis in Paul. For ἔργον can clearly have soteriological connotations (Rom 14:20; 1 Cor 9:1; cf. also Phil 1:22, 2:30). Rather, the apparent difficulty arises from the widespread mundane use of ἔργον ἀγαθόν for good deeds. This seems to exclude an allusion to salvation.

But, as the foregoing examination of 2 Cor 8:9 has shown, Paul can depict salvation as a good work. Other NT writers also characterize salvation by traditional good works. Luke 4:17–21 portrays the ministry of Jesus as fulfilling the promises in Isa 61:1, 2; 58:6 LXX, where examples of good works abound.[225] Jesus brings good news to the poor, proclaims release to the captives and sets free the downtrodden (Luke 4:18; 7:22; Matt 11:5).[226] Messianic salvation includes *divine* fulfillment of such good works, but in a way that surpasses all previous demonstrations of charity.[227] The Matthean and especially the Lukan beatitudes can describe the inbreaking of messianic salvation in terms of divine good works—the poor receive the kingdom, the hungry are satisfied, the mourning are comforted (Luke 6:20–23; Matt 5:3–10). Further, the *Testament of Joseph*, whose record of a series of divinely performed good works has already been noted, also reflects a soteriological understanding of the divine good work. In 1:6 God appears as the Savior, σωτήρ, who bestows χάρις upon the prisoner: ἐν φυλακῇ ἤμην καὶ ὁ σωτὴρ ἐχαρίτωσέ με.[228] These early Christian descriptions of messianic salvation as a divine good work lead us to think that Paul's readers would not have balked at his use of the term ἔργον ἀγαθόν in Phil 1:6 to denote salvation.

In conclusion, Paul asserts his confidence[229] in Phil 1:6 that God will

---

[224] Lohmeyer, *Phil*, 20, 21. Cf. Seesemann, *ΚΟΙΝΩΝΙΑ*, 76.

[225] The same LXX passage from which Jesus quotes in Luke helps provide Matthew with his list of classical works of charity in 25:35–45 (cf. Gundry, *Matt*, 513).

[226] See Wikenhauser, "Liebeswerke," 376, 377.

[227] Correspondingly, it was thought that Christians' good works should also be surpassingly greater: early Christians not only visited and assisted prisoners but even strove to obtain their release (cf. Heb 13:3; *1 Clem* 55:2; v. Harnack, *Mission*, 187–190; Wikenhauser, Liebeswerke," 376, 377).

[228] Charles, *T. 12 Patr.*, 183.; de Jonge, *T. 12 Patr.*, 67f. See also their textual apparata for other readings yielded by some versions. Cf. Eph 1:6 for the use of χαριτοῦν for Christians' salvation.

[229] The perfect tense of πεποιθώς strengthens the note of certainty here (cf. Rom 8:38; see *BDF* §341). Paul's certainty derives from *God's* faithfulness (cf. 2 Cor 1:9;

finish the work of salvation begun in the Philippian Christians.[230] Paul's confidence regarding their final salvation is justified (καθώς ἐστιν δίκαιον ἐμοὶ τοῦτο φρονεῖν ὑπὲρ πάντων ὑμῶν, 1:7).[231] They have given tangible demonstration of their solidarity with the imprisoned apostle in the work of the gospel as his "fellow-sharers of grace" (1:7). Indeed, not only their gifts but also their own suffering as Christians unites them with Paul in the gospel (1:28–30)[232] and points to their future salvation[233] (ἔνδειξις...ὑμῶν δὲ σωτηρίας,...ὅτι ὑμῖν ἐχαρίσθη τὸ ὑπὲρ Χριστου... πάσχειν, 1:28, 29). While the Philippians' lives *justify* Paul's affirmation of their final salvation, he *grounds* continuity in their salvation in the faithfulness of the saving God.[234] "He who began a good work in you will complete it." Paul acknowledges the Philippians' good works (1:3–5) and expects their growth in sanctification (1:9–11),[235] but he bases his confidence of their final salvation not on their continuing to do such works but on God's continuing to do a good work in them.[236]

Gal 5:10; Phil 2:24; 2 Thess 3:4; see Bultmann, πείθω, *TWNT* 6, 6). O'Brien compares the OT expression πέποιθα ἐπὶ τῷ κυρίῳ (*Thanksgivings*, 27).

[230] αὐτὸ τοῦτο in Phil 1:6 refers to what follows (Vincent, *Phil*, 7; O'Brien, *Thanksgivings*, 26; *et al.*). That makes ὅτι epexegetical.

[231] Lohmeyer (*Phil*, 23) and Vincent (*Phil*, 8, 9) correctly see in 1:7 the justification for 1:6, not 1:3–6 (against Gnilka, *Phil*, 48, n. 1). Paul needs to justify his *conviction* regarding the Philippians' future, not his "fatherly sentiments to a favorite child." The following justification (διὰ τό...) does not give the reason for Paul's conviction *that* God will finish the good work begun—this rests securely on God's faithfulness to bring to final salvation those whom God has called (see below). Rather, vv. 7, 8 express why Paul can *apply* this conviction to the *Philippian Christians* (ὑπὲρ πάντων ὑμῶν).

[232] Cf. Gnilka, *Phil*, 101, 102; Vincent, *Phil*, 36.

[233] As does ἀπώλεια, so also the contrasting σωτηρία refers to future, eternal destiny; so Vincent, *Phil*, 35; Gnilka, *Phil*, 100; Lohmeyer, *Phil*, 77.

[234] Martin, *Phil*, 62; O'Brien, *Thanksgivings*, 28; Collange, *Phil*, 46; similarly, Marshall, *Kept*, 107. Bonnard (*Phil*, 17) comments on the effect of the two verbs ἐνάρχεσθαι and ἐπιτελεῖν: "Ils insistent sur la souveraine fidélité de Dieu." Similarly, Gnilka, *Phil*, 46. Some take ἔργον at 1:6 in analogy to the works of creation and affirm the faithfulness of God to the "works of God's hands" which God will not abandon but will bring to completion (so Gnilka, 46; O'Brien,*Thanksgivings*, 27; Eichholz, "Bewahren," 142). Although this observation may be true, it cannot appeal to Phil 1:6, since ἔργον ἀγαθόν does not belong to Pauline creation terminology, and since the thought of a past beginning and future completion of the new creation is absent from Paul's thought. *1 Clement* 33:1ff., on the other hand, uses ἔργα ἀγαθά of the physical creation and makes God's good works exemplary for Christian good works.

[235] Gnilka, *Phil*, 44.

[236] Eichholz, "Bewahren," 142: "Er [Paulus] überantwortet die junge Kirche nicht sich selbst und keiner menschlichen Garantie, auch nicht der Kraft ihres Glaubens, sondern zuerst und zuletzt...eben der Treue Gottes...Das Faktum, das allen anderen Fakten voraufgeht und voraufbleibt, [ist] das Faktum der Treue Gottes." Similarly, Friedrich, *Phil*, 99.

II. TENSION IN CONTINUITY

"Hope That Does Not Disappoint"

Romans 5:1–11. God has begun the good work of salvation in believers, and indeed a fundamental change has already taken place. Summing up Christians' present stance in salvation in Rom 5:1, 2, Paul says, "therefore, being justified by faith,[1] we have[2] peace with God[3] through our Lord Jesus Christ through whom we have received access by faith to this grace in which we now stand."[4] Not only do Christians enjoy the present benefits of salvation. Anticipating its future consummation, they also "boast in hope of the glory of God" (5:2). All have sinned and fallen short of the glory of God (3:23) but God has destined his children to participate in the glory of the Son of God, the risen Lord (see 8:17b, 29, 30c; Phil 3:20, 21; 2 Thess 2:14).[5] Thus Christians hope for the completion of God's saving work already begun in them. "We hope for what we do not see, and wait patiently [for it]" (8:25).[6]

Yet not only time stands between Christian hope and its fulfillment. There are also threats to the realization of that hope. For, although Christians have peace with God, they live in a world which still rises up in rebellion. They belong to God, against whom the world rebels, and are thus themselves stigmatized by this continuing animosity.[7] It touches them in

---

[1] δικαιωθέντες οὖν ἐκ πίστεως sums up Paul's prior discussion of justification by faith (Cranfield, *Rom*, 257; Martin, *Reconciliation*, 137), and leads into the implications of justification (now reckoned to Christians) for the present (Nebe, *Hoffnung*, 125).

[2] In spite of weighty MS support for the cohortative reading ἔχωμεν, most interpreters see superior contextual and theological arguments for the indicative ἔχομεν. See, e.g., Lietzmann, *Röm*, 55; Cranfield, *Rom*, 257, n. 1; Wilckens, *Röm* I, 288; Käsemann, *Rom*, 132, 133.

[3] Peace with God replaces the enmity which existed before (cf. 5:10). Vv. 6–11 interpret this peace as reconciliation with God. Nevertheless, εἰρήνη is a broad term which stands for the blessings of salvation in Christ *in toto* (cf. Wilckens, *Röm* I, 288).

[4] Through the risen Christ, who has entered into the heavenly throne of God, believers now have access to the grace of salvation (cf. Wilckens, *Röm* I, 289).

[5] Cf. Hofius, "Hoffnung," 5; Cranfield, *Rom*, 260.

[6] Cf. 4:18; 12:12; 15:4, 13.

[7] Michel (*Röm*, 179) comments that afflictions characterize the Christian life precisely because of its singularity.

the form of θλίψεις (5:3). This situation of suffering and tribulation introduces tension into the present experience of salvation. In the face of τὰ παθήματα τοῦ νῦν καιροῦ Christians look forward to τὴν μέλλουσαν δόξαν ἀποκαλυφθῆναι εἰς ἡμᾶς (8:18). They groan with the whole creation, awaiting υἱοθεσίαν..., τὴν ἀπολύτρωσιν τοῦ σώματος ἡμῶν (8:23). They long for τὴν ἐλευθερίαν τῆς δόξης τῶν τέκνων τοῦ Θεοῦ (8:21), which contrasts to the present "slavery to corruption." Christians thus hope that, in spite of present afflictions, they will attain final salvation.

Is this hope justified? Paul affirms that it is: "Hope does not disappoint" (5:5).[8] Paul's language reflects the OT conviction that God does not let those who trust in God suffer disappointment (Pss 21:6; 24:3, 20; 118:114, 116; Isa 28:16 LXX).[9] καταισχύνειν alludes to the eschatological quandary of being "put to shame" (Rom 9:33; 10:11), the final day of reckoning when God will "put to shame" the wise and the strong (1 Cor 1:27).[10] The final judgment will reveal whether hope has been futile or not. With this decisive event in mind, Paul refutes the possibility that Christian hope set upon the eschatological manifestation of the glory of God as the crowning moment of salvation[11]—καυχώμεθα ἐπ' ἐλπίδι τῆς δόξης τοῦ Θεοῦ (5:2)—will turn out to be empty. "Daß die Glaubenden nicht der Verurteilung zum Tode, sondern dem Freispruch zum Leben in Herrlichkeit entgegengehen, das ist der Inhalt ihrer heilsgewissen Hoffnung."[12]

Paul's statement that "the love of God has been poured out in our hearts through the Holy Spirit given to us" (v. 5b) grounds the assertion that "hope will not disappoint" (v. 5a).[13] ἡ ἀγάπη τοῦ Θεοῦ denotes God's love of us, not our love of God, as vv. 6–8 make clear.[14] ἐκκέχυται, which describes the "outpouring" of God's love, expresses unbounded fullness.[15]

---

[8] Because hope is here clearly related to the future, eschatological fulfillment of salvation, as the context makes obvious, the future reading, καταισχυνεῖ, would make the same point.

[9] See Wolter, *Rechtfertigung*, 150, 151; also, Michel, *Röm*, 180; Cranfield, *Rom*, 262.

[10] Käsemann, *Rom*, 135; Wilckens, *Röm* I, 292; Nebe, *Hoffnung*, 129, 130.

[11] So Wolter, *Rechtfertigung*, 151, 152. ἐλπίς does not refer to human hopes in general but to the hope which is a corollary to faith in Christ, with Michel, *Röm*, 180, n. 17; Cranfield, *Rom*, 262, n. 1.

[12] Hofius, "Hoffnung," 5.

[13] ὅτι in v. 5 introduces the ground for v. 5a, not v. 3a, with Cranfield, *Rom*, 262. Cf. the association of Spirit and hope in 15:13.

[14] With Käsemann, *Rom*, 135; *et al.*; against Augustine (*Exp. quar. prop. ex ep. ad Rom.* §52.6, CSEL 84, p. 34), who takes ἡ ἀγάπη τοῦ Θεοῦ as an objective genitive. Most modern interpreters agree that the genitive is subjective.

[15] Cf. Behm, ἐκχέω,*TDNT* 2, 469; Wolter, *Rechtfertigung*, 159.

The sheer magnitude of God's gift provides abundant reason for confidence in the fulfillment of Christian hope. The perfect tense of ἐκκέχυται suggests that the outpouring of God's love is only the beginning of an ongoing enjoyment of the benefits of this love by Christians as God continues to accomplish their salvation.[16] Paul will develop the theme of divine love as the ground of Christian hope christologically in the following verses. But first he associates it with the Spirit. The precise relationship between ἡ ἀγάπη τοῦ Θεοῦ and τὸ πνεῦμα ἅγιον in v. 5b is difficult to determine. Does the Holy Spirit enable believers to ascertain God's love as God's saving power which guarantees the final realization of Christian hope?[17] Or does the Spirit as the gift of God's love represent the divine pledge (cf. 8:23; 2 Cor 1:22; 5:5) of Christians' full salvation, which God is sure to fulfill?[18] Both views provide confirmation of the statement "hope will not disappoint." Thus, whether Paul is appealing to believers' subjective grasp—through the Spirit—of divine love as the guarantee of their hope, or the objective guarantee of the indwelling Spirit in whom God has poured out his love toward them, his point still stands: those who hope in the glory of God will not be put to shame in the eschatological test because God's love forms the sure foundation of their hope.[19]

While v. 5b supports the certainty of Christian hope pneumatologically, vv. 6–10 give further, christological grounds for hope.[20] This second argument rests on the objective manifestation of God's love prior to and apart from any subjective appreciation of its significance.[21] Paul interprets Christ's death as the demonstration *par excellence* of God's love (v. 8a).[22]

---

[16] Käsemann, *Rom*, 135.

[17] So, e.g., Michel, *Röm*, 180, 181; Cranfield, *Rom*, 263 with n. 2; Käsemann, *Rom*, 135.

[18] Barrett, *Rom*, 104; Wilckens, *Röm* I, 29; cf. Käsemann, *Rom*, 135, 136. Wolter (*Rechtfertigung*, 167) suggests that Paul here transfers the familiar role of the Spirit—as a pledge—to the love of God, whose concrete manifestation is the Spirit. The love of God then becomes the "ἀρραβών des eschatologischen Heils der Zukunft."

[19] Wolter, *Rechtfertigung*, 164.

[20] Hofius, "Hoffnung," 5: "*Begründet* ist die in Gewißheit erhoffte Heilsvollendung in der Heilstat Gottes in Jesus Christus (V. 6–10. 12–19)." Cf. Nebe (*Hoffnung*, 136), who sees 5:6–11 to support the trustworthiness of the future-oriented salvation of Christians described in 5:1–5. (The future orientation of salvation is also expressed in 5:6–11: σωθησόμεθα and καυχώμενοι.)

[21] Cf. Barrett's (*Rom*, 107) comparison of the two arguments: The manifestation of God's love is through a historical event; the application of it is by the Holy Spirit (v. 5)." Cf. also Martin, *Reconciliation*, 142.

[22] Michel, *Röm*, 182. Bindemann (*Hoffnung*, 91) notes that Paul grounds hope in the past, the Christ-event, in contrast to Jewish apocalyptic, where hope is primarily tied to God's future intervention.

He points to the greatness of divine love demonstrated on the cross as proof
that Christians will not perish in the eschatological manifestation of divine
wrath.[23] Divine love exceeds even the supreme display of human love—to
die for the just or good person (v. 7)[24]—for Christ died "while we were still
weak, at the right time for the ungodly" (v. 6). In v. 8 Paul repeats the point
for emphasis: "Christ died for us when we were still sinners." Paul wants to
draw special attention to the timing of this demonstration of God's love. It
occurred at the least likely moment: when we were sinners, ungodly, weak.
This time, however, was the "right time," the time of desperate human
need.[25] Moreover, God demonstrated God's love at the highest imaginable
cost, the shedding of Christ's blood (ἐν τῷ αἵματι αὐτοῦ, v. 9), the death
of God's own Son (διὰ τοῦ θανάτου τοῦ υἱοῦ αὐτοῦ, v. 10). Thus the
greatest gift of love was made to the least likely candidates.

Theologically, Paul is saying that God's love in Christ is characterized
by grace. Because it has this quality, it reaches out to those who do not de-
serve it.[26] Neither is it motivated by anything good in us, nor is it hindered
by our unworthiness and hostility.[27] And because divine love is essentially
gracious, it knows no bounds. Nothing, then, can thwart God's saving love.
It follows that God's gracious love is determinative not only for the beginning of God's dealings with us, but clear through to the end. The expression of divine love in the death of Christ thus has a significance which
overarches salvation from its present manifestations in justification and
peace with God to its future completion in glorification. This is precisely
the significance of divine grace toward believers in v. 2. There Paul says
that by faith in Christ Christians gain access to grace and now "stand"
(ἑστήκαμεν) in grace (v. 2). This metaphor for the present situation of
believers connotes stability. The perfect tense, ἑστήκαμεν, implies that
Christians continue to stand in grace.[28] Paul can also use ἵστημι (and
πίπτειν) for the outcome of the final judgment (14:4b).[29] To stand on that
day is to be found justified by God's grace and so qualified for final salvation.[30] Thus already in v. 2 Paul alludes to the significance of divine grace
for final salvation: Christians "stand in grace" clear up to their vindication

---

[23] Barrett, *Rom*, 107; Michel, *Röm*, 183.

[24] Paul may be alluding here to the Hellenistic discussion of the question, when is
dying for someone else merited (see Michel, *Röm*, 181 with n. 20).

[25] Cf. Martin, *Reconciliation*, 146, 147.

[26] Michel, *Röm*, 182.

[27] Gaugler, *Röm* I, 116; Leenhardt, *Rom*, 80.

[28] Schlatter, *Gerechtigkeit*, 176, 177.

[29] Wilckens, *Röm* I, 290. Cf. 1 Cor 10:12; Eph 6:11.

[30] Wilckens, *Röm* I, 290.

in the final judgment. According to Paul, grace will never cease to govern God's dealings with believers.[31] And for this very reason Christian hope will not disappoint, "weil es eben Gottes Gnade ist, auf die der Christ hofft."[32]

In 5:9, 10 Paul draws out the significance of God's gracious love as the guarantee that Christian hope will not disappoint. "Having now been justified by his blood, how much more shall we be saved through him from the wrath; for if, while we were enemies, we were reconciled to God through the death of his Son, how much more, having been reconciled, shall we be saved by his life." With the help of these two arguments *a maiori ad minus*, he shows that God's accomplishment of the scarcely imaginable feat of demonstrating love toward rebellious sinners in the cross of Christ guaran‑ tees the future salvation of those who are God's own people in fulfillment of their hope.[33] For those who will benefit from the completion of the work of salvation centered in the cross are no longer "sinners" but "justified," not "enemies" but "reconciled." Moreover, the consummation of salvation is not through the Son's death but his life: σωθησόμεθα ἐν τῇ ζωῇ αὐτοῦ (v. 10). Since God's saving love is already seen to exceed all expectation, no room for doubt about Christians' final destiny remains.[34] Thus, looking back to the cross, Christians see there a reason to look forward with confi‑ dence to the realization of the hope of salvation.[35]

Because Christian hope will not be put to shame, Paul can make it the object of boasting: καυχώμεθα[36] ἐπ' ἐλπίδι τῆς δόξης τοῦ θεοῦ (5:2).[37] Only a hope which is certain can be a hope in which we boast.[38] And only hope in God can fulfill this criterion. Christians' boast can there‑ fore rightly be said to be in God, who fulfills hope: καυχώμενοι ἐν τῷ θεῷ (v. 11; cf. Phil 3:3; Gal 6:14; 1 Cor 1:31; 2 Cor 10:17). Paul discredits

---

[31] Michel, *Röm*, 178.

[32] Wilckens, *Röm* I, 292.

[33] Cf. Martin, *Reconciliation*, 146. Cf. the argument in Col 1:22, where the purpose (or result) of Christ's reconciling death is the completion of Christians' salvation: "to present you holy and blameless and beyond reproach before him." There παραστῆσαι refers to the time of Christ's parousia (Bruce, *Col*, 79, n. 184; cf. the eschatological meaning in Col 1:28; Rom 14:10; 2 Cor 4:14; 11:2; Eph 5:27). Bruce (*Col*, 79) com‑ ments: "The pronouncement of justification made in the believer's favor here and now anticipates the pronouncement of the judgment day."

[34] σῴζειν here refers to final salvation from the eschatological manifestation of di‑ vine wrath, with Findeis, *Versöhnung*, 272; Mattern, *Gericht*, 59–61.

[35] Cf. Findeis, *Versöhnung*, 275.

[36] Indicative (not subjunctive) in parallelism to ἔχομεν (v. 1); with Cranfield, *Rom*, 259.

[37] Cf. Wolter, *Rechtfertigung*, 152.

[38] Cf. Schlier, *Röm*, 143.

all other objects of boasting (4:2, 3; 1 Cor 1:29; 3:21; Phil 3:3), which amount to self-glorying, in particular, Jewish boasting in the law and in (special privilege before) God (cf. 2:23, 17).[39] By contrast, Christians boast appropriately in God and God's saving deeds.[40] For God's work is a worthy object of praise and confidence. Christian confidence with respect to the outcome of salvation can thus express itself in joyful boasting[41] which is not oriented toward human performance but toward God's fulfillment of God's saving purpose. Hope is thus not only the object of Christian boasting; the certainty of Christian hope makes it also the reason for boasting.[42]

The certainty of the fulfillment of Christian hope relativizes present suffering. Paul now states the flip side of the thought that believers boast in hope of the glory of God: οὐ μόνον δέ, ἀλλὰ καὶ καυχώμεθα ἐν ταῖς θλίψεσιν (5:3). Afflictions are in a secondary sense also the object[43] of Christian boasting when seen as occasions for the demonstration of God's power to confirm Christian hope. In this light, the threat to completion of salvation posed by present suffering retreats.[44] Paul shows that God incorporates even these obstacles into the purpose of salvation which God is working out in Christians' lives.[45] Indeed, severe afflictions signalled the approaching end and the bliss of the kingdom to Jews and to Paul alike.[46] For Christians, afflictions herald the consummation of salvation. But they are more than *signs* of the imminent completion of salvation. Through afflictions God continues God's work of salvation by bringing about in believers endurance, provenness, and hope (5:3, 4).[47] These by-products of the process of undergoing present afflictions foreshadow the final manifes-

---

[39] Bultmann, καυχάομαι, *TDNT* 3, 648, 649.

[40] Wilckens, *Röm* I, 290; Cranfield, *Rom*, 164, 165.

[41] Cranfield (*Rom*, 259, 260) compares καυχάομαι with ἀγαλλιᾶν and χαίρειν. Paul is thinking of the exultation which not only took place during corporate worship (so Michel, *Röm*, 131) but which was a fundamental characteristic of Christian life (with Cranfield, *Rom*, 260).

[42] Schlier, *Röm*, 144.

[43] ἐν more probably indicates the object of boasting (so also 5:11; 1 Cor 1:31; 3:21; 2 Cor 10:17; 12:9; Gal 6:13; Phil 3:3), as does ἐπί in v. 2, rather than the circumstances in which boasting takes place (with Cranfield, *Rom*, 260; Käsemann, *Rom*, 134). On the positive appreciation of suffering in Judaism, see, further, Michel, *Röm*, 178 with n. 7; Nebe, *Hoffnung*, 128.

[44] Wilckens, *Röm* I, 292: "Es gibt keinerlei Macht des Widerspruchs, die das, was die Gnade in Christus bewirkt *hat*, für den Glaubenden ernsthaft und mit dem Erfolg seines 'Fallens' in Frage stellen kann."

[45] Nebe, *Hoffnung*, 127: "Vorausgesetzt ist dabei ein übergeordneter Heilsbereich, der sich von der Gegenwart bis in die eschatologische Zukunft erstreckt."

[46] Barrett, *Rom*, 104.

[47] Michel, *Röm*, 179. These human virtues are, from the perspective of divine working in believers, gifts of God (cf. Käsemann, *Rom*, 135).

tation of Christians' provenness and the fulfillment of their hope at the last day. As faith is tested through suffering and proved genuine, Christian hope does not fade but is confirmed in spite of and even through present trials.[48] Afflictions thus serve to increase certainty of final salvation as Christians see God confirming them in salvation even now.[49] Similarly, the apostle boasts in his "weaknesses" through which divine power unto salvation comes to expression in his evangelistic ministry (2 Cor 11:23–30; 12:9, 10). Elsewhere Paul shows that afflictions are taken up into God's saving purpose as indications of Christians' solidarity with the Son of God who suffered and "was raised through the glory of the Father" (6:4).[50] Sharing in the sufferings of Christ, those who belong to Christ will also share in Christ's glory. Thus, Christians can meet present afflictions with the certainty that they do not call into question the realization of hope. Therefore they can also boast in afflictions with the "confidence of the victor."[51]

In conclusion, Christian hope has a sure foundation in the gracious love of God proven in the cross of Christ, made known through the Holy Spirit, and confirmed in Christian experience. Thus hope will not disappoint at the last day. These grounds for Christian hope give rise to confidence of final salvation, which expresses itself in the form of boasting. A sure hope enables Christians to boast even in present afflictions. Though afflictions introduce tension into Christian experience, they do not destroy continuity in salvation. For God's love can and has overcome even greater obstacles to salvation. Thus God will not allow hope to be dashed but will fulfill it. Christians' boast is therefore ultimately in God, who makes hope certain. For Paul hope is not hopefulness, but confidence that salvation will certainly move forward finally to reach its goal in spite of the obstacles in its way.[52]

---

[48] Wilckens, *Röm* I, 292; Balz, *Heilsvertrauen*, 61.

[49] Wilckens, *Röm* I, 292.

[50] See, further, pp. 61, 62 below. Paul also sees his apostolic sufferings to have this significance, cf. 2 Cor 4:10, 11.

[51] Käsemann, *Rom*, 134.

[52] Käsemann, *Rom*, 134; Nebe, *Hoffnung*, 135. Cf. Calvin, *Rom, ad loc.*: "Paul's meaning is that, although believers are now pilgrims on earth, yet by their confidence they surmount to the heavens, so that they cherish their future inheritance in their bosoms with tranquility."

Victory in Trials and Tribulation

Romans 8:28, 35–39. Paul announced the theme of present suffering as
characteristic of Christian experience in Rom 5:1–11. In 8:35–39 he develops it in relation to the question of continuity and tension in salvation. The
θλίψεις mentioned at 5:3 are now named individually: tribulation, hard-
ship, persecution, famine, nakedness, danger, the sword (8:35). Paul's list
of afflictions resembles apocalyptic characterizations of the end times.[53]
Yet he is probably thinking in particular of *Christian* experience: "It does
not concern the person who is exposed to the incalculable whims of chance,
but the follower of Jesus who is stigmatized by the cross."[54] Paul can describe his own life as a Christian and apostle of Christ similarly (cf. 2 Cor
4:7–12; 6:4–10; 11:23–33).[55] That Paul has in mind the sufferings of believers is clear from his quotation of Ps 43:23 LXX at 8:36. The psalm
speaks of the suffering of faithful martyrs: "For your sake we are put to
death the whole day, we are reckoned as sheep for slaughter." Because
Christians' sufferings too are ἕνεκεν σοῦ—for Christ's sake—the OT
martyr psalm[56] is applicable to them.[57] The path of salvation which believers tread is thus a path of suffering.

Not only the natural forces mentioned in 8:35 threaten Christians. They
are also vulnerable to powers greater than themselves—life and death,
angels and rulers, things present and things to come, powers, height and
depth, and other creations (8:38, 39).[58] Christians live in a world of superhuman forces which oppose God and threaten his people. They seem to be
at the mercy of these powers.

The fact that Christians face such adversity raises the question whether
it can separate them from God's love, the power of their salvation.[59] Paul

---

[53] Paulsen, *Römer 8,* 172, 173, in criticism of Münderlein, "Interpretation," 138ff.
Cf. *2 Apoc. Bar.* 27.
[54] Käsemann, *Rom,* 249. Similarly, Hofius, "Hoffnung," 5: "Verfolgungsleiden."
Barrett (*Rom,* 173) refers to the possible suffering of the Roman church through events
connected with the Edict of Claudius (on this possibility, see further, Bruce, "Christianity," 316–318) as well as through the general unpopularity of Christians in the Roman Empire.
[55] Cranfield, *Rom,* 440; Barrett, *Rom,* 173.
[56] On the use of Ps 44:22 in the literature of Judaism, see Paulsen, *Römer 8,* 173.
[57] Paul introduces the quotation with καθὼς γέγραπται, which indicates that what
follows supports the preceding.
[58] Bruce (*Rom,* 179) identifies both natural and supernatural forces in Paul's list
(8:35, 38, 39). On the meanings of the threats in 8:38, 39, see Cranfield, *Rom,* 441–444;
Wilckens, *Röm* II, 176, 177. On the traditional character of 8:38, 39, see Schille, "Liebe
Gottes," 238–244; Paulsen, *Römer 8,* 174, 175.
[59] In our text, as in Ps 44:22, the suffering of believers raises the question of their

has already begun to answer that question by relativizing present sufferings when he says that they are incomparable in weight to the future glory (8:18). Further, he has noted that the Spirit as the firstfruits of salvation even groans with Christians in suffering while interceding before God on their behalf (8:26). Though the present is a time of adversity and vulnerability, believers are not abandoned to their own resources but receive the Spirit's help in their weakness.

These statements set the stage for Paul's ultimate denial of the power of adversity over Christians in his defiant rhetorical question, "who can separate us from the love of Christ?" (8:35). He lists the various evils which assail believers and the superhuman powers beyond their control. Then he repeats, this time with even more conviction, "I am persuaded" ($\pi\acute{\epsilon}\pi\epsilon\iota$-$\sigma\mu\alpha\iota$[60]) that neither these "nor any other created thing can separate us from the love of God in Christ Jesus our Lord" (8:39). He frames the lists of antagonists in 8:35–39 with these two negations of the possibility that Christians can become separated from divine love, as if to express in the very structure of the text that these threats are contained by the love of God. Though Christians must endure suffering in the present time, God's love never leaves them. Nothing can break its power. Paul's denial is both emphatic and comprehensive. Each designation of the superhuman powers threatening Christians is negated by $o\ddot{v}\tau\epsilon$, which produces the strongest possible refutation of the possibility of separation. The paired contrasts—death and life,[61] angels and rulers,[62] things present and things to come,[63] height and depth—suggest the complete range of superhuman forces. As if these contrastive pairs left anything out, Paul adds $o\ddot{v}\tau\epsilon$ $\tau\iota\varsigma$ $\kappa\tau\acute{\iota}\sigma\iota\varsigma$ $\acute{\epsilon}\tau\acute{\epsilon}\rho\alpha$.[64] The denial is utterly comprehensive. $\tau\iota\varsigma$ $\kappa\tau\acute{\iota}\sigma\iota\varsigma$ $\acute{\epsilon}\tau\acute{\epsilon}\rho\alpha$ not only confirms the comprehensiveness of the list but also hints that these powers are by nature impotent to sever Christians from God's love. For they are only created things, and thus subject to the Creator.[65] They are under the

---

future destiny and God's commitment to them (cf. Hengel, *Atonement*, 7).

[60] On the force of this perfect, see Cranfield, *Rom*, 441; Michel, *Röm*, 284; Käsemann, *Rom*, 250.

[61] Cf. 1 Cor 3:22.

[62] Cranfield (*Rom*, 442) sees a contrast between benevolent and malevolent spiritual cosmic powers. $\delta\upsilon\nu\acute{\alpha}\mu\epsilon\iota\varsigma$ is unpaired and is probably another angelic designation (443).

[63] Cf. 1 Cor 3:22.

[64] Cranfield, *Rom*, 444.

[65] Wilckens, *Röm* II, 177: "Mächte und Gewalten ausserhalb der Schöpfermacht Gottes gibt es nicht." Schlier, however, sees a limited comprehensiveness: "Es gibt... keine $\kappa\tau\acute{\iota}\sigma\iota\varsigma$, die den Menschen der Liebe Gottes entreißen könnte, wenn sich der Mensch selbst nicht von ihr scheidet" (*Röm*, 281). But Paul is denying precisely this

rule of Christ, whose cosmic rulership is alluded to in 8:34 (Ps 110:1): "Χριστὸς [Ἰησοῦς]...ὃς καί ἐστιν ἐν δεξιᾷ τοῦ Θεοῦ. Following the psalmist, Paul brings out the meaning of exaltation as victory over the powers at enmity with God.[66] Because Christ rules over all creation (cf. 1 Cor 15:24–28; Rom 14:9), Christians too are victorious over the antagonistic forces of the created world.

Thus, though Christians endure the sufferings of the present time, Paul can say, "in all these things we more than conquer through him who loved us" (8:37). It is the ones who suffer for Christ, ironically, who are the victorious.[67] By unmasking the threats which Christians face and revealing that they have no power to separate from the love of God, Paul shows that even in suffering Christians triumph. Their victory consists in remaining in the love of God amidst tribulation.[68] Moreover, this victory is total: they "super-triumph" (ὑπερνικῶμεν). The prefix ὑπέρ intensifies the meaning of νικᾶν to indicate the thoroughness of the victory.[69] Paul further emphasizes its thoroughness by saying that we more than conquer ἐν τούτοις πᾶσιν. "All these things" refers to the seven forms of tribulation mentioned in 8:35. The number seven and the wide variety in the list suggest the same comprehensiveness already noted in 8:38, 39. Every kind of Christian suffering is included. Where tribulation abounds, there abounds still more the victory of remaining in the love of God.[70] For it is no tenuous cord which snaps under pressure but a bond which cannot be severed.

Paul's affirmation of Christian victory in present suffering (ἐν τούτοις πᾶσιν ὑπερνικῶμεν, 8:37) is anticipated in 8:28: πάντα συνεργεῖ εἰς ἀγαθόν. Since πάντα at 8:37 stands for adversities, it is likely to have the

---

possibility when he says that natural and superhuman forces *which could influence Christians against God* have no power to separate them from God's love (see Schmithals, *Anthropologie*, 188; Leenhardt, *Rom*, 135). Moreover, a human being is also a κτίσις, indeed, a καινή κτίσις (2 Cor 5:17). If not even the forces of the fallen creation can separate Christians from God's love, how can the new creation do so? Finally, Paul himself has already contradicted Schlier's argument at 5:10 by showing that God's love does not stop at the point of human enmity toward God but, in glaring disregard of it, moves forward to accomplish salvation for God's very enemies.

[66] Paulsen, *Römer 8*, 170, following Schweizer, *Erniedrigung*, 148.

[67] Käsemann, *Rom*, 250: "Standing beneath the cross marks the position of the conquerors." Similarly, Fuchs, *Freiheit*, 122.

[68] Thüsing, *Per Christum*, 219; Wilckens, *Röm* II, 175; similarly, Michel, *Röm*, 283. Paul's affirmation of victory in 8:37 provides the answer to 8:35, "who shall separate us from the love of Christ?," so Spicq, *Agape* I, 254.

[69] Cranfield, *Rom*, 441.

[70] ἐν ("in all these things") indicates that the victory comes as Christians meet tribulation, not by evading tribulation (Cranfield, *Rom*, 440, 441).

same connotation at 8:28.[71] Indeed, immediately prior to v. 28 Paul has spoken of the suffering which characterizes present Christian existence (see esp. 8:18, τὰ παθήματα τοῦ νῦν καιροῦ). Thus when Paul says, "all things work together for good," he must have in mind the adversities which *seem* to work against the good of Christians.[72] J. C. Bauer points to a parallel from the *Sayings of Ahikar* which depicts the outcome of distresses in a similar way: "The righteous among men, all who meet him are for his help."[73] He argues that in this saying "es handelt sich...um Dinge, Bedrängnisse, Leiden, Schicksalsschläge" which, as *inimici nolentes*, turn out for the good of the righteous.[74]

But does Rom 8:28 give a more sober estimation of the victory in suffering affirmed a few verses later? Paul claims that adversities lead to good "for those who love God and are called according to his purpose." His formulation raises the question whether the designation of the recipients of the promise as τοῖς ἀγαπῶσιν τὸν Θεόν implies a condition for its fulfillment.[75] B. Mayer suggests: Christians "werden auf Grund ihrer Liebe das Heil sicher erlangen und alles muß ihnen deshalb dazu dienen. Dabei wird aber auch die Mahnung enthalten sein, daß es gerade jetzt, in den Leiden und Verfolgungen, auf ihre Liebe ankommt."[76] Mayer supports his view by pointing to Deuteronomic tradition, in which the belief in divine election stands side by side with the command to love God (Deut 10:12–15). But in fact Paul uses the designation "those who love God" for believers as a *terminus technicus* from Deuteronomic tradition to denote the godly person.[77] The term became a formal appellation parallel to φοβούμενοι τὸν Θεόν.[78] In Paul it simply designates Christians.

---

[71] Cf. Cranfield, *Rom*, 428; Käsemann, *Rom*, 250.

[72] Cranfield, *Rom*, 428; Wickens, *Röm*, II, 162; Käsemann, *Rom*, 243; Balz, *Heilsvertrauen*, 104; Dinkler, "Prädestination," 248; Larsson, *Christus*, 294; Michel, *Röm*, 276. Cf. also Calvin, *Rom, ad loc*8; Wiederkehr, *Berufung*, 156; Dodd, *Rom*, 280; Fuchs, *Freiheit*, 113. It seems unlikely that Paul intended πάντα to include also one's own sins (so in patristic exegesis). For the hardships suffered for Christ's sake are in view ("the cross"; so Calvin, *Rom, ad loc*.). But neither is it likely that Paul thought Christians' sins could negate the promise that all things work together for good, since it is made to τοῖς κατὰ πρόθεσιν κλητοῖς οὖσιν, i.e., to those called apart from their merits.

[73] Cowley, *Aramaic Papyri*, 218, col. 1, line 167. On the OT-Jewish character of the tradition Paul has taken up in 8:28a, see Michel, *Röm*, 275, 276.

[74] Bauer, "Rom 8:28," 106.

[75] So, e.g., v. d. Osten-Sacken, *Römer 8*, 65: "Diese Wirkung "aller Dinge" [ist] aber abhängig von denen, die sie betreffen."

[76] Mayer, *Heilsratschluß*, 149; cf. *ibid*, 146ff., 152.

[77] With Balz, *Heilsvertrauen*, 104, 105.

[78] Spicq, *Agape* I, 248; Nygren, *Röm*, 247; Fuchs, *Freiheit*, 113.

This understanding of the expression is supported by the fact that Paul does not characteristically describe Christians as "those who love God." The designation occurs again only in a quotation at 1 Cor 2:9, which "vigorously emphasizes that salvation is the work of God alone."[79] Instead of our love of God, Paul prefers to speak of God's love toward us (e.g., Rom 5:5, 8; 8:35, 37, 39).[80] "Diese 'Liebe Gottes in Christus Jesus'...ist für Paulus...eine so überwältigende Realität, daß er im allgemein davor zurückscheut, dasselbe hohe Wort als Bezeichnung für unsere Liebe zu Gott anzuwenden."[81] Rather Paul is prone to call Christians ἀγαπητοί θεοῦ, beloved *by* God (Rom 1:7; cf. also Rom 9:25; 1 Thess 1:4; 2 Thess 2:13; also Col 3:12). The multiple references to God's steadfast love in Romans 8 (see vv. 35, 37, 39) reflect Paul's characteristic emphasis.

Paul consistently pairs the designation ἀγαπητοί θεοῦ and its equivalents with the motifs of divine election and calling (cf. Rom 1:7; 1 Thess 1:4; 2 Thess 2:13; also Col 3:12) and thereby shows that those motifs strongly color his understanding of God's love.[82] Pauline practice is reversed in Rom 8:28, however, where the motif of calling (τοῖς κατὰ πρόθεσιν κλητοῖς οὖσιν) is paired with that of human love of God (τοῖς ἀγαπῶσιν τὸν θεόν). But if τοῖς ἀγαπῶσιν τὸν θεόν is a *terminus technicus*, as argued above, this text is not at odds with Pauline thought. The further designation of the recipients of the promise as τοῖς κατὰ πρόθεσιν κλητοῖς οὖσιν confirms that Paul does not intend to make love toward God a condition for the fulfillment of the promise.[83] Instead, the coupling of the motifs of human love for God and divine calling according to God's eternal counsel in 8:28 shows that this calling is effectual.[84]

For those who love God and are called according to God's purpose, i.e., Christians, all adversities assist[85] toward "good" (ἀγαθόν). ἀγαθόν here means the ultimate good: salvation (cf. Rom 3:8; 10:15).[86] In particular,

---

[79] Conzelmann, *1 Cor*, 64. Bauer ("Rom 8:28," 106–112) explains Paul's apparently deliberate change of Isa 64:3 LXX from τοῖς ὑπομένουσιν ἔλεον to τοῖς ἀγαπῶσιν αὐτόν: "So vollzieht Paulus bewußt auch in den gewählten Termini die Umwertung des Gerechtigkeitsideals."

[80] See further, Goppelt, *Theologie*, 464.

[81] Nygren, *Röm*, 246; similarly, Wiederkehr, *Berufung*, 155.

[82] Michel (*Röm*, 286) comments that "für Paulus geliebt sein soviel heißt wie berufen und erwählt sein." Similarly, Spicq, *Agape* I, 258; Stauffer, ἀγαπάω, *TDNT* 1, 50.

[83] Wilckens, *Röm* II, 162; Schille, "Liebe Gottes," 231; Barrett, *2 Cor*, 169; v. d. Osten-Sacken, *Römer 8*, 66; Hofius, "Hoffnung," 9.

[84] Cf. Hofius, "Hoffnung," 9: "Wir lieben ihn einzig deshalb, weil er uns zu solchen Liebenden erwählt und berufen hat."

[85] συνεργεῖ means "assist, help on, profit," not "work together"; see Cranfield, *Rom*, 428; Michel, *Röm*, 275.

[86] Grundmann, ἀγαθός, *TDNT* 1, 17; Hofius, "Hoffnung," 9; see, further, commen-

ἀγαθόν stands for salvation in its full and completed form which will follow the present time of suffering according to 8:17–25.[87] This eschatological salvation is here otherwise called δόξα (8:18, 21), ἀπολύτρωσις (8:23), and ζωή (8:6, 10).[88] 8:28 thus pictures salvation as a sequence beginning with God's eternal purpose, followed by God's calling, and culminating in the "good" of final salvation. This sequence is repeated in a similar fashion in the "golden chain" of 8:29, 30, where God predestinates, calls, and finally glorifies believers. By attributing to *God* the progress of salvation toward its goal in 8:29, 30 Paul strengthens the difficult affirmation in 8:28 that all *adversities* assist toward final salvation. The latter is true because (n.b. the introductory ὅτι at 8:29) adversities have no power to thwart God's initiative in accomplishing final salvation.[89] O. Hofius remarks fittingly, "Gott führt uns in allem und trotz allem zum verheißenen Heil, weil er in Treue seinen ewigen Heilsratschluß zum Ziel führt."[90]

Not only does tribulation not prevent the "good" of salvation from coming about. It can even have a positive function for Paul: it can actually help Christians toward the goal.[91] For, according to the divine plan of salvation history, the period of eschatological suffering will usher in the fulfillment of salvation.[92] The positive relationship between suffering and future glorification came to expression in 8:17c: εἴπερ συμπάσχομεν ἵνα καὶ συνδοξασθῶμεν. There Paul assures Christians suffering for Christ that they will indeed be glorified. For they not only suffer *for Christ*—they also suffer *with Christ* (συμπάσχειν; cf. Phil 3:10; 2 Cor 1:5). Union with Christ accounts for the positive connection between suffering and glorification. Glorification does not follow suffering as the reward merited. Rather glorification is the implication of being a co-heir with Christ: "heirs of God, and co-heirs with Christ, since we suffer with [Christ], so that we might also be glorified with [Christ]."[93] Paul's statement mirrors "the order

---

taries. For Jewish parallels, see Michel, *Röm*, 276.

[87] See commentaries. Some interpreters include present salvation in ἀγαθόν (e.g., Käsemann, *Rom*, 244).

[88] Fuchs, *Freiheit*, 113; Schlier, *Röm*, 278; Spicq, *Agape* I, 249; v. d. Osten-Sacken, *Römer 8*, 278; Dinkler, "Prädestination," 248.

[89] Schmithals, *Anthropologie*, 171.

[90] Hofius, "Hoffnung," 9.

[91] Cf. Calvin, *Rom, ad loc.*

[92] V. d. Osten-Sacken, *Römer 8*, 277: "Die...Zielgerichtetheit aller Dinge (zum Guten) ist jetzt Umschreibung der eschatologischen Finalität des Leidens." On the similar function of tribulation in Luke-Acts, see Brown, *Apostasy*, 124, 125.

[93] Cf. the eschatological understanding of "inheritance" in apocalyptic literature (e.g., 4 Ezra 8:52; 2 Apoc. Bar. 14:12, 13.; see Bindemann, *Hoffnung*, 38).

which the Lord follows in ministering salvation to us, rather than its cause."[94] Those who are "co-heirs with Christ" (8:17b) will follow Christ's path of suffering and also of glorification. Glory is their inheritance as co-heirs; it is a gift of grace based on God's power and appointment; it is not their payment (cf. Gal 3:18).[95] This "Schicksalsgemeinschaft"[96] with Christ transforms the significance of present tribulation from being a threat to constituting a sure sign of final salvation.[97]

What God accomplished for the Son God will also do for God's children, for God "predestined [them] to be conformed to the image of his Son that he might be the first among many brothers" (8:29). Paul makes God's action toward Christ paradigmatic for Christians: "If the Spirit of the One who raised Jesus from the dead dwells in you, the One who raised Christ from the dead will make alive also your mortal bodies through his Spirit who indwells you" (8:11). While oneness with Christ *implies* the glorification of presently suffering Christians, God's power is the efficient *cause* of their participation in glory. The statement "we suffer with [Christ] so that (ἵνα) we might be glorified with [Christ] (8:17c)" does not reveal the subjective motive of the sufferers but the objective connection, according to God's purpose, between suffering and glorification.[98] Paul can say that "all things assist toward good" for believers because he knows that God is working out God's saving purpose even through their tribulation. Whether or not the subject of συνεργεῖ in 8:28 is πάντα,[99] or rather an implied divine subject,[100] it is clear that Paul understands the positive relation of suf-

---

[94] Calvin, *Rom, ad loc.* Some see εἴπερ συμπάσχομεν in 8:17c to introduce a condition or an indirect exhortation (Michaelis, πάσχω, *TDNT* 5, 925, 926; Kuss, *Röm,* 607; Käsemann, *Rom,* 229). εἴπερ can, however, introduce a fact (see, e.g., Rom 3:30; 8:9; 2 Thess 1:6; *BDF* §454, 2). The resulting translation, "seeing that we suffer," is favored by the context, which has numerous references to the present reality of Christian suffering (see esp. 8:18, 35–37). By linking glorification and suffering Paul intends to assure suffering Christians that they will participate in glory; he does not intend to speak tenuously about their final salvation (v. d. Osten-Sacken, *Römer 8,* 143; cf. Barrett, *Rom,* 165; Larsson, *Christus,* 295, 296; Wilckens, *Röm* II, 138; Hauck, κοινός, *TDNT* 3, 806).

[95] Cf. Leenhardt, *Rom,* 123, 124; Foerster, κλῆρος, *TDNT* 3, 782.

[96] Michel, *Röm,* 262; Bindemann, *Hoffnung,* 40.

[97] Cranfield, *Rom,* 407; Wilckens, *Röm* II, 152, 175; Michel, *Röm,* 262; Schlier, *Röm,* 255; Spicq, *Agape* I, 255. Balz (*Heilsvertrauen,* 122) comments that sufferings "... haben...keinen Stellenwert mehr außer dem einen, die Glaubenden durch Leiden ihrer eschatologischen Existenz zu vergewissern."

[98] Cranfield, *Rom,* 408, following Lagrange, *Rom,* 203.

[99] So Cranfield, *Rom,* 427, 428; *et al.* See his discussion of the various possibilities, 425–428.

[100] So Hofius, "Hoffnung," 9; Lagrange, *Rom,* 214; *et al.*

fering to salvation to result from God's activity.[101]

In 8:37 also Paul understands the good outcome of suffering to be a divine work. Christians triumph in tribulation διὰ τοῦ ἀγαπήσαντος ἡμᾶς. "It is not through any courage, endurance, or determination of our own, but through Christ, and not even by our hold on Him but by His hold on us, that we are more than conquerors."[102] The designation of Christ as "the one who loved us" stresses divine steadfastness in the accomplishment of Christians' salvation. The one who now makes us conquer in tribulation is the same one who loved us by dying for us (cf. ὁ ἀγαπήσας, Gal 2:20).[103] Paul attributes to Christ both the past and continuing accomplishment of our salvation by drawing out the significance of Christ's love unto death on the cross as victory over the powers of sin and death. Christians' triumph over these powers, the source of their present suffering, is implicit in Christ's death for them. The victory which suffering Christians have through Christ will culminate in the final subjection of the forces whose power the cross has definitively crushed.

Through Christ Christians are victorious in tribulation. This victory is nothing other than not being separated from the love of Christ. The implicit denial of the rhetorical question at 8:35, "who can separate us from the love of Christ?," is reaffirmed positively in the acclamation at 8:37, "in all these things we more than conquer through the one who loved us" (8:37).[104] The one who loved us keeps us in his love.[105] To remain in Christ's love is nothing less than to continue in salvation. For, as we have seen, Paul understands divine love soteriologically.[106] The one who loved us demonstrated that love by giving himself for our salvation (cf. Gal 2:20, ...τοῦ ἀγαπήσαντός με καὶ παραδόντος ἑαυτὸν ὑπὲρ ἐμοῦ).[107] Similarly, Paul can describe Christ's death as a demonstration of God's love:

---

[101] Cranfield, *Rom*, 428, 429; Leenhardt, *Rom*, 132; v. d. Osten-Sacken, *Römer 8*, 278, 279.

[102] Cranfield, *Rom*, 441. Käsemann's (*Rom*, 247) comment that "...those who hold to him are upheld by him" goes beyond the text.

[103] The aorist participle ἀγαπήσαντος alludes to the event of Christ's death (Cranfield, *Rom*, 441). The reference to Christ's love in τοῦ ἀγαπήσαντός με at Gal 2:20 is interpreted soteriologically in the parallel designation παραδόντος ἑαυτὸν ὑπὲρ ἐμοῦ.

[104] Spicq, *Agape* I, 254.

[105] τοῦ ἀγαπήσαντός at 8:37 leads us to take Χριστοῦ in the phrase ἀγάπης τοῦ Χριστοῦ at 8:35 as a subjective genitive (with Calvin, *Rom*, ad loc.; Spicq, *Agape* I, 253; et al.). Since Paul attributes the victory of not being separated from divine love to Christ, there is no hidden exhortation not to separate oneself from Christ's love. On this fault in the patristic interpretation, see Romaniuk, *L'Amour*, 14, 15.

[106] Michel, *Röm*, 282; Stauffer, ἀγαπάω, *TDNT* 1, 50; Schmithals, *Anthropologie*, 197; Romaniuk, *L'Amour*, 182.

[107] Cf. Cranfield, *Rom*, 441; Schlier, *Röm*, 278.

συνίστησιν δὲ τὴν ἑαυτοῦ ἀγάπην εἰς ἡμᾶς ὁ Θεός, ὅτι ἔτι
ἁμαρτωλῶν ὄντων ἡμῶν Χριστὸς ὑπὲρ ἡμῶν ἀπέθανεν (Rom 5:8). In
8:32 God delivered up the Son for us (ὑπὲρ ἡμῶν πάντων παρέδωκεν
αὐτόν), an act which manifests divine love, as 5:8 makes explicit.[108] Both
the love of God and the love of Christ are characterized as the divine power
which accomplishes Christians' salvation.[109] When Paul raises the issue of
separation from the "love of Christ" (8:35) or from the "love of God in
Christ Jesus" (8:39), he is thus posing a soteriological question. Does
present tribulation have the power to wrest Christians away from divine
love as the power of their salvation?

The question, "who can separate us from the love of Christ?," thus asks
whether the love of God, not only then on the cross but also now in the
period of eschatological suffering, will continue to be the power of salvation for Christians.[110] Will believers remain in the love of God and by that
love attain to final salvation? Paul affirms that nothing can separate them
from divine love. Through the one who loved them they are kept in his
saving love and can confidently anticipate the fulfillment of their hope of
salvation. Paul does not picture salvation as a possession which Christians
have to preserve through the eschatological test—they are clearly no match
for the powers against them—but as the fruit of God's powerful, saving
love, which God's love continues to preserve for them as they endure suffering.[111] The inseverable bond of God's love thus qualifies the significance of their suffering and tribulation for continuity in salvation:[112] these
antagonistic powers cannot bring about the loss of salvation.[113] In confrontation with divine love, they prove impotent to destroy Christians' hope of
final salvation.[114] Indeed, all adversities assist toward final salvation as
they testify to the believer's unity with Christ and usher in the eschatologi-

---

[108] Spicq, *Agape* I, 252; Romaniuk, *L'Amour*, 219. Findeis (*Versöhnung*, 294) notes
the similarity in argumentation in Romans 5 and 8 regarding divine love as the foundation of Christian certainty of salvation.

[109] Wilckens, *Röm* II, 178. For Paul, divine love is an activity centered in the death
of Jesus. Käsemann (*Rom*, 247) describes it as "the ongoing action of one who effects
salvation on earth." Schmithals (*Anthropologie*, 197) uses the expression "Ereignis der
Liebe."

[110] Cf. Schmithals, *Anthropologie*, 188; Balz, *Heilsvertrauen*, 117: "Das Stichwort
χωρίζειν...zeigt, daß es um...das Bleiben im Heil Gottes [geht]."

[111] Goguel ("Assurance," 105) sees the objective ground for Christians' assurance of
salvation to be the omnipotence of God and the proof of God's redemptive will in the
delivering up of God's Son to death.

[112] Balz, *Heilsvertrauen*, 122; Bauer, "Rom 8:28," 111; Spicq, *Agape* I, 254.

[113] Contrast Marshall, *Kept*, 123: "Persecution and tribulation may cause believers to
fall away."

[114] V. d. Osten-Sacken, *Römer 8*, 27.

cal defeat of the forces of suffering and tribulation. Christians thus conquer in all adversity by remaining in the love of God, the power of their salvation. Their victory in tribulation is "geradezu der inmitten der jetzigen Bedrängnis beginnende eschatologische Sieg."[115] In conclusion, in the face of present threats to salvation, God's love in Christ guarantees continuity.

Salvation at the Last Judgment

Romans 8:31–34. In addition to the present tribulations which Christians experience there is also the prospect of future eschatological judgment which threatens to disrupt the continuity in their salvation. Christians are not exempt from the future day of reckoning, "for we must all appear before the judgment seat of Christ" (2 Cor 5:10; cf. Rom 14:10). In Rom 8:31–34 Paul confronts this final threat to salvation.[116] Paul conjures up a judgment scene in these verses by posing questions that fit that context. "Who is against us?" "Who will call out a charge against God's elect?" "Who is the one who will condemn us?"[117] Paul also uses the appropriate judicial terminology. The enemy envisaged in τίς καθ' ἡμῶν, (v. 31) may or may not be the judicial opponent who appears in v. 33.[118] There ἐγκαλεῖν denotes the accusation made in court (Acts 19:38, 40; 26:2, 7).[119] Does Paul think of Satan taking up the role of accuser here (cf. Job 1:9–11; 2:1–5; Zech 3:1; Rev 12:10)?[120] ἐντυγχάνειν (v. 34) describes the activity of the defense. Christ performs this function (cf. 1 John 2:1; Heb 7:25).[121] κατακρίνειν (v. 34) refers to a negative outcome of the trial, while δικαιοῦν (v. 33), used forensically (see also 3:4; 1 Cor 4:4; 1 Tim 3:16),

---

[115] Thüsing, *Per Christum*, 219.

[116] Rom 8:31–34 envisages the future eschatological judgment, so Michel, *Röm*, 281, 282; Wilckens, *Röm* II, 174; Calvin, *Rom, ad loc.*; Schille, "Liebe Gottes," 233; *et al.* Some include present judgment (Lagrange, *Rom*, 219; v. d. Osten-Sacken, *Römer 8*, 313; *et al.*).

[117] The future participle, κατακρινῶν, is to be preferred over the present, κατακρίνων, at 8:34 in view of the parallel future tense of ἐγκαλέσει at 8:33 (Cranfield, *Rom*, 438).

[118] Cranfield (*Rom*, 435) thinks that 8:31 pictures general opposition and that the image of the trial does not arise until 8:33, while others (Michel, *Röm*, 214; Fuchs, *Freiheit*, 115; Leenhardt, *Rom*, 134; Schlier, *Röm*, 276; *et al.*) see the judgment scene to begin at 8:31.

[119] Wilckens, *Röm* II, 172.

[120] So Cranfield, *Rom*, 438, n. 3; Leenhardt, *Rom*, 134. Cf. Schmithals, *Anthropologie*, 184.

[121] Cf. 8:26, where ὑπερεντυγχάνειν denotes the Spirit's activity.

indicates a positive verdict.[122] Both terms suggest the definitive nature of the verdict. Final salvation is at stake.

Paul leaves no doubt in our minds about the outcome of the judgment, however. Both the questions themselves, as rhetorical questions which vigorously dispel doubt,[123] and the accompanying explanations[124] show that he anticipates the judgment to wind up in Christians' favor. The syllogism in 8:31b—εἰ ὁ Θεὸς ὑπὲρ ἡμῶν, τίς καθ᾽ ἡμῶν,— puts the imaginary opponent in a ridiculous position. For the judge takes party with the accused: God is "for us."[125] The description of God as ὑπὲρ ἡμῶν recalls his intervention for our salvation. God "did not spare his own Son but gave him up *for us* all" (ὑπὲρ ἡμῶν πάντων, 8:32).[126] If God once intervened for our salvation, will God not certainly do so again?[127] Paul again makes his point with a rabbinic *qal waḥomer* argument: since God has made the far costlier sacrifice of God's own Son, God will not fail in any further way to accomplish our salvation (cf. 5:8–10). It remains for God only to "give us freely (χαρίσεται) all things with him [Christ]," for God has already "given him up (παρέδωκεν) for us all" (8:32).[128] With πάντα (God "will give us all things") Paul emphasizes the completeness of salvation which he reasons to follow from God's sacrifice of the Son.[129] χαρίζεσθαι alludes to the consistent graciousness of God's dealings with us as yet another reason for the confident outlook on the judgment. The completion of salvation is by grace—God "will *freely give* (χαρίσεται) us all things"—just as salvation begins with grace.[130] Θεὸς ὑπὲρ ἡμῶν with its far-reaching implications which come to expression in the text thus functions as a "warrant for the certitude of full salvation."[131]

In 8:33 Paul gives yet another indication that God the Judge takes party with the defendants, Christians, which will result in a favorable outcome of

---

[122] Wilckens, *Röm* II, 172.

[123] Schille, "Liebe Gottes," 233, 234; Cranfield, *Rom*, 434–439; *et al.*

[124] We ought not to take vv. 33, 34 as made up entirely of questions but as having a combination of questions and affirmations (so, Nestle's punctuation; on the problem, see Cranfield, *Rom*, 437, 438).

[125] εἰ does not suggest uncertainty, but introduces a fulfilled condition (Cranfield, *Rom*, 435).

[126] On the allusion to Gen 22:16, see N. Dahl, "Atonement," 15–29.

[127] Cf. v. d. Osten-Sacken, *Römer 8*, 51.

[128] The parallelism in meanings of the verbs is intentional (cf. Cranfield, *Rom*, 437).

[129] πάντα has a soteriological nuance here whether it refers to the fullness of salvation (so, Cranfield, *Rom*, 437; Dahl, "Atonement," 18; Michel, *Röm*, 280; *et al.*) or the universe as the sphere of Christ's dominion in which Christians will share (cf. 1 Cor 3:21–23; so Wilckens, *Röm* II, 174).

[130] Cf. Schmithals, *Anthropologie*, 182.

[131] Dahl, "Atonement," 17.

the judgment. τίς ἐγκαλέσει κατὰ ἐκλεκτῶν Θεοῦ; The defendants are none other than the ἐκλεκτοὶ Θεοῦ. This designation recalls the earlier pre-destinarian vocabulary, οὓς προέγνω, καὶ προώρισεν (8:29). Paul now wants to reemphasize the significance of election for final destiny. The very ones whom God has foreknown, predestinated to be conformed to the image of God's Son, called, justified, and set on the path to final glorification in 8:29, 30 now appear before the bar of judgment in 8:33.[132] We see again, as we did in the previous verses, that God's eternal purpose in electing them includes the completion of their salvation (see also 2 Thess 2:13, 14; 1 Thess 5:9).[133] God's elective purpose takes precedence over other factors in the context of the last judgment.[134]

But it is not as though the divine Judge simply overlooks accusations against the elect. "God is the one who justifies" them. In the cross of Christ God was shown to be δίκαιον καὶ δικαιοῦντα τὸν ἐκ πίστεως Ἰησοῦ (3:26). Now that God has reckoned to Christians righteousness by faith in Jesus Christ, no accusation against them can incriminate them. They have "vollgültige Rechtfertigung."[135] Calvin sums up this thought well in his comments on 8:33: "The devil, to be sure, accuses all the godly; and the law of God itself and their own conscience also reprove them. But none of these have any influence upon the judge who justifies them."[136] The present tense of the participle in Θεὸς ὁ δικαιῶν indicates the continuing validity of Christians' justification. In Rom 8:33 we thus find the answer to the question which I. H. Marshall poses at the beginning of his investigation of perseverance and falling away in Paul's epistles: "Does the verdict that we have been justified by grace through faith mean that we are certain to be justified on the day of judgement or must there remain an element of

---

[132] Cranfield, *Rom*, 438; Wilckens, *Röm* II, 174; Paulsen, *Römer 8*, 174; Schmithals, *Anthropologie*, 184; Michel, *Röm*, 281.

[133] Against Sanday-Headlam, *Rom*, 220. See the discussions of these parallels in chap. I.

[134] In 1 Enoch also the ἐκλεκτοὶ will be saved in the final judgment (1:7–9; 45:3–6; 50:1, 2; 62:8, 13). In contrast to Paul, however, the mark of election in 1 Enoch is righteous conduct (see, e.g., 94:4; contrast Rom 9:16 and context). There because the elect have followed the path of righteousness they will be saved at the judgment (see 48:7; 103:3, 4). Carson (*Divine Sovereignty*, 68) comments that in intertestamental apocalyptic literature "merit theology transforms election into a divine choice explicitly grounded on human righteousness and worth...the very term 'elect' undergoes a shift in semantic value, and as an adjective it becomes a synonym for 'righteous'." Paul distances himself from this understanding of election in Rom 8:33 by immediately pointing to "God who justifies."

[135] Balz, *Heilsvertrauen*, 118; similarly, Wilckens *Röm* II, 174.

[136] Calvin, *Rom, ad loc.*; similarly, Schmithals, *Anthropologie*, 184.

doubt until the final sentence of acquittal or of guilt has been passed?"[137] Paul leaves no room for doubt. Rather, "Paul never contemplates a reversal of justification or an overturning of either legal acquittal or royal amnesty (Rom. 8:33–34; Gal 5:5)."[138]

By v. 33b Paul has already moved from the stage of hearing the case— τίς ἐγκαλέσει... (v. 33a)—to that of giving the verdict: Θεὸς ὁ δικαιῶν. Justification of the believer by faith in Christ is the criterion of salvation at the judgment, just as it is at present. For emphasis, Paul confirms the verdict of justification by denying its opposite in the rhetorical question, τίς ὁ κατακρινῶν; (8:34a), which negates the possibility of condemnation.[139] The absence of grounds for accusation precludes a verdict of condemnation. Paul then goes on to support his point: "Christ Jesus is the one who died" (v. 34b). The κατάκριμα due us (5:16, 18) fell upon the crucified Christ: "Sending his Son in the likeness of sinful flesh and for sin, God condemned (κατέκρινεν) sin in the flesh" (8:3). Thus Paul can assure believers already, "there is therefore now no κατάκριμα for those who are in Christ Jesus" (8:1).[140]

Not only the salvific work of the earthly Christ but also that of the exalted Christ makes condemnation of Christians *post Christum crucifixum* impossible.[141] Paul's argument moves forward (μᾶλλον δέ).[142] Christ is not only ὁ ἀποθανών. Christ is also [ὁ] ἐγερθείς, ὃς καί ἐστιν ἐν δεξιᾷ τοῦ Θεοῦ, ὃς καὶ ἐντυγχάνει ὑπὲρ ἡμῶν (8:34). Christians have an intercessor who enjoys divine recognition: God vindicated Christ by raising him from the dead and seating him in the position of highest authority at God's right hand.[143] Christ intercedes for his own as Lord of the universe, Lord even over all the powers which are antagonistic toward believers. Christians will not be condemned in the last judgment, for their risen and exalted intercessor pleads with authority before God on their behalf that he himself bore their judgment of condemnation.[144] "Der Glaubende hat vor dem Gericht Gottes einen Fürsprecher, dem auch Gott nicht widersprechen kann; denn er bringt Gottes eigenes Tun vor Gottes

---

137 Marshall, *Kept*, 100.

138 Martin, *Reconciliation*, 153. Cf. Stuhlmacher, "Gerechtigkeitsanschauung," 92: "Die durch das Endgericht hindurchtragende Glaubensgerechtigkeit ist die von Gott kraft der Fürbitte des gekreuzigten und auferstandenen Christus aus Gnade zugesprochene Gerechtigkeit."

139 Cf. Isa 50:8 LXX: ἐγγίζει ὁ δικαιώσας με· τίς ὁ κρινόμενός μοι;

140 Cf. Wilckens, *Röm* II, 174; Lagrange, *Rom*, 219.

141 Cf. Wilckens, *Röm* II, 174.

142 Käsemann, *Rom*, 248.

143 Cf. Calvin, *Rom*, ad loc.

144 Wilckens, *Röm* II, 175; Balz, *Heilsvertrauen*, 120, 121.

Angesicht. Er appelliert an den Gott, der ihn in den Tod dahingab, weil er für den Menschen war; wie sollte er nun gegen diesen sein, ihn verurteilen können."[145]

In conclusion, Christians face the prospect of judgment, accusation, and condemnation which threaten their final salvation. But this prospect should not strike fear in their hearts.[146] The last judgment will turn out in their favor. For the outcome will not depend on their own merits. Indeed, it is a highly unusual judgment which Paul pictures here. Justice is satisfied, to be sure. But God justifies the *ungodly* on the basis of *faith* in Jesus Christ whom God delivered up for their justification. *Grace* is the motivating principle of God's relation to the accused. God treats them not "impartially" but as God's *elect*, predestined to final salvation. God hears the intercession of God's own *Son* on their behalf, who is seated at God's right hand. "La justification n'est pas seulement une sentence rendue par un juge; elle est le pardon accordé par un père."[147] In short, this judge is "for us." The outcome of the judgment is already obvious. Paul envisages the last judgment in this way not because he fails to take it seriously, but because Christians enter the judgment as those for whom judgment has essentially already taken place. In the cross of Jesus Christ God has already given the definitive word of acquittal for those who believe.[148] The last judgment will bring this verdict to the light of day and expose the threats to undo it as impotent.

"God Is Faithful!"

For Paul there is continuity in Christians' salvation because of divine intervention to that end. Even in eschatological tribulation and judgment God will intervene to overcome obstacles to God's continued work of salvation in believers. God will finish the good work begun in them. The presupposition of Paul's argumentation is God's faithfulness. This presupposition, which lies at the bottom of the passages already analyzed in Part One, is made explicit in a number of texts which directly link the future fulfillment of Christians' salvation, notwithstanding threats to it, to God's

---

[145] Schmithals, *Anthropologie*, 186. Cf. 1 John 2:1, 2.

[146] Calvin, *Rom*, *ad loc.*: "The substance of the argument is that we are not only freed from terror by available remedies when we come to the judgement seat of God, but that God comes to our aid beforehand, so that he may better provide for our confidence."

[147] Leenhardt, *Rom*, 80, 81.

[148] Fuchs (*Freiheit*, 120) points to a "vergangenes Eschaton" in Jesus' death and resurrection.

faithfulness. In these texts Paul draws attention to God's faithfulness with
the acclamation, πιστὸς ὁ Θεός, sometimes varying the divine title (1 Cor
1:9; 10:13; 1 Thess 5:24; 2 Thess 3:3).[149] His concise but triumphant faithfulness sayings serve the purpose of boosting Christians' confidence regarding their future destiny. These sayings make explicit how Paul understands the faithfulness of God to ensure continuity in salvation. Two leading questions are pursued in the following analysis of the faithfulness sayings. How does Paul link present and future aspects of salvation by the
motif of divine faithfulness, and what significance does he attribute to
God's faithfulness in the face of threats to Christians' salvation?

2 Thessalonians 3:3; 1 Corinthians 10:13. In 2 Thess 3:3 and 1 Cor
10:13 Paul acclaims God's faithfulness in time of eschatological testing
and tribulation. The period of the end-time is characterized by intensified
evil (2 Thess 2:9–12).[150] πονηροὶ ἄνθρωποι hinder the word of the Lord
(3:1, 2). Christians themselves are endangered by ὁ πονηρός (3:3).[151] Paul
has already expressed his concern over the threat to the Thessalonians'
endurance in faith and love posed by their persecutions (cf. 1:3, 4; 1 Thess
3:2–5). Yet he assures his readers that they will not become victims of the
evil one: πιστὸς δέ ἐστιν ὁ κύριος, ὃς στηρίξει ὑμᾶς καὶ φυλάξει
ἀπὸ τοῦ πονηροῦ (3:3).[152] The affirmation of divine faithfulness stands in
contrast to human faithlessness mentioned in v. 2 (οὐ γὰρ πάντων ἡ
πίστις).[153] The Lord's faithfulness manifests itself in guarding[154] Christians from ὁ πονηρός; they will not be at the mercy of the evil one (cf.

---

[149] I will not include 2 Cor 1:18 in the discussion since it lacks the reference to the
future common to the other faithfulness sayings which makes them significant for the
discussion of perseverance. On other differences between 2 Cor 1:18 and the texts analyzed here, see v. d. Osten-Sacken, "Gottes Treue," 182. The Pauline faithfulness sayings might be connected with similar Jewish blessings (see Sanders, "Transition," 348–
362; v. Unnik, "Reisepläne," 215–234). But v. d. Osten-Sacken is skeptical (181) and
decides rather for an independent creation of these faithfulness sayings for use in the
Christian community as eschatological paraclesis (192).

[150] Bruce, *Thess*, 200; cf. Best, *Thess*, 328.

[151] On the eschatological connotations of πονηρός, see Best, *Thess*, 327, 328.

[152] πονηροῦ could be either masculine or neuter here. Perhaps the interpretation "the
evil one" provides a better counterpart to ὁ κύριος in this verse (so Bruce, *Thess*, 200).
The activity of Satan comes up also in 2:9; 1 Thess 2:18; 3:5. For ὁ πονηρός as a personal designation of the devil, see Matt 13:19, 38; Eph 6:16; 1 John 2:13, 14; 5:18, 19).

[153] Frequently noted by commentators. The inexactness of the contrast is generally
noticed: lack of human πίστις is unbelief, whereas divine πίστις is faithfulness.

[154] For φυλάσσειν for God's protection of God's people from evil, cf. Pss 120:7;
140:9 LXX.

Matt 6:13).[155] For the Lord will faithfully "strengthen" them. στηρίζειν presupposes a situation in which strengthening is necessary in order for faith to withstand (see 1 Thess 3:2, 3; Acts 14:22; 1 Pet 5:10; Luke 22:32; cf. 1 Thess 3:13).[156] στηρίζειν appears together with παρακαλεῖν in 2:17, where both verbs denote divine actions. There divine strengthening and encouragement enable believers to maintain their Christian identity "in every good work and word," i.e., to stand firm while undergoing tribulation.[157] The effect of this divine aid will not be significantly different in 3:3.[158] Thus Paul encourages Christians facing threats of escalated evil that they will not be at the mercy of their opponents but that the Lord will faithfully strengthen and guard them from failure to believe and act according to the gospel. His confidence is in the Lord (πεποίθαμεν δὲ ἐν κυρίῳ ἐφ' ὑμᾶς, 3:4), for the Lord is faithful.[159]

Similarly, in 1 Cor 10:13 Paul acclaims God's faithfulness to Christians in the eschatological test. τὰ τέλη τῶν αἰώνων have come upon the Corinthians (10:11). The dawn of the end-time brings near the great πειρασμός in which believers will be subject to intense testing and tribulation.[160] The eschatological πειρασμός is so severe, Paul implies, that it would be beyond believers' power to withstand (ὑπὲρ ὃ δύνασθε, v. 13), were it not for God's intervening limitation of the trial.[161] In view of its severity, Paul issues a word of comfort—πιστὸς ὁ θεός—since only divine intervention makes the final test bearable. The Corinthians can have confidence in

---

[155] There is no reason to assume, as does v. Dobschütz (*Thess*, 307), that Paul means God protects believers from inner (i.e., ethical) dangers while permitting them to undergo outer dangers (i.e., persecution).

[156] Harder, στηρίζω, *TDNT* 7, 656: "The effect or aim of strengthening is the impregnability of faith in spite of the troubles which have to be endured."

[157] Not "moral confirmation," (so Harder, στηρίζω, *TDNT* 7, 656), for στηρίξαι ἐν παντὶ ἔργῳ καὶ λόγῳ ἀγαθῷ in 2:17 (to which Harder appeals) makes word (i.e., faithful testimony) as well as deed the product of divine strengthening. Both authenticate Christian profession in the context of persecution.

[158] Harder (στηρίζω, *TDNT* 7, 656) interprets στηρίζειν at 3:3 in the light of παρακαλεῖν at 2:17.

[159] On the continuation of the theme of confidence in 3:4, see Bruce, *Thess*, 200.

[160] Hahn, "Teilhabe," 163; Synofzik, *Gerichtsaussagen*, 25. Paul has the period of eschatological horror and tribulation in view (see Seesemann, πεῖρα, *TDNT* 6, 28–32). This use of the vocabulary of testing in 1 Cor 10:13 matches that in the framework of apocalyptic thought for the period of the eschatological distress. The "hour of testing" (ὥρα τοῦ πειρασμοῦ) is coming to "test" (πειράσαι) the inhabitants of the earth (Rev 3:10). Believers will be "tested" (πειρασθῆτε) through Satan's onslaughts (Rev 2:10). Possibly eschatological also, πειρασμός in the sixth petition of the Lord's prayer, Matt 6:13; cf. Luke 11:4. Cf. Kuhn, "New Light," 95; Seesemann, πεῖρα, *TDNT* 6, 31.

[161] Barrett, *1 Cor*, 229; Hahn, "Teilhabe," 163; Seesemann, πεῖρα, *TDNT* 6, 29.

God to see them through the eschatological test.[162]

Paul goes on in the same verse to show how divine faithfulness will manifest itself. God will enable believers to endure the test (τοῦ δύνασθαι ὑπενεγκεῖν). They will be able to endure because God will not permit the testing to exceed their power of resistance: ὅς οὐκ ἐάσει ὑμᾶς πειρα-σθῆναι ὑπὲρ ὃ δύνασθε. When the test comes (σὺν τῷ πειρασμῷ),[163] God will supply τὴν ἔκβασιν τοῦ δύνασθαι ὑπενεγκεῖν. ἔκβασις here could mean "end" (cf. Heb 13:7) and refer to the eschatological act of redemption.[164] Thus with the provision of the ἔκβασις God will set a temporal limit to the πειρασμός, which will thereby be bearable.[165] The testing period will not last longer than the faithful can endure.[166] Alternatively, ἔκβασις can be defined as "way out."[167] In that case Paul's meaning would be that God will provide the means for Christians to endure testing successfully.[168] Whether we take ἔκβασις as "end," or "way out," God's provision of the ἔκβασις and God's disallowing the test to exceed the possibility of endurance manifest God's faithfulness to keep Christians from failing the eschatological test.

Christians' successful endurance of eschatological testing comes by God's faithful provision. In 1 Cor 10:13 Paul makes *God's* work prominent. God "will not allow" (οὐκ ἐάσει) unbearable testing; God "will provide" (ποιήσει) the escape; God will "enable" (δύνασθαι) to endure. Believers are the objects of divine intervention and aid. Paul even omits ὑμᾶς in the infinitive construction τοῦ δύνασθαι ὑπενεγκεῖν, so that the focus

---

[162] Jeske, "Rock," 251; similarly, Hahn, "Teilhabe," 164. Contrast Klauck, *Herrenmahl*, 256, n. 94.

[163] For this temporal interpretation of σὺν τῷ πειρασμῷ, see Kuhn, "New Light," 109; Hahn, "Teilhabe," 164; cf. Conzelmann, *1 Cor*, 169, n. 48. Alternatively, the phrase can be taken together with the verb ("along with the temptation he will provide..."); but in no case does Paul trace the testing to God, as he does the ἔκβασις (correctly, Conzelmann, 169).

[164] Jeske, "Rock," 251; Synofzik, *Gerichtsaussagen*, 25; Conzelmann, *1 Cor*, 169; cf. Hahn, "Teilhabe," 164, 165. If ἔκβασις refers to eschatological redemption, we could translate "good end" (cf. BAGD, s.v. ἔκβασις; Weiß, *1 Kor*, 255).

[165] This interpretation of ἔκβασις makes τοῦ δύνασθαι an ecbatic infinitive. If the ἔκβασις is the eschatological act of redemption, it makes most sense to understand the bearableness of the testing in terms of a limitation of its length, not its degree of severity. For how could final redemption make the testing less severe in degree?

[166] Cf. the similar thought in Mark 13:19, 20.

[167] So, e.g., Barrett, *1 Cor*, 229.

[168] This interpretation of ἔκβασις makes τοῦ δύνασθαι a telic infinitive. Robertson and Plummer (*1 Cor*, 209) see in the imperative φεύγετε at v. 14 the key for the interpretation of ἔκβασις as "way out." Flight would then be the means of successful endurance of testing in this context where Christians face the temptation of idolatry.

remains on divine action.[169] Similarly, the parallel text, Rom 14:4 shows a strikingly exclusive interest in God's enabling the believer to "stand firm": σταθήσεται δέ, δυνατεῖ[170] γὰρ ὁ κύριος στῆσαι αὐτόν. σταθήσεται is an eschatological future in view of the implicit reference to the judgment in the following clause, which states that the Lord will make the servant stand firm (in the judgment).[171] Other NT uses of πειρασμός/πειράζειν for the eschatological test also emphasize God's role in believers' successful endurance of the test: οἶδεν κύριος εὐσεβεῖς ἐκ πειρασμοῦ ῥύεσθαι (2 Pet 2:9); κἀγώ σε τηρήσω ἐκ τῆς ὥρας τοῦ πειρασμοῦ (Rev 3:10). The comment of C. Wolff accurately reflects Paul's emphasis in 1 Cor 10:13: "V. 13b stellt dann sogleich sicher, daß es hier letzlich nicht auf menschliche Tüchtigkeit ankommt, sondern auf Gottes Treue, die den Glaubenden vor dem Abfall bewahren und zur Vollendung führen will."[172]

Yet Paul's promise in v. 13b is preceded by a warning in v. 12: "Let him who thinks he stands beware lest he fall." Interpreters have tried to resolve the tension in various ways.[173] Some explain that Paul must be addressing two different groups. In their opinion, he issues a warning to the overconfident "strong" in v. 12, whereas in v. 13 he supplies encouragement to the despondent "weak."[174] But the text gives no indication of a change in addressees. Rather, the whole of chap. 10 shows concern for those with an over-confident carelessness.[175] Alternatively, C. K. Barrett attempts a synthesis of vv. 12 and 13 by weakening the force of the promise in the light of the warning: "If they do not exert all their power, they may succumb."[176] God's faithfulness means that God "will never allow it to become impossible...to resist."[177] While it is true that Paul exhorts his readers to resist temptation actively, his emphasis nevertheless falls on God's action for the sake of their successful endurance of the test. God's role cannot be reduced to God's passive allowing of only a bearable degree of testing. God also supplies the ability to stand firm. Without divine enabling there can be no talk of human exertion.

It is possible, however, to take the warning and promise to have the

---

[169] Cf. the variant reading with ὑμᾶς.

[170] Here also δύναμαι for divine action.

[171] With Michaelis, πίπτω, *TDNT* 6, 165; Grundmann, στήκω, *TDNT* 7, 648f.

[172] Wolff, *1 Kor*, 48, 49.

[173] Seesemann (πεῖρα, *TDNT* 6, 29) thinks v. 13b "hardly fits the context." Weiß (*1 Kor*, 256) suggests a possible gloss.

[174] Seesemann, πεῖρα, *TDNT* 6, 29; Hahn, "Teilhabe," 162; Bornkamm, "Herrenmahl," 140; similarly, Robertson and Plummer *1 Cor*, 208.

[175] Perrot, "Exemples," 441; similarly, Walter, "Christusglaube," 427.

[176] Barrett, *1 Cor*, 229.

[177] Barrett, *1 Cor*, 229.

same addressees, yet not weaken the force of either. In anticipation of the positive effect of the warning at v. 12 and the Corinthians' standing firm in undivided loyalty to Jesus Christ, in v. 13b Paul wants to inspire in them the proper attitude with which they have to live out their Christian lives in the time of eschatological testing. Fear and uncertainty is no substitute for over-confident carelessness. Instead Christians should trust in God while they attend to the task of not falling. God's faithfulness in the face of great trials is the source of their victory and so of their comfort.[178] Thus Paul *consoles* the Corinthian Christians who *take heed* of his warning against "falling."[179]

The faithfulness sayings in 2 Thess 3:3 and 1 Cor 10:13 thus supply encouragement for Christians whose salvation is threatened in the eschatological distress. This period of intense evil and testing will not inevitably end in failure and loss of salvation. Rather, God's faithfulness provides the guarantee that God will continue God's saving work in believers even through the time of greatest danger to its completion. Endurance of eschatological testing does not depend on what is humanly possible but on God's fulfillment of God's promise.

1 Thessalonians 5:23, 24. For Paul the beginning of salvation and its completion are inseparably linked by the faithfulness of the saving God. When the apostle considers his converts' present stance in salvation, therefore, the thought of the consummation of their salvation is not far away. It is not surprising, then, that both thoughts often appear in Paul's acclamations of God's faithfulness. In 1 Thess 5:24 Paul incorporates into the faithfulness saying itself both a reference to God's previous saving work in Christians and a reference to God's future completion of their salvation: πιστὸς ὁ καλῶν ὑμᾶς, ὃς καὶ ποιήσει. ὁ καλῶν ὑμᾶς is a circumlocution for Θεός. The present tense of the participle καλῶν shows that

---

[178] The promise of divine faithfulness, however, does not exclude the possibility that those who think they stand will in fact fall. On this possibility and its significance for perseverance, see pp. 120-130 below. Cf. Marshall (*Kept*, 107), who comments that the promises of divine faithfulness "do not rule out the possibility that a person may rebel against God and refuse His protection. The faithfulness of God does not rule out the possibility of the faithlessness of men."

[179] Cf. Conzelmann (*1 Cor*, 167), who thinks that Paul has targeted both warning and consolation to one group, namely, the strong as the whole Corinthian community whose members are in danger of becoming idolaters because of over-confidence. Conzelmann resolves the tension in this view by suggesting that Paul intends to undermine the subjective attitude of the carefree Corinthians by revealing their objective situation, which includes objective grounds for comfort as well as fear (169, n. 46).

God "stands in a permanent relation to these Thessalonians" (see also 2:12).[180] Thus Paul even makes the divine title communicate the continuity in God's saving action toward the Thessalonians as the giver of salvation. The designation of God as ὁ Θεὸς τῆς εἰρήνης at v. 23 also suggests that God's relation to the Thessalonians will be characterized by God's ongoing work of salvation in them, for God is the God of "peace," an "all-encompassing term for salvation" (cf. 1:1; Rom 2:10; 8:6; 14:17).[181]

"The one who calls" them is thus faithful to the intent to accomplish their salvation, "and will do [it]." The καί joining the two parts of the saying is not merely connective but introduces a conclusion: "The one who calls you is faithful, *thus* he will do it." The particle "zeigt den inneren Zusammenhang des göttlichen Handelns an."[182] The divine attribute πιστός is thus reflected in the divine action displaying faithfulness, ποιήσει.[183] "It is not that he called them once...and has left them to their own devices thereafter."[184] Paul omits the object of ποιήσει, however, and fails to specify how God's faithfulness will manifest itself.[185] The missing link is supplied by the preceding verse.[186] In this wish-prayer,[187] Paul asks that God wholly sanctify the Thessalonian Christians (ἁγιάσαι[188] ὑμᾶς ὁλοτελεῖς[189]) and keep them blameless (ἀμέμπτως...τηρηθείη, cf. 3:13)[190] in every aspect: spirit, soul, and body (ὁλόκληρον ὑμῶν τὸ πνεῦμα καὶ ἡ ψυχὴ καὶ τὸ σῶμα)[191] at[192] the parousia. By completely sanctifying

[180] Best, *Thess*, 244. On the implications of divine calling in 1 Thess 2:12, Best comments: "They will attain to the kingdom and glory even though their walk is not always worthy of God" (108).

[181] Marshall, *Thess*, 161. Cf. Bruce, *Thess*, 129: "the sum total of gospel blessings." Similarly, v. Dobschütz, *Thess*, 228.

[182] V. d. Osten-Sacken, "Gottes Treue," 182.

[183] Cf. Morris, *Thess*, 183.

[184] Best, *Thess*, 244.

[185] Rigaux, *Thess*, 601.

[186] V. d. Osten-Sacken, "Gottes Treue," 182; v. Dobschütz, *Thess*, 230.

[187] Cf. the wish-prayers in 3:11–13; 2 Thess 3:5.

[188] Both the fundamental notion of sanctification as "setting apart" and the idea of holiness of character, which follows from it, are present in ἁγιάζειν here (Morris, *Thess*, 180; Marshall, *Thess*, 161).

[189] ὁλοτελεῖς denotes the thoroughness of God's sanctifying work. This theme receives further emphasis in ὁλόκληρον and the three-fold reference, τὸ πνεῦμα καὶ ἡ ψυχὴ καὶ τὸ σῶμα (see below with n. 191; Bruce, *Thess*, 129).

[190] ἀμέμπτως—blame*less*—here reiterates the basic negative meaning of ἁγιάζειν, "to set apart from all that is profane." V. Dobschütz (*Thess*, 229) explains ἁγιάζειν in this way rather than giving it an ethical sense. In the chiastically constructed 1 Thess 5:23, ἁγιάσαι ὁλοτελεῖς corresponds to ἀμέμπτως τηρηθείη. On the construction, see Best, *Thess*, 243.

[191] ὁλόκληρον reinforces the thought in ὁλοτελεῖς by explicating the object of sanctification—ὑμᾶς—to be the whole human person, namely, "your spirit and soul and

believers, God ensures that in every respect they will be shown to belong to God at that event.[193] The completion of the process of sanctification already begun is in view (so also, 3:13).[194] The acclamation, "he who calls you is faithful, and will do [it]," thus expresses Paul's conviction that his wish-prayer will be heard.[195] Paul knows that God will faithfully carry out God's saving purpose toward the Thessalonians—which has become manifest already in their calling—by sanctifying them entirely.[196] At the parousia the finished divine work of Christians' salvation will be manifest in their perfect sanctification. Because God is faithful, Paul encourages, God will complete the salvation begun in their calling.[197]

1 Corinthians 1:8, 9. 1 Cor 1:9 also combines the motifs of divine faithfulness and calling: πιστὸς ὁ Θεός, δι᾽ οὗ ἐκλήθητε εἰς κοινωνίαν τοῦ υἱοῦ αὐτοῦ Ἰησοῦ Χριστοῦ τοῦ κυρίου ἡμῶν. Paul connects the promise of God's faithfulness with Christians' calling into fellowship with Christ. The κοινωνία which issues from God's calling[198] is personal association with Christ, not the experience of mystical communion.[199] The fullness of the title "his Son, Jesus Christ, our Lord" suggests that fellowship with Christ includes sharing in Christ's relation to the Father as Son (for we are "predestinated to be conformed to the image of his Son," Rom 8:29)

---

body" (Best, *Thess*, 244). ὁλόκληρος can also have a cultic sense describing animals suitable for sacrifice, Josephus *Ant*. 3.278f.

[192] ἐν stands for εἰς.

[193] Cf. Rigaux, *Thess*, 601, who also comments that Christians could despair of sanctification if left simply to their own resources. See, further, Marshall, *Thess*, 162: "In the last analysis the believer's standing with God at the parousia rests on the work of Christ rather than on any achievement of his own (even though it is the work of God within him), and for Paul believers already are sanctified through Christ when they are converted. The call to full sanctification must be taken with all seriousness, but it cannot and must not be transformed into a doctrine of final salvation by works."

[194] Bruce, *Thess*, 129; Marshall, *Thess*, 161.

[195] Morris, *Thess*, 182.

[196] V. Dobschütz, *Thess*, 230; Rigaux, *Thess*, 601; Best, *Thess*, 244. V. d. Osten-Sacken ("Gottes Treue," 184) comments: "Die erfolgte Zuwendung Gottes in der Berufung, d.h. in der Taufe, wird sich ihrem eigenen Ziel gemäß in der Bewahrung der Berufenen bis zur eschatologischen Offenbarung Jesu Christi erweisen."

[197] Weiß, *1 Kor*, 11: "Die Zuversicht gründet sich auf das, was die Christen schon erlebt haben, die Berufung—in ihr liegt die Gewähr der Vollendung." Cf. 2 Tim 2:13 for the thought that God's faithfulness to Christians does not depend on their faithfulness to him.

[198] δι᾽ οὗ refers to the subject of the action, not the agent of calling.

[199] Barrett, *1 Cor*, 39, 40; Grosheide, *1 Cor*, 32; Conzelmann, *1 Cor*, 29.

and in Christ's exalted position over creation as Lord (for we are Christ's fellow-heirs; cf. Rom 8:17).[200] This fellowship which believers enjoy with Christ is thus a fellowship which "exists now and extends to eternity."[201] κοινωνία so understood presupposes the thought of God's faithfulness.[202] Because the God who called Christians into fellowship with Christ is faithful, that fellowship is certain to continue and reach its climax when Christ comes again.[203]

God's calling of believers into fellowship with Christ makes Christian existence fundamentally oriented toward the coming of Christ to consummate God's saving work. In 1:7 Paul describes believers as ἀπεκδεχόμενοι τὴν ἀποκάλυψιν τοῦ κυρίου ἡμῶν Ἰησοῦ Χριστοῦ. The "revelation" of Christ here is Christ's manifestation in the parousia,[204] which ushers in the fulfillment of Christians' hope (cf. Rom 8:23–25; 1 Cor 15:22, 23, 51, 52).[205] God's faithfulness ensures that their anticipation will not come to nought. Indeed, the acclamation πιστὸς ὁ θεός provides a climax to Paul's thanksgiving (1:4ff.) for the beginning and completion of the salvation of those who are awaiting the revelation of Christ (1:7).[206] Here Paul gives thanks not only that the "testimony of Christ has been confirmed (ἐβεβαιώθη) in you" (1:6),[207] but also that God "will confirm (βεβαιώσει) you to the end" (1:8). Not only was the "grace of God given to you in Christ Jesus" so that "you abound" and "are lacking in no gift" (1:4, 5, 7); the Corinthians also will be "blameless on the day of our Lord Jesus Christ" (1:8).[208]

By characterizing Christ's coming as the time of consummation of salvation for believers Paul asserts that they will stand in the last judgment. For Christ will come as judge.[209] ἡ ἡμέρα τοῦ κυρίου ἡμῶν Ἰησοῦ

---

[200] Cf. Schlatter, *Bote*, 66; Barrett, *1 Cor*, 40; also Grosheide , *1 Cor*, 32; Fascher, *1 Kor*, 87.

[201] Robertson and Plummer, *1 Cor*, 8; cf. Schlatter, *Bote*, 66; Fascher, *1 Kor*, 85.

[202] Barrett, *1 Cor*, 40.

[203] Schlatter, *Bote*, 65.

[204] For this use of ἀποκάλυψις, cf. 2 Thess 1:7; 1 Pet 1:7, 13; 4:13; also Luke 17:30.

[205] Barrett, *1 Cor*, 39.

[206] V. d. Osten-Sacken ("Gottes Treue," 197) notes a connection between the faithfulness sayings and early Christian expectation of the parousia and concludes that the situation characterized by the expectation of the parousia is the *Sitz im Leben* of the faithfulness sayings.

[207] βεβαιοῦν is used here with a view to the founding and development of the church (Conzelmann, *1 Cor*, 27).

[208] Paul's thought moves easily from endowment with spiritual gifts to eschatological completion of salvation, for "the present working of the Spirit in the community is a foretoken of the future" (Conzelmann, *1 Cor*, 28).

[209] On the association of the parousia or revelation of Christ with the last judgment,

[Χριστοῦ] signifies the judgment day (1:8; cf. 3:13; 4:5).[210] On this day, Paul claims, those who have been called into fellowship with Christ will be blameless: ἀνέγκλητοι ἐν τῇ ἡμέρᾳ τοῦ κυρίου ἡμῶν Ἰησοῦ [Χριστοῦ]. The eschatological context makes ἀνέγκλητοι forensic.[211] Paul's formulation here recalls Rom 8:33 where, in the imaginary judgment scene, none can "call out a charge (ἐγκαλέσει) against God's elect." In 1 Cor 1:8 also those who have "been called" (ἐκλήθητε, v. 9)[212] will not be counted unrighteous.[213] Paul presupposes the validity of justification by faith for the final judgment.[214]

God will establish (βεβαιώσει) believers as blameless.[215] This establishment in salvation ensures their withstanding the last judgment.[216] God establishes them ἕως τέλους. Though this expression can mean "entirely," the preceding temporal reference (ἐν τῇ ἡμέρᾳ τοῦ κυρίου...) makes the interpretation, "to the end of the world," more likely.[217] Throughout the period of awaiting the revelation of the Lord Jesus Christ and up until the day of the Lord Jesus Christ, God will establish Christians. Paul is expressing not his wish here but his certainty.[218] This certainty is seen in his choice of the verb βεβαιοῦν, which in commercial usage refers to making a legally binding guarantee.[219]

The reason for Paul's certainty of God's confirmation of believers until

---

cf. Best, *Thess*, 152; v. d. Osten-Sacken, "Gottes Treue," 193.

[210] Barrett, *1 Cor*, 39.

[211] Conzelmann, *1 Cor*, 28. The term refers not to moral perfection but to the irreproachability which comes from having the righteousness of Christ (Barrett, *1 Cor*, 39).

[212] Conzelmann, *1 Cor*, 29. Perhaps there is an intentional play on the words ἐκλήθητε at v. 9 and ἀνέγκλητοι at v. 8.

[213] Cf. v. d. Osten-Sacken, "Gottes Treue," 184: "Bewahrung vor den Sünden...insofern eben die Verfehlungen den Grund zur Anklage, zum Vorwurf bilden würden."

[214] Barrett, *1 Cor*, 39.

[215] It is more likely that ὅς as the subject of βεβαιώσει in v. 8 refers to θεός of v. 4 and v. 9 (so, Conzelmann, *1 Cor*, 28; Fascher, *1 Kor*, 86) than to Χριστός of v. 7 (so Barrett, *1 Cor*, 39). In 2 Cor 1:21 also God is the one who confirms believers (ὁ βεβαιῶν). There too, βεβαιοῦν is linked with juridical and soteriological terms (Conzelmann, *1 Cor*, 27, n. 29; cf. Windisch, *2 Kor*, 71).

[216] Fascher, *1 Kor*, 86: "Die Gefahr des Abgleitens in das Gericht wird ja durch den θεός βεβαιῶν gebannt werden."

[217] So Conzelmann, *1 Cor*, 28; v. d. Osten-Sacken, "Gottes Treue," 179; Barrett, *1 Cor*, 39; Bachmann, *1 Kor*, 41; see, further, Windisch, *2 Kor*, 57–59.

[218] With Conzelmann, *1 Cor*, 28; Fascher, *1 Kor*, 86.

[219] With Schlier, βέβαιος, *TWNT* 1, 603. On the meaning of βεβαιοῦν in commercial usage, see Schlier, 602. For the NT use of βέβαιος and cognates with the connotations found in commercial usage, cf. Heb 2:2, 3; 6:16; Phil 1:7; 1 Cor 1:6; Mark 16:20 (see Schlier, 603).

the end lies in v. 9: πιστὸς ὁ θεός.[220] The structure of the faithfulness saying in 1 Cor 1:8, 9 is opposite that in 1 Thess 5:24. There ὃς καὶ + future tense appears after πιστός ὁ θεός, whereas here it appears before.[221] Paul's meaning is nevertheless clear. He wants the Corinthians to anticipate the coming judge with all confidence of a favorable outcome in spite of their many failures in the Christian life, which the whole first epistle to the Corinthians reflects. Though circumstances in Corinth leave much to be desired, Paul's hope is firm. "The goal (of acceptance at the day of Christ) is sure, notwithstanding man's unfaithfulness...because God...is faithful."[222]

In conclusion, the faithfulness sayings put the promise of God's faithfulness in the context of the eschatological distress and the following climactic events of the parousia and the day of the Lord. God will faithfully enable believers to endure the severe testing associated with the end times. God will guard and protect them so that they will continue to maintain their Christian identity in faith and practice instead of succumbing in the onslaughts of evil. Paul acclaims God's faithfulness to establish believers to the end, irreproachable in the day of the Lord, wholly sanctified, and kept blameless in every respect at the parousia. He thus attributes final salvation to God's faithful fulfillment of the saving work God has already begun. G. C. Berkouwer's comment is appropriate here: "His faithfulness does not depend on our faithfulness, nor on anything that is or will be present in us. There is rather a 'nevertheless', an 'in spite of'. Viewed from one side it is unmotivated and incomprehensible."[223] God's faithfulness is thus a guarantee of continuity in salvation, which not only makes Christians able to withstand eschatological tribulation but also puts their final salvation on sure ground.

---

[220] Grosheide, *1 Cor*, 31.

[221] For this and other formal observations on the faithfulness sayings, see v. d. Osten-Sacken, "Gottes Treue," 183.

[222] Barrett, *1 Cor*, 39 (cf. 2 Tim 2:13). Similarly, Orr and Walther, *1 Cor*, 145, 146: "Regardless of failure, backsliding, and corruption they will not be blamed *on the day of the Lord*...here he states unconditionally that they will be blameless in the final evaluation." Indeed, as Bachmann (*1 Kor*, 50) observes, the thanksgiving (1:4–9) lacks any reference to the readers' own behavior in response to the grace of God. He also notes that 1 Cor 1:4–9 has not merely an innocent group of Corinthians in view but the whole church; furthermore, the tone is sincere, not ironical (49).

[223] Berkouwer, *Faith and Perseverance*, 222.

CONCLUSION TO PART ONE

Preliminary conclusions from the exegetical studies in Part One of this investigation can now be drawn. In Chapter I we saw how Paul relates the various aspects of God's saving work in believers to the consummation of their salvation. A continuity in the divine work of salvation emerges in which a particular aspect of salvation is seen to imply the succeeding ones. The culmination of salvation, described as glorification, obtaining glory or salvation, or conformity to the image of the Son of God, is portrayed as the sure end of this process. Paul argues in two principal ways for the certain realization of believers' full salvation. First, he points to the aspects of salvation which have already been realized in their lives. God has given them the Spirit, who indwells them as the "firstfruits" of salvation and serves as a "deposit" or guarantee, both of which metaphors guarantee God's completion of their redemption. They are sealed with this same Spirit and thus belong to God and come under divine protection with a view to the accomplishment of their full salvation. Further, God has called and justified them. Final salvation is the goal of these divine initiatives. And, according to Paul, the goal which God has set out to fulfill, God will also finish. By portraying salvation as God's work, and by affirming that God will indeed not leave the "good work" already begun unfinished but will faithfully complete it in Christians' lives, Paul undergirds the certainty of final salvation.

Second, Paul draws attention to the eternal divine initiatives in salvation: divine election, foreknowledge and predestination. He shows that these initiatives also have the final salvation of Christians as their ultimate goal. The completion of salvation is thus part of God's eternal will. In this way Paul lifts the matter of final salvation above the uncertainties of temporal events and into the realm of the reality to which history will ultimately fully conform.[1] God's eternal purpose is the reality upon which Christian faith and hope is based. Therefore Paul directs Christians to ponder their final salvation in the light of God's eternal counsel and so look forward to it as a certainty.

In summary, Paul conceives of the consummation of Christians' salvation as the ultimate goal both of God's present saving action toward them and of God's eternal purpose concerning them. And Paul portrays this goal as certain to reach fulfillment because it depends on God's faithful, continued action toward this end according to the working out of God's eternal purpose.

---

[1] Cf. Coenen, "Elect," *NIDNTT* 1, 542.

In Chapter II we saw, however, that the process of consummating the work of salvation is more like an obstacle course than a downhill ride to the finishline. For the destiny of Christians does not go unchallenged in a world opposed to God's purposes. The powers of evil in the form of afflictions and trials threaten continuity in their salvation. Christians face such antagonism in particular during the period of the eschatological distress through the last judgment. But Paul assures them that these threats will not succeed in cutting them off from the hope of salvation. Divine faithfulness guarantees continuity in salvation despite threats to it. Because God is faithful God will complete the work of salvation begun in Christians. God's faithfulness includes enabling them to endure severe testing and intensified evil. Through divine strengthening and protection they will not finally succumb to evil but will maintain their Christian identity in word and deed. God will provide the way out of this crisis, which will thus issue in final salvation. At the day of Christ God will further manifest God's faithfulness by confirming the blamelessness of those have believed in Jesus Christ. They are bound together in lasting fellowship with the Son of God, whose righteousness will be reckoned to them also in the judgment. They belong to God, who sanctifies them entirely in view of Christ's return to judge the world. In faithfulness God will complete the goal of believers' calling by consummating their salvation.

In his acclamations of God's faithfulness Paul attributes continuity in salvation to the faithfulness of the saving God. Paul thinks of divine faithfulness in salvation christologically as God's love in Jesus Christ. This love which was made manifest in the gift of God's Son guarantees continuity in salvation. By arguing christologically for continuity in salvation Paul is able to understand continuity in terms of the overcoming of obstacles to salvation. For, when Jesus died on the cross, God's love gained the victory over the powers of sin and death which contest salvation. The love of God in Christ Jesus is the power of Christians' salvation in the face of their own impotence against these adversaries. Paul affirms that nothing—be it a human or superhuman power—can wrest believers away from God's love which won their salvation. For no hindrance to salvation is stronger than divine love, whose surpassing power is displayed in the delivering up of God's own Son for sinners. Not even God's "enemies" in their rebellion against God could stop God from reconciling them to God. From this supreme demonstration of divine love Paul concludes that nothing can prevent the consummation of salvation for those who have accepted the gift of God's Son by faith and are justified. This loving God has shown in Christ that God is "for us" and will show it again in the final judgment by delivering a favorable verdict confirming Christians' justification. In that climactic event, "the one who loved us" will again intervene for our salvation, as he did on the cross, now as the exalted Son of God, interceding on our behalf and appealing to his own definitive provision for sin, which is the evidence of his all-powerful love. In the meantime, as believers confront present afflictions, the Spirit testifies in them of the divine love lavished on them as the promise of certain final salvation.

Up against God's faithfulness and love, present afflictions and tribulation fail to make Christians' hope of final salvation less sure. Thus they cannot pose a deadly threat. But not only does Paul relativize their negative significance. He also views them positively in the light of the certainty of believers' final salvation. All adversities are caught up into God's overarching purpose of salvation and made to contribute to it. In suffering, Christians manifest their unity with Christ, a sign that they also share Christ's destiny of glorification. Seen in this way, afflictions are even the proper object of "boasting," for they provide occasions for God to work out God's saving intent, as the fruits of suffering in the lives of Christians also manifest.

In conclusion, Paul gives clear and ample evidence of his view that Christians' salvation is certain to reach completion. This thought is integral to his understanding of individual salvation. Though threats to the consummation of Christians' salvation may and will appear, they cannot *successfully* challenge it. God's faithfulness and love make divine triumph the unquestionable outcome. For Paul, certainty of final salvation rests on God's continued intervention to that end.

PART TWO

CONDUCT AND FALLING AWAY

In the texts analyzed in Part One Paul portrays Christians' salvation as having certain continuity based on God's continuing, faithful intervention toward the full accomplishment of God's saving purpose which has become manifest in Christians' present salvation. Does this promise of final salvation hold true without qualification? Or is it conditional upon appropriate behavior? Paul expects Christians not to "continue in sin" but to "walk in newness of life" and to "present [their] members as slaves of righteousness unto sanctification" (Rom 6:1, 4, 19). And, as those led by the Spirit, they truly can practice righteousness, for they are freed from sin, which took advantage through the law and produced failure in the struggle against the flesh (Rom 6:22; 7:7–24; 8:2, 4). Nevertheless, Paul must confront persistent and grievous sin in his churches. A number of examples of such confrontation have in the history of exegesis frequently been taken to offer evidence that Christians' ethical failure can cost them their eschatological inheritance. In Part Two these texts will be studied in order to determine what implications, in Paul's mind, ethical failure can have for continuity in Christians' salvation.

III. "DESTRUCTION" OF THE WEAK

In 1 Corinthians 8:7–13 and Romans 14:1–23 Paul addresses a problem which arises when Christians have different opinions on whether they are free to eat certain foods: when believers who claim no such freedom observe fellow Christians exercising freedom, the former might be led to eat the food which their conscience does not allow them. As a result of this self-contradictory behavior, a person can be "destroyed" (ἀπόλλυμι). Although there are differences between Paul's presentations of the basic problem in 1 Corinthians 8 and Romans 14,[1] both passages share the most basic elements important for the present study—exercising freedom to eat food against one's convictions and being "destroyed"—as well as some secondary motifs.[2] This parallelism justifies their joint treatment here. The two passages are significant for the discussion of continuity in salvation since they raise the question of the detrimental consequences for a Christian who sins wittingly. I will seek to answer the following questions raised by these passages. What is the nature of the destruction of the believer who violates her conscience? Is destruction definitive or not, and why?[3]

First the problem must be defined more precisely. In the Roman and Corinthian communities, members differ in their assessment of certain foods. Some "have γνῶσις/πίστις" (1 Cor 8:10; Rom 14:22) and so partake freely of foods considered by others (the "weak," Rom 14:1, 2; 1 Cor 8:9) as κοινόν (Rom 14:14) or εἰδωλόθυτον (1 Cor 8:7). According to Paul, however, freedom in regard to foods, though in and of itself

---

[1] In Romans 14 the issue is the purity of foods, whereas in 1 Corinthians 8 Paul discusses foods as εἰδωλόθυτον. In the Corinthians discussion the συνείδησις is supposed to check behavior whereas in Romans actions should spring ἐκ πίστεως.

[2] These common motifs will become apparent in the following discussion.

[3] I will not discuss the final destiny of the Christian who *influences* another to sin wittingly. Paul does not apply the language of destruction to this person. He only says that by "sinning against the brothers" one "sins against Christ" (1 Cor 8:12). And Paul gives no reason to conclude that sinning against Christ brings on any sort of destruction (contrast Marshall, *Kept*, 113; Wolff, *1 Kor*, 15; Conzelmann, *1 Cor*, 150, n. 40). We may not read Matt 18:6, 7 par. into the Pauline context (against Wolff, *1 Kor*, 13).

legitimate (1 Cor 8:7, 8; Rom 14:14), cannot be exercised indiscriminately. Those who partake freely should not by their example serve as a catalyst for others to transgress their conscience when it forbids them to eat.[4] *All* who exercise freedom in regard to foods must have the accompanying conviction of the rightness of their action. Otherwise they "stumble" (προσ- κόπτειν, Rom 14:21; πρόσκομμα, Rom 14:13, 20; 1 Cor 8:9; σκάνδαλον, Rom 14:13; σκανδαλίζειν, 1 Cor 8:13), are "condemned" (κατακρίνειν, Rom 14:23), and "destroyed" (ἀπόλλυμι, Rom 14:15; 1 Cor 8:11; κατα- λύειν, Rom 14:20). Do these consequences of acting against one's convictions entail loss of salvation?

The vast majority of commentators think that Paul is contemplating this possibility.[5] E. Gaugler comments: "Der Schwache verliert sein Heil, wenn er sein Gewissen vergewaltigt."[6] The use of the verb ἀπόλλυμι in this context seems to support this view, for in Paul it typically connotes eternal ruin (see Rom 2:12; 1 Cor 1:18, 19; 15:18; 2 Cor 2:15; 4:3; 2 Thess 2:10). Thus O. Michel, for example, judges: "Im Anschluß an einen bestimmten jü- dischen Begriff bedeutet ἀπόλλυμι hier: 'in Sünde verstricken, das eschato- logische Leben zerstören, den Glauben zunichte machen'."[7]

But, considering the degree of seriousness of the sin, this judgment seems unduly severe. Can it really be that Paul warns against eternal de- struction for an act contrary to an *overscrupulous, misguided* Christian con- science, an act in and of itself *permissible* for Christians? Indeed this inter- pretation appears to some to require qualifications. "It would be wrong to think that a single act of sin is going to cost him [the weaker Christian] his soul."[8] It seems easier to some interpreters to speak here in terms of a pro- cess: "Eine Untreue, so klein sie auch aussehen mag, trennt den Gläubigen von seinem Herrn.... Damit beginnt der geistliche Tod, und wenn dieser Zu- stand fortdauert und sich befestigt, was in einem solchen Fall unvermeid- lich ist, so führt dies schließlich zum ewigen Verderben."[9] Further, it seems

---

[4] In Rom 14:22, 23 the terms διακρίνεσθαι and πίστις are used in connection with the assessment of foods. This activity is associated with the συνείδησις in 1 Cor 8:7, 10, 12.

[5] See Conzelmann, *1 Cor*, 149, n. 38; *et al.*

[6] Gaugler, *Röm* II, 347.

[7] Michel, *Röm*, 433. See also Schlier, *Röm*, 414; Cranfield, *Rom*, 715; Müller, *Anstoss*, 41; Fee, *1 Cor*, 387; Godet, *1 Kor* II, 14; Wolff, *1 Kor*, 14.

[8] Marshall, *Kept*, 113.

[9] Godet, *1 Kor* II, 14. It should be noted that this view does not presuppose that the weak Christian has *already* suffered definitive destruction and that 1 Cor 8:11 and Rom 14:15 thus provide examples of Christians who have actually lost salvation. Indeed, this judgment would not be allowed on grammatical grounds. Paul uses the present tense of ἀπόλλυμι indicating linear action. A process of destruction is in view. (Cf. the present

like the application of "destruction" terminology here borders on exaggeration. The choice of strong words leads I. H. Marshall to suggest that Paul "is pressing his point to the limit...in order to stress the enormity of the act" of sin. Marshall then softens the predicted destruction to an "ultimate possibility," though not an "unreal one."[10] These two qualifications—the strong terminology is emphatic and the damage is progressive—render less unpalatable the interpretation that the weak Christian becomes subject to a destruction which is eternal for violating the conscience in relation to foods. But this thought is unusual enough, to say the least, to warrant thorough re-examination and an investigation of alternatives. In the following discussion I will try to establish the meaning of ἀπόλλυμι as applied to believers who transgress the judgment of their conscience in amoral matters. How does the context illumine the meaning of the verb as used in 1 Corinthians 8 and Romans 14? What expressions parallel ἀπόλλυμι and illumine its meaning? What in the context contrasts with ἀπόλλυμι? What other texts shed light on the interpretation of ἀπόλλυμι?

The NT occurrences of ἀπόλλυμι (active: "destroy;" middle: "perish"[11]) as a theological term for eternal destruction do not provide any parallels to the proposed possibility of falling *from salvation* to destruction: salvation is never followed by destruction. And in one occurrence this possibility is explicitly denied: at John 10:28 Jesus affirms that his sheep οὐ μὴ ἀπόλωνται εἰς τὸν αἰῶνα and that "no one shall snatch them out of my hand."[12] The view that the weak *Christian* in 1 Corinthians 8 and Romans 14 who sins against her conscience can perish ultimately would introduce a thought foreign to and even in contradiction with NT usage of ἀπόλλυμι.

Furthermore, in every NT occurrence of ἀπόλλυμι for definitive destruction of persons the context confirms this meaning, when not obvious, by explicit contrastive and parallel motifs: salvation, faith, repentance, the

---

tenses of parallel verbs in both passages, especially κατάλυε in Rom 14:20; the variant reading ἀπολεῖται at 1 Cor 8:11, which has the future tense, could have arisen out of an eschatological understanding of destruction). Further, the outcome of the process is uncertain. Thus Paul can exhort, "Stop destroying...!" (Rom 14:15). The destruction is both incomplete and reversible (Orr and Walther, *1 Cor*, 232). Contrast the absence of a suggestion of reversal in the progressive destruction of unbelievers at 1 Cor 1:18; 2 Cor 2:15; 4:3, where Paul uses the present participle ἀπολλυμένοις to denote "perish" in the ultimate sense.

[10] Marshall, *Kept*, 113.

[11] The active voice appears in Rom 14:15 and the passive voice in 1 Cor 8:11.

[12] The one exception—καὶ οὐδεὶς ἐξ αὐτῶν ἀπώλετο εἰ μὴ ὁ υἱὸς τῆς ἀπωλείας—because it *is* an exception, requires a justification: ἵνα ἡ γραφὴ πληρωθῇ (John 17:12).

notion of eternality or final judgment (see Rom 2:12; 1 Cor 1:18; 15:18; 2 Cor 2:15; 4:3; 2 Thess 2:10; Matt 10:28; Luke 19:10; John 3:16; 10:28; 12:25; 17:12; Jas 4:12; 2 Pet 3:9).[13] Without illumination by the context the meaning of ἀπόλλυμι in these instances would remain unclear since there would be no way of distinguishing it from other meanings of the verb.[14] What light does the context shed on the meaning of ἀπόλλυμι in 1 Corinthians 8 and Romans 14? Does the context in these cases point toward the meaning "eternal destruction"?

In Rom 14:15 and 1 Cor 8:11 Paul protests the destruction of the weak Christian by appealing to Christ's dying for that person: ὑπὲρ οὗ (or δι' ὃν) Χριστὸς ἀπέθανεν. Many take Paul to be putting forward a contrast between salvation and destruction: Christ died to *save* the weak Christian, but a loveless fellow Christian *destroys* the weak person, i.e. negates the effectiveness of Christ's death.[15] But does not Paul mean to contrast two types of *behavior* toward the weak rather than the *effects* of this behavior?[16] After all, ἀπόλλυμι has no counterpart—"save," or the like—in the text. Paul states rather that Χριστὸς ἀπέθανεν, which contrasts with οὐκέτι κατὰ ἀγάπην περιπατεῖς (Rom 14:15) and ἁμαρτάνοντες εἰς τοὺς ἀδελφούς (1 Cor 8:12). That is, Christ's dying contrasts to the enlightened Christian's eating food which provokes another to sin.[17] Of course, these two types of behavior do have different effects. But that is not what Paul is driving at. Rather, his point lies in the difference between the two types of behavior themselves. J. A. Bengel captures the attitudes behind such radically different actions: "Do not make more of thy food than Christ did of his life."[18] The point of the contrast lies in the recognition of the value of the other. Christ's self-sacrifice reveals the "divine measure of the worth of a human being."[19] Paul inspires the offenders to curtail their freedom for the sake of their fellow Christians by arguing how the cross makes these weaker ones indeed "worthy" of such love. Instead of a destruction-salvation contrast in Paul's christological reference, therefore, we

---

[13] Cf. the contextual contrasts and parallels with ἀπώλεια in Rom 9:22; Phil 1:28; 3:19; 1 Tim 6:9; Heb 10:39; 2 Pet 3:7.

[14] E.g., "kill," "die," "ruin," "lose," "pass away;" see BAGD, s.v. ἀπόλλυμι.

[15] Murphy-O'Connor, "Freedom," 29; Robertson and Plummer, *1 Cor*, 172; Barrett, *1 Cor*, 196; Maly, *Gemeinde*, 118; Merk, *Handeln*, 123; Nababan, *Bekenntnis*, 95.

[16] Cf. Schlatter, *Bote*, 265, 266; Fee, *1 Cor*, 388.

[17] The destruction wrought is repeatedly traced to the exercise of freedom to eat: διὰ βρῶμα..., τῷ βρώματι..., ἕνεκεν βρώματος... (Rom 14:15a, 15b, 20; see also Rom 14:21, 23; 1 Cor 8:11, 13).

[18] Bengel, *NT Commentary* II, 150.

[19] Bruce, *Rom*, 252.

ought to see a comparison of divine love with human neglect of love.[20]

Do we, however, find a destruction-salvation contrast in Rom 14:20: μὴ ἕνεκεν βρώματος κατάλυε τὸ ἔργον τοῦ Θεοῦ? If ἔργον τοῦ Θεοῦ refers to individual salvation or the work of Christ on the cross, the danger of destroying this work would parallel the idea that the strong Christians are demolishing the efficacy of Christ's death for the weak.[21] But it is not clear whether Paul means ἔργον τοῦ Θεοῦ to refer to salvation or to the church as God's "building" (1 Cor 3:9).[22] The concern for mutual edification in the kingdom life in Rom 14:17–19 speaks for the latter. Another factor which lessens the likelihood of a destruction-salvation contrast in Rom 14:20 is that in the NT καταλύειν lacks the connotations of final destruction frequently present in ἀπόλλυμι. In Gal 2:18 Paul can even contemplate building up (οἰκοδομῶ) the things he tore down (κατέλυσα). καταλύειν in and of itself therefore cannot suggest the eternal destruction of τὸ ἔργον τοῦ Θεοῦ.

The wider context discloses the intended contrast to the destructive effect of indiscriminate exercise of Christian freedom. Paul advocates edification instead of destruction:[23] διώκωμεν καὶ τὰ τῆς οἰκοδομῆς τῆς εἰς ἀλλήλους (Rom 14:19)...ἕκαστος ἡμῶν τῷ πλησίον ἀρεσκέτω εἰς τὸ ἀγαθὸν πρὸς οἰκοδομήν (15:2).[24] The call to mutual edification at v. 19 is complemented by the prohibition of "destroy[ing] the work of God on account of food" at v. 20. In 1 Cor 10:24 a similar exhortation to "seek τὸ τοῦ ἑτέρου" surfaces in another discussion about freedom regarding food. Paul there reminds his readers that οὐ πάντα οἰκοδομεῖ (1 Cor 10:23) and warns them of the harmful consequences which their eating

---

[20] Paul's parenetic appeal to his own example of voluntary self-restriction in his apostolic ministry—μὴ ζητῶν τὸ ἐμαυτοῦ σύμφορον ἀλλὰ τὸ τῶν πολλῶν, ἵνα σωθῶσιν (1 Cor 10:33; cf. chap. 9)—might be taken as advice to curtail freedom to eat for the sake of another's *salvation*. But that application presses the parallel too far. For Paul seeks to save those who do not yet believe, whereas those who have "knowledge" regarding food have a responsibility toward their fellow Christians. The principle of self-restriction for the sake of the other applies both to evangelism and community life. The effects of this practice may differ in their respective settings, "toward Jews and Greeks" or "toward the church of God" (1 Cor 10:32). In either case, Paul can say, "whether you eat or drink or whatever you do, do all to the glory of God" (1 Cor 10:31).

[21] Nababan (*Bekenntnis*, 97) sees this to be the connection between the two statements about destruction.

[22] For the latter view, see Käsemann, *Rom*, 378; Lietzmann, *Röm*, 117; Schlier, *Röm*, 417.

[23] Edification of the individual, here, the "weak" Christian, is one aspect of the edification of the church as the "work of God."

[24] Cambier ("Liberté," 73, n. 31): "L'image de la déstruction est sans doute inspirée par le terme 'édification mutuelle' (14,19)."

freely may have. Furthermore, when Paul uses οἰκοδομεῖν ironically at 1 Cor 8:10[25] for "building up" the "weak" conscience to eat meat sacrificed to idols, he concludes that quite the reverse of edification results: ἀπόλλυ ται γὰρ ὁ ἀσθενῶν ἐν τῇ σῇ γνώσει (1 Cor 8:11). This so-called edification parallels the "puffing up" (φυσιοῦν) which comes through knowledge. For precisely that, he says, is what knowledge does,[26] whereas love "builds up" (οἰκοδομεῖ, 1 Cor 8:1). Because the strong "do not walk according to love," which edifies, they "are destroying the one for whom Christ died" (Rom 14:15) instead of building their fellow Christian up. In 2 Cor 10:8; 13:10 Paul achieves the contrast to οἰκοδομή with another term for destruction, καθαίρεσις.[27] His apostolic ἐξουσία is given "for building up and not tearing down." Christian freedom, which Paul also calls ἐξου σία (1 Cor 8:9), must also serve to build up and not destroy. The suggestion that Paul intends to contrast "destruction" with "edification" when discussing the matter of food thus receives support both from the context and from parallel texts.[28]

An enjoinder toward edification of one's fellow Christian (and thus toward love) in one's use of Christian freedom with respect to food reflects Paul's general concern for mutual edification which is especially evident in 1 Corinthians (see 14:3–5, 12, 17, 26; 12:7). Whereas the improper use of spiritual gifts can simply deprive the church of edification (1 Cor 14:17) —and thus frustrate the purpose of spiritual gifts—the unloving practice of Christian freedom can actually destroy the work of God. In both cases Paul sees a hindrance to edification. The second instance not only deters but actually works the opposite of edification: destruction.

In summary, in 1 Corinthians 8 and Romans 14 Paul does not set up a contrast between the destruction terminology applied to the Christian who acts against her convictions, on the one hand, and salvation terminology, on the other. Rather, in both the immediate and wider contexts of Rom 14:15 and 1 Cor 8:11 a contrast between destruction and edification becomes obvious. This contrast suggests a weaker meaning for "destruction." I will now try to define this weaker meaning of ἀπόλλυμι more precisely and establish whether it can be substantiated sufficiently.

As already noted, the view that Paul is referring to a destructive process, not full and immediate destruction, makes better sense of the two texts

---

[25] So Furnish, *Love Command*, 114.

[26] Furnish (*Love Command*, 112) thinks that the "puffing up" of knowledge (ἡ γνῶσις φυσιοῖ) hurts not only the individual but also relationships in the community.

[27] Cf. the contrast ἀπόλλυμι/ἀνοικοδομεῖν in Jer 1:10 LXX.

[28] Cf. Merk, *Handeln*, 130.

under consideration.[29] The weaker meaning for ἀπόλλυμι suggested by the context must therefore connote partial destruction.

But where would this process of destruction end? What kind of destruction is in view? Our answer to this question ought to take into account Paul's other descriptions of the adverse effects which the careless exercise of freedom has upon the weak. Paul says that the "brother is caused to stumble" (1 Cor 8:13; cf. 8:9; Rom 14:13, 20, 21). The one who partakes οὐκ ἐκ πίστεως sins (Rom 14:23) and as a result his weak conscience "is defiled" (μολύνεται, 1 Cor 8:7). The conscience suffers a blow (τύπτοντες ...τὴν συνείδησιν, 1 Cor 8:12) and the weak one "is made to sorrow (λυπεῖται, Rom 14:15). What kind of damage do these expressions suggest? What is their relationship to destruction (ἀπόλλυμι)? What contrasts does Paul set up to these other adverse effects, and can these contrasts shed light on the fundamental contrast between destruction and edification?

The statement ὁ ἀδελφός σου λυπεῖται in Rom 14:15 refers to a *sub-jective* condition. Grief (λύπη) now characterizes the weak Christian's psychological state instead of joy (χαρά), which should prevail in the kingdom of God (Rom 14:17). "Food and drink," in which the kingdom of God does not consist, as Paul explicitly denies (Rom 14:17), have become a source of sorrow for the weak. For, led by the example of others, they transgress their conscience and suffer the pain of a defiled conscience: ἡ συνείδησις αὐτῶν...μολύνεται (1 Cor 8:7).[30] But the pangs of conscience lead to more than remorse. The overscrupulous conscience condemns those who disregard its guiding function: ὁ δὲ διακρινόμενος ἐὰν φάγῃ κατακέκριται, ὅτι οὐκ ἐκ πίστεως (Rom 14:23).[31] The victim of self-condemnation

---

[29] See above, pp. 86, 87 with n. 9.

[30] Pierce, *Conscience*, 78; Jewett, *Terms*, 424. Wilckens (*Röm* III, 92) interprets Rom 14:15 in parallel fashion: "Sie fügen seinem Wahrheitsbewußtsein Schmerzen zu."

[31] The passive voice of κατακέκριται leaves the subject of the action unidentified. Some interpreters assume that we have here a divine passive (e.g. Michel, *Röm*, 439; cf. Käsemann, *Rom*, 379). Nevertheless, word usage shows that κατακρίνειν can have a human subject (so Matt 12:41, 42; 20:18; 27:3; Mark 10:33; 14:64; Luke 11:31, 32; John 8:10; Rom 2:1; Heb 11:7), and need not refer to the eschatological judgment (see preceding references except Matt 12:41, 42). The context of κατακέκριται at Rom 14:23 clearly allows that the implied subject is human and that the passive verb refers to self-condemnation. The whole passage is concerned with the subjective state of the person who acts contrary to personal convictions. The view that Paul has self-condemnation in mind can draw further support from the contrast he sets up between "the one who does not judge himself" (ὁ μὴ κρίνων ἑαυτόν) and the one who "is condemned" (κατακέκριται). The opposite of "not judging *oneself*" is "being judged" *by oneself*. Sinning by failing to act out of faith (cf. 14:23b, "everything that is not from faith is sin") can bring on this self-condemnation. Rom 2:1 provides a parallel for the possibility of self-condemnation: σεαυτὸν κατακρίνεις. Although initially we might have

contrasts with ὁ μὴ κρίνων ἑαυτὸν ἐν ᾧ δοκιμάζει (Rom 14:22). The latter alone enjoys the blessedness of inner peace: μακάριος ὁ μὴ κρίνων ἑαυτὸν ἐν ᾧ δοκιμάζει (Rom 14:22).[32] If one acts against one's convictions, however, one's integrity and well-being are threatened in a fundamental way. Sir 14:1, 2 pronounces a strikingly parallel blessing on the person who avoids the grief and self-condemnation which arises from sin:

μακάριος ἀνήρ, ὃς οὐκ ὠλίσθησεν ἐν τῷ στόματι αὐτοῦ
καὶ οὐ κατενύγη ἐν λύπῃ ἁμαρτιῶν ·
μακάριος οὗ οὐ κατέγνω ἡ ψυχὴ αὐτοῦ,
καὶ ὃς οὐκ ἔπεσεν ἀπὸ τῆς ἐλπίδος αὐτοῦ.

Paul appears, however, not to limit the damage incurred by the weak Christian to a worsened subjective condition. She suffers an objective setback in the Christian life also.[33] Though she may not have sinned by "the letter of the law"—for, οὐδὲν κοινὸν δι' ἑαυτοῦ (Rom 14:14)—she will nevertheless have sinned by violating her convictions. For πᾶν δὲ ὃ οὐκ ἐκ πίστεως ἁμαρτία ἐστίν (Rom 14:23). Even a misinformed conscience may not be transgressed without incurring objective guilt. The weak Christian regresses as a Christian by not letting πίστις (conviction before God in 14:23, as in 14:22[34]), through the guidelines of conscience, determine her behavior.

The sin consists not in the act of eating itself but in violating one's convictions, or acting without πίστις. For Paul this battle is internal, having to

---

expected κατακέκριται at Rom 14:23 to be a divine passive and speak of God's condemnation on the erring believer, we are finally led to call that view into question because of the theological difficulties it poses in the light of texts like Rom 8:1—οὐδὲν ἄρα νῦν κατάκριμα τοῖς ἐν Χριστῷ Ἰησοῦ. It is also hard to explain how divine condemnation can result from a simple act not grounded in faith, *not* from an absence of faith altogether. It thus seems much less problematic to regard the weak Christian not as an apostate but merely a hypocrite.

[32] With Barrett (*Rom*, 267): "Once this man's faith and reason have affirmed a course of action he does not waver: happy is he in that he does not." Behind the makarism stands Paul's concern for the subjective state of the weak.

[33] Cf. Eckstein, *Syneidesis*, 241. In 2 Cor 2:6–11 Paul pictures the compounding of subjective and objective damage when a person sins and becomes overwhelmed by excessive sorrow, and when Satan, taking advantage of the situation, then wreaks more damage.

[34] Cf. Gaugler (*Röm* II, 357, 358): "Alle Erklärungen, die annehmen, dass auch hier vom Heilsglauben gesprochen werde, tragen zu viel ein und wirken künstlich.... Es geht aber nicht um die Frage, ob der Täter überhaupt Glauben habe oder nicht, sondern ob er bei seinem Handeln die Gewißheit besitzt, Gott auf seiner Seite zu haben oder nicht.... Es ist eindeutig an die Gewißheit gedacht, die aus der lautern Überzeugung stammt, in Einheit mit der eigenen, persönlichen Führung zu handeln."

do with motives, not external, having to do with absolute right or wrong. The weak Christian thus does not become an idolator[35] by eating food she regards as εἰδωλόθυτον. Rather, the one who is weak sins by failing to live from faith. Paul describes this sinning metaphorically as "stumbling" (προσκόπτει, Rom 14:21) over a "stumbling block" put in the way by those who practice their freedom (τιθέναι πρόσκομμα, Rom 14:13). The weak Christian is "caused to fall" (σκανδαλίζειν, 1 Cor 8:13) when others set up an occasion of offense (τιθέναι σκάνδαλον, Rom 14:13).[36]

---

[35] Against Fee, *1 Cor*, 387, 381; v. Soden, "Sakrament," 243; Wolff, *1 Kor*, 149; Sanders, *Law*, 110. Fee's view that 1 Corinthians 8 discusses the question of attending cultic meals (as in 10:14–22), not merely eating sacrificial food sold in the marketplace, leads him to take idolatry to be the reason for the destruction of the weak Christian. Fee is aware that his reconstruction faces the difficulty that in chap. 8 Paul argues against the Corinthians' behavior not because it is idolatrous, but because it is not loving (363, n. 23). If idolatry really is in question, surely Paul would not have failed to prohibit their practices as *inherently* wrong, and not merely as detrimental for weaker fellow-Christians. When Paul explicitly prohibits participating in demon worship at cultic meals in chap. 10, he does so on the grounds that such behavior is inherently idolatrous. Fee tries to get around this difficulty by saying that (a) Paul's argument follows the course of the Corinthians' argument (in their letter in which they insist on their "right" to go to the temples based on their "knowledge" which "builds up"), and that (b) Paul generally begins with the indicative rather than the imperative (390, 391; 363, n. 23). But the textual data seem to me to indicate that, at least with reference to the weak Christian's behavior, Paul is not discussing idolatry in chap. 8. Although Paul speaks of the Christian with knowledge "lying in an idol's temple" (ἐν εἰδωλείῳ κατακείμενον, 8:10a), the weak Christian who sees this behavior is said to "be built up to eat the things sacrificed to idols" (οἰκοδομηθήσεται εἰς τὸ τὰ εἰδωλόθυτα ἐσθίειν, 8:10b), a description which does not necessarily include participation in idolatrous cultic meals but can simply refer to the eating of marketplace food (see BAGD, s.v. εἰδωλόθυτος; so Acts 15:29, 21:25; 1 Cor 10:28 in the textual witnesses C D F G ψ𝔐). At 8:8 Paul affirms that eating as such neither helps nor harms spiritually, a statement which does apply to the eating of marketplace food, but not to the eating of sacrificial meat in the context of pagan worship (as he makes clear in chap. 10). The eating of sacrificial meat by the weak Christian, however, can in fact produce spiritual harm. But the problem Paul outlines here falls short of a description of idolatry and its consequences. The weak Christian's behavior produces a defiled conscience: ἡ συνείδησις αὐτῶν ἀσθενὴς οὖσα μολύνεται (8:7c). For that person does not have "knowledge" (8:7a) that idols have no real existence (8:4–6) and continues to be influenced by a former pagan attitude toward idol meat as sacrificed to a real god (τινὲς δὲ τῇ συνηθείᾳ ἕως ἄρτι τοῦ εἰδώλου ὡς εἰδωλόθυτον ἐσθίουσιν, 8:7b). Paul implies that if one has knowledge, no problems of conscience result from eating marketplace food; the behavior in question here is amoral. Indeed, the fact that Paul portrays the weak Christian as *still bothered* by the associations of sacrificial meat with idolatrous practices makes it unlikely that the weak Christian is on the verge of eating food sacrificed to idols and falling into idolatry. It is the Christians with knowledge who must be warned against idolatry: they *underestimate* the danger of idolatry, and their free and easy use of the pagan temples puts them in danger of having fellowship with demons, so that they must "flee idolatry!" (10:14).

[36] On the parallelism of πρόσκομμα and σκάνδαλον, see Wilckens, *Röm III*, 90; Müller, *Anstoss*, 32.

Some take the σκάνδαλον/πρόσκομμα metaphors to indicate the danger of losing salvation or faith.[37] In the NT this terminology can carry such connotations (Matt 5:29, 30; 13:21 par.; 18:6–9 par.; 24:10; 26:33).[38] But σκάνδαλον and σκανδαλίζειν also appear in contexts which do not suggest more than the idea of provocation to sinful behavior (2 Cor 11:29; 1 John 2:10; Matt 16:23).[39] In 2 Cor 11:29 this type of σκάνδαλον threatens the "weak" Christian: τίς ἀσθενεῖ καὶ οὐκ ἀσθενῶ; τίς σκανδαλίζεται καὶ οὐκ ἐγὼ πυροῦμαι; The weak, in Paul's view, were especially endangered by a σκάνδαλον, which might seduce them to sin.[40] He contrasts *his* treatment of the weak, which takes into account their vulnerability— accommodation (ἀσθενῶ)—with the behavior of *others*, who cause them to sin (σκανδαλίζεται) and who feel the barbs of Paul's criticism for doing so.[41] It makes more sense to interpret the metaphors of the σκάνδαλον and πρόσκομμα in 1 Corinthians 8 and Romans 14 in the light of 2 Cor 11:29 than to draw upon their occasional connection with idolatry and apostasy in the OT and Judaism,[42] especially since Paul does not view the weak, who follow the example of the strong, as idolaters but hypocrites.[43]

1 John 2:10, 11 also uses σκάνδαλον in a way which does not connote more than an "occasion to sin." The context reveals a concern for loving mutual Christian relations which parallels that in 1 Corinthians 8 and Romans 14. The one who loves a fellow Christian remains in the light and there is no σκάνδαλον in that person. By contrast, the one who hates a fellow Christian is in darkness (1 John 2:10, 11). In both Johannine and Pauline contexts mutual love translates into practical avoidance of σκάνδαλα in community life.[44] ἀπρόσκοποι in 1 Cor 10:32 also seems to refer to the avoidance of common pitfalls instead of to eternal perdition.[45]

---

[37] E.g., Nababan, *Bekenntnis*, 94; Stählin, σκάνδαλον, *TDNT* 6, 752. The NT, however, does not use πρόσκομμα or προσκόπτειν of believers except in Romans 14 and 1 Corinthians 8.

[38] The question whether these texts see loss of faith as permanent remains open. The σκάνδαλον/πρόσκομμα metaphors can also signify unbelievers' failure to come to faith (e.g., Rom 9:32, 33; 11:9).

[39] Possibly also Rom 16:17.

[40] On 2 Cor 11:29, see Plummer, *2 Cor*, 331.

[41] Similarly, in Lev 19:14 LXX, one should not place an obstacle (σκάνδαλον) in the way of the blind, for they too are at a disadvantage in overcoming it.

[42] On this background, see Müller, *Anstoss*, 32–37.

[43] See above, pp. 93, 94 with n. 35.

[44] Cf. Ps 49:20 LXX.

[45] See Eckstein, *Syneidesis*, 245. It is also significant that Stählin, who argues that the σκάνδαλον/ πρόσκομμα terminology suggests "eternal loss" in 1 Corinthians 8 and Romans 14, distinguishes διὰ προσκόμματος in Rom 14:20 from the rest of the occurrences of the term. The phrase means "with a disturbed...conscience," he says, and does

Thus the σκάνδαλον/πρόσκομμα language in 1 Corinthians 8 and Romans 14 says simply that an occasion for sin has been set up. The terms themselves do not tell us *what* is the nature of the sin. The context must provide this information. And, as Rom 14:23b reveals, the sin consists in acting out of step with conscience-approved πίστις. The notions of "stumbling" and "causing to sin" allude to the objective spiritual damage incurred by the weak when they sin in this way. Finally, the expression τύπτειν τὴν συνείδησιν may refer to disabling the function of the conscience[46] which is necessary for responsible behavior before God. This injury would also entail objective consequences.

In summary, the contexts of the destruction terminology in Romans 14 and 1 Corinthians 8 reveal two forms of damage incurred by the weak: a subjective form consisting in grief and deep self-deprecation, and an objective form consisting in concrete sin, resultant guilt and possible incapacitation to behave consistently with one's beliefs. None of Paul's descriptions of the negative consequences born by the weak when they follow the example of the strong—stumbling, sinning, sorrow, defiling and wounding of the conscience, self-condemnation—necessarily entails loss of salvation or complete dissolution of a relationship to God. They thus do not provide a reason to interpret ἀπόλλυμι as eternal destruction. The thought of final perdition goes beyond the implications of the objective and subjective damage suggested by the various expressions Paul employs in the context. How then do these other expressions which denote the weak Christian's subjective and objective decline illuminate the meaning of ἀπόλλυμι?

Since the structure of Rom 14:15 creates a parallel between the destruction of the weak Christian (ἀπόλλυε) and that person's being made to sorrow (λυπεῖται), it appears that destruction consists at least partly in the subjective consequence of sorrow.[47] The two verse halves of 14:15 correspond to each other in a number of ways. In each, βρῶμα serves as the occasion for sorrow (διὰ βρῶμα...λυπεῖται) or destruction (τῷ βρώματι... ἀπόλλυε). The behavior of the Christian who has knowledge and eats— "you are no longer walking according to love"—contrasts to the loving action of Christ toward the weak Christian—"for whom Christ died."[48] The sequence of thought in the two verse halves is also parallel: (1) occasion

---

not refer to falling in faith, as προσκόπτειν in 14:21 (σκάνδαλον, *TDNT* 6, 757).

[46] Jewett, *Terms*, 425. Stählin (τύπτω, *TDNT* 8, 268) speaks of actual damage in relation to one's existence before God.

[47] Cf. the connection between ἁμαρτίαι and λυπεῖσθαι in Lam 1:22 LXX.

[48] For the interpretation of Christ's death as an act of love, cf. Rom 5:8 (on that verse, see pp. 51-53 above).

(food), (2) damage (sorrow, destruction), (3) type of behavior toward the fellow Christian (love, neglected or practiced).

But does not "grieve" (λυπεῖν) dilute the meaning of "destroy" (ἀπόλλυμι) in an unacceptable way?[49] On the contrary, the LXX does not hesitate to use ἀπόλλυμι for the effect of sorrow and other forms of psychological distress: καὶ λύπην μακρὰν ἀπόστησον ἀπὸ σοῦ · πολλοὺς γὰρ ἀπώλεσεν ἡ λύπη (Sir 30:23; cf. also vv. 21–25). By contrast, εὐφροσύνη and ἀγαλλίαμα enrich human life (v. 22). Sorrow is inferior to them because οὐκ ἔστιν ὠφέλεια ἐν αὐτῇ (v. 23). The whole thought pattern very much resembles Paul's in Romans 14: one must strive for that which brings benefit and avoid destruction; sorrow works damage but joy and peace belong to the godly life. Another passage in Sirach uses ἀπόλλυμι in a subjective sense in a context whose vocabulary and themes mirror Paul's discussion of the destruction of the weak believer. Sir 20:21, 22 sets up a contrast between the person who is hindered from sinning (κωλυόμενος ἁμαρτάνειν) and thus spared the pain or remorse (οὐ κατανυγήσεται) and the person who destroys his life through shame (ἀπολλύων τὴν ψυχὴν αὐτοῦ δι' αἰσχύνην). The latter recalls the Christian who is destroyed in the Pauline passages. Although Paul, for the sake of a parenetic point, puts the blame on the strong, who "have knowledge," he surely holds the weak responsible too; a Christian can bring destruction on herself. As does Sirach, so also Paul traces the destruction to sin (ἁμαρτάνειν, ἁμαρτία) and pictures it as subjective (remorse, shame).

These uses of ἀπόλλυμι in the LXX for what might best be called "existential destruction" are by no means isolated instances. Wisdom literature employs the term with this implication liberally. People invite "destruction" upon themselves with their tongues (Sir 22:27), foolishness (Prov 5:23), or evil (Prov 19:9; Sir 6:4). Others can "destroy" someone by their wrath (Prov 15:1) or double-mindedness (Sir 28:13). An evil-doing woman "destroys" her husband (Prov 12:4), and a sinner will "destroy" much good (Eccl 9:18). And things such as wine (Sir 31:25), gold (Sir 8:2) or a bribe (Eccl 7:7) have the power to "destroy" a person. In these occurrences of ἀπόλλυμι "destruction" results from the disintegration of moral or psychological values and poses a fundamental existential threat to a person. The LXX thus provides parallels for Paul's use of ἀπόλλυμι to denote existential destruction with both subjective and objective dimensions. This type of destruction falls short of final perdition.

---

[49] Eckstein (*Syneidesis*, 249), for example, pleads against a weakened meaning of ἀπόλλυμι.

To some extent, the secondary literature on 1 Corinthians 8 and Romans 14 attests the validity of the interpretation of ἀπόλλυμι in those passages as existential destruction. H. Conzelmann notes the use of ἀπόλλυμι elsewhere for destruction of one's humanity,[50] though he assigns it the meaning "eternal damnation" in the Pauline context.[51] Commenting on Rom 14:15, E. Käsemann speaks of "the violating of humanity,"[52] while C. E. B. Cranfield sees "the actual destruction of his [the weak person's] integrity as a Christian."[53] So also R. Jewett describes the results of acting against one's conscience as the "destruction of personality" and "inner disunity—schizophrenia."[54] Only F. F. Bruce, however, clearly rejects the eschatological interpretation of ἀπόλλυμι in favor of the "existential" one: "It is not the man's eternal perdition, but the stunting of his Christian life and usefulness by the 'wounding' of his 'conscience when it is weak' that Paul has in mind."[55] This explanation has the most in its favor, as the findings of the foregoing analysis indicate: (1) NT usage of ἀπόλλυμι does not encompass and even conflicts with the idea that the saved may finally suffer eternal destruction; (2) in Romans 14 and 1 Corinthians 8 Paul intends to contrast ἀπόλλυμι not to salvation but to edification; (3) the other adverse effects suffered by the weak which parallel ἀπόλλυμι are forms of subjective and objective "destruction" which fall short of final perdition; (4) the fact that the LXX uses ἀπόλλυμι for existential destruction when associated with the related motifs of sorrow, joy, benefit, sin and remorse makes it not unlikely that Paul has the same type of destruction in mind in 1 Cor 8:11 and Rom 14:15, where those motifs also appear.

In conclusion, the destruction of the weak Christian presents an obstacle to Christian sanctification, not to final salvation. In the passages considered Paul pleads for mutual relations in the church which do not threaten but encourage the individual life of faith in its various manifestations.

---

[50] Epictetus *Dis.* II.9.3: ὅρα οὖν μή τί πως ὡς θηρίον ποιήσῃς · εἰ δὲ μή, ἀπώλεσας τὸν ἄνθρωπον.

[51] Conzelmann, *1 Cor*, 149, n. 38.

[52] Käsemann, *Rom*, 376. Nevertheless, he also gives the verb eschatological significance.

[53] Cranfield, *Rom*, 714, n. 3. Yet on p. 715, n. 2 he interprets ἀπόλλυμι as the bringing about of eschatological ruin.

[54] Jewett, *Terms*, 423, 425.

[55] Bruce, *Cor*, 82. Cf. Grosheide (*1 Cor*, 197), who takes ἀπόλλυμι as "come to sin," or "not to show oneself as a Christian."

IV. PUNISHMENT OF THE DISOBEDIENT

To "Eat" and "Drink" Judgment

1 Corinthians 11:27–34. The dangers of participating inappropriately in the Lord's Supper of which Paul warns the Corinthians have an ominous ring: "become guilty of the body and blood of the Lord" (11:27), "eat and drink judgment" (11:29), "come together for judgment" (11:34). What do these expressions mean, and what implications do they have for the Corinthians' final salvation? How does the judgment of Christians to which Paul refers relate to God's condemnation of the world (11:32)? Is final condemnation presented as a real danger for the guilty Corinthians too?

The motif of judgment strongly colors 1 Cor 11:27–34. Paul employs a number of (often similar) terms to announce this motif: ἀναξίως, ἔνοχος, δοκιμάζειν, κρίμα, διακρίνειν, κρίνειν, παιδεύειν, κατακρίνειν.[1] He takes advantage of the different nuances these terms for judgment have.[2] δοκιμάζειν and διακρίνειν denote the act of judging or determining by applying one's critical faculties. ἔνοχος and ἀναξίως describe what is characterized by failure to apply these critical faculties and thus comes under judgment. Paul uses κρίνειν, κρίμα and παιδεύειν to denote God's judgment of the Corinthians. κατακρίνειν stands for God's sentence of final condemnation.[3]

The problem Paul addresses in 1 Cor 11:27–34 arises from the Corinthians' failure to "judge" themselves and the "body." Paul must thus command self-testing (δοκιμαζέτω δὲ ἄνθρωπος ἑαυτόν, 11:28) and warn against not correctly assessing the "body" (μὴ διακρίνων[4] τὸ σῶμα,[5] 11:29). For some, however, the warnings come too late. Their inappropriate

---

[1] This passage gives us an example of paranomasia, the recurrence of the same word or word stem in close proximity (see *BDF* §488, 1b); see Mattern, *Gericht*, 99.

[2] Mattern, *Gericht*, 102.

[3] See BAGD, s.v. κατακρίνω.

[4] See BAGD, s.v. διακρίνω, 1.c.β. The meaning of διακρίνειν at v. 29, as at v. 31, is "assess" (cf. 1 Cor 14:29; Matt 16:3). Differently, Büchsel, κρίνω, *TDNT* 3, 946, with nn. 4, 7.

[5] σῶμα means here either the eucharistic bread or the church as Christ's body. See the commentaries.

(ἀναξίως[6]) participation in the Lord's Supper has already called forth divine judgment—they are κρινόμενοι (11:32)! Had they "judged" themselves before partaking in the meal, they could have avoided God's judgment: εἰ δὲ ἑαυτοὺς διεκρίνομεν, οὐκ ἂν ἐκρινόμεθα (11:31).[7]

What is the nature of this divine judgment? As Paul's present and imperfect indicatives (κρινόμενοι, ἐκρινόμεθα) show, it is a judgment which has already begun and continues to strike the Corinthian community. It is thus a presently[8] ongoing judgment, as distinct from the strictly future eschatological judgment according to works, which Christians also await (cf. 2 Cor 5:10). When Paul warns against "coming together for judgment (ἵνα μὴ εἰς κρίμα συνέρχησθε, 11:34) he presumably means a divine judgment which strikes in the here and now.[9] Earlier in the chapter he criticized the Corinthians for their misbehavior in a similar way: οὐκ εἰς τὸ κρεῖσσον ἀλλὰ εἰς τὸ ἧσσον συνέρχεσθε (11:17). The benefit which those gathered around the Lord's table could have obtained was forfeited, for the κυριακὸν δεῖπνον had become an ἴδιον δεῖπνον. Their perverted celebration could evoke only judgment, as it did.

Thus it is evident that Paul considers the Corinthians to be *presently* judged by God. 11:29, however, has been taken to refer to eternal judgment: "The one who eats and drinks without discerning the body eats and drinks judgment to himself."[10] In support of this view, elsewhere Paul uses κρίμα for the last judgment (Rom 2:2, 3; 3:8).[11] The force of this argument is weakened, however, by the fact that Paul's other uses of κρίμα for the last judgment are arthrous, whereas 1 Cor 11:29, 34 has an anarthrous κρίμα .[12] Still it is contested that the future tense of ἔνοχος ἔσται in 11:27 presupposes a future judgment: whoever eats the bread and drinks the cup of the Lord inappropriately *will be* guilty of the body and blood of the Lord. If ἔσται is an eschatological future,[13] v. 27 would mean, "der wird

---

[6] ἀναξίως refers to the manner of participation, not the ethical state of the participant (Klauck, *Herrenmahl*, 324; *et al.*). On this question, see also Synofzik, *Gerichtsaussagen*, 55.

[7] Wolff (*1 Kor*, 94) correctly takes the admonishment to self-examination to concern behavior associated with the Lord's Supper.

[8] Cf. Wolff, *1 Kor*, 95.

[9] On συνέρχεσθαι εἰς as introducing a result, see BAGD, s.v. συνέρχομαι, 1.a. On the use of συνέρχεσθαι as a *terminus technicus* for gathering for worship, see Käsemann, "Abendmahlslehre," 21; Hofius, "Herrenmahl," 374, n. 15.

[10] So Delling, "Abendmahlsgeschehen," 329; Theissen, "Integration," 312.

[11] Delling, "Abendmahlsgeschehen," 329.

[12] Wolff, *1 Kor*, 94, 95.

[13] So Käsemann, "Abendmahlslehre," 23; Delling, "Abendmahlsgeschehen," 329; Neuenzeit, *Herrenmahl*, 228. Similarly, Grosheide, *1 Cor*, 274.

sich im Endgericht als schuldig gegenüber Leib und Blut erweisen."[14] Thus ἔνοχος ἔσται would parallel a future notion of κρίμα in 11:29.[15] But it is more likely that Paul intends ἔσται as a *futurum intensivum*.[16] The Septuagintal parallels with ἔνοχος ἔσται in the apodosis (Gen 26:11; 1 Macc 14:45; Josh 2:19), influenced by Greek formulations of "holy law," speak in favor of this interpretation.[17] In these clauses, explains K. Berger, "handelt es sich nicht um Aussagen über zukünftiges—'immanentes' oder eschatologisches—Geschick, sondern um Schulderklärungen und damit um Belehrungen oder Proklamationen, die den forensischen Bereich berühren."[18] The context shows the Corinthians to have *already* become guilty of[19] the body and blood of the Lord for participating inappropriately in the Lord's Supper and held accountable for their misconduct: ἐν τούτῳ οὐκ ἐπαινῶ (11:22).[20] Their present guilt and accountability gives rise to Paul's admonitions for amendment in 11:28, 33, 34. Thus it seems best to take ἔνοχος ἔσται as a proclamation of incurred guilt with a *futurum intensivum*.

If then ἔνοχος ἔσται is not an eschatological future, the crucial prop in the argument for a future κρίμα in 11:29 falls down.[21] The anarthrous use of κρίμα in this verse and the use of the cognates κρινόμενοι and ἐκρινόμεθα for already ongoing judgment combine to militate convincingly against a future understanding of κρίμα. Thus Paul warns the Corinthians not against being found guilty at the last judgment but against present judgment for their wrong actions.[22]

---

14 Delling, "Abendmahlsgeschehen," 329.

15 So Delling ("Abendmahlsgeschehen," 329): "Dieses Verständnis des ἔνοχος ἔσται läge durchaus auf der Linie dessen, was sich als Deutung für κρίμα in V. 29 nahelegt."

16 Cf. *BDF* §362. So Conzelmann, *1 Cor*, 202; Wolff, *1 Kor*, 94.

17 For the same influence in other NT passages, cf. Matt 5:21, 22; Jas 2:10; see also the variant reading for Mark 3:29. K. Berger has shown that no proper correspondance to the LXX's formulation with ἔνοχος ἔσται in the apodosis exists in the MT and that the influence on NT writers is Greek rather than OT-Jewish ("Sätze," 35–38). Contrast Wolff, *1 Kor*, 94; similarly, Delling, Abendmahlsgeschehen," 329, n. 11.

18 Berger, "Sätze," 35.

19 ἔνοχος here takes the genitive of the law or value against which one has transgressed (Hanse, ἔχω, *TDNT* 2, 828).

20 Correctly, Wolff (*1 Kor*, 94): "Das Schuldigwerden...ist ja ein mit dem unangemessenen Verhalten bereits gegebener Tatbestand." So also Hofius, "Herrenmahl," 374, n. 20; Synofzik, *Gerichtsaussagen*, 82.

21 Cf. Hofius ("Herrenmahl," 374, n. 20): "ἔνοχος ἔσται ist nicht als eschatologisches Futur zu deuten und als 'Gerichtsdrohung' auf das Endgericht zu beziehen."

22 Correctly, Hofius ("Herrenmahl," 374, n. 21): "κρίμα V. 29.34 meint nicht das Endgericht, sondern die gegenwärtig erfolgende 'Verurteilung' und 'Bestrafung', die dem frevelhaften Verhalten auf dem Fuße folgt."

In the light of this evidence, E. Käsemann's view that Paul develops a dialectical interpretation of the Lord's Supper in 1 Cor 11:27ff. as evoking judgment in both its future and present forms[23] also suffers. Against this view, the text does not speak clearly of a future judgment of the guilty Corinthians. Moreover, the Corinthians' present judgment differs *in kind* from the future judgment which, according to Käsemann, will also fall upon guilty participants. Käsemann himself describes the present judgment as " 'pädagogisches' Werk der Gnade, die dem zukünftigen Gericht entreißt."[24] Here he is alluding appropriately to 11:32: "Being judged (κρινό-μενοι) by the Lord, we are chastised (παιδευόμεθα) so that we might not be condemned (κατακριθῶμεν) with the world." Paul divides the two judgments into different categories, pedagogical judgment and final condemnation, rather than aligning them. Indeed, he explicitly juxtaposes the two forms of judgment: παιδευόμεθα ἵνα μή...κατακριθῶμεν. The contrasting objects of the two judgments reinforce their juxtaposition: present pedagogical judgment has fallen upon the *church* ("we are chastised"), whereas the *world* is destined for final condemnation ("...that we might not be condemned with the world").[25] Käsemann obscures the radical differences in the two judgments when he says, "Im Sakrament wird in gewisser Weise schon gegenwärtig, was am jüngsten Tage sich enthüllt."[26] His position seems illogical on the basis of his own reading of the text. He himself, it appears, would have to conclude that God's present *judgment* on Christians contrasts to their final *salvation*, not prefigures their future judgment.

In summary, the language of judgment employed in this passage denotes two kinds of judgment which differ in time of execution, nature and object. Paul uses the verb κρίνειν here not for eternal damnation[27] but for present pedagogical judgment on the church in contradistinction to the final condemnation to come upon the world. The noun κρίμα denoting the Corinthian Christians' judgment (11:29, 34) has the same connotations as its cog-

---

[23] So Käsemann ("Abendmahlslehre," 25, 27): "Gericht ereignet sich schon gegenwärtig beim Vollzug des Herrenmahles, wurde dort (sc. in V. 29) in gewissem Gegensatz zu der Aussage von V. 27 mit ihrem eschatologischen Futur festgestellt.... Es geht dem Apostel offensichtlich darum, den Korinthern jene Dialektik aufzudecken, die mit dem Sakrament gesetzt ist."

[24] Käsemann, "Abendmahlslehre," 27.

[25] Käsemann instead sees the judgment of the church and the world as parallel, in contrast to Paul's formulation: Christ is the "letzten Richter,... der in seiner Gemeinde schon heute handelt, wie er der Welt gegenüber am jüngsten Tage handeln wird" ("Abendmahlslehre," 26).

[26] Käsemann, "Abendmahlslehre," 24.

[27] Conzelmann, *1 Cor*, 203.

nate κρίνειν here. It does not refer to eschatological judgment.[28] We can therefore conclude that the expression "eat and drink judgment to oneself" warns against temporal judgment which is pedagogical in nature and diametrically opposed to final condemnation. Paul does not suggest that certain Corinthian Christians will reap the judgment of eternal damnation for their wrong behavior at the Lord's Supper. None of the judicial terms in this passage supports such an idea.

Rather, the context suggests that the judgment upon the one who eats and drinks without rightly assessing the body consists in subjection to corporeal punishments. Paul notes the numerous illnesses and deaths in the Corinthian community at the time of writing: ἐν ὑμῖν πολλοὶ ἀσθενεῖς καὶ ἄρρωστοι καὶ κοιμῶνται ἱκανοί (11:30). He gives the reason for these physical afflictions (διὰ τοῦτο ἐν ὑμῖν...) in the preceding verse: ὁ γὰρ ἐσθίων καὶ πίνων κρίμα ἑαυτῷ ἐσθίει καὶ πίνει μὴ διακρίνων τὸ σῶμα (11:29). Some Corinthians have fallen ill or died as a result of eating and drinking "judgment" to themselves.[29] The judgment struck in their physical members. We need not presuppose some magical effect of the eucharistic elements as a φάρμακον θανασίας.[30] But neither do the sicknesses and deaths have merely natural causes (here, for example, gluttony).[31] For they result from divine chastening (ὑπὸ [τοῦ] κυρίου παιδευόμεθα (11:32).[32] God has dealt out corporeal punishments as the "material consequences of guilt"[33] for defiling the Lord's Supper.

Some interpreters take these physical sufferings to represent God's judgment of the *whole* community, not individual guilty members: the suffering of individual members is unrelated to their personal guilt or innocence in the celebration of the eucharist. Rather Paul wants to portray the community as under judgment for wrongly tolerating the inappropriate participation of some members.[34] This view allows for a future judgment of

---

[28] Klauck, *Herrenmahl*, 326; Morris, *1 Cor*, 164; Robertson and Plummer, *1 Cor*, 252.

[29] V. 30 concretizes v. 29. Against Delling ("Abendmahlsgeschehen," 330): "Krankheit und Tod sind nicht Vollzug dieses Spruches."

[30] With Gundry (*ΣΩΜΑ*, 237, 67) and Conzelmann (*1 Cor*, 203), who argue that Paul stresses the manner of participation in the Lord's Supper, not the nature of the elements. Against Lietzmann, *Kor*, 59. Conversely, appropriate participation does not make the elements a φάρμακον ἀθανασίας (cf. Ign. *Eph.* 20:2). See Gundry's arguments, *ΣΩΜΑ*, 237, 238.

[31] Bruce, *Cor*, 115; Morris, *1 Cor*, 164.

[32] Morris, *1 Cor*, 164. Similarly, Bornkamm, "Herrenmahl," 170.

[33] Conzelmann, *1 Cor*, 203. Similarly, Synofzik, *Gerichtsaussagen*, 52.

[34] So Delling, "Abendmahlsgeschehen," 330. Similarly, Conzelmann, *1 Cor*, 203, n. 115; Bornkamm, "Herrenmahl," 170; Wolff, *1 Kor*, 95.

the guilty individuals who have misused the Lord's Supper but not necessarily suffered the physical afflictions now manifest in the community. But, not only is the thought of a clearly future judgment of the guilty Corinthians absent. Paul also does not appear to suggest that the *community's* guilt is the reason for the suffering of physical disorders. To be sure, in the larger context Paul expresses his concern for the life of the whole ἐκκλη̄ σία, but he does not leave the impression that he considers the entire community to be at fault for this particular problem. Rather, he distinguishes the "approved" (δόκιμοι) from the unapproved, who become manifest as such by separating themselves into factions (σχίσματα, αἱρέσεις, 11:18, 19).[35] The unapproved fail to behave in a truly Christian manner as befits those who partake of the Lord's Supper.[36] Paul lists their offenses in 11:21, 22[37]

---

[35] The δόκιμοι can already be distinguished from the ἀδόκιμοι, even before the final judgment (with Fee, *1 Cor*, 538, 539, w. n. 37). The Corinthians had divided into factions presumably along the lines of wealth and social position (Morris, *1 Cor*, 159; Barrett, *1 Cor*, 261). The σχίσματα of 1:10ff. however have a different source (with Hofius, "Herrenmahl," 374f.).

[36] Barrett, *1 Cor*, 262. Hofius ("Herrenmahl," 407) explains: "Wer wirklich weiß, was die beiden das Mahl umgebenden und es in seinem Wesen qualifizierenden sakramentalen Akte bedeuten, der kann sich also prinzipiell nicht so verhalten, wie die von Paulus getadelten Korinther es tun; und wer sich so verhält, der gibt damit zu erkennen, daß er nicht weiß und bedenkt, was jene Akte bedeuten." The use of the term δόκιμος (11:19; see pp. 219–221 below) and the reference to present σχίσματα and αἱρέσεις (11:18, 19), which prefigure the eschatological separation of the wheat and the tares (see, further, Fee, *1 Cor*, 538, 539 with n. 38), seem to suggest that at this stage in the argument Paul suspects the guilty Corinthians of false profession of Christian faith. Cf. Bruce, *1 Cor*, 114, 115: "Such 'unworthy' eating or drinking was possible only for a Christian whose behaviour belied his profession" (similarly, Fee, *1 Cor*, 562, 538, 539). But, insofar as Paul begins his argument in this way, he does not continue in the same vein. Though the δόκιμος terminology reappears later, it seems unrelated to the question of false profession. The context of 11:28 implies that the self-examination demanded of the Christian there (δοκιμαζέτω δὲ ἄνθρωπος ἑαυτόν) "will be specially directed to ascertaining whether or not he is living and acting 'in love and charity' with his neighbours" (Bruce, *1 Cor*, 115; similarly, Fee, *1 Cor*, 562). Genuineness of profession of faith is not specifically put to the test. Further, Paul does not require the expulsion of the trouble-makers from the church, as he demanded in chap. 5 in the case of the fornicator, who was apparently a mere "so-called brother" and should be "cast out" (5:11-13). Instead he charges the Corinthians to satisfy their hunger at home before they "come together" (11:34)—presumably for the Lord's Supper—and to "receive one another when you come together to eat" (11:33; on ἐκδέχεσθαι at 11:33 as "receive someone [by showing hospitality]," see Hofius, "Herrenmahl," 388–390). He wants the schismatics to continue participating in the fellowship—including the eucharist—yet without a factious spirit and without despising the church by putting to shame the have-nots (11:22). In other words, Paul expects the offenders to reform within the context of the church as genuine Christians. He implies here what he will make clear at the end of the chapter, namely, that they are children of God who are subject to the Lord's chastisement (ὑπὸ [τοῦ] κυρίου παιδευόμεθα, 11:32a). They suffer divine judgment pres-

and issues them commands in 11:33, 34. The victims of these offenses—
those who go hungry, the have-nots (11:21, 22)—escape unscathed by criticism.[38] Thus it appears that Paul intends his readers to take the sicknesses
and deaths in their community as manifestations of God's judgment on
guilty *individuals*.[39]

The guilty Corinthians' present judgment therefore takes the form of
corporeal afflictions. But what is the relation of this judgment to their final
destiny? Does Paul think those who suffer temporal punishment will escape
final condemnation, or might they still be excluded from salvation? As already noted, the two judgments are explicitly juxtaposed in 11:32: κρινόμενοι...παιδευόμεθα, ἵνα μὴ σὺν τῷ κόσμῳ κατακριθῶμεν. Interpreters often take chastisement to be the *means* of escape from final condemnation: through pedagogical judgment final condemnation is forestalled.
How? Paul could not have attributed atoning value to present suffering, as
in Judaism, without exposing himself to the charge of theological inconsistency.[40] Did he, however, think that pedagogical judgment can prevent final condemnation by evoking penitence and amendment? Does Paul intend
us to presuppose an intermediate stage, viz., repentance, which occurs after
chastisement and thus prevents condemnation? If so, repentance from the
sin committed would be a necessary prerequisite for escape from condemnation. Paul's use of παιδεία to describe pedagogical judgment here favors
this possibility. For the OT-Jewish παιδεία tradition features amendment
as the goal of chastisement (cf. *Ps. Sol.* 10:1–3; Jer 31:18, 19).[41] The NT

---

ently so as to be spared condemnation with the world (11:32b; see pp. 111, 112 below).
At the end of his discussion of the problem Paul still addresses the whole church as
ἀδελφοί μου (11:33). In conclusion, Paul does not appear to resolve the problem of
abuse of the Lord's Supper in Corinth by ferreting out falsely professing Christians.

[37] For a discussion of theories of reconstruction of the Corinthian celebration of the
Lord's Supper on the basis of 1 Cor 11:17–34, see Hofius, "Herrenmahl." On the precise nature of the offenses of the guilty members, which appear even more abominable
in his reconstruction, see *ibid.*, 384–390.

[38] The second person plural in 11:22 refers obviously to the offenders only. Contrast
5:1–5, where Paul considers the whole community guilty of pride (πεφυσιωμένοι, 5:2)
for tolerating the sexual offender. Yet even there God's judgment does not fall on the
community at large. How much less likely, therefore, that the sicknesses and deaths in
chap. 11 represent God's judgment on the whole community, whose general guilt is not
even implied.

[39] With Bruce, *Cor*, 115; Synofzik, *Gerichtsaussagen*, 52; Robertson and Plummer,
1 Cor, 254; Moule, "Judgment," 473; Schlatter, *Bote*, 329; Lampe, "Discipline," 347,
348.

[40] Marshall, *Kept*, 115. Contrast Sanders, *Palestinian Judaism*, 516, 517. For the
atoning value of chastisements in Judaism, see Sanders, *ibid.*, 168–172.

[41] Moore, *Judaism* 2, 252, 255. See also Str-B 3.445. On suffering as educative

picks up this feature in its use of the παιδεία motif as remedial in intent (cf. Rev 3:19; Tit 2:12; 1 Tim 1:20). Paul's exhortations in 1 Cor 11:28, 33, 34 also suggest his anticipation of the Corinthians' amendment.

If repentance from their particular misconduct were a necessary prerequisite for the Corinthians to escape condemnation, then those who had already died through divine judgment without having the opportunity to repent would be unable to escape condemnation. The chastisement of death, which Paul names in addition to illness and weakness (11:30), may not have left room for subsequent repentance.[42] Does premature physical death here then foreshadow eternal death? Does death represent not really a chastisement but a judgment in the ultimate sense?

Against that view, Paul makes no distinction between death and weakness or illness as divine chastisement. All these forms of chastisement, apparently, are pedagogical κρίμα which is consistent with exemption from final condemnation.[43] Paul's choice of the verb κοιμᾶν to denote the Corinthians' deaths confirms that a chastising death need not connote final condemnation. For the NT reserves this term for the deaths of those who will be raised to new life and whose physical deaths are thus—not just euphemistically—a "falling asleep."[44] Even if the guilty had failed to repent before death, therefore, their physical deaths would not have entailed eschatological or spiritual death.[45] Repentance is not mentioned as a prerequisite for exemption from final condemnation. For these reasons also it is inadvisable to postulate that the Corinthians' premature deaths were "the ultimate stage in an unsuccessful process of discipline" and on that basis to suggest that this passage provides "definite examples of people

---

punishment since the time of the Maccabees, see Bertram, παιδεύω, *TDNT* 5, 610.

[42] A post-mortal repentance (as Weiss, *1 Kor*, 292, suggests) "hat keinen Anhaltspunkt bei Paulus" (Mattern, *Gericht*, 101; so also, Filson, *Recompense*, 87). The possibility of a death-bed repentance (cf. Marshall, *Kept*, 115) is highly speculative. So also is Lampe's solution: "Paul envisages a divine sentence of death which continues to take effect even after illness has induced the offender to come to a better mind" ("Discipline," 348).

[43] For death as a form of divine chastisement in the LXX, cf. Ps. 6:2, 6: "Lord, do not punish (ἐλέγξῃς) me in your rage, or chastise (παιδεύσῃς) me in your anger, ...for in death there is none who remembers you, in Hades who will confess you?" Cf. Ps. 37:2; Jer 10:24 LXX.

[44] 1 Thess 4:13–15; 1 Cor 15:6, 18, 20, 51; John 11:11; Matt 27:52; Acts 7:60; 13:36; 2 Pet 3:4. See also *Herm. Sim.* 9.16.3, 5–7; Ign. *Rom* 4:2; 2 Macc 12:45. Unclear, 1 Cor 7:39. So Bruce, *Cor*, 116; Robertson and Plummer, *1 Cor*, 253; Didier, *Désinteressement*, 43 with n. 16.

[45] Against Marshall, *Kept*, 115, 116; Lampe, "Discipline," 348; Grosheide, *1 Cor*, 276; similarly, Roetzel, *Judgment*, 124, n. 4.

who 'fell asleep' and thus forfeited their salvation."[46]

We cannot adequately explain the relation between the two judgments by the theory that repentance induced by pedagogical judgment prevents final condemnation. Rather, the Corinthians' chastisement itself, apart from any accompanying connotations of atonement for sin or the remedial effect of repentance, implies their exemption from final condemnation. Paul sees κρίμα or παιδεία and κατάκριμα as mutually exclusive categories. The objects of God's pedagogical judgment are *ipso facto* not objects of God's final condemnation. By interpreting the temporal punishments of the guilty Corinthians as divine chastisement, Paul does not leave the question of their exemption from final condemnation open but confirms that very exemption. His warnings against present judgment, however, do not thereby become innocuous.

The thesis that the two types of divine judgment are mutually exclusive categories gains support from the similar understanding of divine παιδεία in OT-Jewish tradition, as the following excursus will reveal.

Excursus: Divine Chastisement in OT-Jewish Thought and the NT. In biblical thought, divine chastisement is not proper to sinners in general. As the literal meaning of the verb παιδεύειν, "treat as a child," suggests, it applies to God's children, God's people. Yahweh appears as the father who chastises his son Israel (Deut 8:5; Prov 3:11, 12; Wis 11:10). Chastisement marks the true children of God and distinguishes them from illegitimate children: εἰ δὲ χωρίς ἐστε παιδείας ἧς μέτοχοι γεγόνασιν πάντες, ἄρα νόθοι καὶ οὐχ υἱοί ἐστε (Heb 12:8). The suffering of divine chastisement is appropriate for those who enjoy a unique relation to God as God's elect children.[47] In fact, O. Michel comments on 2 Macc 6:12–17: "Aus der Erwählung Israels folgt *notwendig* Recht und Gnade der Züchtigung" (italics mine).[48] Subjection to divine chastisement aligns God's children with God's Son, Jesus Christ, who by subjecting himself to suffering models the behavior characteristic of true children (Heb 12:2–4).[49] Chastisement marks those God loves: "Whom the Lord loves he chastens" (Prov 3:12 LXX; Rev 3:19; cf. Sir 18:13, 14). In fact, chastisements were taken

---

[46] Marshall, *Kept*, 115, 116. Mattern (*Gericht*, 103) and Roetzel (*Judgment*, 139) consider the possibility that the church fail to repent through chastisement and thereby join the world in going to a destiny of condemnation.

[47] Bertram, παιδεύω, *TDNT* 5, 607, 611. Cf. Philo, *De cong*.177.

[48] Michel, *Heb*, 297.

[49] Bertram, παιδεύω, *TDNT* 5, 622.

as such clear expressions of divine love that in Judaism a separate category—"chastisements of love"—existed for afflictions brought on apart
from any guilt whatsoever and originating wholly in God's compassion.[50]
Thus it could truly be said, "Blessed is the one whom you chasten, O Lord"
(Ps 94:12; cf. Job 5:17), for chastisements testified to God's love and one's
own status as a child of God.

The interpretation of sufferings as tokens of divine love and a unique relation to God as God's children made sense of the otherwise incongruous
phenomenon that God's own people undergo suffering presently while the
nations escape it. In the words of 2 Maccabees: "In the case of other nations, the Sovereign Lord in his forbearance refrains from punishing them
till they have filled up their sins to the full, but in our case he has determined otherwise, that his vengeance may not fall on us in afterdays when
our sins have reached their height" (6:14, 15).[51] And even if the nations are
sometimes said to experience God's kindness in the form of present punishment, this is quite different from divine chastisement of true children.
God's mercy, which extends to all creation, prompts God to admonish
(νουθετεῖς) in the present even those who do not belong to God's people
(Wis 12:2; Sir 18:13). In this way God refrains from bringing upon them a
"once-for-all" annihilation for their sins at the end and instead causes them
to perish gradually (Wis 11:23; 12:2, 8; cf. 2 Macc 6:13), thereby giving
them room for repentance (Wis 12:10). Nevertheless, such display of divine mercy in punishment does not match that shown to God's true children so as to put the nations on an equal level with them. Rather, if kindness characterizes even God's punishment of the nations, how much more
merciful is God's chastisement of God's own children—for God punishes
their enemies "10,000 times more" than God's children (Wis 12:21, 22).[52]
God's wrath toward God's own sinful people serves to admonish them (εἰς
νουθεσίαν, Wis 16:6), yet it does not continue to the uttermost (οὐ μέχρι
τέλους ἔμεινεν ἡ ὀργή σου, Wis 16:5). On the contrary, it endures a
short while (πρὸς ὀλίγον, Wis 16:6; cf. 18:20–25), only to be followed by
mercy: "He will chastise (μαστιγώσει) us on account of our unrighteousness and then be merciful again" (Tob 13:5, cf. vv. 2–16; similarly, Lam
3:31–33). "Never does he remove his mercy from us, chastising (παιδεύων)

---

[50] Cf. Moore, *Judaism* 2, 256.

[51] *APOT* 1, 140.

[52] Cf. Michel, *Heb*, 297. *2 Apoc. Bar.* 13:9 makes the point that being God's children is no ground for exemption from affliction; rather, God "afflicted them as his
enemies, because they sinned." The author, however, careful to maintain a difference in
God's treatment of children as opposed to enemies, quickly qualifies this affliction as
"chastening that they may be sanctified" (13:10).

with calamity, he will not forsake his people" (2 Macc 6:16). "Wholly to root out and destroy them is not permitted" (*As. Mos.* 12:12). Rather, "if you consider that you have now suffered those things for your good that you may not finally be condemned and tormented, then you will receive eternal hope" (*2 Apoc. Bar.* 78:6). By contrast, "pitiless wrath to the uttermost" comes on the enemies of God's people (Wis 19:1). Although the nations may suffer present chastisement for their sin (νουθετηθέντες), this suffering does not exempt them from "the uttermost penalty" (τὸ τέρμα τῆς καταδίκης, Wis 12:26, 27). They shall face a "judgment worthy of God" (ἀξίαν Θεοῦ κρίσιν, 12:26). Even their coming to acknowledge the true God through punishment, whom they formerly refused to know, does not help (Wis 12:27). Although in principle gradual punishment leaves room for repentance, God knows the minds of the unrighteous: they will never change (12:10).

Even though God may punish the nations as well as God's people, this does not erase the distinctions between them. The author of Wisdom brings out the disparity between God's children and their enemies by explaining how water turned to blood for the Egyptians, chastening them with thirst; but the same element, water, flowed from the rock for the Israelites and quenched their thirst: "By what things their foes were punished, by these they in their need were benefited" (11:2–14). And although Israel experienced the same chastisement as Egypt did, the author insists on a difference: the Egyptians did not thirst in the same manner as the righteous (11:14). Similarly, God used the same means, small animals, to nourish Israel, on the one hand, and to torment the Egyptians, on the other. God fed Israel in the wilderness with quail but sent a plague of vermin on Egypt (16:1–4). In spite of the fact that "in the actualities of life prior to the last judgment it is not easy to distinguish the chastisement of the righteous from judgment on the wicked,"[53] the author of Wisdom regards this distinction as essential.

Although the terminology sometimes overlaps, a clear contrast between the divine response to the sin of God's children and to that of the nations emerges. *Ruth Rab.* (Proem III) records the belief that God cannot destroy God's children (as God might the nations), nor take them back to Egypt, nor exchange them for another people; so God chastises them. Wis 11:9, 10 expresses this contrast using language which strongly resembles Paul's in 1 Corinthians 11 (n.b. the following highlighted words). Comparing Israel

---

[53] Bertram, παιδεύω, *TDNT* 5, 610.

in the wilderness and the Egyptians, the author says:

> ὅτε γὰρ ἐπειράσθησαν, καίπερ ἐν ἐλέει παιδευόμενοι,
> ἔγνωσαν πῶς μετ' ὀργῆς κρινόμενοι ἀσεβεῖς ἐβασανίζοντο ·
> τούτους μὲν γὰρ ὡς πατὴρ νουθετῶν ἐδοκίμασας,
> ἐκείνους δὲ ὡς ἀπότομος βασιλεὺς καταδικάζων ἐξήτασας.[54]

Wisdom has καταδικάζειν for the condemnation of the ungodly (cf. also 12:27, καταδίκη) where Paul has κατακρίνειν for the condemnation of the world at 1 Cor 11:31. Both authors use the milder verb παιδεύειν (also νουθετεῖν in Wisdom 11) to denote God's treatment of God's people. Both want to distinguish God's chastising judgment on the disobedient children of God from God's final judgment on sinful humanity outside the family of God. It looks as if both Paul and the author of Wisdom were influenced by a tradition concerned to interpret correctly the sufferings of God's people.[55] These sufferings are, in the words of 2 Maccabees, μὴ πρὸς ὄλεθρον, ἀλλὰ πρὸς παιδείαν (6:12), in contrast to the afflictions of the ungodly.

Significant differences, then, set God's chastisement of God's people apart from divine judgment of the nations, who, like illegitimate children, technically belong outside the realm of chastisement. For true children, chastisement is 10,000 times less severe, only temporary, and followed by mercy. Why do these limitations characterize God's chastisement of God's own people but not others? In the tradition the reason lies not in the repentance of God's people through the experience of chastisement. Though the chastisement should lead them to remember God's "oracle" and "the commandment of the law" (Wis 16:6, 11), the achievement of this goal is not stated to be the reason for the final outcome, mercy, instead of total destruction. Rather, just as the impetus for God's chastisement of God's children lies in their status as elect, so also it is this status with its implications which apparently dictates limitations to the chastisement. "With how great carefulness you judged (ἔκρινας) your sons, to whose fathers you gave oaths and covenants of good promise" (Wis 12:21; cf. also *As. Mos.* 12:13 for the significance of divine oaths and covenants for chastisement). When the plague struck Israel, Aaron intervened and "by a word he subdued the minister of punishment, by bringing to remembrance oaths and covenants made with the fathers" (Wis 18:22). He used his priestly service, prayer and atonement with incense, as a weapon (18:21). And his priestly attire on which was pictured the glory of the fathers and divine majesty

---

[54] Cf. Wis 12:22, where παιδεύειν and κρίνειν denote the milder punishment of God's people in contrast to God's more severe punishment of their enemies.

[55] For the relation of Paul to Wisdom, cf. Larcher, *Sagesse*, 14–20.

won the battle for him (18:24). The special status of God's people as elect children tempers divine response to their sinful behavior. Condemnation is inappropriate to, indeed inconsistent with, this status. Thus God responds with παιδεία to the sin of God's people, as a father mercifully chastises a child instead of meting out the full punishment deserved (*2 Apoc. Bar.* 79:2).[56]

In the light of the foregoing excursus, it can be said that Paul's thought in 1 Cor 11:27–34 runs parallel to the OT-Jewish tradition of divine παιδεία. Both Paul and this tradition distinguish between two kinds of divine punishment which differ in nature, object[57] and (at least in principle) time of execution. Exemption from present suffering characterizes the nonelect, whose destiny is condemnation. But divine chastisement is appropriate for God's children. Their relation to God as elect (through the covenants established with the fathers) exercises a limiting influence on the punishment meted out to them. God's children will not be condemned. Repentance itself, though the goal of chastisement, does not appear to be what effects this limitation of their punishment. Rather, election prevents God's punishment of God's children from resulting in annihilation deserved for transgressions. Thus in 1 Cor 11:32 the chastised Corinthians and the unchastised world bound for condemnation fall into two, non-overlapping categories. The present punishments of illness, weakness and death among the Corinthians prove them to be God's children,[58] who suffer divine chastisement now instead of being swallowed up in the world's destiny in the final act of judgment.

The negative conjunction ἵνα μή, which connects the two verbs παιδεύειν and κατακρίνειν in 11:32, expresses their relationship as mutually exclusive categories of judgment. When ἵνα is used to introduce a logical result it produces exactly this sense. C. F. D. Moule identifies a number of ἵνα clauses which he considers probably "logically consecutive."[59] For example, Gal 5:17 and 1 Thess 5:4 both use a ἵνα clause to express the

---

56 Cf. Moore, *Judaism* 2, 252; Bertram, παιδεύω, *TDNT* 5, 606.

57 Whereas divine παιδεία is applied corporately in the OT-Jewish tradition, Paul speaks of chastisement of individuals. This common difference between OT and NT thought, however, ought not to prevent the tradition from illuminating Paul's meaning.

58 Similarly, Bruce (*1 Cor*, 116): "[As in Wis 11:10], so here the fact that the people warned are chastened is a token of their being true children of God."

59 Moule, *Idiom*, 142, 1.i. (Luke 9:45; Gal 5:17; 1 Thess 5:4; 1 John 1:9; Gen 22:14 LXX). Elsewhere in Paul and the NT ἵνα can substitute for an infinitive of result when the result is not actual (*BDF* §391, 5; cf. also 2 Cor 1:17; John 9:2; Rev 9:20; so BAGD, s.v. ἵνα, II.2.).

exclusive relation of two propositions.[60] Taking ἴνα μή at 1 Cor 11:32 likewise to introduce a logical result would produce the following meaning: "We who have fallen under judgment are chastised by the Lord; thus (or, it follows that) we will not be condemned with the world."

The same ἴνα μή construction appears in the parallel text, 2 Macc 6:12–16. Here the author affirms the Jews' exemption from divine vengeance against sins which will have reached their peak in the last days. They will be exempt for God chastises them presently, unlike the other nations:

> "Our people were being punished by way of chastening and not for their destruction (μὴ πρὸς ὄλεθρον, ἀλλὰ πρὸς παιδείαν) ...so that (ἴνα μή) his vengeance may not fall on us in afterdays when our sins have reached their height."[61]

1 Clement uses a similar ecbatic construction to express the result of divine chastisement: πατὴρ γὰρ ἀγαθὸς ὢν παιδεύει εἰς τὸ ἐλεηθῆναι ἡμᾶς διὰ τῆς ὁσίας παιδείας αὐτοῦ (56:16; cf. vv. 3–16).

How then will the guilty Corinthian Christians escape final condemnation with the world? Interpreting their present punishment as divine chastisement (παιδευόμεθα), Paul follows the OT-Jewish tradition of divine παιδεία in seeing exemption from final condemnation to be the implication of Christians' present suffering for sin. Paul even implies that the chastisement of premature physical death can mark one out as a child of God who does not share the world's destiny. The Corinthian Christians who became guilty of the body and blood of the Lord by participating inappropriately in the Lord's Supper and who were chastised with physical death will, in the end, be saved.[62] Paul does not make repentance from a sin for which a Christian incurs temporal judgment pivotal for escape from final condemnation. Rather, Christians' relation to God as God's children is here presented as definitive for their final destiny.

---

[60] So on Gal 5:17, Bruce, *Gal*, 244, and Oepke, *Gal*, 175.

[61] *APOT* 1, 140.

[62] With Lietzmann, *Kor*, 60: "Von κρίνεσθαι, der 'zeitlichen' Strafe unterscheidet... der Apostel hier das κατακρίνεσθαι, die Vernichtung, welcher 'die Welt' anheimfallen wird.... Also auch der gezüchtigte, ja mit dem Tode bestrafte Christ wird am Ende gerettet werden vgl. 3:15 5:5." Similarly, Wolff, *1 Kor*, 96: Christus "handelt auch an der 'unwürdigen' Gemeinde, erhielt ihr (und damit eben auch den Kranken und Verstorbenen) durch das Gericht hindurch das gewährte Heil, bewahrt sie davor, der 'Welt' (das heißt den gottlosen Menschen; vgl 1,20; 2,12) gleich zu werden...und dadurch dem endgültigen Verdammungsurteil anheimzufallen." *Ibid*: "Wie in 10,12f., so wird auch jetzt ebenfalls einer möglichen Resignation oder Heilsunsicherheit gewehrt." Cf. Jer 30:11; 46:28: "For I am with you to save you; I will make an end of all the nations where I have scattered you, I will not make an end of you, only discipline you in moderation, so as not to let you go entirely unpunished." Cf. also Heb 12:10, 11.

Deliverance to Satan

1 Corinthians 5:1–5. In 1 Corinthians 5 Paul deals with another instance of sinful behavior in the Corinthian community, a flagrant case of sexual misconduct: "Someone has his father's wife" (5:1). The Corinthians have not reacted as they ought ("You are puffed up! Shouldn't you rather have been filled with grief?", 5:2; "Your boasting is not good!," 5:6). The church may not allow this kind of persistent sinful conduct in its midst. Disciplinary action toward the offending member is in order. This discipline involves excommunication: "The one who has done this thing [must] be removed from your midst" (5:2). More enigmatically, Paul formulates that the appropriate thing to do is to "deliver such a one to Satan for destruction of the flesh" (5:5). Does this fate which the culprit has invited upon himself suggest loss of salvation? What can this text tell us about the implications for continuity in salvation which Paul attributed to blatantly sinful lifestyles of people in the church?

The misconduct of the Corinthian man is of the most serious kind. Paul terms it πορνεία, meaning here a specific kind of sexual immorality,[63] incest. This church member was living with his "father's wife" in an enduring sexual relationship.[64] A stigma attached to this behavior not only in early Christian circles influenced by their OT-Jewish heritage but also among pagans of the day, to which Paul alludes in 5:1: τοιαύτη πορνεία ἥτις οὐδὲ ἐν τοῖς ἔθνεσιν. Both the OT and Roman law prohibited a man's having sexual relations with his father's wife.[65] The sin and the church's attitude toward it is thus absolutely appalling.

In the interests of the church and the sinner himself, Paul outlines the long overdue steps which must be taken. While Paul's main concern appears to be preserving the purity of the community (see esp. 5:6–8),[66] the matter to which we will devote most of our attention is the destiny of the sinner. The man must "be taken out of your midst" (5:2) and "deliver[ed]... to Satan for destruction of the flesh" (5:5). The severity of this punishment seems to indicate the gravity of the sin. What exactly do these measures entail? What significance do they have for the eternal destiny of the man?

The answer to the second question lies more readily at hand. For Paul

---

[63] See BAGD, s.v. πορνεία.

[64] On this meaning of ἔχειν, see Fee, *1 Cor*, 200, 278 with n. 49; BAGD, s.v. ἔχω, I.2.b.

[65] See Lev 18:7f.; 20:11 LXX; for other Jewish and Greco-Roman material, see Fee, *1 Cor*, 200, n. 24; Forkman, *Limits*, 141 with n. 134.

[66] Cf. Fee, *1 Cor*, 215, 197; Grosheide, *1 Cor*, 131.

states explicitly the purpose of the man's deliverance to Satan for the destruction of the flesh: ἵνα τὸ πνεῦμα σωθῇ ἐν τῇ ἡμέρᾳ τοῦ κυρίου (5:5). The final salvation of the sinner is not excluded; on the contrary, it is the very goal of punishment.[67] How the punishment can have this salvific effect is not immediately apparent. I will pursue that point later in the discussion. Before proceeding further, however, I want to establish that the deliverance to Satan for the destruction of the flesh is motivated by the goal of the sinner's salvation, not the certainty of his condemnation. Paul gives us no grounds here to say that he thought particularly grievous sins disqualify in principle from final salvation.

Paul's formulation of the goal of the disciplinary measure, however, does not necessarily convey that it will achieve its intended effect. The ἵνα of 5:5 could be ecbatic or final. Is the final salvation of the sinner an open question for Paul? If so, on what would it depend? Or if salvation is the certain outcome of the process, how are we to understand the relationship between punishment and salvation?

First I will discuss the possibility that the ἵνα of 5:5 is ecbatic and that Paul expresses confidence in the final salvation of the sexual offender. This view could appeal to the similar argumentation in 11:27–34. There the Corinthian Christians who have become guilty of profaning the Lord's Supper

---

[67] The expression ἵνα τὸ πνεῦμα σωθῇ denotes the salvation of the man. Paul elects the term τὸ πνεῦμα here for the sake of contrast with σάρξ, which will be destroyed (εἰς ὄλεθρον τῆς σαρκός). τὸ πνεῦμα must be taken as an anthropological designation here (so also 2 Cor 2:13; 7:1, 13; 1 Cor 16:18; Rom 8:16; Gal 6:18; Phil 4:23; Phlm 25; cf. Col 2:5; Heb 4:12; see Gundry, *SŌMA*, 48, 49, 141). The other views are too problematic. τὸ πνεῦμα as the divine Spirit (so v. Campenhausen, *Authority*, 134, 135, n. 50, following Bornkamm; also Yarbro Collins, "Excommunication," 260) can hardly be saved (with Sand, *Fleisch*, 143; Mattern,*Gericht*, 105; MacArthur, "Spirit," 251). τὸ πνεῦμα as the portion of God's Spirit which constitutes the new "I" given by God (so Schweizer, πνεῦμα, *TDNT* 6, 435) contradicts Pauline usage characterized by careful distinction of the divine and the human spirit (cf. Rom 8:15, 16; 1 Cor 2:11; with Gundry, *SŌMA*, 141, 142). τὸ πνεῦμα as the whole human person living under the influence of the Spirit (so Cambier, "Chair," 228) also contradicts Pauline usage characterized by restriction of the term to an aspect of human personhood or an external influence (with MacArthur, "Spirit," 251, 252). Taking τὸ πνεῦμα as an anthropological term does not require us to think that the spirit of the man will be saved *at the expense of the physical body*, in contradiction to the doctrine of the bodily resurrection elucidated in chap. 15. Rather Paul finds the term τὸ πνεῦμα appropriate probably because it can denote "the condemned person insofar as he will exist after his death in the realm of the dead" (MacArthur, "Spirit," 253 with n. 22; he compares 1 Enoch 22:3–13; Sir 9:9; Luke 24:37, 39; 1 Pet 3:19; ruaḥ in *b. Ber.* 18c; 4 Ezra 7:100 [see also ibid., 256, n. 25]). The phrase ἵνα τὸ πνεῦμα σωθῇ ἐν τῇ ἡμέρᾳ τοῦ κυρίου in 1 Cor 5:5b would not therefore convey the "manner of the duration of his [the sinner's] eternal life," but "what will be the mode of being in which he faces judgment and finds approbation on the day of the Lord" (253).

are subject to divine punishment which does not exclude but includes their final salvation. "Being judged by the Lord we are chastised so that (ἵνα) we might not be condemned with the world" (11:32). ἵνα there introduces the logical result.[68] These two texts have in common not only the motifs of sinful behavior, punishment, and salvation, and similar formulations expressing the relation between punishment and salvation with a ἵνα-clause. The nature of the punishments in 11:30—physical sickness and death—also parallel ὄλεθρος τῆς σαρκός in 5:5 as most commonly interpreted, namely, as a reference to physical suffering or death.[69] Further, neither text explicitly mentions repentance as necessary to the sinners' attainment of final salvation.

Nevertheless, there are important differences between the two texts. Paul attributes the temporal judgment suffered by the profaners of the Lord's Supper to the Lord himself: κρινόμενοι δὲ ὑπὸ [τοῦ] κυρίου (11:32).[70] By contrast, the man guilty of incest is "deliver[ed] to Satan (τῷ σατανᾷ) for destruction of the flesh" (5:5). The παιδεία-terminology used at 11:32 leads us to interpret the punishments suffered in that context in terms of the OT-Jewish divine παιδεία tradition as fatherly chastisements of God's children which show them to be exempt from eschatological condemnation with the world.[71] That terminology, however, is missing in chap. 5. Instead Paul goes on in 5:11 to speak of the πόρνος not as a child of God but as a "so-called brother" (ἀδελφὸς ὀνομαζόμενος). He classes the so-called brother who is a πόρνος with other sinners in a vice catalogue (5:11), i.e., among those who, as he will say in another vice list at 6:9, 10, "will not inherit the kingdom of God." The πόρνος belongs to the world (cf. 5:10), and if he somehow finds himself within the church, he is to be judged and cast out (ἐξάρατε τὸν πονηρὸν ἐξ ὑμῶν αὐτῶν, 5:13). For the church must judge οἱ ἔσω (5:12). Fellowship in the church is not for the vice-doers of the world. Paul prohibits such people in the ranks of the church: μὴ συναναμίγνυσθαι πόρνοις (5:9, 11). Further, he excludes them from a specific form of church fellowship: τῷ τοιούτῳ μηδὲ συνεσθίειν (5:11). That is, he bars πόρνοι from partaking in the Lord's Supper, if not also from other meal fellowship with Christians.[72] This prohibition stands in stark contrast to the closing instruction in chap. 11, where

---

[68] See the discussion of 11:27–34 on pp. 99–112 above.
[69] So Meeks, *Urban Christians*, 130; Lampe, "Discipline," 349, 351; Gundry, ΣΩΜΑ, 143; Roetzel, *Judgment*, 121; Barrett, *1 Cor*, 126; MacArthur, "Spirit," 250; Havener, "Curse," 341; Morris, *1 Cor*, 88.
[70] So also implicitly in the divine passives at 11:31, 32, ἐκρινόμεθα, παιδευόμεθα.
[71] See excursus on pp. 107-111 above.
[72] See p. 117 below.

the offenders who are being chastised by the Lord are thoroughly and expressly included in the church's gathering for worship, including the meal fellowship around the Lord's table: "So then my brothers, when you come together to eat, receive one another. And if anyone is hungry, let him eat at home, so that you might not come together for judgment" (11:33, 34a). In conclusion, Paul does not view the cases of the profaners of the Lord's Supper and the man guilty of incest as parallel.[73] The punishments meted out in both instances have different significance and therefore the relation of punishment to final salvation is not the same. The discipline of the offender in chap. 5 is not divine chastisement and does not imply his exemption from condemnation as a child of God. Rather, as 5:9–13 (which is a continuation of the argument in 5:1–8)[74] makes clear, Paul considers the fornicator to be a falsely professing Christian who is yet outside the kingdom and who belongs to the world. The goal of his punishment—"that the spirit might be saved at the day of the Lord"—is not certain to come about.[75] Final salvation is a possibility, but not a foregone conclusion.

What then is the significance of the punishment with respect to the final salvation of the sinner? How can the possibility of salvation be realized? In order to answer these questions we must first come to a clearer understanding of the nature of the punishment itself.

The offender was to be formally and practically excluded from the life of the church. The Corinthians should have already expelled the member who was guilty of incest: ...ἵνα ἀρθῇ ἐκ μέσου ὑμῶν ὁ τὸ ἔργον τοῦτο πράξας (5:2b). Since they had not yet, Paul issues the commands in 5:13, ἐξάρατε τὸν πονηρὸν ἐξ ὑμῶν αὐτῶν, and 5:7, ἐκκαθάρατε τὴν παλαιὰν ζύμην.[76] Removing the incestuous man from their midst and

---

[73] With Fee, *1 Cor*, 211, 212.

[74] Correctly, Fee, *1 Cor*, 220–221; similarly, Grosheide, *1 Cor*, 127. Fee notes the following connections between the two sections: "(1) The matter of associating with one who is sexually immoral is both the point of their 'misunderstanding' of the previous letter and of their present 'boasting' with a well-known *pornos* ('sexually immoral person') in their midst. (2) The clarification in v. 11 intends to forbid any kind of association with a man who calls himself a *brother* but who is a *pornos*, which is precisely what vv. 1–8 are all about. (3) The paragraph, and therefore the whole section, concludes with a citation of Deut. 17:7, which explicitly repeats the injunctions of vv. 2, 5, and 7."

[75] Contrast Goguel (*Primitive Church*, 234), who says that the sinner's premature death substitutes for eternal condemnation in 1 Cor 5:5, though he calls this an improvisation.

[76] The Corinthians should have realized their responsibility to excommunicate this erring member because Paul had already written to them "not to associate with fornicators," as he reminds them at 5:9. They had misinterpreted his instruction (perhaps deliberately; see Fee, *1 Cor*, 222, 223), as 5:10 implies, and failed to apply the necessary

"cleaning out the old leaven" meant, practically speaking, denying him participation in the fellowship as a member.[77] Paul formulates broadly with his directive "not to associate (συναναμίγνυσθαι) with a so-called brother who is a fornicator" (5:11).[78] Yet the command "not even to eat with such a one" (5:11), probably a reference to Christian fellowship meals, including the Lord's table,[79] suggests that he rules out in particular such forms of fellowship as are appropriate only for members (that is, people whose Christian profession appears genuine). Others should be excluded for they are "stains on your love-feasts" (οἱ ἐν ταῖς ἀγάπαις ὑμῶν σπιλάδες, Jude 12). Table fellowship in the early church, which went hand in hand with the celebration of the Lord's Supper,[80] presupposed the participants' full acceptance in the fellowship of the saints in Christ (cf. Gal 2:12 and context; 1 Cor 10:16, 17). Because the offender's behavior called his profession into question, he had to be expelled and treated as an unbeliever.[81]

A formal expulsion of the Corinthian man was to take place. Paul apparently envisions it as "a community action, carried out in the context of the Spirit, where 'you and my S/spirit are assembled together, along with the power of the Lord Jesus'."[82] Paul describes the proceeding as "deliver[ing] such a one to Satan" (5:5).[83] The parallel παρέδωκα τῷ σατανᾷ at 1 Tim

---

discipline. But now Paul makes perfectly clear how they are to put into practice this principle of not associating with fornicators, namely, by excommunicating the sexual offender: "Now I have written to you not to associate with any so-called brother who is a fornicator...not even to eat with such a one...cast out the fornicator from your midst!" (5:11–13).

[77] Fee, *1 Cor*, 226: the man should be "excluded from the *community* as it gathers for worship and instruction." The metaphor of removing the leaven obviously has this implication in this context (correctly, Fee, *1 Cor*, 216).

[78] On the use of the same verb in the prohibition of associating with idlers in the church at 2 Thess 3:14, see Marshall, *1 2 Thess*, 227, 228.

[79] Cf. Fee, *1 Cor*, 226. The question is whether Paul's prohibition includes also private meals.

[80] Cf. 1 Cor 11:25a, which presupposes a meal between the partaking of the two elements, bread and wine, as Hofius argues ("Herrenmahl," 376–384).

[81] Cf. the instructions Jesus gives concerning the persistently disobedient in the church in Matt 18:15–17: "...if he doesn't listen to the church, let him be to you as a Gentile and a tax-collector." By contrast, the command "not to associate" (μὴ συναναμίγνυσθαι) with idlers subject to church discipline at 2 Thess 3:14 does not preclude their being admonished as fellow Christians (νουθετεῖτε ὡς ἀδελφόν, 2 Thess 3:15). Fee (*1 Cor*, 226, n. 35) comments "that the parallel [with 1 Cor 5:11] is not exact, and that the discipline may be more drastic here than in Thessalonica."

[82] Fee, *1 Cor*, 206. Fee argues on pp. 205, 206 with n. 44 against Conzelmann (*1 Cor*, 97) for an understanding of the grammar that takes the action to be communal and not Paul's alone.

[83] Paul's expression παραδοῦναι τῷ σατανᾷ has been compared to ancient curse

1:20 for the expulsion of Hymenaeus and Alexander from the church suggests that the formula was technical.[84] It presupposes the notion that Satan as ruler of this world holds sway over those outside the church (2 Cor 4:4; Eph 2:2). Unbelievers find themselves in the sphere of Satan's authority and activity. The incestuous man's formal expulsion from the community of the saints by deliverance to Satan gave formal recognition to the fact that he belonged to this other sphere.[85] It is doubtful that the phrase has in mind more than that, e.g., a special consignment to Satan which subjected the man to extraordinary affliction.[86] Nor can it be said that the express purpose of deliverance to Satan was the "destruction of the flesh" ("in the sense of personally handing the man to Satan to 'go to work on him,' as it were"[87]). The express purpose is salvation ($\H{\iota}\nu\alpha...\sigma\omega\theta\hat{\eta}$, 5:5).[88] Destruction of the flesh is simply the consequence ($\epsilon\H{\iota}\varsigma$ $\H{o}\lambda\epsilon\theta\rho\text{o}\nu$ $\tau\hat{\eta}\varsigma$ $\sigma\alpha\rho\kappa\text{ó}\varsigma$) of deliverance to Satan.[89] Paul's language does not exclude a Satanic attack on the man, but neither does it demand one.[90]

---

formulas common in both pagan and Jewish milieux (see Forkmann, *Limits*, 143; Deissmann, *Light*, 302–303; Yarbro Collins, "Excommunication," 255). Fee (*1 Cor*, 208) argues, however, that the only truly parallel use of such language, namely, for expulsion from a religious community, is found in 1 Tim 1:20. We can compare the similar language used in Job 2:6 LXX ($\epsilon\H{\iota}\pi\epsilon\nu$ $\delta\grave{\epsilon}$ $\H{o}$ $\kappa\acute{\upsilon}\rho\iota\text{o}\varsigma$ $\tau\hat{\omega}$ $\delta\iota\alpha\beta\acute{o}\lambda\omega$, $\H{\iota}\delta\text{o}\grave{\upsilon}$ $\pi\alpha\rho\alpha\delta\acute{\iota}\delta\omega\mu\acute{\iota}$ $\sigma\text{o}\iota$ $\alpha\grave{\upsilon}\tau\acute{o}\nu$); but a material parallel is doubtful (see discussion below).

[84] Fee, *1 Cor*, 208; Kelly, *Pastorals*, 58.

[85] Contrast Bruce (*Cor*, 54, 55), who assumes that the man is a believer over whom "Satan normally has no power," and explains that therefore "a deliberate act of delivery to Satan is necessary."

[86] With Fee, *1 Cor*, 209. Various arguments against the view that $\pi\alpha\rho\alpha\delta\text{o}\hat{\upsilon}\nu\alpha\iota$ $\tau\hat{\omega}$ $\sigma\alpha\tau\alpha\nu\hat{\alpha}$ refers to expulsion have been put up: (1) Lampe ("Discipline," 352) argues that neither Paul nor other NT writers conceive of the expulsion of impenitent sinners in terms of deliverance to Satan. But this argument is not persuasive, and 1 Tim 1:20 seems to speak against it. (2) MacArthur ("Spirit," 249) does not want to equate $\pi\alpha\rho\alpha\text{-}\delta\text{o}\hat{\upsilon}\nu\alpha\iota$ $\tau\hat{\omega}$ $\sigma\alpha\tau\alpha\nu\hat{\alpha}$ with excommunication since Satan can exercise power even over those within the church (cf. 2 Cor 12:7; 1 Thess 2:18). But this argument seems to ignore that "deliverance" to Satan goes beyond mere vulnerability to Satanic activity which may characterize church members. When we realize that delivering the man to Satan acknowledges his exclusion not merely from the church but from the sphere of salvation, we need find no other "severer" sentence in the expression $\pi\alpha\rho\alpha\delta\text{o}\hat{\upsilon}\nu\alpha\iota$ $\tau\hat{\omega}$ $\sigma\alpha\tau\alpha\nu\hat{\alpha}$. Contrast Bruce, *Cor*, 55; also, Gundry, *ΣΩΜΑ*, 143; Conzelmann, *1 Cor*, 97.

[87] Fee *1 Cor*, 209. Against Grosheide, *1 Cor*, 123.

[88] Satan is thus only indirectly the agent of the realization of the purpose of salvation. On Satan as God's agent in Jewish thought, see Thornton, "Satan," 152.

[89] For this use of $\epsilon\H{\iota}\varsigma$, see BAGD, s.v. $\epsilon\H{\iota}\varsigma$, 4.e. With Fee, (*1 Cor*, 209 with nn. 66, 67), who argues that when he wants to express a double purpose, Paul uses two final (verbal) clauses, not a purpose clause coupled with a prepositional phrase introduced by $\epsilon\H{\iota}\varsigma$ as here (see, e.g., 1 Cor 1:28, 29; 2 Thess 1:11, 12; 2 Cor 8:14; 1 Cor 4:6; 7:5; Rom 7:4; 15:16).

[90] With Fee, *1 Cor*, 209.

The "destruction of the flesh" which results from deliverance to Satan has been understood in two ways. Taking σάρξ in an anthropological sense to refer to the physical body, most interpreters see ὄλεθρος as physical suffering or even death.[91] The competing view takes σάρξ as a theological term meaning the human sin-bent self, and sees the destruction of the sinner's lust and pride to result through deliverance to Satan.[92] Whether the process is physical, or spiritual or both, Paul imagines the "destruction of the flesh" to move the sinner toward the goal of final salvation. It is not hard to see how the destruction of pride and lust could contribute to this goal. The same effect, repentance, could however conceivably come also through physical suffering. Perhaps it is impossible to say with certainty which consequence of expulsion from the church, Paul hopes, will spur the sinner on to spiritual transformation, but such repentance and conversion is doubtless the key to the reversal of the man's fate.[93] Elsewhere also church discipline is thought to produce sorrow leading to repentance (cf. 2 Cor 2:6, 7).[94] Thus, although Paul here omits to mention the sinner's repentance as the desired effect of discipline or presupposition of his final salvation, it is understood.[95] If Paul considers the offender not to be a genuine Christian, as I have argued that the rest of chap. 5 reveals, his final salvation is unthinkable apart from repentance and conversion.[96] The salvation of the incestuous man thus depends on the success of the process of discipline in

---

[91] For σάρξ as the body or the bodily aspect of human existence, see BAGD, s.v. σάρξ, 2. Cf. 2 Cor 7:1, 5; 5:16; Gal 4:13, 14; also Eph 2:15; 5:29, 31; Col 2:1, 5; 1 Tim 3:16. The connotations of ὄλεθρος, frequently associated with physical suffering and death (cf. Philo, *spec. leg.* I.160; III.147; IV.127; Wis 1:12, 18:13; 1 Thess 5:3; 4 Macc 10:15), support this understanding. Satan's agency in the destruction of the flesh may also speak in favor of a physical interpretation (for Satanically inflicted physical suffering, cf. Acts 10:38; Ign. *Rom.* 5:3; Heb 2:14; 2 Cor 12:7).

[92] Cambier, "Chair," 228; Mattern, *Gericht*, 106; Sand, *Fleisch*, 144, 145. Cf. Thiselton, "ΣΑΡΞ," 204–228. Marshall (*Kept*, 114) suggests the destruction of both the physical flesh and the "lower nature."

[93] The notion that the man could atone for his sin through suffering is unpauline and cannot explain the possibility of a reversal of his fate. See above, p. 105 with n. 40.

[94] 2 Cor 2:11 may suggest that Satan plays a role in the process of sorrow-producing discipline referred to in 2:6, 7. Nevertheless, the discussions in 1 Corinthians 5:1–5 and 2 Cor 2:5–11; 7:12 do not seem to reflect the same case; see Furnish, *2 Cor*, 163–166.

[95] With Marshall, *Kept*, 114; Lampe. "Discipline," 349, 351; Gundry, *ΣΩΜΑ*,143; Sand, *Fleisch*, 145; Cambier, "Chair," 227; Käsemann, Sätze," 74; Fee, *1 Cor*, 213; Grosheide, *1 Cor*, 129, 130. Against Conzelmann, *1 Cor*, 98, n. 40; Forkmann, *Limits*, 146; Havener, "Curse," 341, 338; Mattern, *Gericht*, 107; Synofzik, *Gerichtsaussagen*, 56.

[96] While Paul can express confidence of final salvation apart from repentance from a particular sin committed in the case of *Christians* who have suffered God's temporal judgment (11:32), theologically it is impossible for him to do so in the case of falsely professing Christians subjected to punishment.

inducing repentance and conversion.[97] The fact that Paul speaks of salvation "on the day of the Lord" does not imply that he could not be saved before then, if he repented and converted. Rather, Paul chooses this expression for salvation, which stresses its eschatological quality, in order to convey that the punishment does not have to be the *final* word on the sinner's destiny.[98] Instead, present punishment opens up the possibility of future salvation. When the church exercises its responsibility to "judge those inside" (5:12) and expels the fornicator from the church, he has conceivably more incentive to repent and be saved, whereas "the fornicators of this world" merely await the final judgment when "God will judge those outside" (5:13). Thus, although the judgment experienced by the incestuous man differs from the chastisement of God's children, which shows their exemption from condemnation (see 11:27–34), it still gives him an advantage over those outside the church, as Paul sees it.[99] There is a distinct hope that the disciplined falsely professing Christian will be saved.

Should the man not "be saved on the day of the Lord," however, because he did not repent and convert, no loss of salvation would have taken place. 1 Corinthians 5 rather illustrates that Paul recognizes the possibility of false profession and does not base certainty of final salvation on church membership.

Beware Not to Fall!

1 Corinthians 10:12. In 1 Cor 10:12 Paul issues an ominous warning: ὥστε ὁ δοκῶν ἑστάναι βλεπέτω μὴ πέσῃ. H. Conzelmann suggests that "the statement provokes the question as to the possibility of assurance of salvation."[100] Does the metaphor "fall" (πίπτειν) refer to losing salvation or faith?[101] What can precipitate such falling? In the following analysis

---

[97] Since the discipline has this remedial character (with Morris, *1 Cor*, 89; Thornton, "Satan," 151; against Barrett, *1 Cor*, 126), it is unlikely that destruction of the flesh, if meant in a physical sense, could denote immediate death. The fact that Paul prohibits associating and eating with fornicators at 5:11 also speaks against the possibility of an immediate punitive death (Fee, *1 Cor*, 210, 212).

[98] Similarly, Fee, *1 Cor*, 213.

[99] Grosheide (*1 Cor*, 130) comments on 5:13: "To the church God gives the grace of exercising discipline which serves to warn sinners. They that are without lack that grace so that they come at once before the judgment of God, not having any benefit at all."

[100] Conzelmann, *1 Cor*, 168, n. 43.

[101] So Marshall, *Kept*, 116; Grosheide, *1 Cor*, 226; Walter, "Christusglaube," 427; Wolff, *1 Kor*, 48; Roetzel, *Judgment*, 172; Hahn, "Teilhabe," 157, 158; Galley, *Heilsgeschehen*, 16; Weiß *1 Kor*, 250; Dugandzic, *'Ja' Gottes*, 244; Klauck, *Herrenmahl*, 252;

of the warning in its context I will attempt to answer these questions and show the significance of this text for Paul's understanding of continuity in salvation.

The warning at 10:12 occurs in a lengthy discussion of meat sacrificed to idols begun at 8:1 (περὶ δὲ τῶν εἰδωλοθύτων...).[102] The "strong" in Corinth apparently insisted on, among other things, their freedom to "lie in an idol's temple" (8:10), i.e. to participate in pagan cultic meals.[103] But Paul sees therein the danger of idolatry, as he makes clear in chap. 10. He explains why taking part in such meals is tantamount to idolatry (even though an idol has no real existence and sacrificial meat is nothing) in 10:15–21. Therefore the over-confident Corinthians should not go to the temples; rather they should "flee idolatry" (10:14). Paul wants them to learn a lesson from the wilderness generation, who "sat down to eat" in the presence of the golden calf, thereby committing idolatry,[104] and suffered the consequences: μηδὲ εἰδωλολάτραι γίνεσθε καθώς τινες αὐτῶν... (10:7, 8).[105] The Corinthians should heed Paul's warning lest they too "fall" (10:12).[106]

Paul does not yet pronounce judgment on the Corinthians as idolaters. In contrast to the discussions on the incestuous man in chap. 5 and the profaners of the Lord's Supper in chap. 11, they are so far not judged guilty, therefore, punishment is still a possibility to be avoided. They are now in

Barrett, *1 Cor*, 224; Käsemann, "Abendmahlslehre," 18, 19; Davidson, *Typology*, 291.

[102] On the disputed question of the relation of the various parts of Paul's argument concerning εἰδωλόθυτα in 8:1–11:1, see Fee, "*Εἰδωλόθυτα*."

[103] Cf. Fee, *1 Cor*, 359–362. The Corinthians probably thought of their attending cultic meals merely as an occasion for social intercourse but not for religious worship. On the disputed significance of pagan cultic meals, see the discussion in Willis, *Idol Meat*, 17–61; Horsley, *New Documents*, 5–9.

[104] Fee (*1 Cor*, 454) points out that Paul quotes the portion of the OT narrative (Exod 32:6b LXX) which specifically indicates that the Israelites committed idolatry by participating in a cultic meal in an idol's presence. The form of the Corinthians' temptation to commit idolatry is exactly parallel.

[105] For the use of the wilderness generation motif in Paul and early Christian and Jewish literature, see Wiebe, *Wüstenzeit*. 1 Cor 10:11—"these things were written down for our instruction (νουθεσία)"—shows that Paul does not ascribe a typological significance to the Israelites in the technical-hermeneutical sense, as though the wilderness generation's fate will inevitably befall the Corinthians. Rather he uses τυπικῶς/τύποι in a moral sense (cf. Conzelmann, *1 Cor*, 167, 168; Weiß, *1 Kor*, 254, n. 1; Dugandzic, *'Ja' Gottes*, 247).

[106] The warning is against idolatry and its consequences, as the verses which immediately precede and follow show. ὥστε introduces the warning at 10:12 and refers back to the illustration of the idolatrous Israelites (Barrett, *1 Cor*, 228). διόπερ heading 10:14–22 ties the argument to flee idolatry closely to the preceding section and and thus to the warning at 10:12 (see Moule, *Idiom*, 164). Cf. Léon-Dufour, *Partage*, 240.

the danger zone and must turn away and flee. Otherwise they might "become idolaters" (10:7) and might "fall" (10:12).

Therefore the question wanting an answer here is how Paul understands the potential fall on account of idolatry in relation to the salvation of the Corinthians who might succumb. First we must determine the nature of the punishment which will befall those who become idolaters. This task is not an easy one, for Paul's allusions to the consequences of idolatry are vague. What exactly does the metaphor "fall" mean? What aspect of the idolatrous wilderness generation's punishment does Paul find parallel to this "falling"? Then we must ask what implications for salvation Paul attributes to the punishment. Does "falling" exclude one from salvation? What does the Israelites' punishment imply about their "salvation"? Wherein would the parallel with the Corinthians consist? What is the significance for salvation of the forceful affirmation of God's faithfulness in testing at 10:13b? Finally, is it clear that Paul's concern is that the Corinthians might *lose* salvation? How do Paul's descriptions of the person warned as ὁ δοκῶν ἑστά- ναι (10:12), and of the guilty Israelites as those with whom "God was not pleased" (οὐκ...εὐδόκησεν ὁ Θεός, 10:5) help us answer that question?

Paul uses a metaphor to express the danger facing the Corinthians who want to attend the pagan cultic meals: "Let him who thinks he stands beware lest he fall" (10:12). What does such language mean here? The verb πίπτειν as well as its mate ἵστημι have already appeared in the discussion, namely, in connection with the Israelites' folly. Describing their idolatry and fornication, Paul quotes Exod 32:6 LXX: ἐκάθισεν ὁ λαὸς φαγεῖν καὶ πεῖν καὶ ἀνέστησαν παίζειν (10:7).[107] Then he notes their punishment: καὶ ἔπεσαν μιᾷ ἡμέρᾳ εἴκοσι τρεῖς χιλιάδες (10:8). Paul takes up the pair of contrasting verbs describing the OT idolaters, πίπτειν and (ἀν)ίστημι, and applies them to the NT counterpart in 10:12. πέσῃ in the warning to the Corinthians echoes ἔπεσαν in the description of the Israelites' punishment.[108] Does Paul want his readers to interpret their potential "falling" as the same kind experienced by the Israelites? The latter died in the wilderness. πίπτειν at 10:8 is a euphemism for death (cf. Luke 21:24; Heb 3:17 [here referring to the wilderness generation]; Job 14:10 LXX; Amos 7:17 LXX).[109] Does it have the same connotations at 10:12?[110]

---

[107] On παίζειν for sexual play, see Perrot, "Exemples," 450, n. 10; Meeks, "And Rose up to Play," 70.

[108] Contrast Michaelis (πίπτω, *TDNT* 6, 164, n. 21), who thinks the recurrence of πίπτειν in v. 12 is not intentional parallelism.

[109] The author of Hebrews also uses πίπτειν both for death in the wilderness (3:17) and for the danger facing Christians who imitate the wilderness generation (4:11).

[110] Perrot ("Exemples," 441) notes the double use of (ἀν)ίστημι as significant for

If the description of the wilderness generation's punishment in 10:5–10 is decisive for the meaning of "falling" in the Corinthians' case, the most ready conclusion to draw is that Paul has in mind physical punishment, in particular, death. The summary description of the Israelites' punishment in 10:5 indicates physical death: κατεστρώθησαν γὰρ ἐν τῇ ἐρήμῳ. The description of each particular sin and its consequent punishment makes the same point: they "fell" (v. 8), "were destroyed by the serpents" (v. 9), and "were destroyed by the destroyer" (v. 10). Thus E. P. Sanders concludes: "The force of the typological argument is that those who commit idolatry will be killed."[111] But most modern-day interpreters largely fail to draw the implications of Paul's emphasis on the physical nature of the Israelites' punishment when they interpret the Corinthians' danger. The Corinthians themselves, however, most probably did not miss the point. They have already heard Paul speak of the punishment of the fornicator in 5:5 in such a way as to make it seem physical in nature: "deliver such a one to Satan for destruction of the flesh."[112] He even uses cognates when he describes both punishments: ὀλοθρευτής (10:10) recalls ὄλεθρος (5:5). Further, the profaning of the Lord's Supper has brought on physical illness and even death as chastisement (11:30–32), as Paul is about to declare. The metaphorical πίπτειν at 10:12 therefore probably connotes a physical type of punishment. If they become idolaters, the Corinthians will expose themselves to the danger of punitive suffering or death.

But is that all? Did not the Israelites who died in the wilderness also fail to reach the promised land and thus do not they represent the danger of idolaters' exclusion from salvation? Do not they function as examples of people who do not "run so as to obtain" the eschatological prize, as Paul urges the Corinthians to do in 9:24?[113] This is the significance usually attributed to the OT example.[114] Paul makes no reference to this aspect of the OT people's punishment in 10:1–10, yet one might argue that the point is implicit.[115] G. Fee understands the warning in 10:12 to "mean that the

---

Paul's comparison of Israel and the Corinthians. Cf. Rom 14:4, where the synonyms, στήκειν and ἑστάναι, contrast to πίπτειν (see BAGD, s.v. ἵστημι, II.1.d.)

[111] Sanders, *Law*, 110. Similarly, Perrot, "Exemples," 443: "Les Corinthiens sont endanger de mort."

[112] See treatment of 1 Cor 5:5 on pp. 113-120 above.

[113] So Fee, *1 Cor*, 442.

[114] So, e.g., Barrett, *1 Cor*, 223; Grosheide, *1 Cor*, 226; Wolff, *1 Kor*, 48; Neuenzeit, *Herrenmahl*, 46. Contrast Sanders, *Law*, 110: "We probably should not read 1 Corinthians 10 as implying that the act of eating at an idol's table leads to damnation." Contrast also Michaelis, πίπτω, *TDNT* 6, 165.

[115] Heb 3:16–18 mentions both death in the wilderness and failure to enter God's

Corinthians, too, as Israel, may fail of the eschatological prize, in this case eternal salvation."[116]

Some considerations lend support to this view. πίπτειν can have an eschatological sense connoting exclusion from salvation (Rom 11:11; Heb 4:11) or connoting judgment (Rom 14:4; Jas 5:12). The verb appears together with ἴστημι at Rom 14:4 with this sense. The contrasting verb ἴστημι often serves as a figure for salvation or eschatological steadfastness and triumph, either explicitly—"stand in grace" (Rom 5:2; cf. 1 Pet 5:12), "...in faith" (2 Cor 1:24), "...in the gospel" (1 Cor 15:1)—or implicitly (Rom 11:20; 14:4; Rev 6:17; Jude 24; Eph 6:13, 14; Col 4:12). Not only word usage gives support to this view. The vice list at 6:9, 10 excludes idolaters along with other sinners from salvation: they "will not inherit the kingdom of God." In 10:6–10 Paul describes the wilderness generation as guilty of two of these vices characteristic of the unsaved: the Israelites became πόρνοι and εἰδωλολάτραι. This description suggests that their punishment involved exclusion from salvation.[117] When Paul exhorts the Corinthians not to imitate the Israelites' fornication and idolatry (μηδὲ εἰδωλολάτραι γίνεσθε...μηδὲ πορνεύωμεν, 10:7, 8), he seems to be implying that they too would be excluded from salvation.

Thus one can argue that Paul's warning against falling at 10:12 may refer not only to a physical kind of punishment, but also to exclusion from salvation. That possibility raises another question, however: does Paul think the Corinthians who sin in the manner of the Israelites will *forfeit* salvation?[118] Not necessarily. For he does not so judge in the case of the man who was guilty of fornication in chap. 5. This person did not lose salvation but proved by his behavior to be a mere "so-called brother" (5:11) and so lost only the outward status of one saved (through expulsion from the church, cf. 5:5).[119]

Does Paul reckon similarly with the possibility of false profession when dealing with the matter of idolatry in chap. 10? Paul has already listed the

---

"rest" as the punishment of the disobedient wilderness generation. Paul, however, is known to exercise considerable freedom in his use of OT texts, adapting or assigning new meanings (see Hab 2:4 at Rom 1:17; Gal 3:11), allegorizing (see Gen 16:15; 17:16 at Gal 4:21ff.), or wresting them from their original context (see Deut 25:4 at 1 Cor 9:9). On this matter see, further, Fitzmeyer, "Pauline Theology," 802.

[116] Fee, *1 Cor*, 459.

[117] Paul is considerably more positive when he speaks about Israel's final destiny in Romans 9–11. See treatment of that passage on pp. 161–195 below.

[118] Lietzmann (*Kor*, 47) thinks that Paul sees the danger of a "Rückfall ins Heidentum."

[119] See pp. 113–120 above.

εἰδωλολάτρης along with the *πόρνος* in the vice catalogue at 5:10, 11 which describes the kind of person with whom Christians ought not to associate or eat (*μὴ συναναμίγνυσθαι...μηδὲ συνεσθίειν*, 5:11), i.e. have Christian fellowship, because that person is merely an *ἀδελφὸς ὀνομαζό μενος*. Paul recognizes that there are people in the church who falsely profess Christian faith, and that these people, like *οἱ ἄδικοι* (6:9, 10), *ὁ κόσμος, οἱ ἔξω*, (5:10–13), are (and have been so far) excluded from salvation. Their persistently sinful behavior and the punishment it provokes betrays them to be such.[120] The question is whether Paul portrays the Corinthians or the wilderness generation in this way.

The Israelites who wandered through the wilderness experienced prefigurations[121] of the sacraments of baptism and the Lord's Supper, explains Paul, when God manifested God's presence and power among God's people in the cloud and the parting of the Red Sea.[122] "All our fathers were under the cloud and all passed through the sea. And all were baptized into Moses in the cloud and in the sea. And all ate the same spiritual food and all drank the same spiritual drink" (10:1–4a). Through a five-fold repetition of *πάντες* Paul emphasizes that participation in these "sacraments" was the common experience of the members of God's people. They all at least appeared to be recipients of salvation. Yet their destiny was not the same: "But with *most of them* God was not pleased, for they were scattered over the desert" (10:5). For not all proved to be God's obedient children: "*Some of them*" (*τινες αὐτῶν*) became idolaters, "*some of them* fornicated," "*some of them* tested," "*some of them* grumbled" (10:7–10). These "were scattered over the desert," "fell," "were destroyed," (10:5, 8, 9, 10). In what respect are the Israelites who partook the "sacraments" yet "fell" a type of the Corinthians? What is the point of the strong contrast[123] between the "all" who partook the "sacraments" and the "some" who were punished? Why is participation in the sacraments no good indication of one's destiny?

G. Fee answers that the Israelites' behavior invited God's judgment and

---

[120] It is true that Paul can make comparisons between the behavior of the unrighteous vice-doers and that of his readers (see 1 Cor 6:7–10). But his purpose does not seem to be to warn Christians against losing salvation by their sinful conduct. He rather reminds them that this way of life belongs to their pre-Christian past, so that they ought to behave differently as Christians (6:11). Or he draws the conclusion that a vice-doer in the church is merely a "so-called brother" (5:11). See the discussions devoted to these texts in the present study.

[121] Conzelmann, *1 Cor*, 166.

[122] On the similarities between Paul's and Wisdom's spiritualized descriptions of events in the wilderness, see Feuillet, *Christ*, 87–111.

[123] So Conzelmann, *1 Cor*, 167.

resulted in the "forfeiture of election—despite their privileges."[124] The same will happen to the Corinthians who do not heed Paul's warning. The sacraments will not protect them any more than they protected the disobedient Israelites.[125] Fee sees the motif of election in the expression οὐκ εὐ- δοκεῖν ὁ Θεός. The verb can have the meaning "decide in favor of, elect" (so, christologically, at Mark 1:11 par.; Matt 12:18; 17:5; 2 Pet 1:17).[126] But, against Fee, its converse, εὐδοκεῖν with a negation, could not for Paul mean reversal of election resulting in its forfeiture. Divine election stands (cf. Rom 11:1, 2; 8:29, 30, 33)!'Αλλ' οὐκ ἐν τοῖς πλείοσιν αὐτῶν εὐ- δόκησεν ὁ Θεός at 1 Cor 10:5 must refer to the rejection of those not chosen (to enter the promised land), if the verb has more than a merely affective sense here.[127] At Heb 10:38 (citing Hab 2:4 LXX) the one who shrinks back (before the imminent end) God rejects (οὐκ εὐδοκεῖν ἐν), but ὁ δὲ δίκαιός μου ἐκ πίστεως ζήσεται. O. Michel comments: " 'Mein Gerechter' ist der von Gott erwählte, Gott zugehörige, bewährte Gerechte."[128] The unbeliever, the unrighteous, the nonelect is rejected.

Paul's meaning seems to be that, whereas God's great works in Israel's history manifesting God's redemptive purpose for God's people benefited them all,[129] when it came time to fulfill God's promise of a "land flowing with milk and honey," those chosen to receive the promise were separated from the rest when the latter fell away from faith in and worship of the one true God and received their due punishment.[130] In that the Israelites could

---

[124] Fee, *1 Cor*, 450.

[125] According to Fee (*1 Cor*, 443), Paul's argument presupposes that the Corinthians had "a somewhat magical view of the sacraments... [and argued for their] security through the sacraments, which so identified them as Christians that attendance at the idol temples was immaterial." On the Corinthian error, cf. Conzelmann, *1 Cor*, 169, n. 46; Wolff, *1 Kor*, 57; Lietzmann, *Kor*, 46; Davidson, *Typology*, 291. Insofar as an over-realized eschatology characterized Corinthian theology (so Thiselton, "Realized Eschatology," 510–526; also Moule, "Judgment," 467, 468, followed by Roetzel, *Judgment*, 142), it may have contributed to the problem Paul addresses here.

[126] See Legasse, εὐδοκέω, *EWNT* 2, 188; Schrenk, εὐδοκέω, *TWNT* 2, 737.

[127] For the definition of οὐκ εὐδοκεῖν as "reject," see Schrenk, εὐδοκέω, *TWNT* 2, 737; Wolff, *1 Kor*, 43. For οὐκ εὐδοκεῖν in the sense of failure to choose, cf. Ps 151:5 LXX. For the affective sense, cf. Jer 14:10, 12 LXX; Sir 34:19. At Sir 45:19 οὐκ εὐδοκεῖν expresses God's dissatisfaction with the Israelites in the wilderness, which results in their death.

[128] Michel, *Heb*, 363.

[129] Grosheide, *1 Cor*, 220: "All Israelites enjoyed that favor of God [the pillar of cloud]. Even so when they passed through the Red Sea there was no distinction between believers and unbelievers: the entire nation safely reached the other shore."

[130] Cf. Grosheide (*1 Cor*, 222): "*God was not well pleased* refers to the fact that God, though granting His blessings to the entire nation at the beginning of the wilderness journey, in the end gave that kind of blessings to only a few."

all point to external signs of being God's people-on-the-way-to-the-promised-land, yet some of them proved themselves not to be genuine recipients of the promise, they function as τύποι of the Corinthians. The Corinthians as a church represent God's people who participate in the gifts of salvation which God has given to the church. They also are awaiting the fulfilment of God's promise to consummate God's redemptive purpose now that the ends of the ages have come. The Corinthians must not, however, take for granted that because they are "church members" they will enjoy in this consummation.

Does Paul's description of the Corinthians fit this characterization of the typological significance of the wilderness generation as illustrating the nature of the outward manifestation of the people of God as a mixed community? Once we read Paul's warning to the Corinthians at 10:12 with this hypothesis in mind, the answer jumps out at us right from the text. Paul formulates, ὥστε ὁ δοκῶν ἑστάναι βλεπέτω μὴ πέσῃ. He describes the person warned as "he who thinks he stands" or "he who seems to stand." Paul does not assume or declare the one addressed here to have salvation already. Instead his formulation almost seems to challenge any such claim. At the very least, he is withholding his opinion about the matter, for he does not address his warning to ὁ ἑστηκώς. Therefore, insofar as πίπτειν in Paul's warning suggests more than a physical punishment, we should take it to refer not to losing salvation but to losing the appearance of salvation. To paraphrase Paul's meaning according to this interpretation: 'let the one who appears to be saved (by virtue of being a partaker of the Lord's Supper) beware that she does not behave like a non-Christian (in committing idolatry) and fall under judgment, thereby disproving her Christian profession!' The temptation of idolatry will divide the true from the false.[131]

Paul has shown that the Corinthians are by no means already past the danger point. Rather, the eschatological test is ahead of them. The temptation of idolatry must be taken with all seriousness. The Israelites faced this

---

[131] The notion of false profession is at home in this context which is characterized by eschatological motifs and language . The Corinthians find themselves in a situation of eschatological testing. "The ends of the ages have come upon [them]" (10:11). They face πειρασμοί (10:13). For the eschatological separation of the true from the false, cf. the Gospel of Matthew. When Christ comes as judge, he will put the sheep on his right, and the goats, whom he "never knew," on his left (Matt 25:31–46). In anticipation of that final separation, however, the trials and persecution which precede the end already begin to distinguish genuine believers from falsely-professing ones. Nondisciples ("dogs," "swine") who have crept into the church will, under pressure, turn against true disciples and "tear you to pieces" (Matt 7:6; see Gundry, *Matt*, 122, 123). False Christs and false prophets will arise in those days (Matt 24:24, par.; 24:11).

same temptation while they were still in the wilderness and fell without reaching the promised land. It could happen also to the Corinthians. They are no better situated than were the Israelites. Will they stand the test?

After the warning to alert those who take their Christian profession so lightly that they may be in danger of disproving it and/or suffering physical punishment comes a promise to encourage those who, as a result of the warning, are overwhelmed by the prospect of eschatological testing and failure.[132] Though "most" of the Israelites fell, failure is not inevitable. "God is faithful, and he will not allow you to be tested beyond what you are able to withstand, but when the test comes will provide the way of escape so that you may be able to endure it." (10:13). Christians will succeed in withstanding the test because of God's faithfulness. They will not be exempt from testing, but they will be enabled to endure it; God will provide a way out. In God lies their hope face to face with eschatological testing.[133]

G. Fee limits the promise of God's faithfulness to "ordinary trials"— "God will help them through such"—from which he excludes the temptation to attend idol feasts, saying that "there is no divine aid when one is 'testing' Christ in the way they currently are doing (v. 9)."[134] In his view 10:13 gives no encouragement to the Corinthians in their present dilemma. But this view makes 10:13 sit even more oddly in its context: it makes Paul follow his warning with a promise which does not even pertain to the problem at hand. Further, against Fee, Paul does not take care to distinguish the test of idolatry, which presents the danger of falling (10:12), from the

---

[132] δέ at 10:13b introduces a contrast. The encouragement does not come until v. 13b (with Hahn, "Teilhabe," 163; against Grosheide, *1 Cor*, 227; Davidson, *Typology*, 178, 179; Robertson and Plummer, *1 Cor*, 208).

[133] Apart from divine intervention, the πειρασμός would be impossible to endure, cf. above, p. 71 with n. 161. The test is eschatological, yet we need not limit it to "the *one* eschatological act of salvation" (so Conzelmann, *1 Cor*, 169), for Paul's acclamation of God's faithfulness is meant to encourage the Corinthians (upon whom the "end of the ages have come") in their *present* test.

[134] Fee, *1 Cor*, 460. Fee argues that attendance at idol feasts, which the Corinthians "were haughtily doing as their 'right'," does not fit the description of the ανθρώπινος πειρασμός which threatens to "overtake" or "befall" (εἴληφεν) them apart from their willing or doing (*1 Cor*, 460). But this reasoning seems simplistic: temptation can be enticing as well as threatening; it can appear harmless as well as dangerous. Paul here tries to bring the Corinthians to recognize that attending idol feasts is not an innocent exercise of their Christian freedom but a risky challenge of the Lord himself: "Or do we provoke the Lord? We are not stronger than he, are we?" (10:22). The test of idolatry has befallen them unawares. Fee, however, seems in the end to find Paul's encouragement to be relevant to the test of idolatry after all: "By persisting in attendance at the cultic meals with pagan friends they have put themselves in grave danger of 'falling'; but the 'temptation'...to do so as part of the 'trial' of their new life in Christ is not of such a nature that they must succumb to it" (461).

πειρασμός which God will enable believers to withstand (10:13). It seems rather that Paul means to give a double-edged message on a single problem to one and the same audience:[135] although the Corinthians face the very temptation the Israelites did,[136] idolatry, they ought not to fall (warning!) and they will not inevitably fall (promise!). Fee's argument that there is no divine aid for the present test in which they are 'testing' Christ does not stick, for to 'test' Christ is to have already failed the test; divine aid can obviously only be for helping one not to fail the test, in this case, helping the Corinthians not to become idolaters by frequenting the idol feasts. That step is one they should not make—thus the warning—not one they have already made. Paul can give an encouraging promise for the same situation to the same audience because he wants to attribute a positive response to the warning, which demonstrates authenticity of faith, to God's faithfulness in providing a way out.

The promise of divine enablement in testing here bears some resemblance to the notion in the synoptic tradition that God will intervene in the great tribulation, which is so severe that "unless those days had been cut short, no life would have been saved" (Matt 24:21, 22). There God acts "for the sake of the elect." Given the use of a "faithfulness saying" in 1 Cor 10:13, with which Paul characteristically combines election terminology (cf. 1 Thess 5:24; 1 Cor 1:9),[137] the idea of God's faithfulness to his elect will not be far from Paul's mind here. The promise therefore has its proper place in this context beside the warning. It serves to strengthen genuine believers confronted with the temptation of idolatry. God will enable them to resist it. They should therefore "flee idolatry" and so prove to be the elect.

In conclusion, Conzelmann's verdict stands: Paul does not deny the possibility of assurance of salvation here.[138] Rather, he prompts his readers to apply themselves to the salvation proffered, to adhere to Christ not only by

---

[135] On the question whether the warning and the promise are addressed to the same or two different groups, see pp. 73, 74 above.

[136] Paul explicitly parallels the Corinthians' temptation with that of the wilderness generation (10:6–10), as if he wants his readers to know that, though they may think themselves spiritually wise (φρόνιμοι, 10:15), they can be tempted and even fall like others. "These things happened typologically and were written down for our instruction" (10:11). 10:13a probably also intends to affirm the similarity between the Corinthians' and the Israelites' situation: "No test has come upon you except that which is ἀνθρώπινος ("a test common to humanity," 10:13a). For this meaning of ἀνθρώπινος, see Barrett, *1 Cor*, 228, 229). Alternatively, ἀνθρώπινος means "humanly bearable" (so, Jeremias, ἄνθρωπος, *TWNT* 1, 367; Wolff, *1 Kor*, 48; Conzelmann, *1 Cor*, 169; Lietzmann, *Kor*, 47; Weiß, *1 Kor*, 255) and 10:13a together with 10:13b gives assurance that falling in the test of idolatry is not inevitable.

[137] On the faithfulness sayings in Paul , see pp. 69-79 above.

[138] Conzelmann, *1 Cor*, 168, n. 43.

having κοινωνία with him through the sacraments but also by refusing κοινωνία with demons through pagan cultic meals (10:16–21). By honoring the exclusive bond of fellowship with Christ and withstanding the test of idolatry through the faithful enabling of God the Corinthians' assurance of salvation—and the authenticity of their Christian profession—will be confirmed.

V. EXCLUSION OF EVILDOERS
FROM THE KINGDOM

In 1 Cor 6:9, 10 and Gal 5:19–21 Paul lists the practices which characterize people (or the people as characterized by their practices) who will
not inherit the kingdom of God. Catalogues of vices and virtues such as we
find in these texts were widely used in the ancient world.[1] Paul is taking up
a rhetorical device probably well known to his readers.[2] What use does he
find for the vice list and traditional language about inheriting the kingdom
of God where these appear together in his epistles?[3] Do they serve as a
warning to Christian readers lest they too might be excluded from the
coming kingdom[4] because of ethical failure? E. P. Sanders softens the
impact of this common interpretation by commenting that the vice lists are
traditional and that Paul simply repeats the standard line here without
necessarily implying that Christians who commit such sins will be
condemned.[5] Or does the traditional material have a different function in
Paul's argument? In the following discussion of 1 Cor 6:9–11 and Gal
5:19–21 I will attempt to answer these questions by analyzing each passage
in context, comparing Pauline and other NT uses of the same material, and
reflecting on its *Sitz im Leben* in early Christianity.

---

[1] See Wibbing, *Lasterkataloge*, 14–76; Vögtle, *Lasterkataloge*, 56–120; Kamlah,
Form, 39–175.

[2] See also the Pauline vice catalogues in Rom 1:29–31; 13:13; 1 Cor 5:10, 11; 2 Cor
12:20, 21. Cf. also Eph 4:31; 5:3–5; Col 3:5, 8; 1 Tim 1:9, 10; 2 Tim 3:2–5; Tit 3:3;
Matt 15:19; Mark 7:21, 22; 1 Pet 2:1; 4:3, 15; Rev 9:21; 21:8; 22:15.

[3] On the plurality of functions of ethical lists in antiquity, see Betz, *Gal*, 282. For
Pauline use of the traditional language about inheriting the kingdom of God, cf. also
1 Cor 15:50; Eph 5:5. On the Deuteronomic prehistory of the expression "inherit the
kingdom," see Windisch, "Sprüche," 167. On the relation of Paul's use of the expression to synoptic tradition (Matt 5:20; 25:34), see Vögtle, *Lasterkataloge*, 43. On the expression in rabbinic literature, see Gager, "Diversity," 333. The language is also at
home in apocalyptic thought (cf. Rev 21:7; 4 Ezra 7:17).

[4] βασιλεία τοῦ θεοῦ is future at 1 Cor 6:9, 10; Gal 5:21 (so also, e.g., 1 Cor 15:50;
2 Tim 4:18; Matt 6:10; Luke 11:2). See Barrett, *1 Cor*, 140; Merk, *Handeln*, 73, 74.

[5] Sanders, *Law*, 109.

1 Corinthians 6:9–11. The vice list and tradition about not entering the kingdom of God in 1 Cor 6:9, 10 occur in a discussion of the community's responsibility to judge matters of morality that come up in its midst. The Corinthians had failed in this respect and instead were submitting to the judgment of non-Christian judges in the secular courts.[6] Paul reprimands them not only for this: they should not be behaving immorally in the first place! Wrongdoing and wrongdoers in the fellowship are not to be tolerated. The church must take its responsibility with respect to immorality within its ranks seriously.

In 6:2–6 Paul supports his first criticism expressed in 6:1. Christians should not be judged before unbelievers but before the saints because of the impending eschatological reversal of relationships.[7] "Do you not know that the saints will judge the world?... Do you not know that we will judge angels? How much more matters pertaining to this life" (6:2, 3). His point has even more force in view of the evidence for such a reversal of relationships already, namely, in the church: judges of earthly things have no authority in the church, whereas the Christian σοφός does (6:4, 5).

The argument of 6:9–11 supports Paul's second criticism expressed in 6:7, 8:[8] "It is already defeat for you to have lawsuits at all with one another. Why do you not rather suffer wrong? Why not rather be defrauded. But you wrong and defraud, and brothers at that." Vv. 9–11 show why Christians should not exhibit unrighteous behavior at all (in which case no judgment would be necessary).[9] Here Paul appeals to familiar Christian tradition:[10] "Or don't you know that the unrighteous will not inherit the kingdom of God? Don't be deceived! Neither fornicators nor idolaters nor adulterers nor the effeminate nor homosexuals nor thieves nor covetous people nor drunkards nor slanderers nor robbers will inherit the kingdom of God. And some of you were such as these. But you were washed, but you were sanctified, but you were justified in the name of the Lord Jesus Christ and in the Spirit of our God."[11]

---

[6] Paul does not tell us exactly what the Corinthians were feuding over. He says simply that were wronging (ἀδικεῖτε) and defrauding each other (ἀποστερεῖτε). On the precise behavior involved, see Richardson's suggestions in "Judgment."

[7] On this idea elsewhere, see Meurer, *Recht*, 143, 144.

[8] On the question whether the vice catalogues in 1 Corinthians 5, 6 are intrinsically connected to the epistolary situation of the letter or are merely traditional, see Zaas, "Catalogues," who makes a case for the former view.

[9] Kamlah (*Form*, 11) describes 6:9–11 as "die Grundlegung der Weisung, die in den vorangehenden Versen ausgesprochen war."

[10] On the traditional character of vv. 9–11, see pp. 139–141 below.

[11] Richardson ("Judgment," 42) and Dinkler ("Problem," 173) see an intentional connection between vv. 9, 10 and the preceding verses. This suggestion is substantiated

There is no doubt that Paul intends vv. 9–11 to exercise a reforming influence on his readers' conduct. He draws implicit parallels between their wrong behavior and the behavior of those who, according to the vice list, are excluded from the future kingdom.[12] Some church members are acting unrighteously (ἀδικεῖτε, v. 8) as do "the unrighteous" (ἄδικοι, v. 9), whose behavior is characterized in the vice list.[13] The Corinthians defraud others (ἀποστερεῖτε, v. 8) as the thieves, robbers, and greedy persons in the catalogue prey on others for personal gain (v. 10). The question is, however, what motivation for improved conduct do these verses supply? Paul's meaning in this regard is not perfectly clear. As E. Kamlah observes, the vice list here has a mediate rather than an immediate function in the parenesis: it *describes* (in the third person) who is excluded from the kingdom. Usually interpreters take the vice list and saying about exclusion from the kingdom of God in 6:9, 10 to motivate the readers by evoking fear of losing salvation. Can those who do the works of the unrighteous expect not to share their destiny? Paul seems to be warning heirs of the kingdom of God that they effectively change their status as heirs and thus forfeit their inheritance of the kingdom by living like those excluded from the kingdom.[14] In Kamlah's words: "Der Paränese dient er [der Lasterkatalog], indem er droht: Wer sich diesen Ungerechten anschließt, ist mit ihnen vom Reiche Gottes geschieden."[15] Further, for E. Dinkler exclusion of the unrighteous

---

by the use of parallel terminology (ἀδικεῖν, vv. 7, 8, and ἄδικος, v. 9) and similar motifs (fraud, v. 8, greed and theft, v. 10). Richardson ("Judgment," 44–46) sees sexual overtones in these terms and argues that 6:1–11 fits well in 5:1–7:40, where Paul handles sexual matters. Similarly, Lietzmann (*Kor*, 26) finds 6:9–11 appropriate as a transition to 6:12–20, where Paul discusses the problem of πορνεία mentioned in the vice list (v. 9). Repetition of the rhetorical device ἢ οὐκ οἴδατε (6:2, 3, 9) also links 6:9, 10 to what precedes (Richardson, "Judgment," 42). Cf. Kamlah, *Form*, 11: "durchgehender diatribischer Stil."

[12] Cf. Vögtle, *Lasterkataloge*, 31; Bailey, "Foundation," 28. Because vice lists varied significantly in their content, an author's choice of certain terms over others, despite their being conventional, could reveal that author's special interests. Nevertheless, Paul preserves here numerous basic features of the conventional vice list which have no direct relation to the problem of legal disputes in Corinth (so Easton, "Lists," 5; Kamlah, *Form*, 115). On vice list terminology, see Wibbing, *Lasterkataloge*, 87, 88. Zaas ("Catalogues") pleads for taking the Pauline vice catalogue as "*both* traditional *and* related to its epistolary context" (623), and builds a case for this view on 1 Corinthians 5 and 6.

[13] Vögtle (*Lasterkataloge*, 39) thinks ἀδικεῖτε at v. 8 may have influenced the choice of the term ἄδικοι at v. 9.

[14] Richardson, "Judgment," 42 with n. 18; Dinkler, "Problem," 173; also Grosheide, *1 Cor*, 140; Fascher, *1 Kor*, 171; Vischer, *Auslegungsgeschichte*, 19.

[15] Kamlah, *Form*, 11. See also Haufe, "Reich Gottes," 468; Merk, *Handeln*, 93; Gager, "Diversity," 334; Dinkler, "Problem," 173; Marshall, *Kept*, 112; Grosheide, *1 Cor*, 140; Easton, "Ethical Lists," 5.

Corinthians from salvation is not a mere threat but already a fact: "Dies ist keine Hypothese, sondern war bereits eingetreten in Korinth, wenigstens bei manchen ($\tau\iota\nu\acute{\epsilon}\varsigma$)."[16] The prospect of eternal loss for overstepping the boundaries of appropriate Christian conduct[17] is thus supposed to serve as a motivation for the Corinthian Christians to reform.

For I. H. Marshall this explanation of the way the vice list and the prediction of wrongdoers' exclusion from the kingdom of God could motivate behavioral change is the obvious one: "It is plain that he [Paul] is here issuing a stern warning to the members of the church about the possible outcome of their action."[18] One can argue, however, that in several respects this meaning is not so plain. First, on this view Paul says in the same breath both that the Corinthian Christians will judge the world and angels (see 6:2, 3) and that these believers are in danger of not inheriting the kingdom.[19] Paul has exposed the sin of bringing legal suits between Christians before pagan judges as contrary to Christians' eschatological position of *superiority* to unbelievers; he presupposes the Corinthians' eschatological triumph in 6:2, 3. Can he then reverse himself in 6:9 and suggest that they might not triumph after all at the last day? Even E. Dinkler thinks that 6:2 and 6:9 express the *same* thought in positive and negative forms: the saints will judge the world at the last day; by contrast, $o\iota$ $\mathring{\alpha}\delta\iota\kappa o\iota$ will not inherit the kingdom of God.[20]

Second, the text does not compel us to the view that Paul threatens his readers here with loss of their eschatological inheritance. Even the words $\mu\mathring{\eta}$ $\pi\lambda\alpha\nu\mathring{\alpha}\sigma\theta\epsilon$ do not lead unambiguously to this interpretation. In the NT the reason for this exhortation is always found in the immediately following thought.[21] Vv. 9b, 10, however, do not say that the *Corinthians* are in danger of losing their inheritance[22] but that "the unrighteous"[23] will not inherit the kingdom.

---

[16] Dinkler, "Problem," 173. Against this view, see Barrett, *1 Cor*, 140.

[17] For this characterization of the problem, see Kamlah, *Form*, 11. The important question of defining ethical boundaries for qualification for inheritance in the kingdom as presupposed in this view—precisely what actions disqualify?—is not discussed in the literature and points to a difficulty in this view. For an example of this ambiguity, see Marshall, *Kept*, 112: "They may go *so far* (italics mine) in wrongdoing that they are liable to exclusion from the kingdom."

[18] Marshall, *Kept*, 112.

[19] The apocalyptic tradition in Dan 7:22 LXX that the saints "will be given the judgment" links this event with the occasion of their inheritance of the eschatological kingdom.

[20] Dinkler, "Problem," 187.

[21] Braun, $\pi\lambda\alpha\nu\acute{\alpha}\omega$, *TWNT* 6, 245. See Gal 6:7; 1 Cor 15:33; Jas 1:16; cf. 1 John 3:7.

[22] Against Dinkler, "Problem," 173; Merk, *Handeln*, 94.

[23] In Paul, $\mathring{\alpha}\delta\iota\kappa o\varsigma$ as a noun occurs only at 1 Cor 6:1, 9.

Could it be, however, that Paul presupposes the Corinthians might become ἄδικοι and therefore issues them an indirect warning (in the third person)? This assumption is problematic. The designation ἄδικοι belongs to conventional terminology used in vice lists (cf., e.g., Luke 18:11), where it denotes unbelievers. In keeping with this conventional usage, in the present context οἱ ἄδικοι is synonymous with οἱ ἄπιστοι. The parallel phrases ἐπὶ τῶν ἀδίκων (6:1) and ἐπὶ ἀπίστων (6:6) show this synonymity. The view that Paul warns the Corinthian Christians indirectly not to become ἄδικοι, however, requires the term to change meanings in the context: whereas it refers strictly to unbelievers at 6:1, at 6:6 it would have to mean "wrongdoers including believers."[24] Since such a change in meaning is doubtful,[25] the Corinthians could be included in οἱ ἄδικοι only if they are not Christians at all but actually ἄπιστοι. Does the Corinthians' behavior make their Christian profession questionable to Paul? This may be true of a minority, as we will see below. Here, nevertheless, although Paul castigates the Corinthians for behaving unrighteously (ἀδικεῖν, 6:7, 8), he speaks of them as οἱ ἅγιοι (6:1, 2) instead of ἄδικοι. The antithetical parallelism between ἐπὶ τῶν ἀδίκων and ἐπὶ τῶν ἁγίων at 6:1 confirms that Paul intends primarily to contrast his Christian readers with non-Christians. These unbelievers are simply called ἄδικοι in order to highlight their unrighteous behavior as detailed in the vice list.[26] Insofar as Paul intends this designation to include his readers, he must be thinking only of a minority who are not genuine Christians.

"Don't be deceived!" therefore implies not that Christians who behave unrighteously might fail to inherit the kingdom, but that unbelievers as "the unrighteous" (perhaps even though they may find themselves within the fellowship of the church) will not inherit the kingdom. Paul wants to make the point that since the unrighteous have no share in the future kingdom, conduct typical of them should not characterize those *who will inherit the kingdom*. As he did in 6:2, 3, so also in 6:9, 10 Paul argues from *eschatological* destiny to *present* conduct.[27] The realization that the destinies of believers and unbelievers are opposite provides the motivation for reformed conduct. Thus Paul stresses cognizance of the difference of unbelievers'

---

[24] For this problematic view, see Barrett, *1 Cor*, 140; Richardson, "Judgment," 42.

[25] Even Dinkler ("Problem," 173) concludes: "Mit diesen ἄδικοι müssen wie in V. 1 die Ungläubigen gemeint sein."

[26] Against Barrett (*1 Cor*, 140), who gives the term οἱ ἄδικοι a "strictly moral sense."

[27] On the way Paul applies this eschatological argument, see Merk, *Handeln*, 92, in criticism of Dinkler, "Problem," 187.

destiny: ἢ οὐκ οἴδατε... (v. 9a).[28] The vice list and tradition on exclusion from the kingdom serve to reinforce against the prospect of decay behavioral distinctions between Christians and the non-Christian world by educating Christian readers.[29] Paul's words threaten only those who are not genuine believers.[30]

And it is possible that he does intend to threaten some Corinthians whose conduct makes him suspect false profession of faith. He has just spoken of the "so-called brother (ἀδελφὸς ὀνομαζόμενος) who is a fornicator, etc.," i.e., a Christian in name only, whom the church should not tolerate within its fellowship (μὴ συναναμίγνυσθαι), rather must "cast out" (ἐξάρατε, 5:11–13). The Corinthians actually have such a person in their midst (cf. 5:1, ἐν ὑμῖν πορνεία), and in 5:1–5 Paul has instructed the church to deal with the guilty member accordingly. This man is apparently an unbeliever, for he is "deliver[ed] to Satan for the destruction of the flesh," an unlikely predication of Christians, who are under Christ's rule.[31] The "unrighteous" inside the church are as much unbelievers as the

---

[28] Contrast Braun, πλανάω, *TWNT* 6, 246. See Eph 5:5, 6 for a similar interest in knowing (τοῦτο γὰρ ἴστε γινώσκοντες) and not being deceived (μηδεὶς ὑμᾶς ἀπατάτω) about the exclusion of wrongdoers (in a vice list!) from the kingdom (οὐκ ἔχει κληρονομίαν ἐν τῇ βασιλείᾳ τοῦ Χριστοῦ καὶ Θεοῦ).

[29] 1 Cor 6:9, 10 could also support Paul's point in 6:1 that the church, not the secular courts, should judge the wrong conduct of its members. It makes little sense for the Corinthians to be judged now by people who will not inherit the kingdom of God but will even be judged at the last day (cf. 6:2) and who themselves practice vices and are thus quite unfit to decide moral matters between Christians. Some of the Corinthians may have once been like these unrighteous, but they are so no longer. They have a better destiny and a better moral quality of life (although Paul qualifies this point at 6:7, 8). Therefore, those who have no part in this new way of life and destiny should not be put in a position of authority over Christians in deciding their conflicts—if Christians must press charges against each other at all!

[30] Paul's assertion of the eschatological demise of the unrighteous, which serves to reinforce the difference in the saints' destiny, can be compared with the use of *Unheilsdrohungen* disguised as *Heilszusprüche* in OT judgment language (e.g., Hos 5:12ff.; 13:7, 8; Isa 7:5–9; Westermann, *Grundformen*, 147 with n. 25) and apocalyptic literature (e.g., 1 Enoch 94:1ff.; 2 *Apoc. Bar.* 54:17, 18). C. Münchow (*Ethik*, 127) comments on this phenomenon in apocalyptic contexts: "So werden auch die Weherufe nicht mehr in ihrer eigentlichen Funktion, sondern mit einer neuen Intention als Heilszusage und Aufmunterung der Gerechten verwendet. Die Formulierung ethischer Sachverhalte *per negationem* ist folglich als eine besondere Form der Heilszusage an die Gerechten anzusehen, die nicht zu den Sündern gehören.... Die aus der Prophetie übernommene Anklage hat also nun den Sinn, die Gerechten zu stärken und zu trösten." The apocalyptic color of 1 Corinthians 6—seen in the saints' judgment of the world and angels, the dualistic view of the righteous and the unrighteous (see Münchow, *Ethik*, 126), and the language of "the kingdom of God"—makes a comparison with this phenomenon in apocalyptic attractive.

[31] See discussion of this text on pp. 113–120 above.

"unrighteous" outside. Both are subject to judgment, and the present judgment of the church on οἱ ἔσω lays bare their true colors (5:12, 13a).[32] Perhaps Paul has the same "insiders" partly in mind in the next chapter when he speaks of the destiny of the unrighteous (6:9, 10). 2 Cor 12:21 also shows that Paul can single out a minority in the Corinthian community who are not true Christians, for they "have sinned previously and have not repented from the impurity and fornication and licentiousness which they have done."[33] Apparently the Corinthian church attached too little importance to the implications of conduct for the genuineness of professed faith and had thus welcomed into its fellowship those who did not truly belong. Paul exhorts them in 2 Cor 6:14–7:1, "don't be yoked together with unbelievers" and urges them to practice righteousness instead.[34]

1 Cor 6:9–11 is one of a series of attempts by Paul to reinforce behavioral distinctions between believers and unbelievers which had apparently eroded in the Corinthians' minds. W. Meeks observes that the discussion of lawsuits in 6:1–8 "illustrates [the Corinthians'] confusion about the lines dividing 'inside' from 'outside.' "[35] The clear-cut distinctions in Paul's terminology in 6:1–11—οἱ ἅγιοι and ἀδελφοί contrast with οἱ ἄδικοι, οἱ ἄπιστοι, and ὁ κόσμος— ensure that the forgotten contrasts will not escape the readers here.[36]

I have already noted that Paul reinforces the distinctions between the saints and the world by pointing to their different future eschatological roles in 6:2, 3. He also contrasts the two groups according to present distinctions: even now in the context of the church pagan judges are lightly esteemed (οἱ ἐξουθενημένοι, 6:4), whereas the Christian σοφός enjoys high regard and is thus in a position to arbitrate between Christians (6:5).

Finally, Paul illustrates the difference between the saints and the world from the perspective of the past: at conversion, the Corinthians parted ways with the non-Christian world. The difference between οἱ ἅγιοι and οἱ ἄδικοι is precisely the difference between the pre-conversion ("once") and

---

[32] But, whereas οἱ ἔξω God will judge (finally), there is some hope that those who experience judgment now by the church will repent, be converted and saved at the last. See pp. 119, 120 above.

[33] Especially the terminology used here suggests that Paul suspects that they falsely profess faith; see text below, pp. 221–224.

[34] Uncertainty regarding the original context of this passage does not prevent it from shedding light on the situation in Corinth.

[35] Meeks, *Urban Christians*, 129.

[36] Cf. Kamlah (*Form*, 11–13) on the "Gegenüberstellung von Heiligen und Ungerechten." Kamlah (12) traces the separation of people into two categories (ἄδικοι, ἅγιοι) to apocalyptic dualism.

post-conversion ("now") identity of the Corinthians themselves,[37] a difference established in the act of baptism:[38] καὶ ταῦτά τινες ἦτε · ἀλλὰ
ἀπελούσασθε, ἀλλὰ ἡγιάσθητε, ἀλλὰ ἐδικαιώθητε ἐν τῷ ὀνόματι
τοῦ κυρίου Ἰησοῦ Χριστοῦ καὶ ἐν τῷ πνεύματι τοῦ θεοῦ ἡμῶν
(v. 11). The allusion to baptism[39] makes Paul's argument from the past also
a sacramental argument[40] and thus gives it added force. By recalling the
vivid experiences of conversion and baptism, Paul reinforces known distinctions between the Corinthians and οἱ ἄδικοι. Because the Corinthians
are no longer οἱ ἄδικοι ("you were such as these...") but have broken with
the past through conversion and baptism and have a new identity, they
ought not to continue in their old ways.[41] The "once-now" pattern thus does
not call into question the Corinthians' salvation but is "ausschließlich an
der Versicherung des Heiles interressiert..., wenn es Sünde und heidnischen
Wandel der Vergangenheit zuweist."[42]

In summary, the motivation for truly Christian conduct derives from the
realization that one is divorced from the former existence and has em-
barked upon a new one with a new future to which different behavior is
appropriate. I have pointed out that throughout 6:1–11 Paul argues for
reformed behavior by encouraging a distinctly Christian self-understanding
in his readers. He summons them to behavior consistent with their true
identity both now and at the last day. The view that Paul does *not* threaten
his readers with exclusion from the kingdom of God in vv. 9, 10 (except of
course those readers who are unbelievers, if any) therefore fits well in the
context.

---

[37] On the "once-now" pattern, see Tachau, '*Einst*,' 83, 84. Significant for our understanding of Paul's argument in 1 Corinthians 6 is Tachau's comment: "Der entschei-
dende Aspekt beim Schema ist der Kontrast" (109).

[38] See Kamlah, *Form*, 12; Tachau, '*Einst*,' 83. For the view that baptismal parenesis
was the *Sitz im Leben* of the NT catalogues, see Kamlah, 38.

[39] The allusion to baptism is made clear in the choice of terminology, see Tachau,
'*Einst*,' 83; Kamlah, *Form*, 12 with n. 2.

[40] Cf. Dinkler, "Problem," 173; Conzelmann, *1 Cor*, 137.

[41] Vögtle (*Lasterkataloge*, 11) identifies this "antithetische Spannung, welche die
christliche Gegenwart und die vorchristliche Vergangenheit als absolute Gegensätze
kennzeichnet und deshalb ein Motiv zum sittlichen Handeln abgibt" as typical of the
Pauline and deuteropauline parenetic vice lists. See Schweizer ("Ethical Patterns," 196)
for the view that our text functions as a reminder of the break with past sins. See also
Lietzmann, *Kor*, 26; Tachau, '*Einst*,' 83. Rather than warning against overestimation of
baptism (so Dinkler, "Problem," 190; Merk, *Handeln*, 94; cf. Héring, *1 Cor*, 45), the
text seems to ascribe great significance to baptism as the point of departure from a life
according to the flesh. It is more likely that the Corinthians suffered from a *failure* to
reflect on the behavioral implications of their new existence rather than from a misinterpretation of that existence in a libertinistic sense (contrast Tachau, '*Einst*,' 128).

[42] Tachau, '*Einst*,' 112, 113.

Furthermore, it is not surprising that Paul uses a vice list and a saying about exclusion from the kingdom to reinforce a distinctively Christian self-understanding in his Gentile readers. For the repudiation of pagan vices and their implication of exclusion from the coming kingdom (and similar motifs) played a role in the instruction of early Christian converts. These themes belonged to Paul's own standard missionary teaching.[43] Consequently, he can remind his readers that he "said before" (Gal 5:21; 1 Thess 4:6) and "wrote to you" (1 Cor 5:9, 11) and that "you know" (1 Cor 6:9; 1 Thess 4:2) what things characterize those who will not inherit the kingdom. Such teaching functioned to impress upon new converts behavioral norms which distinguished them from unbelievers. They were made to realize that they had left behind the things that characterize "the heathen who do not know God" (1 Thess 4:5). Insistence on the absence of vices (in particular, fornication, idolatry, and greed) also typified the self-understanding of Hellenistic Judaism (cf. Wis 14:12; *Ep. Jer.* 4, 5; *T. Dan.* 5:5–7).[44]

Further evidence that denunciation of vices and their final outcome served the formation of a distinct Christian self-consciousness comes from the related tradition in early Christianity of the "two ways." This tradition contrasts the practice of righteousness (the "way of life"), which ends in final blessedness, with the practice of unrighteousness (the "way of death"), which ends in final destruction. The *Didache* makes both the vices and virtues of the two ways explicit (see *Did* 2–5). The recitation of these descriptions of both ways belonged to the initatory rite of baptism: "Having first rehearsed all these things, baptize..." (*Did* 7:1).[45] M. J. Suggs thus describes the function of the "two ways" genre as "intensifying in-group/out-group consciousness" and "serv[ing] the distinction between 'we' and 'they' in terms of which the movement can establish its youthful identity."[46] The use of the "two ways" tradition in connection with baptism in the *Didache* parallels 1 Cor 6:9–11 and gives us reason to think that Paul was trying to reestablish the new self-understanding which the Corinthians had initially gained. His application of the vice list to the Corinthians' present situation long after their conversion seems to have the same purpose as in its initiatory setting.[47]

---

[43] See Schweizer, "Ethical Patterns," 195; Vögtle, *Lasterkataloge*, 19.

[44] Schweizer, "Ethical Patterns," 195.

[45] Suggs, "Two Ways" (see esp. 72).

[46] Suggs, "Two Ways," 73. Suggs allows that the tradition could be adapted to serve other needs, as it in fact was during and after the community's transition to a stable, institutional existence.

[47] Contrast Schweizer, "Ethical Patterns," 196: "The function of the traditional list

Many of the same features characterize the use of traditional vice lists elsewhere in Paul and the NT. Vices typify the heathen (Rom 1:28–31; 1 Tim 1:9, 10; 1 Pet 4:3; Rev 9:21; 21:8) or describe the former lives of pagan Christians (Eph 5:7, 8; Col 3:7; Tit 3:3; 1 Pet 4:3). They should not, however, characterize the present lives of people in the church (1 Pet 4:3; 2 Cor 12:20, 21; 1 Cor 5:10, 11). For the "putting off" of such practices (Rom 13:12; Col 3:8; cf. Eph 4:31, 22–24) is appropriate to baptism (Tit 3:3–5; cf. 1 Pet 2:1). Joining with evildoers in their works is ruled out because for Christians vices belong to the past.[48] In fact, Paul suspects church members who practice vices of never having truly converted (2 Cor 12:20, 21).[49] They are "brothers" in name only (ἀδελφὸς ὀνομαζόμενος, 1 Cor 5:11). Wrongdoing is inconsistent with the present identity of believers as "saints": "It is fitting to saints" (πρέπει ἁγίοις) that vices "not be named among you" (Eph 5:3).[50] Instead, their καινὸς ἄνθρωπος, "created according to God," determines the works they should "put on" (Eph 4:24ff.; Col 3:10ff.). This necessary consistency between identity and behavior should be evident to Christians, "for you know this" (Eph 5:5), namely, that the same consistency in identity and behavior is found in those outside the eschatological community: people who "have no inheritance in the kingdom" invariably practice what is inappropriate for the kingdom (fornication, uncleanness, covetousness, and idolatry, Eph 5:5). Their destiny also corresponds to their identity and behavior: "For on account of these things [vices] the wrath of God is coming upon the sons of disobedience" (Eph 5:6). "Those who do such things are worthy of death" (Rom 1:32); their part will be the "second death" (Rev 21:8); they will remain "outside" the "city" (22:15). By contrast, Christians await not wrath but salvation. Their future part implies that their conduct should differ from that of evildoers: "For our[51] salvation is nearer now than when we believed.... Therefore let us put off the works of darkness" (Rom 13:11, 12; cf. 1 Thess 5:8, 9). In

---

of vices has totally changed with Paul; no longer does it distinguish the perfect church from the imperfect world; on the contrary, it serves to remind the church of the fact that vices, which it thinks to have left behind for ever, easily creep back." See further, Haufe, "Reich Gottes," 467–472, on the *Sitz im Leben* of the Pauline sayings on the kingdom of God and the vice lists.

[48] Wibbing, *Lasterkataloge*, 112; also Tachau, 'Einst,' 130.

[49] See pp. 221–225 below.

[50] Similarly, Wisdom rejects wrongdoing as inconsistent with the status of God's people. In the context of a vice catalogue (14:25, 26) the author says, οὐχ ἁμαρτησόμεθα δέ, εἰδότες ὅτι σοὶ λελογίσμεθα (15:2).

[51] The decision whether to take ἡμῶν with σωτηρία or ἐγγύτερον in Rom 13:11 affects Paul's basic meaning very little: the proximity of fulfillment of Christians' eschatological hope (not its uncertain fulfillment) should motivate them to good conduct.

Rom 13:11–14 Paul supports his argument against the practice of vices (see the list in v. 13) not by threatening his readers with exclusion from the kingdom (or with subjection to the coming wrath),[52] but by noting the increasing nearness of their salvation. "The day is near," final salvation is at the doorstep (13:12); the only appropriate behavior is therefore to "walk decently as in the day" (13:13).

In summary, Paul as well as other NT writers use the vice list genre in a way compatible with the interpretation of 1 Cor 6:9–11 for which I have argued. Eph 5:3, with the phrase καθὼς πρέπει ἁγίοις in conjunction with a vice list, showed most clearly the NT tendency to view Christian behavior as rooted in a correct Christian self-perception, which the polemic against vices primarily intends to reinforce. Paul's allusion to baptism as the point of breaking away from pagan vices in 1 Cor 6:11 constitutes just such an attempt to motivate reformed behavior by heightening his readers' consciousness of their distinctive Christian identity.

The results of this investigation of 1 Cor 6:9–11 can be summarized as follows. In this text Paul intends to motivate the readers to reform their conduct chiefly by reeducating them about the fundamental distinctions between the saints and the world, which make distinctions in practice imperative. The function of the vice list and tradition about inheriting the kingdom of God here corresponds to wider Christian use of this traditional material. This view allows us to account for various features in Paul's argument: the stark contrast between the saints and the unrighteous and their eschatological roles, the relegation of vices to the period before conversion and baptism. Vv. 9, 10 , however, may function in a secondary way to motivate behavioral change by warning those in the Corinthian church whose unrighteous conduct betrays them as unbelievers that they will not inherit the kingdom of God. The larger context provides parallels for the idea that Paul suspects a minority in Corinth to be falsely professing "Christians" who must repent and whose salvation is yet future.

Galatians 5:19–21. In Gal 5:19–21 also Paul draws on the conventional vice list and traditional language on inheriting the kingdom of God. Here most interpreters discover "a plain warning that if a Christian lives according to the flesh, he may in the end be excluded from the kingdom."[53]

---

[52] Although the predictions of judgment connected with vice lists generally refer explicitly to Non-Christians, 1 Thess 4:6 is vague.

[53] Marshall, *Kept*, 112; similarly, Bruce, *Gal*, 250; Sanders, *Palestinian Judaism*, 517, 518; Oepke, *Gal*, 180; Eckert, *Verkündigung*, 142; cf. Mattern, *Gericht*, 133.

Sometimes, however, the observation is made that the vice list in 5:19–21a has no explicitly parenetic application but a more descriptive character.[54] Nevertheless, its location in the "parenetic section" of the epistle[55] undoubtedly accounts for the most common view today that Paul's purpose in 5:19–21 is "to enforce the exhortation of v. 13b, not to convert their liberty into an occasion to the flesh."[56] That is, a parenetic function is commonly attributed by implication to the vice list and to the prediction of evildoers' exclusion from the kingdom of God in Gal 5:19–21:[57] these verses should motivate the Galatians to avoid the works of the flesh in order not to lose their eschatological inheritance. In order to assess this understanding of the function ascribed to 5:19–21 by the context, we must gain a good grasp of the content and purpose of the context itself. To do so, I will pursue the following primary questions: What prompts Paul to deal with the problem of the flesh in relation to Christian freedom here? And how does he deal with this problem?

Various occasions for the composition of 5:13ff. have been suggested. The explanation that Paul customarily includes an ethical section at the end of his epistles[58] is unsatisfactory. It does not account for the extraordinary length of Paul's discussion on the "flesh" nor his continuation of the polemic regarding the law.[59] It is more probable that the situation in the Galatian churches provoked Paul to write this passage.

W. Lütgert's 1919 essay, *Gesetz und Geist*, made famous the view that some Galatian Christians were actually using their freedom as an "opportunity for the flesh"[60] and thus invited Paul's "Angriff"[61] in Gal 5:13ff. Lütgert sought to prove the existence of an actual front with libertinistic tendencies in Galatians.[62] Others took up this suggestion and elaborated on it.[63] But evidence for such a front is neither clear nor compelling.[64]

---

[54] See Kamlah, *Form*, 16; Mußner, *Gal*, 379; similarly, Vögtle, *Lasterkataloge*, 10.

[55] For a discussion on the disputed beginning of the parenesis, see Merk, "Beginn," who sees it to begin at 5:13 (104).

[56] Burton, *Gal*, 304.

[57] See Betz, *Gal*, 285.

[58] So Bonnard, *Gal*, 108; Ridderbos, *Gal*, 197.

[59] On this polemic, see pp. 145–151 below.

[60] Lütgert, *Gesetz und Geist*, 16, 17. He follows de Wette, who refers to these people as "die freiere Paulinische Christen." Similarly, Lightfoot, *Gal*, 208.

[61] Lütgert, *Gesetz und Geist*, 15.

[62] Lütgert (*Gesetz und Geist*, 9–13) appeals to 5:15, 20; 4:21; 5:4; 6:1 as indications of two Galatian fronts.

[63] E.g., Ropes, *Singular Problem*; Schmithals, "Häretiker," 25–67 (see esp. 55, 56).

[64] Lagrange, *Gal*, 144: "Rien n'indique qu'il y ait eu un parti de fidèles versant dans la license sous prétexte de liberté." See also Eckert, *Verkündigung*, 133–136; Mußner, *Gal*, 373, 374; *et al.*

Others, however, posit instead of a libertinistic front as such a problem with libertinistic behavior in the Galatian churches. The phenomenon of ethical excesses evoked Paul's discussion of the flesh, they propose.[65] But this view is not easy to defend either. The vice list in 5:19–21a is traditional[66] and should not be confused with a "chronique scandaleuse"[67] of the Galatian churches. Even the terms designating interpersonal discord (ἔρις, ζῆλος, θυμοί, ἐριθεῖαι), which are sometimes taken to reveal the particular form of the Galatians' fleshliness,[68] seem "formelhaft":[69] they appear in other lists (cf. 2 Cor 12:20, 21; Rom 1:29–31; 1 Tim 6:4) and possibly owe their mention to the fact that they have similar meanings.[70] The closing reference to τὰ ὅμοια τούτοις (5:21) gives the list a much more general tone—it could just as easily have been submitted to other churches.[71] The reference to not inheriting the kingdom of God (5:21) also shows Paul's heavy indebtedness to tradition here and thus warns against a simple identification of the vice list with the concrete situation in Galatia.[72]

Interpreters have exercised caution in reconstructing the circumstances in Galatia by means of other data in the context as well. The allusion to inner-church disputations in 5:15 is hyperbolic—"bite...devour...consume each other"—and does not give a clear picture of the Galatians' actual behavior.[73] Perhaps we should understand the protasis ("if you bite ..."), though grammatically a *realis*,[74] as exaggerated preaching style.[75] The similar prohibition of unpeaceful relations among Christians—μὴ γινώμεθα κενόδοξοι, κτλ, (5:26)—could refer to potential developments,[76] not actual circumstances. Paul's instruction on how to deal with transgressions of community members (6:1) does not necessarily presuppose a more serious problem with the flesh than do Paul's ethical admonitions in general. It is mere conjecture to conclude from this verse that "flagrant

---

[65] See, e.g., Betz, *Gal*, 8; tentatively, Jewett, "Agitators," 211; Vögtle, *Lasterkataloge*, 30; Oepke, *Gal*, 168.

[66] Only the terms διχοστασία and αἵρεσις fail to appear in the other NT vice lists (Wibbing, *Lasterkataloge*, 95).

[67] Oepke, *Gal*, 171; followed by Mußner, *Gal*, 374; contrast Schmithals, "Häretiker," 55, 56.

[68] See Bruce, *Gal*, 250.

[69] Wibbing, *Lasterkataloge*, 97.

[70] Wibbing, *Lasterkataloge*, 96.

[71] Mußner, *Gal*, 374; Eckert, *Verkündigung*, 139.

[72] Eckert, *Verkündigung*, 139.

[73] See Betz, *Gal*, 277.

[74] Paul has εἰ with the indicative; see *BDF* §372.

[75] Mußner, *Gal*, 373, 374; cf. Eckert, *Verkündigung*, 135, n. 6.

[76] So Mußner, *Gal*, 396. For the use of γίνεσθαι for persons' or things' changing their nature or entering a new condition, see BAGD, s.v. γίνομαι, 4.

misconduct by Christians must have been one, or even the major, problem of the Galatians."[77] In fact, the absence of instructions for punishment of the transgressor in chap. 6, the stress on gentleness in the rebuke (6:1), and the immediate shift in attention to the "spiritual" rebuker, who receives a special exhortation (σκοπῶν σεαυτόν),[78] suggest that Paul was *not* addressing the problem of flagrant misconduct in the Galatian churches.

Thus it is doubtful that ethical excesses had already reached a proportion that could have called for Paul's lengthy treatment of the flesh in Gal 5:13ff. Certainly the Galatians did fall prey, as other Christians, to the desire of the flesh (cf. 5:16), and their particular pitfall may have been a "quarrelsome spirit."[79] But even granted this problem, it alone could not account for the amount of attention devoted to the problem of the flesh here. In short, little speaks for the theory that actual gross misuse of freedom as an opportunity for the flesh by the readers occasioned Paul's composition of Gal 5:13ff.

Did Paul compose this section, then, in view of the possible, if not actual, misuse of Christian freedom? And if so, why did Paul deem it necessary to argue against such potential misuse? Should we understand Paul's excursus on Christian ethics as "walking by the Spirit" primarily as an outgrowth of his "bisherige, prononciert einseitige Verneinung des Gesetzes,"[80] i.e., as the next logical step in his argument in Galatians? Or does something in the Galatians themselves evoke his comments? The urgency and concreteness which characterize his argument in 5:13ff. suggest the latter. What then in the Galatian Christians prompts Paul to speak against misuse of freedom? It has often been claimed that Paul's readers are ethically uncautious and need his warning against the danger of gratifying the flesh under the ongoing influence of their pagan background.[81] Thus, predisposed to ethical laxity, and as converts to Paul's law-free gospel, they would have easily fallen prey to libertinism.

But this characterization does not fit the picture of the Galatians Paul gives us in his epistle. He portrays them as attracted to the law and sensitive to the practical obligations of the Christian life (as they perceived them), not ethically naive or disinterested. M.-J. Lagrange ventures to attribute their attraction to the law to their desire for regulations and to their

---

[77] Betz, *Gal*, 273.

[78] Noted by Betz himself, *Gal*, 296, 297.

[79] So Bruce, *Gal*, 25.

[80] So Eckert, *Verkündigung*, 134; tentatively, Mußner, *Gal*, 367, n. 10.

[81] By pagan background is meant either so-called typical Gentile ethical degeneracy (so, e.g., Oepke, *Gal*, 168) or a Hellenistic association of the Spirit with ethical irrelevance (Jewett, "Agitators," 210, 211).

aspiration to practice the good, whose parameters they found traced by the law.[82] Their openness to circumcision (cf. 5:3) and to other aspects of law-keeping (cf. 4:10)[83] reveal more of a tendency to slavish legalism (5:1) than to pagan immorality. The "Galatians" presupposed by those who think Paul is anticipating a problem with libertinism in 5:13ff. are, from the perspective of their characterization in the rest of the epistle, very strangely out of character. We ought instead to take the addressees of 5:13ff. as the same ethically sensitive Christians we have already encountered.[84] The fact that Paul argues against libertinism is not reason enough to suppose that his readers were prone to it.

The occasion for 5:13ff. which Lütgert rejected and which constituted the dominant view in his day was opposition to Paul's law-free gospel as promoting ethical irresponsibility.[85] Yet this view corresponds best to the situation and characterization of the Galatians. J. Eckert judges it still to be "nicht ausgeschlossen."[86] H. Lietzmann speaks with greater certainty, formulating in explicit contradiction of Lütgert's view: Paul "zeigt den Galatern v. 13–6,10, daß die evangelische Freiheit vom Gesetz mit nichten, wie die Judaisten behaupten, eine Freiheit zum Sündigen ist."[87] Similarly, C. Holsten superscribes the section 5:13–24 "Rückweis der anklage der judaisten, dass die freiheit vom gesetze eine freiheit zur sünde sei."[88]

It is quite plausible that Paul's gospel was disparaged by the false teachers in Galatia and those under their influence. H. D. Betz comments: "His [Paul's] 'freedom from the law' must have seemed to them [the opponents] to be committing those who followed Paul to the realm of 'Beliar' and turning Christ into a 'servant of sin.' Faced with such a peculiar dilemma, the Galatians must have taken very seriously what these opponents of Paul had to say."[89] And indeed, as M.-J. Lagrange reminds, "c'était le reproche

---

[82] Lagrange, *Gal*, 144. He continues: "L'apôtre montre ici comment ces instincts généreux trouvent leurs satisfaction dans la vie chrétienne."

[83] Even if the Galatians had not yet contemplated keeping the whole law (cf. 5:3), this need not point to a merely superficial ethical concern.

[84] Not only does the two-front theory collapse (see pp. 142-144 above). Also inappropriate to Paul's characterization of the Galatians is Mußner's view (*Gal*, 367, n. 10) that Paul is fighting "nicht gegen zwei Fronten, sondern gegen zwei Gefahren, die den galatischen Gemeinden drohten: einmal gegen die nomistische, zum andern gegen die libertinistische Gefahr." See also Jewett, "Agitators," 210; Schlier, *Gal*, 242.

[85] See Lütgert, *Gesetz und Geist*, 14–16; also Ropes, *Singular Problem*, 16.

[86] Eckert, *Verkündigung*, 134. Cf. Mußner, *Gal*, 14: "Und auch die Ethik des Briefes könnte mit der Lehre der Gegner zusammenhängen, weil Paulus eine Ethik der Freiheit lehrt."

[87] Lietzmann, *Gal*, 39.

[88] Holsten, *Evangelium* I.1, 125. So also, e.g., Sieffert, *Gal*, 314, 315.

[89] Betz, *Gal*, 9; see also *idem*, "Defense of the Spirit," 105, 107.

ordinaire qu'on faisait à la doctrine de Paul (Rom. III,8; VI,1); il était bon de ne pas paraître l'ignorer."[90] In fact, Paul has already defended himself against an apparent criticism of his law-free gospel in Gal 2:17: ἆρα Χριστὸς ἁμαρτίας διάκονος; μὴ γένοιτο.[91] From the epistle to the Romans we know that the slogan οὐκ ἐσμὲν ὑπὸ νόμον ἀλλὰ ὑπὸ χάριν (6:15b) could be misconstrued to support sinful behavior (τί οὖν, ἁμαρτήσωμεν...; Rom 6:15a; cf. 6:1) and that Paul had to defend himself against such misinterpretations of his gospel: καὶ μὴ καθὼς βλασφημούμεθα καὶ καθώς φασίν τινες ἡμᾶς λέγειν ὅτι ποιήσωμεν τὰ κακά, ἵνα ἔλθῃ τὰ ἀγαθά (3:8).[92] Whether or not Paul is responding to already voiced criticisms in Gal 5:13ff. or simply anticipating them, the crucial point is that he is *defending* his position to ethically sensitive Christians, not trying to stir his readers from ethical slumber. Paul here addresses Christians influenced by Judaizing teaching to the extent that they could have suspected him, or did suspect him, of giving free rein to the flesh or of offering an inferior means of dealing with it.[93] Therefore, Paul had to defend his emphasis on freedom,[94] proving that it was not compatible with the flesh, by developing an ethic of the Spirit as a viable alternative to the law.

Even interpreters who do not describe the whole section beginning at 5:13 as a defense take Paul to defend himself at particular points against criticisms from the legalistic camp. R. Jewett cannot ignore the fact that in 5:13–6:10 "there are answers to questions raised by the nomistic flux."[95] D. Guthrie gives an example: "The fruit of the Spirit [5:22, 23] is...the positive answer to the legalist's challenge."[96] On 5:24 F. Mußner comments that "es deutlich um die Abwehr eines möglichen Einwands geht."[97] On the latter verse, C. Holsten, who espouses the view that Gal 5:13ff. is a defense, makes an even stronger statement: in saying that Christians "have

---

[90] Lagrange, *Gal*, 145.

[91] Mußner, *Gal*, 14, 176, n. 42; also Lietzmann, *Gal*, 16.

[92] On Paul's refutation of accusations in Romans, see Jeremias, "Gedankenführung," 269–271.

[93] Betz (*Gal*, 273) suggests that the Galatians were already looking for a solution to the problem of transgressions when the false teachers came along. Alternatively, did the false teachers make them aware of the problem before presenting their solution? In any case, by the time Paul wrote Galatians, his converts were inclined to adopt an ethic based on law.

[94] The word ἐλευθερία itself at 5:13 signals the continuation of the polemic against the Judaizing tendency in Galatia (cf. 5:1; 2:4). Cf. Eckert, *Verkündigung*, 132.

[95] Jewett, "Agitators," 210.

[96] Guthrie, *Gal*, 150.

[97] Mußner, *Gal*, 390; similarly, Eckert, *Verkündigung*, 141.

crucified the flesh" Paul "hat...den gegengrund der judaisten gegen die freiheit seines evangeliums entkräftet, dass diese freiheit one gesetz eine freiheit des fleisches sei (v. 13)."[98]

The interpretation of 5:13ff. against the backdrop of a Judaizing influence yields a consistent picture of the addressees and eliminates the need for a two-front theory, for which evidence is lacking. F. Sieffert sums up: "Diese Ermahnungen richten sich...in erster Linie nicht etwa an solche unter den Lesern, welche in direktem Gegensatze gegen die Gesetzesgerechten die paulinische Lehre von der Gesetzesfreiheit falsch übertreiben und zur Beschönigung ihrer sittlichen Zügellosigkeit missbrauchen, sondern an dieselben Judaisierenden, denen die bisherige Begründung und Empfehlung der Gesetzesfreiheit galt, nämlich an solche, welche mit Beobachtung äusserer Satzungen sich unter das mos. Gesetz stellen, ...während sie der paul. Lehre die Konsequenz sittlicher Zügellosigkeit vorwerfen."[99] This view frees us from the problem of explaining how "a group exhibiting such a marked tendency toward pneumatic libertinism would at the same time be in danger of nomism."[100] On the basis of the data of the epistle we can reconstruct only a marked tendency toward legalism.[101]

A closer look at Paul's arguments in 5:13ff. supports this view of the passage as a defense to ethical rigorists skeptical of Pauline freedom from the law. For the points Paul puts forward in favor of his ethic of the Spirit seem tailored to people inclined to hold up the law as a standard of Christian behavior. Indeed, as H. D. Betz remarks, the Galatians addressed in the parenetic section are "preoccupied with circumcision and Torah;" that "issue...looms largest in their minds."[102] It is precisely the "Gesetzeswilligen,"[103] not the ethically naive, to whom Paul turns in 5:13ff.

To those who want to keep the law, Paul portrays his ethic of mutual service through love ($\delta\iota\grave{\alpha}$ $\tau\hat{\eta}\varsigma$ $\dot{\alpha}\gamma\acute{\alpha}\pi\eta\varsigma$ $\delta o\upsilon\lambda\epsilon\acute{\upsilon}\epsilon\tau\epsilon$ $\dot{\alpha}\lambda\lambda\acute{\eta}\lambda o\iota\varsigma$, 5:13b) as the fulfillment of the law: "For the whole law is fulfilled in one word, 'You shall love your neighbor as yourself' " (5:14).[104] From this perspective

---

[98] Holsten, *Evangelium* I.1, 129. Cf. his comments on 5:16 (126).

[99] Sieffert, *Gal*, 314, 315.

[100] Jewett's ("Agitators," 212) formulation of the problem. He finds the Galatians' motive for lawkeeping in their "desire to gain the final level of perfection" and their "instinctive respect for the cosmic powers."

[101] Similarly, Bruce, *Gal*, 240: "The danger of unrestrained licence is touched on but briefly in the letter to the Galatians: it was the danger from the opposite extreme that currently presented the greater threat to them."

[102] Betz, *Gal*, 275. Jewett ("Agitators," 210) argues that "the ethic arrayed against libertinism was phrased as a replacement of the law."

[103] Eckert, *Verkündigung*, 134.

[104] Cf. Lietzmann, *Gal*, 39; Lightfoot, *Gal*, 208.

even legalists could not consider his emphasis on Christian freedom as ethically irresponsible.[105] Rather, Paul's single command does the job of the whole law. Therefore his ethic is not inferior.[106]

In 6:2 Paul supports his ethic of loving mutual service with a similar argument geared toward those sympathetic to the law. "Bear one another's burdens and so fulfill the law of Christ." The language and thought have polemical overtones: "Paul is compelled to defend himself against the accusation of 'lawlessness' " [107] before the "lawful." Whatever the unusual expression νόμος τοῦ Χριστοῦ means as a characterization of Paul's ethic,[108] Paul's affirmation was sure to ring true to the law-oriented Galatian Christians. Paul thus talks their language to win them over to his ethic.

The same motive must lie behind Paul's choice of the word δουλεύειν to describe his view of the practical obligations of Christian faith: διὰ τῆς ἀγάπης δουλεύετε ἀλλήλοις (5:13b). δουλεύειν has only negative connotations in the rest of the epistle, where it refers to the slavery of legalism (4:25; cf. δουλεία, 4:24; 5:1) or bondage in a pre-Christian state (4:8, 9). But it takes on a quite positive sense when referring to the love Christians "owe" one another (5:13).[109] F. F. Bruce explains Paul's meaning: "It is as though he said, 'If you must live in slavery, here is a form of slavery in which you may safely indulge—the slavery of practical love for one another.' "[110]

Paul again draws the law into his argument when he shows that his ethic of the Spirit does not lead to violation of the law: the "fruit of the Spirit" is not transgression of the law—κατὰ τῶν τοιούτων[111] οὐκ ἔστιν νόμος (5:22, 23)—as some who associate the Spirit with libertinism might think. Moreover, Paul's ethic of the Spirit succeeds so well against the flesh that

---

[105] Hofius ("Gesetz," 281) interprets 5:14 against the background of Paul's defense against his opponents "daß Leben unter der Herrschaft des Geistes *alles andere* ist als Leben im Widerspruch zu der guten, sich in der Tora gültig bekundenden Rechtsforderung Gottes." Cf. Barrett, *Gal*, 55.

[106] It is often noted that Paul puts the law in a positive light in 5:14. In so doing he is not re-establishing the law (cf. 2:18, 21) but playing on his readers' sympathies to the law in order to win them over to his ethic, which he can characterize as the fulfillment of the law.

[107] Betz, *Gal*, 300, 301.

[108] See Stuhlmacher's discussion, "Gesetz," 156ff.

[109] Mußner, *Gal*, 368.

[110] Bruce, *Gal*, 241. Similarly, Lightfoot, *Gal*, 208. Bruce finds a similar meaning in 6:2: "If you must live under law..." (241).

[111] The view that τοιούτων here is masculine, not neuter, does not change the force of κατὰ τῶν τοιούτων οὐκ ἔστιν νόμος as a denial that Paul's ethic of the Spirit is inferior to an ethic based on law.

it fully replaces the law.[112] Those "led by the Spirit" resist the desire of the flesh (5:16) and "are not under law": εἰ δὲ πνεύματι ἄγεσθε, οὐκ ἐστὲ ὑπὸ νόμον (5:18). These points are clearly aimed at readers who embrace the law as their ethical guide.[113]

Thus the Galatians' attraction to the law accounts not only for the continuation of the discussion as such regarding the law in 5:13ff.[114] but also for the surprisingly *positive* overtones of the law in this passage. Paul's argumentation in Gal 5:13ff. presupposes a law-oriented, ethically sensitive readership.

Paul does not confine himself, however, to arguments which play on the readers' attraction to the law. He also confronts them with the potential harm of law-keeping. It erodes relationships in the community (cf. 5:15, 26).[115] It leads to the despising of transgressors and to an attitude of spiritual superiority (cf. 6:1–4).[116] One might almost say that Paul portrays slavery to the law, not freedom from the law, as providing an "opportunity (ἀφορμή) for the flesh" (5:13b). Paul in fact says so plainly in Rom 7:8, 11, where sin takes the ἀφορμήν...διὰ τῆς ἐντολῆς and produces all ἐπιθυμία (cf. Gal 5:16, 24). Paul's law-critical argumentation in Gal 5:13ff. presupposes an ethically rigorous readership. H. Lietzmann observes: "6,1 warnt Pls die 'Pneumatiker' vor Hochmut, aber mit dem Hinweis, sie sollten einen Übertreter der Moralgesetze nicht verachten, denn sie könnten ja auch selbst einmal in die gleiche Lage kommen. Das ist kein Argument gegenüber Libertinisten, denen an Moral nichts liegt, sondern nur gegenüber Gesetzesleuten, die sich in ihrer Tugend sicher und erhaben fühlen."[117]

By reminding the Galatian Christians of their responsibility to "serve one another through love" (5:13b), which seems to be their ethical blind spot as legalists, Paul takes the offensive in the argument. Lütgert finds this clear polemic against wrong conduct problematic for the view that in 5:13ff. Paul is defending his theology against the criticism that it gives the flesh free rein: "Damit wird die Deutung der Stelle widerspruchsvoll, denn einerseits soll eine Anklage zurückgewiesen und andrerseits dieselbe

---

[112] Paul here pictures the law as "überflüssig" rather than "notwendig" (Eckert, *Verkündigung*, 141; Betz, *Gal*, 289; similarly, Sieffert, *Gal*, 328).

[113] This point is expressed or presupposed in the comments of Mußner, *Gal*, 378; Betz, *Gal*, 281.

[114] Cf. Guthrie, *Gal*, 149.

[115] Bruce, *Gal*, 257; Lightfoot, *Gal*, 209. Many interpreters surmise that these references to unpeaceful mutual relations reflect an atmosphere of law-keeping, although they may not indicate disputes about the law itself.

[116] Lietzmann, *Gal*, 39.

[117] Lietzmann, *Gal*, 39.

Anklage an dieselbe Adresse zurückgegeben werden."[118] On the contrary, the contradiction lies not in the argument incorporating both polemic and defense with respect to ethical laxity[119] but in the theology and praxis of the Galatians and the false teachers in their midst (cf. 6:13). Those who equate Paul's law-free gospel with ethical licence fail themselves to meet the ethical demands of the law: love![120] Pointing out this weakness in his accusers' position strengthens Paul's defense by undermining their claim to an ethically superior position. Further, his command to "serve one another in love" not only prepares for the implicit criticism of legalistic loveless-ness but also shows that Paul does not think freedom from law does away with ethical responsibility. And insofar as the Galatian Christians follow this injunction, their actual conduct will contribute to Paul's defense.[121]

In 5:13ff. Paul's primary aim is not to instill an ethical awareness in his readers but to *reorient* their already sensitized consciences. They intend to resist the flesh. Paul shows them a superior way. He promises[122] them success "by the Spirit": πνεύματι περιπατεῖτε καὶ ἐπιθυμίαν σαρκὸς οὐ μὴ τελέσητε (5:16). His way—the Spirit—is better suited to the task because "the flesh sets its desire against the Spirit and the Spirit against the flesh, for these two are opposed to each other" (5:17). That is, the Spirit, not the law, is the perfect weapon against fleshly desires.[123] Did the Gala-tians assume instead a law-flesh antithesis? Did they even align the Spirit with the flesh?[124] Against such misconceptions Paul supports the Spirit-flesh antithesis by contrasting the behavior consistent with each.[125] "The works of the flesh" are plainly opposite to "the fruit of the Spirit" (5:19–23). By constructing the list of "the fruit of the Spirit" with three sets each having three manifestations of the Spirit Paul makes it clear that where the Spirit moves "there is no room left for the opposite, the manifestation of

---

[118] Lütgert, *Gesetz und Geist*, 15. Similarly, Schmithals, "Häretiker," 58.

[119] For the combination of polemic and defense, see also 2 Cor 13:5–10, where both polemic and defense refer to the same thing: the authenticity of self-claims (to apostle-ship and to Christian profession; see pp. 217–225 below).

[120] Cf. Sieffert, *Gal*, 316.

[121] Cf. Lietzmann, *Gal*, 39.

[122] Bruce (*Gal*, 243), Betz (*Gal*, 278), and Schlier (*Gal*, 248) interpret οὐ μὴ τελέσητε as the expression of a promise. οὐ μὴ with the subjunctive is "the most defi-nite form of negation regarding the future" (*BDF* §365).

[123] In Rom 7:15–23, too, the law is impotent to produce the good. Both passages have the motif of not doing the good one *wants* to do (Gal 5:17c; Rom 7:15b). Both also presuppose a situation in which the law functions as the ethical norm.

[124] Sieffert (*Gal*, 323) formulates the Judaizing objection: "Ein nicht durch das Ge-setz bestimmtes Christenleben werde von dem nichtchristlichen Leben sich garnicht deutlich unterscheiden lassen."

[125] See Burton, *Gal*, 303; Sieffert, *Gal*, 323.

evil ('the works of the flesh')."[126] Finally, it should be evident to those who "live by the Spirit" that the Spirit will also guide them to appropriate behavior: εἰ ζῶμεν πνεύματι, πνεύματι καὶ στοιχῶμεν (5:25).[127] In 5:13ff. Paul gives his readers ample reason to base their ethic on the Spirit instead of the law. His whole argument assumes their sensitivity to Christian ethical obligations.

In summary, in Gal 5:13ff. Paul defends freedom from the law according to his gospel against the caricature of that freedom as an "opportunity for the flesh." For his readers, or at least his Judaizing opponents in Galatia, apparently criticize Paul's law-free gospel for this seeming weakness. Law-keeping seemed more attractive to the Galatian Christians. Behavioral norms mattered to them. They took a serious attitude—more serious than Paul, as they probably perceived it—toward the practical implications of their faith. And now Paul must convince them that "walking by the Spirit" is an ethically responsible way to live the Christian life. This reconstruction of the situation which occasioned Gal 5:13ff. best fits the argument in the rest of the epistle and illuminates the textual data significantly better than other views.

If Paul is defending his law-free gospel against ethical rigorists who suspect him of promoting ethical laxity in 5:13ff., what does the vice list and saying about exclusion from the kingdom of God contribute to his argument? Since Paul is addressing people who take the practical obligations of their faith so seriously as to begin keeping the law, it would seem odd for him to issue them a *warning* against exclusion from the kingdom for the practice of vices. Even if there were unpeaceful mutual relations among the Galatian Christians,[128] this failure alone would not provide enough reason for Paul to threaten them with exclusion from the kingdom and recount to them a long list of other disqualifying vices. Thus the vice list and saying about exclusion from the kingdom of God do not belong to Paul's offensive arguments which expose the weakness in his accusers' theology and praxis and in this way contribute indirectly to his defense.

How then could Paul have meant Gal 5:19–21 to strengthen his defense directly against the legalists' criticism that Pauline "freedom" was a disguised "opportunity for the flesh"? F. Mußner notes that the vice list beginning in v. 19 has an introduction, φανερὰ δέ ἐστιν, which shows the list not to have an explicitly parenetic function.[129] Paul wants not simply to

---

[126] Betz, *Gal*, 33.
[127] N.b. Paul's repeated use of πνεύματι here (5:16, 18, 25).
[128] On this problem, see p. 143 above.
[129] Mußner, *Gal*, 379.

name particular "works of the flesh,"[130] but to emphasize that they "are evident."[131] As H. D. Betz suggests, we could almost add to Paul's introduction the words "without law": the works of the flesh are evident as such without law.[132] Indeed, v. 18 closes on the same note of the unnecessisariness of the law: εἰ δὲ πνεύματι ἄγεσθε, οὐκ ἐστὲ ὑπὸ νόμον. And Paul uses the expression φανερόν ἐστιν in Rom 1:19 to describe the "self-evident" knowledge of God that even pagans have *without law* (cf. 2:14, 15). So then, if no one needs the law to recognize the works of the flesh, dispensing with the law does not make one any less ethically informed and prepared to resist the flesh. Adherents to the law have no monopoly on knowledge of the works of the flesh. In that respect, Paul's law-free gospel is not inferior as the Galatians suppose.

Nor can it be called inferior in a second respect: his gospel takes account of the consequences of practicing the works of the flesh. Like the vice list, the prediction of the final destiny of vice-doers which follows in v. 21 has an introduction: προλέγω ὑμῖν, καθὼς προεῖπον ὅτι.... Paul does not simply repeat tradition here[133] that οἱ τὰ τοιαῦτα πράσσοντες βασιλείαν Θεοῦ οὐ κληρονομήσουσιν. More important, he indicates the relation of that tradition to *his* teaching: it belongs now as always to his catechetical instruction (προλέγω ὑμῖν, καθὼς προεῖπον...). Paul's double affirmation produces a very strong statement of his agreement with the tradition.[134]

A. Oepke suggests that Paul is reminding the Galatians of the tradition they had received from him because "aktuell bleibt diese Gerichtsansage auch für gläubige Leser."[135] But, after examining the argument in 5:13ff. and the picture of the readers in the rest of the epistle, it is hard to believe that Paul intends these verses to function as a warning to the Galatian Christians. Instead, 5:19–21 may represent the readers' own beliefs. "There is no reason to believe that the Galatians took transgression lightly. On the contrary, they must have been quite concerned that such instances would

---

[130] The final, generalizing καὶ τὰ ὅμοια τούτοις at v. 21 suggests that the explicit mention of individual vices itself is not so important.

[131] Here φανερός refers to the present time; cf. Rom 1:19; 1 Cor 11:19; Phil 1:13.

[132] Betz, *Gal*, 283; similarly, Lagrange, *Gal*, 149.

[133] On the traditional character of statements about exclusion from the kingdom of God, see Schlier, *Gal*, 255; Mußner, *Gal*, 384.

[134] Cf. similar double affirmations in 2 Cor 13:2; Gal 1:9; 1 Thess 4:6; Phil 3:18. Paul may be following a "set style of quoting what the individual himself has stated previously" (Betz, *Gal*, 284). Paul can also simplify the quotation formula and achieve the same emphatic effect in other ways (cf. 1 Thess 3:4; 2 Thess 2:5).

[135] Oepke, *Gal*, 180; similarly, Mußner, *Gal*, 383; Betz, *Gal*, 285, n. 13; *et al.*

destroy their hope of salvation in Christ."[136] But, they might have wondered, did Paul's law-free gospel run parallel to the slippery slope which leads to destruction? By affirming that his teaching incorporates the tradition of exclusion from the kingdom of God for practicing fleshliness, Paul proves that his teaching does not promote ethical laxity. F. Sieffert sees this to be Paul's intention in vv. 19–21. Commenting on the prediction of vicedoers' exclusion from the kingdom, he says: "Ist das die Lehre des P., wie er sie auch in Galatien verkündet hat, dann ergibt sich die Verdächtigung derselben Seitens der gal. Judaisten als einer zu unsittlichen Konsequenzen führenden als völlig unbegründet."[137] Whether or not the Galatians had in fact already heard this tradition from Paul—the ὑμῖν is missing after προεῖπον[138]—others had. Thus, by showing the continuity in his teaching against the works of the flesh, Paul clears himself of potential charges of propounding freedom as an opportunity for the flesh. Even Paul's clothing his defense in the language of tradition[139] instead of in characteristically Pauline terminology would surely have worked to his advantage under the assumption that the Galatians respected this tradition. The Galatians' opinion of Paul must have improved when they heard "that he considers his view of Christian ethics to be part of the tradition of the church, a tradition in which the Galatians themselves stand."[140]

In summary, Paul needed to remind the Galatians not of the content of the tradition—in order to warn them—but of the fact that he taught it, in agreement with their convictions, in order to defend his gospel as being opposed to the flesh. Thus Gal 5:19–21 strengthens Paul's defense in 5:13ff. Paul does not use the vice list and tradition concerning exclusion from the kingdom of God to call into question the final salvation of his readers.

Gal 6:6–10, which continues the antithesis between the flesh and the Spirit, can be understood in much the same way. Paul's elaboration on the proverb of sowing and reaping looks to many like a reference to the Galatians' possible loss of salvation: "He who sows to his own flesh will reap corruption from the flesh, but he who sows to the Spirit will reap eternal

---

[136] Betz, *Gal*, 273.

[137] Sieffert, *Gal*, 326.

[138] Betz thinks they had (*Gal*, 284). Mußner is not sure (*Gal*, 383).

[139] βασιλεία [τοῦ θεοῦ] is traditional and occurs infrequently in Paul (Rom 14:17; 1 Cor 4:20; 6:9, 10; 15:24, 50; Gal 5:21; 1 Thess 2:12; 2 Thess 1:5). The meaning of κληρονομεῖν here stands out from Paul's other uses of its word group in Galatians (cf. 3:18, 29; 4:1, 7, 30). πράσσειν is also traditional (cf. its use in connection with catalogues in Rom 1:32; 2 Cor 12:21). So Betz, *Gal*, 284 with nn. 125–129.

[140] Betz, *Gal*, 285, 286.

life from the Spirit" (6:8).[141] But it could easily be interpreted instead as another attempt by Paul to align his ethic of the Spirit with familiar ethical teaching from Hellenistic-Jewish tradition[142] and so counteract criticism that his gospel leads to ethical irresponsibility. As he showed in 5:22, 23 that the fruit of the Spirit does not violate the law, here he states positively and even more forcefully that sowing to the Spirit results in a harvest of eternal life.[143] On sowing to the flesh, he actually sides with the ethical rigorists: it brings a bad harvest of "corruption."[144] The significance which F. Mußner attributes to these thoughts supports the view that their function in chap. 6 is polemical: "Der Apostel ist, so zeigt sich deutlich, trotz seiner Rechtfertigungslehre kein Vertreter eines geistlichen Quietismus. Vielmehr treibt gerade seine Rechtfertigungslehre zu äußerster Aktivität, so paradox das auch aufs erste klingen mag."[145] We can take Paul's practical instruction in 6:6–10, therefore, to have a polemical character: he is continuing his defense of the ethical integrity of Spirit-led Christian behavior. This is not to ignore Paul's parenetic interests—in v. 6 he exhorts the readers to contribute to the material needs of Christian teachers[146] and not to provide exclusively for their own "flesh," i.e., physical welfare.[147] But since Paul presupposes the Galatians were already "doing good" in this way (6:9),[148] and since the passage has polemical overtones, there is little reason to see in 6:8 a warning to the Galatians against losing their salvation.

---

[141] See, e.g., Betz, *Gal*, 308, 309; Marshall, *Kept*, 112.

[142] Cf. Betz, *Gal*, 307.

[143] Bruce (*Gal*, 265) connects "sow to the Spirit" with the "fruit of the Spirit."

[144] Most interpret φθορά eschatologically; but see Burton (*Gal*, 342) for the possibility of a temporal, physical meaning.

[145] Mußner, *Gal*, 406, 407.

[146] Some take ἐν πᾶσιν ἀγαθοῖς to mean both material and spiritual goods. On both possibilities and the Hellenistic background of this maxim, see Betz, *Gal*, 304–306.

[147] Burton (*Gal*, 341); he notes the contrasting uses of σάρξ in 5:13–24.

[148] "Let us not grow weary of doing good" (6:9) presupposes their practice of good (so Betz, *Gal*, 309).

CONCLUSION TO PART TWO

The findings of the exegetical analyses undertaken in Part Two can be summarized as follows. For Paul, continuity in salvation does not make Christian conduct irrelevant. Rather, Paul argues ardently against immoral behavior on the part of believers, yet not saying that such behavior leads to loss of salvation. Christians' ethical failure has other negative consequences and implications.

Paul considers the conduct of believers so important that he instructs them how to act even when amoral matters are in question, as the discussion of 1 Cor 8:7–13 and Rom 14:1–23 revealed. Christians are free in regard to food, for example, but they must not exercise that freedom in violation of their conscience. No action which is unaccompanied by the conviction of its rightness is allowed. Neglecting this rule has the consequence of "destroying" the "weak" believer in an existential sense, i.e., causing a breakdown of Christian character and identity formed by adherence to Christian values.

Questions of morality exercise Paul yet more. Criticizing the Corinthians for profaning the Lord's Supper, he declares that when they take the elements in this way they "eat and drink judgment" to themselves (1 Cor 11:29). Paul interprets the illnesses and deaths in their midst as the evidence of God's punishment of disobedient individuals. They have experienced the consequences of their ethical failure already in their present bodily existence. The prospect of temporal punishment for misconduct is obviously not to be taken lightly, nevertheless, it does not introduce doubt with regard to Christians' final salvation. On the contrary, Paul sees in such temporal judgment of Christians a confirmation of God's intention to spare God's children from final condemnation, which is reserved for the world. God chastises Christians now instead of condemning them in the final judgment (1 Cor 11:32). Present judgment is thus compatible with God's intent to save them at the day of Christ.

Some ethical failure is so serious, however, that it can call into question the genuineness of one's Christian profession. 1 Cor 5:1–5 relates how a certain church member engaged in a heinous form of fornication must be expelled from the Corinthian fellowship and delivered to Satan (whose realm is outside the church), where the man apparently truly belongs, since his behavior is entirely incompatible with Christian faith. This person ought to be considered a "so-called brother" and still a candidate for salvation ("... the spirit might be saved," 5:5) rather than an apostate. 1 Cor 10:12 suggests that the sin of idolatry also calls into question the authenticity of professed faith in Christ. The Corinthians will become idolaters if they yield to the temptation to frequent the pagan cultic meals. Paul warns the one who "thinks he stands" or "seems to stand," i.e., to be saved: he may "fall," i.e., lose the outward status or appearance of salvation. Exclusive worship of the one true God, not mere routine partaking of the sacraments, marks out the truly saved from the rest. Further, Paul suggests both in the case of fornication and idolatry that falsely-professing Christians are distinguished from the genuine not only by such unchristian behavior but also by some form of physical suffering accompanying their undoing. Paul does not, however, interpret suffering in this case as God's fatherly chastisement of God's children but as Satanic affliction of the unrighteous. There is apparently hope that this suffering will play a positive, remedial role in the life of the falsely-professing Christian and thus move that person on, in the end, to salvation.

Paul thus judges immorality to be totally incompatible with the Christian life and faith. To reinforce this basic truth he can take up a traditional vice list and characterize the vice-doers named in it as people who are excluded from the kingdom of God in contrast to Christians who are heirs of the kingdom, bearers of the Spirit, justified and sanctified (1 Cor 6:9–11; Gal 5:19–25). In 1 Corinthians 6 Paul uses this reasoning as a parenetic device to get his readers to conform their conduct to their new identity and destiny in Christ (although Paul may also intend to expose a minority in the church as yet unconverted, and call them to repentance and salvation). The vice list illustrating the incompatibility of immorality and Christian faith in Galatians 5, however, has a different function, a polemical one. Paul is trying to convince his readers that he himself takes Christian conduct seriously (as they do) and that his ethic of the Spirit solves rather than aggravates the problem of the flesh. He thus shows here that he holds the traditional view: those who practice vices will not inherit the kingdom of God. He has taught this view all along; no one can accuse him of encouraging libertinism. Thus neither 1 Cor 6:9, 10 nor Gal 5:19–21 has the purpose of warning Christians against loss of salvation because of immoral behavior.

E. P. Sanders has analyzed Paul's view of the significance of ethical failure by Christians in relation to their continuance in salvation. He concludes that "Paul thought that salvation basically depends on membership in the in-group," but that "within that context deeds still count" and can call forth divine punishment. In Sanders' view Paul thinks that "remaining in the in-group is conditional on behavior"—including repentance from sin—

and is made possible by the atonement which comes through punishment.[1] Sanders has correctly seen that Paul is deeply concerned with the ethical behavior of his converts and that immorality can provoke punishment. But we need to make some finer distinctions when discussing the implications of ethical failure for final salvation. In the foregoing exegetical analyses of the same passages which Sanders considers I have noted that Paul does not make Christians' final salvation dependent on their repentance from post-conversion sins, though he by all means views their repentance as desirable. Moreover, Paul traces continuance in salvation in spite of transgressions not to atonement through suffering but to the new relationship of erring Christians to God: they are God's children, as seen by the nature of their punishment—parental chastisement. They are objects of the Father's love, which accounts both for their punishment and their final inheritance of salvation. But according to Paul it is also possible to lose one's membership in the "in-group" on account of immoral conduct, namely, by falsifying one's Christian profession by one's behavior. This can happen in the case of "grievous" sins. But when this happens, continuity in actual salvation is not interrupted. To say that "remaining in the in-group is conditional on behavior" is not the same as saying that remaining in *salvation* is conditional upon behavior. Sanders' statement is true but perhaps too obvious to be helpful, once we acknowledge that for Paul the "in-group" is a mixed community not to be identified with the elect or the justified.

What then is the significance of ethical failure for continuance in salvation in Paul's mind? Without belittling the importance he attributes to Christian conduct—we have noted the signficance of wrong conduct as an indicator of the inauthenticity of Christian profession, an occasion for divine chastisement of believers and a cause of regression in sanctification—we can justifiably draw the conclusion that Paul does not think Christians' ethical failure results in exclusion from final salvation.[2] Rather, in dealing with sinful behavior in his communities Paul does not contradict his fundamental affirmation of the continuity in believers' salvation. The verdict οὐδὲν ἄρα νῦν κατάκριμα τοῖς ἐν Χριστῷ Ἰησοῦ (Rom 8:1) holds true in spite of their ethical failure.

---

[1] Sanders, *Law*, 111.

[2] Sanders, whose thesis stresses the significance of behavior for "staying in," nevertheless comes to a similar conclusion: "It is difficult in Paul to determine what, if anything, will permanently exclude and condemn a member of the group.... There is no deed which necessarily leads to the condemnation of a believer, although Paul appears to waver with regard to food offered to idols" (*Law*, 111).

PART THREE

FAITH AND FALLING AWAY

In Part One the various interconnected divine initiatives were analyzed that Paul portrays as together making up the one divine work of salvation in Christians and constituting its completeness. God's faithfulness to finish the work of salvation in believers, despite obstacles to the realization of that goal, manifests itself in the interconnectedness of God's saving initiatives. In Part Two the potential obstacle to God's faithful accomplishment of God's purpose posed by Christians' ethical failure was seen not to prevent this purpose from coming to fulfillment, in Paul's view. The final part of this study will deal with the Pauline texts which seem to present another obstacle to attainment of final salvation, namely, lack of faith in the gospel. Does the apostle think that continuity in a Christian's salvation depends on that person's positive relation to the gospel through faith? Is constancy in faith a criterion of the certain consummation of one's salvation?

The question of Israel immediately arises. Given the rejection of the gospel by God's elect people and their present exclusion from salvation, must it be concluded that divine election of Israel does not necessarily entail salvation? What are the implications for professing Christians? Can they fall away from salvation through lapses in faith, so that the divine work of salvation begun in God's foreknowledge and election is cut short in their lives? How can such alienation from the gospel's promises come about and what significance would it have for Paul's view of continuity in salvation?

VI. ISRAEL, THE GENTILES,
AND THE GOSPEL

Israel's Unbelief

Romans 9–11. As seen in Part One, Paul gives election great significance for continuity in salvation. The electing God is committed to fulfill the purpose of election: to complete the salvation of the elect. God's faithfulness guarantees that election will lead to this goal. Paul cannot ascribe this significance to election for Christians, however, without addressing the apparent contradiction between *Israel's* election and virtually complete exclusion from salvation in Jesus Christ, a contradiction which was painfully obvious in his day. The fact that God's *elect people* Israel stood, by and large, outside the community of the saved was in tension with the claim that God will faithfully carry out God's intention in the election of Christians.[1] Paul's argument in Romans shows that he fully recognizes this tension, for he puts his lengthy treatment of the problem of unbelieving, excluded Israel in Romans 9–11 immediately after his strongest affirmation of the significance of election for Christians' salvation in Rom 8:28–39. The terminology and motifs common to 8:14–39 and 9:4–13—sonship (or children of God),[2] glory,[3] calling,[4] election,[5] divine predestination,[6] and divine love[7]—confirm that the two passages are tied together in an attempt to resolve the tension. In chaps. 9–11 Paul proceeds to clear up potential confusion or objection concerning the implications of election in chap. 8 raised by the problem of elect but unbelieving Israel. How can election guarantee salvation if even God's elect people Israel fail to participate in

---

[1] Cf. Aageson, "Scripture," 288.
[2] Cf. 8:14–17, 19, 21, 23 and 9:4, 7–12.
[3] Cf. 8:18, 30 and 9:4.
[4] Cf. 8:28, 30 and 9:7, 12; 11:29.
[5] Cf. 8:33 and 9:11; 11:28.
[6] Cf. 8:28, 29, 30 and 9:11; 11:2.
[7] Cf. 8:35, 39 and 9:13; 11:28.

the Messianic community of salvation? Indeed, by preaching a gospel that excluded unbelieving Israel from salvation, has not Paul implied that Israel's election was nullified? And if election can be nullified, how can it provide any guarantee for salvation?[8] In Romans 9–11 Paul explains the nature of Israel's election and the relationship between that election and the Jews' present exclusion from salvation and hope of future salvation. After examining Paul's argument concerning Israel's election and its implications for the salvation of Israel, I will consider the implications of Romans 9–11 for continuity in Christians' salvation.

In three rounds Paul knocks down three false inferences from his gospel of salvation by faith in Jesus Christ, inferences which could have easily come from the mouths of his opponents in the synagogue.[9] To them Paul was an apostate and a heretic for proclaiming salvation through Jesus, a salvation which had essentially bypassed Israel. In self-defense Paul declares his deep grief over his unbelieving fellow Jews and a wish that, even at his own expense, he could benefit them (9:1–3).[10] In defense of his gospel Paul denies that "the word of God" (concerning Israel) has collapsed (9:6a), that "God has rejected his people" (11:1), and that "Israel has stumbled so as to fall" (11:11).

---

[8] Beker ("Faithfulness," 14) explains: "If it could be argued that God has rejected the people of the election, Israel, and that therefore God's promises to Israel have become null and void, how are the Gentiles to trust the confirmation of these promises to them through God's righteousness in Christ?... In other words, the gospel cannot have any authentic validity or legitimacy apart from the people of Israel because the theological issue of God's faithfulness (Rom 3:3) and righteousness determines the truth of the gospel."

[9] Paul has already engaged in dialogue with the synagogue in chaps. 2, 3, 4; see Wilckens, *Röm* I, 93, 122, 131, 154, 155, 161, 244, 280, 281. Chaps. 9–11 ought to be read against the background of this debate which overarches the epistle, as well as in the context of the theological development of Paul's argument to Christian readers in Rome, in particular, chap. 8. On the connection to the previous chapters, see Hofius, "Evangelium," 299, 300.

[10] Interpreters often take 9:3 (ηὐχόμην γὰρ ἀνάθεμα εἶναι αὐτὸς ἐγὼ ἀπὸ τοῦ Χριστοῦ ὑπὲρ τῶν ἀδελφῶν μου τῶν συγγενῶν μου κατὰ σάρκα) to express Paul's willingness to change places with his unbelieving fellow Jews. This interpretation implies that unbelieving Israel is now ἀνάθεμα. In their view, ὑπὲρ τῶν ἀδελφῶν μου means "in place of my brothers" (see BAGD, s.v. ὑπέρ, 1.c). But ὑπέρ could be used here simply as "for, on behalf of, for the sake of" (see BAGD, s.v. ὑπέρ, 1.a). It can have this sense after expressions of suffering, dying, devoting oneself, etc. (e.g., Rom 5:7a, b; 16:4; see BAGD, s.v. ὑπέρ, 1.a.ε.). Thus Paul could simply be confessing how great a sacrifice he would make in order to help his fellow Jews—he would even become ἀνάθεμα...ἀπὸ τοῦ Χριστοῦ, if that could benefit them. Elsewhere Paul states his readiness to endure suffering for the benefit of the Gentiles; in fact he has done so (with ὑπέρ, see 2 Cor 12:15; cf. Eph 3:1, 13; Col 1:24). We need not suppose, therefore, that Paul considers the unbelieving Jews presently ἀνάθεμα. Moreover, this supposition

Paul sets the stage for the rebuttal of the first false inference drawn from his gospel by listing the magnificent privileges of election which have been bestowed upon Israel: the honored title "Israelites," sonship, the glory of the divine presence, the covenants, the giving of the law, cultic service, the promises, and the privilege of being descendants of the fathers and ancestors of the Messiah (9:4, 5; cf. Eph 2:12). Ironically, however, Israel is excluded from the gift which surpasses all others: participation in the salvation which has come in Jesus Christ. This tragedy appears to imply the collapse of the "word of God." "But," formulates Paul, "it is not so that the word of God has fallen" (9:6a). The introductory formula, οὐχ οἷον δὲ ὅτι shows that Paul wants to avert a false conclusion from the preceding verses.[11] The fact that Israel has been largely excluded from salvation might cast doubt on the continuing validity of Israel's election which brought the nation their great privileges. Does God's withholding the privilege of salvation in Christ have this negative implication for Israel's election? If so, the "word of God," namely, the OT substantiation of God's elective grace toward the chosen people through its record of their privileges,[12] would have lost its validity. Thus Paul's gospel would imply that Israel's election is a thing of the past and that God's word, to which it witnesses, is unreliable.

But Paul denies such an inference. In support of his denial he argues, οὐ γὰρ πάντες οἱ ἐξ Ἰσραὴλ οὗτοι Ἰσραήλ (9:6b). Some confusion exists over the meaning of this argument. What is the Ἰσραήλ to which not all οἱ ἐξ Ἰσραήλ belong? Paul cannot mean to exclude some Israelites from Ἰσραήλ *as the elect people of God*. For he has just affirmed that the privileges of national election belong even to his unbelieving kinspeople (9:4, 5).[13] Israel's election to be the people of God remains unchanged. Thus

---

would conflict with Paul's subsequent affirmation that Israel is still God's elect people; see p. 163 below.

[11] Cf. Steiger, "Schutzrede," 52; Murray, *Rom* II, 8; *BDF* §304.

[12] Cf. τὰ λόγια τοῦ θεοῦ, 3:2. See Wilckens, *Röm* II, 192 with n. 848. The majority of commentators interpret ὁ λόγος τοῦ θεοῦ at 9:6a in terms of αἱ ἐπαγγελίαι at 9:4. But there is little reason to limit the meaning of ὁ λόγος τοῦ θεοῦ to one of the nine privileges mentioned (for a broader definition, see Piper, *Justification*, 32, 33; Mayer, *Heilsratschluß*, 169, 170). Cranfield (*Rom*, 473) and Sanday and Headlam (*Rom*, 240) interpret ὁ λόγος τοῦ θεοῦ in terms of God's elective purpose. This makes good sense since ἵνα ἡ κατ' ἐκλογὴν πρόθεσις τοῦ θεοῦ μένῃ at 9:11 apparently forms the antithesis to the negated inference in 9:6a that the "word of God has fallen" (so Piper, *Justification*, 33).

[13] The lasting significance of Israel's privileges is implied by the present tense of εἰσιν at 9:4 (Mußner, *Traktat*, 46). Cf. Eichholz (*Theologie*, 292): "immer noch verliehene Privilegien." De Villiers ("Salvation," 201) concludes that these privileges of

Ἰσραήλ at 9:6bβ does not denote the elect people. Rather, it denotes *the community to whom salvation has come through the Messiah*, to whom the promise has been fulfilled.[14] The Jews who have rejected the gospel of Jesus Christ are excluded from this group. Only those who have believed in Christ and been justified by faith have received the promised blessings. The designation ὁ Ἰσραήλ τοῦ Θεοῦ at Gal 6:16 probably also denotes the community of those who are saved through faith in Christ.[15] Although Paul continues to use the title Ἰσραήλ in such a way that it includes the unbelieving Jews,[16] it is also an appropriate designation for the "people of God" who have welcomed the Messiah and received the promised salvation.[17] Thus the sense of 9:6b is as follows: it is no argument against the reliability of God's word that not all members of the elect people belong to the other people of God made up of the *present* beneficiaries of Messianic salvation.

With this explanation of Paul's terminology in 9:6b, we can now seek to understand how in 9:7–10:21 he justifies the statement, "not all who are 'from Israel' are 'Israel'." Paul justifies his claim at 9:6b in two ways: from the perspective of (1) Israel's relation to the gospel and (2) God's sovereignty in his dealings with Israel. This justification is indeed necessary. For a Jewish reader would have looked with suspicion on Paul's argument against the unreliability of God's word. By denying to the elect people as a whole a necessary place in present salvation based on their election through Abraham, and by implying that this expected honor has been usurped by the Gentiles, who, along with a handful of Jews, make up the "Israel" which is the Messianic community of salvation, Paul contradicts Jewish self-understanding. The Jews considered themselves to have priority in receiving salvation by virtue of their physical descent from Abraham, the father of the elect nation.[18] How could Messianic salvation have bypassed them and come first to the Gentiles? According to the tradition of the

---

Israel "indicate the continuing fact of their election."

[14] Cf. Hofius ("Evangelium," 301), who describes the Ἰσραήλ of 9:6bβ as the "*Heilsgemeinde* 'Israel', an der sich die Verheißung erfüllt." He nevertheless includes in this "Israel" only the *Jewish* Christians, i.e., ἡ ἐκλογή (11:7a; see his n. 15). Cf. Paul's use of the ethnic term Ἰουδαῖος at 2:28, 29 in a double sense denoting both physical descent and spiritual relation to God.

[15] Cf. Sanders, *Law*, 174; Gutbrod, Ἰσραήλ, *TDNT* 3, 387, 388; Luz, *Geschichtsverständnis*, 269; cf. Hofius, "Evangelium," 301, n. 15.

[16] For Ἰσραήλ as the unbelieving Jews, see 9:31; 10:19, 21; 11:7. For Ἰσραήλ as the whole nation, see 9:6bα, 27a; 11:25, 26; 1 Cor 10:18.

[17] Gutbrod (Ἰσραήλ, *TDNT* 3, 387, 388) notes that the title cannot be transferred to the new community at the expense of the old.

[18] Cf. Gutbrod, Ἰσραήλ, *TDNT* 3, 360. On the later expression of this expectation in rabbinic literature, see Sanders, *Palestinian Judaism*, 147–150.

eschatological pilgrimage of the nations to Zion, the Jews entered into the blessings of salvation brought by the Messiah, and only after them, the Gentiles. The claim that all physical Israelites do not constitute the Messianic community of salvation which has now been inaugurated denies a fundamental Jewish hope. But not only did Paul's gospel contradict Jewish priority. It seemed to exclude Israel altogether from salvation. First Paul deals with the issue of priority, the problem created by the coming of salvation first to the Gentiles. Later he tackles the question of the extent of Israel's exclusion from salvation: Is it thoroughgoing? Is it lasting?

In 9:7–10:21 Paul gives a justification of the elect people's present exclusion from salvation. This section explains the statement in 9:6b in the two ways noted. Paul's argument presents faith in Jesus Christ as the *sine qua non* for enjoyment of the blessings of Messianic salvation. Participation in salvation brought by the Messiah depends not on physical but spiritual descent from Abraham (9:7, 8). Thus, though Israel is still God's elect people, only the "children of promise" (9:8), who have the faith of their father Abraham, have become members of the other "Israel" to which the promised salvation has come. The "children of the flesh" (9:8) are not automatically included in the present community of salvation.

Paul's ennumeration of examples from Israel's own history in 9:7–13 substantiates that the sovereign God consistently disregards physical descent in God's gracious dealings with humankind. God's call is not based on physical descent from Abraham, for though Isaac and Ishmael were both born to Abraham, God said, ἐν Ἰσαὰκ κληθήσεταί σοι σπέρμα (9:7). Jacob and Esau, both born to Isaac, were in the womb of one woman at the same time—a gripping picture of their equality with regard to physical Abrahamic descent—yet it is written, τὸν Ἰακὼβ ἠγάπησα, τὸν δὲ Ἡσαῦ ἐμίσησα (9:13). Just as election is not ἐξ ἔργων ἀλλ' ἐκ τοῦ καλοῦντος (9:12), so God's elective purpose remains rooted in God's sovereign will (ἵνα ἡ κατ' ἐκλογὴν πρόθεσις τοῦ θεοῦ μένῃ, 9:11b). For Paul, this means that God deals sovereignly even with God's elect people Israel by including some in the community of salvation while excluding others. From the perspective of the history of God's dealings with the chosen people, therefore, Paul can show that Israel's present exclusion from salvation is not inconsistent with their election. In the present time God's sovereignty in relation to God's people has come to expression in God's omitting to call the majority of them to faith in the gospel.

The use of καλεῖν in both OT examples noted above is striking since Paul likes to employ this verb for the divine initiative at conversion resulting in faith in the gospel (cf., e.g., Rom 8:28, 30; 1 Thess 5:24; 2 Thess

2:14).[19] The double appearance of the term here suggests that Paul intends the OT examples of "calling" in disregard of physical descent to justify God's disregarding Israel's national election through Abraham in presently omitting to call the majority of the Jews to salvation in Jesus Christ. As in Israel's history, so now in the age of Messianic salvation, God's call disregards physical descent. Paul's gospel is in line with the OT on this point, not in contradiction with it. In this way Paul substantiates his affirmation that the word of God has not fallen with the exclusion of elect Israel from the present community of salvation. Israel's divine election, to which the OT record of Israel's unique privileges testifies, has continuing validity, so long as false inferences regarding Israel's present participation in salvation are not drawn. The OT record itself precludes the over-interpretation of election through Abraham in this sense.

With the help of OT examples, Paul has demonstrated that unbelieving Israel's election, though continuingly valid, does not automatically imply their calling to present salvation. In the next major section (9:30–10:21) he shows how his fellow Jews' exclusion from present salvation is appropriate in the light of their behavior toward the gospel.[20] They stumbled over the stone of stumbling (9:32), sought to establish their own righteousness (10:3), and did not obey the gospel after hearing and knowing it (10:16, 18, 19).[21] Their reaction to the gospel is consistent with their exclusion. This section thus illuminates the statement, "not all who are 'of Israel' are 'Israel'," by pointing to the Jews' self-exclusion from present salvation. Whereas Israel is seen to reject the gospel, God is portrayed as graciously extending welcoming hands the whole day long to a disobedient and stiff-necked people (10:21).[22] Therefore, when Paul begins to attack the second false inference from his gospel—God has not rejected God's people, has God?—in the next round of his argument (11:1–10) his readers are already prepared for the implied negative answer to this rhetorical question.[23] How

---

[19] Cf. Lagrange, *Rom*, 231.

[20] Paul will later attribute the Jews' rejection of the gospel to divine hardening (11:7). On the relation of God's hardening to Israel's rejection of the gospel, see Hofius, "Evangelium," 303.

[21] See, further, Hofius, "Evangelium," 298, 299.

[22] Müller (*Gerechtigkeit*, 38) describes 10:21 as a "Gerichtswort." But the verse should be taken instead as a testimony to God's faithful love, which, however, does not exclude God's freedom to harden God's people, cf. 11:7ff.

[23] οὖν at 11:1 connects the new section especially to the immediately preceding remarks (with Munck, *Christus*, 80; Plag, *Wege*, 32); n.b. the obvious contrast between divine welcome (10:21) and divine rejection (11:1). But οὖν also links 11:1ff. to the entire preceding section (9:30–10:21) in view of the contrast between God's supposed rejection of Israel and Israel's actual rejection of the gospel.

could one suppose that the God with arms outstretched to God's people has rejected them? Far from implying rejection, the gospel issues a welcome to Israel as to "everyone who believes" (10:11).[24]

By 11:1 Paul has dealt with the anticipated Jewish objection that his gospel disregards Israel's priority in salvation (over the Gentiles), and he has already begun addressing the more fundamental objection that his gospel denies Israel a place at all in salvation. In 9:6a Paul affirmed that Israel's election to salvation is not nullified, putting Israel forever beyond hope of salvation; for "the word of God has not fallen." Now he goes on to oppose a second erroneous interpretation of Israel's present exclusion from salvation.

In one breath, he both formulates and denies the false inference—μὴ ἀπώσατο ὁ Θεὸς τὸν λαὸν αὐτοῦ (11:1a). As if he could not state his meaning too strongly, Paul follows the rhetorical question with μὴ γένοιτο. His formulation mirrors 1 Sam 12:22 and Ps 93:14 LXX: οὐκ ἀπώσεται κύριος τὸν λαὸν αὐτοῦ. He substitutes the future ἀπώσεται with the aorist ἀπώσατο, however, and thus makes Rom 11:2a confirm the fulfillment of the OT promise.[25] In light of this OT allusion it becomes clear that the false inference is "tantamount to asking, 'has God broken His explicit promise not to cast off His people?'."[26] The strength of the OT promise thus gives additional force to Paul's denial. God has not rejected Israel but has remained faithful according to the promise.

Not only God's faithfulness to God's promise militates against Israel's rejection. Also Israel's unique relationship to God as "his people" makes their rejection unthinkable. For to be God's people is to be "foreknown" by God: τὸν λαὸν αὐτοῦ ὃν προέγνω (11:2). Divine foreknowledge refers to God's election in eternity of a people to be set apart for God.[27] That is,

---

[24] Had some inferred from Paul's gospel that God had to reject God's people because they did not believe? (so Sanday and Headlam, *Rom*, 307). Or did some suppose Paul to think that Israel's unbelief resulted from God's supposed rejection? (so Munck, *Christus*, 80). In any case, Paul gives no place to the inference that God has rejected Israel.

[25] The promise in 1 Sam 12:22 occurs after Israel rejected God as their king. Its original setting thus makes the OT promise even more applicable to the present context in which Israel has rejected the Messiah. In the OT, God punished, but did not reject, Israel (cf. Jer 38:37 LXX [= 31:36 MT]). Cf. Strathmann, λαός, *TWNT* 4, 36.

[26] Cranfield, *Rom*, 544; similarly, Gaugler, *Röm* II, 158; cf. Wilckens, *Röm* II, 236.

[27] Cf. Deut. 4:37; 7:6; 14:2; Ps 134:4 LXX. ὃν προέγνω does not allude to God's prior knowledge of his people's deeds and character, against Chrysostom, *Hom. in ep. ad Rom.*, 577. For a discussion on the possible implications of the prefix προ-, see Munck, *Christus*, 82, n. 139. Dreyfus ("Passé," 142) sees in 11:2 the strongest evidence in Romans 9–11 for the election of the whole people, though he later claims that Israel as a whole was never elect (144).

Israel's election is inherent to their identity as the people of God. Election is the inalienable privilege of God's people. In this light the incongruity of the idea that God has rejected God's people becomes clear.[28] Divine foreknowledge of Israel thus provides an additional ground for Paul's denial in 11:1a that God has rejected his people.[29]

Paul finds yet another reason why God cannot have rejected Israel: the existence of a faithful remnant (11:1b–6). The Jews who have believed in Christ constitute this remnant. They prove that God has clearly not rejected Israel; otherwise no Israelites would have a share in Messianic salvation.[30] Paul himself belongs to this remnant made up of Jewish Christians: καὶ γὰρ ἐγὼ Ἰσραηλίτης εἰμί, ἐκ σπέρματος Ἀβραάμ, φυλῆς Βενιαμίν (11:1b). Paul's pointing to himself as an example of the remnant is rhetorically highly effective: "Eindringlicher kann man rhetorisch und dialektisch nicht verfahren—leiblich eintretende Vernunft."[31] Paul's use of his own example buttresses his argument in still another way. It shows the ridiculousness of the inference that Paul's gospel leaves no more room for Israel in salvation history—if Paul did imply this, he would exclude *himself* (11:1b).[32]

Furthermore, God has always preserved a faithful remnant among Israel. So Paul can link the present remnant with the one in OT times. In chap. 9 he interprets the Jewish Christian minority ("whom he has called...from the Jews," 9:24) according to the prophetic word that "a remnant (ὑπόλειμμα)

---

[28] Cf. Gaugler (*Röm* II, 163): "Mag Israel ihn zurückstossen, er verstösst nie mehr, was er einmal in seiner Liebe 'erkannte'."

[29] Cranfield, *Rom*, 545; Mayer, *Heilsratschluß*, 247. The argument that divine foreknowledge precludes rejection does not contradict 9:7–13, where Paul emphasizes God's sovereignty in dealing with God's elect people. In the earlier passage Israel is not rejected but excluded from *present* participation in salvation. Käsemann (*Rom*, 299) summarizes: Election "does not establish human claims, but it allows no escape from the divine claim which is raised with it." On the relation of the two passages, see Munck, *Christus*, 82, in dialogue with Jülicher; cf. also Zeller, *Juden*, 127, 128.

[30] Munck (*Christus*, 81): "Die christlichen Juden verbürgen, daß die Gesamtheit des Volkes nicht verstossen sein kann." Zeller (*Juden*, 128, n. 193, following Schrenk) suggests that Paul picks up the positive aspect of the remnant concept seen in postexilic and Qumran thought in which "die Übriggebliebenen...bestätigen...die unaufgebbare Zuwendung Gottes zu seinem Volk" (128, 129). Paul, however, gives the remnant a completely different significance for the rest of the people than was attributed to the remnant in Qumran, see below with n. 38.

[31] Steiger, "Schutzrede," 54.

[32] The suggestion that Paul points to his own example because of his prior resistance to Christ in order to make plausible the salvation of the now resistant majority (so Munck, *Christus*, 81; Vischer, "Geheimnis," 114; similarly, Käsemann, *Rom*, 299) probably sees more in the text than is actually intended. Cf. Gaugler's reservations, *Röm* II, 161.

will be saved" and that "the Lord Sabaoth has left you a seed" ($\sigma\pi\acute{\epsilon}\rho\mu\alpha$, 9:27–29). The remnant of Elijah's time also parallels the present faithful minority (11:2b–4). Although the whole nation of Israel appeared to Elijah to have apostatized, God had kept "seven thousand who have not bowed the knee to Baal" (see 1 Kgs 19:10–18 LXX).[33] Paul comments: "So also in the present time there is a remnant..." (11:5).

The remnant throughout the ages demonstrates that human apostasy and divine judgment do not imply the rejection of God's people. Rather, God preserves a remnant in demonstration of God's lasting commitment to God's people. The continued existence of a remnant thus testifies to the ongoing significance of Israel's divine election.[34] Through the remnant, God's people survives and their unique relation to God is maintained. But God's commitment extends to the whole people Israel, not merely to the individuals who make up the remnant. The number seven thousand, referring to the remnant in Elijah's time, reflects not merely a traditional estimate of the number of Israelites who remained faithful, but also makes the remnant a symbol for the whole people, given the connotations of completeness attaching to the number seven and its multiples in the Bible and Judaism.[35] Moreover, Paul describes the remnant as $\kappa\alpha\tau$' $\grave{\epsilon}\kappa\lambda o\gamma\grave{\eta}\nu$ $\chi\acute{\alpha}\rho\iota$-$\tau o\varsigma$ $\gamma\acute{\epsilon}\gamma o\nu\epsilon\nu$ (11:5). God's commitment to Israel is not "through works," but "by grace" (11:6). If God's grace is what accounts for the present salvation of a remnant, then there is hope for the unbelieving majority.[36] The remnant thus inspires hope for all Israel both as a symbol of the whole people and as the creation of God's elective grace.[37]

God has not rejected Israel. Not even the unbelieving Jews—as opposed to the believing remnant—have been cast aside.[38] In 11:7 Paul offers an alternative explanation of Israel's present condition. God has saved the

---

[33] On God's judgment, rather than annihilation, of God's people, cf. Isa 46:3, 4. See, further, Günther and Krienke, "Remnant," *NIDNTT* 3, 252, 253.

[34] Clements, "Remnant," 118.

[35] Cf. Cranfield, *Rom*, 546–548; Luz, *Geschichtsverständnis*, 80.

[36] Cranfield, *Rom*, 547, 548; Munck, *Christus*, 83, 84; Michel, *Röm*, 340.

[37] Johnson ("Romans 11," 94) contrasts the significance of the remnant in chap. 11 as a symbol of hope for Israel with its significance in chap. 9 as a symbol of judgment on Israel. In the context of chap. 11 the remnant cannot be interpreted as a sign that God has faithfully saved part of Israel while rejecting the rest.

[38] Contrast Plag (*Wege*, 33): "Also sind die anderen...von Gott verworfen." Contrast also the sharp dissociation of the remnant and the rest of Israel in the DSS: *only* the remnant, not the rest, is truly elect and constitutes the community of salvation to whom the promises will be fulfilled (on this contrast, see Hofius, "Evangelium," 304–306, who refers correctly to the following references: 1QS 1:8, 10; 7:10, 12; 1QH 2:12; 6:8; 4QpPs37 2:5; 3:5; 4:11f.; 1QpHab 10:13).

remnant,[39] but the rest he has hardened: ἡ δὲ ἐκλογὴ ἐπέτυχεν· οἱ δὲ λοιποὶ ἐπωρώθησαν.[40] οὐκ ἀπώσατο ὁ Θεὸς τὸν λαὸν αὐτοῦ at 11:2, therefore, cannot mean "God has not *fully* rejected his people, as if a limited rejection had occurred.[41] For none have been rejected; rather, some have been hardened. The LXX, which Paul quotes here, consistently uses ὁ λαός for the whole people.[42] Word usage also, therefore, speaks against diluting the term to mean a part of God's people which has been spared rejection.

Two further points can be made in criticism of the view that God has partially rejected Israel. Paul does not use ὃν προέγνω which modifies λαός at 11:2 in a restrictive sense, as if to say that within the people of God there is a "foreknown people," and that this special foreknown group alone has not been rejected.[43] For God's foreknowledge connotes God's general election of Israel to be God's people.[44] Therefore, ὃν προέγνω must refer to the whole people in 11:2. ὃν προέγνω gives a ground ("God has not rejected his people, whom he foreknew"), not a restriction ("God has not rejected his people whom he foreknew"). The parallelism of 11:1a, where Paul uses the unqualified λαός αὐτοῦ in affirming that God has not rejected God's people, and 11:2a also speaks against a restrictive understanding of ὃν προέγνω[45] Further, although Paul identifies the Jewish remnant alone as ἡ ἐκλογή at 11:7,[46] he still considers Israel as a whole elect, as has already been observed. In keeping with his tendency to reserve election terminology for Christians, whose election has become manifest in their calling to present salvation, however, he uses ἐκλογή with its Christian connotations for the Jews who believe in Christ.[47] In summary, Paul claims

---

[39] Plag (*Wege*, 32, 33) says misleadingly that the remnant *still possesses* salvation, which implies that οἱ λοιποί have lost it and that Paul considers Israel's salvation "numerisch veränderlich" (so Plag).

[40] The OT quotations in 11:8–10 show ἐπωρώθησαν to be a divine passive. See Wilckens (*Röm* II, 238) and Cranfield (*Rom*, 551) against the interpretation "they hardened themselves."

[41] Against Schlier, *Röm*, 321; Plag, *Wege*, 32; Calvin, *Rom, ad loc.*

[42] Dreyfus, "Passé," 142.

[43] This is a common patristic interpretation.

[44] See above, p. 167 with n. 27.

[45] Cranfield, *Rom*, 545.

[46] Wilckens (*Röm* II, 238) argues correctly that ἡ ἐκλογή at 11:7a refers to Jewish Christians (also Käsemann, *Rom*, 300), not the Gentiles as elect, since ἡ ἐκλογή contrasts with οἱ λοιποί at 11:7b, which refers to the Jews who did not "attain." The abstract ἡ ἐκλογή stands here for the concrete οἱ ἐκλεκτοί and is better suited for stressing the ground for attainment—divine election, not human merit (Calvin, *Rom, ad loc.*; Sanday and Headlam, *Rom*, 318). Similarly, Gaugler, *Röm* II, 173.

[47] Cf. Dreyfus, "Passé," 141.

that God has hardened, not rejected Israel, not even partially.

The argument that God has hardened Israel provides further explanation for 9:6b. "Not all who are 'of Israel' are 'Israel'," for God has hardened those Jews who are not included in the present community of the saved. These hardened ones are the ones whom God has omitted to call to faith in the gospel, or, as Paul can also describe them, those who have rejected the gospel in unbelief. Paul can explain the exclusion of the greater part of God's people Israel from present salvation from more than one perspective—Israel's response to the gospel, and God's sovereign dealings with Israel. Both of these perspectives illuminate the meaning of 9:6b, which pertains to the present situation of Israel. And both perspectives figure in his explanation of the final destiny of Israel, as will be seen.

Paul substantiates[48] the claim, οἱ δὲ λοιποὶ ἐπωρώθησαν, by referring to God's hardening of Israel in OT times: "God gave them a spirit of numbness..." (11:8–10). These examples from scripture provide Paul with a precedent for the divine hardening which has fallen over Israel and thus make plausible his explanation of Israel's present state. But, though he has distinguished between rejection and hardening and shown that God has hardened Israel before, Paul has still not made clear the relationship between Israel's divine hardening and divine election. How are they compatible, whereas rejection and election are not? Paul addresses these matters in 11:11–32.

In this section Paul argues against the mistaken conclusion that the hardened majority within Israel is permanently excluded from salvation.[49] In so doing, he refutes the third of three false inferences from his gospel addressed in Romans 9–11. The third false inference is couched in the rhetorical question, "they have not stumbled so as to[50] fall, have they?" (11:11a).[51] "Stumbling" refers to the Jews' antagonistic reaction to the gospel as at 9:32 ("they stumbled over the stone of stumbling..."). The noun τὸ παράπτωμα αὐτῶν ("their trespass") in 11:11b expresses the same action denoted by the verb ἔπταισαν ("they stumbled") in 11:11a,[52]

---

[48] The quotations in 11:8–10 are introduced by καθὼς γέγραπται...καὶ Δαυὶδ λέγει.

[49] Cf. Aageson, "Scripture," 282; Cranfield, *Rom*, 549; Michel, *Röm*, 338.

[50] The ἵνα is ecbatic, see Cranfield, *Rom*, 554, 555; Sanday and Headlam, *Rom*, 321. Although a final ἵνα is grammatically possible, it makes no sense here, for the activity of stumbling has no express purpose.

[51] The third person plural denotes οἱ λοιποί of 11:7 who are under divine hardening (11:8–10).

[52] Some take τὸ ἥττημα αὐτῶν at 11:12 as "failure," in which case it would also denote the same action as "they stumbled." See Cranfield's discussion of the possible meanings of these terms (*Rom*, 555–557).

viz., the Jews' rejection of the gospel.[53] "So as to fall" ($\ell\nu\alpha\ \pi\epsilon\sigma\omega\sigma\iota\nu$) suggests that this "stumbling" over Christ as the "stone of stumbling" has lasting implications: Israel will not recover from their failure; their "falling" puts them beyond hope of salvation in Christ.[54] $\pi\ell\pi\tau\epsilon\iota\nu$ elsewhere can have these definitive connotations which the context gives it here.[55]

But Paul's rhetorical question denies that Israel's "stumbling" has such definitive consequences. And his following exclamation, $\mu\dot{\eta}\ \gamma\epsilon\nu o\iota\tau o$, adds emphasis to that denial. Rather ($\dot{\alpha}\lambda\lambda\dot{\alpha}$, 11:11b), Paul continues, introducing an alternative interpretation of Israel's "stumbling," it has had a positive effect. "By their transgression salvation [came] to the Gentiles...their transgression was riches for the world and their reduction was riches for the Gentiles" (11:11, 12); "their cutting off was reconciliation for the world" (11:15). This effect of the Jews' stumbling has positive significance not only for the Gentiles but also for the Jews themselves. Paul makes two points in this regard. First, the Gentiles' salvation will stir up the Jews' "jealousy" when they realize that the eschatological community of salvation is coming into being in the church,[56] and they will seek the same salvation which the Gentiles did. This will happen in fulfillment of Deut 32:21 LXX, which Paul has quoted in 10:19 ($\dot{\epsilon}\gamma\dot{\omega}\ \pi\alpha\rho\alpha\zeta\eta\lambda\dot{\omega}\sigma\omega\ \dot{\upsilon}\mu\dot{\alpha}s\ \dot{\epsilon}\pi'\ o\dot{\upsilon}\kappa\ \dot{\epsilon}\theta\nu\epsilon\iota...$). Paul hopes that his own ministry will contribute to the Jews' "jealousy" for salvation (11:14). His longing to "save some of them" is further proof that he does not consider the hardened majority permanently excluded from salvation.[57] But even more significantly, Paul's formulation in 11:11, $\epsilon\dot{\iota}s\ \tau\dot{o}\ \pi\alpha\rho\alpha\zeta\eta\lambda\dot{\omega}\sigma\alpha\iota\ \alpha\dot{\upsilon}\tau o\dot{\upsilon}s$, expresses the *divine* intention that the Gentiles' salvation will result in that of more Jews through their growing "jealous."[58] Paul thus begins to portray God's hardening of the Jews as a foil for God's continued mercy toward them.

The Jews' stumbling has benefited the Gentiles by opening the door to salvation for them. Moreover, Paul anticipates a further benefit which the Gentiles will gain through the Jews. The coming benefit will even surpass in greatness that already won, because it will have a surpassingly greater cause. "If their transgression was riches for the world and their reduction,

---

[53] Cranfield, *Rom*, 557; Schlier, *Röm*, 328.

[54] Cf. Steiger ("Schutzrede," 54): "...solche die verstockt bleiben."

[55] Cf., e.g., Isa 8:15; 24:20 LXX; *Ps. Sol.* 3:10. See Cranfield, *Rom*, 554, 555; Hofius, "Evangelium," 306, 307 with n. 35. Nevertheless, in 11:22 Paul switches to the weak meaning of $\pi\ell\pi\tau\epsilon\iota\nu$, where it does not imply that "the ones who have fallen" suffer lasting consequences. See below, p. 200 with n. 245.

[56] So Wilckens, *Röm* II, 250.

[57] Cf. v. Kölichen, "Zitate," 55.

[58] Cranfield, *Rom*, 556.

riches for the Gentiles, how much more their fullness.... For if their cutting off was reconciliation for the world, what [will] their reception [be] but life from the dead?!" (11:12, 15).[59] That second, greater cause of the Gentiles' benefit will be not the Jews' rejection of the gospel but τὸ πλήρωμα αὐτῶν (11:12), in other words, their πρόσλημψις (11:15) by God. While explaining what second, greater benefit will come to the Gentiles through the Jews, Paul has again revealed his hope concerning the hardened Jews.

The content of this hope is expressed in the terms τὸ πλήρωμα αὐτῶν and ἡ πρόσλημψις. The latter term refers to God's final acceptance of presently unbelieving Israel[60] after their time of being put aside, ἡ ἀπο- βολὴ αὐτῶν.[61] τὸ πλήρωμα αὐτῶν indicates the scope of this acceptance. Like τὸ πλήρωμα τῶν ἐθνῶν at 11:25,[62] the Jews' πλήρωμα at 11:12 is best taken to connote wholeness in contrast to incompleteness. It is the antonym to ἥττημα as "reduction."[63] In the conversion of the unbelieving Jewish majority and their reunification with the believing remnant salvation will come to the "fullness" of Israel.[64] Thus the future πλήρωμα will en- compass more than the few already believing Jewish Christians and the additional converts Paul hopes to make through his preaching of the gospel (11:14).[65] It will include all appointed to salvation in Israel.

Israel's πλήρωμα will result in ζωὴ ἐκ νεκρῶν (11:15). This statement of the result of Israel's salvation sheds light on that salvation itself. For ζωὴ

---

[59] Paul argues *a minori ad maius* (Wilckens, *Röm* II, 243).

[60] Cranfield, *Rom*, 562.

[61] Gaugler, *Röm* II, 186.

[62] τὸ πλήρωμα τῶν ἐθνῶν at 11:25 refers to the eschatological measure of the Gentiles and corresponds to πᾶς Ἰσραήλ as the "whole nation." These two observa- tions point to its quantitative sense. See Wilckens, *Röm* II, 243; cf. Stuhlmann, *Eschato- logische Maβ*, 186.

[63] With Wilckens, *Röm* II, 243 with n. 22; Hofius, "Evangelium," 307, 308.

[64] For this quantitative understanding of πλήρωμα at 11:12, see Wilckens, *Röm* II, 243. Others take it not quantitatively but qualitatively as denoting conversion. For rep- resentatives of both views, see Stuhlmann, *Eschatologische Maβ*, 185, nn. 19, 20. Since παράπτωμα and ἥττημα are correlates to πλήρωμα in 11:12, their meanings are brought to bear on the question whether πλήρωμα is quantitative or qualitative. ἥττημα can be taken either quantitatively ("fraction") or qualitatively ("failure"). παράπτωμα however cannot be understood quantitatively. But, in spite of its formal correspondence to πλήρωμα, there need not be a material correspondance which would force us to take πλήρωμα too in a qualitative sense. Instead it has been suggested that ἥττημα, which can have quantitative and qualitative meanings, both picks up the qualitative aspect of the preceding παράπτωμα and introduces a quantitative aspect in preparation for the following (quantitative) πλήρωμα (Stuhlmann, *Eschatologische Maβ*, 185, 186).

[65] Since the Jews converted through the Gentile mission constitute only a small group (τινὰς ἐξ αὐτῶν, 11:14), it is unlikely that Paul expects the salvation of the full number of Israel to come about in this way (Luz, *Geschichtsverständnis*, 393).

ἐκ νεκρῶν most probably refers to the general resurrection.[66] This interpretation fits Paul's argument that the second benefit the Gentiles will receive through the Jews will be greater than the first.[67] For resurrection from the dead will usher in the consummation of the salvation begun in the first benefit, ἡ καταλλαγή and ὁ πλοῦτος κόσμου/ἐθνῶν.[68] In 8:23 Paul described that consummation as ἡ ἀπολύτρωσις τοῦ σώματος. Here, in a similar way, he anticipates "life from the dead" as God's final work of salvation.[69] The time of Israel's πλήρωμα, therefore, will be the time of completion of salvation. The salvation of now hardened Israel will fall together with the eschatological events of the last days. Israel's "fullness" and "acceptance" will be the "Stoß, der das Endheil ins Rollen bringt."[70]

In summary, in 11:11–15 Paul begins to show that God's hardening of Israel does not imply permanent exclusion from salvation but is temporally limited.[71] He foresees instead Israel's future participation in salvation. They will become "jealous" for the salvation they see among the Gentiles. The "fullness" of the Jews will join in this salvation through God's final "acceptance." Because of its temporariness, divine hardening of the Jews, which resulted in their present exclusion from salvation, does not contradict their election as the people of God, which implies the accomplishment of God's saving purpose toward them.

With the help of an extended metaphor, the olive tree, in the next section (11:16–24) Paul illustrates how Israel's hardening and present exclusion from salvation can—and will—be reversed.[72] Paul is not only defending his gospel against a false inference here; he is also attacking an erroneous view actually held by his Gentile readers in Rome.[73] The boastful Gentile

---

[66] So Cranfield, *Rom*, 563; Vischer, "Geheimnis," 122; Wilckens, *Röm* II, 245; Hofius, "Evangelium," 317.

[67] Since ζωὴ ἐκ νεκρῶν is a benefit the *Gentiles* will receive, the term cannot refer to *Israel's* spiritual vivification. Anyway, Israel's spiritual vivification (ἡ πρόσλημψις or τὸ πλήρωμα αὐτῶν) is the cause of ζωὴ ἐκ νεκρῶν and thus will have occurred prior to it (Zeller, *Juden*, 241; Schrenk, *Weissagung*, 68, n. 41).

[68] Because the second benefit will be greater than the first, ζωὴ ἐκ νεκρῶν cannot refer simply to a further spiritual vivification of the Gentiles (Zeller, *Juden*, 241). Anyway, the "fullness of the Gentiles" will have already "come in" (11:25), making a further spiritual vivification of the Gentiles unnecessary (see Cranfield's criticisms, *Rom*, 526, 527; contrast Plag, *Wege*, 34).

[69] ζωὴ ἐκ νεκρῶν is more than a temporal reference (as if equal to ἀνάστασις ἐκ νεκρῶν), with Zeller, *Juden*, 243; cf. Schlier, *Röm*, 329.

[70] Schrenk, *Weissagung*, 34. Cf. Vischer, "Geheimnis," 123.

[71] With Hofius, "Evangelium," 308.

[72] Similarly, Hofius, "Evangelium," 310.

[73] Ὑμῖν δὲ λέγω τοῖς ἔθνεσιν (11:13) begins the direct address to the Gentile readers which is sustained through v. 31.

Christians apparently assume that the Jews, whose empty place on the olive tree they have filled, are permanently cut off from salvation (11:23, 24). But Paul proves them wrong in a number of ways.

The olive tree, a familiar designation for the people of God in the OT and Judaism,[74] represents the community of the saved. The present constitution of the olive tree matches that of Ἰσραήλ at 9:6bβ as the community of participants in Messianic salvation.[75] Paul admits that God has pruned[76] some branches of the tree—the unbelieving Jews (11:17)—in order to graft in branches from the wild olive—Gentile believers (11:19). But the original branches, though now pruned, can be grafted in the olive tree again.[77] Paul mentions such a regrafting three times (11:23a, 23b, 24). Further, he provides reasons to expect it to take place.

First, even the wild olive branches were grafted in the cultivated olive and made to share its root, though they did not belong to it by nature (11:24a).[78] W. Vischer calls the "Widernatürliche in diesem Gleichnis gerade die Spitze."[79] If even the unexpected has taken place, how much more plausible is the regrafting of the original branches in the olive, Paul argues *a minori ad maius*.[80] But not only the *fact* of the wild olive branches' engrafting in the cultivated olive tree serves to suggest the future regrafting of the natural branches. The *purpose* of the wild branches' engrafting does also. The engrafting of wild olive shoots *was* undertaken in the ancient world, namely, when a well-established tree failed to produce a proper yield, and with the single purpose of *rejuvenating* the ailing tree.[81] Paul's reference to this procedure thus does not reveal his ignorance of arboriculture but his clever allusion to a familiar practice in order to "stress God's intention to save Israel."[82] These human practices and natural processes, of course, are meant to portray the working of divine grace and power in

---

[74] Jer 11:16; Hos 14:6; *b. Men.* 53b. See Maurer, ῥίζα, *TWNT* 6, 985, 986; Behm, ἄμπελος, *TDNT* 1, 342.

[75] Cf. Hofius, "Evangelium," 308: "Der 'edle Ölbaum'...meint die Heilsgemeinde Israel, d. h. das Ἰσραήλ von 9, 6bβ."

[76] On the divine passives in 11:17–24, see Rengstorf, "Gleichnis," 157, n. 4.

[77] By contrast, in actual practice, pruned branches were normally cast into the fire (see Rengstorf, "Gleichnis," 154).

[78] παρὰ φύσιν contrasts with κατὰ φύσιν (11:20, 24). Cranfield (*Rom*, 571, 572) explains: "It is the grafting of a branch on to a tree to which it does not belong by nature which is being characterized as contrary to nature."

[79] Vischer, "Geheimnis," 126. Cf. Schrenk, *Weissagung*, 33.

[80] Jeremias, "Römer 11, 25–36," 193.

[81] Baxter and Ziesler ("Arboriculture," 26) have rightly pointed to Columella, *De re rustica* 5.9.16 for this practice.

[82] Baxter and Ziesler, "Arboriculture," 29.

salvation history.[83] And since only God's sovereign grace has made the Gentiles' salvation possible, it is even more likely than the metaphor itself can suggest (on the basis of natural law) that that same grace and power will come to the Jews' aid, resulting in their salvation.[84] Indeed, Paul makes it known that not only does God's engrafting the Gentiles reveal God's intention to regraft the Jews but also that "God is able to graft them in again" (11:24).

This confident assertion[85] of God's power to restore the pruned olive branches apparently guards against the supposition that disobedient and hardened Israel can never regain its place among God's people. It seems that Gentile Christians, who had not been cut off from the olive tree, considered pruning an irreversible procedure. Once severed from the root, the Jews would remain forever outside of salvation. Paul strongly disagrees. And in principle it is impossible for the Gentile church, which draws its own life from God's grace toward sinners, to think the Jews beyond reach of this grace.[86] Driving home his point that the Jews' hardening is not irreversible, Paul affirms not only that God is able, moreover, he *will* graft the broken off branches back in the olive tree: οἱ κατὰ φύσιν ἐγκεντρισθή σονται τῇ ἰδίᾳ ἐλαίᾳ (11:24b).[87] This unambiguous assertion of Israel's future salvation forms the climax of Paul's argument using the olive tree metaphor.

Although Paul gives weighty reasons for the Jews' future regrafting in the olive tree, he does not neglect the problem of their unbelief in the gospel. "And they too, if they do not continue in unbelief, will be grafted in" (11:23). Thus they will not become part of the olive tree as unbelievers but only as believers in Jesus Christ. Their incorporation into the community of salvation implies their salvation by faith in Christ.[88] In summary, the metaphor of the olive tree illustrates that Israel's present exclusion from

---

[83] Cf. Hahn, "Römer 11.26a," 226.

[84] Paul plays up the Jews' relation "by nature" to the "olive tree" in order to deflate the pride of Gentile Christians, whose relation is "unnatural" (Müller, *Gerechtigkeit*, 44). The Jews' natural relation to the olive tree, however, does not give them a right to be regrafted in. God's power and kindness alone accounts for their, as for the Gentiles', grafting in the olive tree. Thus Paul's argument from the Jews' *natural* relation to the olive tree can be attributed to his polemic against Gentile Christian pride (cf. Zeller, *Juden*, 244).

[85] So Michel, *Röm*, 352, n. 33.

[86] Wilckens, *Röm* II, 249. God's δύναμις is concretely his power to justify sinners by his grace (cf. Zeller, *Juden*, 244, 245).

[87] Hofius ("Evangelium," 310) observes the advance in Paul's argument ("zwei sich steigernde Sätze").

[88] See Wilckens, *Röm*, 250; Käsemann, *Rom*, 310; Zeller, *Juden*, 245; Müller, *Zuvorersehung*, 49.

salvation is not irreversible. Just how the change in their hardened state will come about, Paul goes on to reveal.

In 11:25–32 Paul's argument regarding Israel's destiny in Romans 9–11 comes to a climax. With a specificity and clarity greater than in his previous statements, here he claims that "all Israel will be saved" (11:26a). In support of this dramatic claim he elucidates the nature and purpose of the divine hardening over Israel. He also relates God's election of Israel to the final purpose of saving God's people. Paul's argument at this juncture is more compelling than ever because it is based on τὸ μυστήριον τοῦτο (11:25), known only through divine impartation.[89] Paul closes his defense of God's faithfulness toward unbelieving but elect Israel with the weightiest of all arguments.[90]

Whereas Paul has earlier implied that the partial hardening over unbelieving Israel[91] is temporary, now he unreservedly states that the hardening will last only until the "fullness of the Gentiles comes in": πώρωσις ἀπὸ μέρους τῷ Ἰσραὴλ γέγονεν ἄχρι οὗ τὸ πλήρωμα τῶν ἐθνῶν εἰσ ἔλθῃ (11:25b).[92] Borrowing from Jewish apocalyptic thought, Paul uses the idea of a *numerus iustorum*, which must be complete before the promise comes to fulfillment.[93] The full number[94] of elect Gentiles must "enter" by participating in the salvation inaugurated by the Messiah.[95] This salvation

---

[89] Bornkamm, μυστήριον, *TDNT* 4, 823; Hofius, "Evangelium," 310.

[90] See Siegert, *Argumentation*, 172.

[91] ἀπὸ μέρους is adnominal to πώρωσις and alludes to the limitation of the hardening to οἱ λοιποί (cf. 11:7; cf. also 11:17, τινες τῶν κλάδων ἐξεκλάσθησαν); see Hofius, "Evangelium," 312.

[92] Stuhlmann (*Eschatologische Maß*, 183) observes: "In der Limitierungsaussage liegt das Novum gegenüber dem Vorangehenden und darum die Spitze des Prophetenspruchs." Cf. Munck, *Christus*, 99; Zeller, *Juden*, 251. On possible OT sources of Paul's notion of a limited duration of Israel's hardening, see Hofius, "Evangelium," 323; Kim, *Origin*, 96.

[93] For a fuller explanation of the *numerus iustorum*, see Stuhlmann, *Eschatologische Maß*, 169. For its use, see esp. 4 Ezra 4:33–37. For other NT uses of the notion of the "eschatological measure," consult Jeremias, "Römer 11, 25–36," 196, 197.

[94] πλήρωμα has a quantitative sense (see Mayer, *Heilsratschluß*, 283). It means "the complete number pre-determined by God from among the Gentiles" (with Gaugler, *Röm* II, 204; Schrenk, *Weissagung*, 34; Mayer, 283; Hofius, "Evangelium," 313; somewhat differently, Schlier, *Röm*, 339). Although we cannot rule out the possibility that this fixed number might be identical with the sum of the whole (with Barrett, *Rom*, 223), the term itself is numerically ambiguous, for its numerical value is known only by the electing God (cf. Schlier, 339). Thus we ought not to interpret πλήρωμα as "all the Gentiles" or even as "a great number of Gentiles" ("Vielzahl," so Hahn, 229). πλήρωμα gets its plenitude not from its size as such but from the fact that it contains the entire number fixed by God (so Ponsot, "Tout Israël," 411; cf. Gal 4:4).

[95] The context makes it clear that to "enter" means to participate in Messianic salvation. Cf. Wilckens, *Röm* II, 254, 255; Hofius, "Evangelium," 313. For the figurative

of the fullness of the Gentiles will signify the completion of God's redemptive work among them and the turning point in God's dealings with Israel.[96] Thus Israel's hardening will last only "until the fullness of the Gentiles comes in."[97]

"Until," or ἄχρι οὗ, has more than simply temporal significance here. Paul does not want merely to foretell the sequence of events leading up to Israel's salvation. He is also interested in illuminating the relationship between these events. He has already shown how Israel's exclusion from salvation facilitated the inclusion of the Gentiles (11:11, 12, 15). Indeed, therein lay its very purpose (11:19). Israel's hardening is thus inherently instrumental. Having served its purpose of facilitating the Gentiles' salvation, therefore, the hardening will cease.[98] It is thus correct to see a final aspect in ἄχρι οὗ and translate: "until the reaching of the goal when."[99] With the accomplishment of its purpose, Israel's hardening will end and the once hardened Jews will enter through the open door to salvation.[100]

The revelation that the hardening over Israel will be lifted is the stepping stone to the climax of Paul's argument: "All Israel will be saved"

---

meaning of εἰσέρχεσθαι as "share in something," see BAGD, s.v. εἰσέρχομαι, 2.a.

[96] Paul has radically altered the Zion tradition which he draws upon with the term εἰσέρχεσθαι (see Käsemann, *Rom*, 312; Stuhlmacher, "Römer 11, 25–32," 560, 561; Hofius, "Evangelium," 313; cf. Stuhlmann, *Eschatologische Maß*, 166; Jeremias, "Römer 11, 25–36," 197; Wilckens, *Röm* II, 255 with n. 1145). He reverses the order in this tradition, so that the Jews follow the Gentiles in salvation. Hofius ("Evangelium," 324) suggests Isa 59:19, 20; 45:14–17, 20–25; Mic 4:1–8 as possible sources of inspiration for this reversal. But, though transformed in his hands, the tradition retains its original intention of affirming Israel's salvation (Stuhlmann, 167, 168, 172).

[97] Could Paul's pessimistic outlook on the Jews in 1 Thess 2:16—ἔφθασεν δὲ ἐπ' αὐτοὺς ἡ ὀργὴ εἰς τέλος—parallel Rom 11:25 by suggesting a temporal limitation to the divine judgment on the Jews? If εἰς τέλος is taken restrictively and translated "until the end" (see BAGD, s.v. τέλος, 1.d.γ.; so Synofzik, *Gerichtsaussagen*, 36), the limitation of divine wrath to the period preceding the eschatological climax would liken the limitation of divine hardening to the time of the Gentiles' salvation ("until the fullness of the Gentiles comes in"). The passages are already linked by their common use of the motif of the eschatological measure (ἀναπληροῦν, 1 Thess 2:16, and πλήρωμα, Rom 11:25; see Synofzik, *Gerichtsaussagen*, 35, 36). Differences in tone can be attributed to the contrasting contexts: opposition to Paul's Gentile mission in 1 Thessalonians 2 and Paul's hope of Israel's salvation in Romans 11 (see Kim, *Origin*, 98). 1 Thess 2:16 thus may not reflect an earlier stage in Paul's thinking (for representatives of this view, see Kim, 98, n. 3) or be simply a late anti-Jewish interpolation (for representatives of this view, see Kim, 98, n. 4). The question is nevertheless difficult to decide.

[98] Cf. Stuhlmann, *Eschatologische Maß*, 184.

[99] So Jeremias, "Römer 11, 25–36," 196; cf. Hofius, "Evangelium," 312, 313; *idem*, "Bis daß er kommt," 439–441. Cf. 1 Cor 11:26; 15:25; Luke 21:24.

[100] Kim (*Origin*, 97) thinks that Isa 6:13 may have helped Paul to infer Israel's eventual salvation from the limited duration of Israel's hardening.

(11:26a). The limited duration of Israel's hardening makes such a claim plausible. 11:25b, which supplies the information on the temporariness of the hardening, therefore functions as the logical prerequisite to the statement, "all Israel will be saved."[101] It thus seems good to take καὶ οὕτως in 11:26a, as logical or inferential[102] (while the temporal connotations are supplied by the context, not καὶ οὕτως[103]). "Die Worte καὶ οὕτως πᾶς Ἰσραὴλ σωθήσεται besagen also, daß die Rettung 'ganz Israels' erst dann erfolgen *kann*, dann aber auch ganz gewiß erfolgen *wird*, wenn das 'Eingehen' der von Gott erwählten Heiden in die Heilsgemeinde Israel zum Abschluß gekommen sein wird."[104]

Some, however, take καὶ οὕτως to indicate the mode of Israel's salvation: "In this way all Israel will be saved." They suggest either that καὶ οὕτως refers back ("rückweisend") to the mode of salvation mentioned in the preceding,[105] or that it refers forward ("vorausweisend") to the mode of salvation mentioned in the following.[106] But both versions are problematic in that they transfer attention away from the *fact* of Israel's future salvation to the *way* it will occur. Paul has not previously stated with great clarity and force *that* Israel will be saved. Thus the reader is not yet prepared for a statement of *how*.[107] Now that Paul has revealed the temporariness of Israel's hardening, would he complicate this opportunity to predict beyond a shadow of a doubt *that* Israel will be saved?[108] The modal view robs πᾶς Ἰσραὴλ σωθήσεται of its climactic character and shifts attention to the

---

[101] Michel, *Röm*, 355. Cf. Siegert's argumentation, *Argumentation*, 172.

[102] Cf. 1 Thess 4:17. Hofius ("Evangelium," 315, n. 74) notes correctly also the following references with καὶ οὕτως in this sense: Sir 32 (35):1; 33 (36):4; 1 Macc 13:47; 4 Macc 1:12; *T. Job* 5:3; *Apoc. Mos.* 37; *Barn.* 7:8; Philogelos §§57, 243 (cf. also 3). See BAGD, s.v. οὕτως, 1.b.; LSJ, s.v. οὕτως, II. Hofius captures the logical meaning of καὶ οὕτως with the translation, "und als das geschehen war, da...," or "und wenn das geschehen sein wird, dann...." Kim (*Origin*, 84) renders "so" or "therefore." See also Michel, *Röm*, 355; Zeller, *Juden*, 251; more vaguely, Murray, *Rom*, 96.

[103] See pp. 180, 181 below.

[104] Hofius, "Evangelium," 315.

[105] Cf. Rom 5:12. For representatives of this view, see Wilckens, *Röm* II, 255, n. 1149.

[106] In this view, καθὼς γέγραπται (with καθώς as a correlative particle) introduces the modus. For representatives of this view, see Wilckens, *Röm* II, 255, n. 1148.

[107] Kim (*Origin*, 83) notes the difficulty in the transition of thought required by the modal view.

[108] Although Paul's earlier assertions of Israel's future salvation (11:11, 12, 15, 24) are clear enough, the assertion in 11:26a has exceeding force because it is based on the revelation of the mystery and is thus not superfluous. Schlier's (*Röm*, 338) overestimation of the sufficiency of the previous assertions that Israel will be saved leads him wrongly to the modal view of καὶ οὕτως.

particular mode of salvation supposedly introduced by καὶ οὕτως.[109] Not only is this shift in focus unexpected—it also seems out of place in Paul's polemic against Gentile Christians. For they disputed not how but whether at all Israel as a whole would be saved.[110]

Other difficulties also militate against the modal interpretation of καὶ οὕτως. The modal view which takes οὕτως as "rückweisend" suffers from the difficulty of finding in the preceding ὅτι-clause (11:25b) a description of how all Israel will be saved.[111] The ὅτι-clause really describes what happens *before* Israel's salvation (namely, their hardening and the Gentiles' salvation), not the event of their salvation itself.[112] The interpretation of οὕτως as "vorausweisend" and correlative with καθώς has been discredited even on formal grounds—inconsistency with Pauline linguistic usage, syntactical considerations, and the unlikelihood that the formal καθὼς γέγραπται is logically connected to καὶ οὕτως.[113] Further, 11:26b, 27 stands in a supportive relationship to 11:26a: καθὼς γέγραπται introduces a ground.[114] Thus the mixed quotation at 11:26b, 27 is meant first and foremost to support the *fact* of Israel's future salvation, the claim of 11:26a.[115] It so happens that this supportive argument suggests the *mode* of Israel's future salvation—through the Redeemer who will come from Zion[116]—though this is not its primary purpose.

Other interpreters take καὶ οὕτως as temporal (= καὶ τότε). Criticism levelled elsewhere against this view has rendered it unpersuasive.[117] Although καὶ οὕτως can have no temporal meaning here, the inference it introduces is nevertheless temporally determined, since the prerequisites

---

[109] See, e.g., Mayer, *Heilsratschluß*, 289, 290; Schlier, *Röm*, 338.

[110] Stuhlmann, *Eschatologische Maß*, 165, n. 11; against Mayer, *Heilsratschluß*, 289.

[111] Hofius, "Evangelium," 314.

[112] Interpreters who describe the modus of Israel's future salvation as "auf unerwartete und paradoxe Weise" (Luz, *Geschichtsverständnis*, 294), or "auf schlechthin wunderbare Weise" (Wilckens, *Röm* II, 255) do not find that description in Paul's text. The reader must reflect on the text in order to find a modus. But, as Kim notes (*Origin*, 84, n. 1), "it is far-fetched to read out of the οὕτως Paul's idea that "Israel wird auf unerwartete paradoxe Weise gerettet'." Even Jeremias, who takes the modal view, translating οὕτως as "solcherart," fails to explain what he thinks this modus is ("Römer 11, 25–36," 198, 199).

[113] See Jeremias, "Römer 11, 25–36," 198; Hofius, "Evangelium," 315 with notes; Mußner, *Traktat*, 243; Müller, *Prophetie*, 226, 227.

[114] Those who take καὶ οὕτως as "rückweisend" share this view of καθὼς γέγραπται.

[115] Kim, *Origin*, 87. Those who take καὶ οὕτως as "rückweisend" agree.

[116] See comments on the mixed quotation at 11:26b, 27 below, p. 185 with n. 150.

[117] For supporters and critics of this view, see Wilckens, *Röm* II, 255, n. 1147.

for the salvation of all Israel are temporally specific. Israel's salvation will occur after the prerequisites for it have been met, i.e., after the fullness of the Gentiles has entered and Israel's hardening has ceased.[118] Nevertheless, Paul's interest here lies in developing a logical argument, not an eschatological timetable.[119] The logical/inferential view of καὶ οὕτως best takes this interest into account and derives most support from the context.

We now arrive at the heart of the mystery: πᾶς Ἰσραὴλ σωθήσεται. In this climactic statement, however, we have to do with a *crux interpretum*. Who is πᾶς Ἰσραήλ? Whose future but certain salvation forces the Gentile Christians to abandon their pessimism about Israel? Whose confidently anticipated redemption will answer the fundamental question of the trustworthiness of God's election? Four dominant interpretations of πᾶς Ἰσραήλ are found in the secondary literature: (1) all the elect Jews and Gentiles,[120] (2) the whole elect remnant from the nation Israel,[121] (3) the whole nation Israel, including every individual member,[122] (4) the whole nation Israel, not necessarily including every individual member.[123] What does the expression πᾶς Ἰσραήλ mean here?

The first view of πᾶς Ἰσραήλ as "all the elect Jews and Gentiles" has the least in its favor. Throughout chaps. 9–11 Ἰσραήλ never has the meaning this view attributes to it at 11:26a.[124] The inclusion of Gentiles with Jews in the term πᾶς Ἰσραήλ is in tension with the sustained contrast of these two groups in vv. 11–32.[125] The improbability that Paul would have used the term Ἰσραήλ with such different meanings side by side in v. 25 (where Ἰσραήλ refers the whole nation Israel) and v. 26, when the context itself suggests no such contrast,[126] but a parallelism,[127] also speaks against view (1).[128]

---

[118] Stuhlmann (*Eschatologische Maß*, 165) sees a "geschichtlichen Prozeß" in 11:25f. and gives καὶ οὕτως "temporalen Nebensinn"; similarly, Hofius, "Evangelium," 315.

[119] Cf. Kim, *Origin*, 85.

[120] E.g., Jeremias, "Römer 11, 25–36," 200; Calvin, *Rom, ad loc.*

[121] E.g., Bengel, *NT Commentary*, 132.

[122] E.g., Kühl, *Theodicee*, 329, 330; cf. Schmidt, *Judenfrage*, 37–41.

[123] E.g., Lagrange, *Rom*, 285; Barrett, *Rom*, 223, 224; Schlier, *Röm*, 340; Käsemann, *Rom*, 313.

[124] The interpretation of Ἰσραήλ at 9:6bβ (see also Gal 6:16) as the present community of the saved (which I favor; see p. 164 above) differs from view (1) in that it excludes the Israelites who are now hardened, though elect. The representatives of view (1), however, (rightly) want to include these Israelites in the πᾶς Ἰσραήλ who will be saved.

[125] Murray, *Rom*, 96.

[126] Compare 9:6b, where the context makes the contrast between the two uses of Ἰσραήλ obvious. Thus 9:6b does not help interpret 11:26a, against Jeremias, "Römer

The last-mentioned argument applies also to the second view of πᾶς Ἰσραήλ as "the whole elect remnant from the nation Israel." Further, this view makes Paul answer a question which he has not even raised—the future of the elect remnant—rather than the one he has raised—the future of the hardened Jews (11:1).[129] Moreover, it would be anticlimactic for Paul to claim simply that a select group of elect will be saved, after he has set the stage for something greater by revealing the temporariness of Israel's hardening. The earlier πρόσλημψις and τὸ πλήρωμα αὐτῶν as well as the olive tree metaphor also make the reader anticipate more. Finally, the fact that the elect remnant will be saved according to view (2) is no argument against Gentile Christians who prided themselves on having supposedly replaced the hardened Jews cut off from salvation.[130] This view does not fit in Paul's polemic.

Views (3) and (4) remain. Both take πᾶς Ἰσραήλ to be the "whole nation Israel." Much speaks in favor of this definition. It preserves a correspondence between Ἰσραήλ in v. 25 as the nation Israel and the same designation in v. 26. This interpretation of πᾶς Ἰσραήλ fits well in Paul's argument regarding unbelieving Israel's salvation because it includes the *hardened* Jews in "all Israel" who will be saved. It also serves Paul's polemic against Gentile Christian pride toward the Jews by affirming the salvation even of the Jews who are now cut off. It takes into account the contrast between ἀπὸ μέρους and πᾶς: *part* of the nation Israel is now excluded from salvation by a temporary hardening but *all* Israel as a nation will be saved once that hardening has ceased.[131] πᾶς Ἰσραήλ as the "whole nation Israel" is thus the sum of the remnant and the "rest" of the Jews who have been subject to divine hardening.[132] Not only the remnant, but "all Israel" will be saved. Thus God will attain his goal of the redemption of his whole people Israel.[133] The word πᾶς is emphatic.[134] The full

---

11, 25–36," 200, n. 35; Ponsot, "Tout Israël," 414; Richardson, *Israel*, 136. See Mußner's helpful comments, "Ganz Israel," 242.

[127] Murray, *Rom*, 96.

[128] See Stuhlmann, *Eschatologische Maß*, 180, for additional arguments.

[129] Mayer, *Heilsratschluß*, 285.

[130] Mayer, *Heilsratschluß*, 285.

[131] There is also an implicit contrast between πᾶς Ἰσραήλ and λεῖμμα (11:5), τὸ ὑπόλειμμα (9:27), cf. Schlier, *Röm*, 340; Hofius, "Evangelium," 316.

[132] So Mußner, "Ganz Israel," 243; Gaugler, *Röm* II, 202; Mayer, *Heilsratschluß*, 288; Dahl, *Studies in Paul*, 153. Paul's thought here parallels 11:12: the reuniting of the unbeliving majority (οἱ λοιποί) with the remnant (ἡ ἐκλογή) will constitute τὸ πλήρωμα αὐτῶν, the full number of Israel (Mußner, 243).

[133] Schrenk (*Weissagung*, 36) comments: "Es ist vielmehr irgendwie Wert darauf gelegt, daß noch einmal das ganze Volk vom Evangelium erfaßt werden soll."

attainment of the divine purpose is foremost in Paul's mind.[135] It shows the thoroughness of God's faithfulness to Israel.[136] Perhaps therein lies the reason Paul does not write καὶ οὕτως οἱ λοιποὶ σωθήσονται, a much less bold claim. With πᾶς Ἰσραήλ, by contrast, he can anticipate the motif of the boundlessness of God's mercy in 11:30–32 and the grandeur of God's gracious designs in 11:33–36. πᾶς Ἰσραήλ σωθήσεται is thus more than the logical inference from the fact that Israel's hardening is temporary. It has the ring of an acclamation:[137] God will save[138] God's *whole* people!

But does πᾶς Ἰσραήλ include each individual Israelite, or is the term used in a general sense allowing for exceptions? In the LXX and early Judaism "all Israel" does not imply numerical completeness, but completeness as a collectivity.[139] The strikingly close parallel to Rom 11:26a in *m. Sanh.* 10:1 goes so far as to name those excluded from this collectivity:

> All Israelites have a share in the world to come, for it is written, *Thy people also shall be all righteous, they shall inherit the land forever*;.... And these are they that have no share in the world to come: ....[140]

Although the earliest kernel of the passage consists simply in the opening statement regarding all Israel, whereas the exceptions which follow constitute later, gradual additions,[141] these additions probably merely serve to bring out the early non-numerical understanding of כָּל־יִשְׂרָאֵל.[142] The OT shows a similar freedom to designate as "all Israel," for example, simply a portion of the twelve tribes (cf. 1 Sam 18:16; 2 Sam 2:9; 3:21; 2 Chr 12:1) or a narrower group with a representative function (cf. 1 Sam 7:5; 11:15; 13:20; 2 Sam 15:6; 18:17; Deut 31:11; Judg 8:27).[143] These parallels thus lend support to the view that πᾶς Ἰσραήλ at Rom 11:26a does not

---

134 Mußner, *Traktat*, 55.
135 Schrenk, *Weissagung*, 37.
136 Cf. Michel, *Röm*, 356, n. 9.
137 Michel, *Röm*, 356.
138 σωθήσεται here is a divine passive.
139 See Siegert, *Argumentation*, 173.
140 Danby, *Mishnah*, 397.
141 See Wilckens, *Röm* II, 256.
142 Jeremias, "Römer 11, 25–36," 199, 200. Cf. Luz, *Geschichtsverständnis*, 290; Sanders, *Palestinian Judaism*, 149.
143 Plag, *Wege*, 47, 48. These parallels, however, do not justify limiting πᾶς Ἰσραήλ in Rom 11:26a to a segment of Israel, such as the non-Christian sector of Israel; against Plag, *Wege*, 47. As already noted, the thrust of Paul's argument is the salvation of Israel as a whole, so that πᾶς Ἰσραήλ is best taken to denote the whole nation. See Mayer's (*Heilsratschluß*, 287) criticisms of Plag's "qualitative" understanding of πᾶς Ἰσραήλ.

necessarily include all individual Israelites.[144] The term can connote completeness in a nonnumerical sense.

Without naming exceptions, therefore, Paul intends the designation "all Israel" to connote this nonnumerical type of completeness, or completeness as a collectivity.[145] At the same time, however, he gains the force of an unqualified statement: "All Israel will be saved."[146] With this formulation Paul directs attention to the destiny of the whole people, not individuals within it. He has already proven that some Israelites, himself included, have been saved. But his final aim is to show God's faithfulness to the people as a whole whom God has elected and will, in the end, bless with salvation through their own Messiah.

On examination, therefore, the view that "all Israel" ($\pi\hat{a}\varsigma$ $\,'I\sigma\rho\alpha\acute{\eta}\lambda$) at Rom 11:26a means the nation Israel as a complete collectivity turns out to be the best. Specifically, this collectivity will consist of the now hardened majority of the Jews and the believing remnant. Whereas at the present time, only a minority of Jewish Christians has participated in salvation and the rest have been hardened, in the future Israel as a whole will join in the salvation inaugurated by the Messiah. From this explanation it also appears that Paul is using the term $\pi\hat{a}\varsigma$ $\,'I\sigma\rho\alpha\acute{\eta}\lambda$ in a temporally limited way: it does not include all generations of Israel but refers specifically to the Jews who have responded to the gospel, either in belief or unbelief, but who will all be saved in the end.[147] To take $\pi\hat{a}\varsigma$ $\,'I\sigma\rho\alpha\acute{\eta}\lambda$ as a temporally limited designation best fits Paul's argument in Romans 9–11. The object of Paul's grief and hope in these chapters is the generation of Israel which largely rejected its own Messiah, not all generations of Israel. He pinpoints the sal-

---

[144] See Müller, *Gerechtigkeit*, 42, n. 87; Hofius, "Evangelium," 317. Some see support for this view of $\pi\hat{a}\varsigma$ $\,'I\sigma\rho\alpha\acute{\eta}\lambda$ in the corollary $\tau\grave{o}$ $\pi\lambda\acute{\eta}\rho\omega\mu\alpha$ $\tau\hat{\omega}\nu$ $\grave{\epsilon}\theta\nu\hat{\omega}\nu$, since it too does not necessarily include all the Gentiles (so, e.g., Schrenk, *Weissagung*, 35). This argument is not compelling, however.

[145] Benoit, "Conclusion," 418; Luz, *Geschichtsverständnis*, 291, 292; Zeller, *Juden*, 253ff.; Käsemann, *Rom*, 313; Schlier, *Röm*, 340, 341. Stuhlmann (*Eschatologische Maß*, 179), by contrast, interprets $\pi\hat{a}\varsigma$ $\,'I\sigma\rho\alpha\acute{\eta}\lambda$ to denote completeness in a numerical sense. He sees the notion of the eschatological measure behind $\pi\hat{a}\varsigma$ $\,'I\sigma\rho\alpha\acute{\eta}\lambda$ and defines it: "Die von Gott bestimmte Anzahl der Heilsempfänger aus dem jüdischen Volk." The context, however, suggests that Paul understood completeness in terms of groups (the remnant plus the hardened rest), not individuals. Correctly, Mayer (*Heilsratschluß*, 288): "Die Formulierung $\pi\acute{\omega}\rho\omega\sigma\iota\varsigma$ $\grave{\alpha}\pi\grave{o}$ $\mu\acute{\epsilon}\rho\sigma\upsilon\varsigma$ $\tau\hat{\omega}$ $\,'I\sigma\rho\alpha\acute{\eta}\lambda$ $\gamma\acute{\epsilon}\gamma\sigma\nu\epsilon\nu$ zeigt, daß Paulus nicht auf den je einzelnen Israeliten sieht, sondern es geht ihm um die Größen, durch die in der Gegenwart Israel beschrieben werden muß: auf der einen Seite um $\tau\grave{o}$ $\dot{\upsilon}\pi\acute{o}$-$\lambda\epsilon\iota\mu\mu\alpha$, $\lambda\epsilon\hat{\iota}\mu\mu\alpha$, $\grave{\epsilon}\kappa\lambda\sigma\gamma\acute{\eta}$ und auf der anderen Seite um $\sigma\acute{\iota}$ $\lambda\sigma\iota\pi\sigma\acute{\iota}$. Beide befinden sich am Ende als $\pi\hat{a}\varsigma$ $\,'I\sigma\rho\alpha\acute{\eta}\lambda$ gerettet."

[146] Luz, *Geschichtsverständnis*, 290; cf. Barrett, *First Adam*, 114.

[147] Cf. 11:28: $\kappa\alpha\tau\grave{a}$ $\mu\grave{\epsilon}\nu$ $\tau\grave{o}$ $\epsilon\grave{\upsilon}\alpha\gamma\gamma\acute{\epsilon}\lambda\iota\sigma\nu$ $\grave{\epsilon}\chi\theta\rho\sigma\acute{\iota}$.

vation of "all Israel" as an event in which those living at the consummation of salvation history will participate:[148] it will happen after the "fullness of the Gentiles has come in" (11:25); it will usher in the general resurrection (11:15). Paul grounds (καθὼς γέγραπται) the claim πᾶς Ἰσραὴλ σωθήσεται with a mixed quotation from the OT describing the work of the redeemer who will come from Zion (11:26b, 27),[149] which can be taken as a reference to Christ at his parousia.[150] πᾶς Ἰσραήλ therefore stands for the whole nation which will see these events come to pass. In a final demonstration of faithfulness to God's elect people, God will save this entire generation of Israel. We ought to take πᾶς Ἰσραήλ therefore as synchronic, not diachronic, in meaning.[151]

In summary, at the climax of Paul's argument in Romans 9–11 he defends God's faithfulness to elect Israel by referring to the salvation of the whole parousia generation, though the prospects of salvation for the now hardened majority seem bleak. Paul's claim has the weight of revealed truth: it is substantiated by a μυστήριον (11:25). Furthermore, it is supported by scriptural testimony (11:26b, 27). Finally, in 11:28–32 Paul offers a theological explanation and justification of his view that his fellow Jews are temporarily hardened but still elect to salvation, as the consummation of salvation history will prove.

This theological argument for Israel's final salvation has actually begun already in 11:16, where Paul draws out the significance of divine election of the fathers for the whole people. Paul develops this point later in 11:28–32, as the similarity in argument of these two texts shows.[152] The metaphor of the olive tree, which he uses in 11:16, however, temporarily sidetracks him into a polemic against prideful Gentile Christians.[153] I will therefore

---

[148] Cranfield, *Rom*, 577.

[149] Cf. Gaugler, *Röm* II, 205.

[150] So Wilckens, *Röm* II, 256; Cranfield, *Rom*, 578; Stuhlmacher, "Römer 11, 25–32," 561; Hofius, "Evangelium" 318; Davies, "Salvation," 27; Mußner, "Ganz Israel," 251. In favor of this view, it has been noted (1) that ὁ ῥυόμενος at 1 Thess 1:10 also refers to Christ at the parousia, and (2) that *b. Sanh.* 98a gives a Messianic interpretation of Isa 59:20, which Paul quotes at Rom 11:26b (Hofius, "Evangelium" 318, n. 83). Hofius (319, 320) concludes Israel's final coming to faith in Christ: "Das dem wiederkommenden Christus begegnende Israel wird also an *ihn* glauben.... Es kommt *nicht* ohne den Glauben an Christus zum Heil" (319, 320). The description of Israel's salvation in 11:25–27 does not contradict other statements about Israel's salvation in chap. 11, which associate it with faith, the Gentile mission, and the holiness of the fathers, against Plag's thesis that 11:25–27 must be a "sekundärer Zusatz" (*Wege*, 60, 61). See Stuhlmacher's criticisms, "Römer 11, 25–32," 562ff.

[151] Nevertheless, see below, p. 188, n. 171.

[152] Cf. Richardson, *Israel*, 129; Dreyfus, "Passé," 143.

[153] The abrupt introduction of the direct address to the readers beginning in 11:17

begin the analysis of Paul's theological explanation and justification of Israel's final salvation by looking at 11:16, then continue with 11:28–32.

Paul cloaks his argument in metaphorical language: "If the firstfruit is holy, so also is the lump, and if the root is holy, so also are the branches" (11:16).[154] Who do these metaphors represent and what does their "holiness" signify? Most interpreters agree that τὸ φύραμα and οἱ κλάδοι stand for the whole nation of Israel. Less clarity prevails, however, about the referents of ἡ ἀπαρχή and ἡ ῥίζα. Most think the "root" is meant to denote the patriarchs,[155] or Abraham, in particular[156] (cf. *Jub.* 1:16; *1 Enoch* 10:16; 93:2–10; *T. Jud.* 24:5).[157] ἡ ἀπαρχή is parallel to ἡ ῥίζα and for that reason is often ascribed the same meaning.[158] The great importance which Paul attaches elsewhere to Israel's relationship to the fathers (cf. 9:5) and to Abraham (cf. 4:12) makes plausible his linking them as "root" and "branches," "firstfruits" and "lump" here. Furthermore, the resulting emphasis on the patriarchs foreshadows 11:28b, where Paul bases Israel's relation to God as ἀγαπητοί on their relation to οἱ πατέρες. Since, as already suggested, 11:28ff. picks up the thought of 11:16, it makes sense to interpret the metaphorical ἡ ἀπαρχή and ἡ ῥίζα in terms of the later οἱ πατέρες. The competing suggestion makes ἡ ἀπαρχή refer to Jewish Christians.[159] But the supporting argument that ἀπαρχή in 16:5 and 1 Cor 16:15 denotes the first converts from an evangelized area[160] has little force.

---

signals the turn in Paul's argument. Klappert (*Jüdische Existenz*, 73) sees here a new "kirchen-kritische" dimension.

[154] As in 11:12, 15, the argument is based on a comparison. But whereas there Paul argued from the good result of something bad to the greater result of something good, now he concludes from the good quality of the first the good quality of the rest.

[155] E.g., Wilckens, *Röm* II, 246, n. 1101; Sanday and Headlam, *Rom*, 326; Plag, *Wege*, 35; Maurer, ῥίζα, *TWNT* 6, 989.

[156] Rengstorf, "Gleichnis," 138–140; Hofius, "Evangelium," 308.

[157] Barrett (*Rom*, 216) argues that ἡ ῥίζα refers to Jewish Christians (and possibly Christ himself; so also, Proksch, ἄγιος, *TWNT* 1, 107) since Paul discusses the relation of the believing remnant to Israel in this context. Against Barrett, after 11:5, Paul does not speak of the Jewish Christians anymore as a pledge of the salvation of all Israel. 11:14 does not express this hope, and thus cannot support Barrett's view by bridging the gap between 11:5 and 11:16. Furthermore, Barrett's criticism that the relation between Israel and the fathers surfaces only later in 11:28 loses force upon recognition that 11:28ff. is a later continuation of the argument begun in 11:16 (see, further, pp. 188ff. below).

[158] The "firstfruit" (ἡ ἀπαρχή) refers literally to the cake offered to God which is baked from the new dough (see below, n. 161).

[159] So Dodd, *Rom*, 188; Gaugler, *Röm* II, 191; Leenhardt, *Rom*, 161; Bruce, *Rom*, 217; Cranfield, *Rom*, 564.

[160] So Cranfield, *Rom*, 564; Leenhardt, *Rom*, 161. 1 Cor 15:20, where Christ himself is called ἀπαρχή, does not provide enough reason to interpret the word in the same way

For the context of Rom 11:16 simply does not favor this use of ἀπαρχή. Both metaphors, the firstfruit and the root, are best taken to signify the patriarchs.

What does their "holiness" signify? The description ἀγία seems appropriate in the cultic metaphor of the firstfruit offered from the lump of dough,[161] though we do not find the term used in precisely this connection.[162] Paul simply carries over the notion of holiness to a noncultic setting when he speaks of a "holy" root and branches.[163] Holiness refers not to a quality of human origin[164] but, as the cultic connotations suggest, to the quality of being set apart for God. In this sense also Paul can use the term ἀγιοι for Christians (e.g., 1:7), and beseech them to set their bodies apart for God as a θυσία ἀγία (12:1). The patriarchs of the OT are the "holy" firstfruit or root as those set apart[165] by God to be the unique objects of God's election and promise (cf. 9:7–13), the fathers of God's covenant people (9:4, 5; cf. Acts 3:25). This special status is unrelated to their own doing; it originates in divine love (9:12, 13).

By virtue of their relation to the holy patriarchs, their descendants are holy too, Paul argues. The metaphors illustrate this point. The firstfruit, which is set apart for God, represents the whole lump of dough, which thus also belongs to God. And the holy root which supports the branches "nourishes" them with its holiness. Thus the Jews derive the status "holy" from their holy fathers. They can no more be separated from the patriarchs than the firstfruit from the dough, or the root from the branches. Joined together as the beginning to the end,[166] the two through their relationship share the quality of holiness.[167] And since the holiness of the patriarchs signifies their special relation to God through election and the covenants and promises based on it,[168] their descendants partake in this relation to God and its benefits which culminate in the promised salvation.[169]

---

at 11:16 (for this possibility, see Barrett, *Rom*, 216, 217; cf. Cranfield's criticisms, *Rom*, 565).

[161] Cf. Num 15:17–21; cf. Philo *spec. leg.* I.131–144; Josephus *Ant.* 4.71.

[162] Lagrange, *Rom*, 279. Cf. the OT idea that the fruits from trees could be considered "uncircumcised" or, on the other hand, "holy" (ἀγιος) as an offering to God (Lev 19:23–25); see Cranfield, *Rom*, 563; Lagrange, *Rom*, 279; Gaugler, *Rom* II, 191.

[163] Berger, "Abraham," 84. On the notion of the holiness of certain trees in antiquity, see Rengstorf, "Gleichnis," 130.

[164] With Käsemann, *Rom*, 308; Cranfield, *Rom*, 565.

[165] Käsemann, *Rom*, 308: "consecrated" (see also Rengstorf, "Gleichnis," 148).

[166] Michel, *Röm*, 347.

[167] Käsemann, *Rom*, 308; similarly, Rengstorf, "Gleichnis," 129.

[168] Cf. Gaugler, *Röm* II, 192.

[169] Cf. Gen 13:15–17; 17:1–8; 24:7. Wilckens, *Röm* II, 246: "Alle Israeliten sind...

Paul's argument in 11:16 that Israel is holy because the fathers are holy seems to contradict 9:6–13, where physical descent from the fathers is relativized.[170] But in the earlier passage Paul is answering the question why Israel has largely been excluded from present salvation inaugurated through the Messiah, whereas later he addresses the matter of Israel's salvation at the end time after the Gentiles have all been evangelized. Relation to the fathers thus entails Israel's final salvation, though it does not guarantee their enjoyment of salvation presently.[171] When viewed from two different perspectives, therefore, the branches which represent the Jews can be said to be both "holy" and "cut off" from the olive tree.

The picture of branches which are holy, yet now cut off from salvation, anticipates 11:28 and the tension-filled description of Israel there as κατὰ μὲν τὸ εὐαγγέλιον ἐχθροὶ δι' ὑμᾶς, κατὰ δὲ τὴν ἐκλογὴν ἀγαπητοὶ διὰ τοὺς πατέρας. The contrastive construction μέν...δέ highlights the tension in Paul's portrayal of Israel's present position.[172] These contrasting descriptions of Israel arise from two ways of viewing Israel: in relation to τὸ εὐαγγέλιον and in relation to ἡ ἐκλογή. Introduced by κατά, they specify the norm or the ground for the two descriptions of Israel.[173] κατὰ τὸ εὐαγγέλιον the Jews are enemies for the sake of the Gentiles. The contents of the gospel is not meant by τὸ εὐαγγέλιον here. For its contents neither provides a rule by which to consider the Jews enemies nor is it the reason for their enmity.[174] Rather, Paul means that the Jews are enemies for the sake of the *preaching of the gospel* among the Gentiles (δι' ὑμᾶς).[175] As he puts it in 11:30, 31, "you (Gentiles) have been shown mercy through their (the Jews') disobedience...and they have been disobedient to your

geheiligt und haben Teil an der Erwählung der Väter." Cf. Stuhlmacher, "Römer 11, 25–32," 564; Hahn, "Römer 11.26a," 225; Mayer, *Heilsratschluß*, 272; Maurer, ῥίζα, *TWNT* 6, 989; Dahl, *Studies in Paul*, 151.

[170] On these tensions, see Plag, *Wege*, 35; Wilckens, *Röm* II, 246.

[171] Paul's theological justification of the claim πᾶς Ἰσραὴλ σωθήσεται through Israel's relation to the patriarchs could in principle support the salvation not only of the majority in Paul's day, who were hardened to the gospel, but also the Israelites in previous times who fell under God's judgment when only the remnant was spared, even though Paul himself does not proceed to argue on this basis for the salvation of "all Israel" in a diachronic sense.

[172] For the view that 11:28 refers to Israel's *present* position, see Barrett, *Rom*, 224; Mayer, *Heilsratschluß*, 302; Batey, "All Israel," 224.

[173] See BAGD, s.v. κατά 5.d. Cf. Rom 2:7; 8:28; 11:5; 16:26; 1 Tim 1:1; Tit 1:3. Cf. Mayer, *Heilsratschluß*, 251, n. 18.

[174] Cf. Cranfield, *Rom*, 579.

[175] For εὐαγγέλιον with this meaning, see also, 1 Thess 1:5; 1 Cor 9:14b, 18b; 2 Cor 2:12; 8:18; 10:14; possibly, 1 Cor 4:15. Cf. Barrett, *Rom*, 224.

advantage that mercy might be shown to you."[176] "Enemies for the sake of the preaching of the gospel" echoes Paul's earlier explanation that Israel has been hardened for the purpose of the Gentiles' salvation (cf. 11:11, 12, 15, 19, 25).[177] Paul is not merely saying that God has used the Jews' enmity to the Gentiles' benefit; their enmity is also purposed by God, as the context supports.[178] The Jews are "enemies...*on account of you* [Gentiles]" (δι᾽ ὑμᾶς), which implies divine purpose.[179] Paul's parallel description of the Jews as ἀγαπητοί, "beloved by God," suggests that we should take ἐχθροί as "made enemies by God."[180]

But though God himself has ordained the Jews' enmity, they too are not beyond reach of his love. Paul sees the Jews not only as enemies for the sake of the gospel's progress but also as κατὰ τὴν ἐκλογὴν ἀγαπητοί. Though Paul uses ἐκλογή in a narrower sense in 11:7 to refer to the believing remnant (cf. 11:5, λεῖμμα κατ᾽ ἐκλογήν), in 11:28 it refers—more broadly—to God's election of Israel through the patriarchs (διὰ τοὺς πατέρας).[181] Not only "those whom he has called...from the Jews" (9:24) but also the Jews who have been excluded from present salvation belong to God's elect. Paul's very designation for the unbelieving Jews here, ἀγαπητοί, alludes to their election. Because God's love flows out of God's mercy and goodness ἀγαπητοί is not an inappropriate characterization of God's elect.[182] Divine love manifested itself in the election of the patriarchs: τὸν Ἰακὼβ ἠγάπησα (9:13). Even the Gentiles, who did not belong to the elect people (οὐκ ἠγαπημένην), have become "beloved" by election (ἠγαπημένην), "my people," "sons of the living God" (9:25, 26). Just as the designation "beloved" implies salvation in the Gentiles' case, so also in the case

---

[176] On the dative, τῷ ὑμετέρῳ ἐλέει, see Käsemann, *Rom*, 316.

[177] Cf. Schlier, *Röm*, 342; Cranfield, *Rom*, 580; Käsemann, *Rom*, 315.

[178] Foerster, ἐχθρός, *TDNT* 2, 814.

[179] Foerster, ἐχθρός, *TDNT* 2, 814; cf. Mayer, *Heilsratschluß*, 303.

[180] BAGD, s.v. ἐχθρός, 1; Foerster, ἐχθρός, *TDNT* 2, 814; Cranfield, *Rom*, 580; Michel, *Röm*, 357; Lietzmann, *Röm*, 101; cf. Käsemann, *Rom*, 315. Contrast the use of ἐχθρός in Rom 5:10; 1 Cor 15:25, 26. The primary meaning of ἐχθρός at Rom 11:28 is passive, though the active sense, as in the parallels, is not excluded. Here divine *purpose*, but certainly not divine affect, is implied in ἐχθροί, as in ἀγαπητοί (contrast Mayer, *Heilsratschluß*, 302).

[181] See Cranfield, *Rom*, 580. On πατέρας as the patriarchs in 11:28; 9:5; 15:8, see Hofius, "Evangelium," 321, n. 93; *idem*, "Unabänderlichkeit," 144 (following Lietzmann, *Röm*, 89). We ought not to understand διὰ τοὺς πατέρας in terms of the patriarchs' merits (contrast Sanday and Headlam, *Rom*, 337) but in terms of their gracious election by God (correctly, Wilckens, *Röm* II, 258; Käsemann, *Rom*, 315).

[182] Michel, *Röm*, 357. On the OT connection between divine love and election, see Cerfaux, "Privilège d'Israël," 347.

of the Jews.[183] For the election and promises made to the patriarchs and their descendants are for salvation.[184] They who are already "beloved" will yet experience the salvation which God purposes for God's elect. Their status as ἀγαπητοί will not change, divorcing them from that hope of salvation, because it rests on God's election, and because God is faithful to the covenants established with and promises made to the patriarchs (διὰ τοὺς πατέρας).[185] But their status as ἐχθροί will change because it rests on God's salvation-historical purpose for the spread of the gospel among the Gentiles (δι᾽ ὑμᾶς) which has been facilitated by a temporary hardening of the Jews.[186] God's love therefore will overcome the obstacle of the Jews' unbelief, as Paul promises it will overcome every obstacle in 8:31–39, and bring salvation to God's beloved.[187] Then the tension in Israel's double relation to God as ἐχθροί and ἀγαπητοί will be resolved as the temporary gives way to the permanent.[188]

Paul has made the patriarchs the key to his interpretation of Israel as "beloved according to election": God has elected Israel in the patriarchs to salvation. This line of reasoning, however, requires substantiation.[189] Here Paul assumes a necessary connection between the patriarchs' privileged relation to God and their descendants' privilege of being elect and beloved.[190] 11:29 introduces support (n.b. the introductory γάρ) for Paul's claim in 11:28b.[191] The patriarchs can have this significance for Israel in light of τὰ χαρίσματα καὶ ἡ κλῆσις τοῦ θεοῦ, which are ἀμεταμέλητα. God's "gracious gifts" (χαρίσματα)[192] refer most probably to the election of and promise to Abraham and his descendants κατὰ χάριν (4:4, 16; cf. Gal 3:18).[193] With an explicative καί[194] Paul draws particular attention to one

[183] Cf. 8:31–39 for the God's love as the power of salvation.

[184] With Stuhlmacher, "Römer 11, 25–32," 564.

[185] Cf. Dreyfus, "Passé," 143; Mußner, "Ganz Israel," 245; Cranfield, *Rom,* 581.

[186] Cf. Stuhlmacher, "Römer 11, 25–32," 565.

[187] Haacker ("Evangelium," 69) draws a parallel between the Christian's certainty of God's faithfulness in Romans 8 and Israel's certainty in Romans 11.

[188] Cf. Cranfield, *Rom,* 580; similarly, Michel, *Röm,* 357. Contrast Haacker's attempt to resolve the tension ("Evangelium," 71).

[189] Cf. Mayer, *Heilsratschluß,* 304.

[190] Cf. Spicq, "ΑΜΕΤΑΜΕΛΗΤΟΣ," 215, n. 3.

[191] For γάρ (11:29) as supportive of 11:28b, see Hofius, "Unabänderlichkeit," 144; *idem,* "Evangelium," 321; Plag, *Wege,* 315; differently, Luz, *Geschichtsverständnis,* 296, n. 129.

[192] The emphasis falls on the graciousness of God's gifts, so Spicq, "ΑΜΕΤΑΜΕΛΗΤΟΣ," 216, n. 1. Cf. Michel, *Röm,* 358.

[193] So Hofius, "Evangelium," 321; *idem,* "Unabänderlichkeit," 144. Many see in τὰ χαρίσματα the privileges of Israel listed in 9:4, 5 (so Käsemann, *Rom,* 297; Wilckens, *Röm* II, 258; Lagrange, *Rom,* 287; Schlier, *Röm,* 342; Sanday and Headlam, *Rom,* 338).

of these gifts, namely, God's calling, in which divine election comes to expression. He does not have in mind the calling through the preaching of the gospel.[195] For ἡ κλῆσις in a Christian sense applies only to the remnant (9:24). Rather, ἡ κλῆσις harks back to chap. 9, where God as ὁ καλῶν set God's love upon Jacob (9:12, 13) and "called" Abraham's seed through Isaac (9:7)[196] in fulfillment of God's promise (9:9). Israel's privileged relation to God as "beloved" is therefore traced to the calling and other gracious gifts received by the fathers.

The crucial aspect of God's calling and gifts, however, is their permanent character as ἀμεταμέλητα, a juridical term[197] meaning "irrevocable, beyond repentance" (cf. 2 Cor 7:10; Heb 7:21). Paul stresses this quality by positioning the word at the very head of the sentence.[198] In so doing, he intends to throw God's calling and gifts as *irrevocable* into sharp contrast with the *variable* hardening and enmity with God which also presently characterize Israel. God's gifts and calling derive the quality of permanence from their source: they are irrevocable because God, the one who calls and gives, does not go back on God's acts of grace and choice.[199] Paul does not mean that God is juridically bound and for that reason cannot violate the stipulations of the covenant, nor that God's character is immutable and therefore God's gifts cannot change. Rather, God's love holds God to the commitment to God's beloved: "Son amour étant définitif, ses dons le sont également."[200] τὰ χαρίσματα are thus so permanent that even the juridical term, ἀμεταμέλητα, can be applied to them. Paul has indeed made a stupendous claim. "Il va de soi qu'un contrat, une alliance, un testament soient irrévocables, mais il est audacieux de l'affirmer d'un don purement gratuit,

---

But there οἱ πατέρες are counted among the privileges, whereas here the fathers are distinct from τὰ χαρίσματα as their recipients. On the relation of τὰ χαρίσματα and divine election, see Wilckens, *Röm* II, 258.

[194] So Hofius, "Unabänderlichkeit," 144; Michel, *Röm*, 358; Jeremias, "Römer 11, 25–36," 202. Contrast Cranfield, *Rom*, 581, whose argument from the divine calling is not convincing. The explicative καί has a particularizing function, see *BDF* §442,9.

[195] Against Wilckens, *Röm* II, 258. God's call through the gospel results in faith and *present* participation in salvation (cf. 8:28–30).

[196] On God's calling to be a child of Abraham and participate in his election, see Wilckens, *Röm* II, 192.

[197] Spicq, "ΑΜΕΤΑΜΕΛΗΤΟΣ," 215.

[198] Michel, *Röm*, 357.

[199] Sanday and Headlam, *Rom*, 338. Cf. 3:3, 4 (on this text, see Hofius, "Unabänderlichkeit," 145; Käsemann, *Rom*, 315).

[200] Spicq, "ΑΜΕΤΑΜΕΛΗΤΟΣ," 216. Cf. 8:31–39 for the steadfastness of God's love. Käsemann's criticism (*Rom*, 315) of Spicq is unjustified, for though Spicq traces the irrevocable quality of God's gifts to divine love, he relates the term ἀμεταμέλητα correctly to the χαρίσματα mentioned in the text.

d'une faveur non seulement indue, mais que toute la conduite des bénéfici-
aires devrait amener à révoquer. Là est la pointe de l'assertion. Si scandaleuse que paraisse la fidélité de Dieu vis-à-vis d'élus infidèles (cf. II Tim.,
II,13), non seulement il ne se repent pas de ses largesses ou de ses pro-
messes mais celles-ci sont de soi irrémissibles."[201] Thus 11:29 not only
substantiates Paul's claim that the Jews are presently God's beloved. The
verse also shows why they will continue to remain so: God's gifts and
calling are irrevocable.

11:30, 31 strengthen Paul's thesis in 11:28 that the Jews are enemies for
the sake of the gospel's progress among the Gentiles and beloved according
to God's election of Israel through the patriarchs. By bringing out the similarity in God's dealings with the Jews and the Gentiles he makes Israel's
salvation just as plausible as the Gentiles', which has already been put in
motion.[202] Lest one think that God's enemies cannot possibly be God's beloved, Paul refers to the Gentiles as a case in point. "For just as you [Gen-
tiles] were once disobedient to God but now have been shown mercy...so
also they [the Jews] now are disobedient...in order that they might be
shown mercy." The Gentiles have filled both shoes that the Jews now fill in
being both "enemies" and "beloved" of God.[203] The Gentiles' transition
from disobedience to mercy constitutes a precedent for the positive change
anticipated in the Jews' relationship to the gospel of salvation.[204] Thus their
present state of disobedience is no more a hindrance to their final salvation
as God's beloved than was the Gentiles' unbelief.[205] In fact, the Jews "were
disobedient...*in order that* (ἵνα) they might be shown mercy." ἵνα denotes
the divine purpose behind their unbelief,[206] which, as it turns out, has not
negative but positive implications for their final salvation.[207] Further, the
fact that the Jews' disobedience is instrumental—it serves the Gentiles'
reception of mercy (ἠλεήθητε τῇ τούτων ἀπειθείᾳ)[208]—makes it easy to

---

[201] Spicq, "*ΑΜΕΤΑΜΕΛΗΤΟΣ*," 215, 216.

[202] Cf. Siegert, *Argumentation*, 175.

[203] Paul can use both epithets ascribed to the Jews of the Gentiles also (cf. ἐχθροί,
Rom 5:10; ἀγαπητοί, Rom 1:7; cf. 9:25; Eph 5:1).

[204] Disobedience (ἀπειθεία) and unbelief (ἀπιστία) are parallels in Romans 11; see
Käsemann, *Rom*, 316. Cf. 10:16: ἀλλ' οὐ πάντες ὑπήκουσαν τῷ εὐαγγελίῳ.

[205] Plag, *Wege*, 39: "Die analoge Folge von 'apeitheia' und 'eleos' bei den Heiden
schließt das künftige Erbarmen Gottes über Israel nicht aus sondern ein."

[206] On ἵνα as final, see Cranfield, *Rom*, 585. Paul wants to emphasize God's salvific
goal in his dealings with Israel (Hofius, "Evangelium," 322). An ecbatic ἵνα, however,
would not minimize the significance of the statement.

[207] Mayer, *Heilsratschluß*, 306.

[208] On the dative as "heilsgeschichtlich-instrumental," see Wilckens, *Röm* II, 261;
cf. the same use of the dative in 11:11b.

project the replacement of their disobedience with divine mercy.[209] Once the Jews' disobedience has served its purpose in allowing God's mercy to come to the Gentiles, God will bestow God's saving mercy on the Jews too. And indeed. Paul expects the Gentiles' receiving of mercy to trigger God's bestowing of mercy on the Jews: τῷ ὑμετέρῳ ἐλέει ἵνα καὶ αὐτοὶ [νῦν] ἐλεηθῶσιν.[210] τῷ ὑμετέρῳ ἐλέει, placed before the ἵνα-clause for emphasis,[211] impresses on Paul's Gentile readers the interwovenness of their salvation with that of the Jews. They ought to see their own receiving of mercy as a signal of the sure salvation of Israel's unbelieving majority.

Paul not only affirms that God will have mercy on Israel. He says that "they have been disobedient that they might *now* be shown mercy" ([νῦν] ἐλεηθῶσιν). This νῦν in v. 31b seems inconsistent with νῦν ἠπείθησαν in the same verse. Can Israel be simultaneously disobedient and shown mercy? The seeming inconsistency presumably gave rise to the variant readings.[212] We should retain the νῦν, however, as the *lectio difficilior*.[213] What then does Paul mean? He has said that the Gentiles were once (ποτέ) disobedient but now (νῦν) have been shown mercy. Thus the reader expects to hear that the Jews are now disobedient but *in the future* will be shown mercy. Instead Paul claims that they are *now* both disobedient and shown mercy, just as he described the Jews as both ἐχθροί and ἀγαπητοί in 11:28.[214] [νῦν] ἐλεηθῶσιν cannot mean merely that the Jews are now elect and in this way recipients of divine mercy. Since νῦν δὲ ἠλεήθητε denotes the Gentiles' receiving divine mercy which accompanies salvation and faith in Christ, [νῦν] ἐλεηθῶσιν must refer to the Jews' receiving the mercy of salvation. But what justifies the assertion that Israel has *now* received mercy in this sense? Does the existence of a believing remnant justify it (ἐν τῷ νῦν καιρῷ λεῖμμα, 11:5)?[215] It is more likely that Paul is thinking primarily of the now disobedient majority in Israel, since αὐτοί...

---

[209] Cf. 11:25, 26, where Israel's hardening is instrumental and does not preclude final salvation.

[210] Cranfield correctly connects τῷ ὑμετέρῳ ἐλέει with ἐλεηθῶσιν instead of ἠπείθησαν. His view (*Rom*, 583–585) has the following in its favor: (1) it is syntactically possible (cf. *BDF* §475,1), (2) it preserves the 3–3:3–3 correspondance in protasis and apodosis (against Wilckens' objection, *Röm* II, 260 with n. 1168), and (3) it parallels the argument in 11:25, 26.

[211] Cf. *BDF* §475,1.

[212] 𝔓46 A D² F G Ψ 𝔐 latt sy omit νῦν, while 33. 365 pc sa read ὕστερον.

[213] With most interpreters; differently, Wilckens, *Röm* II, 261.

[214] Cf. Steiger, "Schutzrede," 56.

[215] Judant, "Destinée," 109. This interpretation could explain ἐλεηθῶσιν as an ingressive aorist, connoting the begining of God's saving mercy toward the Jews which will culminate with the inclusion of the hardened Jews in salvation when the redeemer comes (11:26, 27).

ἐλεηθῶσιν parallels οὗτοι...ἠπείθησαν, which obviously refers to the unbelieving Jews. νῦν must thus refer to a time period, not a point in time, during which both resistance to the gospel but also God's saving mercy at different points in that period characterize Israel.[216] The "now" during which
both characterize Israel is the era of Messianic salvation beginning with the
gospel events and culminating in the parousia, thus, the "eschatological
now."[217] In the present period of God's gracious dealings with the Gentiles
Paul expects also God's work of mercy in Israel to reach its climax, the
outpouring of mercy on God's people for their salvation. [νῦν] ἐλεηθῶσιν
thus refers to the time when the "fullness of the Gentiles" will attain salvation and "the redeemer will come from Zion to take away ungodliness from
Jacob" and all Israel will be saved.

In 11:30, 31 Paul has shown that even the enemies of God, whether Jew
or Gentile, can be God's beloved, chosen for salvation. Enmity with God
does not cancel out election. Rather, God has given it a place in salvation
history. In 11:32 Paul reveals that an all-encompassing divine purpose lies
behind this seemingly contradictory state of affairs: "For God has shut up
all (τοὺς πάντας)[218] to disobedience in order to have mercy on all." Thus
God is not the one whose promises have failed and whose loyalty has
shifted. God is the one whose faithfulness and purpose make out of human
failure and sin an opportunity to bestow saving mercy. Paul now lets us
understand God's shutting up of Israel to disobedience as "the foil of his
mercy."[219] ἔλεος is the final word for Israel in salvation history.[220] Thus, in
the light of God's saving purpose toward the whole of sinful humanity, Israel's present exclusion from salvation does not cast doubt on the reliability
of divine election, either for Israel or for Christians. Rather Israel's present
state manifests God's sovereignty in carrying out God's elective purpose.
God takes up human unbelief and disobedience and incorporates them in
the faithful fulfillment of God's promises. A correct understanding of election therefore must acknowledge divine sovereignty in affirming God's

---

[216] For νῦν as a time period, see Rom 3:26; 8:18; 11:5; 2 Cor 6:2; probably also
Rom 5:9, 11; 8:1; 16:26; Gal 4:9.

[217] Cranfield, *Rom*, 586; Feuillet, "Espérance," 491. Alternatively, νῦν could express
the certainty and nearness of Israel's reception of the mercy of salvation (Hofius,
"Evangelium," 322; following Jeremias, "Römer 11, 25–36," 203).

[218] The Jews and the Gentiles represent the whole of humanity here, cf. Gal 3:22
(Michel, *Röm*, 358; Käsemann, *Rom*, 316; Mayer, *Heilsratschluß*, 308). The use of the
definite article (τοὺς πάντας) makes it likely that Paul is referring to groups rather
than individuals (Cranfield, *Rom*, 588; cf. *BDF* §275,7).

[219] Barrett, *Rom*, 227.

[220] Schlier, *Röm*, 344.

faithfulness to complete the salvation of the elect.[221]

Paul has warded off three misconceptions about Israel which would impair the reliability of divine election for salvation. He has shown that "the word of God has not fallen (see 9:6)." Israel's present exclusion from salvation does not imply that God has failed in fulfilling God's promises to God's elect people. Rather Israel's exclusion testifies both to the essentiality of faith in Jesus Christ for participation in salvation and to God's sovereignty in fulfilling God's promises in accordance with God's own purposes. Israel's present state of alienation to the gospel does not mean that "God has rejected his people" (11:1). The past and present existence of a believing remnant, God's foreknowledge of God's people, and God's explicit promise not to reject them all provide arguments against their rejection. Thus, although the majority in Israel has not participated in the salvation brought by the Messiah, they have "not stumbled so as to fall" (11:11) definitively away from hope of salvation. Rather, God has hardened Israel temporarily in order to save the Gentiles. Paul envisions the future "acceptance" of the unbelieving Jews by God and their incorporation in "fullness" into the Messianic community of salvation. They too will believe in Jesus as the Christ when the redeemer comes to remove their ungodliness. Then, in the final accomplishment of God's overarching purpose in salvation history to show mercy to all whom God has shut up in disobedience, God will save "all Israel."

Paul's defense of God's faithfulness to God's elect people Israel in Romans 9–11 bolsters his claims regarding the implications of Christians' election in Romans 8. Using the same terminology and motifs, Paul roots the final salvation of Israel in God's foreknowledge, election, calling and love, as he did the salvation of Christians. These divine initiatives guarantee that even in the face of obstacles, including Israel's hardening and unbelief, God's purpose in electing them to salvation through faith in Jesus Christ will reach fulfillment.[222] The case of Israel clarifies, but does not contradict, Paul's view of continuity in salvation.

---

[221] Cf. Evans, "Paul," 570; Cranfield, *Rom*, 586; Barrett, *Rom*, 226; Gaugler, *Röm* II, 209.

[222] Hofius ("Evangelium," 31, 319) takes this redemptive event in fulfillment of OT prophecy as "die in der Segensverheißung von Gen 12, 2f angekündigte *iustificatio impiorum*."

Gentiles' Boasting

Romans 11:17–24. In the course of his discussion of the destiny of God's people Israel, who are elect but have rejected the gospel and been excluded from the salvation which has come in Jesus Christ, Paul enters into a polemic with his Gentile Christian readers in Rome. These Gentile Christians apparently felt superior to the unbelieving Jews since the latter had been "cut off" from the olive tree, whereas they had been grafted into the community of the saved. The Gentiles' observation that "the branches were cut off in order that I might be grafted in" (Rom 11:19), though correct, fostered boasting and self-exaltation (11:18, 20).[223] Paul proceeds to put the Gentile Christians in their place. "Don't boast!" (11:18a). "You do not support the root, but the root supports you" (11:18b). "You stand [only] by faith" (11:20a). "Do not be conceited but fear!" (11:20b). "If God did not spare the natural branches, he will not spare you" (11:21). "You will be cut off [if you do not remain in God's kindness]" (11:22). While trying to establish the faithfulness of God to God's elective purpose for God's people Israel in Romans 9–11, in 11:17–24 Paul appears to introduce doubt regarding Gentile Christians' certainty of perseverance. Is their continuance in salvation endangered, and for what reason?

The "cutting off" (ἐκκόπτεσθαι) and "not being spared" (φείδεσθαι)[224] of the boastful Gentiles represent their possible exclusion from salvation in which they now participate. They were grafted into the olive tree and made to share in the rich root—a metaphor for salvation—as believers in Christ (11:17).[225] But their present boasting threatens their position on the olive tree. For, since salvation is solely by grace, faith is the only mode of participation in salvation: τῇ πίστει[226] ἕστηκας[227] (11:20). The Gentile

---

[223] The prevalence of anti-Semitic sentiment in the Roman world of Paul's day may have encouraged the Gentile Christian attitude toward Jews reflected here (cf. Cranfield, *Rom*, 568). But the primary aspect of this attitude—spiritual pride toward unbelieving Jews who have been "cut off"—is specific to *Christian* Gentiles (cf. Schlier, *Röm*, 333).

[224] The divine passives express God's cutting off and grafting in; see Michel, *Röm*, 351, n. 28.

[225] On the olive tree as a figure of speech for the people of God, see n. 74 above. The "root of fatness" (11:17) stands for the patriarchs, in whom God has elected God's people and who thus bear the promises (Cranfield, *Rom*, 567; Michel, *Röm*, 350).

[226] The datives are modal, with Hofius, "Evangelium," 309, 310. Cranfield (*Rom*, 569, n. 1) illuminates Paul's meaning: "Paul does not think of standing as a reward for faith; and there is no good reason for reading into the other dative the idea of 'as a punishment for'. It is rather by the very fact of their unbelief, and by the very fact of their faith, that the ones are cut off and the others stand." Similarly, Lagrange, *Rom*, 281.

[227] For ἑστάναι used in relation to salvation, see Rom 5:2; 1 Cor 10:12; 15:1; 2 Cor 1:24; cf. 1 Pet 5:12.

Christians owe their position as branches on the olive tree to the kindness, or mercy, of God: ...ἐπὶ δὲ σὲ χρηστότης Θεοῦ (11:22).[228] Therefore they should believe instead of boast. Their boasting appears to displace faith[229] and thus calls into question their perseverance in salvation.[230] By faith they must "remain in [God's] kindness (ἐπιμένειν τῇ χρηστότητι),[231] otherwise you will be cut off" (11:22b).

Paul's attempt to humble his Gentile Christian readers in Rom 11:17–24 thus raises the possibility of their falling away in unbelief. Failure to continue in faith will cause a rupture in the continuity of salvation. Only believers, those who continue to depend on divine grace, will persevere. This passage shows that for Paul perseverance in salvation can be understood only as perseverance in faith.[232]

If the Roman Gentile Christians boast instead of believe, they will be excluded from salvation. The threat to perseverance posed by alienation from the gospel in unbelief is real. But, beyond the present danger, what is

---

[228] Schlier, *Röm*, 334. In the LXX the divine attribute χρηστός denotes God's graciousness and mercy, including the benefits of salvation which they bring (Zmijewski, χρηστότης *EWNT* 3, 1139); see, e.g., Ps 33:9 LXX; Nah 1:7 LXX; Wis 15:1. The term gains a strong christological orientation in Paul, for according to his gospel God's grace has come to supreme expression in Christ (Zmijewski, χρηστότης, *EWNT* 3, 1142; Weiss, χρηστός, *TWNT* 9, 477, 450). The kindness of God thus means mercy and grace for the sinner who has faith in Christ. To believe is to know the kindness of God.

[229] Gaugler, *Röm* II, 195. Cranfield (*Rom*, 569) uses the expression, "fall from faith."

[230] Cf. Sanday and Headlam, *Rom*, 329.

[231] Because "faith [is] living from God's kindness, God's grace," Paul can use τῇ χρηστότητι instead of τῇ πίστει (Cranfield, *Rom*, 570). Cf. the expression ἐπιμένειν τῇ πίστει in Col 1:23. There also there is no participation in salvation apart from persevering faith and and steadfast hope in the gospel. Those who "remain in the faith" and show themselves "well-founded" (τεθεμελιωμένοι) and "firm" (ἑδραῖοι), "not shifting from the hope of the gospel" (μὴ μετακινούμενοι ἀπὸ τῆς ἐλπίδος τοῦ εὐαγγελίου) have assurance of salvation not only now but for the last day: Christ will "present [them] holy and blameless and beyond reproach before him" (1:22). The emphasis on perseverance in faith in the true gospel here may be occasioned by the danger of heretical teaching confronting the Colossian Christians (cf. Martin, *Col*, 59); cf. the occasion and message of Galatians. By straying away from the gospel the Colossians would alienate themselves from their only hope and fall back into the hopelessness of paganism. Cleaving to the gospel, on the other hand, they could anticipate the fulfillment of their hope with certainty. "If the gospel teaches the final perseverance of the saints, it teaches at the same time that the saints are those who finally persevere—in Christ" (Bruce, *Col*, 79). Bruce goes on to imply that professing Christians who fail to persevere in faith betray that they are not among the saints: "Continuance is the test of reality" (79). Nevertheless, Paul does not convey doubt with the words "provided that you continue in the faith..." (1:23), but expects that the Colossians will do so, as the indicative mood following εἴ γε suggests (cf. Martin, *Col*, 59, n. 1; *BDF* §439, 2; 454, 2).

[232] Cf. Wilckens, *Rom* II, 250.

Paul's forecast for his readers' final destiny? If the Gentiles are cut off, can they be grafted in again? What speaks for or against such a regrafting into the olive tree? Unfortunately, here Paul leaves us in the dark. His agenda is not really to discuss the fate of Gentile Christians. He abruptly switches his attention from the Gentile readers to the unbelieving Jews in 11:23, 24[233] and ends the section with an argument for the possibility and the probability that the *Jews* who have been cut off will be grafted in again. Chaps. 9–11 are explicitly concerned primarily with the destiny of Israel. Paul brings up the Gentile Christians' potentially tenuous relation to the olive tree in 11:17–24 in order to illustrate the erroneousness of the Gentiles' attitude toward Israel and her future: "standing" or being on the olive tree, or, on the other hand, being cut off, have nothing to do with merit or demerit but with divine grace and severity; branches are engrafted "in faith" and cut off "in unbelief," not on the basis of deserts.[234] The Gentile Christians should have grasped this principle because it is so obviously true in their case. Their inclusion in salvation is entirely an act of grace; it is completely "unnatural," if you will: "You were cut off from what is by nature a wild olive tree and were grafted contrary to nature into a cultivated olive tree" (11:24). But, by boasting over the branches which have been cut off, the readers show that they have missed the point of Israel's being cut off and their own being grafted in: both are expressions of God's sovereignty, not of human inferiority or superiority. God can cut off branches because God owes no one the gift of salvation; God does not need to spare them.[235] And when God grafts on branches, God does so out of God's merciful kindness. The Gentiles should view Israel's path in the light of God's sovereignty—which illuminates also their own path.[236]

Since Rom 11:17–24 does not aim to explain the destiny of Gentile Christians, the conclusions we can draw from this passage for Paul's understanding of continuity in salvation are limited. While it shows clearly that Paul thought that faith is indispensable for perseverance in salvation, it does not indicate whether Paul feared that a final rupture in the salvation of his readers would take place and thus make the saving work of God in their

---

[233] Cf. Michel, *Rom*, 352.

[234] Cf. Cranfield, *Rom*, 569.

[235] Hofius, "Evangelium," 308. A fitting translation of οὐδὲ σοῦ φείσεται (11:21b), which captures the idea of God's sovereignty, is: "He does not *need* to spare you." I owe this suggestion to Otfried Hofius, who noted the following references for this nuance of the future tense: Matt 15:6; in the LXX, e.g., Ex 22:14; Lev 13:36; Ps 90:5; Sir 34:14.

[236] On the thought of God's freedom here, see Luz, *Geschichtsverständnis*, 279; Wilckens, *Röm* II, 247, 248; Gaugler, *Röm* II, 196.

lives ultimately incomplete. This question is simply beyond the scope of Paul's discussion. We will do best to refrain from drawing Paul's conclusions for him.

Probably the most that can legitimately be said is that the conclusions which Paul himself would draw about the final destiny of the Gentile Christians who are in danger of being cut off in unbelief would be consistent with his stress in Romans 9–11 on God's faithfulness to God's elective purpose.

With respect to Israel, divine faithfulness did not preclude the Jews' being cut off in unbelief (11:20). Yet being cut off from the Messianic community of salvation does not mean that God has nullified their election. Paul has fought hard against this assumption already in chaps. 9–11.[237] The electing God remains faithful to the elect. Paul uses the same metaphor of the root and the branches in 11:16 to express the abiding "holiness" or election of the branches symbolizing the unbelieving Jews: "If the root is holy, so also are the branches." Israel's election remains intact, even in their separation from the people where God is fulfilling God's promises.[238] Paul's argument thus does not support the interpretation that members of God's people have been "shut out of his election."[239]

Rather, ἐκκλείεσθαι signifies a "bestimmten Gerichtsakt"[240] which does not preclude subsequent ἐγκεντρίζεσθαι. For Paul uses the possibility of the Jews' regrafting on the olive tree to argue against Gentile Christian pride over the branches now cut off. Three things show that Israel's being cut off is not inconsistent with their being grafted in again. Their unbelief is not necessarily permanent:[241] "If they do not remain in unbelief, they will be grafted in again" (11:23). Behind their resistance to the gospel lies a temporary hardening imposed by God according to his salvation-historical intention, as Paul reveals in 11:25.[242] The future lifting of this hardening opens up the possibility of Israel's faith and incorporation into the community of salvation. Second, "God is able to graft them on again" (11:23). Paul's forceful affirmation of God's power here may take aim at the false

---

[237] See pp. 163, 187 above.
[238] Cf. Rengstorf, "Gleichnis," 162: "Wer immer zu Abraham gehört, hat also auch an seiner einzigartigen Würde Anteil, und sie geht ihm niemals und unter gar keinen Umständen verloren, selbst dann nicht, wenn der Zustand des Abgetrenntseins von Gott für ihn eintreten sollte."
[239] So Michel, *Röm*, 349.
[240] Michel, *Röm*, 349.
[241] Schlier (*Röm*, 330) sees Israel's unbelief as fundamentally temporary.
[242] Schlier, *Röm*, 330.

assumption that God's exclusion of Israel from salvation is irreversible.[243] But this exclusion is neither irreversible in principle nor, as Paul's third argument shows, is it irreversible in fact. Paul reminds his readers that God displayed God's power to reverse their own destiny as Gentiles who had no part in the people of God. In the Gentiles' case God took branches from the wild olive and grafted them on the cultivated olive. If God did this most unusual feat, how can the regrafting of branches in their own tree lie outside God's power or intention (11:24)? This possibility—more, probability—points to the faithfulness of God as the foundation of the final perseverance of those who are elect to salvation.[244]

Divine faithfulness with respect to Israel also did not preclude God's "severity" toward them. "Behold then the kindness and severity of God: on the ones who fell,[245] severity..." (11:22). ἀποτομία denotes the harshness of a judge[246] or, possibly, of a father.[247] K. Rengstorf argues for the latter, setting Paul's use of ἀποτομία against the background of the familial legal institution, *keṣaṣah*, which corresponds to the Greek ἀποτομία. The close connection in Rom 11:21, 22 between ἀποτομία and the thought of God's "not sparing" (φείδεσθαι) may also strengthen Rengstorf's argument, since Paul's only other use of φείδεσθαι with God as subject refers to the *Father* who "did not spare his own Son" (8:32). An allusion to the *keṣaṣah* would also fit the picture of fluctuation between divine severity and kindness which Paul paints here. For this institution included the possibility of restitution of a family member who underwent a disciplinary separation, pending a transformation in behavior.[248]

Even the elect people therefore can fall under God's severity and not be spared. But severity is reversible.[249] Hope of salvation is in sight for the very ones who have fallen. For they can also experience the kindness of God. God's kindness is not a reward for those who believe but divine grace

---

[243] See Cranfield, *Rom*, 570, 571.

[244] Wilckens, *Röm* II, 249.

[245] In 11:11 Paul denies that the unbelieving Jews "fell" (πέσωσιν), i.e., fell without hope of recovery, and softens their failure to a mere "stumbling" (ἔπταισαν). Thus he cannot mean in v. 22 that οἱ πέσοντες fell *ultimately* (Wilckens, *Röm* II, 242). See, further, above, pp. 171, 172 with notes.

[246] It is common to understand Paul's use of the term here against the background of Jewish wisdom literature in which the themes of God's severity and kindness appear frequently as two aspects of God's character, so, e.g., Köster, τέμνω, *TWNT* 8, 109; Käsemann, *Rom*, 310; Michel, *Röm*, 352.

[247] Rengstorf, "Gleichnis," 158–161.

[248] See Rengstorf, "Gleichnis," 158, 159.

[249] Barrett, *Rom*, 219; similarly, Munck, *Christus*, 98. ἀποτομία, if reversible, cannot then be the result of reprobation. Cf. Lagrange, *Rom*, 282.

itself directed toward the fallen.[250] In kindness God exercizes forbearance toward sinners and thus provides opportunity for repentance (τὸ χρηστὸν τοῦ θεοῦ εἰς μετάνοιάν σε ἄγει, 2:4). The Gentiles became beneficiaries of this kindness when God incorporated them into God's own people by grace.[251] Although the unbelieving Jew "is ignorant" of the intention of God's kindness and "despise[s] the riches of his χρηστότης" (2:4), and in so doing "store[s] up wrath for [him]self" (2:5), God continually reaches out in kindness to save.[252]

God's faithfulness to God's elective purpose for Israel is not contradicted by God's cutting them off and showing them severity. These forms of judgment are reversible, temporary measures. Have the Jews been cut off in unbelief? They will be regrafted in the olive tree in faith and participate in salvation, says Paul here and even more forcefully elsewhere in chap. 11 (cf., e.g., 11:26). Israel's exclusion from salvation is only temporary. God's saving purpose toward Israel will be fully realized.

U. Wilckens concludes on Rom 11:11–24: "Gegenüber der schöpferischen Kraft der Gnade Gottes ist kein menschliches Nein irreversibel."[253] God's faithfulness will triumph. The God who may cut off the boastful Gentile Christians and not spare them, as God did to the unbelieving Jews,[254] is a faithful God who will bring to pass God's elective purpose. As much as Paul knows of a salvation-historical advantage of Israel (cf., e.g., Rom 3:1, 2; 9:4, 5),[255] he also knows that with respect to the justification of the ungodly "there is no distinction" between Jews and Gentiles before God (cf., e.g., Rom 3, 4; Gal 3, 4). Paul's unexpressed opinion about the final destiny of the boastful Gentile Christians would surely have to take into account the faithfulness of the electing God and the equality of Jews and Gentiles with respect to God's saving work in Christ.

---

[250] Cf. Weiss, χρηστός, *TWNT* 9, 450.

[251] Schlier, *Röm*, 335.

[252] Cf. Siotis, *XPHΣTOTHΣ*, 217–219.

[253] Wilckens, *Röm* II, 249. Similarly, Michel, *Röm*, 352.

[254] On the explicit comparison of Jews and Gentiles as objects of God's severity, cf. 11:22: "You also (καὶ σύ) will be cut off."

[255] Cf. Wilckens, *Röm* II, 249.

VII. BELIEVERS' TURNING AWAY

Justification by Law and Falling from Grace

Galatians 5:1–4. The epistle to the Galatians revolves around the problem of Christians' alienation from the gospel. Paul makes this clear at the very outset in 1:6: "I am amazed that you are turning so quickly from the one who called you to another gospel." Then in 5:7, 8 he summarizes the situation in similar terms: "You were running well. Who hindered you from obeying the truth [of the gospel]?[1] This persuasion[2] is not from the one who called you." In the course of his argument, the nature of the false teaching and the consequences for Christians who fall prey to it become evident. Paul finds fault with the opponents' teaching for they require circumcision and law-keeping of Gentile Christians. The Galatian Christians' submitting to these requirements will result in their having no future benefit from Christ, being estranged from Christ, and falling from grace (5:2–4). On the eve of such a tragedy and with the intention of preventing it, Paul writes Galatians.

Why is the false gospel incompatible with Paul's gospel? How is it portrayed as inferior to his gospel? What are the meaning and implications of Paul's statements about the consequences of embracing the false teaching? What measure of hope does Paul retain that the Galatians will not succumb? Finally, what is the relation between the undeniably real danger of falling into false teaching and Paul's hope that the Galatians will not do so?

Paul's previous confrontations—before the epistle to the Galatians—with Judaizers over insistence on Gentile law-keeping help us understand his criticism of the false teaching in Galatia. For Paul's accounts of his visit to Jerusalem (2:1–10) and of the Antioch incident (2:11–14) show that he thought the demand for Gentile circumcision and law-keeping ran contrary

---

[1] $\dot{\alpha}\lambda\dot{\eta}\theta\epsilon\iota\alpha$ in 5:7 is the $\dot{\alpha}\lambda\dot{\eta}\theta\epsilon\iota\alpha$ $\tau o\hat{v}$ $\epsilon\dot{v}\alpha\gamma\gamma\epsilon\lambda\acute{\iota}o v$ of 2:5, 14, namely, the law-free gospel (with Schlier, *Gal*, 236).

[2] $\pi\epsilon\iota\sigma\mu o\nu\acute{\eta}$, which refers to the Galatians' conviction at the time of writing, contrasts to $\dot{\alpha}\lambda\dot{\eta}\theta\epsilon\iota\alpha$ and is derogatory here, connoting the rhetorical gimmickery of the Galatian interlopers (Betz, *Gal*, 265).

to the very "truth of the gospel" (vv. 5, 14). Now the Galatian interlopers, by "compelling"[3] Gentile Christians to be circumcised (6:12),[4] were "hindering [them] from obeying the truth" (5:7). These intruding missionaries threatened afresh the hard-won legacy of freedom Paul had handed down to his Gentile converts (1:8, 9), the freedom from the law which belonged to the core of the gospel.[5] After engineering the triumph of the "gospel of freedom" in Jerusalem and in Antioch, Paul wants the truth to win in Galatia too.[6]

In Galatians Paul reveals why requiring Gentile Christians to be circumcised and keep the law conflicts with the gospel: it contradicts justification by faith.[7] To make this contradiction obvious, Paul explicitly interprets Gentile submission to the law and to circumcision as ἐν νόμῳ δικαιοῦσθαι (5:4). Justification by faith and justification by law are mutually exclusive in Galatians.[8] "Knowing that no one is justified by works of law but only by faith in Jesus Christ, we ourselves have also believed in Christ

---

[3] So also Cephas "compels" the Gentiles to Judaize (ἀναγκάζεις Ἰουδαΐζειν, 2:14).

[4] The extent of obedience to the law they required—or intended to require—is a matter of debate. On this question, see, e.g., Kertelge, "Gesetz," 386.

[5] ἡ ἐλευθερία is integral to ἡ ἀλήθεια τοῦ εὐαγγελίου at 2:4, 5.

[6] Betz sees the three situations as parallel (*Gal*, 261, n. 75). Paul is concerned with personal triumph in these controversies insofar as his own triumph is that of the gospel. He does not oppose false teaching threatening his converts in order to protect his own earthly interests (cf. Betz, *Gal*, 261; see, however, pp. 261–267 above for Paul's hope of God's eschatological commendation). Paul leaves no room for misinterpretation on this point. His formulations reveal that his concern is for the gospel's/truth's sake (2:5, 14, 21) and for his converts' sake (2:5, 14). He rejoices when "Christ is preached," even by those at enmity with him personally (Phil 1:15–18). And he does not hesitate to pronounce even himself ἀνάθεμα, if he should proclaim as the gospel what is contrary to the gospel he has already proclaimed and which is the true gospel (Gal 1:8). Neither the psychological explanation of Paul's struggle against the opponents' message, nor, for that matter, the sociological explanation by Watson (*Paul*), who argues that abandonment of the law was meant to contribute to the establishment of Pauline Christianity as a sect distinct from its Jewish mother community—neither of these explanations does justice to the intensity of the theological concerns at the root of the Galatian controversy with which the epistle throbs.

[7] In other words, with Kertelge ("Gesetz", 385): "Die Verfälschung des Evangeliums...besteht also darin, daß sie die 'Christologie' des Paulus in Frage stell[t]." Similarly, Sanders, *Law*, 159: "If acceptance of the Mosaic law were the crucial point for membership in God's people..., Christ would have died in vain (Gal. 2:21)." Sanders also suggests that Paul thought the requirement of Gentile law observance would put the Gentiles at an unfair disadvantage and perpetuate inequality in the church (153, 154). These difficulties, however, are but undesirable sociological ramifications of requiring Gentile Christians to keep the law (cf. 3:26–29). The theological—more precisely, christological—ramifications exercised Paul to a much greater extent. And rightly so, for the theological error is the root of the others.

[8] Cf. Merk, "Beginn," 85.

Jesus in order that we might be justified by faith in Christ and not by works of law, because by works of law no flesh will be justified" (2:16; cf. 2:17–21; 3:11, 12, 23–26). Faith excludes law-keeping *for justification*.[9] Abraham is the prime example, for he was justified by faith even before the law (3:6, 15–18).[10]

The contradiction was probably not obvious to the Galatians, however. They had apparently been led to believe that faith in Christ and law-keeping went hand-in-hand, indeed, that works of law were a necessary supplement to faith.[11] But for Paul, the marriage could not take place. *Requiring* Christians to keep the law made law-keeping a means of justification. And making the law a means of justification implied that faith alone is insufficient for justification. If faith is insufficient, however, then God's grace is insufficient to justify sinners. But if grace is insufficient, then grace is not grace.[12] Either we can leave everything to the grace of God, or we can leave nothing to it. Paul insists on the former: "I do not nullify the grace of God, for if righteousness is through law, then Christ died needlessly" (2:21).[13] Gentile law-keeping, therefore, cannot be a supplement to faith; it can only be a substitute for faith, and thus for grace.[14]

We are not expressly told the Galatians' motive for wanting to take up law-keeping. E. P. Sanders thinks that the question in Galatians is how to "get in," i.e., whether law observance is a basic requirement for membership in the people of God (*Law*, 19). But the thrust of Paul's argument in Galatians seems to suggest instead that the issue was how to "stay in," to use Sanders' terminology. If it *is* the case that Paul argues against "staying in" by works in Galatians, the epistle contradicts Sanders' basic thesis that "Paul is in agreement with Palestinian Judaism.... Works are the condition of remaining 'in' " (*Palestinian Judaism*, 543). Sanders therefore has much at stake in the matter of whether Paul criticizes getting in or staying in by works in Galatians. Against Sanders, however, Paul's arguments seem directed at the problem of remaining in salvation. His

---

[9] Faith does not exclude good works *for sanctification*, however. Correct conduct is important for Paul as the *implication* and the *new possibility* of salvation by faith, but not as its *basis* (cf. Beker, *Paul*, 245–248). Sanders fails to put Paul's ethical exhortations in proper relation to Christians' salvation and thus misses the distinction between the Pauline imperatives and works of law in Judaism (see *Law*, 98ff.). This superficial paralleling of Paul's ethical demands with those in Judaism arises from—or contributes to—his drawing faulty parallels between their respective soteriologies.

[10] Merk, "Beginn," 85.

[11] Cf. Betz, *Gal*, 261; Kertelge, "Gesetz," 386; Barrett, *Gal*, 15.

[12] Cf. Betz, *Gal*, 261.

[13] Here Paul distantiates himself from the Judaizers, who nullified the grace of God by making law the means of justification (see Maurer, τίθημι, *TWNT* 8, 159).

[14] Sanders misses the whole point when he says that the dispute in Galatians was not "over the necessity to...have faith in Christ... [but] ...whether or not one had to be Jewish" (*Law*, 159). For Paul argues that the necessity of Judaizing *a priori* rules out faith and therefore is unacceptable.

question at 3:3, "having begun by the Spirit, are you going to finish by the flesh?," illustrates this point: here it is taken for granted that the Galatians are members; under debate are their obligations as members (how to "finish"). Similarly, in 5:1 Paul is interested in the *life of salvation* as a life of freedom from law: "*For freedom* Christ has set you free." The fact that in Galatians Paul argues for justification by faith over against law may at first seem to suggest that law observance was being made an entry requirement in Galatia. But Paul argues that justification is by faith in order to conclude how to stay in, not how to get in. For he contends that the Galatians should continue in the same way they started as Christians. In order to stress that they ought to finish by faith, not works, as they have begun, Paul speaks not only of present justification by faith but also of the future, eschatological righteousness which is by faith: ἡμεῖς γὰρ πνεύματι ἐκ πίστεως ἐλπίδα δικαιοσύνης ἀπεκδεχόμεθα (5:5; cf. 2:16d; Rom 3:20, 30; 8:33). In Galatians, therefore, Paul uses the principle of justification by faith to answer the question how a Christian ought to live in anticipation of final salvation. Not works of law but continuance in faith is the certain path from the present justification of believers to their final pronouncement as δίκαιοι at the last judgment (on 5:5, see Stuhlmacher, *Gerechtigkeit Gottes*, 228ff.). Paul agrees with Judaism and his Jewish Christian opponents here in locating justification at the future judgment (see Schrenk, δικαιοσύνη, *TWNT* 2, 210; Betz, *Gal*, 262) only to disagree with them by making justification ἐκ πίστεως Χριστοῦ καὶ οὐκ ἐξ ἔργων νόμου, and in this light a certain, not an uncertain, "hope." In conclusion, Paul's purpose in Galatians is to undermine law-keeping as the way to remain in salvation until its consummation. Even though the Galatians might have become so uncertain about the sufficiency of faith that they thought works of law a membership requirement (though this line of thought contradicts the soteriology of Palestinian Judaism as Sanders presents it, and for him is therefore unlikely to have characterized the Galatians), Paul himself takes their membership by faith as a given and develops an argument for maintaining that membership by faith. Galatians therefore directly addresses the subject of the present investigation: staying in salvation and falling away.

On what basis does Paul interpret the requirement of law-keeping as an affirmation of justification by works? He apparently reasons as follows. The demand that Gentile Christians be circumcised and keep the law can have no rationale other than the one he attributes to it: justification by works of law (5:4). Jewish Christians may circumcise and keep the rest of the law out of respect for their own heritage and not out of necessity. Indeed, by believing in Christ to be justified they have already testified against the possibility of justification by law, which they have kept prior to believing in Christ (2:16).[15] Their law-keeping is evident *not* to serve the

---

[15] Cf. Betz, *Gal*, 261. Because converted Jews had implicitly renounced the law-as-a-means-of-justification, Sanders is wrong to say that "in Pauline theory, Jews who enter the Christian movement renounce nothing" (*Law*, 176). Indeed, Sanders himself makes a fatal qualification of his statement: "The points of the law which must not be accepted as essential to membership in the church may, *if understood differently*, be observed" (176, 177; italics mine).

purpose of attaining justification (ἐν νόμῳ δικαιοῦσθαι).[16] *But Gentiles have no reason to keep the law other than to seek justification by it.* It is thus impossible to assign any other significance to their law-keeping. Thus the requirement of law observance by Christian Gentiles must be rejected for the same reasons that justification by works is rejected as contrary to the gospel.[17] In Galatians Paul lays bare the presuppositions and implications of the false gospel. As he exposes the *inner logic* of his opponents' position, it becomes clear that they are actually advocating justification by works of law, a teaching which stands in fundamental contradiction to the gospel of justification by faith in Christ.[18]

Having identified the nature of the Galatian opponents' false teaching, we now have a framework within which to understand the projected consequences of accepting it. The interlopers' message is not compatible with the gospel. Indeed, it is a ἕτερον εὐαγγέλιον, as Paul calls it (1:6), which is in fact no gospel at all (1:7). By turning to that teaching, therefore, the Galatians turn away from the gospel, indeed, away from God, whose saving word is the gospel. Paul decries their turnabout in penetrating and personal terms: "I am amazed that you are so quickly turning away from the

---

16 Where no soteriological significance is attributed to circumcision, Paul regards it with indifference: "*In Christ Jesus* neither circumcision nor uncircumcision amounts to anything" (5:6a). Correctly, Barrett (*Gal*, 69): "It is circumcision as security, not as for example a national custom, that Paul opposes." Cf. Sanders, *Law*, 159.

17 Cf. Betz, *Gal*, 261: "But Gentiles who have become Christians and who wish to become Jews in addition demonstrate that for them 'grace' and 'Christ' (i.e. the salvation through Christ outside of the Torah) are not sufficient and that to come under the Torah is necessary for their salvation."

18 Paul's opponents in Galatia may or may not have explicitly believed or taught justification by law. Especially now that E. P. Sanders' work has led to the serious revamping of views on the soteriology of Palestinian Judaism, the accuracy of Paul's portrait of his opponents' teaching in Galatians is being called into question. Räisänen ("Legalism," 72, 73), for example, contends that the notion of salvation by works of law, by which Paul characterizes the Galatian interlopers' teaching, cannot be verified by Jewish sources, and thus that "Paul is wrong." But his criticism is not so significant, as a later comment by Räisänen himself supports: Paul "understood the logic of his opponents' position in a different way than they themselves did" (80). In the light of the gospel of Jesus Christ, the Jewish way of salvation, which Paul knew only too well, is exposed as salvation by works, whether or not it was acknowledged as such in Judaism. The accuracy of Paul's characterization of his opponents' soteriology does not stand or fall with the availability of explicit literary testimony to their views. Further, Gundry ("Grace," 1–38) has argued persuasively that Paul was not off target in portraying the Jewish religion as self-consciously a religion of salvation by works, deserving of the description "synergistic." He concludes: "Despite some formal similarities, then, Paul and Palestinian Judaism look materially different at the point of grace and works.... Paul rejected Judaism and Judaistic Christianity...because of a conviction that works-righteousness lay at the heart of Judaism and Judaistic Christianity and that it would corrupt what he had come to believe concerning God's grace in Jesus Christ" (37, 38).

one who called you by the grace of Christ" (1:6).[19] No matter how sincere
their intentions might be, the Galatians are in danger of abandoning the true
gospel, of deserting the one who has saved them through that gospel.

What are the consequences of alienating oneself from the gospel and the
one who calls through the gospel? Far from completing or ensuring salvation—the Galatians' likely intention in heading in a new direction—submission to circumcision and law-keeping will alienate the Galatians from
the salvation which they have already experienced by faith in Christ.[20]

"If you have yourselves circumcised, Christ will not benefit you at all"
(οὐδὲν ὠφελήσει, 5:2). The benefit which the Galatians might think to
derive from circumcision is here played off against the benefits which
Christ bestows.[21] And where Christ benefits, there is salvation. Paul has
just spoken of the benefit of freedom—ἡμᾶς Χριστὸς ἠλευθέρωσεν
(5:1a)—recalling the Galatians' emancipation from "the weak and poor
elements," "those things which by nature are not gods," which they
"served," according to 4:3, 8, 9.[22] Salvation is thus appropriately characterized as freedom here.[23] But not only have they been set free—they are to
remain free: τῇ ἐλευθερίᾳ...ἠλευθέρωσεν.[24] Freedom as the characteristic
of the Galatians' initiation into salvation should be a distinguishing mark of
their entire Christian experience. Christians have the task of preserving
freedom.[25] With the imperative στήκετε οὖν καὶ μὴ πάλιν ζυγῷ
δουλείας ἐνέχεσθε (5:1b) Paul calls them to this task. They will fulfill it
by refusing to have themselves circumcised and keep the law. With πάλιν
Paul draws a parallel between law-keeping for justification and the Gala-

---

[19] Or, "the one who called you by grace, Christ."

[20] Cf. Eckert, *Verkündigung*, 42: "Wer glaubt, über den Weg der Gesetzeserfüllung
das Heil oder auch nur 'mehr Heil' oder Heilssicherheit zu erlangen, erreicht genau das
Gegenteil: er geht seines Heils verlustig, weil er die Gnade Christi (1, 6) verkannte."

[21] Cf. Paul's confirmation of the benefit of circumcision in Rom 2:25; 3:1, 2. This
benefit belongs to those who keep the law, he says here, but trangression of the law nullifies the benefit of circumcision. In Galatians Paul talks about the benefits of *Christ*:
Christian Gentiles will lose them if they submit to circumcision and keep the law in
order to be justified before God.

[22] Cf. the characterization of their pre-Christian state in 1:4.

[23] Cf. Betz's remarks, *Gal*, 255. Cf. Rom 8:2; 6:18, 22.

[24] In the light of ἐπ' ἐλευθερίᾳ ἐκλήθητε at 5:13a, the dative in the construction τῇ
ἐλευθερίᾳ...ἠλευθέρωσεν at 5:1a is best taken as a dative of destination or goal (not
instrumentality), with Betz, *Gal*, 255; Mußner, *Gal*, 342; Eckert, *Verkündigung*, 39. In
both phrases freedom is the present goal of salvation.

[25] Cf. Betz, *Gal*, 256. Though Christians are free, Paul can use the language of slavery to describe their present obligation to Christ, cf. Romans 6. For Paul conceives of
service to Christ as true freedom.

tians' former pagan practices.[26] He relegates both to the same category: ζυγὸς δουλείας.[27] If they choose to live by law, they will have traded one form of slavery for another. They will become like the "children of Hagar," who are in slavery to the law (δουλεύει, 4:21–25) and "will not inherit" the promise, which belongs to the "children of the free" (4:30, 31). By submitting to the Judaizers' demands the Galatians will be as far away from salvation as they were before their conversion.

The future tense of ὠφελήσει (5:2) refers to the loss of Christ's benefit—here, salvation as freedom—upon acceptance of circumcision, not at the future judgment.[28] The context lacks specific references to the coming eschatological events.[29] The reader is left to assume that the future forfeiture of Christ's benefit dates from the time indicated in the subordinate clause (ἐὰν περιτέμνησθε). The aorist tense of κατηργήθητε and ἐξεπέσατε in 5:4, which express parallel consequences of adopting the false teaching, confirms the assumption that Paul is thinking of the immediate consequences of submission to circumcision.[30]

οὐδέν (5:2) emphasizes the extensiveness of the imminent loss of Christ's benefits. Since the gospel excludes living by faith *and* law, it is impossible to derive benefits from both at the same time. Rather, either the Galatians can enjoy Christ's benefits exclusively (without the imagined benefits of the law), or they will lose those benefits entirely. There is no middle ground, no enjoyment of a salvation based on law and grace.[31] The reason for this exclusivity, as 5:3 shows, lies in the fact that "every man who has himself circumcised...is obligated to do the *whole* law."[32] Circumcision is an external ritual symbolizing the acceptance of Judaism and thus the intent to keep the rest of the law.[33] The Galatians have to realize what they are getting into if they have themselves circumcised.[34] The obligation

---

[26] Burton, *Gal*, 271; Sanders, *Law*, 69; *et al.*

[27] Burton, *Gal*, 271. ζυγός is anarthrous, so that law-keeping can be pictured, like heathenism, as just another yoke.

[28] With Sieffert, *Gal*, 299; cf. Eckert, *Verkündigung*, 41, n. 5. Against Schlier, *Gal*, 231. In the NT, ὠφελεῖν often refers to present benefits, sometimes of a spiritual nature (Matt 15:5; 27:24; Mark 5:26; John 6:63; 12:19; Rom 2:25; 1 Cor 14:6; Heb 4:2; 13:9; cf. also *Herm. Sim.* 9.13.2; *Herm. Vis.* 2.2.2; Ign. *Smyrn.* 5:2; contrast Matt 16:26, par.; *Barn.* 4:9; *Did.* 16:2; possibly also 1 Cor 13:3).

[29] Contrast, e.g., Rom 2:13, 16.

[30] Burton, *Gal*, 273. The aorists are proleptic, see Bruce, *Gal*, 231.

[31] Cf. Bruce, *Gal*, 229; Burton, *Gal*, 272.

[32] Cf. Burton, *Gal*, 274.

[33] Betz, *Gal*, 258, 259; Hübner, *Law*, 22. At least the rigorist wing in first century Judaism understood this to be the implication of circumcision; see, further, Betz, 260.

[34] Did the Galatian interlopers have a policy of gradualism in introducing law-keeping into the Galatian churches and were the Galatian Christians thus not informed of the

to do the whole law was not only burdensome, in particular for Gentiles.[35] Paul's point is that the attempt fully to keep the law constitutes an entirely different way of salvation. Circumcision and the obligation of thorough-going law observance which comes with it rule out the benefits of faith in Christ, because they put one on a different path to salvation. Those who obligate themselves to keep the whole law, Paul explains in 5:4, "are seeking to be justified[36] by law."[37] Christ will in no way benefit such people.

Further, the Galatians will trade all the advantages of being in Christ for all the disadvantages of being under law. They will be obligated to do the whole law, but they will not succeed in obeying it perfectly. Lacking perfect obedience, they will not be justified before God.[38] Rather, they will be under a curse (3:10–12). The false teaching which the Galatians are about to accept is not only contrary to the gospel—it is inferior to the gospel. Submitting to the requirement of circumcision and law-keeping will work precisely the opposite of what Christ did for them by redeeming them from the curse of the law (3:13).

Continuing to warn the Galatians of the consequences of alienating themselves from the gospel, Paul says to all who are seeking to be justified by law: $\kappa\alpha\tau\eta\rho\gamma\dot{\eta}\theta\tau\epsilon$ $\dot{\alpha}\pi\dot{o}$ $X\rho\iota\sigma\tauo\hat{\upsilon}$ (5:4).[39] The same construction appears in Rom 7:2, 6 ($\kappa\alpha\tau\dot{\eta}\rho\gamma\eta\tau\alpha\iota$ $\dot{\alpha}\pi\dot{o}$; $\kappa\alpha\tau\eta\rho\gamma\dot{\eta}\theta\eta\mu\epsilon\nu$ $\dot{\alpha}\pi\dot{o}$).[40] There the object of $\dot{\alpha}\pi\dot{o}$ is not $X\rho\iota\sigma\tau\dot{o}\varsigma$ but $\nu\dot{o}\mu o\varsigma$, and the action of $\kappa\alpha\tau\alpha\rho\gamma\epsilon\hat{\iota}\sigma\theta\alpha\iota$ is favorable, not regretable as in Gal 5:4. Paul uses the example of the woman who becomes "free from the law" (7:3) which previously "ruled" (7:1) over her—she could not remarry as long as her husband was alive—in order to illustrate how Christians have "died to the law" which held them in bondage to sin (7:4, 5) and have been joined to Christ with the result of "bear[ing] fruit to God" (7:4; cf 7:6). In other words, Rom 7:2, 6 pictures the reverse of Gal 5:4: the complete end of the law for Christians and their

---

far-reaching implications of circumcision? (see Sanders, *Law*, 29). Or did the Galatians already know, and need to be reminded, that circumcision obligates one to do the whole law? (Betz, *Gal*, 260).

[35] Sanders (*Law*, 29) thinks this is the force of the threat in 5:3. But see continuation of discussion here.

[36] $\delta\iota\kappa\alpha\iota o\hat{\upsilon}\sigma\theta\epsilon$ is a conative present, with Burton, *Gal*, 276.

[37] Cf. Schlier, *Gal*, 231.

[38] According to Sanders, what Paul thought wrong with the law was not that it cannot be kept perfectly but that it was never meant to mediate righteousness. Therefore Paul vetoed Gentile submission to the law (*Law*, 27–29). Gundry, however, delivers a fatal critique of this opinion ("Grace," 12–27).

[39] The aorist is proleptic, with Bruce, *Gal*, 231.

[40] See also *Acts John* 84, where a word play with the active and passive voices of $\kappa\alpha\tau\alpha\rho\gamma\epsilon\hat{\iota}\nu$ occurs.

total incorporation into the rule of Christ.[41]

The context of Rom 7:2, 6 shows that καταργεῖσθαι ἀπὸ τοῦ νόμου results in passivity in relation to the law: the woman no longer does what the law required of her previously. Christians also become inactive[42] in relation to the law, which used to stimulate the "sinful passions at work in our members." They cease to "bear fruit to death" (7:5) and to "serve in oldness of letter" (7:6). Paul's sense of irony may come to play in his choice of the same verb in Galatians, where bondage to the law is also at issue. καταργεῖσθαι ἀπὸ Χριστοῦ in Gal 5:4 might suggest that the Galatians are reduced to inactivity, not in relation to the law, however, but to Christ. Such an expression would catch the attention of the Galatian "activists" and would have been chosen entirely for that reason. If they let the law control their behavior by submitting to circumcision and rigorous law-keeping, Christ will exercise no influence over their lives and thus, in relation to Christ, they will have no obligations, since their activity will be oriented fully to the law.[43] κατηργήθτε ἀπὸ Χριστοῦ in Gal 5:4 envisions a severance of the Galatians' relation to Christ which Paul, playing on the Galatians' attraction to works, characterizes as inactivity. Similarly, Rom 7:1–6 pictures the severance of the woman's and Christians' relationship to the law and focuses on the effect of this severance on a person's activity.

The suggestion that Paul, in deference to the Galatians' interest in works, warns that submitting to the law will render one totally passive in relation to Christ could have not only an ironic sense but also an entirely serious one. Paul's genuine concern is the resulting divorce of Christian conduct from Christ. Paul sees the law and faith as incompatible at this point—as well as for justification—as the parenesis which follows (5:13–6:10) bears out.[44] Christians ought not to take up the law in their fight against the flesh but to walk by the Spirit (see esp. 5:16–18). If separated from Christ they will be unable to submit to the leading of the Spirit of Christ and thus to bear the fruit of the Spirit. The person who becomes circumcised makes the law not only the basis of salvation but also the norm for conduct. He is thoroughly sold into slavery to the law.

καταργεῖσθαι ἀπὸ Χριστοῦ here thus means "to be estranged from Christ, resulting in the complete dissociation of one's activity from Christ."

---

[41] Cf. Käsemann, *Rom*, 189.

[42] Lampe lists, "be idle," as a definition of the passive, καταργεῖσθαι (*LPGL*, s.v. καταργέω, 3).

[43] Käsemann (*Rom*, 187) sees the point of comparison intended in the metaphor in Romans 7 as the principle that "death dissolves obligations valid through life."

[44] On that passage, cf. pp. 142-154 above.

The expression points to a "Herrschaftswechsel," as in Romans 7,[45] which has consequences for conduct. This definition retains the element of ineffectiveness or ceasing to operate which καταργεῖν is recognized to have in the active voice[46] but which interpreters generally ignore in passive usage.[47] The use of καταργεῖσθαι ἀπό in *Acts John* 84 supports this definition. There the command καταργήθητι ἀπὸ τῶν ἐλπιζόντων πρὸς τὸν κύριον, ἀπὸ ἐννοιῶν αὐτῶν... refers to Satan's not exercising influence over Christians. In the edition by Junod and Kaestli, the expression is rendered "Reste à l'écart, loin de...."[48] In Gal 5:4, therefore, Paul chooses the construction καταργεῖσθαι ἀπὸ Χριστοῦ to express the consequence of accepting circumcision in terms which the Galatians, with their great interest in Christian conduct, will take seriously. This consequence is an estrangement from Christ which results in an incongruous attempt to live the Christian life apart from Christ.

Paul adds yet another explanation of the consequence of alienation from the gospel: τῆς χάριτος ἐξεπέσατε (5:4). Here grace is pictured as the sphere of Christian existence, as elsewhere: "this grace *in which you stand*" (Rom 5:2; cf. 1 Pet 5:12). Grace belongs not only at the beginning of Christians' salvation but throughout God's work of salvation to its very completion.[49] The believer's relation to God continues to be characterized by divine grace. Paul's implicit affirmation of grace as the fundament of the Christian life in Gal 5:4 opposes the false teachers' demand that the law fulfill this role. The law threatens to usurp the place of grace in the Galatians' lives. Their present stance in grace may thus be altered: they will fall from grace, if they accept the principle of justification by law.[50] The consequence of embracing the false teaching—"to fall from grace"—is thus not a form of divine punishment.[51] It is itself the enactment of their choice

---

[45] See Michel, *Röm*, 219; Wilckens, *Röm* II, 63.

[46] E.g., Delling (ἀργός, *TDNT* 1, 453) translates, "to make completely inoperative," "to put out of use." See, further, the lexica.

[47] Instead of relating the element of inactivity to the subject of καταργεῖσθαι, Delling relates it to the object of ἀπό: "to take from the sphere of operation (of the law or Christ)" (Delling, *TDNT* 1, 454). So also, Cranfield, *Rom*, 333, n. 3.

[48] Junod and Kaestli, *Acta Johannis*, 288, 289. Lampe gives the definition "excommunicate" for this usage (*LPGL*, s.v. καταργέω, 6).

[49] Berger, χάρις, *EWNT* 3, 1097. Cf. Rom 6:1, 14; 2 Pet 3:18; 2 Tim 2:1; Acts 13:43; Heb 10:29; 12:15; 13:9; also Paul's introductory greetings and closing blessings.

[50] 5:4 pictures the opposite of Rom 5:2 (Bruce, *Gal*, 231).

[51] Divine grace is not "taken from them," rather, they abandon it (correctly, Burton, *Gal*, 277). Burton explains: "For to affirm that their seeking justification in law involved as an immediate consequence the penal withdrawal of the divine grace (note the force of the aorist in relation to the present δικαιοῦσθε...) involves a wholly improbable harshness of conception."

to live by law.[52] Paul does not envision a consequence limited to day to day Christian experience, however, as if it were possible to have a minimum of grace necessary for salvation, yet to live the Christian life by law rather than grace. Just as those who want to live by law are implicitly seeking *justification* by law, so also those who fall from grace relinquish not only the benefits of living in relation to God through his grace but *God's grace as such*, i.e., they relinquish the basis of their salvation.

The Galatians are in danger of removing themselves from the realm of grace by rejecting the gospel of grace, which they will do if they embrace the ἕτερον εὐαγγέλιον based on law. Paul's association of χάρις with sound doctrine or the true gospel here appears elsewhere in the NT (1 Pet 5:12; 2 Pet 3:18; 2 Tim 2:1; Acts 13:43; Heb 10:29; 13:9; Jude 4).[53] Christians thus remain in grace by holding fast the initial message of grace.[54] To depart from the gospel is to endanger one's fundamental existence "in grace." By adding law to grace as the basis of their Christian life, the Galatians will have given up the true gospel and thus their own position in grace. For grace and law cannot be combined; they are two mutually exclusive ways of salvation. This incompatibility of the false teaching and Paul's gospel becomes clear once again in his warning that the Galatians ought not to step outside of grace.

The definite article with χάρις in 5:4 makes us think in particular of the grace proclaimed to the Galatians and received by them at conversion, the grace by which they were called (1:6).[55] This grace, the basis of their initial salvation, they are about to sacrifice. As in 3:1–5, here Paul reminds his readers of their conversion experience to convince them to continue in that same doctrine and the experience of salvation it brought. The grace given them initially must remain the foundation of their Christian existence.

In 5:2–4 Paul has delineated three consequences of alienation from the gospel for those who succomb to the false teaching. Each consequence will manifest itself in loss of the salvation which characterizes the Galatians' present experience. (1) They will lose the benefit of Christ who "set [them] free for freedom" (5:1). (2) They will be cut off from Christ in such a way that their present life and conduct will have no relation to Christ. (3) They will remove themselves from the grace which, from beginning to end, is the

---

[52] Similarly, Barrett (*Gal*, 63): "The man who thinks he can justify himself by his own achievement in obedience to the law proclaims thereby that he has no need of grace and therefore automatically falls out of that relation with God which is defined by grace."

[53] Berger, χάρις, *EWNT* 3, 1097.

[54] Cf. Berger, χάρις, *EWNT* 3, 1098.

[55] Burton, *Gal*, 276.

fundament of salvation. In short, they will trade away their present salvation for a false gospel which offers nothing of what they have received by simple faith in Christ. Paul stresses the immediate consequences of alienation from the gospel of Christ[56]—present loss of salvation—and thereby makes the danger more vivid. Yet the danger encompasses more than present loss. Paul does not come to speak of the eschatological judgment in warning the Galatians; but he surely presupposes that those who become alienated presently from the gospel cannot hope for final salvation. The threat to perseverance is most serious.[57]

Paul writes Galatians to prevent his readers from sacrificing the salvation which is now theirs. The letter comes none too soon: the situation has already reached a critical point. For the Galatians are apparently observing the Jewish calendar (cf. 4:10). But they do not yet seem to have made the decisive step—circumcision—in favor of the false teaching.[58] So Paul hopes to turn the tide with his epistle. He faces the Galatians with the implications of obligating themselves to keep the law. Now that they know how high the stakes are, will they actually continue in the same direction?

Paul not only *hopes* that his warnings and pleadings will evoke the desired response. He claims to "have been persuaded in the Lord concerning you that you will think nothing other" than the truth (5:10). Though he anathematizes the perpetrators of the "other gospel" (1:8, 9) and consigns them to "judgment" (5:10), regarding them as "false brethren" (cf. 2:4), he has confidence that his Galatian converts will reaffirm their acceptance of the gospel he preached to them.[59] Paul's expression of confidence here, as other such expressions in his epistles, resembles conventional Hellenistic epistolary language,[60] but is for that reason no less sincere.[61] Rather, Paul injects new significance into conventional language, just as he fills his conventional epistolary greetings with theological meaning.

Nor ought we to take this proclamation of confidence lightly since it

---

56 Eckert, *Verkündigung*, 40: "unmittelbare Gefahr."

57 Cf. Barrett, *Gal*, 65; Sanders, *Law*, 110.

58 Schlier, *Gal*, 231; cf. Burton, *Gal*, 276.

59 Schlier comments that Paul's confidence "setzt allerdings auch voraus, daß sie noch nicht endgültig eine Entscheidung getroffen haben" (*Gal*, 238). This is saying too little, however. Paul is confident that they *will not* ultimately decide against the truth of the gospel. The perpetrators of the "other gospel" are not former Christians who have defected, and thus possible prototypes of the Galatians, as Schlier suggests, but falsely-professing Christians.

60 See Betz, *Gal*, 266, 267, with nn. 132, 133; also Olson, "Expressions of Confidence," 282–295.

61 Cf. Betz, *Gal*, 267; White, *Body*, 105. Olson ("Expressions of Confidence," 288) takes Gal 5:10 as both sincere and ironic.

comes as somewhat of a surprise after four and a half chapters of impassioned argument revealing a situation in Galatia which, humanly speaking, far from inspires confidence. Paul himself dares to give his expression the strength of the perfect tense: πέποιθα.[62] And there is no necessary contradiction between Paul's firm confidence in 5:10 and the degree of danger in which the Galatians find themselves, according to the epistle.[63] For Paul has a good reason for his more positive tone in 5:10. This reason is found in the words ἐν κυρίῳ.[64] His "confidence arises from his trust in Christ" (cf. 2 Thess 3:4; 2 Cor 3:4)[65] After all Paul's efforts to mend the situation, he acknowledges that the Galatians' destiny does not lie in his hands but the Lord's.[66] And the Lord's faithfulness guarantees the final outcome. "Der κύριος wird sie bei der Wahrheit halten. Ihm gegenüber und seiner Treue gegenüber bedeutet die drohende Gefahr nichts."[67] Paul's own intervention in the matter is not thereby rendered superfluous, however. For God's faithfulness can manifest itself precisely in the effect the apostle's warning and wooing has in the Galatian churches. And indeed Paul must have expected his expression of confidence actually to effect such positive change, as did other Hellenistic writers who made use of such conventional expressions.[68] From the perspective of God's faithfulness, Paul is certain that the Galatians will not finally turn away from the gospel.

This same positive expectation regarding the outcome of God's saving work in the Galatian Christians surfaces briefly in 3:4. Paul poses the question whether they "have experienced[69] so many things in vain" in order to convince them not to give up all they have gained by setting out on a different path. His formulation of the question itself expresses profound incredulity: τοσαῦτα ἐπάθετε εἰκῇ; Paul can hardly entertain the thought that the experiences he has mentioned here—having Christ portrayed crucified before their eyes, the gift of the Spirit, miracles—could lose their grip on

---

[62] See Schlier (*Gal*, 237): "nicht nur ein vages und angestrengtes Vertrauenwollen trotz alles gegenteiligen Augenscheines."

[63] Schlier, *Gal*, 237.

[64] ἐν κυρίῳ modifies πέποιθα, not εἰς ὑμᾶς (with Mußner, *Gal*, 357, *et al*.). Although B omits ἐν κυρίῳ, the omission is likely to be accidental (with Bruce, *Gal*, 235).

[65] Bruce *Gal*, 235.

[66] Betz compares Paul's criticism of confidence in the flesh elsewhere (Phil 3:3, 4; 2 Cor 10:2; cf. Rom 2:19).

[67] Schlier, *Gal*, 238.

[68] Olson, "Expressions of Confidence," 289: "The function is to undergird the letter's requests or admonitions by creating a sense of obligation through praise."

[69] For this meaning of πάσχειν, see BAGD, s.v. πάσχω, 1. For the neutral sense in Gal 3:4 rather than the frequent NT meaning, "suffer," see Betz, *Gal*, 134; Bonnard, *Gal*, 63; Schlier, *Gal*, 124. The choice between meanings does not affect the point in question.

the Galatians. This mood of incredulity in 3:4a leads us to interpret the cryptic εἰ γε καὶ εἰκῇ in 3:4b as a confirmation that it is indeed impossible to believe that such great experiences could have been in vain: "if [at all one] really [can experience such great gifts] in vain."[70] The opposing interpretation—Paul threatens that it was all in vain[71]—seems less likely for being redundant, since Paul's question has already formulated the possibility that it was all in vain. Just as the question in 3:3 does not imply that it is possible to "complete by the flesh" after "having begun by the Spirit"— the proposition is absurd—so the idea that the powerful experiences of conversion could be in vain is unthinkable.[72] From the perspective of the spiritual realities at hand, the coming to pass of the potential dangers is beyond all imagination. In this sense, it is "impossible" that the Galatians will turn from the gospel of their salvation. Here Paul expresses his inner conviction that the situation is indeed not hopeless.[73]

But not the Galatians' experiences as such, rather, the God behind those experiences makes it impossible to believe that they are in vain. Paul traces the Galatians' conversion experiences explicitly to divine working in 3:1–5. Christ was "crucified." God "supplies the Spirit" and "works miracles among [them]." As in 5:10, therefore, so also here Paul (implicitly) expresses "confidence in the Lord" that the Galatians will not succomb to the false teaching and suffer the consequences of this error. For God's faithfulness is greater than is the threat to the Galatians' salvation. Thus Paul's optimism is not born of convention but reality, a reality in which he sees God at work in spite of many human failings.[74] This divine reality takes precedence over any human reality in conflict with it.

In Galatians Paul takes seriously the threat of alienation from the gospel of Christ through the lure of the false gospel. Yet even on the brink of disaster, while issuing stern warnings against loss of salvation, he maintains a divinely-inspired confidence that the worst will not happen. Not even the Galatian controversy blurs his vision of God's faithful continuation of the work of salvation in believers.

---

[70] Cf. the interpretation of Chrysostom, *Comm. in ep. ad Gal.*, *ad loc.*; Luther, *Gal, ad loc.*; Calvin, *Gal, ad loc.*

[71] So Betz,*Gal*, 134, 135; Oepke, *Gal*, 68; *et al.*

[72] Lightfoot (*Gal*, 135): "Εἰ γε leaves a loophole for doubt, and καὶ widens this, implying an unwillingness to believe on the part of the speaker." Similarly, Mußner, *Gal*, 210.

[73] With Bruce, *Gal*, 150; Bonnard, *Gal*, 64; *et al.*

[74] Betz (*Gal*, 267) attributes Paul's optimism more to convention than reality: "Ignoring that the Galatians may have already taken another view, his hope can only be that having read his letter they may change their mind again." Further, Betz strangely interprets ἐν κυρίῳ (5:10) as a *qualification*, not a source, of Paul's confidence.

Failing the Test of Faith

2 Corinthians 13:5. In 2 Cor 13:5 Paul probes the Corinthians' Christian profession as to its genuineness: "Test yourselves [and see] whether you are in the faith; prove yourselves, or don't you recognize this about yourselves, that Jesus Christ is in you?—unless you are unapproved!"[75] To fail the test is to be ἀδόκιμος, "rejected." The word here means "rejected with regard to salvation," as is obvious from the contrasting expressions ἐν τῇ πίστει εἶναι and Ἰησοῦς Χριστὸς ἐν ὑμῖν[76] in the same verse.[77] How might the Corinthians fail the test of salvation? And why does Paul recommend self-testing in this regard?

The context of Paul's injunction to "test yourselves..." is his apostolic defense to the Corinthian opposition. In this epistle Paul wrestles with the problem of his diminished authority in the church at Corinth. He does not measure up to the Corinthians' expectations of an apostle. Compared with the rival apostles, who evince impressive capabilities, Paul comes up short. He lacks letters of commendation (3:1). He is meek when face to face with them (10:1). His speech is contemptible and his personal presence unimposing (10:10; 11:6). He "walks according to the flesh" (10:2). He seems inferior to the other apostles (11:5; 12:11). He does not, as would befit an apostle, accept their remuneration for his preaching (11:7, 9; 12:13). They are looking for proof that Christ is speaking through him (13:3), that he is "of Christ"[78] (10:7). The controversy over Paul's apostolic qualifications in this epistle comes to a climax in chaps. 10–13.[79] Paul concentrates his attempts to regain credibility in the Corinthians' eyes in this section. His final argument for the authenticity of his apostolic claims takes the form of an exhortation to the Corinthians. It is his exhortation to self-testing.

In challenging the Corinthians to test themselves, Paul is not interested in playing tit for tat to redress the balance of accusations which both parties in the controversy have thrown at each other. He is not even interested in seriously questioning the Corinthians' faith. For Paul actually expects them

---

[75] The test determines the quality—genuine or counterfeit—of the thing tested; cf. 2 Cor 8:8; 1 Cor 3:13.

[76] On the meaning of these expressions as descriptions of being "in Christ," see Windisch, *2 Kor*, 420.

[77] For the testing of faith, see 1 Pet 1:7; cf. Jas 1:12.

[78] On this expression, see p. 234, n. 6.

[79] I here presuppose with others that 2 Corinthians 10–13 was originally one literary unit. It is unnecessary for the purposes of the following discussion to address other questions regarding the integrity of 2 Corinthians.

to pass the test.[80] He formulates his question—"don't you know that Jesus Christ is in you?"—in anticipation of their affirmative answer.[81] It thus has the effect of a rhetorical question. Because of this indirect affirmation that their Christian profession is genuine, it is difficult to take the following εἰ μήτι ἀδόκιμοί ἐστε as a serious suggestion.[82] To the degree that the statement points to the real possibility of being ἀδόκιμος, it must refer to a minority in the back of Paul's mind.[83] Paul does not—at least not primarily—intend to elicit from the Corinthians a confession of having failed the test. The self-confident Corinthians would hardly have admitted to being ἀδόκιμοι anyway.[84]

Further, such a confession would not contribute to Paul's argument for his apostleship, the primary concern of chaps. 10–13.[85] On the other hand, the Corinthians' affirmation that they *are* genuine Christians, that they *do* pass the test of faith, *would* contribute to this argument. For if "Jesus Christ is in [them]," it is precisely because of Paul's apostolic activity. Through his evangelistic message the power of God had come to the Corinthians. By means of the apostle's self-giving to "death," "life" now works in them (4:11, 12). The "proof of the Christ speaking in [Paul]" (13:3) lies in the profession of faith made by the proof-seekers: Christ *did* speak through Paul when they heard the gospel and believed.[86] If the Corinthians claim to be δόκιμοι (true Christians), then they must acknowledge Paul as δόκιμος (a true apostle)! If instead they deny that Christ speaks through Paul, they imply that their own "Christenstand" is a sham.[87] Paul has cleverly found the proof of his apostleship on the lips of his very accusers.[88] Paul argues similarly in 3:1–3, where the Corinthians themselves function as Paul's "letter of recommendation" which they seek: ἡ ἐπιστολὴ ἡμῶν ὑμεῖς

---

[80] Cf. Bruce, *Cor*, 254; Tasker, *2 Cor*, 188; Windisch, *2 Kor*, 420.

[81] Cf. Hughes, *2 Cor*, 481. A question with οὐκ anticipates an affirmative answer (*BDF* §427, 2).

[82] Against Windisch, *2 Kor*, 421.

[83] On this possibility, see pp. 223, 224 below.

[84] Bultmann, *2 Kor*, 248.

[85] As Barrett (*2 Cor*, 339) observes, Paul's simultaneous concern is his readers' good, cf. 13:7–10.

[86] Cf. Barrett, *2 Cor*, 339; Hughes, *2 Cor*, 339.

[87] Barrett (*2 Cor*, 338): "For if the Corinthians are Christians, it is through Paul's ministry. To throw doubt on his apostleship and apostolic message is to throw doubt on their own being as Christians; to affirm their own faith is to vindicate the preacher through whom they became believers.... This is why Paul urges the Corinthians to test themselves."

[88] In finding indirect substantiation of his apostleship Paul avoids the self-commendation which his opponents practice (cf. 10:18).

ἐστε...γινωσκομένη καὶ ἀναγινωσκομένη ὑπὸ πάντων ἀνθρώπων.[89]
His apostolic credentials are displayed on the "tablets" of their hearts.
Again in 1 Cor 9:1, 2 Paul points to the Corinthians as τὸ ἔργον μου ἐν
κυρίῳ and ἡ σφραγίς μου τῆς ἀποστολῆς.[90] They, of all people, must
recognize that he is a true apostle (v. 2). How ironic, superfluous and—he
now reveals—self-incriminating that Paul's own converts would require
additional confirmation of his apostleship!

In summary, Paul's ultimate purpose in getting the Corinthians to test
themselves lies in establishing *his own* provenness. He even makes it
explicit that his exhortation to self-testing ought to have this final result:
ἐλπίζω δὲ ὅτι γνώσεσθε ὅτι ἡμεῖς οὐκ ἐσμὲν ἀδόκιμοι (13:6).[91]
Thus, tongue in cheek, he challenges the Corinthians to prove the authenticity of their Christian profession. For he knows what their response will
be.[92] He suggests the preposterous—are they "rejected"?!—in order to provoke them to the most vociferous affirmation of their "provenness." For in
the logic of the argument, the greater the affirmation of the Corinthians'
provenness, the more undeniable Paul's provenness.

Accordingly, the term ἀδόκιμος in this context as applied to the Corinthians means "rejected with regard to salvation *in an unconverted state*." It
cannot mean rejected after conversion, as if Paul were suggesting that the
Corinthians might have fallen away from true faith. For this meaning would
make no sense in Paul's argument. He presupposes that, if the Corinthians
want to call his apostleship into question, they would have to call their conversion into question too. For they would have believed in a fake message
of a fake apostle. The idea that the Corinthians might still be unconverted
(ἀδόκιμοι) serves to discourage them from considering Paul ἀδόκιμος.

The view that ἀδόκιμος referring to the Corinthians means rejected in
an unconverted state fits NT usage of the term. In the NT ἀδόκιμος always
has this association. Those who have an ἀδόκιμος νοῦς "do the things
which are not proper" (Rom 1:28). In their "unfit" state of mind, "they do
not acknowledge (οὐκ ἐδοκίμασαν) God" (Rom 1:28). Here ἀδόκιμος
describes the minds of unconverted pagans. In 2 Tim 3:8 and Tit 1:16 the
term describes professing Christians whose lives radically contradict their
profession. The author of 2 Timothy compares those who are ἀδόκιμοι

---

[89] Cf. Hughes, *2 Cor*, 481.

[90] Cf. Barrett, *2 Cor*, 338.

[91] But he immediately takes back this wish (οὐχ ἵνα ἡμεῖς δόκιμοι φανῶμεν...
ἡμεῖς δὲ ὡς ἀδόκιμοι ὦμεν, 13:7) as it seems to conflict with his abhorrence of self-
defense (cf. 11:1, 16, 17, 30; 12:1, 5, 6, 11, 19).

[92] Barrett, *2 Cor*, 338.

περὶ τὴν πίστιν with Jannes and Jambres, who opposed Moses, because they also "opposed the truth." He calls them, among other things, "men of depraved mind," "lovers of pleasure rather than lovers of God," who "hold to a form of godliness, although they have denied its power" (3:2–5, 8). In v. 6 he identifies them as the false teachers active in Timothy's community. They are the "impostors" (v. 13) who creep into the church in the "last days" (v. 1). The text gives no reason to suppose that these persons were once true Christians and have since fallen away. Rather, they are the types Timothy must "avoid" (v. 5), i.e., not receive into the church.[93] They are described in fundamentally negative terms that suggest why they should be kept out of the church: they have not at all converted to Christianity.

We gain a similar picture of the ἀδόκιμοι from Tit 1:16. They too are linked with false teaching inside the community (vv. 11, 12). They belong to those who "turn away from the truth" (v. 14) and are "defiled and unbelieving" (ἄπιστοι, v. 15). "They profess to know God but by their deeds they deny him," and thus show themselves "ἀδόκιμοι for any good work" (v. 16).[94] They need "severe reproof" in order to arrive at a sound faith (ἵνα ὑγιαίνωσιν[95] ἐν τῇ πίστει, v. 13). Here again, the text gives no indication of a regression from being δόκιμος to becoming ἀδόκιμος. The "unproven" seem to have always had the characteristics of unconverted people. E. Scott comments on Tit 1:16: "The writer has been led to speak generally of all who make profession of religion but who have never really known what it means."[96] The facts that they participate in the community and are subject to its reproof do not necessarily imply a genuine prior conversion. The early church reckoned with the problem of false profession in a "mixed church" (cf., e.g., 1 Cor 5:11–13; Matt 13:24–30, 36–43, 47–50).

Thus the NT uses the designation ἀδόκιμος for people whose lives and beliefs stand in fundamental contradiction to the Christian faith and give no evidence of ever having been compatible with it. Conversely, the NT's failure to apply the term ἀδόκιμος explicitly to *former* Christians suggests its inappropriateness for this use.[97] W. Grundmann assumes too much

---

[93] Scott, *Pastorals*, 120.

[94] In the theology of the Pastorals, the absence of good works reflects the absence of true faith: "Practice is the only confession of faith which has any value" (Scott, *Pastorals*, 161, commenting on Tit 1:16).

[95] The Pastorals often describe the Christian teaching as "sound" (ὑγιαινούσα, cf. 1 Tim 1:10; 2 Tim 4:3; Tit 1:9; 2:1, etc.) in the sense of "correct." Thus for someone to "become sound in the faith" means to embrace Christianity as the correct teaching, i.e. to convert. It does not mean to progress from a worse to a "healthier" stage of faith. Contrast Weiss, *Tim*, 347.

[96] Scott, *Pastorals*, 161.

[97] The use of ἀδόκιμος in 1 Cor 9:27 refers not to loss of salvation but to failing the

therefore when he takes the δόκιμος word group to reflect a "Ringen um die Bewährung...des empfangenen Heiles, um in der Prüfung des Gerichtes als bewährt zu erscheinen."[98] The testing of profession to faith does not require us to presuppose actual prior reception of salvation.

This conclusion might be called into question, however, by 2 Cor 12:21, where Paul speaks of "many who have sinned before and not repented from the immorality, fornication and sensuality which they practiced" (cf. 13:2). I. H. Marshall argues on the basis of this verse that ἀδόκιμος in 13:5 refers to people who might have "lapsed from the faith": "Paul shows that he has in mind those believers who have fallen into sin and have not yet repented. Such people will be disciplined by Paul if they fail to repent."[99]

In fact, however, Paul never indicates that these persons were genuine "believers," though they were apparently in the church.[100] Neither his attempt to evoke their repentance nor his threat to take disciplinary action necessarily presupposes their prior conversion. They presuppose only that the unrepentant participate in the believing community and are thus subject to the standards governing community life.

The interest in the sinners' repentance and the use of the term μετανοεῖν in 12:21 may even indicate the opposite of what Marshall says, namely, that Paul is calling for their *initial* conversion because they have not yet put their lives under the authority of the gospel and thus show themselves to be unbelievers. μετανοεῖν is a *terminus technicus* from early Christian "Bekehrungssprache,"[101] a standard component of evangelistic preaching from John the Baptist through the apostolic age, including Paul's own evangelistic message, according to Luke (Acts 17:30; 26:20; cf. 20:21 with μετάνοια).[102] Repentance forms the precondition for baptism (cf. Acts 2:38).[103] Paul knows of this μετάνοια associated with conversion (Rom 2:4).[104] The fact that he expects the Corinthian intransigents to repent from persistent sin thus speaks as much for their prior failure to convert as for their prior conversion.

The same ambiguity resides in the designation οἱ προημαρτηκότες (12:21; 13:2). Does the προ- refer to sins arising in an already converted

---

test of faithful service. See pp. 233–247 above.
[98] Grundmann, δόκιμος, *TWNT* 2, 259, 260.
[99] Marshall, *Kept*, 122.
[100] Barrett also simply assumes their prior conversion, *2 Cor*, 332.
[101] Georgi, *Gegner*, 233; Bultmann, *2 Kor*, 242; Windisch, *2 Kor*, 411; cf. Merklein, μετάνοια, *EWNT* 2, 1022–1031.
[102] See also Matt 3:2; 4:17; Mark 6:12.
[103] For the expression βάπτισμα μετανοίας, see Mark 1:4; Acts 13:24; 19:4.
[104] Cf. 2 Cor 7:9, 10 for μετάνοια as "remorse" of Christians.

condition prior to Paul's writing 2 Corinthians, or to sins originating in a pagan, pre-Christian state? προαμαρτάνειν can denote the "earlier sins" from which one repents as the preparatory step for baptism. The verb has this sense where it appears together with the notion of repentance in Justin *Apol.* I.61.10: "In order that we do not continue as children of necessity and ignorance, but of deliberate choice and knowledge, and in order to obtain in the water the forgiveness of past sins (ἀφέσεώς τε ἁμαρτιῶν ὧν προη μάρτομεν), there is invoked over the one who wishes to be regenerated, and who is repentant of his sins (τῷ ἑλομένῳ ἀναγεννηθῆναι καὶ μετα νοήσαντι ἐπὶ τοῖς ἡμαρτημένοις), the name of God, the Father and Lord of all; he who leads the person to be baptized to the laver calls him by this name only."[105] Paul's combination of the two terms in 2 Cor 12:21—οἱ προημαρτηκότες καὶ μὴ μετανοήσαντες—recalls this early Christian formula for conversion and thus suggests that "those who have sinned before and not repented" in Corinth are unconverted people.

It is not impossible, on the other hand, that the προ- in προαμαρτάνειν at 2 Cor 12:21 refers simply to some date before the composition of 2 Corinthians 10-13.[106] The sins which were committed "before" are sexual in nature: μὴ μετανοησάντων ἐπὶ τῇ ἀκαθαρσίᾳ, πορνείᾳ, καὶ ἀσελ γείᾳ ᾗ ἔπραξαν (12:21). We know from 1 Cor 5:1–13; 6:12–20 that Paul had already confronted such sexual offenders in Corinth.[107] And at the time he wrote 2 Corinthians 10–13 they are still not few in number (πολλοὺς τῶν προημαρτηκότων[108]), as might be expected from the degeneration of Paul's authority among the Corinthians in the meantime. Perhaps the "earlier sins" denote simply these previous occurences of sexual immorality in the Corinthian community which Paul had judged, yet without complete success.[109]

It is more likely, however, that the unrepentant Corinthians' "earlier sins" reach farther back in time than Paul's own knowledge and criticism

---

[105] Falls, *Justin*, 99–100. See also Josephus *War* I.24.4 §481 for προαμαρτάνειν in connection with repentance in a secular sense. Cf. Windisch, *2 Kor*, 411.

[106] Cf. Lietzmann, *Kor*, 161: "Misstände, die bereits vor der zweiten Anwesenheit des Pls eingetreten waren und deren Beseitigung ihm damals nicht gelungen war."

[107] This type of immorality had become a problem in Corinth even before the opposing missionaries intruded.

[108] The genitive stands for the accusative πολλοὺς τοὺς προημαρτηκότας, cf. Bultmann, *2 Kor*, 241; Windisch, *2 Kor*, 410.

[109] The sins listed in 12:20 have to do with the Corinthians' opposition to the apostle: ἔρις, ζῆλος, θυμοί, ἐριθεῖαι, καταλαλιαί, ψιθυρισμοί, φυσιώσεις, ἀκατα στασίαι. But they are not explicitly among the "previous sins" listed in 12:21 (cf. Barrett, *2 Cor*, 332). Yet even these sins stemming from the antagonism toward Paul may be characteristic of unconverted people; see discussion below.

of them.[110] For, in Paul's thought, ἀκαθαρσία, πορνεία and ἀσέλγεια typically characterize pagans (Rom 1:24), Gentiles (1 Cor 5:1; 1 Thess 4:3, 5; cf. also Eph 4:17, 19) and a state of lawlessness (Rom 6:19). We do not expect to find them in a description of post-conversion behavior in Paul, but pre-conversion behavior. After naming various sexual offenders— πόρνοι, μοιχοί, μαλακοί, ἀρσενοκοῖται—in a list of people who will not inherit the kingdom of God, Paul reminds his Christan readers that they *used to* fall into this category: καὶ ταῦτά τινες ἦτε (1 Cor 6:9–11a; cf. also Col 3:5–7; Tit 3:3). "But," he adds, "you were washed, but you were sanctified, but you were justified in the name of the Lord Jesus Christ" (1 Cor 6:11b). If, for Paul, a life of sexual immorality belongs to the pre-Christian past, what is the status of those in the church who practice sexual immorality? Do they show that they have never managed to "exit" from their pagan lifestyle by repenting, even though they have "entered" the church? H. Windisch thinks that this is the case in 2 Cor 12:21 and concludes: "Dann ist es die erste Buße, die P. von ihnen erzwingen will und von einer eigentlichen 'Buße nach der Taufe' ist keine Rede. In jedem Fall sind diese Sünder als Nochnichtbekehrte betrachtet, die ihr heidnisches Treiben (vgl. auch 1 Petr 4, 1–4) auch nach dem Eintritt in die Gemeinde noch nicht abgelegt haben."[111] The alternative possibility that the sinners named at 12:21 once truly converted and then fell back into former sexual patterns and thus out of a Christian state is less likely, given the occurence of the terms προαμαρτάνειν and μετανοεῖν which together allude to *initial* repentance and conversion.

The mention of unrepentant sexually immoral persons in the Corinthian community at 12:21 thus does not weaken the argument that ἀδόκιμος at 13:5 refers to people who fail the test because they have never converted to Christianity. Rather, it alerts us to the fact that Paul may have thought that some Corinthians would actually fail the test and prove to be "rejected as nonconverts." Although he intended the exhortation to self-testing primarily to motivate the Corinthians to affirm his own provenness as their

---

[110] Lietzmann's argument that baptism had already eradicated the sins prior to entrance into the community (*Kor*, 160) receives just criticism from Georgi, who comments that Paul does not think so "magisch" about baptism (*Gegner*, 233).

[111] Windisch, *2 Kor*, 411. So also Bultmann, *2 Kor*, 242. Similarly, Georgi (*Gegner*, 233), who suggests that 1 Cor 3:3 is a parallel accusation that the immoral Corinthians were never really Christians at all. Cf. Schlatter: "Denn das Verhalten, das aus der Vergebung und Heiligung folgerichtig entsteht, ist die Umkehr, μετάνοια. Blieb sie aus, weil die innere Befleckung aus der heidnischen oder jüdischen Zeit auch in den Christenstand hinüberwirkte, so ergab dies einen unwahren und unwirksamen Christenstand, der nicht auf die Dauer möglich war. Bei dieser Deutung geschieht die von Paulus verlangte μετάνοια zugleich mit der Annahme des christlichen Worts" (*Bote*, 674, 675).

founding apostle, he may have envisioned a secondary effect, that of exposing certain Corinthians' failure to repent and be converted and of reminding them that they will not escape severe discipline (cf. 13:10).

The problem of a minority of unconverted church members in Corinth may be reflected not only in the persistent sexual immorality of some church members but also in the mentality of the opposition to Paul. The Corinthians expect from Paul the signs of an apostle which the rival missionaries in Corinth impressively display. But they find him deficient in this respect.[112] Their game of "testing apostles" resembles the intellectual "marketplace" outside the church where the religious propagandists of their day competed for adherents. D. Georgi has analyzed the phenomenon of religious propagandizing in NT times and has found good reason to consider the methods and evaluation standards of Paul's opponents and their followers in Corinth as one and the same with the practices of religious propagandists and their adherents in Judaism and the Hellenistic world at large. That is, the "pneumatic competition" in Corinth reveals a fundamentally preconversion attitude not only of the rival missionaries but also of some Corinthians themselves insofar as they deny Paul's apostleship and allow themselves to be persuaded by the "false apostles" (11:13). According to Georgi, this spirit of "pneumatic competition" explains why Paul can think "die Korinther seien in Wirklichkeit nie Christen geworden."[113] Those who continue to appraise apostolic claims by non-Christian standards betray that they have not yet recognized the Christ who speaks through his apostle and thereby establishes his apostle's claims as legitimate. They are akin to the ψυχικὸς ἄνθρωπος, who cannot understand or accept the things of the Spirit of God, which only a πνευματικός can do (1 Cor 2:14, 15). If Georgi is right in paralleling the Corinthians' mentality with attitudes and practices in contemporaneous non-Christian religious propagandizing, the possibility of falsely professing, unconverted members of the community in Corinth seems even more likely. Not only unrepentant sexually immoral persons but also Paul's hardest critics in Corinth may not yet have abandoned paganism in their thinking and behavior.

We thus have a two-fold indication that a secondary as well as a primary agenda may lie behind the statement, εἰ μήτι ἀδόκιμοί ἐστε. Besides provoking the majority of Corinthians to affirm that Paul is not ἀδόκιμος (for that would lead to the impossible conclusion that *they* are ἀδόκιμοι), it could also expose a minority of Corinthians who intransigently resist Paul's

---

112 See p. 217 above.
113 Georgi, *Gegner*, 233, 234.

authority as still unconverted. The contextual evidence from 2 Cor 12:21 thus corroborates the interpretation of ἀδόκιμος as referring to those rejected in an unconverted state by making it plausible that some professing Christians in Corinth had actually remained unconverted.

In conclusion, the immediate and larger contexts and the general NT use of ἀδόκιμος support the interpretation of 2 Cor 13:5 as "unless you are rejected as nonconverts." The meaning given to ἀδόκιμος here not only conforms to general NT use of the term but also makes excellent sense in the context of Paul's apostolic self-defense. Understood in this way, the verse not only provides an argument for Paul's apostleship but also, as its secondary function, deals with the suspected pocket of falsely professing Christians in the Corinthian community. In 2 Cor 13:5 then Paul does not suggest that some of his converts in Corinth have lost salvation.[114]

---

[114] Against Barrett, *2 Cor*, 337 (following Kümmel), who is inconsistent with his own understanding of Paul's argument at this point (see n. 87 above).

CONCLUSION TO PART THREE

In Part Three I have sought to define more precisely Paul's understanding of continuity in salvation by discussing the matter of failure to believe in the gospel on the part of those who are elect or professing Christians. The possibility of Christians' alienation from the gospel in 2 Cor 13:5 turns out not to be a warning against loss of salvation. The context shows that ἀδόκιμος can only mean rejection as a nonconvert, and that the exhortation to self-testing has the main purpose of pointing out Paul's own provenness as an apostle and possibly the subordinate purpose of exposing some Corinthians to be falsely professing Christians. In other texts, however, Paul does envision the possibility of lack of faith on the part of the elect and their ensuing alienation from salvation.

After ascribing divine election such importance for continuity in salvation in Romans 8, Paul must provide some explanation of the seemingly contradictory exclusion of God's elect people Israel from the salvation which has come in Christ. In Romans 9–11 Paul argues that Israel's present exclusion—apart from a remnant—is compatible with divine election since election does not entail *automatic* participation in salvation *apart from faith in Christ*. Thus only a *believing* remnant is now included in salvation. Nevertheless, Israel's election as *election to salvation* is still valid. In the end, God will save Israel. And God will save not just a part of God's people but "all Israel." The temporary hardening over Israel (for the sake of the Gentiles' salvation), which accounts for their rejection of the gospel, will be removed and, turning in faith to the gospel through the redeemer who will come and bestow forgiveness, the presently unbelieving Jews will join the believing remnant in salvation. Paul shows in this way that the faithfulness of the electing God still stands. He shows further that faith in Christ is integral to the completion of God's saving purpose for the elect. God's faithful accomplishment of God's purpose includes bringing the elect to faith in the gospel. For only as believers in Christ do the elect receive the fullness of salvation. Israel's unbelief does not rule out the final accomplishment of God's elective purpose. Rather, God's faithfulness makes this purpose certain to be realized.

In the course of his discussion of the destiny of Israel, in Rom 11:17–24 Paul mentions the possibility of the boastful Gentile Christians' alienation from salvation. Gentiles who have been incorporated into the community where God's promises are being fulfilled can also be alienated from salvation in unbelief. For it is true for them too that participation in salvation is only "in faith." Without faith, the Gentiles —like the Jews who are elect—

will be cut off and subject to divine severity. Unfortunately, however, Paul does not develop this point further. He fails to clarify whether he conceives of the potential cutting off of the boastful Gentiles as final or temporary. Instead he abruptly moves on to his main concern, the question of the reintegration of the Jews. There he ends the discussion inspired by the metaphor of the olive tree by noting God's faithfulness and power to carry out God's elective purpose, the stress of the whole of chaps. 9-11.

Although Rom 11:17-24 falls short of telling us explicitly whether Paul thinks a final rupture in the salvation of Christians through unbelief is possible, this text plays a significant role in helping us refine our understanding of Paul's view of continuity in salvation. The fact that God need not spare the branches on the olive tree but can—and does—cut them off shows again that for Paul continuity in salvation is not automatic. Though Paul teaches (materially) a type of perseverance of the saints, he has not made the gospel into a closed system of divine election.

The illustration which Paul chose to denote participation in salvation in Rom 11:17–24—drawing on the root as a branch on the olive tree—could have served him well to describe an automatic notion of perseverance in which the divine clock of salvation simply ticks away in the lives of the elect. For the relationship of a branch to the root is an organic one; the branch draws life from the fatness of the root as the laws of nature run their course. But Paul develops the metaphor in such a way that there is nothing "natural" about the relation of the branches to the root. The branches representing the Gentiles are able to derive nourishment from the root only because they have been grafted into the olive tree. Not only are they grafts; they come from a different kind of tree: they are wild olive branches, not from a cultivated olive tree, and are grafted in παρὰ φύσιν (11:24). Thus their engrafting is even more unnatural. And even the olive tree's very own branches must undergo a special procedure in order to draw life from the root (Paul is speaking here only about the branches which represent the unbelieving Jews, not the believing minority). Although they are branches κατὰ φύσιν, since they have been cut off, they must also be grafted in.

Not only do the branches gain access to the root's nourishment through an unnatural intervention. Once on the tree, their sharing in the root is nothing to take for granted. The branches' further relationship to the root depends not on the course of nature but on the action of the gardener: the one who cut off and engrafted may in the future cut off and engraft again. He is not bound by a process once set in motion; rather, his actions determine the continuing relationship between branches and root. Because of God's doing the branches "stand" or "fall," because of divine "kindness" or "severity."

They do not stand or fall because of their own actions—that is the point of Paul's saying they "stand in faith" and "are cut off in unbelief." Staying on the olive tree is thus not a foregone conclusion. God "need not spare" them. By developing the metaphor of the olive tree in this unexpected way Paul shows that in his view continuity in salvation is not based on inherent necessity but on the continual intervention of God for the sake of the elect.

Behind Paul's depiction of continuity in salvation not as automatic but as dependent on the action of God, who can interrupt it or give it continuity, lies an important theological truth. If the path of the elect to final salvation progressed automatically with no possibility of premature termination, the free grace of salvation would be obscured. For Paul salvation is exclusively by God's sovereign and unconstrained grace from start to finish. God is and God remains the sole and gracious subject of salvation. Therefore perseverance cannot be automatic. Paul's doctrine of salvation excludes the kind of perseverance that amounts to an automatic, closed system of divine election. But if perseverance means that the salvation which is at every moment and in every stage only a work of divine grace is certain to be completed, perseverance is compatible with Paul's doctrine of salvation by grace alone. Paul thus remains true to the gospel by making continuity in salvation a possibility which *will* come to realization rather than a logical necessity.

Perseverance thus depends on God's gracious action toward the elect. The guarantee of final salvation lies in God, not in the elect, not even in a process outside of God which automatically unfolds in their lives. And God is totally free in working out God's saving purpose for the elect; nothing constrains God to save us; God's saving work proceeds entirely from God's gracious character. The possibility of perseverance becomes a reality for the elect because God faithfully continues to act graciously toward them.

For Paul perseverance does not mean that the threat to continuity in salvation is not real—it *is* real. Ruptures in salvation through unbelief can occur. But perseverance means that God continues to give the gift of salvation to those who are repeatedly in danger of losing it, for salvation is by grace alone, and God is faithful. The epistle to the Galatians, which at first appears contrary to the notion of continuity in salvation in that it reveals the possibility of Christians' losing salvation by abandoning faith in the one true gospel, in fact exemplifies this Paul's brand of perseverance. For Galatians shows up divine grace to be the sole fundament of salvation from beginning to end, and faith in God's gracious gift as the sole mode of participation in salvation now til its consummation. Further, Galatians teaches God's faithfulness to overcome the obstacle to perseverance posed by the false gospel which nullifies God's grace and to keep believers from abandoning the gospel of grace in Christ.

To sum up, while Paul recognizes the real danger of exclusion from salvation through absence or abandonment of faith in Christ, his fundamental belief in God's faithfulness accounts for the apostle's hope and even conviction of the final perseverance in faith of the elect, which in his discussions emerges as his dominant perspective. Further, in the light of Paul's affirmations of ultimate continuity in salvation despite possible temporary alienation from the gospel we can say that Paul sees the tension introduced into the process of a person's salvation through unbelief or wrong belief to be highly inappropriate, but not incompatible, with final continuity in salvation. In the end, Paul is confident that God will faithfully complete the salvation begun in the elect. God will do so not apart from their faith in the gospel, but accompanied by their faith, though that faith is not necessarily a constant in the process of salvation, which derives its essential continuity instead from divine initiative.

PART FOUR

FINAL OUTCOME OF MISSION

After having examined Paul's view of continuity in salvation in the light of ethical failure and unbelief or abandonment of the gospel we will look at a last group of texts in which Paul reflects in a deeply personal way on the final outcome of his mission, and addresses the question whether it will end in eschatological success or failure. Paul considers his own final destiny in the texts analyzed in Chapter VIII, and the destiny of his converts in those treated in Chapter XI. Will the outward successes manifested in his apostolic ministry be crowned in glory and triumph on the last day, or will they not last but be unmasked as deceptions and fail to withstand the final test, despite all the effort the apostle has expended?

VIII. PAUL'S HOPE

Passing the Test

1 Corinthians 9:27. In 1 Cor 9:27 Paul uses the term ἀδόκιμος with reference to himself. Here he is concerned not that others might know he *is not ἀδόκιμος*, as in 2 Cor 13:6, 7, but that he might *not become ἀδόκιμος*. He goes to great lengths in order not to become so: ὑπωπιάζω μου τὸ σῶμα καὶ δουλαγωγῶ, μή πως ἄλλοις κηρύξας αὐτὸς ἀδόκιμος γένωμαι.[1] Many have thought that Paul here expresses his fear of being found unqualified for salvation in the final test. The test to which ἀδόκιμος alludes however is not specified.[2] To judge the merits of the interpretation suggested and of alternatives I will examine the Pauline use of δόκιμος terminology, the context and parallels.

Often interpreters as a matter of course take ἀδόκιμος to describe the " 'reprobate'...those who are outside the kingdom of God."[3] The term can have this association in the NT (cf. Rom 1:28; 2 Cor 13:5; 2 Tim 3:8; Tit 1:16). Yet it also occurs without it. In 2 Cor 13:5–7 Paul uses the term with a double meaning. In v. 5 it refers to the Corinthians and means "rejected in the test of faith."[4] In vv. 6, 7, however, Paul applies the term to himself and his fellow-apostles with the meaning "rejected in the test of apostleship."[5] The context makes this clearly the meaning of Paul's self-reference. His refutation, ἡμεῖς οὐκ ἐσμὲν ἀδόκιμοι, counters the Corinthians' accusation that Paul and his companions were in fact ἀδόκιμοι. This accusation

---

[1] The degree of effort Paul makes to pass the test here is appropriate in view of the great significance he ascribes to the Lord's judgment of him; see 1 Cor 4:4, 5. On common elements in 1 Cor 9:1ff. and 4:1ff., cf. Theissen, "Legitimation," 218, 219.

[2] Cf. 2 Cor 13:5; 2 Tim 3:8; 1 Cor 11:19; Rom 1:28; Tit 1:16; Heb 6:8; Jas 1:12 for δόκιμος/ἀδόκιμος in contexts which make clear in what respect one may be approved or unapproved.

[3] See, e.g., Osborne, "Soteriology," 160.

[4] See p. 217 above.

[5] Correctly, Héring: "Il y a cependant une nuance dans la manière dont ἀδόκιμος est employé respectivement aux v. 6 et 7. Dans le cas de l'apôtre il ne s'agit pas d'un examen de conscience, mais d'une preuve de ses capacités, il y a donc presque un jeu de mots" (*2 Cor*, 103, n. 1).

aims not at their profession of Christian faith, as though they were repro-
bates and not true Christians, but at the genuineness of their apostleship.[6]
The Corinthians had put Paul to the test as to whether or not Christ was
speaking through him as an apostle: δοκιμὴν ζητεῖτε τοῦ ἐν ἐμοὶ λα-
λοῦντος Χριστοῦ (13:3).[7] But Paul will not fail the test—even according
to their criteria of true apostleship: ἐὰν ἔλθω εἰς τὸ πάλιν οὐ φείσομαι
(13:2). He can and will, if necessary, demonstrate the kind of apostolic
ἐξουσία which has persuasive power in Corinth. Yet he would rather gain
recognition of his apostleship without having to resort to such severity
(13:10; cf. 10:2). Paul knows that if Christ is truly in the Corinthian believers, they will recognize the same Christ speaking through Paul the apostle
of Christ. So Paul induces them to confirm his apostleship indirectly by
confirming the authenticity of their own faith: ἑαυτοὺς δοκιμάζετε · ἢ
οὐκ ἐπιγινώσκετε ἑαυτοὺς ὅτι Ἰησοῦς Χριστὸς ἐν ὑμῖν, εἰ μήτι
ἀδόκιμοί ἐστε (13:5). Those who do not fail the test of true Christian profession will realize that Paul also does not fail the test of genuine apostleship (13:6).[8] As a result they will drop their charges against him and make
it unnecessary for him to use severity when he comes. Thus Paul and his
companions will appear ὡς ἀδόκιμοι (13:7) on their next visit to Corinth
because they will not (need to) display outwardly impressive signs of apostleship which had an appeal in Corinth (10:7).[9]

Nevertheless, Paul saw his provenness as an apostle to manifest itself in
an entirely different way than the Corinthians did. Though they took offense at the weakness which characterized Paul's apostolic ministry (cf.
10:10; 11:5–7; 12:13),[10] he regarded this very weakness, through which
Christ's power was mightily at work (cf. 4:7, 10, 11; 12:9, 10), as divine
authentication of his apostleship.[11] And it was the divine verdict on his

---

[6] The question whether Paul and his associates or his opponents could rightfully
make the claim Χριστοῦ εἶναι (2 Cor 10:7) also has nothing to do with the genuineness
of their Christian profession. Correctly, Bultmann, *2 Kor*, 189: "Es kann nicht gemeint
sein das gewöhnliche Christsein..., sondern nur etwas Auszeichnendes."

[7] Windisch, *2 Kor*, 417: "δοκιμή...ist hier nämlich ein bestimmter konkreter Erweis
seiner ap. ἐξουσία."

[8] On Paul's argument in 2 Cor 13:5ff., see, further, pp. 217–225 above.

[9] The Corinthians should have remembered that Paul had already performed these
kind of signs among them (12:12).

[10] On the unimposing character of Paul's ministry, see, further, 4:7–12; 6:4–10;
11:23b–33; 12:5, 9, 10.

[11] Cf. Theissen ("Legitimation," 225): "Paulus vertritt dagegen eine andere Form
apostolischer Legitimität, eine funktionale, die er mit Elementen einer charismatischen
verbindet—wobei er gerade sein charismatisches Defizit, seine 'Schwäche' als Zeichen
seiner apostolischen Existenz hervorhebt. Diese beiden Legitimationsformen stehen in
Zusammenhang mit verschiedenen Weisen, den Lebensunterhalt zu bestreiten."

apostleship which truly mattered to Paul. He attached importance neither to self-commendation (cf. 10:18) nor to human commendation (cf. 13:7; 3:1; 1 Cor 4:3–5). Rather, he sought to be δόκιμος in God's eyes: οὐ γὰρ ὁ ἑαυτὸν συνιστάνων, ἐκεῖνός ἐστιν δόκιμος, ἀλλὰ ὃν ὁ κύριος συνίστησιν (10:18).

In summary, in 2 Corinthians Paul applies the terminology of testing—ἀδόκιμος and its cognates—to himself *as an apostle*, not as a professing Christian. Both the content of the Corinthians' accusations and the way Paul defends himself make clear that the authenticity of Paul's apostolic claims is the issue. ἀδόκιμος in Paul's self-references thus does not pertain to the test of faith but to the test of apostleship. Paul hopes the Corinthians will know he does not fail *this* test and will recognize his apostolic authority, so that he will continue to appear "unapproved" by their standards of apostleship.

Elsewhere also Paul uses the terminology of testing for his provenness in apostolic service. Paul defends his apostolic character to the Thessalonians by referring to the divine approval which rests on his apostleship: ἀλλὰ καθὼς δεδοκιμάσμεθα ὑπὸ τοῦ Θεοῦ πιστευθῆναι τὸ εὐαγγέλιον, οὕτως λαλοῦμεν, οὐχ ὡς ἀνθρώποις ἀρέσκοντες ἀλλὰ Θεῷ τῷ δοκιμάζοντι τὰς καρδίας ἡμῶν (1 Thess 2:4). As candidates for public office underwent an evaluation of their capabilities before appointment to office, so also God had tested Paul and his associates and approved them to be commissioned with the task of preaching the gospel.[12] The perfect tense of δεδοκιμάσμεθα indicates the continuing validity of this divine approval.[13] But it is something to be maintained, not taken for granted. Initial approval does not give Paul and his co-workers a *carte blanche* to carry out their commission as they please. Rather, they constantly reckon with God's critical appraisal of their service: ἀρέσκοντες...Θεῷ τῷ δοκιμάζοντι (present tense!) τὰς καρδίας ἡμῶν.[14] This continual subjection to divine testing, the umbrella under which Paul and his associates carry out their apostolic ministry, provides them with a defense against criticisms of their

---

[12] Dibelius, *Thess*, 7; Morris, *Thess*, 72. For δοκιμάζειν as a *terminus technicus* for official testing, cf. Grundmann, δόκιμος, *TWNT* 2, 259, n. 4. For the NT uses of δοκιμάζειν and cognates as testing fitness for a task, cf. 1 Tim 3:10; Phil 2:22; Rom 16:10; 2 Cor 8:22.

[13] Morris, *Thess*, 72.

[14] Grundmann (δόκιμος, *TWNT* 2, 260) comments on 1 Thess 2:4: "Ihr Apostolat gründet in Gottes prüfendem Ratschluß, in der Führung ihres Amtes wissen sie sich unter Gottes prüfenden Augen." For δοκιμάζειν of God's testing people in the LXX, cf. Jer 11:20; 17:10; 20:12; Ps 25:2.

ministry.[15] For no missionaries with erroneous teaching, impure character, deceit, greed and thirst for recognition would receive divine approval as Paul and his companions have, much less, continually seek such approval (2:3, 5, 6). Their seeking divine approval causes them to reject both the dubious practices of wandering sophists, impostors and propagandists of religious cults,[16] and even their own rights as apostles. Lest they be accused of egotistical glory-seeking, they gave up their right to the Thessalonians' special honor as apostles of Christ (2:6, 7).[17] Lest someone suppose they use their missionary activities as a pretext for personal financial gain, they renounced their apostolic right to remuneration for their service and instead worked day and night so as not to burden the Thessalonians financially (2:5, 9). These sacrifices show that they seek divine, not human, approval. Paul turns his consciousness of divine testing and approval throughout his ministry (cf. also 1 Cor 4:1–5; 2 Cor 4:2; 5:9, 10; 10:18) into an argument for the legitimacy of his apostleship. In summary, a survey of Paul's self-references with ἀδόκιμος and cognates has shown that Paul always has in mind the test of his apostleship when he applies the terminology of testing to himself.

2 Tim 2:15 uses the terminology of testing in a similar way. The exhortation to Timothy, σπούδασον σεαυτὸν δόκιμον παραστῆσαι τῷ Θεῷ, does not presuppose the danger of his becoming a reprobate but an unfaithful servant who did not adequately fulfill his calling: he should be approved as an ἐργάτης ἀνεπαίσχυντος. Timothy the missionary,[18] not Timothy the Christian, is pictured standing before God in the eschatological judgment.[19] Not Timothy's conduct in general, but whether he has preached the gospel correctly (ὀρθοτομοῦντα τὸν λόγον τῆς ἀληθείας) will give him cause for shame or confidence. Thus, being δόκιμος depends on having performed his ministry faithfully (cf. Phil 2:22). This verse parallels Paul's application of ἀδόκιμος and its cognates to himself to connote provenness in the test of service.

Not only can we now assert that ἀδόκιμος in 1 Cor 9:27 need not refer to failing the test of faith and have the connotation "reprobate." The fact that no instance of the use of ἀδόκιμος or a cognate referring to Paul re-

---

[15] Frame, *Thess*, 96.

[16] Frame, *Thess*, 94; Theissen, "Legitimation," 213 with n. 1.

[17] ἐν βάρει εἶναι (2:7) could mean "to be burdensome," and refer to Paul's renunciation of his apostolic right to the church's financial support, which comes up in 2:9 (cf. 2 Thess 3:8; 2 Cor 12:16; 11:9; 1 Cor 9:6–12); cf. Frame, *Thess*, 99.

[18] For ἐργάτης with the meaning "missionary," cf. 2 Cor 11:13; Phil 3:2; Holtz, *Pastoralbriefe*, 171.

[19] For the eschatological judgment of Christian service, cf. also 1 Cor 3:13-15; 4:1-5.

lates to the test of faith or salvation, rather, that every instance has to do with his fitness as an apostle raises doubts about the view that ἀδόκιμος in 1 Cor 9:27 means rejected from salvation and suggests instead that it means rejected as an apostle.[20] The larger context favors this view as well, since the meaning "rejected as an apostle" fits nicely in Paul's apology for his apostolic status (which his "weak" behavior has called into question) beginning in 9:1 and extending through the whole chapter.[21] Does the other evidence in the context support the interpretation that Paul's use of ἀδόκιμος in 1 Cor 9:27 corresponds in meaning to his other self-references with ἀδόκιμος, that is, that this verse alludes to the danger of Paul's losing the divine approval on the basis of which he received his apostolic commission and now fulfills it? Most interpreters argue from the context that μή πως... ἀδόκιμος γένωμαι expresses Paul's fear of losing salvation. We now turn to these contextual arguments.

In 9:24–27 Paul develops an athletic metaphor[22] and in the process describes the way in which he attempts to avoid becoming ἀδόκιμος: "Therefore I run in such a way as not without aim, I box in such a way as not beating air; rather I buffet my body and enslave it, lest, after I have preached to others, I myself might become unapproved" (vv. 26, 27). What can we deduce from the metaphor about the nature of the test which Paul wants to pass? What do his "athletic" efforts symbolize?

The metaphor serves to make the point that an athlete must let the goal ahead determine present behavior. Winning depends on rigorous self-control in training (πάντα ἐγκρατεύεται,[23] v. 25). Without it one cannot "run so as to obtain" (οὕτως τρέχετε[24] ἵνα καταλάβητε, v. 24) and be the winner of the prize (v. 24). Paul is like a good athlete. He is not oblivious

---

[20] Pfitzner (*Agon*, 96) interprets ἀδόκιμος at 1 Cor 9:27 in the light of 1 Thess 2:4. It should also be noted here that Paul does not think that those who fail the test of *service* automatically also fail the test of salvation. At 1 Cor 3:15 he envisions the possibility that a Christian servant whose work does not pass the test will nevertheless be saved at the judgment.

[21] For the inclusion of vv. 24–27 in Paul's apostolic self-defense, see below, p. 247 with n. 79.

[22] Diatribists made frequent use of allusions to the athletic world, and with good reason. For their Greek audiences sport formed a part of daily life (Conzelmann, *1 Cor*, 162, n. 31). The metaphor is especially well-chosen here, since the Corinthians hosted the Isthmian games (Reinmuth, "Isthmien," 1474f.). Thus Paul can appeal to their knowledge of the things he is describing (οὐκ οἴδατε ὅτι..., 9:24).

[23] The reference to the training period unnaturally follows the reference to the race (Lietzmann, *Kor*, 44). But Paul does not need a correct chronological sequence in the metaphor in order to illustrate the influence which the goal exercises on the athlete's conduct.

[24] τρέχετε is either imperative or indicative.

of the goal: ἐγὼ τοίνυν οὕτως τρέχω ὡς οὐκ ἀδήλως,[25] οὕτως πυ κτεύω ὡς οὐκ ἀέρα δέρων[26] (v. 26). Rather he is aiming for it! Paul's goal-oriented behavior is pictured not merely as self-renunciation in training (cf. ἐγκρατεύεσθαι, v. 25) but, even more radically, as the self-flagellation of a boxer throwing punches against himself: ὑπωπιάζω[27] μου τὸ σῶμα (v. 27a). The athlete's renunciation of the body's desires could not be pictured more graphically.[28] Here renunciation itself is a contest in which the goal is complete subjection of the σῶμα;[29] Paul wants to make his σῶμα his slave (δουλαγωγῶ[30]). The subjugation of the σῶμα serves the attainment of the goal.

Some have identified Paul's violent battle against his σῶμα in v. 27a with the Christian struggle against sin.[31] They conclude that Paul's fear of becoming ἀδόκιμος in v. 27b is therefore his fear of losing salvation.[32] They appeal to 10:5–22 in support, where the Israelites crave evil in the wilderness and die without reaching the promised land, so that Paul warns

---

[25] ἀδήλως means "aimlessly" (BAGD, s.v. ἀδήλως), not "unsure of the goal." Against the latter meaning, see Robertson and Plummer, *1 Cor*, 196.

[26] ἀέρα δέρων most probably refers to aimless activity, not ineffective activity. For the parallelism of the footrace and the boxing match here suggests that ἀέρα δέρων parallels ἀδήλως in meaning (Pfitzner, *Agon*, 91).

[27] ὑπωπιάζειν at v. 27a, which literally means "hit under the eye" (BAGD, s.v. ὑπωπιάζω), continues the language of prize-fighting from v. 26b.

[28] Weiß (*1 Kor*, 249) does not see a return to the theme of ἐγκράτεια, or preparation for the contest, until δουλαγωγῶ. But ἐγκράτεια itself is a kind of contest between the competitor and his own body with its desires which the athlete must dominate. The boxing metaphor aptly pictures this battle of renunciation. This aptness made the figure of the pugilist more appropriate than that of the runner to describe Paul's own renunciation—therefore the sudden switch in metaphors.

[29] σῶμα here has a "specifically and emphatically physical meaning," according to Gundry, *ΣΩΜΑ*, 186, 187, 161; similarly, Pfitzner, *Agon*, 93.

[30] Godet (*1 Kor II*, 39) suggests that δουλαγωγῶ means "lead as captive" and alludes to the practice of the victor leading the loser around the arena for all the spectators to see: "So führt gleichsam Paulus seinen Leib, nachdem er dessen Widerstand gebrochen, dem Auge der Welt als einen solchen vor, der ihm unterworfen...ist." Weiß (*1 Kor*, 248), however, denies that δουλαγωγῶ fits the metaphor.

[31] E.g., Barrett, *1 Cor*, 218: "Here Paul recognizes the need to beat his body out of its all too ready obedience to sin"; so also Grosheide, *1 Cor*, 216; Robertson and Plummer, *1 Cor*, 197. Marshall (*Kept*, 121) seems to favor this interpretation when he says that Paul could become disqualified from salvation not through poor Christian service but through "failure to withstand the temptations of the body and to keep it under" (as the Israelites failed to keep their bodily passions under control in 10:1–10). "But," Marshall thinks, "there is little doubt that Paul felt no severe temptation from this quarter."

[32] So Grundmann, δόκιμος, *TWNT* 2, 260; Barrett, *1 Cor*, 218; Schlatter, *Bote*, 286; Godet, *1 Kor II*, 40. Marshall (*Kept*, 121) sees only a "theoretical possibility" of Paul's rejection from salvation here.

the Corinthians against following their example.[33] But even I. H. Marshall, who suggests this connection, registers doubts: "it must be admitted that the connexion of thought between chs. 9 and 10 may not be very close."[34] It seems best to take the disputed γάρ in 10:1 as a loose connective[35] rather than as introducing a ground for the preceding.

Although J. Weiß more boldly posits a "sehr gute Beziehung" of 9:24–27 to 10:1–23, in his actual treatment of vv. 24–27 he draws parallels with passages like 4:11ff. and 2 Cor 4:8ff., which describe apostolic suffering (including Paul's labor with his own hands, which further strengthens the parallelism with 1 Cor 9:1–23).[36] In the last analysis, he provides more support for a connection of vv. 24–27 to the previous discussion of Paul's renunciation of his apostolic rights resulting in privation and hard work—a connection which he calls poorer, though does not reject—than to the following discussion in 10:1–23. And in fact Paul does show that he intends vv. 24–27 to be taken with the preceding by his introductory οὐκ οἴδατε ὅτι at v. 24, which indicates continuation of the train of thought from the previous section with a fresh illustration.[37] The parallels Weiß adduces relating the athletic metaphor to Paul's apostolic suffering lead us in the right direction in interpreting Paul's subjugation of his σῶμα.

In 1 Cor 9:24–27 we do not have to do with the "general concept of the Christian's self-discipline"[38] in relation to the temptations of the flesh, which smacks of the now outmoded view that Paul used the athletic metaphor to picture life as a moral *agon*.[39] Rather, Paul is illustrating discipline

---

[33] For a discussion of the significance of 1 Cor 10:1ff. for perseverance, see pp. 120–130 above.

[34] Marshall, *Kept*, 121.

[35] With most commentators (contrast Robertson and Plummer, *1 Cor*, 199).

[36] Weiß, *1 Kor*, 246, 248. Barrett (*1 Cor*, 218) interprets 1 Cor 9:27 in the light of Rom 6:13, 19, where Paul speaks of putting the physical members in the service of righteousness. But that text does not provide a good parallel to 1 Corinthians 9, where apostolic suffering and self-renunciation for the sake of the gospel and evangelism, not righteousness and sin, are in view.

[37] See Pfitzner, *Agon*, 84. Cf. οὐκ οἴδατε ὅτι at 9:13, where it also introduces a new example. οὐκ οἴδατε ὅτι indicates the beginning of the metaphor (Straub, *Bildersprache*, 106).

[38] Against Marshall, *Kept*, 121; similarly, Barrett, *1 Cor*, 218; Héring, *1 Cor*, 103.

[39] See Pfitzner's (*Agon*, 78–81) critique of this older view. Summarizing, he says: "But the above characterisations are guilty of ascribing an emphasis to Paul which is not found in his use of the metaphor, but is largely transplanted over to him from the traditional use of the image or from the motifs which the image of the games suggested to the Greek mind" (80). In fact, when Paul applies such imagery to himself, most often it describes his own ministry in the gospel (cf. Gal 2:2; Phil 2:16; 1 Thess 2:2; contrast Phil 3:12–14). Paul's choice of the term σῶμα points away from the moral *agon*, since σῶμα lacks the negative connotations of σάρξ (Rom 6:6; Col 2:11 are exceptions). Cf.

with regard to the use of Christian rights and freedom, which has been his main concern since 8:1. Like the athlete's practice of ἐγκράτεια, Paul's subjugation of the body consists in renunciation of physical desires which are satisfied through normal, accepted behavior. The athlete was deprived of wine, meat and sexual activity for a ten month training period.[40] Similarly Paul gave up practices to which he had a rightful claim. He renounced his right to marry (9:5) and to receive the Corinthians' financial support (9:12, 15, 18). Instead, he lived on his own meager earnings.[41] Moreover, he so radically limited his freedom in Christ that he became a slave to all (ἐλεύθερος γὰρ ὢν ἐκ πάντων πᾶσιν ἐμαυτὸν ἐδούλωσα..., 9:19) by becoming all things to all people in order by all means to save some (9:22). The use of similar verbs to denote "slavery" in apostolic service in 9:19 (ἐμαυτὸν ἐδούλωσα) and the "enslavement" of the σῶμα in 9:27 (μου τὸ σῶμα...δουλαγωγῶ) is significant. It illustrates Paul's practice of connecting the metaphor to its context through a catchword.[42] As V. Pfitzner observes, "the significance of δουλαγωγῶ is...to be gained from...ἐδούλωσα in v. 19."[43] This parallel and the abundance of references to Paul's renunciation of his rights immediately preceding the athletic metaphor make it most natural to define the attacks of Paul against his σῶμα as his self-subjection to physically trying circumstances as a result of renouncing his apostolic rights and limiting his use of Christian freedom.[44]

9:27a then recapitulates the previous arguments that Paul renounces his apostolic rights (9:1b–18) and Christian freedom (9:1a, 19–22) for the sake of attaining a greater goal.[45] Chap. 9 as a whole, therefore, presents the

---

Godet, *1 Kor* II, 39: "Er sagt nicht: sein Fleisch, als ob er hier das sündige Wesen, das an dem Leib haftet, hervorheben wollte"; cf. also Pfitzner, *Agon*, 92, 93.

[40] Weiß, *1 Kor*, 247 with n. 5.

[41] Perhaps Paul found the comparison with the athlete especially appropriate since like the athlete in training he practiced continence (as a bachelor), and since on account of his meager earnings he presumably did not enjoy a diet including costly meat and wine, the very enjoyments given up by the athlete.

[42] Cf. 2 Cor 3:1–3 with the catchword ἐπιστολή. Straub (*Bildersprache*, 106) comments: "In den meisten Fällen fehlt ein erkennbarer Übergang bei Beginn der Bildrede. Der Verfasser geht ohne weiteres zu ihr über, ein Zeichen, wie eng die Gleichnisse in den Zusammenhang eingebettet sind. Eine Verknüpfung kann jedoch hergestellt werden durch ein Stichwort."

[43] Pfitzner, *Agon*, 93. Contrast 2 Cor 11:20, where Paul's opponents enslave the Corinthians instead of enslaving themselves for the Corinthians' sake as Paul does!

[44] Cf. Dautzenberg: "[σῶμα] steht für den von Natur lebenshungrigen, selbstsüchtigen und machtbewußten [Menschen]" ("Verzicht," 232).

[45] Jeremias ("Chiasmus," 290): "Er [Paulus] gibt zwei Beispiele für seine Verzichtbereitschaft: 1. οὐκ εἰμὶ ἐλεύθερος; (V. 1a)—ausgeführt in V. 19–27, und 2. οὐκ εἰμὶ

apostle as a model of the renunciation motivated by love which is proper to all Christians, a topic which Paul has discussed in chap. 8.[46] It follows that the application of the athletic metaphor to Christians in 9:24, 25 should also not be taken to picture their moral struggle but the contest in which they too engage to subdue the body by renouncing their Christian rights and liberties. The exhortation to follow the apostle and exercise discipline in the use of Christian rights and freedoms repeats itself in 10:23–11:1, where there is also no indication of a moral struggle either on Paul's part or on the part of Christians.[47]

If Paul is like the athlete in that he subjects his physical existence to great trials through renunciation of his rights and freedom, he must also, like the athlete, have a goal which greatly motivates his extraordinary renunciation. Paul names his goal in v. 27b: μή πως ἄλλοις κηρύξας αὐτὸς ἀδόκιμος γένωμαι.[48] Some interpreters correctly define Paul's battle against his σῶμα as renunciation of apostolic rights and Christian freedom, yet interpret ἀδόκιμος to mean loss of salvation.[49] But is it likely that Paul could lose his salvation by exercising his very apostolic *rights* and Christian *freedom* instead of renouncing them?[50] The apostolic right to financial support even rests on a command of Jesus: ὁ κύριος διέταξεν τοῖς τὸ εὐαγγέλιον καταγγέλλουσιν ἐκ τοῦ εὐαγγελίου ζῆν (9:14).[51] And Paul mentions that other apostles make use of their rights in the gospel without this practice calling their salvation into question (9:4–6). Paul's going beyond the call of duty in his apostolic ministry does not mean that

---

ἀπόστολος (V. 1b)—ausgeführt in V. 1c–18."

[46] With Jeremias, "Chiasmus," 289: "Paulus zeigt den Korinthern an seinem eigenen Verhalten, wie ein Christ auf ihm zustehende Rechte verzichten kann"; cf. Pfitzner, *Agon*, 84. Scholars now widely recognize the integral connection of chap. 9 to the context in which it is here embedded, Paul's discussion of meat offered to idols in 8:1–11:1.

[47] In 10:23–11:1 Paul will again plead for voluntary renunciation of Christian rights and freedom (cf. Conzelmann, *1 Cor*, 175). Although all is permitted (10:23), although Christians are free (10:29), they ought to relinquish their freedom when it stands in the way of another's good (10:28, 29; cf. 8:9). As in chap. 9, so also in 10:33–11:1 Paul appeals to his own example of "Verzichtbereitschaft."

[48] Contrast this negative formulation (μή πως) with the positive formulations of the final clauses in vv. 24, 25, but compare the negative formulation in 9:12b (ἵνα μή, cf. 9:15c).

[49] Schlatter, *Bote*, 286; Godet, *1 Kor* II, 39.

[50] In 1 Corinthians 8:7–13 and Romans 14:1–23, the weak Christian who exercises freedom without an accompanying good conscience does not lose salvation but suffers only the existentially destructive consequences of such action, see pp. 85–97 above.

[51] Theissen ("Legitimation," 216) suggests that Paul's very renunciation of financial support in contradiction to Jesus' command (διέταξεν, 1 Cor 9:14) could have made him guilty of mistrusting God's grace in the eyes of some.

he fears for his salvation. For he himself knows that even failure in his ministry would not have put his salvation in the balance. In 1 Cor 3:12–15 he writes that the ἔργον[52] of a συνεργὸς θεοῦ (3:9) may fail the eschatological test of fire without disqualifying the servant from salvation: αὐτὸς δὲ σωθήσεται, οὕτως δὲ ὡς διὰ πυρός (3:15).[53] Even building on the foundation with wood, hay, and straw (3:12) does not disqualify God's servant in the final test. How then will the use of apostolic rights and Christian freedom (9:12b–22) disqualify Paul from salvation?[54]

Nevertheless, does not Paul express concern for his salvation in 9:16c: οὐαὶ γάρ μοί ἐστιν ἐὰν μὴ εὐαγγελίσωμαι? And should not his fear of becoming ἀδόκιμος be interpreted in this light? Paul does in fact imply that resisting the divine compulsion[55] laid upon him to preach the gospel would bring on God's judgment. It is his destiny to preach the gospel, a destiny which he cannot escape—like the prophets of old (cf. Jer 20:9)—without going against the will of God. Paul, however, does not appear to be in danger of resisting this divine necessity to preach the gospel. His struggle is not whether to preach—without question he will do so; he must: ἀνάγκη γάρ μοι ἐπίκειται (9:16b). Rather, Paul's aim is to do more than preach; he endeavors to go beyond the call of duty. He wants to get a reward for his apostolic ministry (μισθός, 9:17, 18), to have a boast that will not be made empty (καύχημα, 9:15, 16a). He assumes salvation. What is in question is the evaluation of his service as an apostle.

Examination of Paul's argument in 9:15–18 shows that the above accurately reflects his line of thought. Paul preaches the gospel in obedience to his divine commission (v. 16b). He does so as a steward who has been entrusted with a charge (v. 17b). It is not his free choice to preach the gospel; he does it ἄκων (v. 17b).[56] And since his preaching is comparable to the

---

[52] The ἔργον in 1 Cor 3:13–15 has been understood either in a general way as "contribution to the life of the church" (Barrett, *1 Cor*, 88; so also Weiß, *1 Kor*, 80: "Gemeindearbeit"; cf. Conzelmann, *1 Cor*, 76: "achievement") or in a more specific way as "die christliche Lehre" (Lietzmann, *Kor*, 17) or the Christian community and its individual members (Schlatter, *Bote*, 134). All relate ἔργον to Christian service. Not the works of a Christian in general but the work of one who builds God's οἰκοδομή, the church, is in view here (correctly, Robertson and Plummer, *1 Cor*, 54). Thus the parallel drawn between Paul's service for the gospel in 1 Corinthians 9 and the Christian service performed by others in 1 Cor 3:12–15 is justified.

[53] σωθήσεται in v. 15 refers to eternal salvation; see commentaries.

[54] Marshall (*Kept*, 121) agrees that if the test of faithful service is in view here "the question of loss of salvation does not arise (cf. 1 Corinthians 3:15)."

[55] The statement ἀνάγκη γάρ μοι ἐπίκειται (9:16b) reveals that Paul understands his preaching as a divine necessity, a destiny given him by God (with Käsemann, *Variation*, 149, 150).

[56] ἄκων does not express lack of motivation but lack of choice. See commentaries.

work of a slave, he cannot boast in it (v. 16a). One gains a reward only by going beyond the call of duty, acting out of free choice, ἑκών (v. 17a).[57] To have a boast or reward Paul must do something not required of him; he must act unconstrained. This he does by giving up his right to financial support through the gospel and offering it free of charge: ἵνα...ἀδάπανον θήσω τὸ εὐαγγέλιον εἰς τὸ μὴ καταχρήσασθαι τῇ ἐξουσίᾳ μου ἐν τῷ εὐαγγελίῳ (v. 18). Paul has given a lengthy confirmation of his apostolic right to "live from the gospel" in 9:1–14. Now he offers a rationale for refusing to use that right. The battle of self-renunciation is so important to him because upon it depends his boast and reward for having served God by his free decision.

The reference to divine judgment in 9:16c therefore does not illuminate the possibility of becoming ἀδόκιμος in 9:27. The latter depends on Paul's success in enslaving his body so as to renounce his rights, not on his willingness to preach. For even if he *has* "preached to others" (ἄλλοις κηρύξας), he could still become ἀδόκιμος (v. 27b). The woe will come if he does not preach; the verdict ἀδόκιμος will come despite his having preached. Instead of anticipating Paul's fear in v. 27, the statement "woe is me if I do not preach" simply illustrates why Paul's mere preaching of the gospel does not qualify him to boast or receive a reward: he *must* preach. Fee observes: "His point is that if his labor is not voluntary, as v. 16 has made clear, then he is not entitled to pay."[58]

9:15–18 nevertheless does seem in a different way to offer some help for interpreting 9:27. The discussion of Paul's reward and boast in the earlier passage introduces into the argument a new dimension in Paul's motivation for renouncing his apostolic rights. Not only does he do so "in order that we might not cause any hindrance to the gospel of Christ" (9:12). A personal interest is also involved: "no one will make my boast empty" (9:15). The personal aspect of Paul's motivation in self-sacrificial service

---

[57] With Conzelmann (*1 Cor*, 158) and Fee (*1 Cor*, 419), v. 17a does not reflect Paul's real situation. Paul is not saying that he preaches voluntarily (ἑκών) even though he is under divine necessity. As Fee argues (419, n. 35), the conditional clause at v. 17a, εἰ γὰρ ἑκὼν τοῦτο πράσσω, though εἰ with the indicative usually expresses a real condition (*BDF* §372), need not be considered a real condition here. Rather it merely sets the stage for the *contrasting* conditional clause at v. 17b, εἰ δὲ ἄκων, which (as the context makes clear) is meant to express Paul's real situation. For the pair of conditional clauses support (γάρ) Paul's statement in v. 16 that his preaching is compulsory, not voluntary. For further discussion of this question, cf. Käsemann, *Variation*, 218–223.

[58] Fee, *1 Cor*, 420. Similarly, Conzelmann (*1 Cor*, 158): "The interest lies not in the theoretic structure of the ἀνάγκη, 'constraint,'but in the practical consequence: only voluntary labor deserves and gains a reward."

surfaces not only in 9:15–18[59] but also in 9:26, 27, where Paul aims not to become ἀδόκιμος.[60] Both passages characterize as self-renunciation Paul's means of attaining his personal goal. Does Paul's aspiration to a καύχημα or μισθός in his apostolic ministry then illuminate the possibility of his becoming ἀδόκιμος? Closer examination of the nature of Paul's καύχημα and μισθός in 9:15–18 will help us determine the relationship to 9:27.

What is the reward or boast which Paul is seeking as an apostle, if it is not obtained through the remuneration of the Corinthians? Certainly not his salvation. For, as noted above, the apostle's salvation does not depend on his sacrificing his apostolic rights. Paul himself offers the explanation that the answer to the question τίς οὖν μού ἐστιν ὁ μισθός; (v. 18a) is nothing other than his offering the gospel free of charge, which he can do by not making use of his right in the gospel (v. 18b).[61] In other words, Paul gets the pay he wants when he takes no μισθός from his hearers. He wants this kind of "remuneration," as he has already indicated, so that, though he is bound to preach, he can still act voluntarily, namely, in preaching *free of charge*. The reward of "no pay" will enable him to boast as one who has acted without constraint (cf. 2 Cor 11:7–10). Ironically, he boasts for having renounced his right, a sign of weakness to others. But Paul's καύχημα is never an occasion for self-glorying (cf. 2 Cor 10:17, 18), rather, for glorying in God, whose power goes to work mightily through human weakness (cf. 2 Cor 12:9).[62] So Paul can boast in his weaknesses (2 Cor 12:5, 9), for thereby he boasts indirectly in the Lord. Paul's intense desire to keep his boast therefore expresses his hope that God's blessing and thus God's favor would manifest itself in his ministry. Paul does not want his boast to become "empty" and his ministry devoid of the signs of divine working. Then his labor would be "in vain" (cf. Phil 2:16; 1 Thess 2:19 with 3:9).[63] Therefore Paul accepts weakness by renouncing his apostolic rights so that God's power can work through him; in this way he endeavors not to make his boast empty. Paul's nonmaterial μισθός and his fear of losing his boast in 9:15–18 therefore clearly have to do with the (true) successfulness of his apostolic ministry.

---

[59] Cf. Nasuti, "Woes," 254.

[60] 1 Cor 9:23 ("in order that I might become a partner with it [the gospel]") focuses more on the progress of the gospel than on Paul's personal interest (see treatment of this verse below, pp. 247–254 below).

[61] Cf. Conzelmann, *1 Cor*, 158.

[62] Cf. Fee, *1 Cor*, 417: his boast is thus "in an indirect way in the gospel itself." Cf. also Nasuti, "Woes," 261: "His real *misthos* lies in the opportunity to share in both the master's work and the fruits of the master's gospel."

[63] Cf. the discussion of Paul's fear of laboring in vain below, pp. 261–271.

After tracing his renunciation of his apostolic rights to his fear of losing his μισθός and καύχημα, Paul shows in 9:19–23 how his personal interests in pursuing a self-sacrificial course in his apostolic ministry ultimately serve the good of others, namely their salvation. Having made this important qualification, Paul then returns to the personal aspect in 9:24–27. The flow of Paul's argument and the parallelism of 9:15–18 and 9:24–27 thus suggest that Paul's fear of becoming ἀδόκιμος pertains to the evaluation of his successfulness as an apostle.[64]

In this case, what is the point of the contrast in v. 27b between Paul's having preached to *others* and the possibility that he *himself* be disqualified? I. H. Marshall has argued that here the salvation of Paul's converts contrasts to his own possible rejection from salvation.[65] In this view, ἄλλοις κηρύξας implies "having brought others to salvation." Indeed, in 9:19–22 Paul has just described the goal of his apostolic activity as the salvation of his hearers.[66] That thought may continue in 9:24–27. Nevertheless, even if it does, a contrast with the apostle's rejection from salvation is not proven. For a meaningful contrast could also be made between Paul's rejection as an apostle and his converts' reception of salvation. In 2 Cor 13:5, 6 Paul creates just such an inexact comparison of his converts' hypothetical rejection as unsaved (εἰ μήτι ἀδόκιμοί ἐστε) and his provenness as an apostle (ἡμεῖς οὐκ ἐσμὲν ἀδόκιμοι).[67] In summary, ἄλλοις κηρύξας does not necessitate taking αὐτὸς ἀδόκιμος γένωμαι as a reference to Paul's loss of salvation.[68]

Further, it could be that ἄλλοις κηρύξας does not denote Paul's having brought others to salvation. κηρύσσειν here may not be used technically, in the sense of proclaiming the crucified and risen Christ.[69] Paul may not have left the athletic metaphor yet. If not, κηρύσσειν alludes to the action of the

---

[64] Similarly, Nasuti, "Woes," 262: "Paul's disciplining and subduing of his own body in v 27...is a specific reference to his refusal to take material recompense from the Corinthians. This is made clear by the second half of the verse, which speaks of the danger of being 'disqualified' after preaching to others. In the context of the present chapter, this can only refer to the receiving of a *misthos* from the Corinthians for his apostolic activity. Even though such a *misthos* is his right, its acceptance would put an obstacle in the path of the gospel and make him a hired person of the Corinthians rather than God's steward and a sharer in the gospel."

[65] Marshall, *Kept*, 121.

[66] Cf. the terms σῴζειν and κερδαίνειν in 9:19–22. On κερδαίνειν as an evangelistic term for "save," see Schlier, κέρδος, *TWNT* 3, 672.

[67] See pp. 218, 219 above.

[68] Thus Pfitzner (*Agon*, 96, 97, n. 4) is correct: "The antique parallels here adduced by Schlatter and Weiß, *ad loc.*, are consequently irrelevant."

[69] For this sense, cf. Rom 10:8, 14, 15; 1 Cor 1:23; 15:11, 12; 2 Cor 1:19; 4:5; 11:4; Gal 2:2; 5:11; 1 Thess 2:9.

κῆρυξ in the games: the κῆρυξ called out the rules and conditions of the games, as well as the qualifications for participating, and the names of the competitors and victors.[70] As a κῆρυξ "[Paul] had instructed others as to the rules to be observed for winning the prize."[71] What rules? What prize? The contest in which Paul invites his readers to participate is, like his own, the subjugation of the body in the renunciation of one's rights and liberties as a Christian for the sake of the good of another. Paul began in chap. 8 by arguing that the strong should give up their right with regard to food so as not to "destroy" the weak. Then in chap. 9 he illustrates such voluntary self-sacrifice by his own example. Now he brings that lesson to a climax by inspiring his readers to strive after an imperishable goal at all costs by practicing radical ἐγκράτεια.[72] The ἄφθαρτος στέφανος and βραβεῖον which will be theirs for such behavior, like Paul's καύχημα, far outweigh in glory the reward enjoyed by exercising one's rights and liberties. The food which they might eat and the remuneration which Paul might receive seem petty in comparison, like the φθαρτὸς στέφανος.[73] Not only ought the Corinthians to understand Paul's forfeiting of his apostolic rights as not inconsistent with his apostolicity; they ought to practice this kind of behavior themselves, for it is desirable for all Christians.

After Paul has announced the rules for obtaining the imperishable crown—which is not identifiable with salvation itself[74]—how ironic it would be if he himself were disqualified from obtaining it. If κηρύξας has a metaphorical sense, ἀδόκιμος too seems to belong to the metaphor.[75] In this word Paul gives expression to his fear of losing divine approval as an

---

[70] See Pfitzner, *Agon*, 94.

[71] Robertson and Plummer, *1 Cor*, 197. This instruction cannot, however, be identified with Paul's kerygma.

[72] Nasuti ("Woes," 262) correctly connects vv. 24–27 with the preceding argument and brings out the close relation of the exhortation to the Corinthians with Paul's personal statements regarding his boast and reward.

[73] Paul argues *a minori ad maius* by contrasting exertion for the victor's perishable pine wreath awarded at the Isthmian games with that for the Christian's imperishable crown (cf. Weiß, *1 Kor*, 247).

[74] The means of attaining the crown or prize—renunciation of Christian rights and liberties—disallows the interpretation that the metaphorical στέφανος and βραβεῖον stand for salvation. Further, στέφανος in the undisputed epistles does not represent salvation but Paul's grounds for eschatological boasting as a servant of God, namely, his converts (1 Thess 2:19; Phil 4:1). Although βραβεῖον can refer to salvation in Paul (see Phil 3:14), its parallelism with στέφανος in 1 Cor 9:24, 25 and the present context favor an alternative meaning. We ought not to take the crown and prize in a crass sense—Paul's definition of his μισθός as "no pay" already guards against such a misunderstanding. Rather, they stand for the glory which comes from having made voluntary sacrifices in the Christian life out of love.

[75] Contrast Pfitzner, *Agon*, 96.

apostle and the empowerment for ministry which such approval guarantees. In order to remain in God's favor (as well as to cooperate fully in the progress of the gospel) Paul offers not only obedience but voluntary sacrifice. He takes no μισθός from the Corinthians for his preaching, though he has a right to, because doing so would disqualify him from the prize for unconstrained service. Paul wants to be as far away as possible from rejection as an apostle. He does so in anticipation of the day when the divine verdict on his apostolic ministry will become manifest, the day of Christ.[76] If the Lord commends him, he will have an eschatological boast.

In conclusion, in keeping with Paul's confidence regarding his salvation elsewhere,[77] 1 Cor 9:27 does not suggest his possible rejection from salvation. Rather, the fact that Paul tries to avoid becoming ἀδόκιμος through self-sacrificial practices in his *apostolic ministry* suggests that the danger he faced was becoming an ἀδόκιμος ἀπόστολος.[78] Thus the term ἀδόκιμος here is used in the same way as elsewhere applied to Paul. V. 27 appropriately concludes Paul's ἀπολογία[79] which began at v. 3 by turning the very practices for which he is judged (ἀνακρίνειν, v. 3) unapproved as an apostle into arguments for his being approved before God as an apostle. Paul does not want to lose this divine approval in his ministry.

Becoming the Gospel's Partner

1 Corinthians 9:23. The preceding discussion of 1 Cor 9:27 led to the conclusion that Paul's attempt not to become ἀδόκιμος has to do with his apostolic ministry, not his salvation: Paul does not want to lose divine approval as an apostle which guarantees the authenticity and effectiveness of his ministry. Now, however, we have to turn our attention to a statement in the context that has seemed to most interpreters to express Paul's attempt to attain final salvation: πάντα δὲ ποιῶ διὰ τὸ εὐαγγέλιον, ἵνα συγκοινωνὸς αὐτοῦ γένωμαι (1 Cor 9:23). The NASB translates: "I do all things for the sake of the gospel, that I may become a fellow-partaker of it." Is Paul after all motivated by his hope of final salvation here?

---

[76] ἀδόκιμος may have eschatological connotations. For Paul's expectation that the Lord evaluate his faithfulness as a steward when he comes, cf. 1 Cor 4:2, 4, 5.

[77] Marshall (*Kept*, 121) notes this confidence. Cf., e.g., Phil 1:21, 23.

[78] Cf. Bauer ("1 Korinther 9, 24–27," 165): "Unser Text ist reiner Aufruf an die, die sich im Dienste Christi wissen, er ist nicht Aufruf zum 'Ringen um die Rettung', jedenfalls nicht um die eigene Rettung."

[79] Pfitzner, *Agon*, 97, 98.

In this view συγκοινωνός αὐτοῦ at 9:23 means "a fellow-partaker of it (the gospel)." τὸ εὐαγγέλιον (the antecedent of αὐτοῦ) is interpreted as "the blessings of salvation promised in the gospel," so that the expression συγκοινωνός αὐτοῦ amounts to "a participant in salvation." But this view is problematic with respect to linguistic usage: εὐαγγέλιον never means "the gospel blessings" in the NT.[80] In 1 Corinthians 9 it denotes the divine power of salvation which Paul preaches (9:12, 14a, 18b) or the activity itself of preaching the gospel (9:14b, 18c).

Another difficulty with the common interpretation of 9:23 arises when we look at the immediate context. Paul attempts to become a συγκοινωνός τοῦ εὐαγγελίου through his self-sacrificial service as an apostle: πάντα δὲ ποιῶ διὰ τὸ εὐαγγέλιον, ἵνα συγκοινωνὸς αὐτοῦ γένωμαι. Interpreters agree that πάντα δὲ ποιῶ διὰ τὸ εὐαγγέλιον at 9:23a refers to Paul's efforts in apostolic ministry.[81] The apostle's service of the gospel would thus form a "condition for his own share in its blessings."[82] But 1 Cor 3:12–15 contradicts the idea of loss of salvation through inadequate Christian service, as has already been noted.[83]

Is there a way out of these difficulties? I will argue for an alternative interpretation of 1 Cor 9:23 by construing the grammar differently. The construction Paul uses here, συγκοινωνός with the genitive αὐτοῦ, can be taken in more than one way. Most interpreters take αὐτοῦ as the object in which Paul hopes to have a share (gen. of the thing shared[84]), and translate, "fellow-sharer in it," which leads to the interpretation already criticized. On the other hand, the genitive with συγκοινωνός can refer to the person with whom one takes part (gen. of person).[85] For example, συγκοινωνούς μου

---

[80] Dautzenberg ("Verzicht," 229) concludes: "Es genügt nicht, die συγκοινωνία am Evangelium mit Lietzmann als Teilhabe an den Heilsverheissungen des Evangeliums zu fassen und in diesem Satz ein Zeugnis der Bescheidenheit des Apostels zu erblicken...." The expression μεταδοῦναι...τὸ εὐαγγέλιον τοῦ Θεοῦ in 1 Thess 2:8 does not mean "am Heilsgut Anteil geben" (against Friedrich, εὐαγγελίζομαι, *TWNT* 2, 730). Rather, the comparison between imparting the gospel, on the one hand, and giving τὰς ἑαυτῶν ψυχάς, on the other hand, shows that τὸ εὐαγγέλιον τοῦ Θεοῦ here refers to the message of the gospel. In other words, Paul and his companions did not limit their ministry to preaching but gave themselves without reserve in service to the Thessalonians. Cf. Frame, *Thess*, 101.

[81] See, further, below, pp. 252, 253 with notes.

[82] Pfitzner, *Agon*, 85; similarly, Schlatter, *Bote*, 284. See commentaries.

[83] See above, p. 242 with notes.

[84] See BAGD, s.v. συγκοινωνός. So in Rom 11:17, συγκοινωνὸς τῆς ῥίζης; Phil 1:7, συγκοινωνούς...τῆς χάριτος. Cf. κοινωνία with the genitive of the thing shared in 1 Cor 10:18; 2 Cor 1:7; 1 Pet 5:1; 2 Pet 1:4.

[85] See *BDF* §182, 1. According to Seesemann (*KOINΩNIA*, 52), the use of κοινωνός with the genitive of person is first attested in the LXX (cf. Prov 28:24; Isa 1:23); cf.

in Phil 1:7 means "my fellow-sharers."[86] So also ὁ ἀδελφὸς ὑμῶν καὶ συγκοινωνός in Rev 1:9 means "your brother and [your] fellow-sharer." The genitive of person with κοινωνός also appears in Matt 23:30; Heb 10:33; 1 Cor 10:20.[87] In short, it is grammatically possible to understand αὐτοῦ at 1 Cor 9:23 as the one *with whom* Paul participates. This would yield the translation, "its [the gospel's] fellow-sharer, partner."[88]

Taking αὐτοῦ at 9:23 as a genitive of person may even be grammatically

---

(συμ)μέτοχος with the genitive of person in Eph 5:7 and Heb 1:9. Cf. Campbell, "κοινωνία," 358, 359.

[86] In Phil 1:7 μου is best taken to modify συγκοινωνούς, not τῆς χάριτος, in view of its position immediately after συγκοινωνούς (cf. Molland, *Euangelion*, 53). Similarly, the genitive in the construction τῇ κοινωνίᾳ ὑμῶν in Phil 1:5 modifies κοινωνίᾳ, not the following designation of the thing shared. By contrast, when Paul uses a genitive to modify the thing shared—and not to modify κοινωνία—he places it not before but immediately after that thing, as in Phil 3:10 (κοινωνίαν [τῶν] παθημάτων αὐτοῦ) or Phlm 6 (ἡ κοινωνία τῆς πίστεώς σου). Cf. Campbell ("κοινωνία," 370) on the word order and meaning of Phlm 6. Phil 1:7 thus has both a genitive of person (μου) and a genitive of the thing shared (τῆς χάριτος).

[87] The use of the genitive of person in κοινωνοὺς τῶν δαιμονίων, 1 Cor 10:20, is contested (Campbell, "κοινωνία," 375–378). The ancient parallels describing pagan sacrificial meals, which provide the background for Paul's instruction, give support to the view that the genitive of person is to be preferred over the genitive of the thing shared here (on these parallels, see Seesemann, *KOINΩNIA*, 52–54; Lietzmann, *Kor*, 49, 50). Paul is alluding to the belief that the participants in a sacrificial meal become *partners* with the god honored on that occasion. This partnership can be thought to arise through the god's role as host and leader at the sacrificial meal. Thus the participants become "Tischgenossen" of the god. BAGD (s.v. κοινωνία 1.a.β) translates 1 Cor 10:20 correctly as "partner w. the demons (in the sacrifices offered to them)." Cf. Gressmann, "κοινωνία," 224–230. In this instance, perhaps "gen. of partnership" instead of "gen. of person" would be a preferable designation.

[88] Molland, *Euangelion*, 53: "der Genosse des Evangeliums, der Mitarbeiter des Evangeliums." Barrett (*1 Cor*, 216) wrongly requires αὐτῷ, instead of αὐτοῦ, for the translation "a partner with the gospel." One might raise the objection that αὐτοῦ must denote the thing shared since the three other NT uses of συγκοινωνός all appear with some specification of the thing shared. This objection, however, can be easily overruled: συγκοινωνός is absolute in 1 Cor 9:23, and thus a designation of the thing shared is omitted, as in the absolute use of κοινωνός in 2 Cor 8:23; Phlm 17 (cf. BAGD, s.v. κοινωνός, 1.d). Moreover, the use of the genitive rather than the dative to designate the fellow-sharer when κοινωνός is used in the absolute—where no genitive of the thing shared appears—speaks in favor of taking the genitive αὐτοῦ modifying the absolute συγκοινωνός in 1 Cor 9:23 as a designation of the fellow-sharer (cf. Campbell, "κοινωνία," 355). Furthermore, even when κοινωνός is not used in the absolute, the thing shared can be omitted (cf. 1 Cor 10:20; Heb 10:33). In such cases, the immediate context makes clear what it is that the κοινωνοί share (cf. Campbell, 353). There is no reason to assume that συγκοινωνός could not also follow this pattern. Thus the omission of the thing shared in 1 Cor 9:23 is not a weakness in the view that the genitive in συγκοινωνός αὐτοῦ is a gen. of person (whether or not συγκοινωνός is absolute).

preferable. For in the NT, the συν- in compound nouns prefixed with this preposition most often refers to the person in the genitive.[89] More significantly, in NT usage the fellow-participants of συγκοινωνός (alluded to in συν-) are always mentioned *immediately* before[90] or after[91] συγκοινωνός. συν- signals interest in the *association* between parties having something in common.[92] This interest in their association apparently leads to the explicit identification of the fellow-participants. We would have to disregard the apparent purpose behind the prefixing of συν- to κοινωνός in 1 Cor 9:23, however, if we were to interpret αὐτοῦ as a genitive of the thing shared ("fellow-sharer *in* the the gospel"). When taken in this way, the construction breaks with NT usage by omitting an explicit identification of Paul's συγκοινωνός.[93] But if we construe αὐτοῦ as a genitive of person, 1 Cor 9:23 conforms to NT usage of συγκοινωνός through the explicit identification of the fellow-participant, here, αὐτοῦ. In this case, Paul uses the construction to highlight his association with the gospel as its κοινωνός.[94]

But does not τὸ εὐαγγέλιον make an unlikely "partner" for Paul? How can Paul be a συγκοινωνός of an impersonal thing? How can αὐτοῦ in this case really be a genitive of person? The grammatical terminology itself may be stretched here, but usage is not. In the LXX there can be κοινωνία not only between persons but also with *personified things*. Wis 8:18 speaks of associating with personified wisdom: ἐν κοινωνίᾳ λόγων αὐτῆς ("in talking with her," sc. Wisdom).[95] Here αὐτῆς, the genitive of person modifying κοινωνία, denotes a personified thing. Similarly, in Wis 6:23 κοινωνεῖν is used with the dative of person referring to personified wisdom:

---

[89] The examples are too many to list. See Robertson and Plummer, *1 Cor*, 58, n. †.

[90] So in Rom 11:17; Rev 1:9.

[91] So in Phil 1:7.

[92] The simple κοινωνός with the gen. of person communicates less interest in the association (cf. Molland, *Euangelion*, 53).

[93] The closest possible alternate identification of Paul's fellow-sharer(s) is τινάς in v. 22b. See Weiß, *1 Kor*, 246: "Das συν- ist im Hinblick auf die τινές geschrieben." The distance of τινάς from συν-, however, makes the connection between them difficult, since elsewhere the referent of συν- is close and obvious.

[94] I will not deal with the interpretation of συγκοινωνός τοῦ εὐαγγελίου as "fellow-sharer in the preaching of the gospel." It does not raise the question of Paul's salvation. Further, the same criticisms I have made against the interpretation "fellow-sharer in the blessings of salvation promised in the gospel" can also be levelled against this other interpretation. Barrett (*1 Cor*, 216) rejects the view which takes εὐαγγέλιον here as "the preaching of the gospel."

[95] Cf. Campbell ("κοινωνία," 360), who commends this translation and points out the meaninglessness of translating: "in having fellowship with her words." The parallel phrase, ἐν συγγενείᾳ σοφίας (v. 17), supports the view that αὐτῆς is a genitive of person.

κοινωνήσει σοφίᾳ.⁹⁶ The idea of partnership with personified things is not unusual in Greek thought, in which the human body and its members, one's material possessions, native country as well as kinsfolk constituted one's κοινωνοί.⁹⁷ Since a κοινωνός need not be a person but can also be a personified thing, as these parallels show, it is conceivable that τὸ εὐαγγέλιον in 1 Cor 9:23 is Paul's partner.

Furthermore, Paul's personification of τὸ εὐαγγέλιον in 1 Corinthians 9 and elsewhere speaks for this view. Paul pictures the gospel as a vital force on the advance (προκοπὴ τοῦ εὐαγγελίου, Phil 1:12);⁹⁸ its progress is not hindered when Paul lies in chains. Similarly, he describes the word of the Lord as running through the world (ἵνα ὁ λόγος τοῦ κυρίου τρέχῃ), being glorified (2 Thess 3:1). The apostle keeps in step with this onward pressing gospel and takes care not to trip it up by putting some obstacle in its path (ἵνα μή τινα ἐγκοπὴν δῶμεν τῷ εὐαγγελίῳ, 1 Cor 9:12).⁹⁹

As the passages just cited show, Paul personifies the gospel precisely when he has his own service for the gospel in view. His missionary activity takes place in the shadow of the energetic working of the gospel itself. This fact becomes especially clear in 1 Corinthians 9. Paul has renounced his apostolic rights, including the right to remuneration for his preaching in Corinth (9:4–18), in order not to impede the progress of the gospel. He asserts: πάντα στέγομεν¹⁰⁰ ἵνα μή τινα ἐγκοπὴν δῶμεν τῷ εὐαγγελίῳ (9:12). Had he accepted payment for his preaching, some hearers might have suspected him of false motives (personal financial gain) or waned in their interest in his message lest they incur an obligation to pay for his

---

⁹⁶ Campbell ("κοινωνία," 359) rightly criticizes the view that σοφίᾳ at Wis 6:23 is a dative of the thing shared (so BAGD, s.v. κοινωνέω), "for the context makes clear that Wisdom is personified, and that the meaning is 'associate with Wisdom'."

⁹⁷ Campbell ("κοινωνία," 354), who refers correctly to Epictetus *Dis.* I.1.9.

⁹⁸ Cf. 2 Tim 2:9, where the word of God is unfettered (ὁ λόγος τοῦ θεοῦ οὐ δέδεται) while the apostle is bound.

⁹⁹ 1 Cor 9:12 has the progress of the gospel in view (so Robertson and Plummer, *1 Cor*, 186). Noting these verses, Friedrich (εὐαγγελίζομαι, *TWNT* 2, 730) comments: "Das Evangelium wird zu einer persönlichen Größe"; similarly, Molland, *Euangelion*, 54. Interpreters also personify the gospel in their comments (cf. Käsemann, "Variation," 235, with n. 78; Dautzenberg, "Verzicht," 219, 120; Pfitzner, *Agon*, 108). The presupposition of Paul's personification of εὐαγγέλιον is his conviction that the gospel is nothing less than the power of God unto salvation (cf. Rom 1:16; 1 Cor 1:18, 24); cf. Friedrich, εὐαγγελίζομαι, *TWNT* 2, 729. Since the gospel which Paul preaches is the very word of God which goes forth in power and in the Holy Spirit (cf. 1 Cor 2:4; 1 Thess 1:5), it can easily take on lifelike characteristics in expression of such divine power. Thus Paul appropriately characterizes εὐαγγέλιον as an active, creative, and advancing force which engages people in its service.

¹⁰⁰ στέγειν here connotes primarily the physical privations and hardships which Paul undergoes (cf. 4:11–13; Barrett, *1 Cor*, 207; Weiß, *1 Kor*, 238).

services (cf. 1 Thess 2:9; 2 Cor 12:13; 11:9–12).[101] Such suspicion or dis-interest would have set up an obstacle between them and the power of God unto salvation, the gospel working through Paul's preaching.[102] Neither has Paul made use of his freedom in Christ (9:19). Instead he has accommo-dated his behavior to the customs of his audience and has thus become all things to all people (9:20–22). This self-enslavement (ἐμαυτὸν ἐδούλωσα, 9:19) to others is in the interest of their salvation: ἵνα πάντως τινὰς σώσω (9:22b; cf. 2 Tim 2:10).

Both Paul's renunciation of his apostolic rights and limitation of his freedom in Christ serve the goal of winning more to Christ (ἵνα τοὺς πλείονας κερδήσω, 9:19). The salvation of οἱ πλείονες is helped by Paul's avoidance of setting up obstacles to the *gospel's* effective working, since it alone is the power of salvation. And when the gospel can advance unhindered, it will bring all the more people into the sphere of salvation. Thus, far from turning his ministry into an obstacle course for the gospel, Paul wants to clear the track of all hurdles in the way of this advancing power of God unto salvation.[103]

Paul summarizes his conduct as an evangelist and the intention behind it in v. 23: πάντα δὲ ποιῶ διὰ τὸ εὐαγγέλιον, ἵνα συγκοινωνὸς αὐτοῦ γένωμαι.[104] πάντα here consists in Paul's renunciation of his apostolic rights (πάντα στέγομεν, 9:12) and the limitation of his freedom in Christ (τοῖς πᾶσιν γέγονα πάντα, 9:22). Paul has to defend this behavior to the Corinthians (cf. 9:3).[105] He is not really acting contrary to the gospel[106]

---

[101] Roberson and Plummer, *1 Cor*, 186; Barrett, *1 Cor*, 207; Dautzenberg, "Ver-zicht," 219; Theissen, "Legitimation," 223, 224.

[102] Correctly, Friedrich (εὐαγγελίζομαι, *TWNT* 2, 729), who sees ἐγκοπὴ τῷ εὐαγγελίῳ as a hindrance to the "Wirksamkeit des Evangeliums," not simply to the preaching of the gospel message.

[103] The idea of partnership with the gospel as a divine power in 1 Cor 9:23 parallels the thought of cooperation with God as a συνεργός elsewhere in Paul. Cf. συνεργὸς τοῦ θεοῦ (1 Thess 3:2; cf. also the variant reading διάκονος τοῦ θεοῦ); θεοῦ...συν-εργοί (1 Cor 3:9, where συν- most naturally alludes to the prior θεός; with Weiß, *1 Kor*, 78); συνεργοῦντες (2 Cor 6:1, where τῷ θεῷ is understood; with Bultmann, *2 Kor*, 168). The equality of the partners in cooperation need not be implied, of course.

[104] See Hauck, κοινός, *TWNT* 3, 805; Wolff, *1 Kor*, 33.

[105] Cf. Moffat, *1 Cor*, 125; Schlatter, *Bote*, 284. Paul's "passive" contribution to the gospel's progress here (through personal sacrifice) highlights the "activity" of the per-sonified gospel itself. In this way Paul defends the legitimacy of his failing to exercise his apostolic rights to Corinthian Christians who have turned skeptical about his apos-tleship. Since Paul here seeks to establish his partnership with the gospel precisely on the basis of his sacrifice, not his achievements, Conzelmann's objection that "συγκοι-νωνός does not denote an active participator" (*1 Cor*, 159, n. 12) does not tell against the translation "the gospel's partner." Paul *refrains* from certain activities which would hinder the gospel. Paul's claim that he strives to become the gospel's partner through

though he relinquishes the very rights and freedom which he has in the gospel (cf. 9:14, 18b). Rather, he is acting διὰ τὸ εὐαγγέλιον (9:23), for the benefit of the gospel's progress.[107] Thus Paul's self-denial, far from giving rise to suspicions about his true apostolicity, authenticates it.[108]

The purpose behind Paul's doing all for the sake of the gospel, ἵνα συγκοινωνὸς αὐτοῦ γένωμαι (9:23b), summarizes his earlier statements of purpose. He has previously stated the intention which underlies the renunciation of his apostolic rights to be his determination not to set up obstacles to the gospel's effective working: ἵνα μή τινα ἐγκοπὴν δῶμεν τῷ εὐαγγελίῳ (9:12b). The motive behind the limitation of his freedom (9:19–22) is materially the same, simply expressed in terms of the result of the gospel's unhindered progress: ἵνα πάντως τινὰς σώσω (9:22b). Because the gospel is the power of God unto salvation Paul can pursue his goal of bringing more people to salvation only through radical cooperation with the gospel as it works. Thus, comments J. Schütz on 9:23, "Paul must mean that he has done all this to become [a] participant in the dynamic character of the gospel—to share in the gospel's *own* work."[109] In other words, Paul's aim is to become the gospel's partner (instead of its antagonist) in bringing people into the sphere of salvation.[110] This aspiration to true partnership with the gospel entails the highest degree of cooperation. From this perspective the apostle's unusual behavior makes good sense.

According to the proposed interpretation of συγκοινωνὸς τοῦ εὐαγγελίου, Paul's rigorous efforts in apostolic ministry do not serve to secure his own salvation but to make him the gospel's partner in fulfillment of his calling. This interpretation has solid support from word usage, grammar, and the context which equals or betters support for the common view.

---

renunciation of his rights and freedom is part of his defense begun in 9:1. The motif of freedom (ἐλεύθερος εἶναι, 9:1, 19) formally links 9:19–23 with the apology (cf. Conzelmann, *1 Cor*, 159).

[106] Theissen, "Legitimation," 216.

[107] Against Robertson and Plummer (*1 Cor*, 193), who interpret διὰ τὸ εὐαγγέλιον as meaning "because the Gospel is so precious to himself."

[108] Cf. Conzelmann, *1 Cor*, 153.

[109] Schütz, *Paul*, 52.

[110] Cf. Molland, *Euangelion*, 54. Cf. the expression, διάκονος [τοῦ εὐαγγελίου], in Eph 3:6, 7 and Col 1:23. Friedrich (εὐαγγελίζομαι, *TWNT* 2, 730) agrees with the translation "Genosse des Evangeliums" in 1 Cor 9:23 but is inconsistent when he interprets the verse to mean that a co-worker with the gospel has no certainty of gaining a share in what he himself has preached. If Friedrich is right in interpreting συγκοινωνὸς αὐτοῦ [i.e., τοῦ εὐαγγελίου] as "Genosse des Evangeliums," the phrase cannot also mean "fellow-sharer in the gospel"; i.e., αὐτοῦ cannot be *both* a genitive of person and a genitive of the thing shared.

Further, in this view Paul's great evangelistic efforts are not reduced to a means to his own salvation, a bothersome implication of the usual interpretation: "P. tue das alles um seines Heiles willen."[111] Indeed, the parallel verse 10:33 shows how unpauline such a thought is by explicitly denying selfish interests in Paul's ministry: μὴ ζητῶν τὸ ἐμαυτοῦ σύμφορον ἀλλὰ τὸ τῶν πολλῶν, ἵνα σωθῶσιν (cf. 10:24).[112] Here Paul restricts his freedom for the sake of the salvation of others and not for his own good. The context of 9:23, which focuses on Paul's laboring for the gospel *at his own expense*, does not permit selfish motives either.[113] Seeing such motives in the idea of Paul striving to become a fellow-sharer in the gospel, J. Weiß finds 9:23 so awkward a conclusion to 9:19–22 that he postulates an interpolation as a transition to the following section.[114] But this move is unnecessary. The view that Paul aims to become a partner with the gospel in the salvation of the world avoids the problems which have long plagued the interpretation of 1 Cor 9:23. This verse thus complements 9:27 by explaining Paul's renunciation of his rights and liberties in terms of his goals as an apostle, not his final salvation.

Attaining the Final Goal

Philippians 3:11, 12. In Phil 3:7–16 Paul stresses the futurity of the consummation of salvation. He does so in an attempt to counteract a perfectionist tendency in Philippi. Paul distantiates himself from the false teachers by firmly disclaiming his own attainment of Christian "perfection":[115]

---

[111] Weiß, *1 Kor*, 246. Conzelmann (*1 Cor*, 161) tries to temper this "utilitarianism" and "extreme religious individualism" by viewing it in the context of other aspects of Paul's soteriology, in particular, the aspect of God's election *sola gratia*. Conzelmann has not, however, thereby resolved the tension in his view. Then, in a more promising suggestion, he points to the link between Paul's "self-consciousness and the task committed to him": "At the Last Judgment [Paul] will have to render account of his work; there he will point to his communities as his legitimation. Verse 23, too, has the community and his own commission in view." This comment takes into account the significance for the eschatological test which Paul ascribes to his apostolic service and still avoids the pitfall of making Paul's salvation explicitly dependent on his service. Yet Paul may not have the eschatological test in mind at all in 9:23. Rather, he may be thinking simply of his present relation to the gospel in his apostolic ministry, as in 9:12.

[112] τὸ σύμφορον τῶν πολλῶν is their salvation, with Conzelmann, *1 Cor*, 179. Robertson and Plummer (*1 Cor*, 225) with no justification read into 10:33 the idea that Paul "seeks his own salvation through the salvation of others."

[113] Cf. Molland, *Euangelion*, 54.

[114] Weiß, *1 Kor*, 246. Barrett (*1 Cor*, 216) also thinks v. 23 is transitionary.

[115] The false teachers in Philippi apparently claimed to have attained perfection

οὐχ ὅτι ἤδη ἔλαβον ἤ ἤδη τετελείωμαι...ἐγὼ ἐμαυτὸν οὐ λογίζομαι κατειληφέναι.[116] Both the introductory οὐχ ὅτι and the terminology apparently borrowed from the opponents make this polemical purpose clear.[117] In contrast to the perfectionists' self-satisfaction, Paul's attitude is one of great expectation as he awaits the *future* completion of salvation. He has a goal: "the resurrection from the dead" (3:11), when salvation will be consummated.[118]

Perfection is thus not a present possession but the object of Paul's hope. But how certain is that hope? Paul expresses his hope of reaching final salvation in two εἰ-clauses which are often taken to indicate not only the futurity of Christian perfection but also Paul's doubt regarding his final destiny.[119] εἰ can be used in expressions of expectation which accompany the action.[120] The two εἰ-clauses in question—εἴ πως καταντήσω εἰς τὴν ἐξανάστασιν τὴν ἐκ νεκρῶν (3:11) and εἰ καὶ καταλάβω (3:12)—will be examined in the following discussion. Do they show that Paul intended to counteract the perfectionism in Philippi by confessing that salvation is unsure as well as unfinished?

Although εἰ καί elsewhere in the NT is followed by the indicative and has a concessive meaning,[121] in Phil 3:12 it appears with the subjunctive and belongs to the εἰ-clauses which communicate expectancy.[122] The

---

(Martin, *Phil*, 151; Lütgert, *Die Vollkommenen*, 30).

[116] The noticeable omission of objects of the verbs λαμβάνειν and καταλαμβάνειν (3:12, 13) strengthens the point that attainment of the goal is future (Pfitzner, *Agon*, 144; *et al.*).

[117] Cf. Gnilka, *Phil*, 198; Beare, *Phil*, 129; Siber, *Christus*, 109. The polemic against the opponents' brand of perfectionism has already begun in 3:2ff., where Paul argues that he can match their perfection in Judaism. But such perfection is "rubbish" in comparison with his goal, the knowledge of Christ (3:8), which characterizes true Christian "perfection" (cf. 3:15).

[118] Cf. also the reference to the resurrection at 3:10. The stress on *future* salvation in the context leads Paul to mention resurrection before suffering and death here: "...to know him and the power of his resurrection and the fellowship of his sufferings, being conformed to his death." Paul's emphasis on a *future* resurrection need not imply that he was countering claims that the resurrection had already taken place. Baumbach ("Zukunftserwartung," 448) sees no reason to presuppose that the resurrection was a point of disagreement between Paul and the opponents at Philippi.

[119] So, e.g., Collange, *Phil*, 118; Koester, "Purpose," 323; Gnilka, *Phil*, 198; Michael, *Phil*, 154.

[120] *BDF* §375.

[121] Cf. 1 Cor 7:21; 2 Cor 4:16; 7:8; 12:11; Phil 2:17; Col 2:5; Heb 6:9; Lk 11:8; 18:4; Mark 14:29. See *BDF* §374.

[122] *BDF* §375 classifies Phil 3:12 as an expression of expectation with εἰ. Perhaps the omission of καί at Phil 3:12 in some MSS can be explained as an attempt to avoid the—here awkward—concessive meaning typical of the construction in the NT.

clause which immediately succeeds διώκω δὲ εἰ καὶ καταλάβω suggests
that Paul does not want to communicate uncertainty about reaching the
goal: κατελήμφθην ὑπὸ Χριστοῦ [Ἰησοῦ]. Paul's pursuit with the expectation of attaining presupposes Christ's grasping him. Paul ties together
closely his own action and that of Christ on him by using the same verb for
both, καταλαμβάνειν: Paul's own seizing (of Christ—or perhaps of full
knowledge of Christ) is put in the context of Christ's prior seizing of Paul.
Can the apostle who is so conscious of being dramatically called and commissioned by Christ[123] totally apart from his own seeking now fail to know
whether he will attain the goal of Christ's very action upon him?

ἐφ' ᾧ introduces κατελήμφθην ὑπὸ Χριστοῦ [Ἰησοῦ] and thus defines
the relationship of its clause to διώκω δὲ εἰ καὶ καταλάβω. A causal ἐφ'
ᾧ, which most interpreters favor,[124] would introduce the reason why Paul
pursues with the expectation of obtaining, namely, because he has "been
obtained by Christ." Because of Christ's prior action toward him, Paul
pursues expecting to obtain. If, on the other hand, ἐφ' ᾧ means "that for
which" Paul has been seized by Christ Jesus, its clause would identify the
goal of Paul's pursuit.[125] Nevertheless, because the goal would be defined
in terms of Christ's action on Paul, the main point of the clause would still
be to show Christ's seizing of Paul as definitive for Paul's own attaining
the goal. M. Goguel comments: "Ainsi, l'effort que le chrétien Paul doit
faire pour parvenir au but, ne dérive pas d'une initiative qui lui appartien-
drait en propre; il est le prolongement et la conséquence d'une initiative
qu'a prise le Christ."[126] Thus εἰ καὶ καταλάβω must communicate expectation *without doubt*, in view of the closely related thought of Paul's
being obtained by Christ. Paul means: "I pursue expecting to obtain...."
G. Baumbach concludes: "Paulus schließt also diesen Abschnitt mit dem
Ausdruck der Erwartung, daß Gott das Werk, das er an ihm bei seiner
'Bekehrung' begonnen hat, auch zur Vollendung bringen werde. Dieses
hoffende Vertrauen auf Gottes Macht und Treue markiert den radikalen Gegensatz zu dem Bewußtsein der vollkommenen Gerechtigkeit aus dem Gesetz, das ihm als Pharisäer bestimmte. So wird das 'allein aus Gnade,' wo-
mit Gottes Ruf an ihm den Anfang machte, auch bis zum Ende festgehal-

---

[123] On the allusion to Paul's conversion and commission here, see Gnilka, *Phil*, 198;
Vincent, *Phil*, 108; Dibelius, *Phil*, 70.

[124] E.g., *BDF* §235, 2; Zerwick, *Biblical Greek*, §127; Pfitzner, *Agon*, 149, n. 1;
Michaelis, *Phil*, 59; Michael, *Phil*, 159; Lohmeyer, *Phil*, 145, n. 1.

[125] So, e.g., Vincent, *Phil*, 108.

[126] Goguel, "Assurance," 108.

ten. Dieses 'allein aus Gnade' verbindet Anfang und Vollendung."[127]

The ϵl in 3:11 is strengthened by $\pi\omega\varsigma$.[128] Here Paul expresses the expectation that he will "attain to the resurrection from the dead." Other expressions of expectation with ϵl $\pi\omega\varsigma$ in the NT (see Rom 1:10; 11:14; Acts 27:12; cf. also 2 Sam 14:15 LXX with v. 16) do not suggest that an element of doubt is inherent to the construction.[129] Rather, it simply communicates hope or expectancy.[130] Further, the Pauline parallels use ϵl $\pi\omega\varsigma$ for expectations of divine working. O. Michel interprets the ϵl $\pi\omega\varsigma$ clause in Rom 11:14, where Paul hopes to "make jealous my kinsfolk and save some of them," as an expression of hope in God's power to save Israel: "Die Möglichkeit, die in ϵl $\pi\omega\varsigma$ angedeutet ist, kann lediglich eine Möglichkeit Gottes sein, nicht aber eine menschliche Absicht...."[131] Paul cannot achieve this goal through his own effort. God must bring it to pass. Paul's formulation of his aim with ϵl $\pi\omega\varsigma$ does not call into question the realization of his hope,[132] but reveals that the expected fulfillment lies with God alone. ϵl $\pi\omega\varsigma$ thus highlights this dependency on God's working out of God's purpose through the apostle.

Likewise, in Rom 1:10 Paul introduces his petition to visit the Roman church with ϵl $\pi\omega\varsigma$ in order to portray this action as a "divine possibility." Paul has long hoped for his planned visit to materialize, but thus far it has been prevented (1:13). Now he prays that at last he "will succeed by the will of God in coming to you." Both the facts that Paul beseeches God ($\delta\epsilon\delta\mu\epsilon\nu\sigma\varsigma$ ϵl $\pi\omega\varsigma$...) and that he acknowledges submissiveness to God's will ($\epsilon\nu$ $\tau\hat{\omega}$ $\theta\epsilon\lambda\eta\mu\alpha\tau\iota$ $\tau\sigma\hat{\upsilon}$ $\Theta\epsilon\sigma\hat{\upsilon}$)[133] indicate conscious dependence on God for the attainment of his goal. Like the salvation of his fellow Jews, the imminent extension of his ministry as far as Rome lies in God's hands. For that reason Paul formulates his hope of coming with ϵl $\pi\omega\varsigma$.

In summary, the parallel uses of ϵl $\pi\omega\varsigma$ in Rom 1:10 and 11:14 suggest that Paul uses this construction to express an expectation whose fulfillment comes from God, not one whose fulfillment is in doubt.[134] This understanding of ϵl $\pi\omega\varsigma$ fits the context of Phil 3:11 well. Here Paul intentionally

---

[127] Baumbach, *Zukunftserwartung*, 447.

[128] Cf. *BDF* §375.

[129] Otfried Hofius brought the reference from the LXX to my attention.

[130] Cf. Barrett, *Rom*, 215; Baumbach, *Zukunftserwartung*, 447. Against Wilckens, *Rom* I, 79.

[131] Michel, *Rom*, 347. Similarly, Schlier, *Rom*, 331.

[132] With Käsemann, *Rom*, 296.

[133] Cranfield (*Rom*, 78) sees ϵl $\pi\omega\varsigma$ to express submissiveness to God's will.

[134] The parallel use of ϵl $\pi\omega\varsigma$ in Acts 27:12 expresses expectation, not doubt, but has no theological implications, in contrast to Pauline usage.

contrasts his attitude toward his final destiny with that of his perfectionist opponents.[135] Whereas they apparently put great stock in their own qualifications and efforts, Paul renounces ἐμὴν δικαιοσύνην and seeks instead τὴν ἐκ Θεοῦ δικαιοσύνην ἐπὶ τῇ πίστει (3:9). Only the righteousness which comes from God can give Paul the assurance that he will "be found in him" at the last day (3:9). After such a confession of utter dependence on God for salvation, Paul's hope of resurrection can hardly rest on his own doing, not even on a possible martyr's death.[136] Rather, Paul looks to God, who alone can raise the dead, for the fulfillment of his expectation that he will attain to the resurrection. In the phrase τὴν δύναμιν τῆς ἀναστάσεως αὐτοῦ at 3:10 Paul views resurrection as a divine act of power. He stakes everything on this power by giving up all things which were "gain" to him (3:7, 8) "in order to know him and the power of his resurrection." By introducing his hope to "attain to the resurrection from the dead" with εἴ πως, Paul removes the realization of this hope from the realm of human possibility and confesses it to be only a "divine possibility." Christian perfection as attainment of the resurrection depends on an act of God. The expectation of obtaining final salvation through the power of God should characterize Christians' attitude toward their final destiny, as it does Paul's.

The εἰ-clauses in Phil 3:11, 12, therefore, do not suggest that Paul doubted his final salvation.[137] They have an entirely different purpose in his argument, as the context and parallels show.[138] Moreover, the immediate and larger contexts[139] give evidence that doubt would contradict Paul's explicit confidence regarding the future. Already in 1:23 he has expressed certainty that his death will entail "being with Christ." In 3:9 he anticipates "being found in Christ," an eschatological expression which connotes final salvation.[140] A few verses later he looks forward to Christ's transformation of "our body of humility to the likeness of his body of glory" when Christ comes (3:21). Elsewhere also Paul speaks with assurance about the resurrection of believers to salvation (e.g., Rom 6:5; 8:11; 2 Cor 4:14).[141] These

---

[135] Cf. Gnilka, *Phil*, 197.

[136] Against Lohmeyer, *Phil*, 138–142.

[137] Correctly, Gnilka, *Phil*, 197; Martin, *Phil*, 150; Bonnard, *Phil*, 67; Calvin, *Phil*, *ad loc.*; Wesley, *Notes*, 537. Vincent (*Phil*, 108) also denies that Paul's pursuit is "prosecuted with any feeling of doubt as to the attainment of its end."

[138] Gnilka (*Phil*, 197) notes that recognizing the polemical function of the εἰ-clause guards against interpreting it wrongly to show Paul's uncertainty about his final destiny.

[139] In drawing arguments from the broader context, I align myself with those who argue for the integrity of Philippians.

[140] Cf. 1 Cor 4:2; Rev 20:15; *Ps Sol* 17:8. So Stuhlmacher, *Gerechtigkeit Gottes*, 99; Gnilka, *Phil*, 193, 194.

[141] Marshall, *Kept*, 119, 120.

kinds of arguments lead I. H. Marshall to the conclusion that "there is...no uncertainty in this passage about Paul's own perseverance in the faith, and this passage must accordingly be removed from any list of passages which express doubt about final perseverance."[142]

Paul argues against perfectionistic theology in Philippi by maintaining that final salvation is yet future, even for the apostle, and that God will bring it about by God's power, not Christians by their deserts. In addition, he wards off the dangers of complacency and irresponsibility resulting from a perfectionistic theology by showing that the futurity of final salvation demands eager "pursuit" of the goal. Paul draws this implication out of the statement, "I have not yet obtained and have not yet become perfect." He continues, "but I pursue" (3:12). In 3:13, 14 he develops the motif of pursuit into the full-blown image of a runner who, "stretching forward to the things ahead,... pursue[s] intently the prize of the upward calling of God in Christ Jesus."[143] Like the athlete, Paul lets the goal ahead determine present conduct.[144] The expectation of attaining that goal does not deflect his interest to things of lesser importance, much less to compromising attitudes or behavior. Instead it rivets his attention on the realization of the goal itself.

Paul pursues τὸ βραβεῖον τῆς ἄνω κλήσεως τοῦ Θεοῦ ἐν Χριστῷ Ἰησοῦ (3:14) The metaphorical description of his goal as God's "upward" calling distinguishes him from the perfectionists. God's calling, not human qualifications, brings salvation.[145] In contrast to the opponents, who "seek τὰ ἐπίγεια" (3:19), Paul sets his sights on the "*upward* (ἄνω) calling."[146] The prize is salvation itself in its consummation, that is, the final salvation attained at the resurrection from the dead, as 3:11 says explicitly.[147]

How does Paul "pursue" this upward calling of God?[148] Paul's athletic imagery has previously been taken to convey moral exertion. V. Pfitzner, in particular, has strongly challenged this interpretation.[149] In the present

---

[142] Marshall, *Kept*, 120. Marshall suggests that Paul was uncertain about the *route* to his final destiny (possible martyrdom), not the destiny itself, however. Cf. Martin, *Phil*, 150. But, as we have seen, the text does not compel us to posit any kind of uncertainty.

[143] On the athletic metaphor, see Pfitzner, *Agon*, 139–156.

[144] On this motif in 1 Cor 9:24–27 see pp. 237, 238 above.

[145] Pfitzner, *Agon*, 150. Similarly, Beare, *Phil*, 130.

[146] On ἄνω, so Pfitzner, *Agon*, 149, following Ewald, *Phil*, 190. So also, Bonnard, *Phil*, 68.

[147] Pfitzner, *Agon*, 154; Beare, *Phil*, 128; Michael, *Phil*, 163; Bonnard, *Phil*, 67; Stauffer, ἀγών, *TWNT* 1, 637.

[148] For διώκειν used elsewhere for zealous pursuit of a good, cf. Rom 9:30, 31; 12:13; 14:19; 1 Cor 14:1; 1 Tim 6:11; 2 Tim 2:22; Hebr 12:14.

[149] *Agon*, 139; also Gnilka, *Phil*, 199. Michael (*Phil*, 154) wrongly cites 1 Cor 9:27

context, commendation of moral endeavor would play right into the hands of those who have confidence in the flesh (cf. 3:3, 4). Rather, instead of glorying in his achievements in Judaism as the opponents do, Paul denigrates what he once considered to be "gain" and embraces the single aim of knowing Christ, the one all-surpassing value (3:5–10).[150] This knowledge of Christ itself leads Paul down the path toward the goal. For to know Christ is to "know...the power of his resurrection and the fellowship of his sufferings, being conformed to his death" (3:10).[151] In the knowledge of Christ Paul finds not only the goal ahead but also the way to it. Suffering and death culminates in resurrection for the one who seeks to know fully the crucified and resurrected Lord. Paul can attain the goal of resurrection only in fundamental unity with Christ through participation in Christ's suffering and death. Paul's apostolic service often took this form.[152] As eager pursuit is appropriate for the runner who hopes to win the prize, so Christlike subjection to suffering is appropriate for the Christian who expects to know the power of Christ's resurrection. This behavior differs radically from the self-glorying of the opponents (3:3, 19). Paul's path of suffering in expectation of attaining the resurrection serves here as an example for all Christians.[153] "As many as are 'perfect,' " he says, filling his opponents' terminology with new content, "should think like this" (3:15).

Fellowship in Christ's sufferings and conformity to Christ's death is not only the appropriate way to "pursue" the goal of resurrection from the dead. It is a way in which Paul finds assurance that he will share in the future resurrection.[154] For the two go hand in hand in Paul's mind: "If we suffer with [Christ], we shall also be glorified with [Christ]" (Rom 8:17). Paul can see this paradoxical unity even in the present: "For we who are living are delivered over unto death on account of Jesus, in order that the life of Jesus might also be manifest in our mortal flesh" (2 Cor 4:11; cf. v. 10). Paul pursues the goal in Phil 3:11, 12 thus not out of fear[155] but in utmost confidence of the final outcome.

---

as revealing the same uncertainty about final salvation that he sees Paul to express in Phil 3:11, 12. He then implies, however, that such self-distrust is invalid (154, 155).

[150] On the polemical context, see Pfitzner, *Agon*, 142.

[151] Beare, *Phil*, 114.

[152] Elsewhere he associates his apostolic sufferings with the sufferings of Christ (cf. 2 Cor 4:10, 11). Cf. Pfitzner, *Agon*, 142, 145; Dibelius, *Phil*, 69; Michaelis, *Phil*, 59.

[153] Cf. Stuhlmacher, *Gerechtigkeit Gottes*, 99; Gnilka, *Phil*, 194; Calvin, *Phil*, *ad* 3:15.

[154] Pfitzner, *Agon*, 146; Hauck, κοινός, *TWNT* 3, 806; Siber, *Christus*, 116; Dibelius, *Phil*, 69.

[155] Correctly, Gnilka, *Phil*, 198.

IX. PAUL'S LABOR AND

CHRISTIANS' FAITH

Paul's consuming desire to fulfill his apostolic calling to the best of his abilities has received attention in the preceding chapter. S. Kim summarizes: Paul "would like to be saved at the last judgment not simply ὡς διά πυρός, not losing the reward of God's commendation."[1] The Lord will judge him as a steward when he comes (1 Cor 4:2–5). And the knowledge that "the work of each will be manifest for the day will make it known" (1 Cor 3:13a) motivates Paul in his ministry. He hopes to maintain divine approval through radical sacrifice for the sake of the gospel and thus ensure God's commendation for his service at the last day. His renunciatory practices serve the greater success of his ministry and in this way too contribute to his gaining God's eschatological commendation. The more positive the results of his ministry, the greater the proof that he has faithfully fulfilled his divine commission. In pursuit of this goal, Paul takes on the task not only of an evangelist but also a pastor who nurtures his converts in the faith, as his epistles amply testify. For his ministry must produce *lasting* fruit to which he can point on the day of reckoning. But Paul does not always express certainty about the long-term effectiveness of his apostolic labor. He voices his concern not to "labor or run in vain" (Phil 2:16; 1 Thess 3:5; Gal 2:2; 4:11) and be forced to stand empty-handed at the final test of Christian service. Does Paul's fear imply the possibility of his converts' falling away? Does Paul manifest such a fear in the expressions "believe in vain" (1 Cor 15:2) and "receive the grace of God in vain" (2 Cor 6:1)? In short, does his confidence that God will complete Christians' salvation break down on the rough turf of the missionfield?

E. P. Sanders comments that such passages as 1 Thess 3:5 and 2 Cor 6:1 "sound ominous, but they are too uncertain to yield sure results."[2] In the

---

[1] Kim, *Origin*, 295. Against Satake ("Apostolat," 105 with n. 1), who comments: "Paulus weiß sein eigenes Heil davon abhängig, daß diejenigen, denen er verkündet hat, wirklich zum Heil gelangen."

[2] Sanders, *Law*, 110.

following pages I will attempt to determine the implications for continuity in salvation of Paul's statements about laboring and believing in vain.

Laboring in Vain

Philippians 2:16; 1 Thessalonians 3:5; Galatians 2:2; 4:11. Paul looks upon the present interim period before the judgment as a time of potential fruitful labor for the gospel (Phil 1:22) which will meet with God's commendation, but also of possible frustration of his labor which will rob him of God's praise. In four texts he contemplates the possibility of having spent his energies for the gospel in vain. He exhorts the Philippian Christians to be "children of God" who will give him cause to boast that he has "not run in vain or labored in vain" (οὐκ εἰς κενὸν ἔδραμον οὐδὲ εἰς κενὸν ἐκοπίασα, Phil 2:16). He recalls his impatience to know how the Thessalonians' faith was faring in persecution "lest the tempter tempted you and our labor toward you might be in vain" (μή πως ἐπείρασεν ὑμᾶς ὁ πειράζων καὶ εἰς κενὸν γένηται ὁ κόπος ἡμῶν, 1 Thess 3:5). The Galatians' attraction to law-keeping, as evidenced by their observance of the Jewish religious calendar (Gal 4:10), makes Paul fear "lest I have labored over you in vain" (μή πως εἰκῇ κεκοπίακα εἰς ὑμᾶς, Gal 4:11). He reminds the same readers how he went up to Jerusalem to make public there "the gospel I preach among the Gentiles...lest I am running or have run in vain" (μή πως εἰς κενὸν τρέχω ἢ ἔδραμον, Gal 2:2). Paul regards the frustration of his apostolic ministry with apprehension. μή πως expresses this element of fear in 1 Thess 3:5; Gal 2:2; 4:11.[3] In Phil 2:16, however, where ὅτι introduces the possibility of laboring in vain, Paul expresses more confidence.

In these formulations Paul designates his missionary toil either with the technical terms κοπιάζειν/κόπος (1 Thess 3:5; Gal 4:11; Phil 2:16)[4] or with the metaphorical τρέχειν (Phil 2:16; Gal 2:2).[5] The prepositional

---

[3] Cf. *BDF* §370. N.b. the emphatic expression of fear in Gal 4:11, φοβοῦμαι ὑμᾶς μή πως.... The view that μή πως εἰς κενὸν τρέχω ἢ ἔδραμον in Gal 2:2 is an expression of implied apprehension prevails over the suggestions that it is a final clause or an indirect question. These alternatives are to be judged inferior on the basis of grammatical considerations and Pauline usage (see criticisms by Burton, *Gal*, 74; Pfitzner, *Agon*, 101; against Sieffert, *Gal*, 90; Oepke, *Gal*, 74).

[4] Cf. Rom 16:6, 12; 1 Cor 3:8; 4:12; 15:10; 16:16; 2 Cor 6:5; 10:15; 11:23, 27; 1 Thess 2:9; 5:12. See v. Harnack, "Κόπος," 1–10.

[5] Cf. 1 Cor 9:26. See Pfitzner, *Agon*, 100.

phrase εἰς κενόν—"in vain, to no purpose"[6] (Phil 2:16; Gal 2:2; 1 Thess 3:5)—or the adverb εἰκῇ[7] (Gal 4:11) expresses the idea of futility. Paul's fear of laboring in vain arises in situations in which his converts' steadfastness in faith is threatened through Satanic onslaughts of persecution (1 Thess 3:3–5) or through false teaching (Gal 4:9–11). Paul apparently does not contemplate a mere temporary wavering in faith but a setback which could make his missionary efforts *ultimately* futile. The consequence of the possible discontinuity in his converts' faith—his labor would have been *in vain*—reveals the far-reaching significance of the danger.

C. Bjerkelund's study, " 'Vergeblich' als Missionsergebnis bei Paulus," confirms that Paul's statements about laboring in vain envision eschatological loss, namely, lack of divine commendation for service at the last day. Bjerkelund gives examples of εἰς κενόν with a pregnant sense[8] in the LXX and midrashic literature which correspond to Paul's usage, in distinction to the formal, mundane meaning common in Hellenistic literature.[9] Isa 49:4, 8 LXX is his key OT text in establishing the eschatological overtones of "laboring in vain." To the Servant who says κενῶς ἐκοπίασα, the Lord answers, "in the day of salvation I have helped you."[10] Paul, who saw his own calling prefigured in that of the Servant,[11] also attributes eschatological implications to his own toiling in vain. Other Septuagintal texts use οὐκ εἰς κενόν or οὐκ κενός in association with the fulfillment of God's promises in the coming world (Isa 45:18; 65:23; Deut 32:47).[12] The midrashic commentaries on some of these occurences of κενός and cognates in the LXX bring out the eschatological overtones even more by relegating what is "in vain" to this age and by associating the coming age with all that is not "in vain."[13] These texts parallel Paul's viewing his labor for the gospel from the perspective of the eschaton. In line with LXX and rabbinic thought, Paul thinks that to labor in vain is to produce nothing of eternal

---

6 BAGD, s.v. κενός, 2.a.b.

7 See BAGD, s.v. εἰκῇ, 2.

8 Cf. Oepke, κενός, *TWNT* 3, 660: κενός and οὐ κενός are "Prädikate für das Widergöttliche und das Göttliche."

9 On the latter, see Schlier, *Gal*, 68, n. 1.

10 Cf. Derrett, "Running," 565.

11 Cf. the allusion to Isa 49:1, 5 LXX in Gal 1:15.

12 Bjerkelund, "Vergeblich," 179–181.

13 See Bjerkelund, "Vergeblich," 181–182. He refers to the midrash on Isa 65:22f.; 49:4; Deut 32:47. See Balz, *Heilsvertrauen*, 39, 40, on the use of κενός and ματαιότης and related words in the wisdom and prophetic literature of the OT for "alles, was Gott fern ist und von ihm deshalb bereits verworfen ist[,]...Vorgänge und Absichten von Menschen, die unter Absehung von Gottes Willen entstehen und deshalb von ihm der Nichtigkeit anheimgegeben sind."

value, of eschatological significance.[14] Consequently, all opportunity for the laborer to "boast" at the day of Christ is removed. The *final* test of Christian service will reveal whether Paul's labor was in vain or not.

In Phil 2:16 the eschatological dimension of Paul's statements about laboring in vain becomes explicit. As he hopes for a successful ministry in Philippi—that "I have not run in vain or labored in vain"—he anticipates the result of being able to "boast[15] at the day of Christ."[16] The relation between his $\kappa\alpha\acute{\upsilon}\chi\eta\mu\alpha$ and not running in vain is denoted by an explicative $\H{o}\tau\iota$.[17] Whether $\H{o}\tau\iota$ introduces the ground or the nature of Paul's boast,[18] it is clear that he sees the consequence of his apostolic work to have eschatological significance. If the exemplary converts described in Phil 2:14–16a do indeed come into being through Paul's ministry, he will have something to boast about when the day of reckoning for God's servants comes.[19] The opposite will be the case, however, if his efforts have no lasting effects in God's kingdom.[20] He would miss God's ultimate approval, having lost his $\kappa\alpha\acute{\upsilon}\chi\eta\mu\alpha$, by laboring in vain.

Paul sees his labor among the Thessalonian Christians also in the framework of its significance for the eschatological test. "For who (is) our hope or joy or crown of boasting[21]—is it not you—before our Lord Jesus at his coming? For you are our glory and joy" (1 Thess 2:19, 20; cf. 3:9; 2 Cor 1:14). Anticipating what his converts will mean for him at the parousia,

---

[14] Bjerkelund, "Vergeblich," 188: "Das paulinische 'vergeblich' dient in seiner Missionsverkündigung dazu, den eschatologischen Ernst zu unterstreichen."

[15] $\kappa\alpha\acute{\upsilon}\chi\eta\mu\alpha$ is the matter or ground of glorying (BAGD, s.v. $\kappa\alpha\acute{\upsilon}\chi\eta\mu\alpha$, 1). Paul, however, does not boast except in the Lord and what he accomplishes through his apostle. Paul sees in his success God's power working through him and thus divine commendation of his ministry (cf. 2 Cor 10:17, 18; 12:9). Gnilka's comment (*Phil*, 153) that Paul's work is from the beginning $\check{\epsilon}\rho\gamma\sigma\nu$ $\Theta\epsilon\sigma\hat{\upsilon}$ (see Phil 1:6) deserves mention here. See, further, Bultmann, $\kappa\alpha\upsilon\chi\acute{\alpha}\sigma\mu\alpha\iota$, *TWNT* 3, 651; Calvin, *1 Thess, ad loc.*; cf. Zmijewski, $\kappa\alpha\upsilon\chi\acute{\alpha}\sigma\mu\alpha\iota$, *EWNT* 2, 689.

[16] $\epsilon\acute{\iota}\varsigma$ $\acute{\eta}\mu\acute{\epsilon}\rho\alpha\nu$ $X\rho\iota\sigma\tau\sigma\hat{\upsilon}$ denotes the time for which the boasting is reserved (Vincent, *Phil*, 70). Cf. Plummer, *2 Cor*, 29: "Paul rather frequently brings in the thought of the Day of the Lord as a sort of test of the value of his missionary work and its results."

[17] Vincent, *Phil*, 70. Pfitzner (*Agon*, 104) comments on Phil 2:16: "Verse 16 expresses the consequences of their faithfulness or lack of faithfulness for Paul's own person."

[18] On the alternatives, see Vincent, *Phil*, 70.

[19] Cf. 1 Cor 3:13–15. Cf. Sanders, *Palestinian Judaism*, 449. Gnilka (*Phil*, 153) sees Phil 2:16 in the context of eschatological testing. Zmijewski ($\kappa\alpha\upsilon\chi\acute{\alpha}\sigma\mu\alpha\iota$, *EWNT* 2, 686) notes the eschatological character of boasting and points to its association with other eschatological terms.

[20] Cf. Lohmeyer, *Phil*, 110.

[21] See 1QS 4:7 for the concepts of crown, joy, glory, etc. with eschatological connotations.

Paul can view them in this light even presently.[22] This thought prefaces Paul's recounting of his great concern for the stability of the Thessalonians' faith which caused him to send Timothy to the afflicted Christians that he might "establish and exhort you in your faith" (3:1–4). An occasion of "testing" made Paul fear that "our labor would be in vain" (3:5). E. v. Dobschütz comments appropriately: "Die Feindschaft Satans richtet sich also in letzter Richtung nicht gegen die Thess., sondern gegen den Apostel."[23] Paul thus feared being robbed of his "hope or joy or crown of boasting... before our Lord Jesus at his coming" if his converts fell in persecution.[24]

The purpose for Paul's visit to Jerusalem in Gal 2:1–10 was to realize his hope not to have run in vain ($\mu\acute{\eta}$ $\pi\omega\varsigma$ $\epsilon\grave{\iota}\varsigma$ $\kappa\epsilon\nu\grave{o}\nu$ $\tau\rho\acute{\epsilon}\chi\omega$ $\mathring{\eta}$ $\ddot{\epsilon}\delta\rho\alpha\mu\rho\nu$, v. 2). A fundamental threat to his whole Gentile mission, past, present and future,[25] motivated Paul to "go up to Jerusalem" and "lay before them the gospel I preach among the Gentiles" (Gal 2:1, 2). The authority of the Jerusalem church could have been used by Judaizing pockets in the early Christian movement to introduce circumcision and law-keeping into Paul's churches as necessary for salvation.[26] But the "apostle of the uncircumcision" would have no eschatological boast in Gentile Christian converts who sought justification by law (cf. Gal 5:4). If his converts were compelled to Judaize (cf. Gal 2:14), he would have labored in vain.[27] Paul does not expect God's commendation for such results. Paul went up to Jerusalem, therefore, not to seek the approval of a higher authority,[28] but to prevent Jerusalem's authority from being played off against his own authority, better put, the authority of the gospel he preached (cf. Gal 1:9).[29]

Paul's fear that opposing forces might gain the backing of the Jerusalem leaders was allayed. He portrays the outcome of the visit as successful: The Gentile Titus was not compelled to be circumcised. The "false brethren"

---

[22] Best, *Thess*, 128, 129.

[23] V. Dobschütz, *Thess*, 138.

[24] Cf. Phil 4:1: "My joy and crown, so stand firm in the Lord!" Best (*Thess*, 128) associates the eschatological note at the end of Philippians 3 with the appellations in 4:1. Similarly, Gnilka, *Phil*, 220, sees an "eschatologische Erstreckung" in the crown motif and draws a comparison with 2:16.

[25] On the significance of the present subjunctive and aorist verbs here, see Pfitzner, *Agon*, 101.

[26] Cf. Lightfoot, *Gal*, 104.

[27] Paul saw the requirement of Gentile circumcision and law-keeping to be a breach with the gospel leading to alienation from salvation; see pp. 203–216 above.

[28] Against Schlier, *Gal*, 68.

[29] Bruce (*Gal*, 109) notes correctly: "It is most unlikely that Paul would have modified his gospel had the Jerusalem leaders *not* approved of it—he had higher authority than theirs for maintaining it unchanged, and 'no one is likely to want the *independence* of his gospel to be confirmed'." Contrast Derrett, "Running," 564, 565.

did not succeed in subjecting them to "slavery." Paul's divine commission
to the Gentiles was recognized (Gal 2:3–10). Through his historic visit,
Paul succeeded not only in subduing the *threat* of the misuse of Jerusalem's authority against his Gentile mission, but also in turning its authority
into an *asset*: the "pillars" actually *supported* his "gospel and apostleship of
uncircumcision."[30] When a concrete instance of the Judaizing threat to his
Gentile converts comes up later in the Galatian churches, Paul appeals to
Jerusalem's recognition of his gospel and commission against the opponents' maligning of these. False teachers may try to cause Paul's labor to
be "in vain," but not with the backing of the church in Jerusalem. The authority of that body could rightfully be mobilized only for the freedom of
the Gentiles to find righteousness without law and thus to bolster Paul's
hope not to "run in vain."[31]

Nevertheless, the cause of Paul's fear that he had labored in vain was
not eradicated. In Galatians the same Judaizing threat has revived this fear:
φοβοῦμαι ὑμᾶς μή πως εἰκῇ κεκοπίακα εἰς ὑμᾶς (4:11). Most interpreters take φοβοῦμαι ὑμᾶς to express Paul's fear *for the Galatians* ("I am
afraid for you")[32] and point to the consequences they will bear if Paul's labor is in vain. But in the NT, the accusative object of φοβεῖσθαι never denotes the one for whose sake one fears, but always what or who inspires
fear.[33] If we follow NT usage, therefore, and take ὑμᾶς to denote the insti-
gator of fear,[34] we find that Paul expresses concern for himself.[35] By observing "days and months and seasons and years" (4:10), the Galatians
make Paul afraid, namely, that his labor will have been in vain, for he will

---

[30] Cf. Betz, *Gal*, 86: "Apparently the matter at stake was to force church authorities
in Jerusalem to give *post factum* approval to the Pauline gospel in the face of heated
opposition, and thereby help to defeat the anti-Pauline forces in Asia Minor." Similarly,
Burton, *Gal*, 72.

[31] Bruce (*Gal*, 109) comments on Gal 2:2: "The approval of those leaders made his
task less difficult and (as here) could serve his apologetic purpose."

[32] See, e.g., BAGD, s.v. φοβέω, 1.a.; Bruce, *Gal*, 207; Betz, *Gal*, 219; Schlier, *Gal*,
207; Sieffert, *Gal*, 255. In support of his translation of φοβοῦμαι ὑμᾶς as "ich bin be-
sorgt um euch," Sieffert (*Gal*, 255) cites Sophocles *OT* 767; Plato *Phaedr.* 239d. But
Sophocles does not use φοβεῖσθαι, rather δέδοικ' ἐμαυτόν. Further, the reference to
Plato (τὸ γὰρ τοιοῦτον σῶμα...οἱ μὲν ἐχθροὶ θαρροῦσιν, οἱ δὲ φίλοι καὶ αὐτοὶ
οἱ ἐρασταὶ φοβοῦνται) does not support his point.

[33] See Matt 10:26, 28b; 14:5; 21:26, 46; Mark 6:20; 9:32; 11:18, 32; 12:12; Luke
1:50; 12:5; 18:4; 20:19; 22:2; 23:40; John 9:22; Acts 5:26; 9:26; 10:2, 22, 35; 13:16, 26;
Rom 13:3; Gal 2:12; Eph 5:33; Col 3:22; Heb 11:23, 27; 1 Pet 2:17; Rev 2:10; 11:18;
14:7; 19:5. The cognate accusatives in Mark 4:41; Luke 2:9; 1 Pet 3:6, 14 form a special
case.

[34] So the NEB: "You make me fear that...." Against Bruce, *Gal*, 207.

[35] Contrast Betz, *Gal*, 219.

not have succeeded in his mission to bring salvation apart from the law to the Gentiles in Galatia. Both main clause (φοβοῦμαι ὑμᾶς) and subordinate clause (μή πως εἰκῇ κεκοπίακα εἰς ὑμᾶς) express the fear of personal loss, which is the primary aspect in the statements about laboring in vain.[36] In summary, the eschatological connotations of laboring in vain are coupled with the present connotations of ineffectiveness in Gal 2:2; 4:11 where Paul focuses on the present success of his mission in the context of the Judaizing opposition.[37]

Thus effective labor for the gospel in Paul's eyes means being able to boast at the day of Christ. Correspondingly, labor in vain signifies loss of that eschatological boast. Paul's statements about laboring in vain express primarily this self-concern. Yet the eschatological nature of the implications of ineffective labor for Paul shows that the implications for his converts are also eschatological: they may be excluded from final salvation.[38] Paul is thus uncertain whether or not some of his converts will be numbered among the saved at the day of Christ. This is the indirect implication of the passages I have considered here. It is hard to say, however, whether his converts' final exclusion from salvation as the implication of Paul's possible labor in vain would imply their apostasy or the falling away of those who falsely professed faith. The statements about laboring in vain themselves do not make this distinction. I will now explore their contexts as well as other passages which reveal Paul's attitude toward his apostolic labor and its effectiveness to see whether they shed any light on this matter.

Paul's consolation in the face of the possible futility of his ministry is the guarantee of success which comes through cooperation with God in the work of salvation. For Paul recognizes that the gospel itself as the divine power of salvation, not the preacher, was the vital force behind the early Christian missionary movement (cf. Phil 1:12; 2 Thess 3:1). Unlike his own efforts, Paul did not call into question the gospel's effectiveness.[39] It is the "power of God unto salvation" (Rom 1:16). It came to the Thessalonians "not by word only but also with power and the Holy Spirit and much persuasion" (1 Thess 1:5). Paul puts his confidence in "the surpassing greatness of the power...from God and not from ourselves" (2 Cor 4:7). As the divine power works, Paul cooperates. He aims to serve the gospel as *it*

---

[36] Or (φοβοῦμαι) ὑμᾶς might be proleptic in anticipation of εἰς ὑμᾶς. So Burton, who translates, "I fear that in vain have I spent my labour upon you" (*Gal*, 234). Cf. *BDF* §476(3). In this case too the fear is primarily self-directed.

[37] For οὐ κενή describing present success in apostolic ministry, see 1 Thess 2:1.

[38] Cf. Satake, "Apostolat," 105, n. 1; Schenk, *Phil*, 223; Betz, *Gal*, 219; Sieffert, *Gal*, 256.

[39] Pfitzner, *Agon*, 104; Oepke, κενός, *TWNT* 3, 660.

accomplishes its task: "I do all things for the sake of the gospel, that I may become its partner" (1 Cor 9:23).[40] He describes himself and other Christian ministers as συνεργοί θεοῦ (1 Cor 3:9; 1 Thess 3:2; cf. 2 Cor 6:1): they "plant" and "water" while God "brings the growth" (1 Cor 3:6). Paul thus understands his apostolic ministry as cooperation with God in *God's* work. He can say, "I worked, but not I, rather the grace of God with me" (1 Cor 15:10; cf. also 2 Cor 3:3; 5:20; 1 Cor 3:5; 16:10).

By contrast, human effort by itself cannot produce success in apostolic ministry. Paul thus does not play the great orator to gain converts: "My message and my preaching did not consist in persuasive words of wisdom" (1 Cor 2:4; cf. 2:1–3). If he preached "with (humanly acquired) wisdom of speech," "the cross of Christ" would "be made void" (κενωθῇ, 1 Cor 1:17). Proclaiming "persuasive words of wisdom" would bring about only "faith... in human wisdom" (1 Cor 2:5). When Paul participates in the divine work of salvation, however, his preaching is accompanied by "the demonstration of the Spirit and power" resulting in "faith...in the power of God" (1 Cor 2:4, 5; see also 1 Thess 1:5). That is, his apostolic activity is not ineffective, nor merely superficially effective. Rather, his hearers receive his message as *God's* word, which, unlike human words, "performs its work in you who believe" (1 Thess 2:13). In the last analysis, Paul attributes his own success to Christ: "I will not presume to speak of anything except what Christ has accomplished through me, resulting in the obedience of the Gentiles by word and deed, in the power of signs and wonders, in the power of the Spirit" (Rom 15:18).

Paul's confidence in the successful outcome of God's saving work through the gospel thus stands side by side with his fear of laboring in vain and losing the attestation to his faithful service which his converts will provide on the day of Christ. His confidence and fear mutually interpret each other. For Paul gains assurance that he is laboring with the gospel, and thus not in vain, when he observes the signs of *divine* working in his converts, and vice versa[41] For example, when the Thessalonians' new faith is tested through persecution Paul's fear of having labored in vain surfaces. But after they have proven steadfast (1 Thess 3:1–8; 1:3), his fear subsides and he grows bold to say, "knowing, brothers, beloved by God, his choice of you" (1:4).

Further, it is no coincidence that in Phil 2:16 the motif of futile service

---

[40] On this verse, see pp. 247–254 above.

[41] Cf. Beardslee, *Achievement*, 65: "He appeals to his success as a sign that God is working through him.... [H]is work has relevance both to the advance of the gospel and to the indescribable new order which God alone can establish."

is not colored by fear but by confidence "*that* I have not run in vain or labored in vain." For Paul sees in the Philippians' Christian faith and life the evidence of God's working and concludes from this the certainty of their final salvation: "I am persuaded of this, that he who began a good work in you will complete it until the day of Christ Jesus" (Phil 1:6).[42]

Phil 2:12, however, appears to be in tension with such confidence. There Paul exhorts Christians: μετὰ φόβου καὶ τρόμου τὴν ἑαυτῶν σωτηρίαν κατεργάζεσθε. P. Ewald explains: "Es kann nur besagen: 'mit Furcht und Zittern' vor einer Pflichtverletzung, die der σωτηρία verlustig machen könnte."[43] Does this comment indeed accurately reflect Paul's meaning?

"Fear and trembling" is a familiar OT and NT expression. In Exod 15:16; Isa 19:16 LXX (cf. Ps 2:11; Dan 4:37a LXX; etc.) φόβος καὶ τρόμος denotes the appropriate attitude of created beings conscious of their weakness and sinfulness before a holy God to whom they owe obedience.[44] The phrase has this sense in Phil 2:12 also. It describes the attitude *before God* in which the readers should "work out [their] salvation."[45] That attitude is to be characterized by *humble dependence and obedient submission*, as the context suggests.[46] Precisely these motifs, humility and obedience, are prominent in the context (cf. 2:2–8, 12a). Further, v. 13, which gives the reason (γάρ) for the exhortation in v. 12, supports this meaning of "fear and trembling": θεὸς γάρ ἐστιν ὁ ἐνεργῶν ἐν ὑμῖν καὶ τὸ θέλειν καὶ τὸ ἐνεργεῖν ὑπὲρ τῆς εὐδοκίας (2:13). Here Paul says that *God* is the true author of every impulse and act in the "working out"[47] of one's salvation[48] for God's good pleasure.[49] That is, not only has God accomplished

---

[42] On this verse, see pp. 33–47 above.

[43] Ewald, *Phil*, 133. Similarly, Vincent (*Phil*, 65); Meyer (*Phil*, 78). Dibelius (*Phil*, 83) finds in 2:12 a Jewish maxim in which μετὰ φόβου καὶ τρόμου expresses uncertainty about attainment of the goal.

[44] Cf. also the expression "fear and trembling" with this sense in *1 Enoch* 13:3; *2 Enoch* 22:10. Otfried Hofius drew these references to my attention.

[45] With Müller, *Phil*, 91; Gnilka, *Phil*, 149. Gnilka argues against reducing the meaning of the phrase φόβος καὶ τρόμος in 2 Cor 7:15 and 1 Cor 2:3 to an attitude toward other human beings, and insists that here "Furcht und Zittern haben mit Gott zu tun" (149; but contrast Eph 6:5). Thus these parallels do not lead us to take φόβος καὶ τρόμος in Phil 2:12 as an attitude toward other human beings (against Barth, *Phil*, 65, 66, 69; Bonnard, *Phil*, 49; Michael, *Phil*, 103; Collange, *Phil*, 98; Martin, *Phil*, 112).

[46] With Müller, *Phil*, 91; Gnilka, *Phil*, 149; Eichholz, "Bewahren," 158.

[47] κατεργάζεσθαι τὴν ἑαυτῶν σωτηρίαν does not mean that Christians themselves have the task of securing their own eternal welfare, but that they are active in the appropriation of the salvation which God has accomplished for them (cf. Müller, *Phil*, 91). Warren ("Work," 125) compares Strabo's use of κατεργασία in *Geo.* III.2.10. Cf. Barth, *Phil*, 64; Dibelius, *Phil*, 83.

[48] Some take σωτηρία here to mean the "spiritual health" of the Christian community at Philippi (e.g., Michael, *Phil*, 101, 102; Martin, *Phil*, 111). But see Marshall's

salvation and freely given it to believers, but God also makes them to appropriate salvation. Christians thus work out their salvation in the knowledge of their utter dependence on God and God's power.[50] Salvation *remains* a gift and does not turn into a human achievement, though it involves human activity.[51] Because the working out of one's salvation is at the same time God's work, that human activity must be characterized by humility and obedience. Calvin explains: "You have...all things from God; therefore be careful and humble."[52] And since salvation even as it is being appropriated is the work of God, Christians do not need to fear losing salvation as they work it out. For God is faithful to carry out God's purpose (cf. 1:6). "Fear and trembling" while working out salvation thus does not consist in apprehension lest one come under the judgment of God and lose salvation.

Instead of suggesting uncertainty about the Philippians' final salvation, Phil 2:12, 13 sheds light on Paul's confidence that his labor toward them will not have been in vain.[53] According to this text, Christians' working out of salvation in their Christian lives gives evidence of *God's continued salvific work* in them. For here Paul sees divine grace and power to be the source of successful Christian living. Divinely-inspired impulses and actions in the Christian life confirm God's faithfulness to God's intent to finish God's salvific purpose begun in believers (cf. 1:6).[54] Thus Paul exhorts

---

criticisms of this view (*Kept*, 124).

[49] εὐδοκία here refers not to human good will (so, Phil 1:15; 2 Thess 1:11) but to divine good pleasure (so also at Matt 11:26; Luke 10:21; Eph 1:5, 9); with Gnilka, *Phil*, 150 with n. 26. The reference to divine good pleasure supports the necessity of humility since "an dem freien Willen Gottes hängt alles" (Barth, *Phil*, 69). Calvin (*Phil, ad loc.*) comments: "This is the true artillery (*machina*) for destroying all haughtiness; this is the sword for killing all pride, when we hear that we are utterly nothing, and can do nothing, except through the grace of God alone...which comes forth from the Spirit of regeneration."

[50] In 1 Cor 2:3–5 the attitude of φόβος καὶ τρόμος is combined with trust in the working of divine δύναμις.

[51] Cf. *Ep. Arist.* 225, where the friendship won (κατεργάζεσθαι) through human effort is called a good gift received from God. Otfried Hofius brought this parallel to my attention.

[52] Calvin, *Phil, ad loc.* Similarly, Eichholz, "Bewahren," 160: "Eben weil Gott alles wirkt, kann der Mensch sein Heil nur 'mit Furcht und Zittern' schaffen" (see also *ibid*, 159). Also Müller, *Phil*, 92; Barth, *Phil*, 69; Friedrich, *Phil*, 112. The phrase μετὰ φόβου καὶ τρόμου is placed forward for emphasis.

[53] Beare, *Phil*, 91.

[54] Paul's thought in the Philippian thanksgiving is similar. The Philippians' "good works" (1:5, 9) bear witness to the accomplishment of the "divine good work" of salvation in them and to God's intent to complete this work (1:6).

Christians to participate actively in the actualization of God's saving purpose toward them; they are not passive. And since their participation shows that God is at work in them completing their salvation according to God's promise, they can work out their salvation not only with humility and obedience but also with joy and confidence in God.

Where God is at work in those who profess faith through the preaching of the gospel, their eschatological destiny is not in doubt.[55] On the other hand, insofar as Paul labors independently of the divine power of salvation, he has reason to fear that the quality of his converts' faith will not pass the test of salvation and he will thus be deprived of his eschatological boast (cf. 1 Cor 3:14, 15).

In conclusion, Paul's laboring in vain has eschatological significance for his converts in that the effects of his ministry—conversion and profession of faith—might not after all be rooted in God's saving power. The salvation of his converts might thus prove to be inauthentic. Alternatively, Paul fears that his converts might become apostates by cutting short the saving work of God begun in their lives. This view, however, is hard to reconcile with Paul's expressions of confidence regarding the successfulness of divine salvific activity. We can more easily account for the combination of confidence and fear in Paul's attitude by tracing potential labor in vain to the apostle's failure to cooperate with the gospel as the power of salvation, and successful apostolic labor to God's faithfulness in the work of salvation—as Paul's own comments frequently lead us to think. Since some ambiguity regarding the interpretation of Paul's statements about laboring in vain remains, however, they cannot be given great weight in determining his view of continuity in Christians' salvation.

Believing in Vain

1 Corinthians 15:2. Paul writes 1 Corinthians 15 to deal with the problem that "some among you say there is no resurrection of the dead" (15:12). Not far into his opening remarks, he suggests the possibility that the Corinthians "believed in vain" (εἰκῇ ἐπιστεύσατε, 15:2c).[56] This

---

[55] In Gal 4:11 Paul comes the closest to expressing doubt about the eschatological destiny of converts whom he considers genuinely Christian. But this verse ought not to be taken in isolation from other statements in Galatians which express confidence regarding continuity in the Galatians' salvation from the perspective of divine working. See the discussion of this point on pp. 214–216.

[56] For a similar expression, cf. Gal 3:4: τοσαῦτα ἐπάθετε εἰκῇ;

possibility would negate the immediately preceding affirmation that they "are being saved through [the gospel] (15:2a)." That is, ἐκτὸς εἰ μὴ εἰκῇ ἐπιστεύσατε formulates the exception to the statement δι' οὗ καὶ σῴζεσθε. In short, Paul asks whether the Corinthians' faith is of the kind which is accompanied by salvation. This passage raises the following questions to be addressed here. What does it mean to believe in vain? How might salvation fail to follow faith in the Corinthians' case?

Various translations of εἰκῇ[57] in 1 Cor 15:2 have been proposed: "without consideration, rashly,"[58] "without reason,"[59] "to no purpose,"[60] and "in vain."[61] Each of these translations, though they have different nuances, suggests the possibility that faith may fail to be accompanied by salvation. It does not appear, however, that Paul is calling the genuineness of his readers' conversion into question.[62] For his opening remarks in vv. 1, 2 and summarizing comment in v. 11 indicate plainly the Corinthians' acceptance of and present stance in the gospel that Paul preached to them.[63] He begins with a *captatio benevolentiae*,[64] to which the exceptive clause, ἐκτὸς εἰ μὴ εἰκῇ ἐπιστεύσατε, forms a contrast. εἰκῇ, therefore, cannot suggest that the Corinthians' faith is inauthentic and for that reason not accompanied by salvation.

Commonly, interpreters identify the problem as the instability of the Corinthians' faith: they might turn away from the gospel and so render their initial faith useless for salvation.[65] In keeping with the NT emphasis on faithfulness to the gospel tradition, here Paul speaks of holding firmly—κατέχειν—to the tradition once delivered (cf. 1 Cor 11:2; Lk 8:15; Heb 10:23), and highlights one fundamental truth from the gospel he preached to them.[66] The resurrection is the particular gospel tenet which the Corinthians must by no means let go (15:3–8). If, on the other hand, they lose

---

[57] Cf. Rom 13:4; Gal 4:11; 3:4; Col 2:18; Matt 5:22 t. r.

[58] BAGD, s.v. εἰκῇ, 4; Robertson and Plummer, *1 Cor*, 332; Weiß, *1 Kor*, 346; Moffat, *1 Cor*, 235.

[59] Schlatter, *Bote*, 394. In his exposition Schlatter also comes close to the meaning "rashly."

[60] Barrett, *1 Cor*, 337.

[61] Grosheide, *1 Cor*, 348; Wolff, *1 Kor*, 149.

[62] Contrast Robertson and Plummer, *1 Cor*, 332.

[63] Cf. Grosheide, *1 Cor*, 347; Conzelmann, *1 Cor*, 250.

[64] Barrett, *1 Cor*, 336; contrast Lietzmann, *Kor*, 76.

[65] Both Barrett (*1 Cor*, 337) and Robertson and Plummer (*1 Cor*, 332, n. t) cite Origen in support of this view.

[66] τίνι λόγῳ εὐηγγελισάμην (v. 2), put forward for emphasis (so Robertson and Plummer, *1 Cor*, 332, *et al.*), shows Paul's interest in the exact form and content of the gospel which the Corinthians should remember and hold fast (Weiß, *1 Kor*, 152). He continues the thought in vv. 3–8: παρέδωκα γὰρ ὑμῖν ἐν πρώτοις....

their grip on the tradition received, they will be excluded from salvation. In this explanation of Paul's meaning εἰ κατέχετε[67] functions as a warning[68] which, if not heeded, negates σῴζεσθε at v. 2.[69] εἰκῇ ἐπιστεύσατε would then describe a conversion which does not last.[70] C. Wolff concludes: "Das Bewahren der vermittelten Überlieferung ist also entscheidend für die eschatologische Rettung."[71]

It is unlikely, however, that the conditional clause, εἰ κατέχετε, suggests why the Corinthians might have believed εἰκῇ, namely, if they fail to hold fast the gospel tradition. Of course, Paul thinks it necessary for the saved to hold fast the gospel.[72] The common interpretation of 1 Cor 15:2 goes astray, however, in assuming that Paul entertains the possibility that his readers might indeed fail to cleave to the gospel. For the conditional clause εἰ κατέχετε is *realis*: the indicative mood after εἰ expresses the expectation that the condition is in fact fulfilled.[73] Paul assumes here that the Corinthians are indeed holding fast the tradition he delivered to them, including the resurrection of Jesus from the dead. Nothing in the text suggests that they openly dispute this piece of tradition.[74] In fact, Paul's argument in chap. 15 presupposes their continuing affirmation of Jesus' resurrection.[75] "If"—as the apostles preached and as the Corinthians believed (15:11)—"Christ...has risen from the dead, how do some among you say that there is no resurrection of the dead" (15:12). Denial of the resurrection of the dead is inconsistent with the Corinthians' belief in Jesus' resurrection according to the gospel.[76] Paul would not have argued this way had the Corinthians already given up belief in Jesus' resurrection. εἰ κατέχετε thus means: "If, as I assume to be the case, you hold fast...." In summary, Paul emphasizes and expounds his readers' firm position *within* the gospel tradition—including the belief in Jesus' resurrection—in order to distance them from the false teaching that "there is no resurrection of the dead." Such a

---

[67] The textual variant, ὀφείλετε κατέχειν (D* F G a b t vg^ms; Ambst), is a secondary improvement on εἰ κατέχετε (Barrett, *1 Cor*, 334, n. 1, *et al.*). *BDF* §478 suggests that εἰ itself is an explanatory gloss.

[68] Marshall, *Kept*, 118.

[69] Weiß, *1 Kor*, 346; Grosheide, *1 Cor*, 348.

[70] Bjerkelund, "Vergeblich," 183.

[71] Wolff, *1 Kor*, 152.

[72] Correctly, Heinrici, *1 Kor*, 473.

[73] See *BDF* §372. So Weiß, *1 Kor*, 346. Wrongly, Wolff, *1 Kor*, 153.

[74] Even the Corinthian group which denies the resurrection of the dead appears to make an exception in the case of Jesus' resurrection, so Spörlein, *Leugnung*, 70.

[75] Cf. Conzelmann, *1 Cor*, 250: "The assertion "you stand" implies that the authority and content of the creed are validly recognized in Corinth. This provides a common basis of argument."

[76] Cf. Grosheide, *1 Cor*, 357.

belief is incompatible with the gospel "in which [they] stand" (15:1).

If Paul thus does not argue that the Corinthians will have believed εἰκῇ if they end up abandoning the gospel, what then does he mean by saying they will have believed εἰκῇ? As I will attempt to show in the following discussion, Paul traces faith which does not bring salvation not to some human failure but to the soteriological impotence of a distorted gospel. He has in mind the case in which the *object* of faith, not its human subject, poses the obstacle to salvation. If one has believed in a *message* which cannot save, which provides no basis for salvation, one has believed εἰκῇ.[77] The Christian gospel would have this fundamental deficiency apart from one of its central tenets, the resurrection of Jesus from the dead. This is Paul's thesis in 1 Cor 15:14, 17–19. If the Corinthians have believed in a resurrectionless gospel, if the gospel tradition that "he was raised on the third day" (15:4) is not true, then there is no basis for their salvation as believers. Then they are not "being saved" (contrast δι' οὗ καὶ σῴζεσθε, 15:2). Then they have believed in vain.[78] A. Schlatter comments aptly: "Vom Wert der Botschaft hängt der des Glaubens vollständig ab.... Wer der Botschaft ihren Inhalt nimmt, nimmt ihn auch dem Glauben. An einen Toten kann sich der Mensch nicht ergeben, von einem Toten kann er nichts erwarten und nichts empfangen."[79]

The denial of the resurrection by some Corinthians called into question the gospel tradition of the resurrection of Jesus. But without Jesus' resurrection, faith is useless. Without the resurrection, further, the gospel is κενός and the preachers of the gospel become ψευδομάρτυρες τοῦ θεοῦ. The statement "Christ has not been raised" opens a Pandora's box of disastrous implications, as Paul reveals in 15:12–19. Paul intends these implications to act as deterrents to the elimination of Jesus' resurrection from the gospel tradition which the Corinthians must hold fast. Among these various implications of the Corinthian heresy, the one which concerns us here is the futility of faith.

Picking up the idea of soteriologically useless faith introduced in v. 2, Paul explains εἰκῇ ἐπιστεύσατε there with the words κενὴ καὶ ἡ πίστις ὑμῶν in 15:14, and ματαία ἡ πίστις ὑμῶν, ἔτι ἐστὲ ἐν ταῖς ἁμαρτίαις ὑμῶν in 15:17. In his repetition of the idea from v. 2 he preserves the πίστις terminology and interprets the adverb εἰκῇ with the adjectives

---

[77] Cf. Godet, *1 Kor* II, 183.

[78] εἰκῇ ἐπιστεύσατε, 15:2c, expresses the opposite of δι' οὗ καὶ σῴζεσθε, 15:2a (an observation made to me by Otfried Hofius).

[79] Schlatter, *Bote*, 405. Cf. Allo, *1 Cor*, 401; Lietzmann, *Kor*, 79; Marshall, *Kept*, 118.

κενός and μάταιος. Paul can also use εἰκῇ and εἰς κενόν interchangeably to describe apostolic labor which bears no eschatologically significant fruit (cf. Gal 4:11; Phil 2:16; 1 Thess 3:5).[80] In the present context he employs the term κενή also with reference to God's grace, which "was not 'without effect' toward me" (15:10). κενή πίστις, then, would be faith which is "empty" in the deepest sense, divorced from divine working and power, without saving significance.[81]

Paul also describes this kind of faith with the word ματαία (15:17), a synonym to κενή here,[82] as it can be elsewhere.[83] The statement ἔτι ἐστὲ ἐν ταῖς ἁμαρτίαις ὑμῶν shows why faith would be characterized by futility: those who believe would not have been forgiven and justified.[84] The guilt and penalty of sin which results in death and condemnation would still define their existence.[85] This thought is stated even more poignantly in the example of believers who have already died. They would have perished definitively (ἀπώλοντο, 15:18), with no hope of salvation.[86] The contrast with σῴζεσθε in v. 2 is obvious.[87] Yet Paul can find even worse words to describe those with a κενή, ματαία πίστις. They are "more pitiable than all people," i.e., even than those who perish outside of Christ, for "in this life [they] have only[88] hoped in Christ" (15:19).[89] "If Christ has not been raised," as Paul says (15:14, 17), we must draw precisely these conclusions for those who have put their faith in him. In short, they would have "believed without reason or result." Their faith would have no basis in God's saving power and thus would be useless. They themselves would not, therefore, be saved.

The exception which Paul says would falsify his affirmation of the Corinthians' salvation, therefore, is not human failure but the failure of a

---

[80] See pp. 262, 263 above.

[81] See BAGD, s.v. κενός, 2.a.α.; Oepke, κενός, *TWNT* 3, 660. Cf. also Rom 4:14, where κεκένωται ἡ πίστις describes the soteriological meaninglessness of faith "if those of the law are heirs." Cf. Bjerkelund's comments, "Vergeblich," 184.

[82] So BAGD, s.v. κενός, 2.a.α.; Oepke, κενός, *TWNT* 3, 660.

[83] Cf. the synonymous parallelism with these terms in Hos 12:2; Job 20:18; Isa 59:4 LXX; *Ep. Arist.* 205; *1 Clem.* 7:2.

[84] Conzelmann, *1 Cor*, 266.

[85] Schlatter, *Bote*, 406; Godet, *1 Kor* II, 193; Allo, *Cor*, 402. Paul here simply presupposes the significance of Jesus' resurrection for the forgiveness of sins and justification of sinners.

[86] For ἀπόλλυμι for definitive destruction, cf., e.g., Rom 2:12; 1 Cor 1:18; 2 Cor 2:15; 4:3; 2 Thess 2:10.

[87] Cf. Wolff, *1 Kor*, 175. Cf. also that contrast in 1 Cor 1:18; 2 Cor 2:15; Phil 1:28.

[88] Against taking μόνον with ἐν τῇ ζωῇ ταύτῃ, see Weiß, *1 Kor*, 355.

[89] On the comparison, see Schlatter, *Bote*, 407.

distorted gospel.[90] To believe εἰκῇ is to base one's hope of salvation on a message which is soteriologically impotent, namely, a "gospel" without the resurrection of Jesus. In 1 Cor 15:2 Paul imagines a situation not in which the Corinthians would have *lost* salvation but in which they *never would have been saved*—in spite of their conversion and faith![91] Paul's use of the present tense in σῴζεσθε[92] shows that he is indeed thinking about the reality of present salvation and not a future loss of salvation. The suggestion that the Corinthians might have believed εἰκῇ and thus might not stand in salvation presently is calculated to provoke their disagreement.[93] The Corinthians themselves know that they "are being saved" and thus cannot have believed "without reason or result."[94] The gospel in which they stand therefore must truly be God's power of salvation through the death and resurrection of Jesus Christ.

In summary, Paul argues that faith in the gospel apart from the reality of Jesus' resurrection has no saving significance. His thesis that a soteriologically effective faith is necessarily grounded in Jesus' resurrection has negative implications for the erroneous denial of the resurrection of the dead, a belief which some Corinthians already espoused. Paul has developed his own domino theory here. Denial of the resurrection of the dead sets the process in motion. The next domino to fall is the resurrection of Jesus, which then knocks down the hope of salvation of those who believe in him. In other words, the logical consequence of the statement ἀνάστασις νεκρῶν οὐκ ἔστιν is denial of salvation through the gospel. The unorthodox Corinthians had pulled the rug out from under their own salvation.[95] Once the implications of their error were exposed, Paul reasoned, the false teaching would no longer have any appeal.

In 2 Cor 13:5 Paul applies the same strategy of unmasking the self-

---

[90] So Heinrici, *1 Kor*, 488: "Das εἰκῇ πιστεύειν (v. 2) hängt dann an den Dingen, die fälschlich verkündigt wurden, und nicht an den Menschen, welche durch eigene Schuld sich die Sicherheit des neuen Lebens verkümmern."

[91] Cf. Weiß, *1 Kor*, 346: "P. ...[will] die Fundamente untersuchen...und [greift] daher [zurück] auf den Moment des Gläubigwerdens."

[92] But not a futuristic present, against Barrett (*1 Cor*, 336) and Robertson and Plummer (*1 Cor*, 331). Cf. the present tense of σῴζεσθαι in 1 Cor 1:18; 2 Cor 2:15.

[93] With Grosheide, *1 Cor*, 348. Paul also provokes his readers to disagreement in vv. 14–19; with Grosheide (359).

[94] Cf. Heinrici, *1 Kor*, 472; Grosheide, *1 Cor*, 348; Schlatter, *Bote*, 409. Weiß (*1 Kor*, 354, 355) calls the similarly provocative statements in vv. 14, 17 *ad hominem* arguments: "Zu gewiß, zu real sind diese Erfahrungen einer neuen, beseligenden Lebensfreudigkeit und Kraft, als daß sie Illusion sein könnten. Sein Argument ist also nur zwingend für Menschen, die eine starke Erfahrung von der Erlösung gemacht haben."

[95] Conzelmann, *1 Cor*, 265: "To dispute one's own resurrection is to abrogate the presupposition of one's own existence, the kerygma and therewith also faith."

incriminating character of a view he wants his readers to reject. The moment the Corinthians pronounce him *ἀδόκιμος* as an apostle, they confess themselves *ἀδόκιμοι* in their Christian profession.[96] Both there and in 1 Cor 15:2 the deterring implication is that the readers were never saved—whether because they were converted by a pseudo-apostle or because they believed in an impotent message.[97] 1 Cor 15:2 does not, then, cast "doubt on the security of the Corinthians' faith."[98] The notion that the Corinthians might have believed *εἰκῇ* is a hypothesis for the sake of argument only. Instead, Paul makes their faith and present stance in salvation a given, and shows the denial of the resurrection to be inconsistent with their saving faith.

Receiving Grace in Vain

2 Corinthians 6:1. In 2 Cor 6:1 Paul pleads with his readers "not to receive the grace of God in vain." The meaning of this appeal to the Corinthian Christians is difficult to discern. This plea must differ from the foregoing one in 5:20, *καταλλάγητε τῷ Θεῷ*, which belongs to Paul's evangelistic message. For the Corinthians had already responded to this call at conversion and so had "received the grace of God."[99] At 6:1 Paul thus does not beseech them to receive the grace of God initially, but not to receive it *εἰς κενόν*. But how might people who are already converts to the gospel make that mistake? Does Paul here entertain the possibility that the Corinthian Christians will not attain final salvation? If so, on what account?

Interpreters commonly trace the possible ineffectiveness of receiving God's grace (implied in the phrase *εἰς κενόν*) to the potential failure of the recipients of that grace themselves. I. H. Marshall comments that "Christians may receive God's grace to no purpose after conversion and so become backsliders."[100] Even though they have accepted instead of rejected grace initially, their acceptance may be shown to be lacking in endurance

---

[96] See p. 218 above.

[97] *εἰ ἐστὲ ἐν τῇ πίστει...εἰ μήτι ἀδόκιμοί ἐστε* (2 Cor 13:5) corresponds to *σῴζεσθε...ἐκτὸς εἰ μὴ εἰκῇ ἐπιστεύσατε* (1 Cor 15:2). N.b. the common use of *πίστις* terminology and conditional clauses in these two texts.

[98] Against Barrett, *1 Cor*, 336. With Bruce, *1 Cor*, 138: "... not that Paul really entertains this [i.e., that they believed in vain] as a serious possibility, but if their denial of the resurrection were carried to its logical conclusion, the denial of the gospel itself, then indeed it would be shown that their belief was fruitless."

[99] Windisch, *2 Kor*, 200. Paul uses *δέχεσθαι* at 2 Cor 6:1 for initial reception of the gospel, as also in 2 Cor 11:4; 1 Thess 1:6; 2:13; 2 Thess 2:10. Cf. Barrett, *2 Cor*, 183; Hughes, *2 Cor*, 219, 220.

[100] Marshall, *Kept*, 119.

and depth.[101] This deficiency can express itself in moral laxity inappropriate to the grace received,[102] or inclination toward a different gospel (cf. 11:4),[103] or even in resistance to the apostle's appeal for personal reconciliation.[104] By contrast, not to receive the grace of God εἰς κενόν would mean to draw the proper practical implications of one's acceptance of God's grace.[105]

Of these commonly suggested ways in which the Corinthians might err, however, only one can draw support from the context. There is no suggestion of either inappropriate behavior or adoption of false teaching here. Such explanations of the cause of the danger are pure speculation. Only the fault of resistance to Paul suits the context. In favor of the view that the Corinthians might receive the grace of God in vain by opposing the apostle, it can be observed that the larger context shows a strong interest in the reconciliation of the Corinthians with Paul. In commending himself as a true servant of God, Paul wants to give the Corinthians an "opportunity to boast in us" (5:12) over against the opposing missionaries. This statement of his purpose leads into a characterisation of his apostolic ministry as (1) for the Corinthians' benefit (5:13, 14) and (2) on God's behalf and in cooperation with God (5:18–6:1a). What an impressive ministry indeed Paul carries out! The word of God and Christ itself comes to expression in Paul's proclamation[106] and works salvation in those who believe. Citing Isa 49:8 LXX, Paul places his own ministry within the eschatological "now," or "the day of salvation," in which the prophetic words are fulfilled (6:2).[107] But, as the servant figure of Isaiah 49, who despairs for having "toiled in vain" (κενῶς ἐκοπίασα, v. 4), Paul had suffered his share of defeat in Corinth.[108] Defending himself to a critical public, Paul explains his apostolic conduct, full of enigmas as it is for the Corinthians, as a thoroughgoing effort not to give offense and thus discredit the ministry (6:3–10). His presentation of his apostolic ministry in this favorable light climaxes in an appeal for personal reconciliation: "Our mouth has spoken freely to you, O Corinthians, our heart is opened wide. You are not restrained by us, but you are restrained

---

[101] Windisch, *2 Kor*, 200.

[102] Bruce, *Cor*, 211; Windisch, *2 Kor*, 200; Schlatter, *Bote*, 569; Plummer, *2 Cor*, 189.

[103] Bruce, *Cor*, 211.

[104] Bruce, *Cor*, 211; cf. Marshall, *Kept*, 119.

[105] So Lattke, κενός, *EWNT* 2, 694; see also Dinkler, "Verkündigung," 182; Bultmann, *2 Kor*, 168.

[106] Bultmann, *2 Kor*, 169; Hofius, "Versöhnung," 10; similarly, Schlatter, *Bote*, 570.

[107] See Schlatter, *Bote*, 570; also Barrett, *2 Cor*, 183.

[108] Plummer, *2 Cor*, 190.

by your own affections. Now in return—I speak as to children—open wide to us also" (6:11–13). In summary, the suggestion that receiving the grace of God in vain has to do with resistance to the apostle, with which the whole context is concerned, enjoys the best support.

R. Bultmann takes the appeal μὴ εἰς κενὸν τὴν χάριν τοῦ Θεοῦ δέξασθαι in conjunction with Paul's effort to reconcile the Corinthians to himself. He explains that Paul exhorts the Corinthian community "daß sie d. Botschaft μὴ εἰς κενόν empfange, indem sie sich klarmacht, daß das Wort des Paulus sie als Christi und Gottes eschatologisches Wort trifft, daß sie sich also als neue Schöpfung versteht und damit das rechte Verständnis des Evangeliums und des Apostels gewinnt—des Apostels, dessen Wirken zur eschatologischen Heilstat gehört."[109] By contrast, to reject Paul is to reject the ambassador of Christ, the one divinely commissioned with the ministry of reconciliation through whom God himself beseeches. And to deny Paul's apostolic preaching is to deny the very salvation-bringing word of God, ὁ λόγος τῆς καταλλαγῆς, spoken through the apostle and thus to alienate oneself from its saving power. "Das rettende, weil die Versöhnungstat wirksam erschließende Evangelium wird...nirgends anders vernommen, als in der apostolischen Verkündigung, die das von Gott 'aufgerichtete' Wort gehorsam...nach-spricht."[110] Rejection of the apostle and his message thus has the same consequences as rejection of God's own reconciling word and work. The expression, "receive the grace of God in vain," envisions the possibility of alienation from God's grace and its effectiveness for salvation by turning away from this grace as present in the apostolic preaching. Paul thus makes clear to the Corinthians who are disenchanted with him the far-reaching implications of dissolving their relationship with the apostle.

But does Paul think the Corinthians might actually fall prey to this danger? To answer affirmatively may be to misinterpret the function of Paul's plea in 6:1b. Paul makes this appeal in the context of his defense of his apostolic ministry and attempt to restore good relations with the Corinthians. This half-verse may contribute to his argument precisely by shocking the readers with unforeseen and unacceptable implications of their resistance to the apostle. Were they really willing to give up the grace of God which had brought them salvation by distancing themselves from its proclaimer Paul? A post-conversion repudiation of God's saving grace *through repudiation of Paul's apostolic preaching* would make initial reception of

---

109 Bultmann, *2 Kor*, 169.
110 Hofius, "Versöhnung," 18.

grace ineffective. It would amount to apostasy from the faith. The Corinthians would hardly have been ready to swallow this bitter pill as the implication of their rejection of Paul. Thus it is conceivable that Paul beseeched the Corinthians "not to receive the grace of God in vain" *for the sake of argument only*, counting on his converts not to deny the gospel of their salvation by denying its minister. Paul argues similarly in 13:5 by forcing those who challenge his apostleship into a self-incriminating position: they themselves would then fail the test of Christian faith as his converts.[111]

Nevertheless, the view that Paul thought the Corinthians might actually repudiate divine grace and apostatize cannot be excluded on the basis of the immediate context. One thing is certain, however: Paul's meaning does not allow for the possibility of Christians' receiving grace in vain through *ethical* failure. The potential cause of alienation from grace here can only be rejection of the gospel as a consequence of rejection of the apostle and the apostolic message. Apart from this important observation, however, the significance of 2 Cor 6:1b for continuity in Christians' salvation must remain ambiguous. For we cannot give a definite answer to the question whether Paul's plea not to receive the grace of God in vain is an expression of his genuine fear or merely a tactic whose effect, he hopes, will be to help mend his relationship with the Corinthians.

---

[111] See, further, pp. 218, 219 above.

CONCLUSION TO PART FOUR

In the texts analyzed in Part Four we have seen Paul reflect on the final outcome of his apostolic mission: what will the last day bring for him and his converts? That day becomes an important source of motivation for Paul in his ministry. He fears failure, on the one hand, and is inspired by the possibility of success, on the other.

So Paul strains toward the goal ahead like an athlete, making all his behavior serve the attainment of the final goal. He goes beyond the call of duty, sacrificing even his apostolic rights and freedom so as to ensure success. Where Paul refers to his own possible failure, however, it does not relate to his salvation but to his apostolic commission. He hopes to receive divine commendation for his service at the last day. Lest he lose divine approval as an apostle and become ἀδόκιμος, Paul conducts his ministry in the most selfless fashion imaginable, subjecting himself to severe physical privations (1 Cor 9:27). Paul aims to become a true partner (συγκοινωνός) of the gospel who cooperates in the divine work of salvation (1 Cor 9:23). He takes care not to hinder its success inadvertently by his behavior.

The same athletic-like concentration on the goal ahead characterizes Paul's attitude toward the future consummation of his salvation. He eagerly anticipates this perfection of God's saving work awaiting him at the resurrection from the dead. Though Christian perfection remains future, it is nonetheless certain. God's own powerful working, which exceeds all human possibilities, guarantees that the apostle will reach the goal. Paul's hope of "attaining" to the resurrection and of "grasping" (Phil 3:11, 12) therefore expresses his dependence on God, not uncertainty of the outcome.

Further, Paul makes his attitude toward final salvation paradigmatic for all Christians: by living in firm hope of future perfection and letting that hope define their present thought and conduct, believers will not become prone to complacency or nonchalance, but with attention fixed on the goal ahead will pursue that goal fittingly. Pursuit takes the form of fellowship with Christ—in suffering now in expectation of sharing the glory of the resurrection of Christ. Against present perfectionism, Paul teaches continuity in salvation based on God's future completion of salvation.

In spite of the great care Paul takes to conduct his apostolic ministry for the maximum benefit of those he evangelizes and nurtures in the faith, he is deeply aware of the possibility that his converts will not stand the final test. The obstacles are formidable. When persecution, testing, and false teaching in conflict with the gospel threaten Paul's converts, he fears that his labor might prove to be "in vain" (Phil 2:16; 1 Thess 3:5; Gal 2:2; 4:11). Instead of producing lasting fruit, his apostolic service would be characterized by futility and, by implication, his seeming converts would have no salvation. Whether failure in the eschatological test should be traced to his converts' false profession or their apostasy from salvation is a question not answered by Paul in these texts. It is possible that his fear of their final rejection comes to expression when he is not yet sure whether or not to attribute his evangelistic "success" to God's calling to faith in the gospel. For Paul's fear seems to give way to confidence when he views the situation from the perspective of God's faithfulness to professing Christians in whom he sees the divine work of salvation taking place. Paul distrusts his own success, but not God's saving power. His confidence in the success of God's saving work through the gospel and his attributing his own success in ministry to divine power may suggest that to "labor in vain" is to labor apart from the gospel and in this way produce works of "wood, hay and straw," which will be consumed by the eschatological test of fire, instead of genuine converts.

Faith as well as labor can be spoken of as ultimately futile. The Corinthians may receive the grace of God in vain (2 Cor 6:1b) if they reject the apostle whom God has entrusted with the message of salvation. It is possible that Paul fears the Corinthians will actually succumb to this danger. Yet his appeal not to receive the grace of God in vain could very well play a different role in his argument: counting on the fact that the Corinthians will not risk forfeiting the grace of God through which they are saved, Paul formulates this hypothetical consequence of their rejection of him as the minister of God's reconciling grace in order to push for a reconciliation between the Corinthians and the apostle. This type of argumentation has its parallels in the Corinthian correspondance itself. In 1 Cor 15:2 the notion of believing in vain is clearly brought up for the sake of argument only. The ineffectiveness of faith for salvation does not result from loss of faith here. Rather, Paul suggests how soteriologically useless a resurrectionless gospel is in order to steer the Corinthians away from this false teaching.

Some of Paul's statements about the possible futility of apostolic labor and Christian faith definitely reveal no fear of Christians' loss of salvation (1 Cor 15:2; Phil 2:16). Yet it is possible to interpret others to portray the real danger of his converts' loss of salvation (Gal 4:11; 2 Cor 6:1). Since, however, it is also possible to interpret these texts as not presupposing final loss of salvation, and compelling arguments for any view are lacking, the texts in question cannot play a decisive role in the discussion of perseverance. By the same token, passages where Paul's meaning is plain ought to take precedence over the ambiguous ones in the attempt to formulate a concluding statement on Paul's view of staying in salvation.

GENERAL CONCLUSION

Final conclusions can now be drawn from the exegetical analyses of the Pauline texts most relevant to the problem of staying in and falling away from salvation. We have uncovered clear and abundant evidence that for Paul sure continuity characterizes the salvation of individual believers. He portrays the various aspects of Christians' salvation as interconnected links of a chain whose last member is glorification, wherein the divine work of salvation reaches its consummation. His characterization of salvation is not, however, open to the misunderstanding or caricature of continuity as a series of logical deductions which guarantees final salvation with mathematical certainty. The repeated intervention of God in human lives is for Paul the key to continuity in salvation (Rom 8:29, 30). God's saving initiatives in history bring to realization the divine purpose existing from eternity to save those God has foreknown and elected (Rom 8:29, 30; 2 Thess 2:13, 14; 1 Thess 5:9), a purpose which includes their final salvation. The certainty of the realization of this saving purpose derives from the character of the author of salvation: God's faithfulness is its guarantee. God will faithfully complete the work of salvation begun in believers (Phil 1:6; 1 Cor 1:8, 9; 1 Thess 5:23, 24). They even have an earnest of God's commitment to carry to fruition God's eternal purpose in their lives, namely, the indwelling Holy Spirit, the pledge of final redemption (Rom 8:23; 2 Cor 1:22; 5:5).

Paul's certainty that God will faithfully accomplish God's purpose to save Christians completely and finally does not mean, however, that he views this process as "automatic." The present is characterized by the eschatological tension. Both the reality of salvation and the power of evil make themselves known. Christians are "saved in hope" (Rom 8:24). They await the completion of their salvation while enduring testing and afflictions in the present. Subjection to antagonistic forces at work in such tribulation can even threaten their salvation. Moreover, they have yet to appear before the judgment seat at which occasion their final destiny will be made manifest. Will they be accused and condemned after all?

It is in the very context of these dangers that Paul affirms the certainty of Christians' final salvation. We discover that Paul views continuity in salvation as the fruit of victory over the obstacles which stand in its way. Christians are more than conquerors in tribulations and will come through the last judgment unscathed (Rom 8:28–39). For the divine triumph over the forces of sin and death which has already taken place on the cross makes possible Christian triumph in present tribulation and the coming judgment. For Paul each new assault on believers by the powers of evil to prevent them from entering into their eschatological inheritance falls within the shadow of the cross. Those who stand under the cross continue to benefit from God's victory on the cross. Suffering thus no longer appears to alienate Christians from salvation but confirms their salvation: in Christ-like suffering, Christians manifest their unity with the Son of God who suffered and was raised in glory and whose destiny the children of God also share (Rom 8:17). Furthermore, God uses afflictions to work out salvation presently in the lives of believers (Rom 5:3, 4).

Paul portrays God's love as the power which has won this all-encompassing victory for Christians. For in the death of Christ divine love is seen to be stronger than all antagonists, whether they threaten from without or within sinful human beings (Rom 5:6–11). God has already proved God's love to such an extent that no doubt can remain about the outcome of subsequent challenges to Christians' salvation. They are no match for the God who is "for us." Because God *is* "for us," because Christ both died and lives to accomplish our salvation, nothing can make retroactive the justification and reconciliation of those who believe in Christ. God's promised faithfulness will be proven as Christians successfully endure eschatological testing and onslaughts of evil (1 Cor 10:13; 2 Thess 3:3) and at the day of reckoning when Christ comes again (1 Cor 1:8, 9; 1 Thess 5:23, 24). Christians' hope, which is fixed on the glory of God at that day, will not disappoint (Rom 5:1–5). Thus, continuity in salvation is won on the battlefield of creaturely rebellion against God through God's mighty and faithful love, not unfolded according to a deterministic plan.

Certainty of final salvation has repercussions on the present conduct of Christians. It ought not and need not foster complacency and carelessness, however. Paul's own life exemplifies the proper influence of this goal which, like a magnet, draws the present attention and energies of Christians to their final destiny (Phil 3:7–16). Further, he shows that it is precisely the continuity in salvation which makes Christian ethics significant. For the fact that Christians *will* inherit the kingdom of God naturally demands conduct which corresponds to their status as children of God and heirs of the kingdom (1 Cor 6:9–11; Gal 5:19–21). Nevertheless, Paul knows that

Christians do not always exhibit this kind of behavior. In fact, he must confront grievous sin in his churches. In arguing vehemently against various forms of misconduct which have arisen he does not threaten Christians with the possibility of losing salvation. Nevertheless, he warns that by their behavior they may regress in their life of faith instead of be built up (1 Cor 8:7–13; Rom 14:1–23). They may invite divine chastisement, even in the form of physical punishment for sin (1 Cor 11:27–34), a punishment which is temporal, not eternal, and marks out even sinful Christians as God's children. For just as a parent punishes a child out of love, so God's chastisement grows out of God's love for God's children, whose sin cannot separate them from this love. Finally, and most ominously, through persistent and grievous sin church members may reveal that they have not yet made the initial step of repentance and conversion (2 Cor 12:20, 21; 1 Cor 5:1–13; 10:1–12), that is, that they are not even saved yet. By contrast, genuinely professing Christians, who are "approved," exhibit the appropriate conduct, which can take the form of recognizing and submitting to the authority which Paul has in the gospel (2 Cor 13:5). Thus in discussing the significance of ethical failure, Paul sticks to his conviction that "there is no condemnation for those who are in Christ Jesus" (Rom 8:1)—not even on account of sinful behavior.

Whereas ethical failure does not exclude true Christians from salvation, according to Paul there is no salvation for those who stand outside the gospel of grace. The salvation which has come in Jesus Christ bypasses even elect Israel who has rejected the gospel (Romans 9–11). Converts to Christianity who abandon faith in the gospel of grace through which they were initially saved can put themselves outside the sphere of its saving power (Gal 5:1–4; Rom 11:17–24).

The reality of the fact that there is no salvation apart from faith in the gospel lends a tone of urgency to some of Paul's statements. The fruit of his apostolic labor must pass the eschatological test (Phil 2:16). His ministry must produce genuine and lasting conversions without which his labor or his converts' faith would be in vain (Gal 2:2; 4:11; 2 Cor 6:1). Present testing, like the test of persecution, serves as a preliminary indicator of the true quality of his converts' faith (1 Thess 3:5). In the event that his efforts have been futile, which the last day will make finally manifest, Paul anticipates loss of God's commendation for his service. Thus, to retain divine commendation, Paul carries out his apostolic ministry with utmost personal sacrifice for the sake of its greater effectiveness (1 Cor 9:23, 27). This manner of service has greater potential effectiveness in that it gives more room for the gospel itself as the divine power of salvation to work. And where God is at work through the gospel Paul preaches, he has full confidence that the results will endure.

Although the situations which threaten Christians' faith in the gospel lead Paul to face them with the real possibility of alienation from salvation, he does not lose his fundamental perspective on the final outcome, which he anticipates to be the full realization of the divine purpose of Christians' salvation. Paul even dares to follow his urgent warning to the Galatians against abandonment of the gospel with an expression of his confidence "in the Lord" of the outcome (Gal 5:10). God will keep believers from ultimately or finally deserting the path of faith in the gospel of grace. Though human faith and behavior is characterized by discontinuity, the faithfulness of God gives continuity to God's saving work in believers. Humanly speaking there is no security or hope of final salvation (Rom 11:17–22), but from the perspective of God's faithfulness Paul can foresee that even alienation from the gospel in unbelief on the part of the elect can be followed by integration into salvation and its blessings in faith (Rom 11:23, 24). Paul's explicit confidence that the danger of falling away in unbelief will be overcome does not always come to expression in his discussions of the problem. But even where not mentioned, it is not inconsistent with his warnings to his converts against abandoning faith.

In Israel's case Paul has similar confidence in divine faithfulness (Romans 9–11). Because he sees God's saving purpose at work in Israel through election, the giving of the promises, and the present salvation of a remnant, Paul can make a case for the future salvation of the unbelieving Jews. Further, the revelation of a "mystery" makes him able to say with utmost certainty and clarity that "all Israel will be saved." But, as with Gentile converts, so also with the Jews, God's work of salvation is not completed apart from faith in Jesus Christ. And, indeed, Paul envisions the turning of now hardened Jews from unbelief to faith in Christ as their redeemer (Rom 11:25–27). Thus, where Paul confronts the danger of alienation from salvation through rejection of the gospel, he shows that even human unbelief cannot separate the elect from God's love, though they may relinquish the gifts of God's grace for a time. Even those who make themselves God's "enemies" by rejecting the gospel remain God's "beloved" to whom God will fulfill the promises made in electing them (Rom 11:28). Nevertheless, Paul cannot imagine the completion of God's saving purpose apart from faith in Christ.

In conclusion, Paul teaches materially a type of perseverance of Christians elected by God and called to faith in Jesus Christ on the basis of their election. Paul is confident that the God who is the author and giver of salvation will also in omnipotent love and unbroken faithfulness finally complete the salvation of those whom God has elected and called and who are "in Christ" by faith as demonstrated by their basic behavioral orientation. And God will do so by overcoming the obstacles to their salvation posed by outward threats or their own ethical failure or even temporary alienation from the gospel through unbelief or wrong belief. Paul's epistles boldly and consistently characterize his view of staying in salvation in this way and do not yield clear or weighty evidence to the contrary.

BIBLIOGRAPHY OF WORKS CITED

Primary Sources

Bible

Biblia Hebraica Stuttgartensia. Ed. K. Elliger and W. Rudolph. Stuttgart: Deutsche Bibelstiftung, 1967/77.
Septuaginta. Ed. Alfred Rahlfs. 2 vols. Stuttgart: Deutsche Bibelstiftung, 1935.
Novum Testamentum Graece. Ed. E. Nestle and K. Aland. Stuttgart: Deutsche Bibelstiftung, ^{26}1979.
The Greek New Testament. Ed. Kurt Aland, *et al.* New York: United Bible Societies, ^{2}1968.

Extracanonical Jewish Literature

Apocrypha and Pseudepigrapha

Black, Matthew, ed. *Apocalypsis Henochi Graece.* PVTG 3. Leiden: Brill, 1970.
Charles, R. H., ed. *The Assumption of Moses.* London, 1897.
— ed. *The Greek Versions of the Testaments of the Twelve Patriarchs.* Oxford: Oxford Univ. Press, 1908; Darmstadt: Wissenschaftliche Buchgesellschaft, 1960.
— ed. *Apocrypha and Pseudepigrapha of the Old Testament.* 2 vols. Oxford: Clarendon, ^{2}1963–64.
— ed. and trans. *The Book of Enoch or 1 Enoch.* Jerusalem: Makor, ^{2}1973.
Charlesworth, James H., ed. *The Old Testament Pseudepigrapha.* 2 vols. Garden City, New York: Doubleday, 1983–85.
Dedering, S., ed. *Apocalypse of Baruch.* Peschitta Institute. Part IV, Fasc. 3. Leiden: Brill, 1973.
Harris, Rendel and Alphonse Mingana, eds. *The Odes and Psalms of Solomon.* 2 vols. Manchester: At the University Press, 1916.
de Jonge, M., ed. *Testamenta XII Patriarcharum.* PVTG 1. Leiden: Brill, 1964.
Kraft, Robert A., ed. and trans. *The Testament of Job: Greek Text and English Translation.* Texts and Translations 5, Pseudepigrapha Series 4. Missoula, Montana: SBL and Scholars Press, 1974.
James, Montague R., ed. *Apocalypsis Baruchi tertia Graece.* In *Apocrypha Anecdota 2.* TextsS 5. Cambridge: Cambridge Univ. Press, 1897.
Junod, Eric and Jean-Daniel Kaestli, eds. and trans. *Acta Johannis: Praefatio, Textus.* CChr SA 1. Turnhout: Brepols, 1983.
Meisner, Norbert, trans. *Aristeasbrief.* In *Unterweisung in erzählender Form.* JSHRZ 2.1, ed. Werner G. Kümmel. Gütersloh: Gütersloher Verlag, Mohn, 1973.
Thackeray, H. St. J., ed. *The Letter of Aristeas.* In H. B. Swete, *An Introduction to the Old Testament in Greek.* Cambridge: Cambridge Univ. Press, 1902.
Tischendorf, Konstantin von, ed. *Apocalypsis Mosis.* In *Apocalypses Apocryphae,* 1–23. Hildesheim: Georg Olms, 1966.
Violet, Bruno, ed. *Die Esra-Apokalypse (IV. Esra): 1. Teil: Die Überlieferung.* GCS 18. Leipzig: J. C. Hinrichs'sche Buchhandlung, 1910.

289

Philo and Josephus

Philo. 10 vols. Loeb Classical Library. 1953–56.
Josephus. 9 vols. Loeb Classical Library. 1956–65.

Qumran Literature

Lohse, Eduard, ed. *Die Texte aus Qumran: Hebräisch und Deutsch mit masoretischer Punktation, Übersetzung, Einführung und Anmerkungen.* Darmstadt: Wissenschaftliche Buchgesellschaft, ³1981.

Rabbinic Literature

Shishshah Sidre Mishnah. 6 vols. Ed. Ch. Albeck. Jerusalem and Tel Aviv, 1958ff.
The Mishnah. Trans. Herbert Danby. London: Oxford Univ. Press, ⁸1964.
Talmud Babli. Ed. Adin Steinsalz. Jerusalem: Institute for Talmudic Publ., 1967ff.
The Babylonian Talmud. Trans. I. Epstein. London: Soncino, 1938.
Sifre on Deuteronomy. Ed. Louis Finkelstein and H. S. Horovitz. New York, 1939.
Der tannaitische Midrasch Sifre Deuteronomium. Trans. Hans Bietenhard. Judaica et Christiana 8. Bern: Lang, 1984.
Midrash Rabbah on the Five Books of the Torah and the Five Megillot . 2 vols. Ed. Romm. Wilna, 1887; rep. Jerusalem, 1961.
Midrash Rabbah. 10 vols. Ed. H. Freedman and Maurice Simon. London and Bournemouth: Soncino, 1959.
Midrash Tehillim. Sammlung agadischer Abhandlungen über die 150 Psalmen. Ed. Salomon Buber. Wilna, 1891; rep. Jerusalem, 1966.
The Midrash on Psalms. 2 vols. Ed. Leon Nemoy, trans. William G. Braude. YJS 13. New Haven: Yale Univ. Press, 1959.

Church Fathers

The Apostolic Fathers. 2 vols. Ed. G. P. Goold, trans. Kirsopp Lake. Cambridge, Mass.: Harvard Univ. Press; London: William Heinemann, 1975.
A Select Library of the Nicene and post-Nicene Fathers of the Christian Church. 14 vols. Ed. Philip Schaff. Series 1. Grand Rapids: Eerdmans, 1979.
Ancient Christian Writers. The Works of the Fathers in Translation. Ed. Johannes Quasten and Walter J. Burghardt. Westminster, Maryland: Newman; London: Longmans, Green and Co., 1949ff.
Augustinus, Aurelius. *De correptione et gratia liber unus.* In *Sancti Aurelii Augustini Opera Omnia* 10.1.915–959. Ed. J.-P. Migne. MPL 44. Paris, 1865.
— *De dono perseverantiae.* In *Sancti Aurelii Augustini Opera Omnia* 10.2.993–1049. Ed. J.-P. Migne. MPL 45. Paris, 1865.
— *Expositio quarundam propositionum ex epistola ad Romanos, epistolae ad Galatas expositionis liber unus, epistolae ad Romanas inchoata expositio.* In *Sancti Aurelii Augustini Opera* 4.1. Ed. Joannis Divjak, CSEL 84. Vienna: Hölder-Pichler-Tempsky, 1971.
Chrysostomus, Johannis. *Commentarius in epistolam ad Galatas.* In *Joannis Chrysostomi Opera Omnia* 10.611–681. Ed. J.-P. Migne. MPG 61. Paris, 1862.
— *Homiliae V in epistolam secundam ad Thessalonicenses.* In *Joannis Chrysostomi Opera Omnia* 11.391–500. Ed. J.-P. Migne. MPG 62. Paris, 1862.
— *Homiliae XXXII in Epistolam ad Romanos.* In *Joannis Chrysostomi Opera Omnia* 9.391–681. Ed. J.-P. Migne. MPG 60. Paris, 1862.
Justin. *Die Apologien Justins des Märtyrers.* Ed. G. Krüger. Kirchen- und dogmengeschichtliche Quellenschriften 1. Freiburg i. B.: Mohr, Siebeck, 1891.

— *Saint Justin Martyr.* Trans. Thomas B. Falls. FC. New York, 1948.

Greek and Roman Literature

Lucius Junius Moderatus Columella. *On Agriculture*. 3 vols. Loeb Classical Library.
Epictetus. *The Discourses as Reported by Arrian. The Manual and Fragments*. 2 vols. Loeb Classical Library.
Justinian. *Edicta*. In *Drei dogmatische Schriften Iustinians*. Ed. Eduard Schwartz. Abt. der Bay. Ak. der Wiss., Philosophisch-historische Abteilung, NT Heft 18. München: Verlag der Bayerischen Akademie der Wissenschaften, 1939.
Philogelos. *Philogelos der Lachfreund, von Hierokles und Philagrios: Griechisch-Deutsch mit Einleitungen und Kommentar*. Ed. Andreas Thierfelder. München: Heimeran, 1968.
Plato. 12 vols. Loeb Classical Library.
Sophocles. 2 vols. Loeb Classical Library.
Strabo.*The Geography of Strabo*. 8 vols. Loeb Classical Library.
Vettius Valens.*Vettii Valentis Antiocheni Anthologiarum libri novem*. Ed. David Pingree. Bibliotheca Scriptorum Graecorum et Romanorum Teubneriana. Leipzig: BSB B.G. Teubner, 1986.

Inscriptions and Papyri

Aramaic Papyri of the Fifth Century B. C. Ed. and trans. Arthur E. Cowley. Oxford: Clarendon, 1923; Osnabrück, 1967.
The Tebtunis Papyri. 3.1, ed. Grenfell, Arthur S. Hunt, J. Gilbart Smyly, 1902; 3.2, ed. Grenfell, Arthur S. Hunt, Edgar J. Goodspeed, 1907.

Other Texts

Die Bekenntnisschriften der reformierten Kirche: in authentischen Texten mit geschichtlicher Einleitung und Register. Ed. E. F. Karl Müller. Leipzig: Deichert'sche Verlagsbuchhandlung, Böhme, 1903.

Exegetical Aids

Aland, Kurt. *Vollständige Konkordanz zum griechischen Neuen Testament unter Zugrundelegung aller modernen kritischen Textausgaben und des Textus Receptus*. 2 vols. Berlin: de Gruyter, 1975ff.
Bauer, Walter. *Wörterbuch zu den Schriften des Neuen Testaments und der übrigen urchristlichen Literatur*. Berlin and New York: de Gruyter, [5]1971.
— *A Greek-English Lexicon of the New Testament and Other Early Christian Literature*. Trans. William F. Arndt and F. Wilbur Gingrich; rev. F. Wilbur Gingrich and F. W. Danker. Chicago and London: Univ. of Chicago Press, 1979.
Blass, Friedrich and Albert Debrunner. *A Greek Grammar of the New Testament and Other Early Christian Literature*. Trans. and rev. Robert W. Funk. Chicago and London: Univ. of Chicago Press, 1961.
Brown, F., S. R. Driver, and C. A. Briggs. *A Hebrew and English Lexicon of the Old Testament*. Oxford: Clarendon, 1953.
Burton, Ernest deWitt. *Syntax of the Moods and Tenses in New Testament Greek*. Edinburgh: T. & T. Clark, [3]1898.
Hatch, Edwin and Henry A Redpath. *A Concordance to the Septuagint and Other Greek Versions of the Old Testament (including the Apocryphal Books)*. 2 vols. Oxford:

Clarendon, 1897; Graz: Akademische Druck- und Verlagsanstalt, 1954.

Lampe, Geoffrey W. H. *A Patristic Greek Lexikon.* Oxford: Clarendon 1961–68.

Liddell, Henry G. and Robert Scott. *A Greek-English Lexicon.* Rev. Henry Stuart Jones. Oxford: Clarendon, ^{9}1958.

Metzger, Bruce M. *A Textual Commentary on the Greek New Testament* . London and New York: United Bible Societies, 1971.

Moule, C. F. D. *An Idiom-Book of New Testament Greek.* Cambridge: Cambridge Univ. Press, ^{2}1977.

Preisigke, Friedrich. *Wörterbuch der griechischen Papyrusurkunden mit Einschluß der griechischen Inschriften, Ausschriften, Ostraka, Mumienschilder usw. aus Ägypten.* Vols. 1–3: 1924–31; vol. 4.1–4 rev. Emil Kießling; Supplement 1.1–3: 1969–71. Berlin and Marburg: Selbstverlag, 1924–71.

Zerwick, Maximilian. *Biblical Greek Illustrated by Examples.* Scripta Pontificii Instituti Biblici. Trans. and rev. Joseph Smith S. J. Rome, 1963.

Secondary Literature

The following books and articles are cited by abbreviated title in the footnotes. The abbreviations used as bibliographical data here conform to the standard system of abbreviations suggested in *JBL* 95 [1976]: 339–344; *Theologische Realenzyklopädie*, Abkürzungsverzeichnis [Berlin: de Gruyter, 1976].

Aageson, James W. "Scripture and Structure in the Development of the Argument in Rom 9–11." In *CBQ* 48 (1986): 265–289.

Allo, E.-B. *Première Epître aux Corinthiens.* EBib. Paris: Librairie Lecoffre, J. Gabalda, 1956.

Bachmann, Philipp. *Der erste Brief des Paulus an die Korinther.* KNT 7. Leipzig and Erlangen: Deichert, ^{4}1936.

Bailey, Kenneth E. "Paul's Theological Foundation for Human Sexuality: 1 Cor. 6:9–20 in the Light of Rhetorical Criticism." In *NESTThRev* 3 (1980): 27–41.

Balz, Horst. *Heilsvertrauen und Welterfahrung: Strukturen der paulinischen Eschatologie nach Römer 8,18–39.* BEvT 59. Göttingen: Vandenhoeck & Ruprecht, 1971.

Barrett, C. K. *A Commentary on the Epistle to the Romans.* BNTC. London: Black, 1957.

— *From First Adam to Last: A Study of Pauline Theology.* London: Black, 1962.

— "Things Sacrificed to Idols." In *NTS* 11 (1964–65): 138–153.

— *A Commentary on the First Epistle to the Corinthians.* BNTC. London: Black, 1968.

— *A Commentary on the Second Epistle to the Corinthians.* BNTC. London: Black, 1976.

— "Romans 9:30–10:21: Fall and Responsibility of Israel." In *Die Israelfrage nach Röm 9–11*, ed. L. de Lorenzi. Monographic Series of 'Benedictina' 3:109–121. Rome: St. Paul's Abbey, 1977.

— *Freedom and Obligation: A Study of the Epistle to the Galatians.* London: SPCK, 1985.

Barth, Karl. *Erklärung des Philipperbriefes.* Zollikon: Evangelischer Verlag, ^{6}1947.

Batey, Richard. " 'So All Israel Will Be Saved'. An Interpretation of Romans 11:25–32." In *Int* 20 (1966): 218–228.

Bauer, Gerhard. "1. Korinther 9, 24–27." In *Herr Tue meine Lippen auf*, ed. G. Eichholz, 2:158–165. Wuppertal and Barmen: Müller, ^{2}1959.

Bauer, J. B. " '...ΤΟΙΣ ΑΓΑΠΩΣΙΝ ΤΟΝ ΘΕΟΝ,' Rom 8:28 (1 Cor 2:9; 1 Cor 8:3)." In *ZNW* 50 (1959): 106–112.

Bauernfeind, Otto. "τρέχω, κτλ." In *TWNT*, ed. Gerhard Friedrich, 8:225–235. Stuttgart: Kohlhammer, 1969.

Baumbach, Günther. "Die Zukunftserwartung nach dem Philipperbrief." In *Die Kirche des Anfangs*, ed. R. Schnackenburg, *et al.*, 435–457. EThSt 38. Leipzig: St. Benno, 1977.

Baumert, Norbert. *Täglich sterben und auferstehen: Der Literalsinn von 2 Kor 4, 12–5, 10*. SANT 34. München: Kösel, 1973.

Baxter, A. G. and J. A. Ziesler. "Paul and Arboriculture: Romans 11.17–24." In *JSNT* 8 (1985): 25–32.

Beardslee, William A. *Human Achievement and Divine Vocation in the Message of Paul*. SBT 21. London, 1961.

Beare, Francis W. *A Commentary on the Epistle to the Philippians*. BNTC. London: Black, 1959.

Behm, J. ἄμπελος. In *TDNT*, ed. Gerhard Kittel, 1:342–343. Grand Rapids: Eerdmans, 1964.

— ἐκχέω, κτλ. In *TDNT*, ed. Gerhard Kittel, 2:467–469. Grand Rapids: Eerdmans, 1964.

Behm, J. and E. Wurthwein, νοέω, κτλ. In*TDNT*, ed. Gerhard Friedrich, 4:948–1022. Grand Rapids: Eerdmans, 1967.

Beker, J. Christiaan. *Paul the Apostle: The Triumph of God in Life and Thought*. Philadelphia: Fortress, [3]1984.

— "The Faithfulness of God and the Priority of Israel in Paul's Letter to the Romans." In *Christians Among Jews and Gentiles: Essays in Honor of Krister Stendahl on His Sixty-fifth Birthday*, ed. George W. E. Nickelsburg with George W. MacRae, 10–16. S. J. Philadelphia: Fortress, 1986.

Bengel, Johann A. *Bengel's New Testament Commentary*. 2 vols. Trans. C. T. Lewis and M. R. Vincent.Grand Rapids: Kregel, 1981.

Benoit, Pierre. "Conclusion par Mode de Synthèse." In *Die Israelfrage nach Röm 9–11*, ed. L. de Lorenzi. Monographic Series of 'Benedictina' 3:216–236. Rome: St. Paul's Abbey, 1977.

Berger, Klaus. "Abraham in den paulinischen Hauptbriefen." In *MTZ* 17 (1966): 47–89.

— "Zu den sogenannten Sätzen heiligen Rechts." In *NTS* 17 (1970): 10–40.

— χάρις. In *EWNT*, ed. Horst Balz and Gerhard Schneider, 3:1095–1102. Stuttgart: Kohlhammer, 1983.

Berkouwer, G. C. *Faith and Perseverance*. Trans. Robert D. Knudsen. Studies in Dogmatics. Grand Rapids: Eerdmans, [3]1979.

Bertram, Georg. ἔργον, κτλ. In *TDNT*, ed. Gerhard Kittel, 2:631–651. Grand Rapids: Eerdmans, 1964.

— παιδεύω, κτλ. In *TDNT*, ed. Gerhard Friedrich, 5:596–625. Grand Rapids: Eerdmans, 1967.

— συνεργός, κτλ. In *TDNT*, ed. Gerhard Friedrich, 7:871–876. Grand Rapids: Eerdmans, 1971.

Best, Ernest. *A Commentary on the First and Second Epistles to the Thessalonians*. BNTC. London: Black, 1972.

Betz, Hans Dieter. "In Defense of the Spirit: Paul's Letter to the Galatians as a Document of Early Christian Apologetics." In *Aspects of Religious Propaganda in Judaism and Early Christianity*, ed. E. Schüssler Fiorenza, 99–114. Notre Dame: Univ. of Notre Dame, 1976.

— *Galatians: A Commentary on Paul's Letter to the Churches in Galatia*. Hermeneia. Philadelphia: Fortress, 1979.

Beyer, Hermann W. βλασφημέω, κτλ. In *TDNT*, ed. Gerhard Kittel, 1:621–625. Grand Rapids: Eerdmans, 1964.

Bindemann, Walther. *Die Hoffnung der Schöpfung: Römer 8,18–27 und die Frage der Theologie der Befreiung von Mensch und Natur*. NStB 14. Neukirchen-Vluyn: Neukirchner Verlag, 1983.

Bjerkelund, Carl J. " 'Vergeblich' als Misionsergebnis bei Paulus." In *God's Christ and his People: Studies in Honour of Nils Alstrup Dahl*, ed. J. Jervell and W. Meeks, 175–191. Oslo: Universitätsforlaget, 1977.

Blevins, James L. "The Problem in Galatia." In *RevExp* 69 (1972): 449–458.

Bohren, R. *Das Problem der Kirchenzucht im Neuen Testament*. Zollikon-Zürich: Evangelischer Verlag, 1952.

Bonnard, Pierre. *L'Epître de Saint Paul aux Philippiens*. CNT 10. Neuchâtel and Paris: Delachaux & Niestlé, 1950.

— *L'Epître de Saint Paul aux Galates*. CNT 9. Neuchâtel and Paris: Delachaux & Niestlé, ²1972.

Bornkamm, Günther. "Herrenmahl und Kirche bei Paulus." In *Studien zu Antike und Urchristentum*. Vol. 2 of his *Gesammelte Aufsätze*, 138–176. BEvT 28. München: Chr. Kaiser, 1959.

— "Der Lohngedanke im Neuen Testament." In *Studien zu Antike und Urchristentum*. Vol. 2 of his *Gesammelte Aufsätze*, 69–92. BEvT 28. München: Chr. Kaiser, 1959.

— μυστήριον, κτλ. In *TDNT*, ed. Gerhard Friedrich, 4:802–828. Grand Rapids: Eerdmans, 1967.

Braun, Herbert. πλανάω, κτλ. In *TWNT*, ed. Gerhard Friedrich, 6:230–254. Stuttgart: Kohlhammer, 1959.

Bring, Ragnar. *Der Brief des Paulus an die Galater*. Trans. Karl-Ludwig Voss. Berlin and Hamburg: Lutherisches Verlagshaus, 1968.

Brinsmead, Bernard H. *Galatians: Dialogical Response to Opponents*. SBL DS 65. Chico: Scholars Press, 1982.

Brown, Schuyler. *Apostasy and Perseverance in the Theology of Luke*. AnBib 36. Rome: Pontifical Biblical Institute, 1969.

Bruce, F. F. "Christianity under Claudius." In *BJRL* 44 (1961–62): 316–318.

— *The Epistle of Paul to the Romans: An Introduction and Commentary*. TNTC. Grand Rapids: Eerdmans, 1963.

— *1 and 2 Corinthians*. NCB. London: Oliphants, 1971.

— *1 and 2 Thessalonians*. WBC 45. Waco, Texas: Word Books, 1982.

— *The Epistle of Paul to the Galatians: A Commentary on the Greek Text*. NIGTC. Exeter: Paternoster, 1982.

— " 'Called to Freedom': A Study in Galatians." In *The New Testament Age: Essays in Honor of Bo Reicke*, ed. William C. Weinrich, 1: 61–71. Macon, GA: Mercer, 1984.

— *The Epistles to the Colossians, to Philemon, and to the Ephesians*. NICNT. Grand Rapids: Eerdmans, 1984.

Büchsel, Friedrich. κρίνω, κτλ. In *TDNT*, ed. Gerhard Kittel, 3:921–954. Grand Rapids: Eerdmans, 1965.

— λύω, κτλ. In *TDNT*, ed. Gerhard Friedrich, 4:328–356. Grand Rapids: Eerdmans, 1967.

Bultmann, Rudolf. καυχάομαι, κτλ. In *TWNT*, ed. Gerhard Kittel, 3:646–654. Stuttgart: Kohlhammer, 1938.

— πείθω, κτλ. In *TWNT*, ed. Gerhard Friedrich, 6:1–11. Stuttgart: Kohlhammer, 1959.

— γινώσκω, κτλ. In *TDNT*, ed. Gerhard Kittel, 1:689–719. Grand Rapids: Eerdmans, 1964.

— "Exegetische Probleme des zweiten Korintherbriefes." In *Exegetica: Aufsätze zur Erforschung des Neuen Testaments*, ed. Erich Dinkler, 298–322. Tübingen: Mohr, Siebeck, 1967.

— λύπη, κτλ. In *TDNT*, ed. Gerhard Friedrich, 4:313–324. Grand Rapids: Eerdmans, 1967.

— *Der Zweite Brief an die Korinther*. Ed. Erich Dinkler. MeyerK 6. Göttingen: Vandenhoeck & Ruprecht, 1976.

Burton, Ernest deWitt. *A Critical and Exegetical Commentary on the Epistle to the Galatians*. ICC. Edinburgh: T. & T. Clark, 1956.

Calvin, Jean. *Institutes of the Christian Religion*. 2 vols. Ed. John T McNeill, *et al.*; trans. Ford L. Battles. Philadelphia: Westminster, 1960.

— *The First Epistle of Paul the Apostle to the Corinthians*. Vol. 9 of *Calvin's Commentaries*, ed. David W. Torrance and Thomas F. Torrance. Trans. John W. Fraser. Grand Rapids: Eerdmans, 1976.

— *The Epistles of Paul the Apostle to the Galatians, Ephesians, Philippians and Colossians*. Vol. 11 of *Calvin's Commentaries*, ed. David W. Torrance and Thomas F. Torrance. Trans. T. H. L. Parker. Grand Rapids: Eerdmans, 1976.

— *The Epistles of Paul to the Romans and to the Thessalonians*. Vol. 8 of *Calvin's Commentaries*, ed. David W. Torrance and Thomas F. Torrance. Trans. Ross Mackenzie. Grand Rapids: Eerdmans, 1976.

Cambier, Jules-Marie. "La chair et l'esprit en 1 Cor. V. 5." In *NTS* 15 (1968–69): 221–232.

— "La liberté chrétienne est et personelle et communautaire." In *Freedom and Love: The Guide for Christian Life (1 Cor 8–10; Rm 14–15).*, ed. L. de Lorenzi. Monographic Series of 'Benedictina' 6:57–84. Rome: St. Paul's Abbey, 1981.

Campbell, J. Y. "κοινωνία and its Cognates in the New Testament." In *JBL* 51 (1932): 352–380.

von Campenhausen, Hans. *Ecclesiastical Authority and Spiritual Power in the Church of the First Three Centuries*. Trans. John A. Baker. London: Black, 1969.

Carson, D. A. *Divine Sovereignty and Human Responsibility: Biblical Perspectives in Tension*. New Foundations Theological Library. Atlanta: John Knox, 1981.

Cerfaux, Lucien. "Le privilège d'Israël selon Saint Paul." In his *Recueil Lucien Cerfaux: Etudes d'exégèse et d'histoire religieuse* 2:339–364. BETL 6/7. Gembloux: Duculot, 1954.

Chrysostom, Helmuth Kittel. *Die Herrlichkeit Gottes: Studien zu Geschichte und Wesen eines neutestamentlichen Begriffs*. Gießen: Alfred Töppelmann, 1934.

Clements, Ronald E. " 'A Remnant Chosen by Grace' (Romans 11:5): The Old Testament Background and Origin of the Remnant Concept." In *Pauline Studies: Essays Presented to F. F. Bruce on his 70th Birthday*, ed. D. A. Hagner and M. J. Harris, 106–121. Exeter: Paternoster; Grand Rapids: Eerdmans, 1980.

Coenen, Lothar and Gerhard Nordholt. "Elect, Choose." In *NIDNTT*, ed. Colin Brown, 1:536–543. Exeter: Paternoster, 1975.

Collange, Jean-François. *L'Epître de Saint Paul aux Philippiens*. Neuchâtel and Paris: Delachaux & Niestlé, 1973.

Conzelmann, Hans. *Grundriß der Theologie des Neuen Testaments*. München: Chr. Kaiser, 1968.

— *A Commentary on the First Epistle to the Corinthians*. Trans. James W. Leitch. Hermeneia. Philadelphia: Fortress, 1975.

Coune, Michel. "Problème des Idolothytes et l'Education de la Syneidesis." In *RSR* 11 (1963): 497–534.

Cranfield, C. E. B. *A Critical and Exegetical Commentary on the Epistle to the Romans*. 2 vols. ICC. Edinburgh: T. & T. Clark, 1975–79.

Dahl, Nils. "The Atonement—An Adequate Reward for the Akedah? Rom. 8:32." In *Neotestamentica et Semitica: Studies in Honour of Matthew Black*, ed E. Earle Ellis and Max Wilcox, 15–29. Edinburgh: T. & T. Clark, 1969.

— *Studies in Paul: Theology for the Early Christian Mission.* Minneapolis: Augsburg, 1977.

Dautzenberg, Gerhard. "Der Verzicht auf das apostolische Unterhaltsrecht. Eine exegetische Untersuchung zu 1 Kor. 9." In *Bib* 50 (1969): 212–232.

Davidson, Richard M. *Typology in Scripture: A Study of Hermeneutical TUPOS Structures.* Berrien Springs, Mich.: Andrews Univ. Press, 1981.

Davies, W. D. "Paul and the Salvation of Israel." In *NTS* 24 (1978): 4–39.

Deissmann, Adolf. *Licht vom Osten: Das Neue Testament und die neuentdeckten Texte der hellenistisch-römischen Welt.* Tübingen: Mohr, Siebeck, [4]1923.

Delling, Gerhard. *ἄρχω, κτλ.* In *TWNT*, ed. Gerhard Kittel, 1:476–488. Stuttgart: Kohlhammer, 1933.

— *et al. ἡμέρα.* In *TWNT*, ed. Gerhard Kittel, 2:945–956l. Stuttgart: Kohlhammer, 1935.

— *ἀργός, κτλ.* In *TDNT*, ed. Gerhard Kittel, 1:452–454. Grand Rapids: Eerdmans, 1964.

— *τέλος, κτλ.* In *TWNT*, ed. Gerhard Friedrich, 8:50–88. Stuttgart: Kohlhammer, 1969.

— "Das Abendmahlsgeschehen nach Paulus." In *Studien zum Neuen Testament und zum hellenistischen Judentum,* ed. Ferdinand Hahn, *et al.*, 318–335. Göttingen: Vandenhoeck & Ruprecht, 1970.

Denton, D. R. "Hope and Perseverance." In *SJT* 34 (1981): 313–320.

Derrett, J. Duncan M. " 'Running' in Paul: The Midrashic Potential of Hab 2, 2." In *Bib* 66 (1985): 560–567.

Dibelius, Martin. *An die Thessalonicher I II. An die Philipper.* Tübingen: Mohr, [3]1937.

Didier, Georges. *Désintéressement du Chrétien: La rétribution dans la morale de saint Paul.* Aubier: Editions Montaigne, 1955.

Dinkler, Erich. "Zum Problem der Ethik bei Paulus. Rechtsnahme und Rechtsverzicht (1. Kor. 6, 1–11)." In *ZTK* 49 (1952): 167–200.

— "Prädestination bei Paulus. Exegetische Bemerkungen zum Römerbrief." In *Signum Crucis: Aufsätze zum Neuen Testament und zur christlichen Archäologie,* 241–269. Tübingen: Mohr, Siebeck, 1967.

— "Die Taufterminologie in 2Kor 1,21f." In *Signum Crucis: Aufsätze zum Neuen Testament und zur christlichen Archäologie,* 99–117. Tübingen: Mohr, Siebeck, 1967.

— "Die Verkündigung als eschatologisch-sakramentales Geschehen. Auslegung von 2 Kor 5l4–62." In *Die Zeit Jesu: Festschrift für Heinrich Schlier,* ed. Günther Bornkamm and Karl Rahner, 169–189. Freiburg, Basel, and Wien: Herder, 1970.

von Dobschütz, Ernst. *Die Thessalonicher–Briefe.* MeyerK 10. Göttingen: Vandenhoeck & Ruprecht, [7]1909, 1974.

Dodd, C. H. *The Epistle of Paul to the Romans.* FB. London: Hodder & Stoughton, 1959.

Donfried, Karl P. "Justification and Last Judgment in Paul." In *ZNW* 67 (1976): 90–110.

Drane, John W. "Tradition, Law and Ethics in Pauline Theology." In *NovT* 16 (1974): 167–178.

— *Paul: Libertine or Legalist? A Study in the Theology of the Major Pauline Epistles.* London: SPCK, 1975.

Dreyfus, François. "Le passé et le présent d'Israël (Rom., 9, 1–5; 11, 1–24)." In *Die Israelfrage nach Röm 9–11,* ed. L. de Lorenzi. Monographic Series of 'Benedictina' 3:131–151. Rome: St. Paul's Abbey, 1977.

Dugandzic, Ivan. *'Ja' Gottes in Christus: Eine Studie zur Bedeutung des Alten Testaments für das Christusverständnis des Paulus.* FzB 26. Würzburg: Echter, 1977.

Dupont, Jacques. *Gnosis: La Connaissance religieuse dans les épîtres de Saint Paul.* Louvain: Universitas Catholica Louvaniensis, 1960.

— "Appel aux faibles et aux forts dans la communauté romaine (Rom 14,1–15,13)." In *Studiorum Paulinorum Congressus Internationalis Catholicus.* AnBib 17:357–366. Rome: Pontifical Biblical Institute, 1961.

Easton, Burton S. "New Testament Ethical Lists." In *JBL* 51 (1932): 1–12.

Eckart, Karl-Gottfried. "Der zweite echte Brief des Apostels Paulus an die Thessaloniker." In *ZTK* 58 (1961): 30–44.

Eckert, Jost. *Die urchristliche Verkündigung im Streit zwischen Paulus und seinen Gegnern nach dem Galaterbrief.* BU 6. Regensburg: F. Pustet, 1971.

Eckstein, Hans-Joachim. *Der Begriff Syneidēsis bei Paulus: Eine neutestamentlich-exegetische Untersuchung zum Gewissensbegriff.* WUNT 2.10. Tübingen: Mohr, Siebeck, 1983.

Eichholz, Georg. "Bewahren und Bewähren des Evangeliums: der Leitfaden von Phil. 1–2." In *Tradition und Interpretation: Studien zum Neuen Testament und zur Hermeneutik,* 138–160. München: Chr. Kaiser, 1965.

— *Die Theologie des Paulus in Umriss.* Neukirchen-Vluyn: Neukirchner Verlag, [3]1981.

Evans, Craig A. "Paul and the Hermeneutics of 'True Prophecy'." In *Bib* 65 (1984): 560–570.

Ewald, Paul. *Der Brief des Paulus an die Philipper.* Rev. Gust. Wohlenberg. KNT 11. Leipzig and Erlangen: Deichertsche Verlagsbuchhandlung, Scholl, [3]1923.

Fascher, Erich. "Zu Tertullians Auslegung von 1 Kor. 5:1–5 (*de pudicitia* c. 13–16)." In *TLZ* 99 (1974) no. 1, cols. 9–12.

— *Der erste Brief des Paulus an die Korinther.* Vol. 1, *Einführung und Auslegung der Kapitel 1–7.* THKNT 7. Berlin: Evangelische, [2]1980.

Fee, Gordon D. "*Εἰδωλόθυτα* Once Again: An Interpretation of 1 Corinthians 8–10." In *Bib* 61 (1980): 172–197.

— *The First Epistle to the Corinthians.* NICNT. Grand Rapids: Eerdmans, 1988.

Feuillet, A. *Le Christ Sagesse de Dieu d'après les Epîtres pauliniennes.* EBib. Paris: Librairie Lecoffre, J. Gabalda, 1966.

— "L'espérance de la conversion d'Israël en Rom. xi,25–32. L'interprétation des vv. 26 et 31." In *De la Torah au Messie: Etudes d'exégèse et d'herméneutique bibliques offertes à Henri Cazelles,* ed. Maurice Carrez, *et al.,* 483–494. Paris: Desclée, 1981.

Fiedler, Peter. "Röm 8 31–39 als Brennpunkt paulinischer Frohbotschaft." In *ZNW* 68 (1977): 23–34.

Filson, Floyd V. *St. Paul's Conception of Recompense.* UNT 21. Leipzig: J. C. Hinrichs, 1931.

Findeis, Hans-Jürgen. *Versöhnung—Apostolat—Kirche: Eine exegetisch-theologische und rezeptionsgeschichtliche Studie zu den Versöhnungsaussagen des Neuen Testaments (2 Kor, Röm, Kol, Eph).* FzB 40. Würzburg: Echter, 1983.

Fitzer, Gottfried. *σφραγίς, κτλ.* In *TWNT,* ed. Gerhard Friedrich, 7:939–954. Stuttgart: Kohlhammer, 1964.

Fitzmeyer, Joseph. "Pauline Theology." In *The Jerome Biblical Commentary,* ed. Raymond E. Brown, *et al.,* 2:800–827. Englewood Cliffs, New Jersey: Prentice-Hall, 1968.

— " 'To Know Him and the Power of his Resurrection.' (Phil 3:10)." In *Mélanges bibliques en homage au R. P. Beda Rigaux,* ed. A. Deschamps and A. de Halleaux, 411–426. Gembloux: Duculot, 1970.

Foerster, Werner. *ἄξιος, κτλ.* In *TDNT,* ed. Gerhard Kittel, 1:379–380. Grand Rapids: Eerdmans, 1964.

— *ἐχθρός, κτλ.* In *TDNT,* ed. Gerhard Kittel, 2:811–815. Grand Rapids: Eerdmans, 1964.

— *et al. κλῆρος, κτλ.* In *TDNT,* ed. Gerhard Kittel, 3:758–785. Grand Rapids: Eerdmans, 1965.

Forkman, Göran. *The Limits of the Religious Community: Expulsion from the Religious Community within the Qumran Sect, within Rabbinic Judaism, and within Primitive Christianity.* ConBNT 5. Lund: CWK Gleerup, 1972.

Frame, James E. *A Critical and Exegetical Commentary on the Epistles of St. Paul to the Thessalonians.* ICC. Edinburgh: T. & T. Clark, [5]1960.

Friedrich, Gerhard. εὐαγγελίζομαι, κτλ. In *TWNT*, ed. Gerhard Kittel, 2:705–735. Stuttgart: Kohlhammer, 1935.

— *Die kleineren Briefe des Apostels Paulus.* NTD 8. Göttingen: Vandenhoeck & Ruprecht, [9]1962.

Fuchs, Ernst. *Die Freiheit des Glaubens: Römer 5–8 ausgelegt.* BEvT 14. München: Chr. Kaiser, 1949.

— "Hermeneutik?" In *ThVia* 7:44–60. Berlin and Stuttgart: Lettner, 1959–60.

Furnish, Victor P. *The Love Command in the New Testament.* Nashville: Abingdon, 1972.

Gager, John G. "Functional Diversity in Paul's Use of End-Time Language." In *JBL* 89 (1970): 325–337.

Galley, Klaus. *Altes und Neues Heilsgeschehen bei Paulus.* Arbeiten zur Theologie I.22. Stuttgart: Calwer, 1965.

Gaugler, Ernst. *Der Brief an die Römer.* 2 vols. Prophezei. Zürich: Zwingli, (vol. 1) 1945, (vol. 2) 1952.

Georgi, Dieter. *Die Gegner des Paulus im 2. Korintherbrief: Studien zur religiösen Propaganda in der Spätantike.* WMANT 11. Neukirchen-Vluyn: Neukirchner Verlag, 1964.

Giblin, C. H. *The Threat to Faith: An Exegetical and Theological Re-Examination of 2 Thessalonians 2.* AnBib 31. Rome: Pontifical Biblical Institute, 1967.

Glombitza, Otto. "Mit Furcht und Zittern. Zum Verständnis von Philip. II12." In *NovT* 3 (1959): 100–106.

Gnilka, Joachim. "Die antipaulinische Mission in Philippi." *BZ* 9 (1965): 258–276.

— *Der Philipperbrief.* HTKNT 10. Freiburg: Herder, [3]1980.

Godet, Frédéric. *Kommentar zu dem ersten Brief an die Korinther.* 2 vols. Trans. P. and K. Wunderlich. Hannover: Meyer, 1886–88.

Goguel, Maurice. "Les fondements de l'assurance du salut chez l'apôtre Paul." In *RHPR* 17 (1938): 105–144.

— *The Primitive Church.* New York: Macmillan Co., 1964.

Goppelt, Leonhard. *Typos: Die typologische Deutung des Alten Testaments im Neuen.* Darmstadt: Wissenschaftliche Buchgesellschaft, 1966.

— *Theologie des Neuen Testaments.* Ed. Jürgen Roloff. Göttingen: Vandenhoeck & Ruprecht, [3]1978.

Gressman, Hugo. " Ἡ κοινωνία τῶν δαιμονίων." In *ZNW* 20 (1921): 224–230.

Grosheide, F. W. *Commentary on the First Epistle to the Corinthians.* NICNT. Grand Rapids: Eerdmans, 1955.

Grundmann, Walter. ἀγαθός, κτλ. In *TDNT*, ed. Gerhard Kittel, 1:10–18. Grand Rapids: Eerdmans, 1964.

— ἀναγκάζω, κτλ. In *TWNT*, ed. Gerhard Kittel, 1:347–350. Stuttgart: Kohlhammer, 1933.

— ἐγκράτεια, κτλ. In *TWNT*, ed. Gerhard Kittel, 2:338–340. Stuttgart: Kohlhammer, 1935.

— δόκιμος, κτλ. In *TDNT*, ed. Gerhard Kittel, 2:255–260. Grand Rapids: Eerdmans, 1964.

— στήκω, κτλ. In *TDNT*, ed. Gerhard Friedrich, 7:636–653. Grand Rapids: Eerdmans, 1971.

— σύν μετά with Genitive, κτλ. In *TDNT*, ed. Gerhard Friedrich, 7:766–797. Grand Rapids: Eerdmans, 1971.

Gundry, Robert H. *ΣΩΜΑ in Biblical Theology with Emphasis on Pauline Anthropology*. SNTS MS 29. Cambridge: Cambridge Univ. Press, 1975.

— *Matthew: A Commentary on his Literary and Theological Art*. Grand Rapids: Eerdmans, 1982.

— "Grace, Works, and Staying Saved in Paul." In *Bib* 66 (1985): 1–38.

Gunther, John J. *St. Paul's Opponents and their Background*. Leiden: Brill, 1973.

Günther, W. and H. Krienke. "Remnant." In *NIDNTT*, ed. Colin Brown, 3:247–253. Exeter: Paternoster, 1978.

Gutbrod, Walter, *et al.* Ἰσραήλ, κτλ. In *TDNT*, ed. Gerhard Kittel, 3:357–391. Grand Rapids: Eerdmans, 1965.

Guthrie, Donald. *Galatians*. NCB. London: Nelson, 1969.

Haacker, Klaus. "Das Evangelium Gottes und die Erwählung Israels. Zum Beitrag des Römerbriefs zur Erneuerung des Verhältnisses zwischen Christen und Juden." In *ThB* 13 (1982): 59–72.

Hahn, Ferdinand. "Das Ja des Paulus und das Ja Gottes. Bemerkungen zu 2 Kor 1 12–2 1." In *Neues Testament und christliche Existenz: Festschrift für Herbert Braun*, ed. Hans Dieter Betz and Luise Schottroff, 229–239. Tübingen: Mohr, Siebeck 1973.

— "Work." In *NIDNTT*, ed. Colin Brown, 3:1147–1152. Exeter: Paternoster, 1978.

— "Teilhabe am Heil und Gefahr des Abfalls. Eine Auslegung von 1 Ko 10,1–22." In *Freedom and Love: The Guide for Christian Life (1 Cor 8–10; Rm 14–15)*, ed. L. de Lorenzi. Monographic Series of 'Benedictina' 6:149–171. Rome: St. Paul's Abbey, 1981.

— "Zum Verständnis von Römer 11.26a: '... und so wird ganz Israel gerettet werden'." In *Paul and Paulinism: Essays in honour of C. K. Barrett*, ed. Morna D. Hooker and S. G. Wilson, 221–234. London: SPCK, 1982.

Hanse, Hermann. ἔχω, κτλ. In *TWNT*, ed. Gerhard Kittel, 2:816–832. Stuttgart: Kohlhammer, 1935.

Hanson, Anthony T. *Studies in Paul's Technique and Theology*. Grand Rapids: Eerdmans, 1974.

Harder, Günther. στηρίζω, κτλ. In *TDNT*, ed. Gerhard Friedrich, 7:653–657. Grand Rapids: Eerdmans, 1971.

von Harnack, Adolf. *Die Mission und Ausbreitung des Christentums*. Wiesbaden: VMA Verlag, [4]1924.

— "κόπος (κοπᾶν, οἱ κοπιῶντες) im frühchristlichen Sprachgebrauch." In *ZNW* 27 (1928): 1–10.

Harnisch, Wolfgang. *Eschatologische Existenz: Ein exegetischer Beitrag zum Sachanliegen von 1. Thessalonisher 4,13–5,11*. FRLANT 110. Göttingen: Vandenhoeck & Ruprecht, 1973.

Hauck, Friedrich. κοινός, κτλ. In *TWNT*, ed. Gerhard Kittel, 3:789–810. Stuttgart: Kohlhammer, 1938.

— μολύνω, κτλ. In *TDNT*, ed. Gerhard Friedrich, 4:736, 737. Grand Rapids: Eerdmans, 1967.

Havener, Ivan. "A Curse for Salvation—1 Corinthians 5:1–5." In *Sin, Salvation and the Spirit*, ed. Daniel Durken. Collegeville, Minn.: Liturgical Press, 1979.

Heinrici, C. F. Georg. *Das erste Sendschreiben des Apostel Paulus an die Korinther*. Berlin: Wilhelm Hertz, 1880.

Hendriksen, William. *Exposition of Philippians*. Vol. 5 of *New Testament Commentary*. Grand Rapids: Baker, 1962.

Hengel, Martin. *The Atonement: A Study of the Origins of the Doctrine in the New Testament*. Trans. John Bowden. London: SCM, 1981.

Héring, Jean. *La première Epître de Saint Paul aux Corinthiens.* CNT 7. Neuchâtel and Paris: Delachaux & Niestlé, 1949.

— *La seconde Epître de Saint Paul aux Corinthiens.* CNT 8. Neuchâtel and Paris: Delachaux & Niestlé, 1958.

Hinz, Christoph. "Bewahrung und Verkehrung der Freiheit in Christo. Versuch einer Transformation von I. Kor 10,23–11,1 (8,1–10,22)." In *Gnosis und Neues Testament,* ed. Karl-Wolfgang Tröger, 405–422. SRTh. Gütersloher Verlag, Mohn, 1973.

Hofius, Otfried. " 'Bis daß er kommt'." In *NTS* 14 (1967–68): 439–441.

— " 'Erwählt vor Grundlegung der Welt' (Eph 14)." In *ZNW* 62 (1971): 123–130.

— "Die Unabänderlichkeit des göttlichen Heilsratschlusses. Erwägungen zur Herkunft eines neutestamentlichen Theologumenon." In *ZNW* 64 (1973): 135–145.

— "Hoffnung und Gewißheit. Römer 8, 19–39." In *Mitarbeiterhilfe* 31 (1976): 3–10.

— " 'Gott hat unter uns aufgerichtet das Wort von der Versöhnung' (2 Kor 5:19)." In *ZNW* 71 (1980): 3–20.

— "Das Gesetz des Mose und das Gesetz Christi." In *ZTK* 80 (1983): 262–286.

— "Das Evangelium und Israel. Erwägungen zu Römer 9–11." In *ZTK* 83 (1986): 297–324.

— "Herrenmahl und Herrenmahlsparadosis. Erwägungen zu 1 Kor 11, 23b–25." In *ZTK* 85 (1988): 371–408.

Holsten, Carl. *Das Evangelium des Paulus.* Vol. 1.1. Berlin: Reimer, 1880.

Holtz, Gottfried. *Die Pastoralbriefe.* THNT 13. Berlin: Evangelische Verlagsanstalt, ³1980.

Horseley, Richard A. "Consciousness and Freedom among the Corinthians: 1 Corinthians 8–10." In *CBQ* 40 (1978): 574–589.

Horsley, G. H. R. *New Documents Illustrating Early Christianity: A Review of the Greek Inscriptions and Papyri Published in 1976.* Vol. 1. North Ryde, N. S. W., Australia: Macquarie University, 1981.

Howard, George. *Paul: Crisis in Galatia: A Study in Early Christian Theology.* SNTS MS 35. New York: Cambridge Univ. Press, 1979.

Hübner, Hans. *Law in Paul's Thought.* Trans. James C. G. Greig. Studies of the New Testament and its World. Edinburgh: T. & T. Clark, 1984.

Hughes, Philip. *Commentary on the Second Epistle to the Corinthians.* NICNT. Grand Rapids: Eerdmans, ³1971.

Iwand, Hans Joachim. *Predigtmeditationen.* Vol. 2. Göttingen: Vandenhoeck & Ruprecht, 1973.

Jeremias, Joachim. ἄνθρωπος, κτλ. In *TWNT*, ed. Gerhard Kittel, 1:365–367. Stuttgart: Kohlhammer, 1933.

— "Die Salbungsgeschichte Mk. 14,3–9." In *ZNW* 35 (1936): 75–82.

— "Chiasmus in den Paulus briefen." In *Abba: Studien zur neutestamentlichen Theologie und Zeitgeschichte,* 276–290. Göttingen: Vandenhoeck & Ruprecht, 1966.

— "Zur Gedankenführung in den paulinischen Briefen." In *Abba: Studien zur neutestamentlichen Theologie und Zeitgeschichte,* 269–276. Göttingen: Vandenhoeck & Ruprecht, 1966.

— "Einige vorwiegend sprachliche Beobachtungen zu Röm 11,25–36." In *Die Israelfrage nach Röm 9–11,* ed. L. de Lorenzi. Monographic Series of 'Benedictina' 3:193–205. Rome: St. Paul's Abbey, 1977.

Jervell, Jacob. *Imago Dei: Gen 1,26f im Spätjudentum, in der Gnosis und in den paulinischen Briefen.* FRLANT 76. Göttingen: Vandenhoeck & Ruprecht, 1960.

Jeske, Richard L. "The Rock was Christ: The Ecclesiology of 1 Corinthians 10." In *Kirche: Festschrift für Günther Bornkamm zum 75. Geburtstag,* ed. Dieter Lührmann and Georg Strecker, 245–255. Tübingen: Mohr, Siebeck, 1980.

Jewett, Paul K. *Election and Predestination.* Grand Rapids: Eerdmans, 1985.

Jewett, Robert. "The Agitators and the Galatian Congregation." In *NTS* 17 (1971): 196–218.

— *Paul's Anthropological Terms. A Study of Their Use in Conflict Settings*. AGJU 10. Leiden: Brill, 1971.

Johnson, Dan. "The Structure and Meaning of Romans 11." In *CBQ* 46 (1984): 91–103.

Judant, D. "A propos de la destineé d'Israël. Remarques concernants un verset de l'épître aux Romains XI,31." In *Divinitas* 23 (1979): 108–125.

Jüngel, Eberhard. *Paulus und Jesus: Eine Untersuchung zur Präzisierung der Frage nach dem Ursprung der Christologie*. HUTh 2. Tübingen: Mohr, Siebeck, 1962.

Käsemann, Ernst. "Die Legitimität des Apostels. Eine Untersuchung zu II Korinther 10–13." In *ZNW* 41 (1942): 33–71.

— "Eine paulinische Variation des 'Amor fati'." In *ZTK* 56 (1959): 138–54.

— "Anliegen und Eigenart der paulinischen Abendmahlslehre." In his *Exegetische Versuche und Besinnungen* 2:11–34. Göttingen: Vandenhoeck & Ruprecht, [3]1964.

— "Sätze heiligen Rechtes im Neuen Testament." In his *Exegetische Versuche und Besinnungen* 2:69–82. Göttingen: Vandenhoeck & Ruprecht, [3]1964.

— *Commentary on Romans*. Trans. Geoffrey Bromiley. Grand Rapids: Eerdmans, 1980.

Kamlah, Ehrhard. *Die Form der katalogischen Paränese im Neuen Testament*. WUNT 7. Tübingen: Mohr, Siebeck, 1964.

Kelly, J. N. D. *A Commentary on the Pastoral Epistles. 1 Timothy, 2 Timothy, Titus.* BNTC. London: Black, 1986.

Kertelge, K. "Gesetz und Freiheit im Galaterbrief." In *NTS* 30 (1984): 382–394.

Kim, Seyoon. *The Origin of Paul's Gospel*. Grand Rapids: Eerdmans, 1982.

Kittel, Gerhard et al. εἰκών. In *TDNT*, ed. Gerhard Kittel, 2:381–397. Grand Rapids: Eerdmans, 1964.

Klappert, Bertold. *Jüdische Existenz und die Erneuerung der christlichen Theologie: Versuch einer Bilanz des christlich-jüdischen Dialogs für die systematische Theologie*. ed. Martin Stöhr. München: Chr. Kaiser, 1982.

Klauck, Hans-Josef. *Herrenmahl und hellenistischer Kult: Eine Religionsgeschichtliche Untersuchung zum 1 Korintherbrief*. NTAbh, N.F. 15. Münster: Aschendorf, 1982.

Klein, William. "Paul's Use of '*KALEIN*': A Proposal." In *JETS* 27(1984): 53–64.

von Kölichen, Johann-Christian. "Die Zitate aus dem Moselied Deut 32 im Römerbrief." In *Theologische Versuche* 5:53–69. Berlin: Evangelische Verlagsanstalt, 1975.

Koester, Helmut. "The Purpose of the Polemic of a Pauline Fragment (Philippians iii)." In *NTS* 8 (1961–62): 317–332.

— τέμνω, κτλ. In *TWNT*, ed. Gerhard Friedrich, 8:106–113. Stuttgart: Kohlhammer, 1969.

Kühl, Ernst. *Zur paulinischen Theodicee: Röm 9–11*. Göttingen: Vandenhoeck & Ruprecht, 1897.

Kümmel, Werner G. *Einleitung in das Neue Testament*. Heidelberg: Quelle & Meyer, [21]1983.

Kuhn, Karl G. "New Light on Temptation, Sin, and Flesh in the New Testament." In *The Scrolls and the New Testament*, ed. Krister Stendahl, 94–113. New York: Harper, 1957.

Kuss, Otto. *Der Römerbrief*. 3 vols. Regensburg: F. Pustet, 1978.

Lagrange, M.-J. *Saint Paul, Epître aux Galates*. EBib. Paris: Librairie Lecoffre, J. Gabalda, [2]1925.

— *Saint Paul: Epître aux Romains*. EBib. Paris: Librairie Lecoffre, J. Gabalda, 1950.

Lampe, G. W. H. *The Seal of the Spirit: A Study of Baptism and Confirmation in the New Testament and the Fathers*. London: Longmans, Green and Co., 1951.

— "Church Discipline and the Interpretation of the Epistles to the Corinthians." In

Christian History and Interpretation: Studies Presented to John Knox, ed. W. R. Farmer, *et al.*, 337–361. Cambridge: Cambridge Univ. Press, 1967.

Larcher, Chrysostome. *Etudes sur le livre de la Sagesse.* EBib. Paris: Librairie Lecoffre, J. Gabalda, 1969.

Larsson, Edvin. *Christus als Vorbild: Eine Untersuchung zu den paulinischen Tauf- und Eikon-Texten.* ASNU 23. Uppsala: C. W. K. Gleerup Lund, 1962.

Lattke, Michael. κενός. In *EWNT*, ed. Horst Balz and Gerhard Schneider, 2:693–695. Stuttgart: Kohlhammer, 1981.

Leaney, A. R. C. " 'Conformed to the Image of his Son' (Rom. VIII. 29)." In *NTS* 10 (1963–64): 470–479.

Légasse, Simon. εὐδοκέω. In *EWNT*, ed. Horst Balz and Gerhard Schneider, 2:187–189. Stuttgart: Kohlhammer, 1981.

Leenhardt, F.-J. *L'Epître de Saint Paul aux Romains.* Neuchâtel and Paris: Delachaux & Niestlé, 1957.

Léon-Dufour, Xavier. *Le partage du pain eucharistique selon le Nouveau Testament.* Paris: Editions du Seuil, 1982.

Lietzmann, Hans. *An die Römer.* HNT 8. Tübingen: Mohr, ⁴1933.

— *An die Korinther.* HNT 9. Tübingen: Mohr, ⁵1969.

— *An die Galater.* HNT 10. Tübingen: Mohr, 1910, ²1923, ⁴1971.

Lightfoot, John B. *Saint Paul's Epistle to the Philippians.* London: Macmillan Co., 1881.

— *Saint Paul's Epistle to the Galatians.* London: Macmillan Co., 1892.

Lohmeyer, Ernst. *Der Brief an die Philipper, an die Kolosser und an Philemon.* MeyerK 9. Göttingen: Vandenhoeck & Ruprecht, ⁸1930, ¹⁴1974.

Lohse, Eduard. *Märtyrer und Gottesknecht: Untersuchungen zur urchristlichen Verkündigung vom Sühnetod Jesu Christi.* FRLANT 64. Göttingen: Vandenhoeck & Ruprecht, ²1963.

Lührmann, Dieter. "Tage, Monate, Jahreszeiten, Jahre (Gal 4:10)." In *Werden und Wirken des AltenTestaments: Festschrift für Claus Westermann zum 70. Geburtstag*, ed. Rainer Albertz, *et al.*, 428–445. Göttingen: Vandenhoeck & Ruprecht; Neukirchen-Vluyn: Neukirchner Verlag, 1980.

Lütgert, Wilhelm. *Die Vollkommenen im Philipperbrief und die Enthusiasten in Thessalonich.* BFCT 13.6. Gütersloh: Bertelsmann, 1909.

— *Gesetz und Geist: Eine Untersuchung zur Vorgeschichte des Galaterbriefes.* BFCT 22.6. Gütersloh: Bertelsmann, 1919.

Luther, Martin *Der Galaterbrief.* Vol. 4 of *D. Martin Luthers Epistel-Auslegung*, ed. Hermann Kleinknecht. Göttingen: Vandenhoeck & Ruprecht, 1980.

Luz, Ulrich. *Römer 9–11 und das Geschichtsverständnis des Paulus.* BEvT 49. München: Chr. Kaiser, 1968.

MacArthur, S. D. " 'Spirit' in Pauline Usage: 1 Corinthians 5.5." In *Studia Biblica 1978*, ed. E. A. Livingstone. JSNTSup 3. Sheffield: Journal for the Study of the Old Testament Press, 1980.

Maier, Gerhard. *Mensch und freier Wille: nach den jüdischen Religionsparteien zwischen Ben Sira und Paulus.* WUNT 12. Tübingen: Mohr, Siebeck, 1971.

Maly, Karl. *Mündige Gemeinde: Untersuchungen zur pastoralen Führung des Apostels Paulus in 1. Korintherbrief.* SBM 2. Stuttgart: Verlag Katholisches Bibelwerk, 1967.

Mare, W. Harold. *I. Corinthians.* The Expositor's Bible Commentary 10. Grand Rapids: Zondervan, 1976.

Marshall, I. Howard. *Kept by the Power of God: A Study of Perseverance and Falling Away.* Minneapolis: Bethany, 1975.

— *1 And 2 Thessalonians.* NCB. Grand Rapids: Eerdmans, 1983.

Martin, Ralph P. *Colossians: The Church's Lord and the Christian's Liberty.* Grand Rapids: Zondervan, 1972.

— *The Epistle of Paul to the Philippians.* NCB. Grand Rapids: Eerdmans, [5]1975.

— *Reconciliation: A Study of Paul's Theology.* London: Marshall, Morgan & Scott, 1981.

Mattern, Liselotte. *Das Verständnis des Gerichtes bei Paulus.* ATANT 47. Zürich and Stuttgart: Zwingli, 1966.

Maurer, Christian. "Grund und Grenze apostolischer Freiheit. Exegetisch-theologische Studie zu 1. Korinther 9." In *Anwort: Karl Barth zum siebzigsten Geburtstag,* ed. Ernst Wolf, 630–641. Zollikon-Zürich: Evangelischer Verlag, 1956.

— ῥίζα. In *TWNT,* ed. Gerhard Friedrich, 6:985–991. Stuttgart: Kohlhammer, 1959.

— τίθημι, κτλ. In *TWNT,* ed. Gerhard Friedrich, 8:152–170. Stuttgart: Kohlhammer, 1969.

Mayer, Bernhard. *Unter Gottes Heilsratschluß.* FzB 15. Stuttgart: Verlag Katholisches Bibelwerk, 1974.

Meeks, Wayne A. " 'And Rose up to Play': Midrash and Paraenesis in 1 Corinthians 10:1–22." In *JSNT* 16 (1982): 64–78.

— *The First Urban Christians: The Social World of the Apostle Paul.* New Haven and London: Yale Univ. Press, 1983.

Mengel, Berthold. *Studien zum Philipperbrief.* WUNT 2.8. Tübingen: Mohr, Siebeck, 1982.

Merk, Otto. *Handeln aus Glauben: Die Motivierungen der paulinischen Ethik.* MThSt 5. Marburg: Elwert, 1968.

— "Der Beginn der Paränese im Galaterbrief." In *ZNW* 60 (1969): 83–104.

Merklein, Helmut. μετάνοια. In *EWNT,* ed. Horst Balz and Gerhard Schneider, 2:1022–1031. Stuttgart: Kohlhammer, 1981.

Meurer, Siegfried. *Das Recht im Dienst der Versöhnung und des Friedens: Studie zur Frage des Rechts nach dem Neuen Testament.* AThANT 63. Zürich: Theologischer Verlag, 1972.

Meyer, Heinr. Aug. Wilh. *Kritisch exegetisches Handbuch über die Briefe Pauli an die Philipper, Kolosser und an Philemon.* Göttingen: Vandenhoeck & Ruprecht, [3]1865.

— *Kritisch exegetisches Handbuch über den ersten Brief an die Korinther.* Göttingen: Vandenhoeck & Ruprecht, [7]1888.

Michael, J. Hugh. *The Epistle of Paul to the Philippians.* MNTC 11. London: Hodder & Stoughton, 1954.

Michaelis, D. Wilhelm. *Der Brief des Paulus an die Philipper.* Leipzig and Erlangen: Deichertsche Verlagsbuchhandlung, Scholl, 1935.

— πάσχω, κτλ. In *TDNT,* ed. Gerhard Friedrich, 5:904–939. Grand Rapids: Eerdmans, 1968.

— πίπτω, κτλ. In *TDNT,* ed. Gerhard Friedrich, 6:161–173. Grand Rapids: Eerdmans, 1968.

— πρῶτος, κτλ. In *TDNT,* ed. Gerhard Friedrich, 6:865–882. Grand Rapids: Eerdmans, 1968.

Michel, Otto. οἶκος, κτλ. In *TDNT,* ed. Gerhard Friedrich, 5:119–159. Grand Rapids: Eerdmans, 1967.

— *Der Brief an die Hebräer.* MeyerK 13. Göttingen: Vandenhoeck & Ruprecht, [7]1936, [13]1975.

— *Der Brief an die Römer.* MeyerK 4. Göttingen: Vandenhoeck & Ruprecht, [5]1955, [15]1978.

Moffat, James. *The First Epistle of Paul to the Corinthians.* MNTC 7. London: Hodder & Stoughton, 1951.

Molland, E. *Das paulinische Euangelion: Das Wort und die Sache.* ANVAO, HF 3:1–

109. Oslo: Dybwad, 1934.

Moltmann, Jürgen. *Prädestination und Perseveranz: Geschichte und Bedeutung der reformierten Lehre 'de perseverantia sanctorum'.* BGLRK 12. Neukirchen: Neukirchner Verlag, 1961.

— "Perseveranz." In *RGG*, ed. Kurt Galling, 5:226–227. Tübingen: Mohr, Siebeck, [3]1986.

Moore, George Foot. *Judaism in the First Centuries of the Christian Era.* 3 vols. Cambridge, Mass: Harvard Univ. Press, 1927–1930.

Morris, Leon. *The First and Second Epistles to the Thessalonians.* NICNT. Grand Rapids: Eerdmans, [4]1970.

— *The First Epistle of Paul to the Corinthians.* NICNT. Grand Rapids: Eerdmans, [7]1975.

Moule, C. F. D. "The Judgment Theme in the Sacraments." In *The Background of the New Testament and its Eschatology*, ed.W. D. Davies and David Daube, 464–481. Cambridge: Cambridge Univ. Press, 1956.

Müller, Christian. *Gottes Gerechtigkeit und Gottes Volk: Eine Untersuchung zu Röm. 9–11.* FRLANT 86. Göttingen: Vandenhoeck & Ruprecht, 1964.

Müller, Jacobus J. *The Epistles of Paul to the Philippians and to Philemon.* NICNT. Grand Rapids: Eerdmans, 1955.

Müller, Karl. *Die göttliche Zuvorersehung und Erwählung in ihrer Bedeutung für den Heilsstand des einzelnen Gläubigen nach dem Evangelium des Paulus.* Halle: Max Niemeyer, 1892.

Müller, Karlheinz. *Anstoß und Gericht: Eine Studie zum jüdischen Hintergrund des paulinischen Skandalon-Begriffs.* SANT 19. München: Kösel, 1969.

Müller, Ulrich B. *Prophetie und Predigt im Neuen Testament: Formgeschichtliche Untersuchungen zur urchristlichen Prophetie.* SNT 10. Gütersloh: Gütersloher Verlag, Mohn, 1975.

Münchow, Christoph. *Ethik und Eschatologie: Ein Beitrag zum Verständnis der frühjüdischen Apokalyptik.* Göttingen: Vandenhoeck & Ruprecht, 1981.

Münderlein, G. "Interpretation einer Tradition. Bemerkungen zu Röm 8,35f." In *KD* 11 (1965): 136–142.

Munck, Johannes. *Christus und Israel: Eine Auslegung von Röm 9–11.* Acta Jutlandica, teol. Ser. 7. Copenhagen: Einar Munksgaard, 1956.

Murphy-O'Connor, Jerome. "Food and Spiritual Gifts in 1 Cor 8:8." In *CBQ* 41 (1979): 292–298.

— "Freedom or the Ghetto (1 Co 8,1–13; 10,23–11,1)." In *Freedom and Love. The Guide for Christian Life (1 Cor 8–10; Rm 14–15)*, ed. L. de Lorenzi. Monographic Series of 'Benedictina' 6:7–38. Rome: St. Paul's Abbey, 1981.

Murray, John. *The Epistle to the Romans.* 2 vols. NICNT. Grand Rapids: Eerdmans, [2]1975.

Mußner, Franz. *Der Galaterbrief.* HTKNT 9. Freiburg: Herder, 1974.

— " 'Ganz Israel wird gerettet werden' (Röm 11, 26)." In *Kairos* N.F. 18 (1976): 241–255.

— *Traktat über die Juden.* München: Kösel Verlag, 1979.

Nababan, Albert E. S. *Bekenntnis und Mission in Römer 14 und 15: Eine exegetische Untersuchung.* Dissertation, Univ. of Heidelberg, 1963.

Nasuti, Harry P. "The Woes of the Prophets and the Rights of the Apostle: The Internal Dynamics of 1 Corinthians 9." In *CBQ* 50 (1988): 246–263.

Nebe, Gottfried. *'Hoffnung' bei Paulus: Elpis und ihre Synonyme im Zusammenhang der Eschatologie.* SUNT 16. Göttingen: Vandenhoeck & Ruprecht, 1983.

Neil, William. *The Epistles of Paul to the Thessalonians.* MNTC. London: Hodder & Stoughton, 1950.

Neuenzeit, Paul. *Das Herrenmahl: Studien zur paulinischen Eucharistieauffassung.* SANT 1. München: Kösel, 1960.

Nieder, Lorenz. *Die Motive der religiös-sittlichen Paränese in den paulinischen Gemeindebriefen: Ein Beitrag zur paulinischen Ethik.* MThS I, Historische Abteilung 12. München: Zink, 1956.

Noack, Bent. *Satanás und Soterίa: Untersuchung zur neutestamentlichen Dämonologie.* Copenhagen: Gads, 1948.

Nygren, Anders. *Der Römerbrief.* Trans. Irmgard Nygren. Göttingen: Vandenhoeck & Ruprecht, 1951.

O'Brien, Peter T. *Introductory Thanksgivings in the Letters of Paul.* NovTSup 49. Leiden: Brill, 1977.

Oepke, Albrecht. κενός, κτλ. In *TWNT*, ed. Gerhard Kittel, 3:659–662. Stuttgart: Kohlhammer, 1938.

— ἀπόλυμμι, κτλ. In *TDNT*, ed. Gerhard Kittel, 1:394–397. Grand Rapids: Eerdmans, 1964.

— *Der Brief des Paulus an die Galater.* THKNT 9. Berlin: Evangelische Verlagsanstalt, [3]1973.

Olson, Stanley N. "Pauline Expressions of Confidence in His Addressees." In *CBQ* 47 (1985): 282–295.

Orr, F. and James A Walther. *1 Corinthians.* AB 32. Garden City, New York: Doubleday, 1976.

Osborne, Grant. "Soteriology in the Epistle to the Hebrews." In *Grace Unlimited,* ed. Clark Pinnock, 144–166. Minneapolis: Bethany, 1975.

von der Osten-Sacken, Peter. *Römer 8 als Beispiel paulinischer Soteriologie.* FRLANT 112. Göttingen: Vandenhoeck & Ruprecht, 1975.

— "Gottes Treue bis zur Parusie. Formgeschichtliche Beobachtungen zu 1 Kor 1:7b–9." In *ZNW* 68 (1977): 176–199.

Outka, Gene. "On Harming Others." In *Int* 34 (1980): 381–393.

Panikulam, George. *Koinonia in the New Testament.* AnBib 85. Rome: Pontifical Biblical Institute, 1979.

Paulsen, Henning. *Überlieferung und Auslegung in Römer 8.* WMANT 43. Neukirchen-Vluyn: Neukirchner Verlag, 1974.

— "Schisma und Häresie. Untersuchungen zu 1 Kor 11,18.19." In *ZTK* 79 (1982): 180–211.

Perrot, Charles. "Exemples du Désert (1 Co. 10.6–11)." In *NTS* 29 (1983): 437–452.

Peterson, E. " Ἔργον in der Bedeutung 'Bau' bei Paulus." In *Bib* 22 (1941): 439–441.

Pfitzner, Victor C. *Paul and the Agon Motif: Traditional Athletic Imagery in the Pauline Literature.* NovTSup 16. Leiden: Brill, 1967.

Pierce, C. A. *Conscience in the New Testament.* SBT 15. Chicago: Alec R. Allenson, 1955.

Piper, John. *The Justification of God: An Exegetical and Theological Study of Romans 9:1–23.* Grand Rapids: Baker, 1983.

Plag, Christoph. *Israels Wege zum Heil: Eine Untersuchung zu Römer 9–11.* Arbeiten zur Theologie 1.40. Stuttgart: Calwer, 1969.

Plummer, Alfred. *A Critical and Exegetical Commentary on the Second Epistle of St Paul to the Corinthians.* ICC. Edinburgh: T. & T. Clark, [2]1925.

Ponsot, Hervé. "Et ainsi tout Israël sera sauvé: Rom., XI,26a." In *RB* 89 (1982): 406–417.

Proksch, Otto. ἅγιος, κτλ. In *TWNT*, ed. Gerhard Kittel, 1:67–116. Stuttgart: Kohlhammer, 1933.

von Rad, Gerhard. "Das Werk Jahwes." In *Gesammelte Sudien zum Alten Testament,* ed. Rudolf Smend, 2:236–244. TB, AT 48. München: Chr. Kaiser, 1966.

Radl, W. *Ankunft des Herrn: Zur Bedeutung und Funktion der Parusieaussagen bei Paulus.* BBE 15. Frankfurt: Lang, 1981.

Räisänen, Heikki. "Legalism and Salvation by the Law." In *Die paulinische Literatur und Theologie,* ed. S. Pedersen, 63–83. Skandinavische Beiträge. Aarhus: Forlaget Aros, 1980.

Reinmuth, Oscar W. "Isthmien." In *Der Kleine Pauly: Lexikon der Antike,* ed. Konrat Ziegler and Walther Sontheimer, 2:1474–1475. München: Alfred Druckenmüller (Artemis), 1979.

Rengstorf, K. H. *Apostolat und Predigtamt.* Stuttgart: Kohlhammer, ^{2}1954.

— "Das Ölbaum-Gleichnis in Rom 11,16ff. Versuch einer weiterführenden Deutung." In *Donum Gentilicum: New Testament Studies in Honour of David Daube,* ed. C. K. Barrett, *et al.,* 127–164. Oxford: Clarendon, 1978.

Richardson, Peter. *Israel in the Apostolic Church.* SNTS MS 10. Cambridge: Cambridge Univ. Press, 1969.

— "Judgment in Sexual Matters in 1 Corinthians 6:1–11." In *NovT* 27 (1983): 37–58.

Ridderbos, Herman. *The Epistle of Paul to the Churches of Galatia.* New London Commentary on the NT 8. London and Edinburgh: Marshall, Morgan & Scott, ^{2}1954.

Rigaux, Beda. *Saint Paul: Les Epîtres aux Thessaloniciens.* EBib. Paris: Lecoffre; Gembloux: Duculot, 1956.

— "L'anticipation du salut eschatologique par l'Esprit." In *Foi et Salut Selon Saint Paul,* ed. Markus Barth *et al.* AnBib 42:101–135. Rome: Pontifical Biblical Institute, 1970.

Robertson A. and A. Plummer. *A Critical and Exegetical Commentary on the First Epistle of St Paul to the Corinthians.* ICC. Edinburgh: T. & T. Clark, ^{2}1975.

Roetzel, Calvin. *Judgment in the Community: A Study of the Relationship between Eschatology and Ecclesiology in Paul.* Leiden: Brill, 1972.

Romaniuk, Kazimierz. *L'Amour du Père et du Fils dans la Soteriologie de Saint Paul.* AnBib 15. Rome: Pontifical Biblical Institute, 1961.

Ropes, James H. *The Singular Problem of the Epistle to the Galatians.* HTS 14. Cambridge, Mass.: Harvard Univ. Press, 1929.

Sand, Alexander. *Der Begriff 'Fleisch' in den paulinischen Hauptbriefen.* BU 2. Regensburg: F. Pustet, 1967.

— *ἀπαρχή.* In *EWNT,* ed. Horst Balz and Gerhard Schneider, 1:278–280. Stuttgart: Kohlhammer, 1980.

— *ἀρραβών.* In *EWNT,* ed. Horst Balz and Gerhard Schneider, 1:379. Stuttgart: Kohlhammer, 1980.

Sanday, William and Arthur Headlam. *A Critical and Exegetical Commentary on The Epistle to the Romans.* ICC. Edinburgh: T. & T. Clark, ^{5}1902.

Sanders, E. P. *Paul and Palestinian Judaism: A Comparison of Patterns of Religion.* Philadelphia: Fortress, 1977.

— *Paul, the Law, and the Jewish People.* Philadelphia: Fortress, 1983.

Sanders, J. A. *Suffering as Divine Discipline in the Old Testament and Post-Biblical Judaism.* Rochester, New York: Colgate Rochester Divinity School, 1955.

Sanders, J. T. "The Transition from Opening Epistolary Thanksgiving to Body in the Letters of the Pauline Corpus." In *JBL* 81 (1962): 348–362.

Satake, Akira. "Apostolat und Gnade bei Paulus." In *NTS* 15 (1968–69): 96–107.

Schenk, Wolfgang. *Die Philipperbriefen des Paulus.* Stuttgart: Kohlhammer, 1984.

Schille, Gottfried. "Die Liebe Gottes in Christus. Beobachtungen zu Rm 8 31–39." In *ZNW* 59 (1968): 230–244.

Schippers, Reinier. "Seal." In *NIDNTT,* ed. Colin Brown, 3:497–501. Exeter: Paternoster, 1978.

Schlatter, Adolf. *Erläuterungen zum Neuen Testament.* 2 vols. Stuttgart: Calwer, 1923.

— *Paulus, der Bote Jesu: Eine Deutung seiner Briefe an die Korinther*. Stuttgart: Calwer, [4]1969.

— *Gottes Gerechtigkeit: Ein Kommentar zum Römerbrief*. Stuttgart: Calwer, [5]1975.

Schlier, Heinrich. βέβαιος, κτλ. In *TWNT*, ed. Gerhard Kittel, 1:600–603. Stuttgart: Kohlhammer, 1933.

— κερδός, κτλ. In *TWNT*, ed. Gerhard Kittel, 3:671–672. Stuttgart: Kohlhammer, 1938.

— ἐλεύθερος, κτλ. In *TDNT*, ed. Gerhard Kittel, 2:487–502. Grand Rapids: Eerdmans, 1964.

— *Der Brief an die Galater*. MeyerK 7. Göttingen: Vandenhoeck & Ruprecht, [10]1949, [14]1971.

— *Der Apostel und seine Gemeinde*. Freiburg: Herder, 1972.

— *Der Römerbrief*. HTKNT 20. Freiburg: Herder, 1977.

— *Der Philipperbrief*. Einsiedeln: Johannes Verlag, 1980.

Schmidt, Karl L. *Die Judenfrage im Lichte der Kap. 9–11 des Römerbriefes*. Theologische Studien 13. Zollikon-Zürich: Evangelischer Verlag, [2]1947.

— ὁρίζω, κτλ. In *TDNT*, ed. Gerhard Friedrich, 5:452–456. Grand Rapids: Eerdmans, 1967.

Schmithals, Walter. "Die Häretiker in Galatien." In *ZNW* 47 (1956): 25–67.

— *Die theologische Anthropologie des Paulus: Auslegung von Röm 7,17–8,39*. Stuttgart: Kohlhammer, 1980.

Schnackenburg, Rudolf. *Das Heilsgeschehen bei der Taufe nach dem Apostel Paulus: Eine Studie zur paulinischen Theologie*. MThS.H 1. München: Chr. Kaiser, 1950.

— *Der Brief an die Epheser*. EKKNT 10. Zürich: Benziger; Neukirchen-Vluyn: Neukirchner Verlag, 1982.

Schneider, Johannes. ὀλεθρεύω. In *TDNT*, ed. Gerhard Friedrich, 5:167–171. Grand Rapids: Eerdmans, 1967.

Schramm, Tim. σφραγίζω. In *EWNT*, ed. Horst Balz and Gerhard Schneider, 3:756–758. Stuttgart: Kohlhammer, 1983.

Schrenk, Gottlob and Gottfried Quell. δίκη, κτλ. In *TWNT*, ed. Gerhard Kittel, 2:176–229. Stuttgart: Kohlhammer, 1935.

Schrenk, Gottlob. εὐδοκέω, κτλ. In *TWNT*, ed. Gerhard Kittel, 2:737–748. Stuttgart: Kohlhammer, 1935.

— *Die Weissagung über Israel im Neuen Testament*. Zürich: Gotthilf Verlag, 1951.

Schubert, Paul. *Form and Function of the Pauline Thanksgivings*. Berlin: Alfred Töpelmann, 1939.

Schütz, John H. *Paul and the Anatomy of Apostolic Authority*. SNTS MS 26. Cambridge: Cambridge Univ. Press, 1975.

Schweizer, Eduard. *Erniedrigung und Erhöhung bei Jesus und seinen Nachfolgern*. ATHANT 28. Zürich: Zwingli, 1955.

— et al. πνεῦμα, κτλ. In *TWNT*, ed. Gerhard Friedrich, 6:330–450. Stuttgart: Kohlhammer, 1959.

— "Dying and Rising with Christ." In *NTS* 14 (1967–68): 1–14.

— σάρξ, κτλ. In *TDNT*, ed. Gerhard Friedrich, 6:98–151. Grand Rapids: Eerdmans, 1968.

— σῶμα, κτλ. In *TWNT*, ed. Gerhard Friedrich, 7:1024–1091. Stuttgart: Kohlhammer, 1964.

— "Christianity of the Circumcised and Judaism of the Uncircumcised." In *Jews, Greeks, and Christians: Religious Culture in Late Antiquity*, ed. Robert Hammerton-Kelly and Robin Scroggs, ed 245–260. Leiden: Brill, 1976.

— "Traditional Ethical Patterns in the Pauline and Post-Pauline Letters and their Development (Lists of Vices and House-Tables)." In *Text and Interpretation: Studies in the New Testament Presented to Matthew Black,* ed. Ernest Best and R. McL. Wilson, 195–209. Cambridge: Cambridge Univ. Press, 1979.

Scott, E. F. *The Pastoral Epistles.* MNTC. London: Hodder & Stoughton, [7]1957.

Seesemann, Heinrich. *Der Begriff KOINΩNIA in Neuen Testament.* Gießen: Alfred Töpelmann, 1933.

— πεῖρα, κτλ. In *TDNT,* ed. Gerhard Friedrich, 6:23–36. Grand Rapids: Eerdmans, 1968.

Selwyn, Edward G. *The First Epistle of St. Peter.* London: Macmillan, [2]1949.

Senft, Christophe. *La première Epître de Saint Paul aux Corinthiens.* Neuchâtel and Paris: Delachaux & Niestlé, 1979.

Siber, Peter. *Mit Christus Leben.* Zürich: Theologischer Verlag, 1971.

Sieffert, Friedrich. *Der Brief an die Galater.* MeyerK 7. Göttingen: Vandenhoeck & Ruprecht, [6]1880, [9]1899.

Siegert, Folker. *Argumentation bei Paulus.* WUNT 34. Tübingen: Mohr, Siebeck, 1985.

Siotis, Markos A. "La *'XPHΣTOTHΣ* de Dieu selon l'Apôtre Paul." In *Paul de Tarse: Apôtre du notre Temps,* ed. L. de Lorenzi. Monographic Series of 'Benedictina' 1:201–232. Rome: St. Paul's Abbey, 1979.

von Soden, Hans. "Sakrament und Ethik." In *Urchristentum und Geschichte: Gesammelte Aufsätze und Vorträge,* ed. Hans von Campenhausen, 1:239–275. Tübingen: Mohr, 1951.

Spicq, Celas. *Agape dans le Nouveau Testament: Analyse des textes.* 3 vols. EBib. Paris: Gabalda, 1958–59.

— "*AMETAMEΛHTOΣ* dans Rom., XI,29." In *RB* 67 (1960): 210–219.

— " *'AΠAPXH'.* Note de Lexicographie Néotestamentaire." In *The New Testament Age: Essays in Honor of Bo Reicke,* ed. William C. Weinrich, 2:493–502. Macon, GA: Mercer, 1984.

Spörlein, Bernhard. *Die Leugnung der Auferstehung: Eine historisch-kritische Untersuchung zu 1 Kor 15.* BU 7. Regensburg: F. Pustet, 1971.

Staab, Karl. *Die Thessalonicherbriefe.* RNT 7. Regensburg: F. Pustet, 1959.

Stählin, Gustav. προσκόπτω, κτλ. In *TDNT,* ed. Gerhard Friedrich, 6:745–758. Grand Rapids: Eerdmans, 1968.

— σκάνδαλον, κτλ. In *TDNT,* ed. Gerhard Friedrich, 7:339–358. Grand Rapids: Eerdmans, 1971.

— τύπτω. In *TDNT,* ed. Gerhard Friedrich, 8:260–269. Grand Rapids: Eerdmans, 1972.

Stauffer, Ethelbert. ἀγών, κτλ. In *TWNT,* ed. Gerhard Kittel, 1:134–140. Stuttgart: Kohlhammer, 1933.

— βραβεύω, κτλ. In *TWNT,* ed. Gerhard Kittel, 1:636–637. Stuttgart: Kohlhammer, 1933.

— et al. ἀγαπάω, κτλ. In *TDNT,* ed. Gerhard Kittel, 1:21–55. Grand Rapids: Eerdmans, 1964.

Steiger, Lothar. "Schützrede für Israel, Römer 9–11." In *Fides pro mundi vita: Hans-Werner Gensichen zum 65. Geburtstag,* ed. Theo Sundermeier, 44–58. Gütersloh: Gütersloher Verlag, Mohn, 1980.

Strack, Hermann and Paul Billerbeck. *Kommentar zum Neuen Testament aus Talmud und Midrasch.* 4 vols. München: C. H. Beck'sche Verlagsbuchhandlung, 1956–61.

Strathmann, Hermann and Rudolf Meyer. λαός. In *TWNT.* Ed Gerhard Friedrich, 4:29–57. Stuttgart: Kohlhammer, 1942.

Straub, Werner. *Die Bildersprache des Apostels Paulus.* Tübingen: Mohr, 1937.

Stuhlmacher, Peter. *Gerechtigkeit Gottes bei Paulus.* FRLANT 87. Göttingen: Vandenhoeck & Ruprecht, 1965.

— "Erwägungen zum Problem von Gegenwart und Zukunft in der paulinischen Eschatologie." In *ZTK* 64 (1967): 423–450.

— "Zur Interpretation von Römer 11,25-32." In *Probleme biblischer Theologie: Festschrift für Gerhard von Rad zum 70. Geburtstag*, ed. Hans W. Wolff, 555-570. München: Chr. Kaiser, 1971.

— "Das Gesetz als Thema biblischer Theologie." In *Versöhnung, Gesetz und Gerechtigkeit: Aufsätze zur biblischen Theologie*, 136-165. Göttingen: Vandenhoeck & Ruprecht, 1981. (= 251-280, 1978).

— "Die Gerechtigkeitsanschauung des Apostels Paulus." In *Versöhnung, Gesetz und Gerechtigkeit: Aufsätze zur biblischen Theologie*, 87-116. Göttingen: Vandenhoeck & Ruprecht, 1981.

Stuhlmann, Rainer. *Das eschatologische Maß im Neuen Testament.* FRLANT 132. Göttingen: Vandenhoeck & Ruprecht, 1983.

Suggs, M. Jack. "The Christian Two Ways Tradition: Its Antiquity, Form and Function." In *Studies in New Testament and Early Christian Literature*, ed. David E. Aune, 60-74. NovTSup 33. Leiden: Brill, 1972.

Synofzik, Ernst. *Die Gerichts- und Vergeltungsaussagen bei Paulus: Eine traditionsgeschichtliche Untersuchung.* Göttinger theologische Arbeiten 8. Göttingen: Vandenhoeck & Ruprecht, 1977.

Tachau, Peter. *'Einst' und 'Jetzt' im Neuen Testament: Beobachtungen zu einem urchristlichen Predigtschema in der neutestamentlichen Briefliteratur und zu seiner Vorgeschichte.* FRLANT 105. Göttingen: Vandenhoeck & Ruprecht, 1972.

Tannehill, Robert. *Dying and Rising with Christ: A Study in Pauline Theology.* BZNW 32. Berlin: Alfred Töppelmann, 1967.

Tasker, R. V. G. *The Second Epistle of Paul to the Corinthians: An Introduction and Commentary.* TNTC. London: Tyndale, [5]1969.

Theissen, Gerd. "Legitimation und Lebensunterhalt. Ein Beitrag zur Soziologie urchristlicher Missionare." In *Studien zur Soziologie des Urchristentums.* WUNT 19:201-230. Tübingen: Mohr, Siebeck, 1979.

— "Soziale Integration und sakramentales Handeln: Eine Analyse von 1 Cor. XI 17-34." In *Studien zur Soziologie des Urchristentums* WUNT 19:290-317. Tübingen: Mohr, Siebeck, 1979.

— "The Strong and the Weak in Corinth: A Sociological Analysis of a Theological Quarrel." In *The Social Setting of Pauline Christianity: Essays on Corinth*, ed. and trans. John H. Schütz, 121-143. Philadelphia: Fortress, 1982.

Thiselton, Anthony C. "The Meaning of ΣΑΡΞ in 1 Corinthians 5:5: A Fresh Approach in the Light of Logical and Semantic Factors." In *SJT* 26 (1973): 204-228.

— "Realized Eschatology at Corinth." In *NTS* 24 (1978): 510- 526.

Thompson, P. "Philippians ii.12." In *ExpTim* 34 (1923-24): 429.

Thornton, Timothy C. G. "Satan—God's Agent for Punishing." In *ExpTim* 83 (1972): 151-152.

Thüsing, Wilhelm. *Per Christum in Deum: Studien zum Verhältnis von Christozentrik und Theozentrik in den paulinischen Hauptbriefen.* NTAbh, N.F. 1. Münster: Aschendorff, 1969.

Trilling, Wolfgang. *Der zweite Brief an die Thessalonicher.* EKKNT 14. Zürich: Benziger Verlag; Neukirchen-Vluyn: Neukirchner Verlag, 1980.

van Unnik, W. C. "Reisepläne und Amen-Sagen. Zusammenhang und Gedankenfolge in 2 Korinther 1 15-24." In *Studia Paulina in honorem Johannis de Zwaan septuagenarii*, ed. J. N. Sevenster and W. C. van Unnik, 215-234. Haarlem: Bohn, 1953.

de Villiers, J. L. "The Salvation of Israel according to Romans 9-11." In *Neot* 15 (1981): 199-221.

Vincent, Marvin R. *A Critical and Exegetical Commentary on the Epistles to the Philippians and to Philemon.* ICC. Edinburgh: T. & T. Clark, [5]1955.

Vischer, Lukas. *Die Auslegungsgeschichte von 1. Kor. 6,1-11: Rechtsverzicht und*

Schlichtung. BGE 1. Tübingen: Mohr, 1955.

Vischer, W. "Das Geheimnis Israels. Eine Erklärung der Kapitel 9–11 des Römerbriefes." In *Judaica* 6 (1950): 81–132.

Vögtle, Anton. *Die Tugend- und Lasterkataloge im Neuen Testament.* NTAbh 16. Münster: Aschendorff, 1936.

Walter, Nikolaus. "Christusglauben und heidnische Religiösität in paulinischen Gemeinden." In *NTS* 25 (1979): 422–442.

Warren, J. "Work Out Your Own Salvation." In *EvQ* 16 (1944): 125–137.

Watson, Francis. *Paul, Judaism and the Gentiles: A Sociological Approach.* SNTS MS 56. Cambridge: Cambridge Univ. Press, 1986.

Weber, E. *Das Problem der Heilsgeschichte nach Röm. 9–11. Ein Beitrag zur historisch-theologischen Würdigung der paulinischen Theodizee.* Leipzig: Deichertsche Verlagsbuchhandlung, 1911.

Weber, Otto. "Die Treue Gottes und die Kontinuität der menschlichen Existenz." In *EvT* Sonderheft f. E. Wolff (1952): 131–143.

Weiß, Bernhard. *Die Briefe Pauli an Timotheus und Titus.* MeyerK 11. Göttingen: Vandenhoeck & Ruprecht, [5]1885, [7]1902.

Weiß, Johannes. *Der erste Korintherbrief.* MeyerK 5. Göttingen: Vandenhoeck & Ruprecht, [9]1910.

Weiss, Konrad. χρηστός, κτλ. In *TWNT*, ed. Gerhard Friedrich, 9:472–481. Stuttgart: Kohlhammer, 1973.

Wesley, John. *Explanatory Notes on the New Testament.* 1754.

Westermann, Claus. *Grundformen prophetischer Rede.* München: Chr. Kaiser, [2]1964.

White, John Lee. *The Form and Function of the Body of the Greek Letter: A Study of the Letter-Body in the non-literary Papyri and in Paul the Apostle.* SBL DS 2. Missoula, Montana: Scholars, [2]1972.

Wibbing, Siegfried. *Die Tugend- und Lasterkataloge im Neuen Testament und ihre Traditionsgeschichte unter besonderer Berücksichtigung der Qumran-Texte.* Berlin: Töpelmann, 1959.

Wiebe, Willi. *Die Wüstenzeit als Typus der messianischen Heilszeit.* Dissertation, Univ. of Göttingen, 1939.

Wiederkehr, Dietrich. *Theologie der Berufung in den Paulusbriefen.* SF, N.F. 36. Freiburg, Schweiz: Universitätsverlag Freiburg, 1963.

Wikenhauser, Alfred. "Die Liebeswerke in dem Gerichtsgemälde Mt 25,31– 46." In *BZ* 20 (1932): 366–377.

Wilckens, Ulrich. *Der Brief an die Römer.* 3 vols. EKKNT 6. Zürich: Benziger Verlag; Neukirchen-Vluyn: Neukirchner Verlag, 1978–1982.

Willis, Wendell Lee. *Idol Meat in Corinth: The Pauline Argument in 1 Corinthians 8 and 10.* SBL DS 68. Chico: Scholars, 1985.

Windisch, Hans. *Taufe und Sünde im ältesten Christentum bis auf Origenes.* Tübingen: Mohr, 1908.

— "Die Sprüche vom Eingehen in das Reich Gottes." In *ZNW* 27 (1928): 163–192.

— *Der Zweite Korintherbrief.* MeyerK 6. Göttingen: Vandenhoeck & Ruprecht, 1970, [9]1924.

Wolff, Christian. *Der erste Brief des Paulus an die Korinther.* Vol 2. *Einführung und Auslegung der Kapitel 8–16.* THKNT 7. Berlin: Evangelische Verlagsanstalt, 1982.

Wolter, Michael. *Rechtfertigung und zukünftiges Heil: Untersuchungen zu Römer 5, 1–11.* BZNW 43. Berlin and New York: Walter de Gruyter, 1978.

Yarbro Collins, Adela. "The Function of Excommunication in Paul." In *HTR* 73 (1980): 251–263.

Zaas, Peter S. "Catalogues and Context: 1 Corinthians 5 and 6." In *NTS* 34 (1988): 622–629.

Zahn, Theodor. "Altes und Neues zum Verständnis des Philipperbriefes." In *ZkWL* 6 (1885): 182–202.

Zeller, Dietrich. *Juden und Heiden in der Mission des Paulus: Studien zum Römerbrief.* FzB 1. Stuttgart: Verlag Katholisches Bibelwerk, ²1976.

Zerwick, Max. *Der Brief an die Galater.* Düsseldorf: Patmos, 1964.

Zimmerli, Walther. *Ezechiel.* BK.AT 13.1. Neukirchen: Neukirchner Verlag, 1969.

Zmijewski, Josef. καυχάομαι, κτλ. In *EWNT*, ed. Horst Balz and Gerhard Schneider, 2:680–690. Stuttgart: Kohlhammer, 1983.

— χρηστότης. In *EWNT*, ed. Horst Balz and Gerhard Schneider, 3:1139–1144. Stuttgart: Kohlhammer, 1983.

INDEX OF REFERENCES TO
BIBLICAL AND OTHER ANCIENT SOURCES

Bible

Old Testament

Genesis
12:2, 3 *195 n. 222*
13:15–17 *187 n. 169*
16:15 *124 n. 115*
17:1–8 *187 n. 169*
17:16 *124 n. 115*
22:14 *111 n. 59*
22:16 *66 n. 126*
24:7 *187 n. 169*
26:11 *101*

Exodus
15:16 *269*
18:20 *34*
22:14 *198 n. 235*
32:6 *121 n. 104, 122*

Leviticus
13:36 *198 n. 235*
18:7, 8 *113 n. 65*
19:14 *94 n. 41*
19:23–25 *187 n. 162*
20:11 *113 n. 65*

Numbers
15:17–21 *187 n. 161*

Deuteronomy
4:37 *167 n. 27*
7:6 *167 n. 27*
7:6–8 *16 n. 40*
8:5 *107*
10:12–15 *59*
10:15 *16 n. 40*
14:2 *167 n. 27*
17:7 *116 n. 74*
25:4 *124 n. 115*
26:18 *16 n. 40*
31:11 *183*
32:21 *172*
32:47 *263*

Joshua
2:19 *101*

Judges
8:27 *183*

1 Samuel
7:5 *183*
11:15 *183*
12:22 *167, 167 n. 25*
13:20 *183*
18:16 *183*

2 Samuel
2:9 *183*
3:21 *183*
14:15, 16 *257*
15:6 *183*
18:17 *183*

1 Kings
19:10–18 *169*

2 Chronicles
12:1 *183*

Job
1:9–11 *65*
2:1–5 *65*
2:6 *118 n. 83*
5:17 *108*
14:10 *122*
20:18 *275 n. 83*

Psalms
2:11 *269*
6:2 LXX *106 n. 43*
6:6 LXX *106 n. 43*
21:6 LXX *50*
24:3 LXX *50*
24:20 LXX *50*
25:2 LXX *235 n. 14*
33:9 LXX *197 n. 228*
37:2 LXX *106 n. 43*
43:23 LXX *56*
44:22 *56 nn. 56 & 59*
49:20 LXX *94 n. 44*
90:5 LXX *198 n. 235*
93:14 LXX *167*
94:12 *108*
110:1 *58*
111:9 LXX *37*
118:114 LXX *50*
118:116 LXX *50*
120:7 LXX *70 n. 154*
134:4 LXX *167 n. 27*
140:9 LXX *70 n. 154*
151:5 LXX *126 n. 127*

Proverbs
3:11, 12 *107*
5:23 *96*
11:24 *37*
12:4 *96*
15:1 *96*
19:9 *96*
22:8a, 9 LXX *37*
25:21, 22 *36 n. 170*
28:24 *248 n. 85*

Ecclesiastes
7:7 *96*
9:18 *96*

Isaiah
1:23 *248 n. 85*
6:13 *178 n. 100*
7:5–9 *136 n. 30*
8:15 *172 n. 55*
19:16 *269*
24:20 *172 n. 55*
28:16 *50*
44:3 *30 n. 140*
44:5 *30 n. 140*
45:14–17 *178 n. 96*

Isaiah (cont.)
45:18 *263*
45:20–25 *178 n. 96*
46:3, 4 *169 n. 33*
49:1 *263 n. 11*
49:4 *263, 278*
49:5 *263 n. 11*
49:6 *21*
49:8 *263, 278*
50:8 *68 n. 139*
58:6 *46*
59:4 *275 n. 83*
59:19 *178 n. 96*
59:20 *178 n. 96, 185
n. 150*
61:1, 2 *46*
63:16 *17*
64:3 LXX *60 n. 79*
65:23 *263*

Jeremiah
1:10 *90 n. 27*
10:24 *106 n. 43*
11:16 *175 n. 74*
11:20 *235 n. 14*
14:10 *126 n. 127*
14:12 *126 n. 127*
17:10 *235 n. 14*
20:9 *242*
20:12 *235 n. 14*
31:18, 19 *105*
38:37 LXX *167 n. 25*
46:28 *112 n. 62*

Lamentations
1:22 *95 n. 47*
3:31–33 *108*

Ezekiel
9:4–6 *31, 31 n. 144*

Daniel
4:37a LXX *269*
7:22 *134 n. 19*

Hosea
5:12ff. *136 n. 30*
12:2 LXX *275 n. 83*
13:7, 8 *136 n. 30*
14:6 *175 n. 74*

Amos
7:17 *122*

Micah
4:1–8 *178 n. 96*
6:8 *34*

Nahum
1:7 *197 n. 228*

Habakkuk
2:4 *124 n. 115, 126*

Zechariah
3:1 *65*

New Testament

Matthew
3:2 *221 n. 102*
4:17 *221 n. 102*
5:3–10 *46*
5:20 *131 n. 3*
5:21 *101 n. 17*
5:22 *101 n. 17, 272
n. 57*
5:29, 30 *94*
6:1 *37*
6:1–4 *36 n. 170*
6:10 *131 n. 4*
6:13 *71, 71 n. 160*
6:25–33 *36*
7:6 *127 n. 131*
10:26 *266 n. 33*
10:28 *88, 266 n. 33*
11:5 *46*
11:26 *270 n. 49*
12:18 *126*
12:41, 42 *91 n. 31*
13:19 *70 n. 152*
13:21 *94*
13:24–30 *220*
13:36–43 *220*
13:38 *70 n. 152*
13:47–50 *220*
14:5 *266 n. 33*
15:5 *209 n. 28*
15:6 *198 n. 235*
15:19 *131 n. 2*
16:3 *99 n. 4*
16:23 *94*
16:26 *209 n. 28*
17:5 *126*
18:6, 7 *85 n. 3*
18:6–9 *94*
18:15–17 *117 n. 81*

19:4 *17*
20:18 *91 n. 31*
21:26 *266 n. 33*
21:46 *266 n. 33*
23:30 *249*
24:10 *94*
24:11 *127 n. 131*
24:21, 22 *129*
24:24 *127 n. 131*
24:34 *131 n. 3*
25:31–46 *127 n. 131*
25:35, 36 *36 n. 170*
25:35–45 *46 n. 2٤* `
26:33 *94*
27:3 *91 n. 3*
27:24 *209 n. 28*
27:52 *106 n. 44*

Mark
1:4 *221 n. 103*
1:11 *126*
3:29 *101 n. 17*
4:41 *266 n. 33*
5:26 *209 n. 28*
6:12 *221 n. 102*
6:20 *266 n. 33*
7:21, 22 *131 n. 2*
9:32 *266 n. 33*
10:33 *91 n. 3*
11:18 *266 n. 33*
11:32 *266 n. 33*
12:12 *266 n. 33*
13:19, 20 *72 n. 166*
14:29 *255 n. 121*
14:64 *91 n. 3*
16:20 *78 n. 219*

Luke
1:50 *266 n. 33*
1:53 *36*
2:9 *266 n. 33*
4:17–21 *46*
6:20–23 *46*
7:22 *46*
8:15 *272*
9:45 *111 n. 59*
10:21 *270 n. 49*
11:2 *131 n. 4*
11:4 *71 n. 160*
11:8 *255 n. 121*
11:31, 32 *91 n. 31*
12:5 *266 n. 33*
12:22–31 *36*

17:30 *77 n. 204*
18:4 *255 n. 121, 266
 n. 33*
18:11 *135*
19:10 *88*
20:19 *266 n. 33*
21:24 *122, 178 n. 55*
22:2 *266 n. 33*
22:32 *71*
23:40 *266 n. 33*
24:37 *114 n. 67*
24:39 *114 n. 67*

John

1:1, 2 *17*
3:16 *88*
6:63 *209 n. 28*
8:10 *91 n. 31*
9:2 *111 n. 59*
9:22 *266 n. 33*
10:28 *87, 88*
11:11 *106 n. 44*
12:19 *209 n. 28*
12:25 *88*
15:16 *21, 21 n. 79*
17:12 *87 n. 12, 88*

Acts

2:38 *221*
3:25 *187*
5:26 *266 n. 33*
7:60 *106 n. 44*
9:26 *266 n. 33*
10:2 *266 n. 33*
10:22 *266 n. 33*
10:35 *266 n. 33*
10:38 *119 n. 91*
13:16 *266 n. 33*
13:24 *221 n. 103*
13:26 *266 n. 33*
13:36 *106 n. 44*
13:43 *212 n. 49, 213*
13:47 *21*
14:22 *71*
15:29 *93 n. 35*
17:30 *221*
19:4 *221 n. 103*
19:38 *65*
19:40 *65*
20:21 *221*
21:25 *93 n. 35*
24:17 *38 n. 180*
26:2 *65*

26:7 *65*
26:20 *221*
27:12 *257, 257 n. 134*

Romans

1:7 *16, 60, 124 n. 115,
 187, 192 n. 203*
1:10 *257*
1:13 *257*
1:16 *251 n. 99, 267*
1:19 *152, 152 n. 131*
1:24 *223*
1:28 *219, 233, 233 n. 2*
1:28–31 *140*
1:29–31 *131 n. 2, 143*
1:32 *140, 153 n. 139*
2:1 *91 n. 31*
2:2, 3 *100*
2:4 *201, 221*
2:5 *21, 201*
2:7 *11, 33, 37, 188
 n. 173*
2:8 *21 n. 84, 37*
2:10 *12, 33, 75*
2:12 *86, 88, 275 n. 86*
2:13 *209 n. 29*
2:14, 15 *152*
2:16 *209 n. 29*
2:17 *34, 54*
2:19 *215 n. 66*
2:23 *54*
2:25 *208 n. 21, 209
 n. 28*
2:28, 29 *164 n. 14*
3:1, 2 *201, 208 n. 21*
3:3 *162 n. 8, 191
 n. 199*
3:4 *65, 191 n. 199*
3:8 *60, 100, 146*
3:20 *206*
3:23 *49*
3:26 *67, 194 n. 216*
3:30 *62 n. 94, 206*
4:2, 3 *54*
4:4 *190*
4:5 *39 n. 182*
4:11 *31 n. 144*
4:12 *186*
4:14 *275 n. 81*
4:16 *190*
4:17 *39 n. 182*
4:18 *49 n. 6*

4:24 *39 n. 182*
5:1–5 *284*
5:1–11 *49–56*
5:2 *11, 124, 196
 n. 227, 212, 212 n. 50*
5:3 *56*
5:5 *45, 60*
5:6–11 *284*
5:7 *162 n. 10*
5:8 *60, 64, 94 n. 48*
5:8–10 *66*
5:9 *21 n. 84, 194
 n. 216*
5:10 *58 n. 65, 189
 n. 180, 192 n. 203*
5:11 *194 n. 216*
5:12 *179 n. 105*
5:12–19 *51 n. 20*
5:16 *68*
5:18 *68*
6:1 *83, 146, 212 n. 49*
6:2 *148*
6:3–5 *9*
6:4 *55, 83*
6:5 *258*
6:6 *239 n. 39*
6:8 *22*
6:13 *239 n. 36*
6:14 *212 n. 49*
6:15 *146*
6:18 *208 n. 23*
6:19 *83, 223, 239 n. 36*
6:22 *83, 208 n. 23*
7:1–6 *210, 211*
7:4 *118 n. 89*
7:7–24 *83*
7:8 *149*
7:11 *149*
7:15–23 *150 n. 123*
7:21 *33 n. 156*
8:1 *68, 92 n. 31, 157,
 194 n. 216, 285*
8:2 *83, 208 n. 23*
8:3 *68*
8:4 *83*
8:6 *61, 75*
8:9 *62 n. 94*
8:10 *61*
8:11 *29, 29 n. 130, 39
 n. 182, 62, 258*
8:14–39 *161, 161
 nn. 1–7*

Romans (cont.)
8:15, 16   *114 n. 67*
8:17   *11, 18 n. 55, 19,*
   19 n. 66, 49, 61, 62,
   62 n. 94, 77, 260, 284
8:17–25   *61*
8:18   *11, 19, 50, 57, 59,*
   61, 62 n. 94, 194
   n. 216
8:18–25   *28*
8:21   *11, 50, 61*
8:23   *11, 27–29, 50, 51,*
   61, 174, 283
8:23–25   *77*
8:24   *283*
8:25   *49*
8:26   *57, 65 n. 121*
8:28   *9, 13 n. 29, 58–*
   62, 165, 188 n. 173
8:28–30   *18 n. 55, 191*
   n. 195
8:28–39   *161, 284*
8:29   *62, 76*
8:29, 30   *9–14, 15, 16*
   n. 41, 49, 67, 126, 283
8:30   *19, 165*
8:31–34   *65–69*
8:31–39   *190, 190*
   n. 183, 191 n. 200
8:32   *64, 200*
8:33   *13 n. 29, 78, 126,*
   206
8:34   *58*
8:35–39   *16, 56–65*
8:38   *46 n. 229*
9:1–3   *162*
9:3   *162 n. 10*
9:4   *161 nn. 2 & 3, 163,*
   163 nn. 12 & 13, 187,
   190 n. 193, 201
9:4–13   *161*
9:5   *163, 187, 189*
   n. 181, 190 n. 193,
   201
9:6   *162–65, 167, 171,*
   175, 175 n. 75, 181
   nn. 124 & 126, 195
9:6–13   *188*
9:7   *191*
9:7–12   *161 nn. 2 & 4*
9:7–13   *168 n. 29, 187*
9:7–10:21   *164–67*

9:9   *191*
9:11   *9, 161 n. 6, 163*
   n. 12
9:12   *191*
9:13   *161 n. 7, 189,*
   191, 239 n. 37
9:16   *67 n. 134*
9:22   *88 n. 13*
9:23   *19*
9:24   *168, 189, 191*
9:25   *60, 189, 192*
   n. 203
9:26   *189*
9:27   *182 n. 131*
9:27–29   *169*
9:30   *259 n. 148*
9:31   *164 n. 16, 259*
   n. 148
9:32   *94 n. 38, 171*
9:33   *50, 94 n. 38*
10:8   *245 n. 69*
10:11   *50*
10:14   *245 n. 69*
10:15   *60, 245 n. 69*
10:16   *192 n. 204*
10:19   *172*
11:1   *126, 162, 182,*
   195
11:1ff.   *166 n. 23*
11:1–10   *167–71*
11:2   *9, 126, 161 n. 6*
11:5   *182 n. 131, 186*
   n. 157, 188 n. 173,
   189, 193, 194 n. 216
11:7   *164 nn. 14 & 16,*
   166 n. 20, 177 n. 91,
   189
11:7ff.   *166 n. 22*
11:9   *94 n. 38*
11:11   *124, 162, 178,*
   179 n. 108, 189, 192
   n. 208, 195, 200
   n. 245
11:11–15   *171–74*
11:11–24   *201*
11:11–32   *171, 181*
11:12   *37 n. 174, 178,*
   179 n. 108, 182
   n. 132, 186 n. 154,
   189
11:14   *186 n. 157, 257*
11:15   *178, 179 n. 108,*

   185, 186 n. 154, 189
11:16   *28, 185–88, 199*
11:16–24   *174–77*
11:17   *185 n. 150, 248*
   n. 84, 250 n. 90
11:17–22   *286*
11:17–24   *196–201,*
   226, 227, 285
11:19   *178, 189*
11:20   *124*
11:21   *198 n. 235*
11:22   *172 n. 55,*
   200 n. 245, 201 n. 254
11:23, 24   *179 n. 108,*
   286
11:25   *173, 189, 199*
11:25, 26   *164 n. 16,*
   173 n. 62, 174 n. 68,
   177–85, 193 nn. 209
   & 210
11:25–27   *286*
11:25–32   *177*
11:26   *193 n. 215, 201*
11:27   *180, 185, 185*
   n. 150, 193 n. 215
11:28   *161 n. 7, 184*
   n. 147, 286
11:28–32   *185–95*
11:29   *161 n. 5*
11:30–32   *183*
11:31   *174 n. 73*
11:33–36   *183*
12:1   *187*
12:12   *49 n. 6*
12:13   *259 n. 148*
12:19   *21 n. 84, 36*
   n. 170
12:20   *36 n. 170*
13:3   *33, 34, 266 n. 33*
13:4   *272 n. 57*
13:11   *140, 140 n. 51*
13:11–14   *141*
13:12   *140*
13:13   *131 n. 2*
14:1–23   *85–97, 155,*
   241 n. 50, 285
14:4   *52, 73, 122*
   n. 110, 124
14:9   *58*
14:10   *53 n. 33, 65*
14:17   *75, 153 n. 139*
14:19   *259 n. 148*

14:20 *34, 45, 46*
15:2 *89*
15:4 *49 n. 6*
15:8 *189 n. 181*
15:13 *49 nn. 6 & 13*
15:16 *118 n. 89*
15:18 *268*
15:24 *36 n. 170*
15:26 *42 n. 207*
15:28 *40, 41 n. 195*
16:4 *162 n. 10*
16:5 *186*
16:6 *262 n. 4*
16:10 *235 n. 12*
16:12 *262 n. 4*
16:17 *94 n. 39*
16:26 *188 n. 173, 194
n. 216*

1 Corinthians
1:2 *20*
1:4 *44, 78 n. 215*
1:4–8 *77*
1:4–9 *79 n. 222*
1:5 *37 n. 174*
1:6 *78 n. 219*
1:7 *44, 77, 78 n. 215*
1:8 *32, 44*
1:8, 9 *76–79, 283, 284*
1:9 *10, 70, 129*
1:10ff. *104 n. 35*
1:17 *268*
1:18 *86, 87 n. 9, 88,
251 n. 99, 275 nn. 86
& 87, 276 n. 92*
1:19 *86*
1:20 *112 n. 62*
1:23 *245 n. 69*
1:24 *251 n. 99*
1:27 *16 n. 41, 50*
1:28 *16 n. 41, 118
n. 89*
1:29 *54, 118 n. 89*
1:31 *53, 54 n. 43*
2:1–5 *268*
2:3 *269 n. 45*
2:3–5 *270 n. 50*
2:4 *251 n. 99*
2:7 *9 n. 3, 16*
2:9 *60*
2:11 *114 n. 67*
2:12 *112 n. 62*

2:14, 15 *224*
3:3 *223 n. 111*
3:5–9 *268*
3:8 *262 n. 4*
3:9 *89, 242, 252 n. 103*
3:12–15 *242, 242
n. 52, 248*
3:13 *78, 217 n. 75, 261*
3:13–15 *45, 236 n. 19,
242 n. 52, 264 n. 19*
3:14 *271*
3:15 *112 n. 62, 237
n. 20, 242 nn. 53 &
54, 271*
3:21 *54, 54 n. 43*
3:21–23 *66 n. 129*
3:22 *57 n. 63*
4:1ff. *233 n. 1*
4:1–5 *236, 236 n. 19*
4:2–5 *247 n. 76, 258
n. 140, 261*
4:3–5 *235*
4:4 *65, 233 n. 1*
4:5 *78, 233 n. 1*
4:6 *118 n. 89*
4:11ff. *239*
4:12 *262 n. 4*
4:15 *188 n. 175*
4:20 *153 n. 139*
5:1 *136, 223*
5:1–5 *105 n. 38, 113–
20, 136, 155*
5:1–8 *116, 116 n. 74*
5:1–13 *222, 285*
5:5 *112 n. 62, 123*
5:6–8 *113*
5:7–7:40 *133 n. 11*
5:9 *115, 116 n. 76, 139*
5:9–13 *116*
5:10 *115, 116 n. 76,
131 n. 2, 140*
5:10–13 *125*
5:11 *115, 116 n. 74,
117 n. 81, 120 n. 97,
124, 125 n. 120, 131
n. 2, 139, 140*
5:11–13 *104 n. 36, 117
n. 76, 136, 220*
5:12 *115, 120, 137*
5:13 *115, 116, 120,
120 n. 99, 137*
6:1 *132, 134 n. 23,*

*135, 135 n. 25, 136
n. 29*
6:1–8 *137*
6:1–11 *133 n. 11, 138*
6:2 *133 n. 11, 134,
135, 136 n. 29, 137*
6:2–6 *132*
6:3 *133 n. 11, 134,
135, 137*
6:4 *137*
6:5 *137*
6:6 *135*
6:7 *132, 133 nn. 11 &
13, 135, 136 n. 29*
6:7–10 *125 n. 120*
6:8 *132, 133, 133
nn. 11 & 13, 135, 136
n. 29*
6:9, 10 *115, 124, 125,
153 n. 139*
6:9–11 *131–41, 156,
223, 284*
6:11 *20, 20 n. 68, 125
n. 120*
6:11–20 *133 n. 11*
7:5 *118 n. 89*
7:21 *255 n. 121*
7:39 *106 n. 44*
8:1 *121, 240*
8:1–11:1 *241 n. 46*
8:4–6 *93 n. 35*
8:7–13 *85–97, 155,
241 n. 50, 285*
8:9 *241 n. 47*
8:10 *121*
9:1 *45, 46, 219, 237,
240 n. 45, 253 n. 105*
9:1ff. *233 n. 1*
9:1–14 *243*
9:1–18 *240, 241 n. 45*
9:2 *219*
9:3 *247, 252*
9:4–6 *241*
9:4–18 *251*
9:6–12 *236 n. 17*
9:9 *124 n. 115*
9:12 *241 n. 48, 243,
248, 251 n. 99, 252,
253, 254 n. 111*
9:12–22 *242*
9:14 *188 n. 175, 241,
241 n. 51, 248, 253*

1 Corinthians (cont.)
9:15 *241 n. 48*
9:15–18 *242–45*
9:18 *188 n. 175, 248,*
   253
9:19–22 *240, 245*
   n. 66, 252–54
9:19–23 *245, 253*
   n. 105
9:19–27 *240 n. 45*
9:22 *250 n. 93*
9:23 *244 n. 60, 247–*
   54, 268, 281, 285
9:24 *123, 246 n. 74*
9:25 *246 n. 74*
9:24–27 *237–41, 245,*
   246 n. 72
9:26 *244, 262 n. 5*
9:27 *233–47, 259*
   n. 149, 281, 285
10:1ff. *239 n. 33*
10:1–4 *125*
10:1–10 *123, 238 n. 31*
10:1–12 *285*
10:1–23 *239*
10:5 *122, 125, 126*
10:5–22 *238*
10:6–10 *124, 129*
   n. 136
10:7, 8 *121, 122*
10:7–10 *125*
10:9 *128*
10:11 *71, 121 n. 105,*
   127 n. 131, 129 n. 136
10:12 *52 n. 29, 73, 74,*
   112 n. 62, 120–30,
   155, 196 n. 227
10:13 *70, 71–74, 112*
   n. 62, 122, 127 n. 131,
   128, 128 n. 132, 129,
   129 n. 136, 284
10:14 *72 n. 168, 121*
10:14–22 *93 n. 35, 121*
   n. 106
10:15 *129 n. 136*
10:15–21 *121*
10:16, 17 *117*
10:16–21 *130*
10:18 *164 n. 16, 248*
   n. 84
10:20 *249, 249 nn. 87*
   & 88

10:22 *128 n. 134*
10:23 *89*
10:23–11:1 *241, 241*
   n. 47
10:24 *89, 254*
10:28 *93 n. 35*
10:31 *89 n. 20*
10:32 *89 n. 20, 94*
10:33 *89 n. 20, 254,*
   254 n. 112
10:33–11:1 *241 n. 47*
11:2 *272*
11:17 *100*
11:18 *104, 104 n. 36*
11:19 *104, 104 n. 36,*
   152 n. 131, 233 n. 2
11:21 *104*
11:22 *101, 104, 104*
   n. 36, 105 n. 38
11:25 *117 n. 80*
11:26 *178 n. 99*
11:27–34 *99–112,*
   114–16, 120, 285
11:29 *155*
11:30–32 *123*
11:31 *115 n. 70*
11:32 *115 n. 70, 119*
   n. 96, 155
11:33 *36 n. 170*
12:7 *90*
13:3 *209 n. 28*
14:1 *259 n. 148*
14:3–5 *90*
14:6 *209 n. 28*
14:12 *90*
14:17 *90*
14:26 *90*
14:29 *99 n. 4*
15:1 *124, 196 n. 227,*
   272, 274
15:2 *261, 271–77, 282*
15:3–8 *272, 272 n. 66*
15:4 *274*
15:6 *106 n. 44*
15:10 *262 n. 4, 268,*
   275
15:11 *245 n. 69, 272,*
   273
15:12 *245 n. 69, 271,*
   273
15:12–19 *274, 275*
15:14 *276 n. 94*

15:14–19 *276 n. 93*
15:17 *276 n. 94*
15:18 *86, 88, 106 n. 44*
15:20 *28, 106 n. 44,*
   186 n. 160
15:22 *77*
15:23 *28, 29, 77*
15:24 *153 n. 139*
15:24–28 *58*
15:25 *178 n. 55, 189*
   n. 180
15:26 *189 n. 180*
15:33 *134 n. 21*
15:43 *11*
15:49 *10*
15:50 *131 nn. 3 & 4,*
   153 n. 139
15:51 *77, 106 n. 44*
15:52 *77*
16:6 *36 n. 170*
16:10 *268*
16:15 *186*
16:16 *262 n. 4*
16:18 *114 n. 67*

2 Corinthians
1:5 *61*
1:7 *248 n. 84*
1:9 *46 n. 229*
1:14 *44, 264*
1:16 *36 n. 170*
1:17 *111 n. 59*
1:18 *70 n. 149*
1:18–22 *32*
1:19 *245 n. 69*
1:20 *32*
1:21 *30 n. 141, 78*
   n. 215
1:22 *27, 28, 29–33, 51,*
   283
1:24 *124, 196 n. 227*
2:5–11 *119 n. 94*
2:6, 7 *119*
2:6–11 *92 n. 33*
2:12 *188 n. 175*
2:13 *114 n. 67*
2:15 *86, 87 n. 9, 88,*
   275 nn. 86 & 87, 276
   n. 92
3:1 *217, 235*
3:1–3 *218, 240 n. 42*
3:3 *268*

3:4 *215*
3:18 *10, 11, 19*
4:2 *236*
4:3 *86, 87 n. 3, 88, 275
n. 86*
4:4 *10, 118*
4:5 *245 n. 69*
4:6 *10*
4:7 *234, 267*
4:7–12 *56, 234 n. 10*
4:8ff. *239*
4:10 *55 n. 50, 234,
260, 260 n. 152*
4:11 *55 n. 50, 218,
234, 260, 260 n. 152*
4:11–13 *251 n. 100*
4:12 *218*
4:14 *22, 53 n. 33, 258*
4:16 *255 n. 121*
4:17 *11*
5:4 *30 n. 138*
5:5 *27, 29–33,
30 n. 138, 51, 283*
5:9 *236*
5:10 *65, 100, 236*
5:12–14 *278*
5:16 *119 n. 91*
5:17 *58 n. 65*
5:18–6:1 *278*
5:20 *268, 277*
6:1 *252 n. 103, 261,
268, 277–80, 282, 285*
6:2 *194 n. 216, 278*
6:3–10 *278*
6:4–10 *56, 234 n. 10*
6:5 *262 n. 4*
6:10 *37 n. 174*
6:11–13 *279*
6:14–7:1 *137*
7:1 *40 n. 194, 114
n. 67, 119 n. 91*
7:5 *119 n. 91*
7:8 *255 n. 121*
7:9 *221 n. 104*
7:10 *191, 221 n. 104*
7:12 *119 n. 91*
7:13 *114 n. 67*
7:15 *269 n. 45*
8:4 *42 n. 207*
8:5 *37*
8:6 *40, 41 n. 195, 43,
43 n. 211*

8:7 *37 n. 175*
8:8 *217 n. 75*
8:9 *36–38, 42–43, 46*
8:10 *41 n. 195, 43, 43
n. 211*
8:11 *40, 41 n. 195, 43,
43 n. 211*
8:14 *118 n. 89*
8:18 *188 n. 175*
8:22 *235 n. 12*
8:23 *249 n. 88*
9:6 *37*
9:7 *37*
9:8 *33, 34 , 43 n. 211*
9:9 *33, 37, 38*
9:10 *37, 38*
9:11 *37 n. 174*
9:11–13 *44 n. 212*
9:13 *42 n. 207*
9:15 *37 n. 174*
10–13 *217 n. 79*
10:1 *217*
10:2 *215 n. 66, 217,
234*
10:7 *217, 234, 234 n. 6*
10:8 *90*
10:10 *217, 234*
10:14 *188 n. 175*
10:15 *262 n. 4*
10:17 *53, 54 n. 43,
244, 264 n. 15*
10:18 *218 n. 88, 235,
236, 244, 264 n. 15*
11:1 *219 n. 91*
11:2 *53 n. 33*
11:4 *245 n. 69, 277
n. 99, 278*
11:5–7 *234*
11:5–9 *217*
11:7–10 *244*
11:9 *236 n. 17*
11:9–12 *252*
11:13 *224, 236 n. 18*
11:16, 17 *219 n. 91*
11:20 *240 n. 43*
11:23 *262 n. 4*
11:23–30 *55*
11:23–33 *56, 234 n. 10*
11:27 *262 n. 4*
11:29 *94*
11:30 *219 n. 91*
12:1 *219 n. 91*

12:5 *219 n. 91, 234
n. 10, 244*
12:6 *219 n. 91*
12:7 *118 n. 86, 119
n. 91*
12:9 *54 n. 43, 55, 234,
234 n. 10, 244, 264
n. 15*
12:10 *55, 234, 234
n. 10*
12:11 *217, 219 n. 91,
255 n. 121*
12:12 *234 n. 9*
12:13 *217, 234, 252*
12:15 *162 n. 10*
12:16 *236 n. 17*
12:19 *219 n. 91*
12:20 *131 n. 2, 140,
143, 222 n. 109, 285*
12:21 *131 n. 2, 137,
140, 143, 153 n. 139,
221–25, 285*
13:2 *152 n. 134, 221*
13:2–7 *234*
13:3 *217, 218*
13:5 *217–25, 226, 233
n. 2, 245, 276, 277
n. 97, 280, 285*
13:5–7 *233, 233 n. 5*
13:5–10 *150 n. 119*
13:6 *219, 245*
13:7 *33 n. 156, 219
n. 91, 235*
13:7–10 *218 n. 85*
13:10 *90, 224, 234*

Galatians
1:4 *37, 37 n. 176, 208
n. 22*
1:6 *39 n. 182, 203,
207, 208, 208 n. 20,
213*
1:7 *207*
1:8 *204, 204 n. 6, 214*
1:9 *37 n. 176, 152
n. 134, 204, 214, 265*
1:15 *263 n. 11*
2:1–10 *203, 265*
2:2 *239 n. 39, 245
n. 69, 261–63, 266
n. 31, 267, 281, 285*
2:3–10 *266*

Galatians (cont.)
2:4 *146 n. 94, 204 n. 5, 214*
2:5 *203 n. 1, 204, 204 nn. 5 & 6*
2:8 *39 n. 182*
2:11–14 *203*
2:12 *117, 266 n. 33*
2:14 *203 n. 1, 204, 204 nn. 3 & 6, 265*
2:16 *206*
2:17 *146*
2:17–21 *205*
2:18 *89, 148 n. 106*
2:20 *63, 63 n. 103*
2:21 *148 n. 106, 204 nn. 6 & 7, 205*
3:1–5 *213, 216*
3:3 *40, 41 n. 195, 206*
3:4 *215, 215 n. 69, 271 n. 56, 272 n. 57*
3:6 *205*
3:10–12 *210*
3:11 *124 n. 115, 205*
3:12 *205*
3:13 *210*
3:15–18 *205*
3:18 *62, 153 n. 139, 190*
3:22 *194 n. 216*
3:23–26 *205*
3:26–29 *204 n. 7*
3:29 *153 n. 139*
4:1 *153 n. 139*
4:3 *208*
4:7 *153 n. 139*
4:8 *148, 208*
4:9 *148, 194 n. 216, 208*
4:9–11 *263*
4:10 *145, 214, 262, 266*
4:11 *261–63, 266, 267, 271 n. 55, 272 n. 57, 275, 281, 282, 285*
4:13, 14 *119 n. 91*
4:21 *142 n. 62*
4:21ff. *124 n. 115*
4:21–25 *209*
4:22, 23 *45*
4:24 *148*
4:25 *148*

4:30 *153 n. 139, 209*
4:31 *209*
5:1 *145, 146 n. 94, 148*
5:1–4 *203–16, 285*
5:3 *145, 145 n. 83*
5:4 *142 n. 62, 265*
5:5 *68, 206*
5:6 *207 n. 16*
5:7 *20 n. 69, 203, 203 n. 1, 204*
5:8 *39 n. 182, 203*
5:10 *47 n. 229, 214, 214 n. 61, 215, 216, 216 n. 74, 286*
5:11 *245 n. 69*
5:13 *208 n. 24*
5:13ff. *142–54*
5:13–6:10 *211*
5:17 *111, 111 n. 59, 112 n. 60*
5:18 *152*
5:19–21 *131, 141–53, 284*
5:19–25 *156*
5:21 *131 n. 4, 139*
6:1 *142 n. 62, 143, 144*
6:1–4 *149*
6:2 *148 n. 110*
6:6–10 *153, 154*
6:7 *134 n. 21*
6:7–10 *37 n. 178*
6:9 *33 n. 156, 154 n. 148*
6:10 *33 n. 156*
6:12 *204*
6:13 *54 n. 43, 150*
6:14 *53*
6:16 *164, 181 n. 124*
6:18 *114 n. 67*

Ephesians
1:4 *16, 16 n. 41*
1:5 *11 n. 12, 16 n. 41, 270 n. 49*
1:6 *46 n. 228*
1:9 *270 n. 49*
1:11 *16 n. 41*
1:13 *28, 30, 31, 32, 44*
1:14 *24, 27, 30 n. 136, 31, 32, 32 n. 149, 44*
2:2 *118*
2:10 *33 n. 155*

2:12 *163*
2:15 *119 n. 91*
2:27 *53 n. 33*
3:1 *162 n. 10*
3:6, 7 *253 n. 110*
3:13 *162 n. 10*
4:17 *223*
4:19 *223*
4:22–24 *140*
4:24ff. *140*
4:30 *28, 30, 32, 32 n. 149*
4:31 *131 n. 2, 140*
5:1 *192 n. 203*
5:3 *141*
5:3–5 *131 n. 2*
5:3–8 *140*
5:5 *131 n. 3, 136 n. 28*
5:6 *21 n. 84, 136 n. 28*
5:7 *249 n. 85*
5:26 *20*
5:29 *119 n. 91*
5:31 *119 n. 91*
5:33 *266 n. 33*
6:5 *269 n. 45*
6:11 *52 n. 29*
6:13, 14 *124*
6:16 *70 n. 152*

Philippians
1:3 *42, 42 n. 207*
1:3–5 *44 n. 212, 47*
1:3–6 *47 n. 231*
1:4 *45*
1:5 *34, 39, 39 n. 191, 40, 40 n. 191, 42, 42 n. 207, 270 n. 54*
1:6 *33–47, 264 n. 15, 269, 270, 270 n. 54, 283*
1:6–11 *44 n. 212*
1:7 *47, 47 n. 231, 78 n. 219, 248 n. 84, 249, 249 n. 86, 250 n. 91*
1:8 *47 n. 231*
1:9 *270 n. 54*
1:9–11 *44, 45, 47*
1:10 *41 n. 201*
1:11 *43, 43 n. 220*
1:12 *251, 267*
1:13 *152 n. 131*
1:15 *270 n. 49*

1:15–18 *204 n. 6*
1:21 *247 n. 77*
1:22 *46, 262*
1:23 *22, 247 n. 77, 258*
1:28 *88 n. 13, 275*
  n. 87
1:28–30 *47*
2:2–8 *269*
2:12, 13 *39, 269–71*
2:14–16 *264*
2:16 *41 n. 201, 239*
  n. 39, 244, 261–63,
  264 nn. 17 & 19, 265
  n. 24, 268, 275, 281,
  282, 285
2:17 *255 n. 121*
2:22 *235 n. 12, 236*
2:24 *47 n. 229*
2:30 *46*
3:2 *236 n. 18*
3:2ff. *255 n. 117*
3:3 *53, 54, 54 n. 43,*
  215 n. 66, 260
3:4 *215 n. 66, 260*
3:5–10 *260*
3:7–10 *258*
3:7–16 *254, 284*
3:8 *255 n. 117*
3:10 *9, 10, 61, 249*
  n. 86, 255 n. 118
3:11, 12 *254–60, 281*
3:12–14 *239 n. 39*
3:13 *255 n. 116, 259*
3:14 *246 n. 74, 259*
3:15 *255 n. 117, 260*
3:18 *152 n. 134*
3:19 *88 n. 13, 259, 260*
3:20 *44, 49*
3:21 *10, 11, 44, 49,*
  258
4:1 *246 n. 74, 265*
  n. 24
4:10–19 *42*
4:14–20 *42*
4:15 *17, 39 n. 189, 42*
  n. 207
4:17 *43*
4:18 *40*
4:23 *114 n. 67*

Colossians
1:10 *33 n. 155*

1:15 *10*
1:19 *10*
1:22 *53 n. 33, 197*
  n. 231
1:23 *197 n. 231, 253*
  n. 110
1:24 *162 n. 10*
2:1 *119 n. 91*
2:5 *114 n. 67, 119*
  n. 91, 255 n. 121
2:7 *32 n. 151*
2:11 *239 n. 39*
2:18 *272 n. 57*
3:4 *19 n. 63*
3:5 *131 n. 2*
3:5–7 *223*
3:6 *21 n. 84*
3:7 *140*
3:8 *131 n. 2, 140*
3:10ff. *140*
3:12 *60*
3:22 *266 n. 33*
4:12 *124*

1 Thessalonians
1:1 *75*
1:3 *40 n. 191*
1:3–5 *268*
1:4 *16, 16 n. 41, 40*
  n. 191, 60
1:5 *44, 188 n. 175, 251*
  n. 99, 267
1:6 *44, 277 n. 99*
1:10 *21, 21 n. 84, 44,*
  185 n. 150
1:28 *53 n. 33*
2:1 *267 n. 37*
2:2 *239 n. 39*
2:3–9 *236*
2:4 *235, 237 n. 20*
2:7 *236 n. 17*
2:8 *248 n. 80*
2:9 *236 n. 17, 245*
  n. 69, 252, 262 n. 4
2:10–12 *17*
2:12 *18 n. 55, 75, 75*
  n. 180
2:13 *268, 277 n. 99*
2:16 *178 n. 97*
2:18 *70 n. 152, 118*
  n. 86
2:19 *244, 246 n. 74,*

264
2:20 *264*
3:1–4 *265*
3:1–8 *268*
3:2 *71, 252 n. 103*
3:2–5 *70*
3:3 *71*
3:3–5 *263*
3:4 *152 n. 134*
3:5 *70 n. 152, 261,*
  262, 265, 275, 281,
  285
3:9 *244, 264*
3:11–13 *75 n. 187*
3:13 *71, 75, 76*
4:2 *139*
4:3 *223*
4:5 *139, 223*
4:6 *139, 141 n. 52, 152*
  n. 134
4:7, 8 *20 n. 68*
4:13–15 *106 n. 44*
4:17 *22, 22 n. 88, 26,*
  179 n. 102
5:3 *119 n. 91*
5:4 *24, 27 n. 119, 111,*
  111 n. 59
5:5 *24, 27 n. 119*
5:6 *22, 26, 27 n. 119*
5:8 *17, 21, 22, 24, 26,*
  27, 27 n. 119, 140
5:9 *16 n. 41, 17, 18, 19*
  n. 63, 21–27, 67, 140,
  283
5:10 *21, 22, 25, 26, 27*
5:12 *262 n. 4*
5:23, 24 *74–76, 283,*
  284
5:24 *39 n. 182, 70, 79,*
  129, 165

2 Thessalonians
1:1 *15 n. 35*
1:3, 4 *70*
1:5 *153 n. 139*
1:6 *62 n. 94*
1:7 *44, 77 n. 204*
1:10 *18 n. 55, 44*
1:11 *18 n. 59, 118*
  n. 89, 270 n. 49
1:12 *118 n. 89*
2:5 *152 n. 134*

2 Thessalonians (cont.)
2:9 70 n. 152
2:9–12 70
2:10 86, 88, 275 n. 86, 277 n. 99
2:12 20 n. 69, 153 n. 139
2:13 60
2:13, 14 15–20, 67, 283
2:14 18 n. 55, 23, 24, 49, 165
2:15 15 n. 36, 20
2:16 16 n. 37
2:17 33, 34, 71, 71 nn. 157 & 158
3:1 70, 251, 267
3:2 70
3:3 70–71, 74, 284
3:4 47 n. 229, 71, 215
3:5 75 n. 187
3:8 236 n. 17
3:14 117 nn. 78 & 81
3:15 117 n. 81

1 Timothy
1:1 188 n. 173
1:9 131 n. 2, 140
1:10 140, 220 n. 95
1:20 106, 117, 118 nn. 83 & 86
2:10 33 n. 155
3:1 33 n. 155
3:10 235 n. 12
3:16 65, 119 n. 91
5:10 33 n. 155
5:25 33 n. 155
6:4 143
6:9 88 n. 13
6:11 259 n. 148
6:18 33 n. 155

2 Timothy
2:1 212 n. 49, 213
2:9 251 n. 98
2:10 19 n. 63, 252
2:13 76 n. 197, 192
2:15 236
2:21 33 n. 155
2:22 259 n. 148
3:1–8 220
3:2–5 131 n. 2

3:8 219, 233, 233 n. 2
3:17 33 n. 155
4:3 220 n. 95
4:18 131 n. 4

Titus
1:3 188 n. 173
1:9 220 n. 95
1:11–16 220
1:16 33 n. 155, 219, 220 n. 94, 233, 233 n. 2
2:1 220 n. 95
2:7 33 n. 155
2:12 106
2:14 33 n. 155
3:1 33 n. 155
3:3 131 n. 2, 223
3:3–5 140
3:8 33 n. 155
3:14 33 n. 155

Philemon
5 44
6 44, 249 n. 86
17 249 n. 88
25 114 n. 67

Hebrews
1:9 249 n. 85
2:2, 3 78 n. 219
2:14 119 n. 91
3:16–18 123 n. 115
3:17 122, 122 n. 109
4:2 209 n. 28
4:11 122 n. 109, 124
4:12 114 n. 67
6:8 233 n. 2
6:9 255 n. 121
6:16 78 n. 219
7:21 191
7:25 65
10:23 272
10:29 212 n. 49, 213
10:33 249, 249 n. 88
10:38 126
10:39 23 n. 98, 88 n. 13
11:7 91 n. 31
11:23 266 n. 33
11:27 266 n. 33
12:2–4 107
12:8 107

12:10, 11 112 n. 62
12:14 259 n. 148
12:15 212 n. 49
13:2 37 n. 175
13:3 46 n. 227
13:7 72
13:9 209 n. 28, 212 n. 49, 213
13:16 42 n. 207

James
1:12 217 n. 77, 233 n. 2
1:16 134 n. 21
2:10 101 n. 17
4:12 88
5:12 124

1 Peter
1:2 20 n. 68
1:7 77 n. 204, 217 n. 77
1:13 77 n. 204
2:1 131 n. 2, 140
2:8 21
2:9 22 n. 89, 23, 24
2:17 266 n. 33
3:6 266 n. 33
3:14 266 n. 33
3:19 114 n. 67
4:1–4 223
4:3 131 n. 2, 140
4:13 77 n. 204
4:15 131 n. 2
5:1 248 n. 84
5:10 71
5:12 124, 196 n. 227, 212, 213

2 Peter
1:4 248 n. 84
1:17 126
2:9 73
3:4 106 n. 44
3:7 88 n. 13
3:9 88
3:18 212 n. 49, 213

1 John
1:9 111 n. 59
2:1 65, 69 n. 145
2:2 69 n. 145
2:10, 11 94

2:13 17, 70 n. 152
2:14 70 n. 152
3:7 134 n. 21
5:18, 19 70 n. 152

Jude
1 16
4 213
12 117
24 124

Revelation
1:9 249, 250 n. 90
2:10 71 n. 160, 266
  n. 33
3:10 71 n. 160, 73
3:19 106
6:17 124
7:2–8 31
9:20 111 n. 59

9:21 131 n. 2, 140
11:18 266 n. 33
12:10 65
14:17 266 n. 33
19:5 266 n. 33
20:15 258 n. 140
21:7 131 n. 3
21:8 131 n. 2, 140
22:15 131 n. 2, 140

Extracanonical Jewish Literature

**OT Apocrypha and
  Pseudepigrapha**

2 Apocalypse of Baruch
13:9, 10 108 n. 52
14:12, 13 61 n. 93
27 56 n. 53
54:17, 18 136 n. 30
78:6 109
79:2 111

3 Apocalypse of Baruch
15:2, 3 37 n. 178

Apocalypse of Moses
37 179 n. 102

Assumption of Moses
12:12 109
12:13 110

1 Enoch
1:7–9 67 n. 134
10:16 186
13:3 269 n. 44
22:3–13 114 n. 67
45:3–6 67 n. 134
48:7 67 n. 134
50:1, 2 67 n. 134
62:8 67 n. 134
62:13 67 n. 134
93:2–10 186
94:1ff. 136 n. 30
94:4 67 n. 134
103:3, 4 67 n. 134

2 Enoch
22:10 269 n. 44

Epistle of Aristeas
205 275 n. 83
225 270 n. 51

Epistle of Jeremy
4, 5 139

4 Ezra
4:33–37 177 n. 93
6:5, 6 31
7:17 131 n. 3
7:100 114 n. 67
8:51ff. 31
8:52 61 n. 93

Jubilees
1:16 186

1 Maccabees
13:47 179 n. 102
14:45 101

2 Maccabees
6:12 110
6:12–16 112
6:12–17 107
6:13–15 108
6:16 109
12:45 106 n. 44

4 Maccabees
1:12 179 n. 102
110:15 119 n. 91

Psalms of Solomon
3:10 172 n. 55
10:1–3 105
15:6 31

15:10–12 31
17:8 258 n. 140

Sirach
6:4 96
8:2 96
9:9 114 n. 67
14:1, 2 92
18:13 107, 108
18:14 107
22:27 96
24:9 17
28:13 96
30:21–25 96
31:25 96
32:1 179 n. 102
33:4 179 n. 102
34:14 198 n. 235
33:19 126 n. 127
35:7–10 37 n. 177
45:19 126 n. 127

Testament of Job
5:3 179 n. 102

*Testaments of the
  Twelve Patriarchs*

Daniel
5:5–7 139

Joseph
1:5–7 36
1:6 46

Judah
24:5 186

Tobit
12:9 *37*
13:2–16 *108*

Wisdom of Solomon
1:12 *119 n. 91*
6:23 *250, 251 n. 96*
8:17 *250 n. 95*
8:18 *250*
11:2–14 *109*
11:10 *107, 111 n. 58*
11:23 *108*
12:2 *108*
12:8 *108*
12:10 *108, 109*
12:21 *108, 110*
12:22 *108, 110 n. 54*
12:26 *109*
12:27 *109, 110*
14:12 *139*
14:25, 26 *140 n. 50*
15:1 *197 n. 228*
15:2 *140 n. 50*
16:1–4 *109*
16:5 *108*
16:6 *108, 110*
16:11 *110*
18:13 *119 n. 91*
18:20–25 *108*
18:21 *110*
18:22 *110*
18:24 *111*
19:1 *109*

Josephus
Antiquities
4.71 *187 n. 161*

Jewish Wars
I.24.4 §481 *222 n. 105*

Philo
De congressu
177 *107 n. 47*

De specialibus legibus
I.131–144 *187 n. 161*
I.160 *119 n. 91*
III.147 *119 n. 91*
IV.127 *119 n. 91*

Qumran Literature
1QS
1:8, 10 *169 n. 38*
4:7 *264 n. 21*
7:10, 12 *169 n. 38*

1QH
2:12 *169 n. 38*
6:8 *169 n. 38*

1QpHab
10:13 *169 n. 38*

4QpPs37
2:5 *169 n. 38*

3:5 *169 n. 38*
4:11f. *169 n. 38*

Rabbinic Literature
Mishnah
Sanhedrin 10:1 *183*

Babylonian Talmud
Berakoth
18c *114 n. 67*

Soṭah
14a *34*

Sanhedrin
98a *185 n. 150*

Menaḥoth
53b *175 n. 74*

Midrashim
Sifre Deuteronomy
11:22 §49(85ᵃ) *35 n. 164*

Leviticus Rabbah
34:9(131b) *37 n. 177*

Ruth Rabbah
Proem III *109*

Midrash Psalm
25 §11(107ᵃ) *35 n. 164*

Other Early Christian Literature

NT Apocrypha
Acts John
84 *210 n. 40, 212*

Apostolic Fathers
Barnabas
4:9 *209 n. 28*
7:8 *179 n. 102*

1 Clement
7:2 *275 n. 83*
10:7 *37 n. 175*
11:1 *37 n. 175*
12:1–8 *37 n. 175*
33:1 *35, 40 n. 194*
33:1ff. *47 n. 234*
33:2 *35*
33:7, 8 *35*
55:2 *46 n. 227*
56:3–16 *112*
59:4 *35*

Didache
2–5 *139*
7:1 *139*
16:2 *209 n. 28*

Hermas, Shepherd of
Visions
2.2.2 *209 n. 28*

Similitude
9.13.2 *209 n. 28*
9.16.3–7 *106 n. 44*

Ignatius

Ephesians
20:2 *103 n. 28*

Romans
4:2 *106 n. 44*
5:3 *119 n. 91*

Smyrneans
5:2 *209 n. 28*

Patristic Literature

Augustine

De correptione et gratia
XII.33 *9 n. 3*

De dono perseverantiae
9 n. 3

*Exp. quar. prop. ex ep.
ad Rom.* §52.6 *50
n. 14*

Chrysostom

Comm. in ep. ad Gal.
216 n. 70

Hom. in ep. ad Rom.
167 n. 27

Hom. in ep. II ad Thess.
20 n. 71

Justin
Apology I.61.10 222

Greek and Roman Literature

Columella

De re rustica
5.9.16 *175 n. 81*

Epictetus
Dissertations
I.1.9 *251 n. 97*
II.9.3 *97 n. 50*

Justinian

Edicta
13.15 *23 n. 99*

Philogelos
§§3, 57, 243 *179
n. 102*

Plato

Phaedros
239d *266 n. 32*

Sophocles
Oedipus Tyrranos
767 *266 n. 32*

Strabo

Geography
III.2.10 *269 n. 47*

Vettius Valens
85.16 *23 n. 99*

Inscriptions and Papyri

Papyrus Cowley
218 *59 n. 73*

Papyrus Tebtunis
317.26 *23 n. 99*

Printed in the United States
19249LVS00003B/133-156